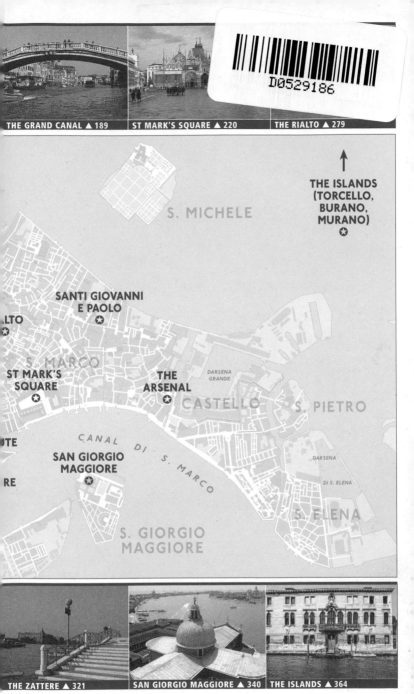

THE GRAND CANAL ▲ 189 **ST MARK'S SQUARE ▲ 220** **THE RIALTO ▲ 279**

S. MICHELE

↑
THE ISLANDS (TORCELLO, BURANO, MURANO) ✪

SANTI GIOVANNI E PAOLO ✪

LTO ✪

S. MARCO

ST MARK'S SQUARE ✪

THE ARSENAL ✪

DARSENA GRANDE

CASTELLO   S. PIETRO

TE

CANAL DI S. MARCO

SAN GIORGIO MAGGIORE ✪

RE

DARSENA DI S. ELENA

S. ELENA

S. GIORGIO MAGGIORE

THE ZATTERE ▲ 321 **SAN GIORGIO MAGGIORE ▲ 340** **THE ISLANDS ▲ 364**

■ **THE FRARI AND SAN ROCCO**
The Gothic basilica is the pantheon of great Venetians. The Scuola San Rocco contains one of the finest collections of paintings in Italy.

■ **THE ACCADEMIA**
The Venetian school in all its splendor, from Bellini to Canaletto.

■ **SANTA MARIA DELLA SALUTE**
The most finely proportioned example of Baroque

architecture, with masterpieces by Titian and Tintoretto.
■ **THE ZATTERE**
This quayside is perfect for strolling, for having lunch in the sun or for visiting Venice's best ice cream parlors.

■ **SAN GIORGIO MAGGIORE**
Palladio's finest church.
■ **THE ISLANDS**
Three faces of the Lagoon: Murano glassblowers, Burano lacemakers and birdsong on Torcello.

VENICE

EVERYMAN GUIDES

● Encyclopedia section

■ **NATURE** The natural heritage: species and habitats characteristic to the area covered by the guide, annotated and illustrated by naturalist authors and artists.

HISTORY The impact of international historical events on local history, from the arrival of the first inhabitants, with key dates appearing in a timeline above the text.

ARTS AND TRADITIONS Customs and traditions and their continuing role in contemporary life.

ARCHITECTURE The architectural heritage, focusing on style and topology, a look at rural and urban buildings, major civil, religious and military monuments.

AS SEEN BY PAINTERS A selection of paintings of the city or country by different artists and schools, arranged chronologically or thematically.

AS SEEN BY WRITERS An anthology of texts focusing on the city or country, taken from works of all periods and countries, arranged thematically.

▲ Itineraries

Each itinerary begins with a map of the area to be explored.

✪ **SPECIAL INTEREST** These sites are not to be missed. They are highlighted in gray boxes in the margins.

★ **EDITOR'S CHOICE** Sites singled out by the editor for special attention.

INSETS On richly illustrated double pages, these insets turn the spotlight on subjects deserving more in-depth treatment.

◆ Practical information

All the travel information you will need before you go and when you get there.

USEFUL ADDRESSES A selection of hotels and restaurants compiled by an expert.

SIGHTSEEING A handy table of addresses and opening hours.

APPENDICES Bibliography, list of illustrations and general index.

MAP SECTION Maps of areas covered by the guide, followed by an index; these maps are marked out with letters and figures making it easy for the reader to pinpoint a town, region or site.

◆ CASTELLO

◆ CASTELLO

Each map in the map section is designated by a letter. In the itineraries, all the sites of interest are given a map reference (for example: **C** B2).

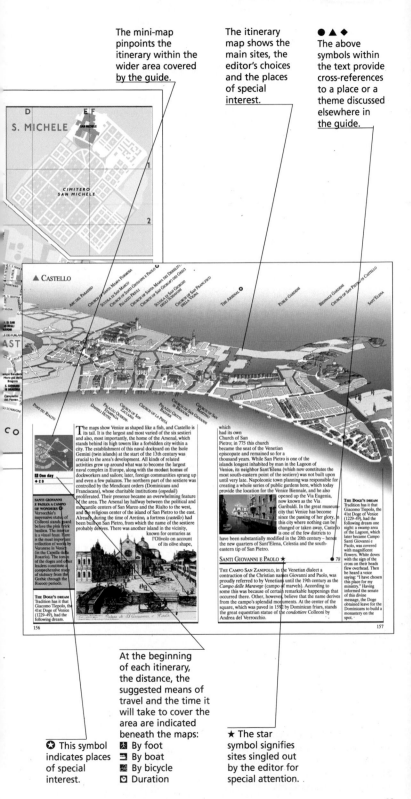

The mini-map pinpoints the itinerary within the wider area covered by the guide.

The itinerary map shows the main sites, the editor's choices and the places of special interest.

● ▲ ◆ The above symbols within the text provide cross-references to a place or a theme discussed elsewhere in the guide.

At the beginning of each itinerary, the distance, the suggested means of travel and the time it will take to cover the area are indicated beneath the maps:
🚶 By foot
🚣 By boat
🚲 By bicycle
🕐 Duration

✪ This symbol indicates places of special interest.

★ The star symbol signifies sites singled out by the editor for special attention.

▲ CASTELLO

The maps show Venice as shaped like a fish, and Castello is its tail. It is the largest and most varied of the six sestieri and also, most importantly, the home of the Arsenal, which stands behind its high towers like a forbidden city within a city. The establishment of this naval dockyard on the Isole Gemini (twin islands) at the start of the 13th century was crucial to the area's development. All kinds of related activities grew up around what was to become the largest naval complex in Europe, along with the modest homes of dockworkers and sailors; later, foreign communities sprang up and even a few palazzos. The northern part of the sestiere was controlled by the Mendicant orders (Dominicans and Franciscans), whose charitable institutions (ospedali) proliferated. Their presence became an overwhelming feature of the area. The Arsenal lay halfway between the political and mercantile centers of San Marco and the Rialto to the west, and the religious center of the island of San Pietro to the east. Already during the time of Aretino, a fortress (castello) had been built on San Pietro, from which the name of the sestiere probably derives. There was another island in the vicinity, known for centuries as l'Olivolo on account of its olive shape, which had its own Church of San Pietro; in 775 this church became the seat of the Venetian episcopate and remained so for a thousand years. While San Pietro is one of the islands longest inhabited by man in the Lagoon of Venice, its neighbor Sant'Elena (which now constitutes the most south-eastern point of the sestiere) was not built upon until very late. Napoleonic town planning was responsible for creating a whole series of public gardens here, which today provide the location for the Venice Biennale, and he also opened up the Via Eugenia, now known as the Via Garibaldi. In the great museum city that Venice has become since the passing of her glory, in this city where nothing can be changed or taken away, Castello is one of the few districts to have been substantially modified in the 20th century – hence the new quarters of Sant'Elena, Celestia and the south-eastern tip of San Pietro.

ONE DAY
◆ C 9

SANTI GIOVANNI E PAOLO A CAMPO OF WONDERS ✪
Verrocchio's impressive statue of Colleoni stands guard before the pink brick basilica. The interior is a visual feast. Here is the most important collection of works by Veronese in Venice (in the Capella della Rosario). The tombs of the doges and other leaders constitute a comprehensive study of statuary from the Gothic through the Rococo periods.

THE DOGE'S DREAM
Tradition has it that Giacomo Tiepolo, the 41st Doge of Venice (1229–49), had the following dream.

SANTI GIOVANNI E PAOLO ★ ● 78

THE CAMPO SAN ZANIPOLO, in the Venetian dialect a contraction of the Christian names Giovanni and Paolo, was proudly referred to by Venetians until the 19th century as the Campo delle Maravege (campo of marvels). According to some this was because of certain remarkable happenings that occurred there. Other, however, believe that the name derives from the campo's splendid monuments. At the center of the square, which was paved in 1592 by Dominican friars, stands the great equestrian statue of the condottiere Colleoni by Andrea del Verrocchio.

THE DOGE'S DREAM
Tradition has it that Giacomo Tiepolo, the 41st Doge of Venice (1229–49), had the following dream one night: a swamp area of the Lagoon, which later became Campo Santi Giovanni e Paolo, was covered with magnificent flowers. White doves with the sign of the cross on their heads flew overhead. Then he heard a voice saying: "I have chosen this place for my ministry." Having informed the senate of this divine message, the Doge obtained leave for the Dominicans to build a monastery on the spot.

156   157

● Encyclopedia section

▲ Itineraries in Venice

◆ Practical information

CANNAREGIO ▲ 135
The Ghetto, at the center of this densely populated *sestiere* (quarter), is full of history, as well as a few ghosts. Other points of interest include the cemetery of San Michele, the Ca' d'Oro, a fine example of Venetian Gothic, and the exuberant Baroque of the Gesuiti.

CASTELLO ▲ 155
A sestiere of contrasts, lying between the Arsenal, which comes to life during the Biennale, and the lively Riva degli Schiavoni, with the Scuola di San Giorgio (paintings by Carpaccio). Devotees of Vivaldi will make the pilgrimage to the Pietà, to experience its superb acoustics at one of the many concerts held there.

SAINT MARK'S SQUARE ▲ 219
Tourists flock to this spot, and not without reason: the piazza and adjacent piazzetta encapsulate the history of Venice: St Mark's Basilica, the campanile, the Doge's Palace, prisons and the Bridge of Sighs more than justify their renown.

SAN MARCO ▲ 257
The southern sweep of the Grand Canal encloses the historical and cultural heart of Venice, with palaces and churches in abundance. The ghost of Casanova pervades the Palazzo Dandolo, once a notorious gambling den, and La Fenice rises from the ashes once more.

SAN POLO ▲ 277
This sestiere centers around the extensive Campo San Polo, where movies are shown in September during La Mostra (bull races were once held there). The Rialto, with its lively market, the House of Goldoni and the basilica of the Frari are the key attractions here.

DORSODURO ▲ 297
A sestiere that seems dedicated to the enjoyment of art (from the collections of the Accademia to the Baroque splendors of Santa Maria della Salute and the Surrealists of the Guggenheim Foundation) as welll as the pleasures of a walk along the Zattere: all part of the Venetian way of life.

SANTA CROCE ▲ 343
Just outside the main tourist areas, this sestiere has an arresting charm, with peaceful piazzas, churches and palazzi along the Grand Canal. Be sure to visit the Fondaco dei Turchi, the Ca' Pesaro, with its remarkable Museum of Oriental art, and the Palazzo Mocenigo.

THE ISLANDS OF THE LAGOON ▲ 353
A true picture of Venice is impossible without a trip out to the Lagoon, which has always been always closely linked to the city's history. The Lido and its beaches and retro palazzi, San Giorgio and its fine Palladian church, Murano and its glassblowers, Burano and its lacemakers, and the other small islands are just a vaporetto ride away.

→ **Numerous specialists and academics have contributed
to this guide. All the information that it contains
has been submitted to them for their approval.**

● Encyclopedia section

■ NATURE
Alberto Giulio Bernstein, Giuseppe
Cherubini (cooperativa Limosa, Venice),
Eleonora Cicotti (Laboratorio di
Ecologia Sperimentale e Acquacoltura,
Rome), Margherita Fusco (cooperativa
Limosa, Venice), Roberta Manzi
(cooperativa Limosa, Venice),
Roberto Rosselli

■ HISTORY AND LANGUAGE
Maria Colombo, Jean-Louis Fournel,
Sabina Vianello

■ CRAFTS & TRADITIONS
Paola Ancillotto, Roberto Fontanari,
Tullio Ortolani, Ugo Pizzarello, Giovani
Roman, Roberto Valese, Giovanni et
Mario Valese, Sabina Vianello

■ ARCHITECTURE
Maroun El Daccache, Dominique
Fernandes, Luciana Miotto,
Silvia Moretti, Loredana Pellarini

■ VENICE AS SEEN BY PAINTERS
Patrick Jusseaux

■ APPENDICES
Maria Grazia Gagliardi,
Donatella Perruccio Chiari

▲ Itineraries in Venice

Caterina Bonomi, Jean-Carlos
Carmigniani, Bruna Caruso, Barbara Di
Maio, Roberto Ellero, Andrea Fabiano,
Jean-Louis Fournel, Chiara Galli Rosso,
Donatella Petruccio Chiari, Giovanni
Roman, Sandra Stocchetto, Pascaline
Vatin Barbini, Sabina Vianello, Jean-
Claude Zancarini, Piero Zanotto

◆ Practical information

Cristina Giussani

EVERYMAN GUIDES

EVERYMAN GUIDES
Published by Everyman Publishers Plc

First published 1993
Further editions, revised and updated:
April 1994, July 1995, March 1999,
August 2000

© 2000 Everyman Publishing Plc

Originally published in France by
Nouveaux-Loisirs, a subsidiary of
Editions Gallimard, Paris, 1992
© 1992 Editions Nouveaux-Loisirs.

Venice – ISBN 1-84159-008-8

TRANSLATED BY
Anthony Roberts

EDITED AND TYPESET BY
Book Creation Services Ltd, London

VENICE
■ **EDITOR**
Laure Raffaëlli
assisted by Frédérique Jubien (Nature),
Corinne Paul
■ **GRAPHICS**
Elisabeth Cohat
■ **PHOTOGRAPHY**
Eric Guillemot, Patrick Léger
■ **MAPS**
Vincent Brunot
■ **ARCHTECTURE**
Bruno Lenormand
■ **ILLUSTRATIONS (Nature)**
Frédéric Bony
■ **PICTURE RESEARCH**
Marie Brandolini D'Adda, William Fischer
■ **LAYOUT**
Riccardo Tremori
■ **RESEARCH**
Gwenhaelle Le Roy

Stefano Barbieri, Jacopo Barovier,
Alberto Bianchi, Maria Raffaella
Caprioglio, Francesco Capuzzo, Giorgio
Ciriotto, Consorzio Venezia Nuova, Gisèle
D'Antony, Gianni De Checchi, Margherita
De Cunzo, Stefania De Marchi, Maddalena
Di Sopra, Ornella Fontanari, Francesca Galli
Aliverti, Donatella Gibbin, Irina Ivancich
Biaggini, Costanza Jori, Maria Teresa
Menotto, Isabelle Caterina Rossato, Marina
Tassinari, Muriel Toso and Ian Littlewood.

All rights reserved. No part of this publication may be reproduced, stored in a retrieval system or
transmitted, in any form or by any means, electronic, mechanical, photocopying, recording or
otherwise, without the prior written permission of the copyright owners.

Printed in Italy by Editoriale Lloyd

EVERYMAN GUIDES
Gloucester Mansions, 140a Shaftesbury Avenue,
London WC2H 8HD
www.everyman.uk.com / guides@everyman.uk.com

Encyclopedia section

The Venetians collected rainwater in deep cisterns dug in the campi of the city. This water was drawn from wells set into each cistern.

Shown here are the wells at San Martino (below) and the Doge's Palace (inset).

The *squeri* built and
maintained Venice's merchant
fleet. Few are left nowadays,
and they are devoted
exclusively to gondolas.
On the left is the former
squero San Nicola.

"The pleasant place
of all festivity,
The revel of the earth,
the masque of Italy."
Lord Byron

A view of the Doge's
Palace from the island
of San Giorgio Maggiore.

CALLE DIETRO
IL CAMPANILE

Needlepoint lacemaking
originated in Venice
during the 16th century
and became a speciality
of the island of Burano.
Today, lacemakers can still
be seen at work in Burano's
streets, sitting in front of
their brightly colored
houses.

Natural History

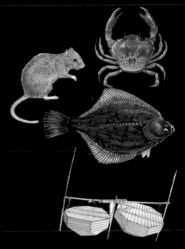

■ THE VENETIAN LAGOON

The Venetian Lagoon extends over 135,903 acres, 123,548 of which are water and 12,355 dry land.

About six thousand years ago, after the last Ice Age, rising water levels created the Venetian Lagoon. Located at the junction of the sea and the river currents of what was once the Po delta, this is a highly complex environment which is probably unique in the world, and includes a wide variety of highly active biological ecosystems. For five centuries now, humans have been working in order to balance their needs with the requirements of nature. The Lagoon is also surrounded by some thirty-one miles of remarkably well preserved coastline.

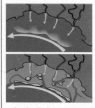

Sand carried down by the rivers and shaped by marine currents eventually formed bands along the coastline, which in due course locked the Lagoon in on itself. Work began in the 14th century to divert the principal rivers emptying into the zone and to block four rivermouths, in order to prevent the clogging of the estuaries. Today the Lagoon is linked to the open sea by just three *bocche di porto* (Lido, Malamocco and Chioggia).

As an area of extraordinary natural wealth, the Lagoon has been much affected by human intervention. Industrial zones and natural preserves now have to survive alongside each other.

The recently enlarged industrial complex of Porto di Marghera is one of the biggest in the Mediterranean, and scarcely a stone's throw from Venice.

The islands, pools and fish farming *valli* ■ *20* (39,535 acres), *barene*, *velme* ■ *19* and canals (96,368 acres) are home to many animal and plant species.

Mestre

Porto Marghera

Canale V. Emanuele III

Canale della Giudecca

La Giudecca

Canale d Malamocc Marghera

BACINO DI MALAMOCCO

BACINO DI CHIOGGIA

16

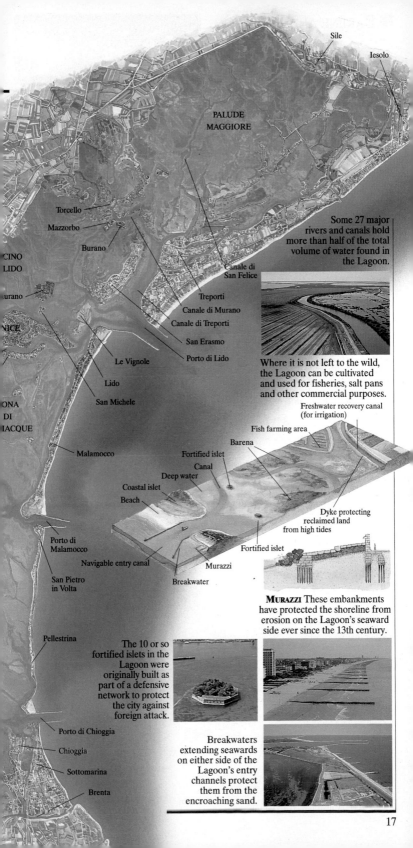

Sile

Iesolo

PALUDE
MAGGIORE

Some 27 major
rivers and canals hold
more than half of the total
volume of water found in
the Lagoon.

Torcello

Mazzorbo

Burano

Canale di
San Felice

Treporti

Canale di Murano

Canale di Treporti

San Erasmo

Porto di Lido

CINO
LIDO

urano

Le Vignole

NICE

Lido

San Michele

ONA
DI
ACQUE

Malamocco

Where it is not left to the wild,
the Lagoon can be cultivated
and used for fisheries, salt pans
and other commercial purposes.

Freshwater recovery canal
(for irrigation)

Fish farming area

Barena

Fortified islet

Canal

Deep water

Coastal islet

Beach

Dyke protecting
reclaimed land
from high tides

Fortified islet

Porto di
Malamocco

Navigable entry canal

Murazzi

San Pietro
in Volta

Breakwater

MURAZZI These embankments
have protected the shoreline from
erosion on the Lagoon's seaward
side ever since the 13th century.

Pellestrina

The 10 or so
fortified islets in the
Lagoon were
originally built as
part of a defensive
network to protect
the city against
foreign attack.

Porto di Chioggia

Chioggia

Sottomarina

Breakwaters
extending seawards
on either side of the
Lagoon's entry
channels protect
them from the
encroaching sand.

Brenta

■ BARENE AND RUSHES

LITTLE EGRET This small member of the heron family is a common sight in parts of the Lagoon where it searches for food.

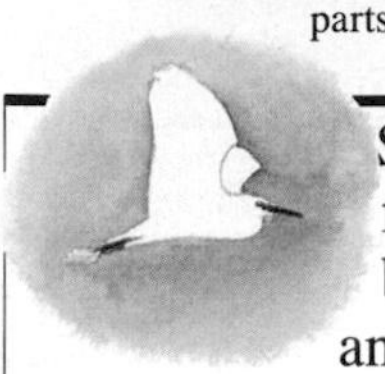

Sea and river currents meet and mingle in the former delta of the River Po, and the resulting brackish water covers the Venetian Lagoon to an average depth of about twenty inches. Clay and sand deposits carried in by both currents have gradually created raised banks called *barene* (salt-flats). These broad, wet expanses are the home to large numbers of water-loving plants and contain food for many species of bird. Near the river estuaries, where the water is less salty, thick rushes grow, providing shelter for much of the Lagoon's bird population.

MARSH HARRIER A tireless hunter of rodents in and around the rushes and *barene*.

BEARDED TIT It can often be seen and heard singing among the rushes.

BITTERN A species of heron that hunts mainly after dark.

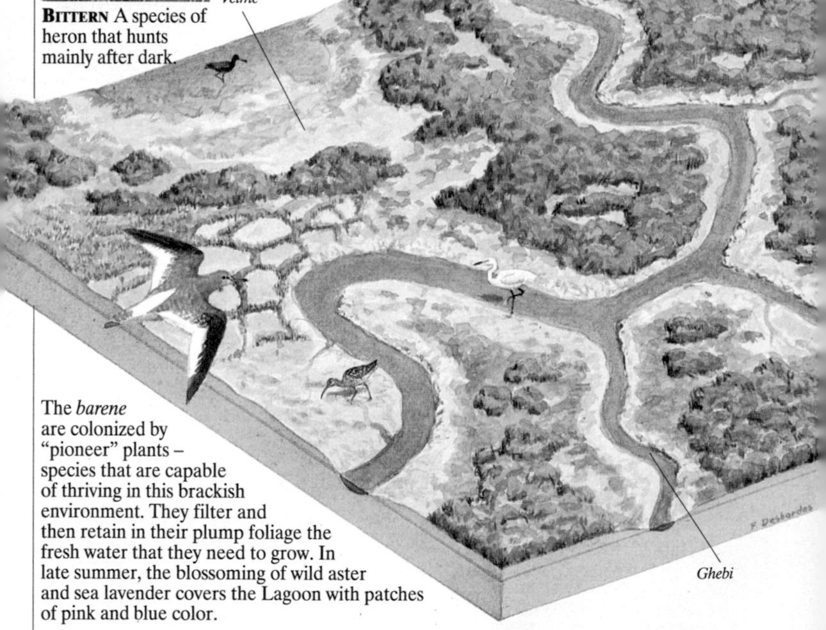

Velme

The *barene* are colonized by "pioneer" plants – species that are capable of thriving in this brackish environment. They filter and then retain in their plump foliage the fresh water that they need to grow. In late summer, the blossoming of wild aster and sea lavender covers the Lagoon with patches of pink and blue color.

Ghebi

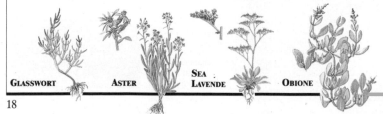

GLASSWORT   **ASTER**   **SEA LAVENDE**   **OBIONE**

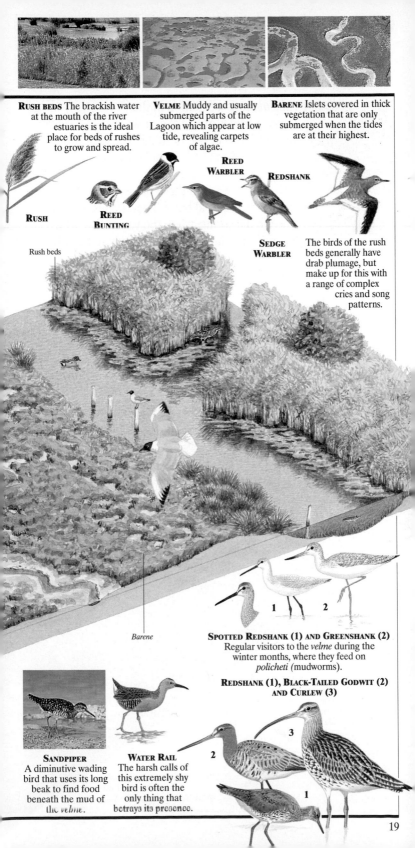

RUSH BEDS The brackish water at the mouth of the river estuaries is the ideal place for beds of rushes to grow and spread.

VELME Muddy and usually submerged parts of the Lagoon which appear at low tide, revealing carpets of algae.

BARENE Islets covered in thick vegetation that are only submerged when the tides are at their highest.

RUSH

REED BUNTING

REED WARBLER

REDSHANK

SEDGE WARBLER

The birds of the rush beds generally have drab plumage, but make up for this with a range of complex cries and song patterns.

Rush beds

Barene

SPOTTED REDSHANK (1) AND GREENSHANK (2)
Regular visitors to the *velme* during the winter months, where they feed on *policheti* (mudworms).

REDSHANK (1), BLACK-TAILED GODWIT (2) AND CURLEW (3)

SANDPIPER
A diminutive wading bird that uses its long beak to find food beneath the mud of the *velme*.

WATER RAIL
The harsh calls of this extremely shy bird is often the only thing that betrays its presence.

19

FISH FARMING

SPOONBILL

This distinctive bird is a common sight in the marshes and around the rush beds and banks of the Lagoon.

The *valli da pesca* cover 21,764 acres of the Lagoon, about a sixth of its total area.

Vallicultura is a tradition in the Lagoon, and is one of the most ancient forms of fish farming. The *valle*, which is entirely man-made, is a banked-up area which is linked to the open Lagoon by a series of channels. Fish locks located at these outlets allow the fish to enter on a seasonal basis. The catches then take place in the spring, when the young fish return to the gulf, and during the winter, when the adults move into the open water to reproduce or in search of warmer currents.

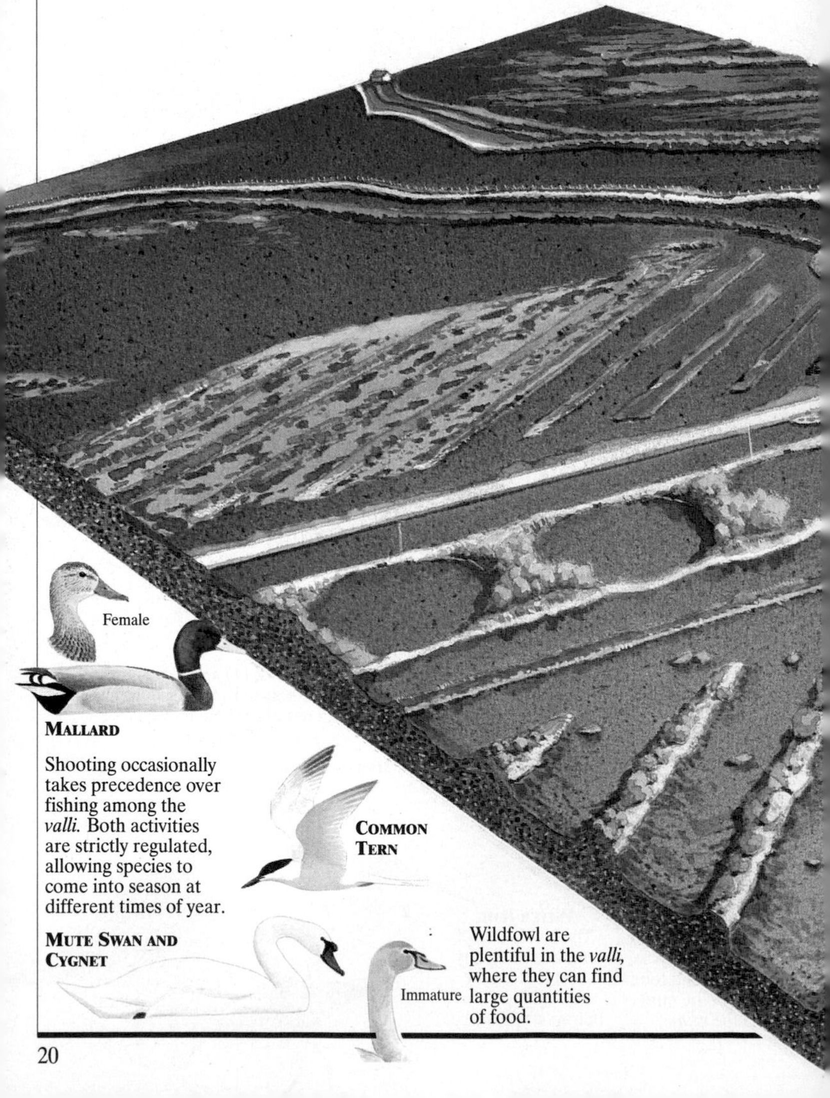

Female

MALLARD

Shooting occasionally takes precedence over fishing among the *valli*. Both activities are strictly regulated, allowing species to come into season at different times of year.

COMMON TERN

MUTE SWAN AND CYGNET

Immature

Wildfowl are plentiful in the *valli*, where they can find large quantities of food.

There are about twenty-four *valli* in the Lagoon, most of which are privately owned. They range in size from 250–750 acres.

1. Parts of the Lagoon in which fish move about freely.
2. Winter ponds and growing ponds.
3. and 4. Fish locks.
5. Sluices, which allow operators to control the water level in the *valle*.

Winter ponds enable the younger fish to survive during the colder months.

The *lavoriero,* or fish lock, is positioned at the neck of the channel linking the *valle* with the Lagoon. It usually consists of two successive dams, which are moveable. The first lock filters out vegetable flotsam, admitting fish only. The second works as a kind of antechamber, from which the fish are graded and directed into different ponds depending on their size.

Baicolere are ponds reserved for young sea bass.

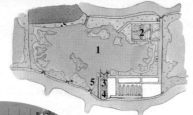

The water in the *valli* requires constant monitoring, with periodical dredging, lock maintenance and regulating of the environment.

FLOUNDER

The average *valle* produces 50 percent eel, 30 percent mullet, 10 percent sea bream, 5 percent sea bass, and 5 percent flounder and other species indigenous to the Lagoon.

■ THE FISH OF THE LAGOON

The sails and rigging of the *bragozzo* used by fishermen on the Lagoon have now been replaced by diesel motors.

The fish sold in the markets of Venice come mostly from the Adriatic Sea. Only a few species remain within the confines of the Lagoon during the summer months, notably eels and mullet. The latter move in shoals along the coastline and come into the Lagoon to feed on the animal and vegetable matter that is their major source of nourishment. The astonishing variety of fishing techniques and fishing vessels generated by Venice is the result of many centuries of experience in managing the Lagoon and its resources.

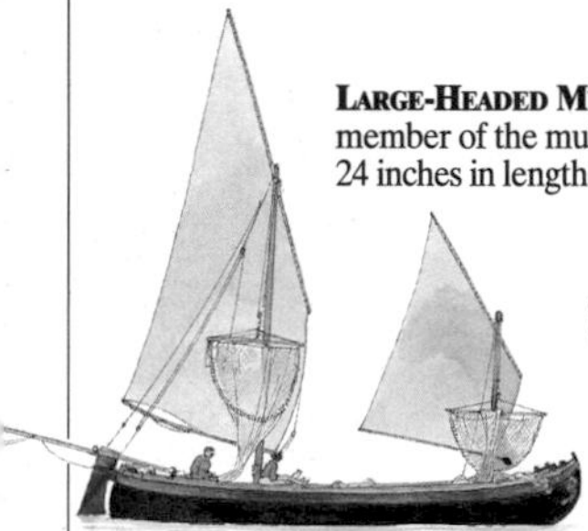

LARGE-HEADED MULLET This most prized member of the mullet family can grow to 24 inches in length

BRAGOZZO The fishing boat of the Lagoon's interior, equipped for harvesting scallops.

GOLDEN MULLET These fish swim into the Lagoon in the winter after reproducing at sea in the fall. They taste less good if caught near a port.

MUSSETTO The young sea mullet, bass and sea bream netted by these vessels are later released into the *valli*.

SQUILL An abundant Lagoon crustacean.

SARDINE AND ANCHOVY Frequently on the menus of Venetian restaurants, these coastal fish are usually netted in the northern Adriatic.

SOLE The fishermen of the Lagoon search for sole at night, attracting them with lamps and then netting or spearing them.

CUTTLEFISH The only member of the squid family found in the Lagoon – and then only if it does not rain, because if the salt content of the water is reduced they head for the open sea. The delicious Venetian dish *spaghetti al nero* is prepared with the ink of the cuttlefish.

SHRIMPS

On nights when the sirocco blows, the surface of the Lagoon glows with a phosphorescent light. At such times, the fish create luminous wakes in the water, making it easy for fishermen with square dipping nets to spot them.

Each species of fish found in the Lagoon is caught in a different manner. One method uses a stationary net, pegged upright with poles, which guides the fish into a central circular pocket net, where they are captured.

HOOP NET Spread at the bottom, the wings of the hoop net guide mullet, sea bass and eels into a pocket at its end.

SEA BASS The fish enters the Lagoon when very young and eventually grows to a length of between 12 and 30 inches.

VIERI
These wicker baskets (*vieri da barca*) hung along the sides of boats allow the Lagoon fishermen to catch crabs as they shed their shells. Crabs with new shells are tender and are something of a delicacy. The largest baskets (below) are known as *vieri da bisatti*.

SEA BREAM Present in the Lagoon from March to November, and caught using either rod and line or nets.

EEL
In the fall, shoals of baby eels move into the Lagoon in the form of translucent elvers. They remain there for between 6 and 12 years before going back to the sea to reproduce.

RED MULLET A sea fish, caught in the Lagoon during the fall.

RED GURNET Lives in open sea, but often caught near ports.

OYSTERS Either dredged from the bottom of the Lagoon, or pulled from the sand by men with rakes.

GREEN CRAB In winter, these crabs reproduce near the open sea, but re-enter the Lagoon with their young from February.

MUSSEL ROPES

MUSSELS
Attached to ropes suspended in the water, mussels are heavily cultivated in the Lagoon.

■ BOLLARDS AND BEACONS

This bollard shrine shows how much the water was an integral part of Venetian life.

The Lagoon of Venice and its maze of waterways would be totally impassable if the navigation channels were not marked out by beacons and bollards, known as *bricole*. These groups of pilings, which are found everywhere in the Lagoon, vary widely in color, shape and number, and follow a precise code of reference. They are much appreciated by the seabird population of this broad and otherwise unrelieved expanse of water. Similarly their submerged parts are home to thriving colonies of animal and vegetable life, with many mollusks and seaweed species sheltering around them.

BRICOLA Made of massive baulks for stability, the *bricole* mark the limits of navigable channels.

DAMA A *bricola* with a tall central baulk. Painted red or green, *dama* mark the entrance of a canal or a junction between two waterways.

Gengiva

PALINA Single pilings which are mostly used as mooring posts in Venice.

COLORED PALINE The colors signify that the *palina* belongs to a specific family.

BARNACLE

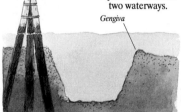

Pilings up to 20 feet long were driven into the Lagoon just behind the *gengiva*, or bank.

RED SEAWEED

ACTINIA The colonies of this star-patterned anemone are cloaked in a shiny gelatinous layer.

ATHERINE FISH This fish lives in sandy coastal areas, but reproduces in brackish water.

The numbers on the *bricole* allow them to be individually identified.

The *bricole* tend to rot quickly and so have to be replaced regularly.

GOBY A very common Lagoon fish, the goby spends the winter months in the mud at the bottom of the canal, where it lays its eggs.

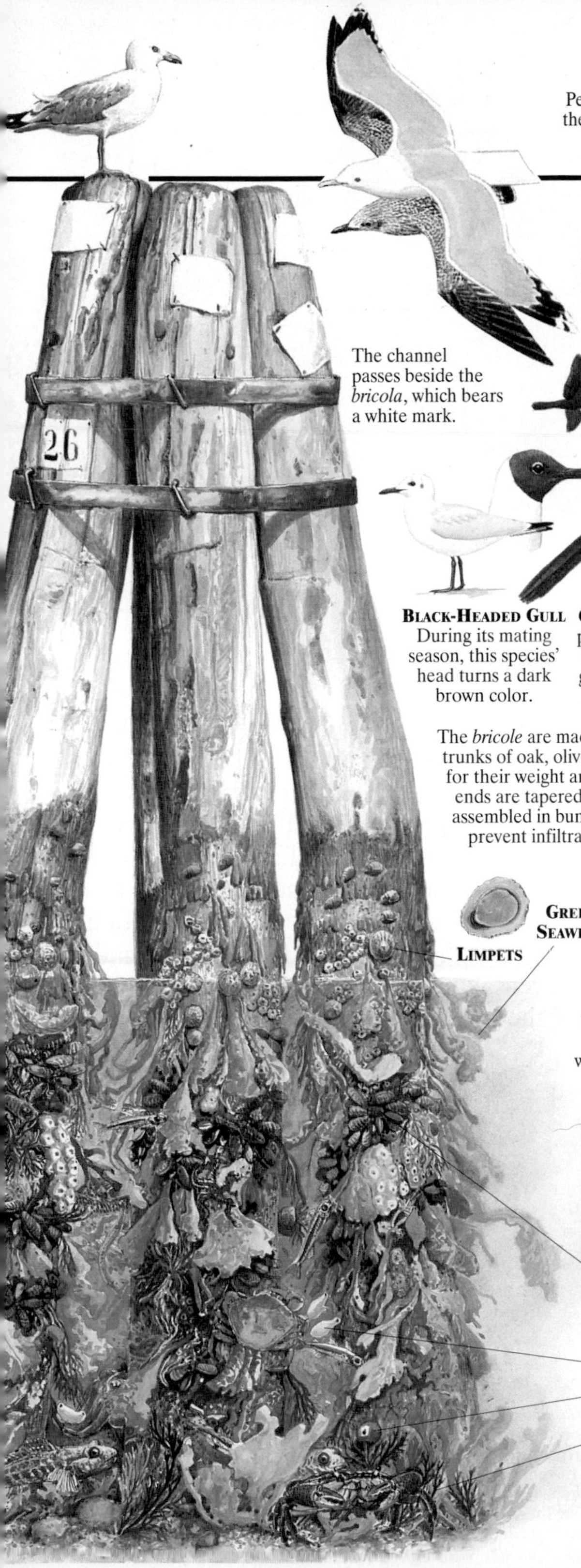

HERRING GULL
Perched on the *bricole,* the gulls patiently await the return of the fishing boats.

The channel passes beside the *bricola*, which bears a white mark.

26

BLACK-HEADED GULL
During its mating season, this species' head turns a dark brown color.

GREAT CORMORANT
A powerful hooked beak and swimming speed give the cormorant an advantage in fishing.

The *bricole* are made out of one or more trunks of oak, olive or chestnut, chosen for their weight and solidity. Their top ends are tapered so that they can be assembled in bunches, then tarred to prevent infiltration by rainwater.

GREEN SEAWEED

LIMPETS

ZOSTERA MARINA
This seaweed, which grows only in clean waters, is recolonizing the Lagoon.

MUSSEL A single mussel may filter as much as 13 gallons of water a day to feed.

ASCIDIAN

SEA ANEMONE

GREEN CRAB

25

Each year, mostly during the winter, Venice is flooded afresh by *acque alte* (high waters). These are exceptionally high tides which pour through the three entrances to the Lagoon and inundate the city. They result from a combination of various natural phenomena: high tides or a new moon, or low atmospheric pressure with a south wind and heavy rain. The level of the *acqua alta* is calculated from the average height of the water at low tide. With an *acqua alta* of three feet, St Mark's Square and parts of the city are under two to sixteen inches of water. Such serious inundations are becoming increasingly frequent. A major engineering program is currently under way to raise the level of the city by at least three feet above the water level at low tide.

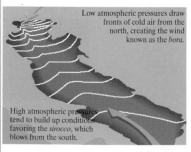

Low atmospheric pressures draw fronts of cold air from the north, creating the wind known as the *bora*.

High atmospheric pressures tend to build up conditions favoring the *sirocco*, which blows from the south.

Because it is a virtually closed sea, the Adriatic is as susceptible to tidal variations (the consequence of the moon's gravitational pull on the oceans) as to the variations of atmospheric pressure which generate high winds. The *sirocco*, a wind blowing out of Syria, pushes the Adriatic towards the Gulf of Venice. The *bora*, a wind from the Hungarian steppes, impedes the tide from flowing back out of the Lagoon. Between them, these two winds are responsible for raising waves more than 8 feet high, and when all these elements combine, an *acqua alta* is unleashed.

Rainwater run-off from St Mark's Square is channeled along a system of drains that flows directly into the Grand Canal. When the water rises in the Lagoon, this process is reversed.

Because the drains are all linked together, the water from the Grand Canal can pour up into the square.

Year by year, the frequency and dimensions of the *acque alte* have steadily increased. During the 1920's, high tides of about 3 feet (24 inches in St Mark's Square) occurred an average of once a year; today the phenomenon is often repeated up to 10 times annually. Among the 15 exceptional *acque alte* recorded since 1867, the worst was in November 1966; in that year St Mark's Square, the lowest point in Venice, found itself under more than 4 feet of water.

Since 1966 research has been carried out with a view to finding ways to protect Venice from flooding. The experimental

module known as MOSE has been set aside for financial reasons, and research into other ways of tackling the problem is under way. If MOSE had been given the go-ahead, the ebb and flow of the tide through the three entry points into the Lagoon would

The compacting of the subsoil (by 10 inches in 24 years) is now a common feature in the oldest quarters of the city – which are also the richest areas from an architectural point of view. Since less water has been taken from beneath the city, to serve the needs of the industrial complex of Porto di Marghera ■ *16*, subsidence has been reduced. The rise in the level of the Adriatic Sea and its seasonal high tides still pose a threat, however.

THE MOSE PROJECT
Here the floodgates are shown in the closed position, preventing the water from entering the Lagoon. When open and regulating the currents back and forth, the floodgates will be completely submerged.

have been controlled by mechanically operated sea-locks Floodgates like the one above would protect the waterways of the Lido, Malamocco and Chioggia.

THE FLORA AND FAUNA OF VENICE

The seaweed on the *bricole* attracts small insects, which are much appreciated by Venetian sparrows.

The labyrinth of Venice's canals, which brings the sea into the very heart of the city, is its most original feature. Green crabs, shrimps, mollusks and several species of fish survive in this brackish environment, adjusting to the rise and fall of the tides. On the surface, between the paving stones of the calli and the stones in the walls, the observant walker can find many different plants that have adapted to this unusual milieu; likewise, the bird population, which thrives in the city's old quarters and hidden gardens.

So large is the city's population of stray cats that an international adoption center for Venetian cats has been set up.

SWIFT
They nest under the eaves of houses.

BLACKBIRD (MALE)

SWALLOW
Mostly to be found on the smaller islands of the Lagoon.

CRYSTHE MARINE
Normally found on sea cliffs, this little plant also grows in the chinks of masonry along the sides of the canals.

FERAL PIGEON
Present in huge flocks not just in St Mark's Square but all over the city.

GREAT TIT

HOUSE SPARROW In contrast to the sparrows of Northern Europe, the race found south of the Alps has a brown head.

The layers of algae and micro-organisms which can be seen along the sides of the canals subject to tidal fluctuations (those in the intertidal zone) testify to one of the richest theaters of biological activity in the Mediterranean.

BROWN RAT
or Sewer Rat.

High water.

Low water.

Alternate layers of sand and clay, topped with a mixture of the two (1000m).

Layer of closely packed clay, or *caranto*.

Superficial layer, mostly detritus.

History

HISTORY OF VENICE

6TH – 10TH CENTURIES   THE FOUNDING OF VENICE

306–37
Reign of Constantine.

330
Transfer of the capital of the Roman Empire to Constantinople.

401
Start of the barbarian invasions.

493–553
The Ostrogoth kings rule in Northern Italy.

554
Justinian, the Byzantine Emperor, restores imperial authority on the peninsula with Ravenna as capital.

The Realtine Islands.

THE ORIGINS. In the 1st century BC, the name *Venetia* designated an administrative region within the Roman Empire, including the present Veneto, Friuli and Trentino areas. In 568 the Lombards encroached from the north and between the 6th and 7th centuries the population of the Veneto (by now a province of Byzantium) was pushed back to the coast and the islands. Conventional wisdom has it that Venice was founded by these forced migrants, but some now think it was already a flourishing Roman port well before then. No one knows for sure.

TOWARDS POLITICAL AUTONOMY. In the 7th century, the Christian patriarch resided at Grado and the Byzantine administration at Heracleia; the latter subsequently moved to Malamocco. Those inhabiting the Lagoon began to elect their own governors, though the links with Byzantium were still close and the Byzantine fleet defended them when the Franks invaded in 810. A pact was made with the Franks and the Lagoon was confirmed as part of the Byzantine Empire.

THE BIRTH OF A STATE. At the same time, the elected governor – or Doge, from the Latin *dux*, or leader – left Malamocco for Rivoaltus in the heart of the Lagoon. In 827 the archipelago came under the religious authority of Aquileia, and found itself again threatened with Frankish domination. Two merchants stole the relics of St Mark the Evangelist and brought them to the Lagoon in 828. Invigorated by this psychological coup, the Realtine Islands achieved religious independence from Grado and established political autonomy. St Mark's emblem, the lion, became the symbol of the new state, and the first stable forms of government were put in place. By the 10th century, the city of Venice had emerged.

11TH – 14TH CENTURIES   A MEDITERRANEAN POWER

727–8
Revolt against Byzantium in Italy.

751
The Lombards occupy Ravenna.

800
Charlemagne is crowned Emperor in Rome.

936
Otho I is crowned Emperor. Italy is assimilated with Germany.

POLITICAL AND ECONOMIC GROWTH. Venice was soon dealing with its former Byzantine masters on equal terms. In return for her financial and military support in the struggle against Islam and the Normans, Venice received commercial advantages in the Byzantine-controlled Orient. Her influence soon spread along the Dalmatian coast, and her war galleys dominated the Adriatic. Like other maritime republics, such as Genoa and Pisa, Venice took advantage of the crusades by supplying ships, food and money to the Christian forces, and opening commercial exchanges around the Mediterranean. By the 12th century, the city's rulers were powerful enough to act as mediators between Pope Alexander III and Emperor Frederick I Barbarossa, who signed

In 828, two merchants from Torcello stole the body of St Mark the Evangelist in Alexandria and brought it home. St Mark became the patron saint of Venice.

a peace treaty in Venice in 1177. In 1204 the Doge Enrico Dandolo took advantage of Constantinople's growing weakness to demand the soldiers of the Fourth Crusade pay for their Venetian transportation by laying siege to the capital of the Eastern Empire. Constantinople fell and another empire was installed, of which the Venetians took the lion's share. But Genoa, envious of the success of its rival, formed an alliance with the deposed Byzantine emperors and reconquered the Eastern Empire in 1261. The Venetians lost a portion of their territory and most of their commercial privileges. After a truce lasting from 1270–90, the struggle with Genoa resumed until 1299, when a fresh peace was concluded. Despite the defeat of the Venetians at the Battle of Curzola in 1298, neither of the adversaries gained a decisive advantage.

THE DEVELOPMENT OF INSTITUTIONS. Meanwhile, economic expansion had modified the social structure of the city. A wave of newly rich families were eager to take their place in government alongside older patrician clans. The quasi-monarchical authority of the Doge was also becoming irksome at a time when free cities were prospering elsewhere in Italy. Councils of "Sages" were set up between 1130 and 1148 to curb the Doge's powers, and in 1172 a committee was formed to monitor his election. But Venice's incessant warfare with Genoa and Constantinople made domestic unity a strong priority, and this probably explains the famous measure of 1297 to "close" the Grand Council, after which only members of families inscribed in the Golden Book (containing the record of births and marriages of the Venetian nobility) could be admitted ● 231. In this way Venice endowed herself with a tightly knit political class, with powerful bodies like the Council of Ten (established in 1310) to complement it.

A DIFFICULT 14TH CENTURY. Venice lost half her population to the Black Death of 1348. A serious economic crisis followed, and Ludwig I of Hungary seized the opportunity to annexe Dalmatia from Venice. At the same time the rulers of Padua and Ferrara, and especially the powerful Viscontis of Milan, began to threaten Venetian interests. The ancestral struggle with Genoa, which had allied itself with Florence, Padua and Hungary, intensified from 1378 onwards.

A THREAT TO SURVIVAL. In 1379, the Genoese fleet penetrated the Lagoon and seized Chioggia, but the Venetian forces made a desperate counterattack which enabled them to conclude a peace at Turin in 1381 and save the situation. The treaty strongly favored Venice's enemies; but Genoa, exhausted by the conflict and wracked by domestic strife, never again posed a serious threat to the Venetians.

EARLY 11TH CENTURY
First Norman invaders appear in Southern Italy and are defeated by the Venetians.

1054
Schism in the East.

c.1080
The principal cities of Northern and Central Italy win their independence: the comuni.

1075
The Turks conquer Jerusalem.

1096–9
The First Crusade.

1154–83
Wars between Barbarossa and the comuni. Treaty of Constantinople in which the freedoms of the comuni are confirmed.

1309–77
The papacy is transferred to Avignon.

15TH CENTURY THE HEIGHT OF VENETIAN POWER

Corfu, a Venetian
possession.

1385–1437
*Hapsburg expansion
into Northern Italy.*

1414–18
*End of the Great
Schism.*

1434
*The Medicis assume
control in Florence.*

1453
*Constantinople falls to
the Ottomans and
becomes Istanbul.*

1488
*Bartolomeo Diaz
reaches the Cape of
Good Hope.*

1492
*Christopher Colombus
discovers America.*

1494
*Charles VIII sets out
to conquer the
kingdom of Naples:
the start of the Italian
Wars.*

The Venetian
conquests.

1494–8
*Piero de Medici leaves
Florence. The
establishment of
Savonarola's
republican government.*

THE DEFENCE OF THE LEVANT.

Venice steadily extended her Mediterranean Empire. Taking advantage of the Genoese decline, she once again took control of the Adriatic, which for many centuries thereafter became known as the Gulf of Venice. Corfu fell in 1386, the Albanian coast submitted a few years later and Dalmatia was finally reconquered between 1409 and 1420. But now another threat was looming in the shape of the Ottoman Empire. The Turkish fleet had been defeated in 1407, but went on to victory in a battle of 1429. The Turkish army captured Constantinople in 1453, advanced into the Balkans, and seized Negroponte (Euboea) from Venice in 1470.

Nevertheless the Republic not only maintained but also strengthened its positions in the eastern Mediterranean, extending its domination to Cyprus in 1489, although fresh defeats by the Turks were in store between 1499 and 1503. In the late 15th century expansionism and the safeguarding of one's own interests could be justified as the defence of Christianity.

THE CONQUEST OF THE MAINLAND.

At the close of the 14th century, Venice formed an alliance with Florence to counter the expansionist politics of the Viscontis in Northern Italy. It was important to keep her powerful Milanese neighbors in their place if Venice was to control the trade routes into Northern Europe and protect the assets of the wealthy Venetian families which had invested in mainland property. But to do so meant she was obliged to abandon her isolation. Although Treviso and the surrounding countryside had been overrun in 1339, Venice's first real effort to extend her authority deep into mainland Italy did not begin until 1404. Within twenty years she had annexed Padua, Vicenza, Verona, Belluna, Feltre and all of Friuli. The Venetian government now divided its activities into two spheres: the *stato da mar* (the colonial sea-state) and the *stato da terra* (the land-state). Venice's advance along the Po valley resumed in 1425–6, and before long the Republic's boundaries had reached the banks of the river Adda, a state of affairs officially sanctioned in 1454 by the Treaty of Lodi. War with Ferrara (1481–4) led to yet another attempt at expansion, which failed in the face of combined resistance from Florence, Milan and Naples. By now, the Italian powers were profoundly suspicious of Venetian ambitions to upset the balance of power and dominate the peninsula: the threat from Milan was forgotten.

Recruitment of sailors for the Venetian fleet.

THE ITALIAN WARS. Taking advantage of the confusion created by the French invasion of Italy in 1494, Venice attempted to seize control of the ports of Apulia and to annexe Pisa, which had risen in revolt against Florence. After this the Republic sought to overrun papal Romagna, and this was the last straw. At Cambrai in 1508 the monarchs of Europe and the Italian city-states formed an alliance against Venice under the aegis of Pope Julius II. The army of the Republic was routed at Agnadello on May 14, 1509; part of Venice's mainland empire was occupied by French and Imperial forces, and the rest rose in revolt. For a few weeks, the fall of the Venetian state appeared inevitable.

16TH – 17TH CENTURIES   A FORCED NEUTRALITY

THE TURNING OF THE TIDE. Thanks to the support of Pope Julius II, who switched alliances as soon as the Papacy was assured of retaining Romagna, Venice was able to take advantage of the rivalries between her Imperial, French and Spanish enemies. By playing off Francis I of France and the Emperor Charles V against each other, within ten years she contrived to regain and consolidate all her lost possessions, relinquishing only Cremona and the Venetian claim to the ports of Apulia.

Pope Julius II.

VENETIAN NEUTRALITY. After this episode, Venice opted for armed neutrality. Over the next two centuries she remained a force to be reckoned with but never again took sides in the quarrels of the great European monarchies.

THE GOLDEN AGE. After Florence and Rome, the Venice of Titian, Tintoretto and Veronese became the third great center of the Italian Renaissance, while the stability of her institutions became a byword in Europe.

RETREAT FROM THE MEDITERRANEAN. The state of Venice's maritime empire was less promising. From the beginning of the 16th century, the islands of the Aegean had been falling into the hands of the Turks. The fruit of a Venetian alliance with Spain and Rome, the victory of Lepanto on October 7, 1571, had no lasting effect and Cyprus was effectively lost. Corsairs on the Bosnian and Dalmatian coasts harried Venetian shipping on the Adriatic, and the

city's resources were steadily depleted by the wars. The government ran deep into debt and had to impose heavy taxes on the economy.

1517
Martin Luther proclaims his reforms.

1519
Charles V is crowned Holy Roman Emperor.

1525
Francis I is defeated at Pavia.

1527
Sack of Rome by the imperial troops.

1530
Venice refuses to acknowledge the dominion of Charles V.

1545
The Council of Trent. Start of the Counter Reformation.

1556
Abdication of Charles V. Italy ceded to Spain.

1559
Treaty of Cateau-Cambrésis: France renounces all claim to Italy.

33

Daniele Manin, leader
of the Venetian
uprising in 1848.

1618–48
*The Thirty Years' War
between the great
European powers.*

Right, a Venetian
plague doctor.

1702–12
*War of the Spanish
Succession between
France and a coalition
of European powers.*

THE START OF A DECLINE. An economic crisis beginning in 1620 followed by the great plague of 1630 heralded the start of an irreversible decline. Europe's commercial focus shifted to the North Sea, the volume of shipping in Venice dropped, and the city's luxury industries began to suffer from French competition. In the 17th century Venice's attempts to influence European politics met with failure, though for a while she held her own against Ottoman encroachment in the East. Her loss of Crete (1645–69) was balanced by the reconquest of Morea and Athens at the end of the century; but both fell back into Turkish hands between 1714 and 1718.

18TH CENTURY   THE DEATH OF THE REPUBLIC

1706–7
*French setbacks in
Italy. Austria conquers
Milan and the
kingdom of Naples.*

1776
*Independence of the
United States.*

1789
*The French
Revolution.*

CRISIS OF CONFIDENCE. The ruinous conflict with the Turks had, on several occasions, obliged the Venetian ruling class to open its ranks to newly enriched families, in exchange for lump payments to the state. However the number of candidates for this honor fell sharply during the course of the 18th century – a sign that confidence was eroding. In fact, the social and political fabric of Venice was in crisis, and the tentative reforms of the second half of the century came too late. Almost inevitably, the Republic was swept away in the turmoil of the Napoleonic Wars.

VENICE, BONAPARTE'S PLAYTHING. Venice's decision in 1793 to adopt a policy of "unarmed neutrality" was such an admission of weakness that in 1796 Napoleon Bonaparte marched into the Veneto, ostensibly to fight the Austrians. In April 1797 he "ceded" part of Venice's territory to the Hapsburgs and then, on May 1, 1797, he declared war on Venice herself. Before long French forces were picketed before the Doge's Palace and Bonaparte was offering peace on his own conditions – with the proviso that the Venetians "reform" their government,

1802
*Napoleon Bonaparte
becomes president of
the Italian Republic.*

which they hurriedly did on May 12. At the subsequent Treaty of Campo Formio, the French abandoned Venice to Austria, whose armies entered the city on January 18, 1798.

19TH CENTURY   FROM AUSTRIA TO ITALY

1804–5
*Napoleon is crowned
Emperor and King of
Italy.*

FOREIGN DOMINATION. Venice was reconquered by French troops in January 1806; the French were driven out again by the Austrians in April 1814. The creation of a free port provided only temporary relief from the city's inexorable decline between 1830 and 1848. An insurrection led by Daniele Manin and Nicolò Tommaseo on May 22, 1848, temporarily expelled

Garibaldi
in Venice.

the Austrians, who responded in 1849 by
laying siege to the city. On August 24,
the provisional government fell,
and the Austrians, returning for
the third time, punished Venice by
stripping her of administrative
authority over the Veneto. Over
the next two decades, Austria
governed the city with
increasing severity.

VENICE REVERTS TO ITALY.

Venice was finally absorbed by
the new Italian monarchy in
1866, when the king received
Venice and the Veneto after the
Austrian defeat at Sadowa, in return for
his support of Prussia.

VENICE IN THE 20TH CENTURY

Venice's spendid isolation was broken by
the construction of a railway bridge (in
1846) and a road bridge (in 1932)
linking the city with the mainland.
Between the end of the 19th century and
the start of the First World War, several attempts
were made to stimulate the Venetian economy by developing
the port, the industrial zone at Mestre and the seaside resort
of the Lido, in addition to the creation of cultural events
such as the Biennale. Between the wars, Venice's trading
economy, centered around the port of Marghera, remained
buoyant. But following the Second World War the attempt to
turn Venice into a modern center, like its neighbors in
Northern Italy, ended in failure. There were numerous
problems; the city's economy was forced to rely on ancillary
activities, and the price of living space became prohibitively
high. The population also
dwindled and aged; the steady
flow of migrants to Mestre and
Marghera turned into a flood. At
the same time the ecological
balance of the Lagoon was
damaged and the phenomenon
of the *acqua alta* attained
disturbing dimensions. The city's
architectural heritage began to
deteriorate rapidly under the
combined assaults of pollution
and heavy canal traffic. Finally,
the plight of Venice began to attract world attention, and in
1973 a special law was passed by the Italian government
which allowed the provision of billions of lire in subsidies.
Nonetheless the fundamental question still remains the
same: should we allow this city, home to 68,000 inhabitants,
to become no more than a huge museum? Should we let
Venice die, or should we make the necessary radical changes
in one of the few great capitals of the past to have survived
the 20th century miraculously intact?

1814–15
*Fall of Napoleon and
restoration of the old
regimes in Italy.*

1831
*Several Italian cities
rebel and Austrian
forces intervene.*

1846–7
*Economic crisis and
famine in Europe.*

1848
*Revolution spreads
throughout Europe.
The first Italian War of
Independence ends
with an Austrian
victory.*

1859
*The second Italian
War of Independence
ends with victory
for the Piedmontese.*

1861
*Proclamation of the
Kingdom of Italy.*

1870
*Rome becomes the
capital of Italy.*

1896–1911
*Conquest of Abyssinia
and Libya by the
Italians.*

1915
*Italy enters the
Second World War
on the side of the
Allies.*

1922
*The march on Rome
and the establishment
of a Fascist regime in
Italy.*

1933
*Hitler seizes power in
Germany.*

1945
*Uprising in Northern
Italy against the
Germans and the
Fascists.*

1946
*Proclamation of the
First Italian Republic.*

35

THE BATTLE OF LEPANTO

In 1570 the Turks attacked Cyprus, a Venetian possession. Christian forces, galvanized by the spirit of the Counter Reformation, responded by forming the Holy League (Venice, Spain and the Papacy) to repel the invader. On October 7, 1571, the Christian fleet engaged the Ottomans off the port of Lepanto on the south-west Hellenic coast. In one of the greatest battles fought in the Mediterranean, the Christian forces crushed an enemy undefeated since 1538.

PHILIP II
On May 19, 1571, the King of Spain, Philip II, joined the Holy League to "bring ruin and destruction upon the Turk", committing his country to fight alongside Venice, Genoa and the Papacy. Philip's brother, Don Juan of Austria, who was a natural son of Charles V, was named commander-in-chief of the allied fleet.

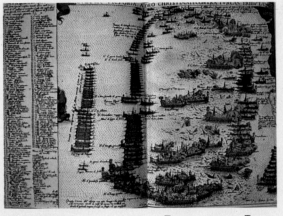

THE DEFEAT OF THE TURKS
The Turkish admiral Ali Pasha underestimated the Christian strength and, against the advice of his squadron commanders, ordered his fleet to leave Lepanto. In the ensuing battle thirty thousand Turks were killed or captured, nine thousand died on the Christian side, and many were wounded, including the Spaniard Miguel de Cervantes, author of *Don Quixote*.

Figures of Moors (in fact, these represent Turkish prisoners in chains) adorning the Morosini galley: after the Battle of Lepanto, it became customary for prisoners to row the galleys of Venice.

LA MERAVIGLIOSA ET IN VITORIA DATA, DA DIO A CHRISTIANI CONTRA TVRCHI ALLI SCOGLI CVRZOLARI L ANO 1571 A 170 O

THE OPPOSING FLEETS

Against the Turks' 230 galleys and 60 galliots, the Christians had only 214 warships, more than half of which came from the Arsenal at Venice. The Christian firepower, however, was vastly superior. To avoid encirclement, the Christian right flank had to spread itself thinly; fortunately the brunt of the action was borne by Don Juan's squadron in the center.

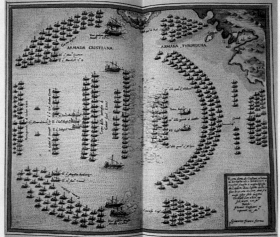

The round ships ▲ *178*, remained in the rearguard while six Venetian galeasses ▲ *180* led the van; these were the only cannon-equipped heavy vessels to be present at the Battle of Lepanto.

THE OTTOMAN SULTAN SELIM II (1524–74)

Selim's attempt to annexe Cyprus in 1570 provoked a Christian retaliation.

PIUS V, INSTIGATOR OF THE LEAGUE

Determined to roll back both the Turkish and Protestant threat to the Roman Church, Pope Pius V moved heaven and earth to form his Holy League. Every soldier who fought under Don Juan's banner of Christ was absolved of all sin by the Pope's special dispensation.

● THE BUCINTORO

The name of "Bucintoro" is probably derived from *bucio*, which was a type of boat used in medieval times: hence *bucio in t'oro* (gilded *bucio*). This Doge's galley was a spectacular symbol of the Serene Republic. It was launched for state visits and other official ceremonies, such as the Doge's marriage with the sea, which took place on Ascension Day. This feast apparently commemorated a 10th-century expedition that was led by the Doge Orseolo II, and which delivered Dalmatia and Istria from the grasp of Slavic pirates and transformed the Adriatic into a Venetian gulf.

THE "OSELLE"
When the last Bucintoro was built at the Arsenal in 1729, the Republic struck an *osella*, or medal. One side of it showed the Doge on his knees before St Mark, the city's patron saint, and the other a picture of the Bucintoro.

THE DOGE'S CORTÈGE
As soon as the ceremony was over, the cortège was reorganized for the procession back from the Lido. Directly astern of the Bucintoro were the most elaborate vessels, belonging to prominent individuals; then came everyone else. Those who had been present at the ceremony joined in the festivities that followed as open-air banquets and parties were held on the islands along the route of the procession.

IMPORTANT VISITORS
The Bucintoro was customarily placed at the disposal of state visitors to Venice. On July 15, 1574, Henry of Valois formally entered Venice aboard the Bucintoro, which carried him up the Grand Canal to the lodgings that had been prepared for him by the Seignory at the Ca' Foscari ▲ *331*.

In 1311, the Senate decreed the construction of a triumphal vessel which would be capable of carrying up to 200 men. The only evidence of how these different Bucintori looked is to be found in engravings, paintings and models; no other trace of them remains. The last Bucintoro was gutted by Napoleon's soldiers in 1798, before being finally scrapped in 1824. Opposite, the prow of a scale model, with the traditional effigy of Justice.

> "It is a kind of galley, covered and gilded. [...] The inside of it is a single, broad cabin, floored with wood, with divans all around and a throne at one end for the Doge."
>
> Charles de Brosses

THE CEREMONY OF THE DOGE'S "MARRIAGE"

Dressed in gold and ermine and wearing his *corno* hat, the Doge was carried by the Bucintoro to the port of San Nicolò di Lido, where he was awaited by the patriarch of San Pietro. He was then "married" to the sea. Throwing a ring into the water, he uttered the words: "We marry you, oh sea, in token of our true and perpetual possession", and invoked God's protection for all who worked on the water.

THE NUPTIAL RING

Legend says the ring was given to the Doge by a fisherman, who himself received it from St Mark. The chronicles record it was the gift of Pope Alexander III to acknowledge the Republic's control of the Adriatic.

SCALE MODEL OF THE LAST BUCINTORO

This model is preserved at the Naval Museum.

It was built by a worker at the Arsenal on the request of a vice-admiral of the Venetian navy, the Marquis Amilcare Paolucci delle Roncole.

39

FRANᶜᵒ MOROSᶦ CAPᶦ GᴺᴬLᴱ CON POCHE GALᴱ E QUATRO NAVI DA LA FUGA A 17 NAVI TURCHEᔆ DA GUERRA, NE FA ROMPERE, E NAUFRAGARE DUE, E NE PRENDE UNA CARICA DI MILIZIE. TERMINA COSÌ LA CARICAᔆ CAPᶦ GᴺᴬLᴱ LA PRIMA VOLTA, E SE NE RITORNA A VENEZIA DOPO ESSERV STATO LONTANO CON L'ARMA IN MANO LO SPAZIO DI 23 ANNI CONTINUI, SENZA MAI RIVEᔆ AE PATRIA NE PUR PER MOᶦ FᴺIL E SUBITO ANZI VIENE SPEDITO PROVᵉᵈ GᴺᴬLᴱ STRAORDᴺ IN FRᵖ PER UNA TENUTA IRRUCIONᵉ ROᴹ IN QUELLA PROVINCIA MAGGIO 1661

FRANᶜᵒ MOROᔆ STATO VICE CAPᶦ DELLE NAVI POI CAPᶦ IN GOLFO E, E ELETTO DOPO CAPᶦ DELLE GALᵉᵉ NELLE ACQUE DI PARISI, E DI NIXIA, OVE SI INCONTRANO LE DUE ARMATE, BENCHE LA TURCA SUPᵉᴿᶦᵒᶦ DEL DOPPIO, DISFA LA GALERA DEL CAPᶦ BASSA, CHE RESTA SOTTOMESSA ROMPE EL ACQUᶦᔆ VNᵉ MAGNA ABBORDA PER VLTIMO CON LA SUA GALEAZZA LA NAVE CAPITANA DI COSTANTINOPOLI GUVERNᵉ DI PIV DI 70 CANNONI, E DOPPO VN SANGUINOSO CONTRASTO LA SOTTOMETTE, FATTO GRAN NUMᵉᵗᵒ DI SCHIAVI, E PRESO VIVO IL CAPO SUPREMO DELL'ARMATA GROSSA NEMICA, DETTO NICOLO Uᶦ NADALINO, FURLANO RINEGATO FAMOSO, CHE SI CHIAMAVA MUSTAFA BASSA QUALᶦ MUORE NELLE CARCᵉᵉᶦ DELLA DOMINANTE. LUGLIO 1651

FRANᶜᵒ MOROᔆ CAPᴺ GᴺᴬLᴱ INSEGUISCE L'ARMATA TURCA, CHE FUGGE SEBENE PIV NUMEROSA ASSAI DELLA VENETA, ARRIVA DUE DELLE PIV GROSSE GALERE, E LE PRENDE. APRILE 1689.

Francesco Morosini (1619–94) was one of the last great admirals of the Venetian Republic. His many naval expeditions were recorded in a series of paintings of the late 17th century, which are now displayed in the Correr Museum (the Morosini Rooms, first floor). His glorious victories and his reconquest of the Peloponnese earned him the title of Doge in 1688.

FRANC. MOROS. K. PROC. E CAP. GNALE ACQVISTA NAVARIN VECCHIO CHE VNA VOLTA DICEVASI IL ZONCHIO FORTEZZA NELA MOREA. E VI PRENDE MONI. DI OGNI GENERE E CANONI DI GRAN NVMERO GIVGNO 1686

FRANC. MOROS SOPRACOMITO NEL PRIMO COMBATTIM MARITIMO NELLA GVERRA DI CANDIA VA PRIMO DI TVTTI AD ASSALTARE LA PIV GRANDE DELLE NAVI TVRCHE NELL ACQVE DI MILO, PER CORRISPONDERE ALL'IMPEGNO PRESO NEL MOTO DA LVI FATTO SCRIVERE SOTTO L'INSEGNA DELLA SVA GALERA, QVALE DICEVA IN CERTAMINE PRIMA. VNA GRANDE BORASCA SEPARA LA BATTAGLIA, CHE CONTINVO MOLTO, E SANGVINOSA OTTOBRE 1645.

FRANCESCO MOROSINI CAP. GNALE ESPVGNA CISME FORTEZZA POSTA IN TERRA FERMA DI RINCONTRO A SCIO, FACENDO CON STRATAGEMA VSCIRE IL PRESIDIO TVRCO DALLA PIAZZA QVALE PERCIO NON POTENDO PIV DIFENDERSI, CEDE. VI ACQVISTA MONIZIONI, BOTTINO CONSIDERABILE, CANNONI DI PIV GENERE IN COPIA. GIVGNO 1689.

● THE VENETIAN DIALECT

**GOLDSMITHS'
EMBLEM**
The goldsmiths (*oresi*
in Venetian) gave
their name to a street
in the Rialto where
their shops were
concentrated ▲ *283*.

PANTALOON
The Venetians owed
their nickname of
pantaloni to a local
saint, St Pantaloon.
This name is also
applied to one of the
masked figures in the
Commedia dell'Arte,
who wears short
trousers, hence the
French name for
trousers,
pantalon.

In the Middle Ages, Italy was divided into
a multitude of states, giving rise to an
enormous diversity of dialects.
With Latin as a common
denominator, the various regions
developed different modes of speech
according to the commercial contacts and
foreign influences to which they were
exposed. Thus the Venetian dialect, which
was used in official documents and for the
composition of literary works, quickly gained
the status of an official language spoken in the
Republic's various colonies. Furthermore Venice
was among the first Italian centers to evolve
family names (from the 11th century). This
system, with characteristic phonetic structures,
was unique in Italy and was universally
respected until the fall of the Republic.

PROPER NAMES

There are many odd features about Venetian
names. Some derive from local distortions of
Italian names, which were then adopted by the Italian
language. Hence Alvise (for Luigi or Ludovico), Tomà (for
Tommaso) and Anzolo (for Angelo). In other cases, a proper
name has served to describe a type of person and has
subsequently been transformed into a common name.
Hence Zani, the Venetian form of Gianni/Giovanni;
In the Commedia dell'Arte this name applied to the
characters of Harlequin and Brighella ▲ *291*.

PLACE NAMES

Apart from a few *vie* driven through the city in the
19th century and given ubiquitous titles like Via
Garibaldi, the streets of Venice mostly have
extremely old and curious names. Some, which hark
back to bygone professions and crafts, occur frequently:
for example, the Calli del Pestrin (milksellers), del Pistor
(bakers), del Frutarol (fruit and vegetable merchants).
Others refer to the original geographical divisions between
various specialized economic activities. Thus the
Fondamenta degli Ormesini of Cannaregio probably owes its
name to the presence of workshops specializing in fabrics
from Hormuz in the Persian Gulf, or perhaps even from the
furs with which the hats of nobles were edged. In the St
Mark's–Rialto zone we find the Frezzerie (arrowsmiths) the
Mercerie (clothsellers) and the Spadaria (swordsmiths).
Venetian street names also preserve the memory of religious
communities, as in the various Calli dei Preti (priests) and
delle Muneghe (nuns); and the vanished influence of great
patrician families who lived in the vicinity, such as Calle
Contarini. Venice's traditionally large foreign contingent is
also reflected in place names such as Calle dei Ragusei
(after emigrants from Raguso, today's Dubrovnik), Calle
delle Turchette ("little Turkish women"), Riva degli
Schiavoni (Dalmatians), Calli degli Armeni
(Armenians) and dei Tedeschi (Germans).

Crafts and traditions

In the first half of the 18th century the graceful and luxurious Rococo style became increasingly popular in Venice, as a reaction against the more formal splendor that dominated the Baroque period. The Republic had begun its slow decline, but the great Venetian families were still embellishing their palaces, particularly the interiors. Rooms became more intimate, and lacquer and fine gilding were the norm for furniture, with swelling, undulating lines, softer hues and a growing preference for flowers and pastel backgrounds over the Baroque chinoiseries.

CONSOLES
The console table was a practical place on which to put things down (gloves, books) temporarily, hence it became known as a *servidor* (servant) in Venice.

LACQUERED FURNITURE ▲ *333*
Prior to the lacquering process, furniture was dressed and polished, then decorated and gilded. Finally it was given 15–20 coats of varnish. Furniture like this served to brighten many a Venetian interior.

ARMCHAIR
The delicate tones of satin and lacquer and the inward-curving lines of this armchair reflect the refined taste of Venetian society.

A lacquered **COMMODE** decorated with flowers and garlands against ivory. Commodes like this, with light backgrounds, were much in demand.

In response to the changing
domestic and social norms,
furniture became increasingly
functional and comfortable.

PIER GLASS-DESK

One of the rare larger
pieces of furniture
produced by the Rococo
style; multifunctional, it
might serve as a
commode, desk or
looking-glass.

SMALL COMMODES could
be adapted to the less
spacious rooms of the 18th
century. In response to a
growing demand for
lacquered furniture, *lacca
povera* ("poor" lacquer)
was developed. This was
basically a painted décor
reproduced on a thin sheet
of paper, then stuck to the
wood and covered with
several coats of varnish.

MIRRORS

The great mirrors of 18th-century Venetian
salons often had rich gilt-wood frames
decorated with carved ribbons and fluting.
Their effect was to scale down the elegant
outlines of furniture and boiseries, by creating
optical illusions (the impression of greater
space) and by reflecting ad infinitum the light
shed by multitudes of wall-brackets.

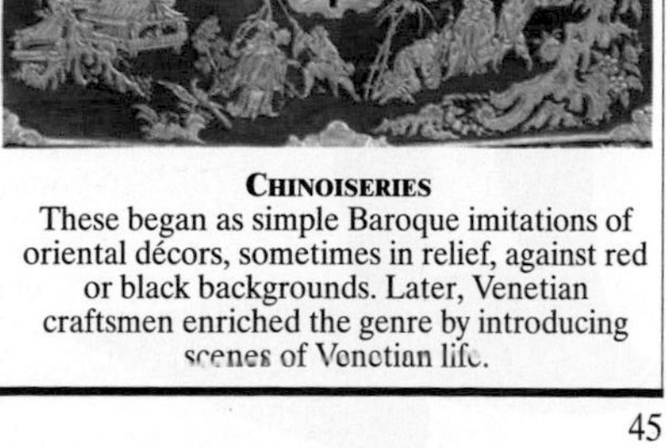

CHINOISERIES

These began as simple Baroque imitations of
oriental décors, sometimes in relief, against red
or black backgrounds. Later, Venetian
craftsmen enriched the genre by introducing
scenes of Venetian life.

In the 18th century, Venetians followed French fashions. Abandoning the rigid outlines of the two preceding centuries, clothes became graceful, sensual and highly colored. Silk was all the rage, often picked out with gold and silver thread and adorned with pearls and precious stones. Dyes took their names from contemporary habits (as in "coffee", Spanish tobacco), or poetry (as in "Angel's feather", a bright Tiepolo red). Pastel tones so dear to the Rococo style were popular, and white predominated in every aspect of human finery. Powder was used to emphasize the pallor of the skin, and jewelry was mainly of diamonds or pearls.

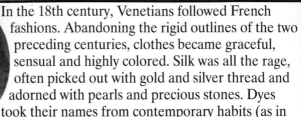

WIGS
Men wore wigs from beginning to end of the 18th century, while women adopted the fashion only after 1750.

THE "VELADA"
Venetian men wore the *velada*, a kind of coat that had much in common with women's clothing, with its tight waist and flared skirts.

SHOES
In the 18th century, Venetian women abandoned the high heels of the 16th century in favour of rather flatter shoes.

MEN'S CLOTHING
The *velada* allowed the shirt and the richly decorated waistcoat to show through. Skin-tight breeches ran down to the knee, and were worn with white silk stockings. Shoes had silver or gold buckles, sometimes set with pearls.

> "The women of Venice are beautiful but, more to the point, they are flirtatious."

Ange Goudar

HAIRSTYLES

In the first half of the 18th century, women wore their hair pulled back with no ornament except perhaps a flower on the left side of the head. Towards the end of the century the fashion returned for more voluminous coiffures, with towering wigs and ribboned bonnets. Depending on the type of bow, ribbon or other decoration, wigs took different names: "à la Turque", "Figaro", "chaste Susan" or "sentimental". In this last example, tiny portraits of dear ones would be pinned to the hair.

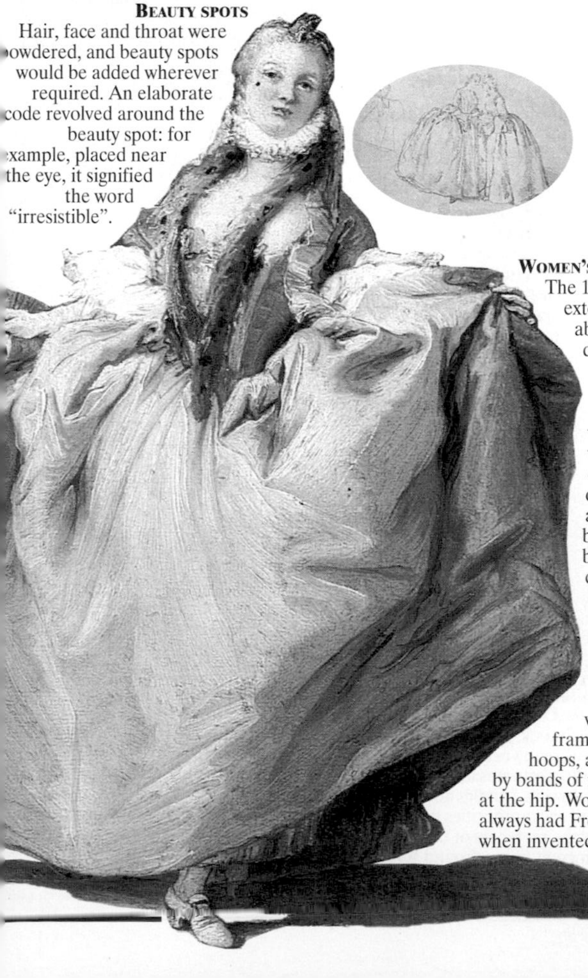

BEAUTY SPOTS

Hair, face and throat were powdered, and beauty spots would be added wherever required. An elaborate code revolved around the beauty spot: for example, placed near the eye, it signified the word "irresistible".

THE TRICORN HAT

A black, three-cornered hat completed a man's coiffure.

WOMEN'S CLOTHING

The 18th-century fashion extolled femininity above all else. The décolleté was low and deep, edged with lace. The corset was stiffened with steel or wooden rods. It cinched the waist down to the hips, and the silhouette ballooned. Skirts bulged outwards like contemporary chests of drawers, so much so that chairs had to be widened to receive them ● *44*. Voluminous hoop-petticoats were worn on a framework of iron hoops, attached to the waist by bands of fabric and padded at the hip. Women's clothes always had French names, even when invented in Venice.

47

● OFFICIAL CEREMONIES

Religious, civil, political and military ceremonies took place in Venice throughout the twelve months of the year. Public buildings were festooned with flags for these occasions; streamers and fabrics from the East were hung across house fronts and palace loggias; porticos and triumphal arches were raised on the city's campi. Citizens participated wholeheartedly in grandiose ceremonials attended by the Doge, and in the various parades and processions through the city. All in all, such events might best be understood as direct celebrations of the spiritual and political life of Venice.

THE DOGE'S CHAPLAIN
The chaplain of St Mark's, bearing his candle, was present in all of the Republic's processions.

RECEPTIONS
Red letter days in the life of the Republic were marked by lavish receptions in honor of ambassadors and European sovereigns visiting the city. A series of memorable parties was given when Henri de Valois came to Venice in July 1574.

PROCESSION TO SAN ZACCARIA
On the first Monday after Easter, the Doge and Seignory proceeded to San Zaccaria to pay homage to the sisters of the convent, who gave up their garden to permit the square to be widened ▲ 172.

THE FEAST OF CORPUS CHRISTI
This ceremony, which took place at the start of June, was renowned for the richness of its costumes and its kaleidoscope of flowers, candles and colors. The religious and civil authorities of the Republic, as well as the members of the scuole, paraded with great pomp around St Mark's Square (seen here at the close of the 15th century) ▲ 296.

THE FESTIVAL OF LA SALUTE

In gratitude to the Virgin for her intervention against the plague of 1630, the Venetians go in procession to the Basilica of La Salute on November 21. On the third Sunday of July, another procession commemorates the end of the epidemic of 1575 at the Church of the Redentore.

For this occasion a pontoon bridge is constructed across the Grand Canal from Santa Maria del Giglio to the Basilica of La Salute.

PROCESSION OF CORPUS CHRISTI

This procession was held more or less under cover, since the cortège (which left the basilica by one door and re-entered it by another) walked under a gallery specially erected for the occasion. A white flag was hung beneath the arcade, which was held up by columns covered in red damask and draped with branches of laurel.

MARITIME PROWESS

The "captain-general of the sea" was chosen by the Grand Council. This nomination to the highest post in the Venetian navy was sealed by the presentation of the commander-in-chief's baton in St Mark's Basilica, after which the captain-general walked in procession to the Piazzetta, with a guard of honor firing a salute over his head. This ceremony, in which the Doge and the Seignory took part, was also an occasion for Venice to celebrate her maritime power.

As part of the Venetian government's deliberate policy to promote "social stability", street entertainments and games were regularly organized in the city, especially at Carnival time. Shows and sports that were thought to build up the citizens' patriotism and fighting spirit were sponsored by the state; but as far as the Venetian populace was concerned, any excuse for a good time was entirely welcome.

THE SKATERS
Very occasionally the Lagoon would freeze over and the canals of Venice would become impassable by boat. At such times, children and young people went about the city on rudimentary ice-skates, probably imitating the ones that the Venetian merchants had seen being used in Northern Europe.

Every February 2, numerous games were organized on Campo Santa Maria Formosa.

CRUEL SPORTS
Two particularly nasty sports were organized at Candlemas. One (on the left in the engraving below) entailed battering a plump white cat to death with one's head while the cat was free to use its claws to defend itself. The cat-killer's skull had to be shaven, whence a Venetian expression (still in use) that roughly translates as "to kill a cat with your shaven head". In another Candlemas event (below right) the competitors leaped from a bridge after a live goose, which was dangled from a balcony by a rope; the winner who managed to grab the wretched creature carried it in triumph through the streets. For bull-baiting, the bull (or ox) was tethered by a rope lashed to its horns, while dogs worried its most vulnerable parts (mostly the ears).

"I was on the Piazzetta and I saw the flight of the angel,
And also the dance of the Moors;
But without you, my dear, I was alone."

IV Foscarini

THE FEAST OF MARDI GRAS ON THE PIAZZETTA

In the background of this painting by Bella are human pyramids and the *svole dell'angelo* (flight of the angel). This latter trick was performed by an acrobat, who slid down a rope from the top of St Mark's campanile to the Doge's Palace, carrying a bunch of flowers for the Doge.

WHEELBARROW RACES

This 18th-century sport was a speciality of Venice's street-sweepers. The first team to cross the finishing line and grab the flag won a cash prize.

STILTS

During Carnival, Venice was haunted by masked men on stilts, who raced around the streets, bestrode the canals, ate their meals on high, and leaned artlessly against the upper balconies of palaces. Probably because of an association of ideas between stilts and crutches, it was popularly believed that to walk on stilts was to attract the evil eye.

Carnival began on Boxing Day, December 26, and reached its climax the day before Ash Wednesday. While it lasted, the law was more or less held in abeyance: the wearing of masks and disguises abolished social divisions for the duration, whereas for the rest of the year the strict orders of precedence observed for official ceremonies did the opposite. During Carnival, the campi, St Mark's Square and the main thoroughfares were thronged with people dancing, singing, carousing and playing games.

The use of masks was so widespread that the maskmakers had their own official artisan status as early as the 15th century.

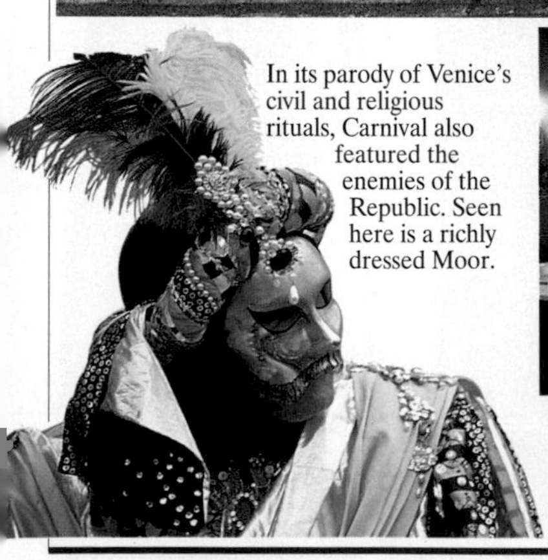

In its parody of Venice's civil and religious rituals, Carnival also featured the enemies of the Republic. Seen here is a richly dressed Moor.

CARNIVAL AT THE CAFÉ FLORIAN
The mask began as a means for nobles to mingl incognito with ordinary citizens in the casini ▲ 2 and theaters. Today, people meet more prosaica in the cafés around St Mark's Square.

Carnival opened with a series of balls on Venice's largest campi; these were followed by spontaneous parties which continued for several weeks until Shrove Tuesday, when the bells of San Francesco della Vigna tolled at midnight to mark the beginning of Lent.

"TABARRO" AND "BAUTO"

The *bauto* was composed of a black silk hood and a lace cape; the costume was completed by a voluminous cloak (*tabarro*) and a three-cornered hat. Wearing *bauto*, *tabarro* and a white mask covering most of the face, one could go anywhere completely incognito.

During Carnival, St Mark's Square was invaded by street vendors selling *frittele* (fritters) and other sweetmeats.

CARNIVAL TODAY

Since 1980, the masks have reappeared in Venice, and 18th-century garments and traditional costumes again mingle with other grotesque disguises. The old custom of giving balls and theatrical performances has been revived, along with an array of ancient Venetian games. On the final day, the effigy of Carnival is burned on St Mark's Square, in accordance with tradition,

THE COMMEDIA DELL'ARTE

Some disguises (in this case, Harlequin) are borrowed from the Commedia dell'Arte, which was played on all the city's campi ▲ 291.

The regattas of Venice began as military exercises for crossbowmen on the Lido and developed into popular events for all Venetians, for whom the sea and everything to do with it was a way of life. The oarsmen of the galleys assigned to transport soldiers to and from St Mark's whiled away the time with races; the government, seeing a convenient way of training the people for war, introduced the first official regatta in about 1300, on the Feast of the Marias ▲ 167. Regattas proliferated and the tradition still continues today, with events held from March to September, in Venice itself and across the Lagoon.

THE HISTORIC REGATTA
After the Bucintoro was scrapped in 1824, it was decided that an annual regatta should be held to preserve the traditions of the Republic.

THE BANNERS
A platform (*machina*) was erected for the judges in front of Ca' Foscari, the traditional finishing line for races. These judges presented the first boats in each category with banners of several different colors (red for the winner).

PAX TIBI MARCE

A DARING COMPETITOR
In 1574, the winner of one of the races, a woman, had to leap from boat to boat to collect her red banner from the judges.

PARADE IN RENAISSANCE COSTUME
Venice's main historic regatta takes place on the first Sunday in September. Large vessels filled with people in costume parade down the Grand Canal, accompanied by a fleet of smaller boats. After this there are four races involving the different types of boats in use on the Lagoon. Opposite, the *bissona Veneziana*, an eight-oared boat featuring the lion of St Mark on its bows.

Right, a *sandalo*, or flat-bottomed boat ● *71*, taking part in the Vogalonga. The two oarsmen row standing up, Venetian style.

THE WOMEN'S RACE
The first women's race took place in 1493, in honor of Beatrice d'Este, the wife of Ludovico il Moro, Duke of Milan. Fifty girls entered this race, which is still run each year.

THE VOGALONGA, OR LONG-DISTANCE RACE
This tremendous event has been organized every year since 1975. On the last Sunday in May, hundreds of boats of all kinds race from St Mark's Basin to Burano and back again, a distance of about 18 miles. The final stretch is through the Cannaregio and Grand Canals, where a huge and enthusiastic crowd awaits the competitors. The Vogalonga is a test of endurance and skill with the oar; entrants train for months in advance around the city's canals.

Once the nobles of Venice had got into the habit of traveling about the city in their own personal gondolas and employing a private gondolier, the latter inevitably became something of a confidante, since he accompanied his master to even the most private rendezvous. Nowadays, the gondoliers still form a "caste" of their own, and the profession is passed down from father to son. Today, the gondola mostly survives as a tourist attraction, and the gondoliers of the city number about four hundred all told.

Gondolas were originally so gaudily decorated that the Republic decreed in 1633 that they should all be painted black.

GONDOLIERS RESTING
A *stazio* is both a mooring place for gondolas and an embarkation point. One of the biggest is near the columns of the Piazzetta, at the feet of which the gondoliers gossip and wait for passengers.

RACING IN THE LAGOON
Gondoliers were able to demonstrate their skill and speed during duck hunts.

A BIZARRE CONSTRUCTION
Since the 19th century the gondola has been designed so that one of its sides is nine inches broader than the other ● 68. Thus the gondola heels and yaws naturally to starboard, but the gondolier, standing in its stern with one leg forward, can right its course with his oar ● 70.

THE GONDOLAS OF THE SUN KING
The Republic of Venice often presented gondolas as gifts to foreign sovereigns and ambassadors. Thus in 1687 Louis XIV of France had no fewer than 15 gondoliers in his service, who were lodged in his "Petit-Venise" on the canal at Versailles.

TRAGHETTI
The traghetti, which are collective gondolas propelled by two oarsmen, provide a ferry service to and fro across the Grand Canal at eight different points.

Black clothes and a red or blue ribboned straw hat make up the uniform of the modern gondolier; formerly he was dressed in much brighter colors.

"FELZE"
This small, cabin-like structure, with a roof like a half-barrel, was usually installed on the gondolas during the winter months. It provided a measure of privacy and warmth for passengers.

1. The glassblower starts by collecting a certain quantity of molten glass on the red hot end of a hollow tube.

2. He lays the tube across a bench, turning it in a wooden mold until the ball of molten glass is round and compact.

5. Using steel pincers, he chokes the collar of the glass ball near the end of the tube.

6. The glass is then reheated and reblown.

9. The glassblower then widens the hollow of the glass and begins the shaping process.

STAGES IN THE MANUFACTURE

11. A second tube is fixed to the inside of the glass, and the first one is detached. The upper part of the glass is now finished.

13. Meanwhile, the glassblower prepares the foot and the stem.

14. A little molten glass is applied to the stem to make it adhere to the upper part of the glass.

Glass is made by the fusion of a mixture based on silica (sand, quartz, sandstone etc.) and alkalis (sodium and potassium).

3. He blows down the tube to pierce the ball, then blows again to form a rough shape.

4. The glassblower continues to rotate his tube to counter the downward-pulling effect of gravity and to stop the glass stretching out.

7. The spherical form is given to the base of the glass and drawn out to a point with the pincers.

8. The point is removed to allow the pincers to be introduced.

OF A WINE GLASS

10. The lip of the glass is widened.

12. The glass is heated once again.

15. The glass is pivoted in the pincers to make sure its alignment is true.

16. The glass is reheated, then finally placed in a special oven to cool.

Venetian lace is made with the needle, although the product is also made with a bobbin at Chioggia and Pellestrina. The Venetian technique of *punto in aria* ▲ *371* first appeared in the mid-16th century; the embroidery technique used until that time still required a canvas backing, which gave a perforated effect. The anonymous invention of *punto in aria* dispensed with this constraint, since a single strand of thread fixed to a piece of parchment served as its support.

The lacemaker arranges the openwork and varies her stitches according to strict conventions imposed by the designer.

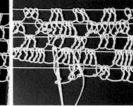

The basic stitch is the simple (or triple gauze) stitch, which produces effects as light as tulle.

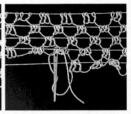

The lacemaker then executes the relief, or alternatively embroiders a thread of greater or lesser thickness.

MOUNTING THE LACE
Several layers of fabric, and then the paper bearing the design to be copied, are spread on a cushion. After passing the stitches through both the paper and the fabric, the design is fixed by running the thread around its contours.

GREEN PAPER is commonly used, as it is less tiring on the eyes.

THE LACEMAKER'S ACCESSORIES
Needles and thread.

THE ROUND CUSHION is mounted on a wooden frame.

The lacemaker attaches her first row of bars to the design.

THE CHAIR
Lacemakers sit on chairs with foot rests, usually facing daylight by the window.

POSTURE
Seemingly made of stone, with only her fingers in constant motion, the lacemaker in her traditional white apron sits for hours at a time, her head bent over her work.

"SAN MARCO" (ARS LAGUNA)
LABORATORIO DI SCIALLI
VENEZIA - Ponte dei Barateri, Calle di Mezzo 4991
Tel. 3617   Tel. 3617

SHAWL FACTORY   SCHALTUCHERSCHULE
Handwork   Handarbeit
ATELIER DE BRODERIES À LA MAIN
Châles

17TH-CENTURY LACE
In the 17th century, Venetian *gros point* lace, thick and modeled against a background of bare stitches, was all the rage. Towards the end of the century, smaller, more delicate patterns came into fashion.

Hanks of thread.

Burano's lacemakers have revived the Venetian lace technique. They also work lace in *Alençon point*, thus perpetuating the finest traditions of their craft, both local and foreign.

When finished, the stitches holding the design are removed, and the lace is separated from it.

The technique of marbling paper originated in Japan around the year 1000, and spread to Persia and Turkey, where craftsmen had the idea of using gum instead of water as a base for the dipping liquid. Known through the Arab world in the Middle Ages, marbling finally reached Europe in the 15th century and, in the 18th century, developed in France, where its former use for holy texts was extended to ordinary bookbindings and boxes. Outside France, marbling largely disappeared with the Industrial Revolution, only to be reborn in Venice during the 1970s.

The technique offers unlimited decorative possibilities, for each sheet of marbled paper is entirely unique.

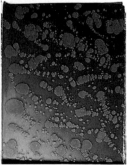

1. Using a brush, droplets of the first color are flicked on to the surface of a colorless, liquid gum. These dilate little by little until they cover the entire surface of the tray.

2. Ox-gall is added to the colors. The second color must contain more gall than the first, so as to push it aside, float and spread. The third contains more than the second, and so on.

3. (Center) Once all the colors have been placed on the liquid surface, they are drawn out in lines with a pointed instrument. After this an upright comb is pulled across them.

4. The comb must be manipulated very slowly, otherwise all the colors risk being displaced.

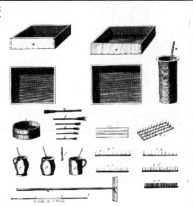

The colors are diluted with water, or oil when the support is a fabric of some kind. Today, turpentine is also used.

The most important tool of the trade is a marbling tray, in which liquid gum and colors are laid. Other tools (brushes, combs, mortar and pestle for pounding the colors to powder) vary according to the technique used.

Alberto Valese working in his shop. It was on his initiative that ancient marbling techniques were revived in Venice in 1970. He has continued to enrich the craft with innovations.

5. The sheet of paper is delicately placed on top of the mixture, taking care that no air is trapped beneath.

6. The sheet is then lifted with extreme care, after which it is hung from a cord or spread out on a table.

The art of metal casting reached its zenith during the Renaissance period, when the taste for bronzes became widespread. Today, the tradition is still maintained by a few old foundries in Venice, which produce objects in copper and bronze. These objects are in many cases beautifully finished sculptures, with forms inspired by the maritime traditions of Venice. Examples are the dolphins that are used to decorate gondolas, and which have long snake-like tails wrapped around tridents.

1. The fusion of the metal takes place at 900°C and lasts between 60 and 90 minutes. The furnace (above) can contain up to 330 lb of metal.

Some palace doors still retain their original bronze handles. These are often extremely refined busts, such as the ones above.

Among the familiar brass objects are these sea-horses, which traditionally decorate the sides of gondolas.

2. The resulting metal is poured into an ingot mold for re-use.

1. PREPARING THE MOLD
The mold containing the model is filled with a fine refractory sand. Once the model has been removed, the form to be reproduced will remain printed on it.

2. POURING THE METAL
The mold is closed, and then the liquid metal is poured in through a tiny hole.

DOOR KNOCKERS
Many of the knockers on Venetian doors are in the form of a lion's head, with a large ring in its jaws. Variations on this theme range from the simple to the highly intricate. Other designs include Moors, grotesque heads, and clowns.

The model below is called a *trevisan*, after a gondolier of that name.

3. REMOVING THE CAST
The inside of the mold has been carefully powdered prior to pouring, to ensure the cast can be easily removed afterwards.

4. FINISHING
After its removal from the mold, the bronze or brass object is finished by hand with a chisel. Finally it is carefully polished.

MOSAICS

The small shards for mosaics are obtained by breaking large plates of colored glass into pieces with a hammer.

Mosaic was a technique of the Greco-Latin era, which was commonly used throughout the Byzantine Empire, and reached a very high level of accomplishment in both Venice and Ravenna. Although no description of it dating from the Venetian-Byzantine period has survived, scholars have been able to work out how it was done from the mosaics of St Mark. The technique of mosaic apparently remained unaltered from antiquity to the Renaissance.

Mosaic craftsmen probably worked from small-scale pictures, taking their cues from the ancient models of Byzantium or from miniatures (as in the Genesis Dome above the narthex of St Mark's). Mosaic work was team work, in which the various tasks were precisely distributed.

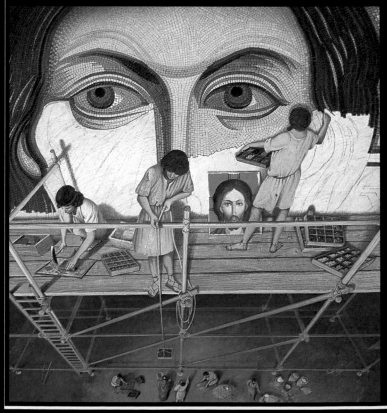

Gold and silver are applied in leaf form to colorless or bottle green cubes, then covered with a thin layer of transparent glass.

Sticking like a skin to a building's interior, mural mosaic work is designed to cover broad surfaces and to be viewed from a distance as an ensemble. This characteristic, like the near invulnerability of mosaic images to the effects of passing time, lends it great symbolic value.

1. First, the surface is covered with either one or two layers of cement, which is scored to make the next layer stick properly.

2. After tracing out the broad lines of the image, a thin layer of mortar is then spread over a part of the surface small enough to be completed in a single day.

3. On the prepared surface, part of the décor is painted, down to the last detail, in the colors to be used.

4. The shards of glass are applied. They are pressed two thirds of their thickness into the mortar, and care is taken to vary the angles of their setting so they will refract light in different ways. The shards must also be placed irregularly, with spaces of varying width between them.

● THE CONSTRUCTION OF A GONDOLA

1. Positioning of the stem and stern of the boat, with three main frame elements of oak. These are the first of the 280 pieces of wood which together make up the gondola.

2. Installation of the *cerchi* (sheathing) on the upper flanks of the gondola. These oak planks are profiled by wetting and gradual warping over a fire of dried rushes.

3. Gradually the other 33 frame elements are added, along with the sides and decking at prow and stern.

4. Finally, thwarts are put in place to strengthen the structure; the shape of the *forcola* and the curve of the hull are adjusted to suit the weight and height of the gondolier.

THE "FERRO"
The *ferro*, or decorative prow of the gondola, is supposed to represent the Doge's hat (or *corno*) ▲ *231* and the six sestieri of Venice. The seventh (on the other side) is supposed to symbolize the Giudecca. In fact, the *ferro* acquired its present form after a long period of evolution. As late as the 17th century, Venetian painters were recording *ferros* on gondolas in the shape of finely wrought crosiers.

THE LAST GONDOLAS
The *squeri*, derived from *squadra* (square), are now rare in Venice. None of them makes more than three or four gondolas a year.

The gondola, a masterpiece of boat building, has a hull thirty-six feet long and less than five feet wide, with only half its bows in contact with the water; hence its floating surface is reduced to a minimum.

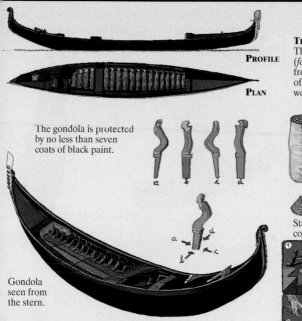

PROFILE

PLAN

The gondola is protected by no less than seven coats of black paint.

Gondola seen from the stern.

THE "FORCOLA"

The rowlock (*forcola*) is carved from a single piece of walnut or cherry wood.

Stages of construction.

The twisted *forcola* is a crucial element of the gondola; its *morso* (notch) is cut so as to cradle the gondolier's oar. The part is cut out with a saw, shaped with a plane and adze, and thoroughly oiled.

THE "SQUERO"

The *squeri*, or gondola yards, are always by the water, with a wooden shed where the boat builders can work in winter and store their tools. The owner usually lives on the floor above, or else in an adjoining building. In front of the buildings a piece of open ground slopes down to the edge of the canal; here the gondolas are worked on during the summer, and construction materials are deposited. Below is the 17th-century Squero di San Trovaso ▲ 324, the oldest in Venice.

THE OAR

The gondolier's oar is made from a single piece of beech, fined down with a drawknife to make a ribbed surface on the blade end, and a round, smooth surface where it works in the rowlock.

Venetian rowing is different from conventional rowing because the oarsman stands upright facing the bows and plies his oar from fore to aft.

Rowing forward.

Gondola stationary, rowing forward.

The gondolier stands upright in the stern of the boat, facing forward.

Pushing the oar backward. To veer left, the gondolier puts extra effort into this stroke.

Movement to stop the gondola.

Rowing forward in narrow canals.

Bringing the oar forward. This corrects the advance of the boat; if the gondolier puts more power into the action, he alters his course to the right.

Rowing backwards.

Rowing by pushing the oar forward.

Before the development of motorized vessels, the Venetian transport system depended on men rowing boats. Since 1975, rowing has become a fashionable pastime and a growing number of races are held.

"DESDOTONA"
Eighteen oars, usually leads parades.

"VOGARIZZO"
A variation on the rowlock for *peate*, or delivery boats.

"CAORLINA"
Rowed by six oarsmen, this boat is a popular feature of the historic regatta.

RACING **"GONDOLINI"**
The star attraction of the historic regatta ● *54*, specifically designed for racing.

"FORCOLA DA REGATA"
Stern rowlock. Being custom-made, no two racing rowlocks are the same.

RACING **"MASCARETA"**
Usually rowed by women. The light, painted hull is characteristic of the Lagoon skiff.

"FORCOLA A DUE MORSI"
Double rowlock, for fishing boats. It is, however, almost never seen on the Lagoon today.

"SANDALO VOGATO ALLA VALESANA"
Here the rower stands inside the boat and rows with crossed oars.

FUNERAL GONDOLA

71

TAXI
Very practical if you are in a hurry, but always the most expensive mode of transport in Venice.

MOTOSCAFO
This craft is smaller than the traditional vaporetto, although Venetians also refer to it by this name.

PUBLIC SERVICES
In Venice, the police, the firemen and the ambulance service all operate by boat. In an emergency, they are not obliged to respect the speed limits on the Grand Canal.

GARBAGE COLLECTORS
Garbage is a major practical problem in Venice. Since everything both arrives in the city and leaves it by boat, the Venetians are obliged to leave their garbage alongside the canals for collection.

VAPORETTO
The term vaporetto applies equally to different three kinds of boats that are in effect floating buses. The VAPORETTO is the slowest, stopping at every halt along the Grand Canal.
The MOTOSCAFO sits lower in the water and, making fewer frequent stops, is a little quicker than the vaporetto.
The MOTONAVE is much larger and bulkier, with two decks. It goes to the more distant islands (such as Lido, Burano, Punta and Sabbioni).

TAXI

POLICE

MOTOSCAFO
DIRECT LINE

AMBULANCE

FIRE BOAT

A.M.I.U.

GARBAGE COLLECTORS

VAPORETTO

> "I lay down to rest, listening to the black boats
> stealing up and down below the window on
> the rippling water, till I fell asleep."
>
> Charles Dickens

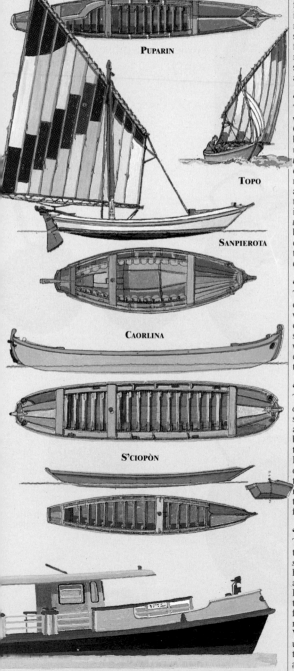

"PUPARIN"

Assymetrical like the gondola, this approximately 30-foot-long vessel owes its name to the lean, raking shape of its stem, and also to the fact that the man rowing it stands on a sort of small platform at the back.

"TOPO"

These sailing boats were developed at Chioggia, where the biggest of them were used for fishing. The *topo* is not entirely decked over; its middle part is left as an open hold so that the fish can be thrown into it. Motorized *topi*, whose size has been modified to enable them to transport goods and cargo, are now used.

"SANPIEROTA"

The *sanpierota* was originally a fishing vessel but, because of its exceptional stability, it is now widely used for excursions around the Lagoon.

"CAORLINA"

The *caorlina* (from *caorle*) is nearly symmetrical in shape and is among the better looking boats to be found on the Lagoon. It was originally designed to pass through the mainland canals, but today it is mostly used for racing.

"S'CIOPÒN"

The full name of this small boat is *sandalo da s'ciopo*, hence the abbreviation *s'cipiòn*. Because it lies low in the water, it was used for shooting (*s'cipiòn* means a duck boat in Venetian). It is still used for negotiating the shallower waters around the Lagoon.

73

● FOOD
SARDE IN SAOR

This very ancient recipe was born of a need to preserve fish for as long as possible; Venetian sailors could take these marinated sardines with them on voyages, as a preventive against scurvy.

2. Brown pinenuts and raisins together in a pan.

1. Fry onions gently in 1 cup of oil until brown and soft.

5. Place a layer of fish on the bottom of a terrine and cover with a layer of the onion mixture.

4. Roll the fish in a plate of flour, then fry. Add vinegar and cook until liquid is reduced.

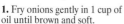

74

> "Looking out, I beheld the Grand Canal so entirely
> covered with fruits and vegetables, on rafts and in
> barges, that I could scarcely distinguish a wave."
>
> William Beckford

INGREDIENTS (for four people)
1½lb of fresh sardines, 2 lb of sweet white onions, 1 cup of virgin olive oil, 1 glass of white wine vinegar, a little flour, a pinch of salt, 2 oz of Smyrna raisins and 1 oz of pinenuts (optional).

Peel the onions and cut finely into rings.

Remove scales from fish, then remove heads and intestines. Wash and drain on paper towels, add salt.

3. Add pinenuts and raisins to onions.

6. Continue adding alternate layers until the terrine is full. Top with onion mixture.

7. Leave in a cool place for at least two days, then serve with grilled polenta.

75

Typical Venetian Products

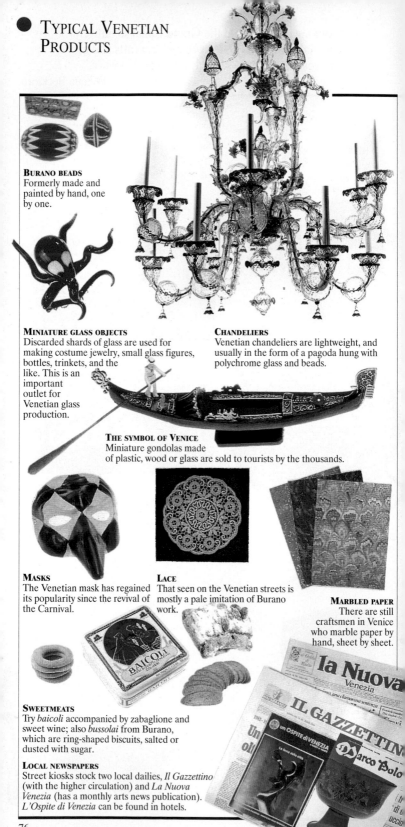

Burano beads
Formerly made and painted by hand, one by one.

Miniature glass objects
Discarded shards of glass are used for making costume jewelry, small glass figures, bottles, trinkets, and the like. This is an important outlet for Venetian glass production.

Chandeliers
Venetian chandeliers are lightweight, and usually in the form of a pagoda hung with polychrome glass and beads.

The symbol of Venice
Miniature gondolas made of plastic, wood or glass are sold to tourists by the thousands.

Masks
The Venetian mask has regained its popularity since the revival of the Carnival.

Lace
That seen on the Venetian streets is mostly a pale imitation of Burano work.

Marbled paper
There are still craftsmen in Venice who marble paper by hand, sheet by sheet.

Sweetmeats
Try *baicoli* accompanied by zabaglione and sweet wine; also *bussolai* from Burano, which are ring-shaped biscuits, salted or dusted with sugar.

Local newspapers
Street kiosks stock two local dailies, *Il Gazzettino* (with the higher circulation) and *La Nuova Venezia* (has a monthly arts news publication). *L'Ospite di Venezia* can be found in hotels.

Architecture

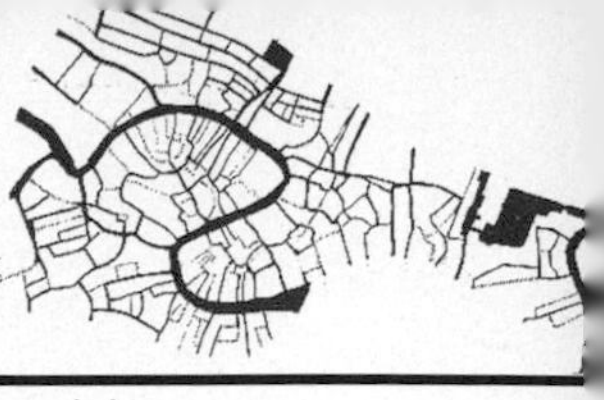

Venice's network
of waterways.

The urban fabric of Venice clearly distinguishes
two separate communication networks – that
of the waterways (canali, rii) and that of
the pedestrian thoroughfares (calli,
piazza, campi, fondamenta, salizzade,
rive and rughe). The choice of network
is governed by the nature of the site
and its formation, for Venice is
essentially a cluster of small
islands joined together by
bridges and separated by
canals and basins.

**OPEN SPACES AND PEDESTRIAN
THOROUGHFARES**

On the islands, a dense maze of
footpaths emerged, mostly regularly
spaced and running at right angles
to the canals, like the teeth of a
comb. Across this network and
parallel to the canals ran the calli,
broken at intervals by larger open
spaces. These were the campi, the
smaller campielli, and the piazza, as
in Piazza San Marco (St Mark's
Square). In time, the pedestrian
thoroughfares and bridges became
a maze of interlinking alleys, and
the cluster of islands became a
real city, regulated by
hierarchy of open spaces –
public campi, semi-private
courtyards and private
gardens.

THE CAMPO
The Venetian campo
varies in form.Campo
Santi Giovanni e Paolo
▲ 157 (right), for
example, is L-shaped.
Sometimes it has canals
running along its edges.
Earlier campi were
paved with bricks in
herringbone patterns
and bordered with
bands of Istrian stone,
but in the 18th century
they acquired hard
stone flags of flint
(*masegni*) which bore
up better under
constant use.

STATUES
Statues placed
in campi, like that
of Colleone ▲ 147,
157, are the exception
in Venice, where the
glorification of the
state mostly took
precedence over
praise of individual
achievement.

THE HOUSES
While patrician palaces and the
mansions of the wealthy
bourgeoisie (notaries, lawyers and
civil servants) gave a hierarchical
flavor to the campi, more modest
dwellings tended to fill in the
narrow spaces behind them.

CANALS AND QUAYS
Indispensable for loading and
unloading goods headed in and out
of the campo's *fondachi* (warehouses), the
side of the campo opening on the canal also
provided the best access to the church, and to
other major buildings around it.

Pedestrian
network.

THE WELLS
There might be
between one and four
cisterns of drinking
water on any given
campo.

CHURCH AND MONASTERY
Each campo has its own church;
most of these churches have façades
fronting a canal. The monastery beside
the church was usually the center around
which the district originally grew up; and this
is one reason why the spacious cloisters of the
Dominican monastery of Santi Giovanni e Paolo
occupy the lion's share of the urban *insula*, so
much so that the projecting church dictates the
shape of the campo.

THE SCUOLA
Sometimes secondary
oratories stood near the
main churches, but more
often there were scuole.

If they were scuole grandi
(here, the Scuola San
Marco ▲ *159*) these
might be as large as the
church itself.

79

● WELLS AND BRIDGES

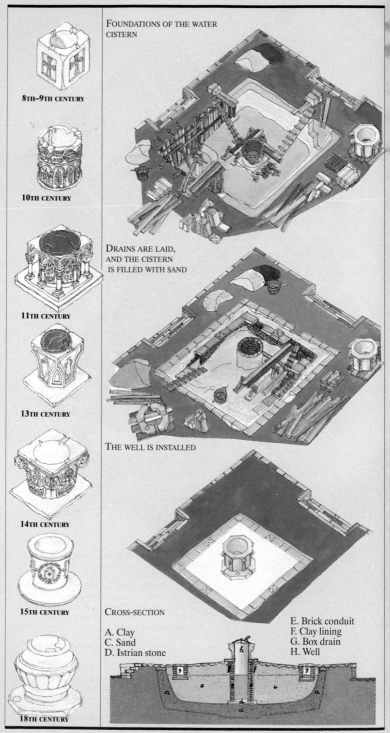

8TH–9TH CENTURY

10TH CENTURY

11TH CENTURY

13TH CENTURY

14TH CENTURY

15TH CENTURY

18TH CENTURY

FOUNDATIONS OF THE WATER CISTERN

DRAINS ARE LAID, AND THE CISTERN IS FILLED WITH SAND

THE WELL IS INSTALLED

CROSS-SECTION

A. Clay
C. Sand
D. Istrian stone

E. Brick conduit
F. Clay lining
G. Box drain
H. Well

> "A realist, in Venice, would become a romantic, by
> mere faithfulness to what he saw before him."

Arthur Symons

THE WELLS

The wells, which performed the essential task of providing Venice with fresh water, were usually privately owned, and they were to be found throughout the city in every campo and thoroughfare. The carved well lip was the only visible feature of what was a complex underground system; beneath the surface, the Venetian well consists of a surrounding 16-foot-deep cistern, with an impermeable clay lining. At the center of this cistern is a shaft with walls of bricks specially made with fissures in their downsides. The cistern is filled with sand, and the rainwater, running through gratings in the pavement of the campo, flows into connected box-drains running around the edge of the cistern. It then filters through the sand until it reaches the central well-shaft.

FOUNDATIONS AND TEMPORARY WOODEN SURROUND

FIRST ELEMENTS OF VAULTING IN ISTRIAN STONE, BRICK VAULTING, AND KEYSTONE

FINISHED BRIDGE, WITH BALUSTRADE AND STEPS

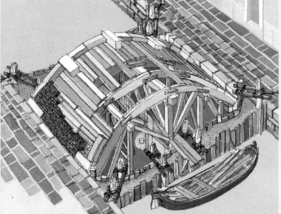

THE BRIDGES

Venice's earlier wooden bridges were soon replaced by stone and brick constructions. The building of these permanent bridges involved a partial emptying of the canal, sinking foundations on either bank, raising a wooden arch on which to mount stones and brick, and constructing steps and parapets on top of these. With only a few exceptions, the bridges of Venice have single, semicircular arches.

In 1033, seventy parishes were established around Venice's churches. These later coalesced into *contrade*, the smallest administrative units of the state framework. By the 18th century there were more than two hundred churches in Venice, ample proof if any were needed of Venetian piety. With their decoration, they served as showcases for the majesty of the state (San Marco ▲ *234*), for the wealth and influence of religious orders (Gesuiti ▲ *152*) or for the glorification of important patrician families (Santa Maria del Giglio ▲ *264*).

THE VENETIAN-BYZANTINE STYLE
The basilica of SANTA MARIA E SAN DONATO ▲ *368* (12th century), famous for its extraordinary octagonal apse, is built on the basilical plan with three naves, as is clear from its restrained three-part exterior in red brick. The vertical thrust of the main body of the building is accentuated by the small double aperture just below the roofline, and by the elegant Lombard blind arches.

Detail of the right pinnacle of the Gothic church of La Madonna dell'Orto ▲ *146*.

Detail from the door of the Baroque Church of the Gesuiti ▲ *152*.

THE GOTHIC STYLE
Like Santi Giovanni e Paolo ▲ *157*, SANTA MARIA GLORIOSA DEI FRARI ▲ *292* was built by a minor religious order. Its traditional three-part façade in brick is studded with the Gothic vocabulary of rosewindow, pinnacles, cornices and elaborate portal. The wavelike line of the coping is similar to that of San Giovanni in Bragora ▲ *176*.

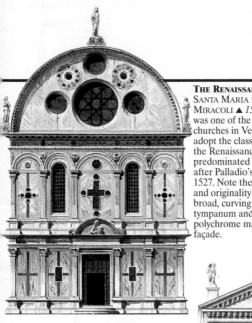

THE RENAISSANCE STYLE

SANTA MARIA DEI MIRACOLI ▲ *151* (1490) was one of the first churches in Venice to adopt the classicism of the Renaissance, which predominated in Venice after Palladio's arrival in 1527. Note the novelty and originality of the broad, curving tympanum and the lush polychrome marble façade.

Detail from the door of the Gesuiti ▲ *152*.

THE PALLADIAN STYLE

SAN GIORGIO MAGGIORE ▲ *340*, one of Palladio's last masterworks, was built in the years after 1565 to plans completed in 1559. Taking his inspiration from the buildings of the ancient world, Palladio skilfully divided the church's façade into two planes and pediments. In this way he achieved the fusion of the classical temple form (on the outside) and the Roman, Latin-cross form (on the inside).

NEO-CLASSICISM

Tommaso Temanza's Church of the MADDALENA (c.1760) is an example of renewed classical severity, in reaction to the current fashion for Baroque. In this adaptation of the classical temple, the architect worked to a centered plan, with a circle on the outside and a hexagon on the inside.

THE BAROQUE STYLE

With the church of the DERELITTI, Longhena abandoned the classical vertical arrangement for a Baroque style influenced by Mannerism.

● CAMPANILES

The campanile is basically a tower-belfry set apart from the main body of the church. Traditionally the tower is square, with an upper, open chamber containing bells. This, in turn, is topped by a conical or pyramidal spire, or an onion-shaped dome. Sometimes a smaller, arcaded campanile will be joined to a church. Those Venetian campaniles which have not been destroyed altogether are today the object of constant restoration work, because their foundations so frequently ≩ subside.

CATHEDRAL OF SANTA MARIA ASSUNTA
(Torcello). This 11th-century campanile is a robust tower cadenced by tall Lombard blind arches. The generous openings of the belfry at its top and its simple, low roof are typical of Venetian-Byzantine architecture.

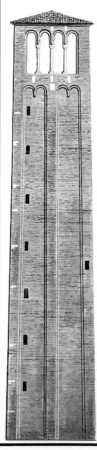

SANTA FOSCA
▲ *145*
The present campanile was built shortly after the collapse of the first bell tower in 1410, and the tower was unaffected by the reconstruction of the church, which was carried out in the late 17th and early 18th centuries. Gothic elements here, such as the double-arched belfry and the four corner pinnacles, are blended with Romanesque holdovers like the Lombard blind arches, reinforcing the body of the tower, and the Byzantine flavor of its dome.

SAN FRANCESCO DELLA VIGNA ▲ *161*
Built between 1571 and 1581, this campanile is like that of St Mark's in that it is made up of three distinct registers. The pyramidal spire, resting on its square base, accentuates the soaring nature of the construction, which is otherwise traditional with classical Renaissance elements.

SAN PIETRO DI CASTELLO ▲ *157, 182*
This campanile, with its original arrangement of two superimposed stone arches, crowned the polygonal base of a dome that is no longer there. It is the only surviving example of its kind in Venice, because the ground was too unstable for weighty construction of this type.

ARCHED BELFRIES
of the sacristy of SANTO STEFANO (above) and of the Church of SANTI GIOVANNI E PAOLO ▲ *157* (left).

BELFRY OF THE ORATORY OF SANT'ANGELO

SANTI APOSTOLI ▲ *150, 198*
The upper parts of this campanile, which was begun in the 15th century, were not completed until between 1720 and 1730. They are separated from the rest of the building by a projecting cornice. The high classical stem, topped by an octagonal tambour and picturesque onion-dome, lends the campanile grace and harmony.

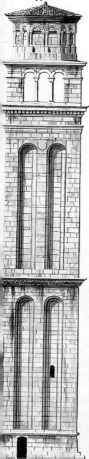

SAN GIACOMO DI RIALTO ▲ *283* is dominated by its bells and by a huge 24-hour clock, which once rang out the hours for the Rialto's merchants

85

From the 13th century onwards, the scuole became the headquarters of the charitable and mutual assistance guilds of Venice. They are most readily identified by their façades, which suggest strictly organized interiors behind them. As a rule, the ground floor of a scuola would be used for religious functions; the chapter room above it was for large assemblies, and it was usually connected to the *sala dell'albergo*, the scuola's treasure house and the meeting place of its dignitaries. Because they were symbols of civic status, prosperity and the power of the guilds, special attention was paid to the decoration of the scuole's exteriors.

SCUOLA DI SAN MARCO ▲ 159
The elegant façade of this scuola is one of the most refined in Venice. The humanist approach of Pietro Lombardo and the marble perspectives which he designed for the ground floor are in marked contrast to Codussi's elaborate coping.

SCUOLA VECCHIA DELLA MISERICORDIA (1450)
Discretion and harmony are the keynotes of this particular façade. The pinnacles, windows and coping all reflect the flamboyance, charm and refinement of Gothic style.

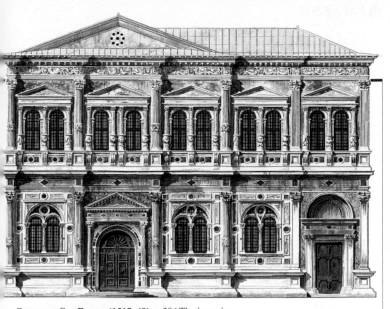

SCUOLA DI SAN ROCCO (1517–49) ▲ *294* The imposing height of this building carries echoes of the triumphalism that was found in ancient Rome. Columns, pilasters and cornices emphasize the composite Codussi-style windows on the lower level and the long pedimented series of double bay windows on the first floor.

SCUOLA DI SAN TEODORO ▲ *275* The balanced composition of this façade, completed by Sardi and Longhena in 1649, perfectly reflects the interior, with its two capacious chambers one above the other.

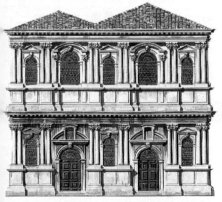

SCUOLA DEI CARMINI ▲ *329* Between 1668 and 1670 Longhena designed the perfect formal symmetry of this façade around the axis of its central bay. The high coping of the upper floor, the grotesque masks on the window arches, and other projecting elements all reflect the taste of 17th-century architects.

SCUOLA DEI BATTILORO E TIRAORO (1711) ▲ *351* The capricious spirit of Rococo predominates in this vividly colored façade.

SCUOLA DELLA CARITÀ This scuola now looks like a Neo-classical, triumphal arch, after Massari failed to complete his 1765 project.

The layout of the Venetian palazzo conforms to certain functional and climatic imperatives. The rooms distributed on either side of a central space (the *portego*) admit the ventilation so essential during periods of humidity or summer heat. The façade, which was usually in three sections, answered both the commercial and residential purposes of the building. The shop areas were on the ground floor, porch or portico areas, offices and archives were between floors, and residential *piani nobili* and *salone* on the upper floor. Servants' quarters were in the attics. Thus the palace served as both a home and a kind of warehouse, or *casa-fontego* ● *104*.

PALAZZO FALIER ▲ *150, 208*
This palace, in the Cannaregio sestiere, belonged in the mid-13th century to the family of the traitor Doge Manin Falier, who is thought to have lived here for several years. A portico on the ground floor reconciled the public and private functions of the building: its façade has many arches on both floors, with windows in the Venetian-Byzantine style and zoomorphically carved Gothic cornerstones.

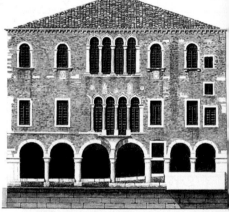

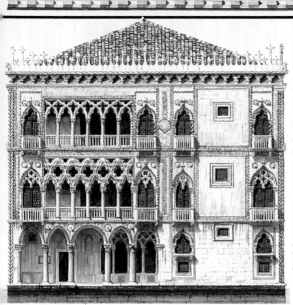

CA' D'ORO ▲ *148, 196*
(Cannaregio). Built
between 1424 and 1434
for the procurator
Marino Contarini on
the foundations of an
earlier palace, this
masterpiece was
originally covered in
gold leaf. Here
Flamboyant Gothic vies
with the refined,
soaring play of pillars
and arches. The
Milanese Matteo
Raverti and the
Venetians Bartolomeo
and Giovanni Bon
planned the Ca' d'Oro
as a blend of the
traditional palazzo,
closed in and compact,
with the freshness and
grace of a façade wide
open to the exterior.
Much of the decorative
repertoire of the
Doge's Palace is copied
from the
Ca' d'Oro.

FONDACO DEI TURCHI ▲ *193, 347–48.* (Santa Croce)
The Ca' Palmieri-Pesaro, which
was built in c.1227, became the
Turks' warehouse in 1621. From
he start it was one of the biggest
palaces on the Grand Canal.

Despite Berchet's misguided
restoration in 1869, the
Fondaco dei Turchi has
remained an important
example of Venetian-
Byzantine civil architecture,
with its two lateral towers
framing the Romanesque
arcades of a portico (on the
ground floor) and a loggia
(on the floor above).

PALAZZO BERNARDO ▲ *204*
(San Paulo) As the epitome of
Flamboyant Gothic (c.1442), the
Palazzo Bernardo has a
symmetrical "triptych" design,
with three levels of bay windows
and colored marbles maximizing
the effect of elevation. The
lateral watergates mean two
families living in the building
can have their own entrances,

PALAZZO VENDRAMIN-CALERGI ▲ *144, 194* (San Marcuola) Designed by Mauro Coducci, this palazzo introduced Tuscan Renaissance sophistication to the Gothic Venice of 1502–4. The usual three-part design is respected, but the twin bay windows, the three classical orders, one on top of the other, the heavily emphasized cornice and the all-stone façade are essentially new.

PALAZZO MALIPIERO-TREVISAN (Castello). Built between 1520 and 1530 by Sante Lombardo, nephew of the more famous Pietro, this palace shows a liveliness of form which is typical of the North Italian Renaissance. The semi-circular arches which crown the windows and doors, the side niches and carefully wrought balconies, all create subtle variations at each level of a classical white façade, the refinement of which is heightened by antique *tondi* in porphyry and green materials. Centered on the building is a small stone bridge, on either side of which are watergates. This bridge links the palace to Campo Santa Maria Formosa ▲ *166*.

PALAZZO TREVISAN ▲ *368* (Murano) Daniele Barbaro was the architect of this 16th-century Palladian building. Here the façade makes use of the play of light and shade to stress its stronger elements – the rich central area, the projecting balcony held up by fluted corbels, the tall niches and masks on the two lower levels, and the extravagent outline of the topmost cornice. The severity and regularity of these contrasts was originally attenuated by the colors of Prospero Bresciano's frescoes.

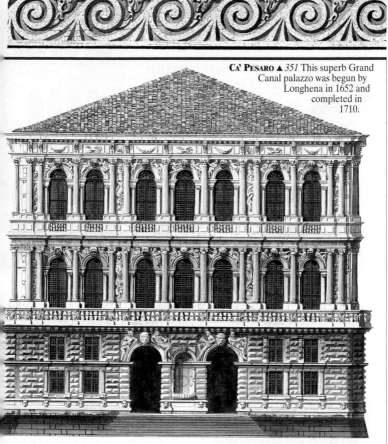

CA' PESARO ▲ *351* This superb Grand Canal palazzo was begun by Longhena in 1652 and completed in 1710.

A triumphalist façade and powerful effects of chiaroscuro make Ca' Pesaro the archetype of a certain aspect of patrician taste, and a masterpiece of Venetian Baroque. Its bossage of diamonds, monstrous heads, *putti* and genies add decorative weight to the more sober elegance of its purely architectural elements.

PALAZZO BELLONI-BATTAGIÀ ▲ *194* Built by Longhena (1645–9), this palazzo in the Santa Croce sestiere is one of the loveliest of its period. The façade is relatively small, but cunningly balanced. The design of it respects the traditional framework by relying on the vertical interplay of Corinthian pilasters on the *piano nobile*. The family coat of arms and Venetian admirals' obelisks, which were commissioned by the owner, blend easily here with the architect's chosen vehicle of expression.

Venetian dwellings are often clustered around an inner courtyard, which is closed off from the outside world and is usually square in shape. From the 13th century, this courtyard commonly depended on a main house, but after the turn of the 16th century it expanded lengthwise to open on to a canal or calle.

GOTHIC HOUSE, RIO MALPAGA (LATE 14TH CENTURY) Located on a narrow islet near San Barnaba ▲ *334*, this building belongs to a group of 60-foot-wide medieval units, by which all the adjoining building sites were strictly regulated. A long courtyard opens onto a major thoroughfare, and the distribution of space follows the Venetian pattern of warehouse on the ground floor, residence above, and loggia under the eaves.

THE VENETIAN-BYZANTINE HOUSE
A number of 13th-century houses around the Campo San Lio have retained their distinctive Venetian-Byzantine character. They are tall, with narrow façades, small windows and ground floors reserved for commercial use.

PALAZZETTO CONSTANTINI (14TH–15TH CENTURY)
Built on the Rio terrà ai Saloni, this little building used to adjoin the Rio terrà dei Catecumeni, which is now filled in. It still has its original wooden Renaissance portico.

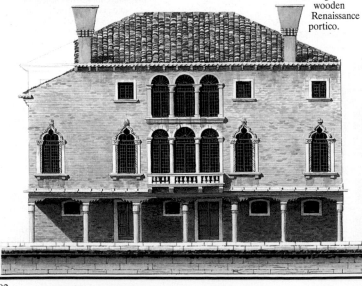

HOUSE ON CAMPO SAN TERNITA (LATE 16TH CENTURY)
A traditional 3-section structure combines with the style of the Renaissance.

BLOCKS OF FLATS BUILT AS LODGINGS FOR RENTAL IN THE CALLE DEL PARADISO (13TH CENTURY)

1171 Commissioned by the Foscari and Mocenigo families, whose coats of arms appear on the Gothic gables, these buildings have first-floor overhangs, which create more space inside without encroaching on the street.

GHETTO NUOVO ▲ *140*
(Cannaregio). Since it
was impossible to
extend the Jewish
quarter beyond the
canals surrounding it,
space had to be
created vertically, by
adding new floors to
existing buildings and
creating communal
areas to be shared by
several blocks. Hence
the unusual tallness
of the Ghetto
structures, which also
show how densely
Venice was populated
in the 16th and 17th
centuries.

**FONDAMENTE
DELLE PROCURATIE
E DEI CERERI**
This complex was
built at the end of
the 16th century in
Venice's poorest
quarter. Most of
the lodgings in it
were apportioned
to indigents free of
charge by the
Procurators of St
Mark, the
government
officers who
administered
charitable
bequests. The
symmetrical
arrangement of
the façade betrays
the equally strict
layout of the
interior.

CALLE DEL TRAGHETTO
(San Marco). This asymmetrical
17th-century palazzetto has its
main entrance and first floor
bay windows grouped to one
side, so that the main reception
room on the upper floor (the
portego) has other rooms on
only one side of it. The whole
building stands on a relatively
high base of Istrian stone,
while the Greek symmetry
of the top floor restores a sense
of vertical balance.

The two substantial wings of the building stand directly on the canal that skirts its island site. Each contains its quota of cheap lodgings overlooking the courtyard, and more expensive ones overlooking the fondamenta, the difference being visible in the façade. A connecting arch lends unity to the ensemble and makes the courtyard a semi-public area.

Chimneys were always an important element of Venetian architecture. The most common is the "inverted bell" type, which has a conical flue top (left). This was eventually supplanted by the cubic flue top, more or less elaborately decorated. In both cases, a frieze of small corbels normally separates the upper and lower sections of the shaft. Some time later, a much more ornate "obelisk" type of chimney came into vogue ● 96.

CAMPO OGNISSANTI
A stone mask is set into the wall of one of the houses overlooking this Dorsoduro campo (16th–17th century)

RIO TERRÀ DEGLI OGNISSANTI
Nothing in the appearance of this substantial building gives any clue to the layout of its interior, except perhaps the two tall chimneys constructed against the façade. These chimneys, which are typical of standard Venetian houses, actually serve two separate lodgings on every floor

OBELISK CHIMNEY Renaissance period, on a house on the Salizzada San Antonin.

CUBE CHIMNEY on a house on Campo San Trovaso. The cap has an elaborate, curving outline (seen below).

INVERTED BELL alongside Rio di Sant'Anna. Variations on this conical silhouette are found all over Venice.

Venice is not built on pilings but on the unstable islets
of the Lagoon. The city's architects had to find specially
adapted ways to give their buildings lightness and flexibility.

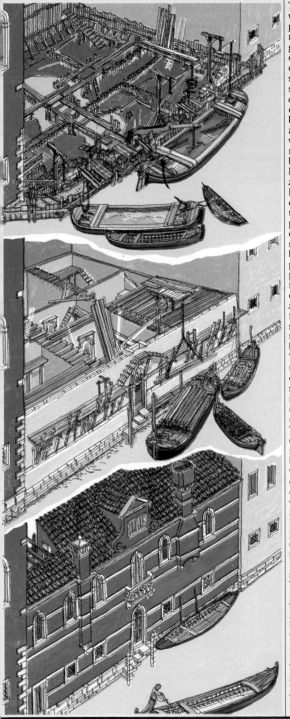

THE FOUNDATIONS
were set on a series of
pilings which were
rammed into the
ground to the depth
of the *caranto*, a layer
of solid clay and sand
some way beneath the
surface. Where the
caranto was too far
down, wooden
barriers were erected
around the site, which
was then drained and
reinforced with
baulks of oak and
larch. After this, a
zattaron would be
laid. This was a kind
of pontoon made of
two layers of larch
planks which were
cemented with a
mixture of stone and
brick. This was a
practice that
prevailed in Venice
from the 16th century
onwards. On the
zattaron rested the
foundations of Istrian
stone, and eventually
the upper parts of the
building.
THE FAÇADES were
usually made of brick,
often left bare but
sometimes rendered
in either pale grey
(*rovigno*) or brick red
(*pastellone*).
THE FLOORS were
constructed in the
normal way using oak
beams and boards,
which were then
covered with a layer
of mortar and spread
with shards of stone
and marble. This final
layer would be firmly
packed down to
create a smooth,
shiny but still
relatively elastic
surface.
THE ROOF was usually
made of Roman tiles,
which were rested on
a layer of flat, hollow
bricks. These tiles
were then set on
rafters. Around the
roof ran the *gorne*,
which were stone
gutters connected
to the drainpipes
which led directly
to the well.

97

CLOCKS AND CLOCKTOWERS

For the Venetians, monumental clocks were vital references which kept them informed of the hour, the movements of the planets, the terrestrial months and the signs of the Zodiac. In the 16th century, the San Marco Clocktower became one of the symbols of the Republic's power; all the major Venice-dominated cities of the mainland were similarly equipped. The mechanisms were regulated seasonally according to a solar hour that varied from forty minutes in summer to eighty minutes in winter. The time was calculated visually, according to the light.

The clocktower (1496–9), which incorporates the gateway between St Mark's Square and the Merceria, has the most beautiful clockface in Venice. The hours, months and phases of the sun and moon are all recorded on it. Studded with stars against a blue background, with the signs of the Zodiac and the planets in relief, the very concept of this tower lends additional force to the majestic beauty of St Mark's. With its face turned to the sea, the clockface is a symbol that is both awe-inspiring and beneficial by turns. For centuries it provided vital information to merchants and ships' crews about to sail from St Mark's Basin bound for the Orient. It was also for centuries a silent witness to grisly public tortures and executions.

Beneath the main clockface is a niche containing statues of the Virgin and Child, on either side of which are small doors. One of these shows the hour in Roman numerals, the other the minutes by multiples of five in Arabic numerals. On Ascension Day, which used to be one of the principal festivals celebrated in Venice, wooden automata representing the Three Kings are trundled out of the doors and pass one by one in front of the Virgin.

The two bronze giants which ring the hours on the top of the clocktower are represented clothed in the skins of wild animals, like the demi-gods of antiquity.

In the Doge's Palace ▲ *224* a single mechanism set into the wall regulates the clockfaces in the Senate and College Chambers. Its workings were devised by Raffaele Penzin in about 1530, and remade after the fire of 1574. The original contraption of wheels and weights was eventually replaced by a regular clock mechanism in 1755. There is a second clockface in the Senate Chamber, decorated with the symbols and signs of the Zodiac, whose usefulness is limited to recording lunar months and the phases of the moon.

The great clock of the Church of San Giacometto di Rialto kept time for the crowds of merchants in the heart of Venice's commercial quarter ▲ *85, 283*.

● ARCHITECTURAL
SHAPES AND STYLES

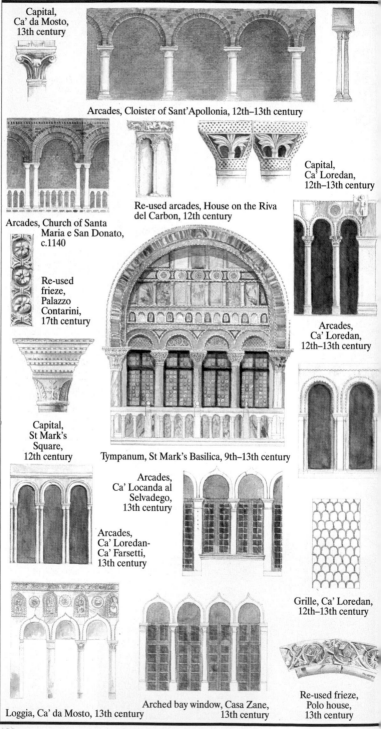

Capital, Ca' da Mosto, 13th century

Arcades, Cloister of Sant'Apollonia, 12th–13th century

Arcades, Church of Santa Maria e San Donato, c.1140

Re-used arcades, House on the Riva del Carbon, 12th century

Capital, Ca' Loredan, 12th–13th century

Re-used frieze, Palazzo Contarini, 17th century

Arcades, Ca' Loredan, 12th–13th century

Capital, St Mark's Square, 12th century

Tympanum, St Mark's Basilica, 9th–13th century

Arcades, Ca' Locanda al Selvadego, 13th century

Arcades, Ca' Loredan-Ca' Farsetti, 13th century

Grille, Ca' Loredan, 12th–13th century

Loggia, Ca' da Mosto, 13th century

Arched bay window, Casa Zane, 13th century

Re-used frieze, Polo house, 13th century

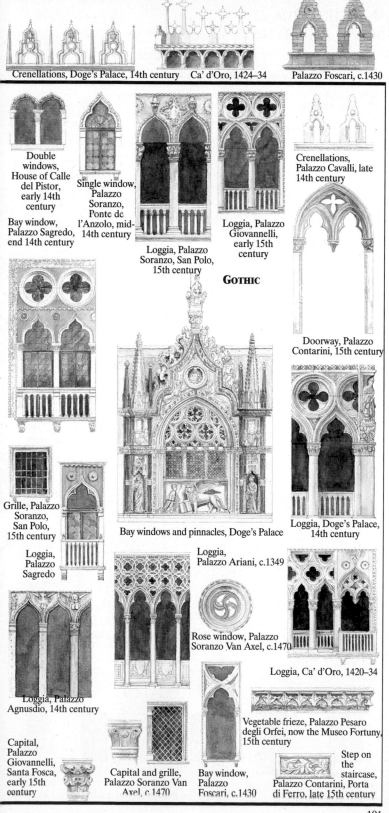

Crenellations, Doge's Palace, 14th century Ca' d'Oro, 1424–34 Palazzo Foscari, c.1430

Double windows, House of Calle del Pistor, early 14th century

Bay window, Palazzo Sagredo, end 14th century

Single window, Palazzo Soranzo, Ponte de l'Anzolo, mid-14th century

Loggia, Palazzo Soranzo, San Polo, 15th century

Loggia, Palazzo Giovannelli, early 15th century

Crenellations, Palazzo Cavalli, late 14th century

GOTHIC

Doorway, Palazzo Contarini, 15th century

Grille, Palazzo Soranzo, San Polo, 15th century

Loggia, Palazzo Sagredo

Bay windows and pinnacles, Doge's Palace

Loggia, Doge's Palace, 14th century

Loggia, Palazzo Ariani, c.1349

Rose window, Palazzo Soranzo Van Axel, c.1470

Loggia, Ca' d'Oro, 1420–34

Loggia, Palazzo Agnusdio, 14th century

Capital, Palazzo Giovannelli, Santa Fosca, early 15th century

Capital and grille, Palazzo Soranzo Van Axel, c.1470

Bay window, Palazzo Foscari, c.1430

Vegetable frieze, Palazzo Pesaro degli Orfei, now the Museo Fortuny, 15th century

Step on the staircase, Palazzo Contarini, Porta di Ferro, late 15th century

101

● ARCHITECTURAL SHAPES AND STYLES

Crenellations, Fondaco dei Tedeschi, 1508   Procuratie Vecchie, 1500–32

RENAISSANCE AND MANNERISM

Double bay window with balcony and bay window, Palazzo Zorzi, 15th century

Staircase, Palazzo Contarini del Bovola, 1499

Single bay window, Palazzo Zen, 1523

Niche, Ponte dei Becchieri, late 15th century

Grille, Palazzo Cappello, Ponte della Canonica, early 16th century

Pediment, Scuola di San Marco, 1490–1533

Bay window and grill, Scuoletta San Rocco, 15th century

Niche, Church of San Giorgio dei Greci, 1539–61

Double bay window with tympanum, Palazzo Vendramin-Calergi, 1504–9

Window with balcony, Palazzo Corner, 1553–6

Window, Palazetto, Via Garibaldi, c.1581

Grille, Palazzo Trevisan, Murano, 16th century

Bay windows with pediments, Palazzo Balbi, 1582–90

Bay window, Palazzo Foscarini, c.1600

Bay window, Palazzo Priuli-Ruzzini, late 16th century

Calle Vendramin, 16th century   Ramo della Pagia, 17th century   Rio della Celestia, 17th century

Arched window with balcony, Procuratie Nuove, 1582–1619

Central bay window, Palazzo Pisani, Santo Stefano, 1614–15

Window, pediment, balcony, Procuratie Nuove, 1582–1619

Window, bay window and balcony, Palazzo Canal, 17th century

Bay windows and balcony, Palazzo Barbaro, 1694

Arched window, balcony, Ca' Pesaro, 1652–82

Door and window, Scuola dei Battiloro e Tiraoro, 1711

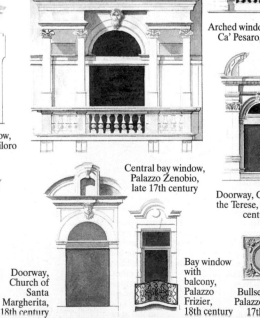

Central bay window, Palazzo Zenobio, late 17th century

Doorway, Convent of the Terese, early 17th century

Doorway, Church of Santa Margherita, 18th century

Bay window with balcony, Palazzo Frizier, 18th century

Bullseye window, Palazzo Labia, late 17th century

103

This idealized representation by Viollet-le-Duc of a Venetian Gothic Palace illustrates the dual function (commercial and residential) of the great patrician house. The French architect has taken certain liberties with the layout of the interior, but in general he has portrayed the salient features correctly ● *88*. The elements of the façade are all carefully detailed. Note particularly the porticos, windows, balconies, loggias, arches, cornices and moldings ● *100* to *103*.

The warehouse area is on the ground floor, with offices and archives at mezzanine level.

The attic area is mostly occupied by kitchens.

One side effect of the sumptuary laws, and the physical constraint of building on pilings, was that three stories was about as high as the Venetians dared go. Here, the main façade presents a stone front to the city, while at the back, a garden, or *cortile*, with a well reminds us that these palazzos were designed to create a hermetic, intimate world of their own.

The ornate *portego* was the largest room on the *piano nobile*, running from one side of the building to the other. Lavish banquets and receptions would be held in this area.

Venice
as seen by painters

"The Grand Canal, the most beautiful thoroughfare in the world that I know of, has the best houses along it, and runs from one end of the city to the other."

Philippe de Commynes

Auguste Renoir (1841–1919) arrived in Venice in late 1881. After visiting Florence, which rather bored him, he was in turn captivated by Venice; nevertheless the paintings that he did here were all of conventional subjects (probably because he badly needed to sell them and raise some money). His *Grand Canal*, which was shown at the 7th Impressionist Exhibition in 1882, received a cold reception, being criticized for its over-careful brushwork which was deemed an unfortunate departure from the naturalness and freshness of his earlier Impressionist work. From the 1870's onward, Renoir belonged firmly to the Impressionist group, which was then revolutionizing painting in general and landscape art in particular. Like Monet, he had

concentrated on light tones, eliminating browns and blacks from his palette. Better than anyone else, he knew how to capture fleeting light effects through the suppleness of his technique. In *Grand Canal*, however, he was accused of freezing this suppleness into a mechanical procedure.

> "When I went to Venice, I discovered that my dream had become – incredibly, but quite simply – my address."
>
> Marcel Proust

Félix Ziem (1821–1911) was successful from 1849. His ability to blend changing skies and glittering water was much admired, as in *Venice: The Doge's Palace* (1). But his art did not develop much after this, and his repertoire remained limited.

JMW Turner (1775–1851) only visited Venice three times, but succeeded wonderfully in evoking the city's atmosphere in paint. With his mastery of watercolor, he caught the subtler effects of Venetian light, which he developed later in oils in his London studio, retaining the watercolor technique. Turner took care to give his canvases of Venice a preliminary coat of white paint. This was a break with the tradition of starting a picture with a backing of red or another dark color. While other painters exploited contrasts of light and shade to construct their forms, Turner concentrated on delicate tonalities of pink, blue and yellow, as in *Leaving for the Ball* (2). Eventually he was painting white on white, a highly innovative practice for the 19th century.

1

2

109

> "We must look at nature purely as a mosaic of different colors, to be imitated one by one in complete simplicity."
>
> Paul Signac

Paul Signac (1863–1935) was influenced early on by the Impressionists; later, after meeting Seurat, he adopted the style of pointillism. This consisted of covering the surface of the canvas with regular dots of color, which created an intense, uniform effect of light, along with a meticulous serenity and calm unknown to art hitherto. A keen sailor who revelled in seascapes, Signac discovered Venice at the end of 1903 and went there again in

1904. He was deeply receptive to the color and oriental flavor of the city, and was fascinated by the mosaics of St Mark's which, he believed, confirmed many of his theories about painting. Signac's experience of Venice yielded canvases such as *The Green Veil* (1).

Henri Edmond Delacroix, known as Henri Cross (1856–1910) was another leading pointillist, but hesitated to go too far in "fracturing" his brushwork – as this watercolor of a *Canal in Venice* shows (2, 3 detail).

1

2   3

Like many other symbolist painters of his generation, Lucien Lévy (alias Lévy-Dhurmer, 1865–1953) was partial to misty atmospheric effects. For him they offered the "only pathway by which the eye might penetrate the world's mysteries"

Venice
as seen by writers

● VENICE AS SEEN BY WRITERS

THE SERENE REPUBLIC

From the 13th century onwards the Venetian Republic was engaged in expanding its control over most of Northern Italy. At the same time it was imposing its authority as a great Mediterranean power, whose empire was acknowledged up to the very rim of the Orient. The stability of Venetian institutions, which remained practically unaltered between 1297 and 1797, was in the eyes of many an ideal of government, and in pre-Revolutionary Europe was something of a political myth.

THE CITY OF THE VENETI

Petrarch (1304–74) first visited Venice in 1354 as the ambassador of Giovanni Visconti, Duke of Milan, and he moved permanently to a palace on the Riva degli Schiavoni in 1362. This palace was given to him by the Republic, in the hope that he would leave his precious library to Venice.

66 The august capital of the Veneti is today the only home of liberty, peace and justice, the only refuge of the good, the only port of destination for those who desire to live well and whose vessels have been tossed and battered by the storms of tyranny and war. Venice is a city rich in gold, but richer still in beauty, mighty in its possessions, but mightier by its virtue, founded on solid marble, but with the yet more solid moral foundation of civil concord, girt about with salt waters, but in the true salt of the spirit how much better encompassed than all others. **99**

PETRARCH, *LETTERS*, 1364

THE DECLINE OF THE REPUBLIC

In 1816, two years after the beginning of Austria's second occupation of Venice and the Veneto, Lord Byron (1788–1824) arrived in the city, newly separated from his wife. Byron moved into the Hotel Gran Bretagna on the Grand Canal, where he lived for the next five years; his profligacy was the talk of the town. In the Fourth Canto of Childe Harold's Pilgrimage, *Byron turns from his fictional Harold character to describe the "dying glories" of Venice.*

I stood in Venice, on the Bridge of Sighs;
A palace and a prison on each hand:
I saw from out the wave her structures rise
As from the stroke of the enchanter's wand:
A thousand years their cloudy wings expand
Around me, and a dying Glory smiles
O'er the far times, when many a subject land
Look'd to the winged Lion's marble piles,
Where Venice sate in state, throned on her hundred isles!

. . . In Venice Tasso's echoes are no more,
And silent rows the songless gondolier;
Her palaces are crumbling to the shore,
And music meets not always now the ear:
Those days are gone – but Beauty still is here.
States fall, arts fade – but Nature doth not die,
Nor yet forget how Venice once was dear,
The pleasant place of all festivity,
The revel of the earth, the masque of Italy.

LORD BYRON, *CHILDE HAROLD*, 1817

A LAMENT

William Wordsworth (1770–1850) took Venice very seriously and reverently; there is little of light-hearted contemporary Venice in his lines as, say, in Byron's Beppo, *a Venetian Story, or Shelley's* Julian and Maddalo. *His private life was troubled after the death of his brother in 1805, and many poems of this period have an elegiac quality. Much of Wordsworth's later work was inspired by his travels in Europe.*

Once did She hold the gorgeous east in fee;
And was the safeguard of the west; the worth
Of Venice did not fall below her birth,
Venice, the eldest child of Liberty.
She was a maiden City, bright and free;
No guile seduced, no force could violate;
And, when she took unto herself a Mate,
She must espouse the everlasting Sea.
And what if she had seen those glories fade,
Those titles vanish, and that strength decay;
Yet shall some tribute of regret be paid
When her long life hath reached its final day:
Men are we, and must grieve when even the Shade
Of that which once was great is passed away.

WILLIAM WORDSWORTH, *ON THE EXTINCTION OF THE VENETIAN REPUBLIC*, 1807

A CITY ON THE WATER

VENICE THROUGH THE EYES OF AN ARTIST

In September 1786, Johann Wolfgang von Goethe (1749–1832), the German poet, novelist and dramatist, left Weimar to travel to Italy. Before moving on to Florence and Naples, he stopped in Venice, keeping a journal which was later to become the basis for his book Italiensche Reise *("Italian Journey").*

❝ My old gift of seeing the world with the eyes of that artist, whose pictures have most recently made an impression on me, has occasioned me some peculiar reflections. It is evident that the eye forms itself by the objects, which, from youth up, it is accustomed to look upon, and so the Venetian artist must see all things in a clearer and brighter light than other men. We, whose eye when out of doors, falls on a dingy soil, which, when not muddy, is dusty, – and which, always colourless, gives a sombre hue to the reflected rays – or at home spend our lives in close, narrow rooms, can never attain to such a cheerful view of nature.

As I floated down the lagoons in the full sunshine, and observed how the figures of the gondoliers in their motley costume, as they rowed, lightly moving above the sides of the gondola, stood out from the bright green surface and against the blue sky, I caught the best and freshest type possible of the Venetian school. The sunshine brought out the local colours with dazzling brilliancy, and the shades even were so luminous, that, comparatively, they in their turn might serve as lights. And the same may be said of the reflection from the sea-green water. All was painted 'chiaro nell' chiaro', so that foamy waves and lightning flashes were necessary to give it a grand finish. ❞

JOHANN WOLFGANG
VON GOETHE,
ITALIENSCHE REISE,
1816

THE SONG OF THE GONDOLIERS

After a quarrel with his first wife, Minna, Richard Wagner (1813–83) fled to Venice with a friend, poet Carl Ritter. He stayed in the Palazzo Giustinian, on the Grand Canal, from August 29, 1858 to March 24, 1859, where he composed the second act of Tristan and Isolde *in solitude. Years later, Wagner returned to Venice, where he died in the Palazzo Vendramin-Calergi. His works of prose were translated into English and published in the 1890's in eight volumes.*

❝ One night, suffering from insomnia, I went out on my balcony at about three o'clock and there heard for the first time the celebrated and ancient song of the gondoliers. It seemed that the first harsh, plaintive cry that echoed through the night's quiet came from the Rialto, about a quarter of an hour's walk away from me. A similar chant answered it from even farther off. This strange, melancholy dialogue continued at intervals, sometimes long intervals, and I was so moved that I could not fix in my memory the few notes, probably very simple ones, that modulated it. Another evening I was able to understand by direct experience the full poetry of this popular air. I was returning late in a gondola, through dark canals; suddenly the moon rose, flooding with light the indescribable palaces and my gondolier, who stood slowly plying his gigantic oar in the stern of the boat. At that moment he uttered a cry like a wild creature, a kind of deep groan that rose in crescendo to a prolonged 'Oh!' and ended with the simple exclamation 'Venezia!' Something else followed, but already the cry had stirred in me so violent a commotion that I forgot the rest. The sensations I experienced at that moment did not leave me throughout my sojourn in Venice; they remained in my mind until I had completed the second act of *Tristan* and may even have suggested the plaintive, trailing clarinet at the beginning of Act Three. ❞

RICHARD WAGNER, *MEIN LEBEN*, 1911

FLOATING IN A GONDOLA

George Eliot (1819–80) was a frequent visitor to Italy throughout her life and its influence can be seen in her work. Her novel Romola *is set in Florence and her poem* The Spanish Gypsy *was inspired by the works of Tintoretto. Seven months before her death, she married her financial adviser, John Walter Cross, whom she had met in Rome. Her letters and journals were edited by Cross and published posthumously in 1885.*

❝ Of all the dreamy delights, that of floating in a gondola among the canals and out of the Lagoon is surely the greatest. We were out one night when the sun was setting, and the wide waters were flushed with the reddened light. I should have liked it to last for hours . . . Another charm of evening was to walk up and down the Piazza of San Marco as the stars were brightening and look at the grand dim buildings, and the flocks of pigeons flitting about them; or to walk on to the Bridge of La Paglia and look along the dark canal that runs under the Bridge of Sighs – its blackness lit up by a gaslight here and there, and the plash of the oar of blackest gondola slowly advancing. ❞

GEORGE ELIOT, *LETTERS AND JOURNALS, 3 VOLS*, 1885

THE VIEW FROM TORCELLO

John Ruskin (1819–1900) had a lifelong interest in landscape painting and between 1834 and 1860 he prepared a five-volume series on Modern Painters*. He spent seven months in Italy researching this series, and wrote passionately of the buildings and the natural beauty of Venice.*

❝ On this mound is built a rude brick campanile, of the commonest Lombardic type, which if we ascend towards evening (and there are none to hinder us, the door of its ruinous staircase swings idly on its hinges), we may command from it one of the most notable scenes in this wide world of ours. Far as the eye can reach, a waste of wild sea moor, of a lurid ashen grey; not like our northern moors with their jet-black pools and purple heath, but lifeless, the colour sackcloth, with the corrupted sea-water soaking through the roots of its acrid weeds, and gleaming hither and thither through its snaky channels. No gathering of fantastic mists, nor coursing of clouds across it; but melancholy clearness of space in the warm sunset, oppressive, reaching to the horizon of its level gloom. ❞

JOHN RUSKIN, *THE STONES OF VENICE*, 1851–3

PROUST IN VENICE

An avid reader of Ruskin, two of whose books he translated into French, Marcel Proust (1871–1922) visited Venice for the first time in 1900.

❝ My gondola followed the course of the small canals; like the mysterious hand of a Genie leading me through the maze of this oriental city, they seemed, as I advanced, to be carving a road for me through the heart of a crowded quarter which they clove asunder, barely dividing with a slender fissure, arbitrarily carved, the tall houses with their tiny Moorish windows; and, as though the magic guide had been holding a candle in his hand and were lighting the way for me, they kept casting ahead of them a ray of sunlight for which they cleared a path.

One felt that between the mean dwellings which the canal had just parted and which otherwise would have formed a compact whole, no open space had been reserved. With the result that the belfry of the church, or the garden-trellis rose sheer above the rio as in a flooded city. But with churches as with gardens, thanks to the same transposition as in the Grand Canal, the sea formed so effective a way of communication, a substitute for street or alley, that on either side of the canaletto the churches rose from the water in this ancient plebeian quarter, degraded into humble, much-frequented mission chapels, bearing upon their surface the stamp of their necessity, of their use by crowds of simple folk, that the gardens crossed by the line of the canal allowed their astonished leaves or fruit to trail in the water and that on the doorstep of the house whose roughly-hewn stone was still wrinkled as though it had only just been sawn, little boys surprised by the gondola and keeping their balance allowed their legs to dangle vertically, like sailors seated upon a swing-bridge the two halves of which have been swung apart, allowing the sea to pass between them.

Now and again there appeared a handsomer building

that happened to be there, like a surprise in a box which we have just opened, a little ivory temple with its Corinthian columns and its allegorical statue on the pediment, somewhat out of place among the ordinary buildings in the midst of which it had survived, and the peristyle with which the canal provided it resembled a landing-stage for market gardeners. **99**

MARCEL PROUST, *A LA RECHERCHE DU TEMPS PERDU*, 1925

DEATH IN VENICE

Death in Venice by Thomas Mann (1875–1955) tells the story of a disillusioned writer, Gustav Aschenbach, who comes to Venice for an extended rest. His meeting with a beautiful young Polish boy awakens in him a mystical joy. Aschenbach is torn between his desire to complete his life's work and his mute and violent passion: meanwhile Venice, the omnipresent backdrop to the story, is in the grip of a cholera epidemic.

66 Tadzio and his sisters at length took a gondola. Aschenbach hid behind a portico or fountain while they embarked, and directly they pushed off did the same. In a furtive whisper he told the boatman he would tip him well to follow at a little distance the other gondola, just rounding a corner, and fairly sickened at the man's quick, sly grasp and ready acceptance of the go-between's role.

Leaning back among soft, black cushions he swayed gently in the wake of the other black-snouted bark, to which the strength of his passion chained him. Sometimes it passed from his view, and then he was assailed by an anguish of unrest. But his guide appeared to have long practice in affairs like these; always, by dint of short cuts or deft manoeuvres, he contrived to overtake the coveted sight. The air was heavy and foul, the sun burnt down through a slate coloured haze. Water slapped gurgling against wood and stone. The gondolier's cry, half warning, half salute, was answered with singular accord from far within the silence of the labyrinth. They passed little gardens, high up the crumbling wall, hung with clustering white and purple flowers that sent down an odour of almonds. Moorish lattices showed shadowy in the gloom. The marble steps of a church descended into the canal, and on them a beggar squatted, displaying his misery to view, showing the whites of his eyes, holding out his hat for alms. Farther on a dealer in antiquities cringed before his lair, inviting the passer by to enter and be duped. Yes, this was Venice, this the fair frailty that fawned and that betrayed, half fairy tale, half snare; the city in whose stagnating air the art of painting once put forth so lusty a growth, and where musicians were moved to accords so weirdly lulling and lascivious. Our adventurer felt his senses wooed by this voluptuousness of sight and sound, tasted his secret knowledge that the city sickened and hid its sickness for love of gain, and bent an ever more unbridled leer on the gondola that glided on before him. **99**

THOMAS MANN, *DEATH IN VENICE*, 1912

VENICE BY NIGHT

Frederick Rolfe, "Baron Corvo", ambivalent English novelist and Catholic convert, spent many years of his life in Venice and died there in 1913.

66 It was unfortunate that his pockets were empty. With threepence, he might have spent the greater part of a cold wet night in a dry warm caffè.

He walked briskly, over the Academy bridge, as far as the Public Gardens eastward. About 23 o'clock, the rain became drizzle. He turned westward, going by Santazustina and Sanzanipolo and millions of little back alleys to the long solitary quay of Santamaria Odorifera, and on through the Ghetto to the three-arched bridge of Cannarezo. There, he turned, crossing the iron-bridge by the station; went round by Santachiara and Santandrea and Sanraffael to the Marittima end of the Zattere. He had walked, so far, as though on definite business; but now he slackened to a leisured dawdle. There was only a night to get through without exciting notice. In the morning, he could arrange better for the future.

The whole quay of the Zattere extended itself before him. He set himself to pace it from end to end. The drizzle ceased, and a warm haze bloomed on the darkness. He kept moving, to dry his drenched clothes.

Midnight sounded, and the stroke of one. The last ferries left the pontoons by the church of the Gesuati . . . On the distant bank of the wide canal of Zuecca, the lengthy line of lights along Spinalonga fluttered like little pale daffodils in a night-mist coloured like the bloom on the fruit of the vine. Great quiet reigned. He prayed, to comfort the minutes as they fled by . . . Dawn, misty, pink and glittering grey like salmon-flesh and scales, came. Very tired and stiff and sodden, he put the night behind him; and crossed Canalazzo, walking by Sanvidal and Sammaurizio and the Piazza to the club. **"**

BARON CORVO, *THE DESIRE AND PURSUIT OF THE WHOLE*, 1934

IMPRESSIONS OF VENICE

CARNIVAL

John Evelyn (1620–1706) is probably best remembered for his Diary, *in which he recounts the details of his travels abroad, providing an invaluable record of the period.*

" 1646. In January Signor *Molino* was chosen *Dodge*, but the extreame snow that fell, & the cold hindred my going to see the solemnity, so as I stirrd not from *Padoa* til *Shrovetide*, when all the world repaire to *Venice* to see the folly & madnesse of the *Carnevall*; The Women, Men & persons of all Conditions disguising themselves in antique dresses, & extravagant Musique & a thousand gambols, & traversing the streetes from house to house, all places being then accessible, & free to enter: There is abroad nothing but flinging of Eggs fill'd with sweete Waters, & sometimes not over sweete; they also have a barbarous costome of hunting bulls about the Streetes & Piazzas, which is very dangerous, the passages being generally so narrow in that Citty: Likewise do the youth of the severall Wards & parrishes contend in other Masteries or pastimes, so as tis altogether impossible to recount the universal madnesse of this place during this time of licence: Now are the great banks set up for those who will play at Basset, the Comedians have also liberty & the *Operas* to Exercise: Witty pasquils are likewise thrown about, & the Mountebanks have their stages in every Corner. **"**

JOHN EVELYN, *DIARY*, 1818

VENICE IN SPRING

Georges Sand (1804–76) left her husband in 1831 and embarked on a life as a writer. Venice is at the center of several of her works, such as the prose poem entitled Lettres d'un Voyageur.

" You can't imagine what Venice is like at present, my friend. When you

119

saw those ancient pillars of Greek marble whose colour and shape reminded you of bleached bones, she hadn't yet discarded the mourning drapes she puts on in winter. Now the spring has blown an emerald dust over all that. The base of the *palazzi*, where oysters used to cling to stagnant moss, are covered in mosses of tender green, and the gondolas glide between two carpets of velvety, beautiful verdure, while the sound of the waves languidly dies away in the foam of their wake. All the balconies are covered with vases of flowers, and the flowers of Venice, planted in a warm soil and blossoming in a humid atmosphere, have a freshness, rich texture and languid air which makes them resemble the women of this clime, whose beauty is as dazzling and as shortlived. Brambles twine around each pillar and hang their garlands of tiny pink and white rosettes from the black wrought-iron balconies. **99**

GEORGES SAND, *LETTRES D'UN VOYAGEUR*, 1837

SAINT MARK'S SQUARE

Guy de Maupassant (1850–93) thought Venice would be a place of surpassing grandeur; he was surprised to arrive there and find the city "resembled a bibelot" threatened by time.

66 I had dreamed of a great city filled with immense palaces, such is the renown of this antique queen of the seas. Amazingly, everything is tiny, tiny, tiny! Venice is no more than a bibelot, an old, charming, bibelot d'art, poor, ruined, but proud with a great sense of her former glory. Everything here is ruinous, on the point of crumbling into the water that floats this poor, worn city on its surface. The facades of the palaces are ravaged by time, stained by humidity, eaten up by the leprosy which destroys stone and marble. Some lean slightly to the side; they are ready to fall, tired of standing so long on their pilings.

I shall not speak of the Venice that everyone else has described. Piazza San Marco resembles Place du Palais Royal in Paris; the façade of the church looks like the pasteboard front of a café-concert; but the inside of it is everything one imagined and is moreover absolutely beautiful. The penetrating harmony of the lines and the colour tones, the glinting soft light of the old gold mosaics in the midst of austere marbles, the marvellous proportions of the vaults and the distances, something of divine discovery in the whole basilica, and in the very sunbeams which become calm and religious around its pillars, in the sensations it casts like beams upon the spirit through the eye: all these things make St Mark's the most completely admirable thing on earth. **99**

GUY DE MAUPASSANT, *GIL BLAS*, 1851

THE SPECTACLE OF VENICE

Edward Gibbon (1737–94) author of History of the Decline and Fall of the Roman Empire, *was not impressed by Venetian architecture.*

❝ The spectacle of Venice afforded some hours of astonishment and some days of disgust. Old and in general ill-built houses, ruined pictures, and stinking ditches dignified with the pompous denomination of canals; a fine bridge spoilt by two rows of houses on it, and a large square decorated with the worst architecture I ever yet saw. ❞

EDWARD GIBBON, *MISCELLANEOUS WORKS*, 1796

THE EFFECTS OF VENICE

Born in Orel, in central Russia, Ivan Turgenev (1818–83) was the first major Russian writer to find success in the rest of Europe. He lived mostly in Western European countries, and his writing examines the social, political and philosophical issues of the times.

❝ No one who has not seen Venice in April knows the full, the indescribable charm of that magical city. The gentleness and softness of spring are to Venice what the bright sun of summer is to majestic Genoa, what the gold and purple of autumn are to that grand old man among cities, Rome . . .
'Venice is dying, Venice is deserted' – so her inhabitants will tell you; but it may be that in the past she lacked such charm as this, the charm of a city fading in the very culmination and flowering of its beauty. No one who has not seen her, knows her: neither Canaletto nor Guardi (not to speak of more recent painters) was able to record the silvery delicacy of her air, her vistas, so near and yet so fugitive, her marvellous harmony of graceful lines and melting colours. To the visitor, soured and broken by life, Venice has nothing to offer; to him she will be bitter as the recollection of early unrealized dreams are bitter. But for him who still has strength and confidence within him, she will be sweet; let him bring his happiness to her and expose it to her enchanted skies, and, however radiant his happiness may be, she will enrich it with her own unfading light. ❞

TURGENEV, *ON THE EVE*, 1859

COLLECTING MEMORIES

Besides novels, short stories, plays and essays, Henry James (1843–1916) wrote several books of "sketches" based on his extensive travels through Europe. His views about the effects of Venice on visitors seem the opposite to those of Turgenev.

❝ I know not whether it is because San Giorgio is so grandly conspicuous, but with a great deal of worn, faded-looking brickwork; but for many persons the whole place has a kind of suffusion of rosiness. Asked what may be the leading colour in the Venetian concert, we should inveterately say Pink, and yet without remembering after all that this elegant hue occurs very often. It is a faint, shimmering, airy, watery pink; the bright sea-light seems to flush with it and the pale whiteish-green of lagoon and canal to drink it in. There is indeed a great deal of very evident brickwork, which is never fresh or loud in colour, but always burnt out, as it were, always exquisitely mild.
Certain little mental pictures rise before the collector of memories at the simple mention, written or spoken, of the places he has loved. When I hear, when I see, the magical name I have written above these pages, it is not of the great Square that I think, with its strange basilica and its high arcades, nor of the wide mouth of the Grand Canal, with the stately steps and the well-poised dome of the Salute; it is not of the low lagoon, nor the sweet Piazzetta, nor the dark chambers of St Mark's. I simply see a narrow canal in the heart of the city – a patch of green water and a

surface of pink wall. The gondola moves slowly; it gives a great smooth swerve, passes under a bridge, and the gondolier's cry, carried over the quiet water, makes a kind of splash in the stillness. A girl crosses the little bridge, which has an arch like a camel's back, with an old shawl on her head, which makes her characteristic and charming; you see her against the sky as you float beneath. The pink of the old wall seems to fill the whole place; it sinks even into the opaque water. Behind the wall is a garden, out of which the long arm of a white June rose – the roses of Venice are splendid – has flung itself by way of spontaneous ornament. On the other side of this small water-way is a great shabby façade of Gothic windows and balconies – balconies on which dirty clothes are hung and under which a cavernous-looking doorway opens from a low flight of slimy water-steps. It is very hot and still, the canal has a queer smell, and the whole place is enchanting.

It is a fact that almost every one interesting, appealing, melancholy, memorable, odd, seems at one time or another, after many days and much life, to have gravitated to Venice by a happy instinct, settling in it and treating it, cherishing it, as a sort of repository of consolations; all of which to-day, for the conscious mind, is mixed with its air and constitutes its unwritten history. The deposed, the defeated, the disenchanted, the wounded, or even only the bored, have seemed to find there something that no other place could give. 〞

HENRY JAMES, *ITALIAN HOURS*, 1909

LINGERING IMPRESSIONS

Hugh Honour's Companion Guide to Venice *was first published in 1965, and has since become one of the standard reference works on the city. He lives in Tuscany.*

〝 When the moment for departure comes, the impressions which are strongest in the memory are more likely to be of the city and the lagoon than of its artistic treasures. No cicerone can indicate, no guide-book can predict, what these will be. It may be no more than a glimpse through an escutcheoned gateway to a cortile hung with washing, or the elation on emerging from a long dark calle on to a smiling fondamenta. A wedding party in a train of gondolas, a greengrocer and a porter abusing each other in the sibilant dialect of Goldoni's pantaloons, a gondolier polishing the brasswork on his boat, an old woman crouched in devotion in some quiet cool church where a Bellini Madonna stares down in compassion, the flicker of candles before a shrine illuminating the carved marble flowers of a Tullio Lombardo, or perhaps some sight as simple as a cat sunning itself on an old well-head, or a pair of pigeons silhouetted against the sky on one of those arches which thrust the palaces apart across some narrow calle. Though they may be sinking, the buildings of Venice will see out our time; but such scenes as these, which form an essential part of the memory of every lover of Venice, neither will nor can be quite the same again. 〞

HUGH HONOUR, *THE COMPANION GUIDE TO VENICE*, 1965

LIFE IN VENICE

COURTESANS AND DESPERATE VILLAINS

Thomas Coryate (c.1577–1617) was well known in his day as an eccentric character. In 1608 he travelled through France, Italy, Switzerland, Germany and Holland, most of the journey being undertaken on foot. An amusing account of his travels, entitled Coryate's Crudities, *was published in 1611.*

❝As for the number of these Venetian Cortezans it is very great. For it is thought there are of them in the whole City and other adjacent places, as Murano, Malomocco, &c. at the least twenty thousand, whereof many are esteemed so loose, that they are said to open their quivers to every arrow. A most ungodly thing without doubt that there should be a tolleration of such licentious wantons in so glorious, so potent, so renowned a city . . . For so infinite are the allurements of these amorous Calypsoes, that the fame of them hath drawen many to Venice from some of the remotest parts of Christendome, to contemplate their beauties, and enjoy their pleasing dalliances. And indeede such is the variety of the delicious objects they minister to their lovers, that they want nothing tending to delight. For when you come into one of their Palaces (as indeed some few of the principallest of them live in very magnificent and portly buildings fit for the entertainement of a great Prince) you seeme to enter into the Paradise of Venus.❞

❝There are certaine desperate and resolute villaines in Venice, called Braves, who at some unlawfull times do commit great villainy. They wander abroad very late in the night to and fro for their prey, like hungry Lyons, being armed with a privy coate of maile, a gauntlet upon their right hand, and a little sharpe dagger called a stiletto. They lurke commonly by the water side, and if at their time of night, which is betwixt eleven of the clocke and two, they happen to meete any man that is worth the rifling, they will presently stabbe him, take away all about him that is of any worth, and when they have thoroughly pulled his plumes, they will throw him into one of the channels: but they buy this booty very deare if they are after apprehended. For they are presently executed.❞

THOMAS CORYATE,
CORYATE'S CRUDITIES, 1611

MORALITY

Lord Byron maintained a regular correspondence with his good friend and publisher, John Murray, throughout the five years that he spent in Italy. By all accounts, he had rather a riotous time in Venice in 1817.

❝The general state of morals is much the same as in the Doges' time; a woman is virtuous (according to the code) who limits herself to her husband and one lover; those who have two, three or more are a little wild; but it is only those who are indiscriminately diffuse and form a low connection such as the Princess of Wales with her courier who are considered as overstepping the modesty of marriage. In Venice the nobility have a trick of marrying with dancers or singers; and truth to say the women of their own order are by no means handsome; but the general race, the woman of the second and other order, the wives of Advocates, merchants and proprietors and untitled gentry are mostly bel'sangne and it is with these that the more aleatory connections are usually formed: there are also instances of stupendous constancy. I know a woman of fifty who never had but one lover, who dying early she became devout renouncing all but her husband: she piques herself as may be presumed upon this miraculous fidelity, talking of it occasionally with a species of misplaced morality which is rather amusing.❞

LORD BYRON,
LETTER TO JOHN MURRAY, JANUARY 2, 1817

● VENICE AS SEEN BY WRITERS

THE EASTERN INFLUENCE
Son of a Lord Mayor of London, William Beckford (1759–1844) was a wealthy traveler and collector of paintings and curios. He is remembered chiefly for an oriental tale entitled Vathek, *but he also wrote two travel books, including* Dreams, Waking Thoughts and Incidents. *This was originally suppressed by the author in 1783 and republished in a revised edition in 1834.*

❝I like this odd town of Venice, and find every day some new amusement in rambling about its innumerable canals and alleys. Sometimes I pry about the great church of St Mark, and examine the variety of marbles and mazes of delicate sculpture with which it is covered. The cupola, glittering with gold, mosaic, and paintings of half the wonders in the Apocalypse, never fails to transport me to the period of the Eastern empire. I think myself in Constantinople, and expect Michael Paleologus with all his train. One circumstance alone prevents me observing half the treasures of the place, and holds down my fancy just springing into the air: I mean the vile stench which exhales from every recess and corner of the edifice and which all the incense of the altars cannot subdue. When no longer able to endure this noxious atmosphere, I run up the campanile in the Piazza, and seating myself amongst the pillars of the gallery, breathe the fresh gales which blow from the Adriatic; survey at leisure all Venice beneath me, and its azure sea, white sails, and long tracks of islands shining in the sun. Having thus laid in a provision of wholesome breezes, I brave the vapours of the canals, and venture into the most curious and murky quarters of the city, in search of Turks and Infidels, that I may ask as many questions as I please about Cairo and Damascus.**❞**

WILLIAM BECKFORD, *DREAMS, WAKING THOUGHTS AND INCIDENTS*, 1783

THE SMELL OF VENICE
Three years after her husband Henry Thrale's death, Hester Thrale (1741–1821) married an Italian musician named Gabriel Piozzi, amid much opposition from family and friends (including Dr Johnson). She published several books of poems and anecdotes.

❝But it is almost time to talk of the Rialto, said to be the finest single arch in Europe, and I suppose it is so – very beautiful, too, when looked on from the water, but so dirtily kept and deformed with mean shops, that, passing over it, disgust gets the better of every other sensation. The truth is, our dear Venetians are nothing less than cleanly. St Mark's Place is all covered over in a morning with chicken-coops, which stink one to death, as nobody, I believe, thinks of changing their baskets; and all about the ducal palace is made so very offensive by the resort of human creatures for every purpose most unworthy of so charming a place, that all enjoyment of its beauties is rendered difficult to a person of any delicacy, and poisoned so provokingly, that I do never cease to wonder that so little police and proper regulation are established in a city so particularly lovely to render her sweet and wholesome.**❞**

HESTER PIOZZI,
OBSERVATIONS AND REFLECTIONS, 1789

CANAL BATHING

Rome, Naples, Florence and Milan were all dear to the French novelist Stendhal (1783–1842), but Venice ultimately left him cold. Nevertheless, in July 1815 he seems to have seriously entertained the idea of moving there with his mistress Angela Pietragrua; but his schemes came to nothing, and he left Venice on 9 August.

❝ On 22 July 1815, at six thirty, I arrived in Venice by the mail-boat from Padua, dying of sleep and a trifle irritated by a brainless fat German, a merchant from Trieste, with a red cross. So was Baron Lepreux. People like this German, because of the ordinariness of their ideas, are on a level with Italian society and to begin with seem quite agreeable. At Milan, Lepreux was put out of countenance by the number of houses to which the man went.

I retired to bed on arrival at thc Regina d'Inghilterra. When I came out again, at 11 o'clock, the first person I came across was Valdramin, who suggested a sea-bathe in the middle of the Giudecca Canal; he had a little ladder attached to the side of his boat. It was exceedingly pleasant and probably very healthy.

When we got back we wrote a letter together to Gina to tell her what a mistake she made by preferring that wretched hole Padua to Venice, which despite all its misfortunes is still one of the most agreeable cities in Europe. **❞**

STENDHAL, *JOURNAL*, 1801–15

SWIMMING THE GRAND CANAL

Byron was a keen swimmer and regularly covered considerable distances.

❝ In 1818 the chevalier Mengaldo (a Gentleman of Bassano) a good swimmer, wished to swim with my friend Mr Alexander Scott and myself. As he seemed particularly anxious on the subject, we indulged him. We all three started from the island of the Lido and swam to Venice. At the entrance of the Grand Canal, Scott and I were a good deal ahead, and we saw no more of our foreign friend, which however was of no consequence, as there was a gondola to hold his clothes and pick him up. Scott swam on past the Rialto when he got out less from fatigue than from chill, having been for hours in the water without rest of stay except what is to be obtained by floating on one's back, this being the condition of our performance. I continued my course on to Santa Chiara, comprising the whole of the Grand Canal/beside the distance from the Lido, and got out where the laguna once more opened to Farina. I had been in the water by my watch without help or rest and never touching ground or boat four hours and twenty minutes . . . I crossed the Hellespont in one hour and ten minutes only. **❞**

LORD BYRON, *LETTER TO JOHN MURRAY*, FEBRUARY 21, 1821

ITALIAN FOOD

Elizabeth David (1913–91) wrote about food and cookery in a style that was both passionate and poetic. She was interested in the culture of food and the country which produced it, and embraced regional cookery rather than haute cuisine.

❝ Of all the spectacular food markets in Italy, the one near the Rialto in Venice must be the most

125

● VENICE AS SEEN BY WRITERS

remarkable. The light of a
Venetian dawn in early
summer – you must be about at
four o'clock in the morning to
see the market coming to life – is so
limpid and so still that it makes every separate
vegetable and fruit and fish luminous with a life of its
own, with unnaturally heightened colours and clear stencilled
outlines. Here the cabbages are cobalt blue, the beetroots deep rose, the
lettuces clear pure green, sharp as glass. Bunches of gaudy gold marrow-flowers
show off the elegance of pink and white marbled bean pods, primrose potatoes,
green plums, green peas. The colours of the peaches, cherries, and apricots, packed
in boxes lined with sugar-bag blue paper matching the blue canvas trousers worn by
the men unloading the gondolas, are reflected in the rose-red mullet and the
orange *vongole* and *cannestrelle* which have been prised out of their shells and
heaped into baskets. In other markets, on other shores, the unfamiliar fishes may
be vivid, mysterious, repellent, fascinating, and bright with splendid colour; only in
Venice do they look good enough to eat. In Venice even ordinary sole and ugly
great skate are striped with delicate lilac lights, the sardines shine like newly-
minted silver coins, pink Venetian *scampi* are fat and fresh, infinitely enticing in the
early dawn.

The gentle swaying of the laden gondolas, the movements of the market men as
they unload, swinging the boxes and baskets ashore, the robust life and rattling
noise contrasted with the fragile taffeta colours and the opal sky of Venice – the
whole scene is out of some marvellous unheard-of ballet. **99**

ELIZABETH DAVID,
ITALIAN FOOD, 1954

THE CATS

Jan Morris is the author of a prodigious number of travel books, and has writtten about many of the world's great cities. Among these works is her classic guide to Venice, which was published in 1960.

66 For myself, I love the cats of Venice, peering from their pedestals,
sunning themselves on the feet of statues, crouching on dark staircases to escape
the rain, or gingerly emerging into the daylight from their fetid subterranean lairs.
Shylock defined them as 'necessary and harmless', and Francesco Morosini, one of
the great fighting Doges, thought so highly of them that he took one with him on
his victorious campaigns in the Peloponnese.

There are few more soothing places of refuge than a Venetian garden on a blazing
summer morning when the trees are thick with green, the air is heavy with
honeysuckle, and the tremulous water-reflections of the canals are thrown
mysteriously upon the walls. The rear façade of the palace before you, with its
confusion of windows, is alive with gentle activity. On the top floor an elderly
housekeeper lowers her basket on a string, in preparation for the morning mail.
From a lower window there issues the harsh melody of a housemaid's song as she
scrubs the bathroom floor. In the door of the ground-floor flat a girl sits sewing, in
a black dress and a demure white apron, with a shine of polished pans from the
kitchen lighting her hair like a halo. From the canal outside comes a pleasant buzz
of boats, and sometimes the throaty warning cry of a bargee. On a neighbouring
roof-garden an artist stands before his easel, with brush in one hand, coffee-cup in
the other.

And dotted all about you in the grass, in attitudes statuesque and contented, with
their tails tucked around them and the eyes narrowed in the sunshine, one licking
his haunches, one biting a blade of grass, one intermittently growling, one twitching
his whiskers – all around you sit the cats of the garden, black, grey or obscurely
tabby, like bland but scrawny guardians. **99**

JAN MORRIS,
VENICE, 1960

TOURISM

Pietro Aretino (1492–1556) wrote several comedies and satires. Here he writes to his landlord in Venice.

❝ It seems to me, Honoured Sir, that I would commit the sin of ingratitude if I did not repay with praise some part of the debt which I owe to the heavenly situation of your house . . . Certainly its builder chose the finest position on the Canal. And since that Canal is the patriarch of all others and since Venice is a female pope among cities, I can truthfully say that I enjoy both the fairest highway and the most joyous view in the world. Whenever I look out of my windows at that time when the merchants foregather I see a thousand persons in as many gondolas . . . To my left I behold the much frequented Bridge and the warehouses of the German traders. There are grapes in the barges below, game of all kinds in the shops and vegetables laid out on the pavements. There is no need for me to long for meadows watered by streams when I can marvel at dawn over waters covered with an endless variety of merchandise, each article in its due season.

What sport it is to watch those who bring in great quantities of fruit and vegetables handing them out to others who carry them to their appointed places! All is tumult and bustle, except where about a score of sailing-boats laden with melons are moored together, making a sort of island to which crowds hurry off to count, sniff and weigh, so as to test the quality of the goods. Of the ladies, gleaming in gold and silk and jewels, though they are mere housewives, I will not speak, lest I grow tedious with the description of such pomp and circumstance. But what makes me roar with laughter are the whistles, catcalls and jeers directed by the boatmen at those whose rowers are not equipped with scarlet hose.

And who would not laugh till he cried at the sight of a boatload of Germans who had just reeled out of a tavern being capsized into the chilly waters of the Canal? ❞

PIETRO ARETINO, *LETTER*, 1529

A COSMOPOLITAN CITY

Following his father's death in 1640, John Evelyn spent a lot of time traveling in Europe until 1652, when he married and decided to settle in England.

❝ Nor was I less surprised with the strange variety of the several nations seen every day in the streets and piazzas; Jews, Turks, Armenians, Persians, Moors, Greeks, Schiavonians some with their targets and buckles, and all in their native fashions, negotiating in this famous Emporium which is always crowded with strangers . . . It was evening, and the canal where the Noblesse go to take the air, as in our Hyde Park, was full of ladies and gentlemen. There are many dangerous stops, by reason of the multitudes of gondolas ready to sink one another; and indeed they affect to lean them on one side, that one who is not accustomed to it, would be afraid of oversetting. Here they were singing, playing harpsichords, and other music, and serenading their mistresses; in another place racing and other pastimes on the water, it being now exceeding hot. ❞

JOHN EVELYN,
DIARY, 1818

ECHOES

Mary McCarthy, American novelist and critic, spent a winter in Venice in the early 1960s. In her classic Venice Observed, *she applied an ironic objectivity to her subject and its people, pointing out that in addition to building the loveliest city on earth, the Venetians invented income tax, statistical science, the floating of government stock, state censorship, anonymous denunciations (the Bocca del Leone), the gambling casino – and the ghetto.*

❝ When the Venetians stroll out in the evening, they do not avoid the Piazza San Marco, where the tourists are, as the Romans do with Doney's on the Via Veneto. The Venetians go to look at the tourists, and the tourists look back at them. It is all for the ear and eye, this city, but primarily for the eye. Built on water, it is an endless succession of reflections and echoes, a mirroring. Contrary to popular belief, there are no back canals where a tourist will not meet himself, with a camera, in the person of the other tourist crossing the little bridge. And no word can be spoken in this city that is not an echo of something said before. 'Mais c'est aussi cher que Paris!' exclaims a Frenchman in a restaurant, unaware that he repeats Montaigne. The complaint against foreigners, voiced by a foreigner, chimes querulously through the ages, in unison with the medieval monk who found St Mark's Square filled with 'Turks, Libyans, Parthians, and other monsters of the sea'. Today it is the Germans we complain of, and no doubt they complain of the Americans, in the same words. Nothing can be said here (including this statement) that has not been said before. One often hears the Piazza described as an open-air drawing-room; the observation goes back to Napoleon, who called it 'the best drawing-room in Europe'. A friend likens the ornamental coping of St Mark's to sea foam, but Ruskin thought of this first '. . . at last, as if in ecstasy, the crests of the arches break into a marbly foam, and toss themselves far into the blue sky in flashes and wreaths of sculptured spray . . .' Another friend observes that the gondolas are like hearses: I was struck by the novelty of the fancy until I found it, two days later, in Shelley: 'that funereal bark'. Now I find it everywhere. A young man, boarding the vaporetto, sighs that 'Venice is so urban', a remark which at least sounds original and doubtless did when Proust spoke of the 'always urban impression' made by Venice in the midst of the sea. And the worst of it is that nearly all these clichés are true. It is true, for example, that St Mark's at night looks like a painted stage flat; this is a fact which everybody notices and which everybody thinks he has discovered for himself. I blush to remember the sound of my own voice, clear in its own conceit, enunciating this proposition in the Piazza, nine years ago. ❞

MARY MCCARTHY, *VENICE OBSERVED*, 1961

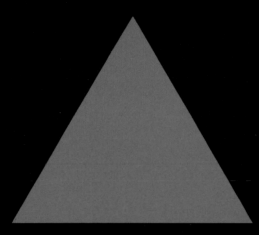

Itineraries in Venice

▲ Gondolier at the landing stage.

Taxi launches. ▼

▲ Gondolas on the Grand Canal.

Acqua alta and white tulle.▼

▲ Ponte degli Scalzi on the Grand Canal.

▲ St Mark's Square in the snow.　　Café Quadri on St Mark's Square. ▼

▲ Riva degli Schiavoni.

Taxi on the Grand Canal.　　　　　　Fishing boats. ▼

▲ General view of Torcello.

Torcello. ▼

▼ Fishing nets in the Lagoon.

Cannaregio

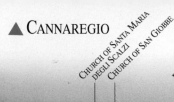

CHURCH OF SANTA MARIA DEGLI SCALZI
CHURCH OF SAN GIOBBE
PALAZZO LABIA
GHETTO ✪
CHURCH OF SANTA DEI SERVI

SANTA LUCIA STATION
CHURCH OF SAN SIMEONE PICCOLO
CHURCH OF SAN GEREMIA
CHURCH OF SAN MARCUOLA
PALAZZO VENDRAMIN-CALERGI
CHURCH OF SANTA MAR DELLA MADDALEN

"The gateway to Venice, after all, is neither the station nor the Piazzale, but the Grand Canal before us, churned by propellers, turbulent as a great river."
Fernand Braudel, *Venise*

Santa Lucia Station.

Immediately outside the railway station lies Cannaregio, the first of the six sestieri of Venice. Situated at the northwest end of the city, this is the second largest sestiere after Castello ▲ *155*, covering an area of 150 hectares. Nearly a third of the population of Venice is concentrated here, amounting to more than twenty thousand people. There are two theories about the origins of the name Cannaregio; according to one, it comes from *Canal regio* (the Royal Canal), meaning the broad waterway which once provided convenient access to the city from the mainland, by prolonging the lagoon canal of San Secondo (which runs parallel to the railway bridge). The other hypothesis is that the word derives from the reeds and canes which used to abound in this area. In any case, a system of straight, parallel canals, with long fondamenta abutting southwards and linked by calli, criss-cross this zone of workmen's houses interspersed with magnificent palaces. To the south, behind the palaces of the Grand Canal, a wide street known as the Strada Nuova was built at the end of the last century. Now pedestrianized, this street runs from the station to the Campo Santi Apostoli, crossing the sestiere from one side to the other and adopting a number of different names as it goes. Few people lived in this sestiere until the 11th century, and it seems to have taken form only gradually, as the process of draining and consolidating the site progressed. From the 15th century onwards, Cannaregio was a definable quarter, though it was still peripheral to Venice proper. Before the railway bridge and the station were built, manufacturing was the principal industry in the district, despite attempts to create a new area of growth with the Fondamente Nuove. A similar project in the 16th century, the draining of the Sacca della Misericordia, was also never realized.

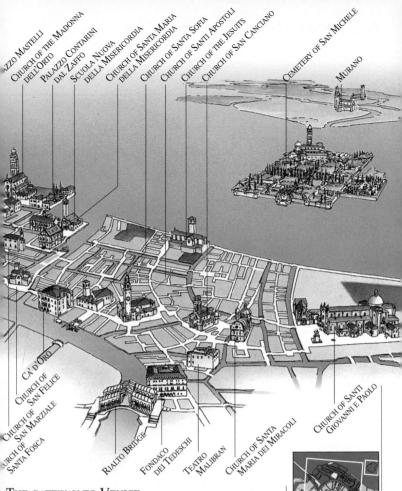

THE GATEWAY TO VENICE

PONTE DELLA LIBERTÀ. Built by the Austrians 50 years after the Treaty of Campo Formio in 1797 ● *34, 243*, to link Venice with Milan. The railway bridge ended the thousand-year separation from the mainland and shook the city's economy as Venice, already in the throes of the industrial revolution, saw its dependence on the mainland grow ever larger.
SANTA LUCIA STATION. The present station dates from 1955, but still bears the name of the Renaissance church demolished in 1861 to make way for it. Opposite is the green dome of the Church of San Simeone Piccolo.

🗓 **Half a day**

◆ A C

BRIDGES TO VENICE
The Austrians conceived a project for a bridge between Mestre and Venice as early as 1814, but it was not until 1846 that construction of the Ponte della Libertà was finally begun. The span of this new viaduct was almost 11,500 feet, and it included 222 stone arches. In 1933, the Ponte delle Littorale was opened. This bridge, designed by Umberto Fantucci, was built in less than two years by the Eugenio Miozzia.

THE CHURCH OF THE SCALZI. Almost adjoining the station is a church commissioned from Longhena by the Discalced (barefoot) Carmelite order. This Baroque building was constructed between 1660 and 1680. The Carmelites brought an image of the Virgin from the island of Lazzaretto Vecchio ▲ *384*; at that time the image was known as that of Santa Maria di Nazaretta, and the new church was then named after it. The façade, by Giuseppe Sardi, dates from 1680, and one of the vaults was decorated with a fresco by Tiepolo, the *Trasporto della Casa del Loveto* (1743–5). This vault was destroyed by an Austrian bomb on the night of October 27, 1915. Only two fragments remain, and these are preserved with Tiepolo's original sketch at the Accademia. The church's other fresco by Tiepolo, the *Gloria di Santa Teresa,* on the lower right-hand side of the church, was not damaged by the bomb. The second chapel on the left-hand side contains the tomb of Lodovico Manin, the last doge of Venice. (Take the Lista di Spagna, formerly the site of the Spanish Embassy, to Campo San Geremia, one of the few piazzas that has four separate wells.)

Ponte delle Guglie.

A WAY INTO VENICE
Before the construction of the bridge, the Cannaregio canal provided the main means of access to Venice: all traffic from the mainland had to pass by way of San Giuliano and Lizza di Fusina (today's Marghera). Fusina, at the mouth of the Brenta, was the scene of constant comings and goings, with vessels carrying provisions to the city. Until the 19th century, the waterway was kept open, even when sea-traffic to St Mark's Basin was jeopardized by the spread of the marshes and *barene* (mudflats) ■ *18,* in the 16th century. At that time, boats had to have empty barrels lashed to their sides, to reduce their draft and enable them to unload directly on the wharves.

FROM SAN GEREMIA TO SAN GIOBBE

THE CHURCH OF SAN GEREMIA. The present church was built in the mid-18th century by Carlo Corbellini, who took as his model the Greek Cross floorplan of the Church of La Salute ▲ *318*. Apart from several Baroque altars, the main point of interest is Palma the Younger's *Madonna Assisting at the Coronation of Venice*. The left-hand extension of the church was modified to house the relics of the Sicilian martyr St Lucia after the destruction of the church named after her. Beside the adjoining Fondamenta Labia is one of Venice's oldest campaniles, which dates from the 12th–13th century.

PALAZZO LABIA. Beside the campo, right next to the church, is the Palazzo Labia, one of the most imposing palazzi in Venice. It was built between the late 17th and early 18th centuries by the Labia, a family of rich Catalan merchants who were admitted to the Venetian Patriarchate in 1646 in exchange for a large donation to support Venice's war in Crete ● *34*. They commissioned Giambattista Tiepolo to decorate the main room on the first floor. Although the

theme is the life of Cleopatra, the real subject is the pomp of
the Venetian aristocracy, which Tiepolo depicted with great
verve. (From here, take the Salizzada San Geremia and, just
before the Ponte delle Guglie, turn left into the Fondamenta
Venier then into the Fondamenta Savorgnan.)

PONTE DELLE GUGLIE. This stone bridge, across the
Cannaregio canal, replaced a wooden one in 1580.
It takes its name from the obelisks that stand
at either end, and occupies a key position
between the Grand Canal and the
Lagoon. Only three waterways in
Venice have the status of canal – the
Giudecca, the Cannaregio and the
Grand Canal – the rest being
known as *rii*. Most of Venice's food
supplies would arrive along the
Cannaregio canal. On the other side
of the bridge, on the Rio terrà San
Leonardo, there is an attractive flower,
vegetable and fish market.

THE CHURCH OF SAN GIOBBE. This church was
begun in 1450 by Antonio Gambello, among others, and its
construction was continued little by little as donations were
raised to pay for it – notably a bequest from the Doge
Cristoforo Moro. When Pietro Lombardo took over the
project in 1470, he decided to alter much of its original style
in order to accommodate some pure Renaissance elements in
the portal, the decoration of the dome of the choir, and also
in the MARTINI CHAPEL, whose vault is covered with shiny
terracotta that came from the workshop of the Florentine
sculptor Luca della Robbia. (Cross over the PONTE DEI TRE
ARCHI, a 17th-century structure which is unique in Venice,
since arches like these would have hindered the barge traffic.)
On the Fondamenta di Cannaregio stands Giuseppe Sardi's
PALAZZO SURIAN-BELLOTTO, in which the French
Ambassador, de Montaigu, stayed during the 18th century,
accompanied by his secretary, Jean-Jacques Rousseau.
(Follow this *fondamenta* in the direction of the Ponte delle
Guglie, in the Fondamenta Pescaria, and turn left in the Calle
del Forno or the Calle di Ghetto Vecchio, into the Ghetto.)

THE GOLDEN PLATES
At a banquet which he
held for his fellow
patricians, Gian
Francesco Labia had
the dinner served on
golden plates. When
they had finished
eating, he apparently
hurled the plates into
the canal, with the
remark "*Le abia, o
non le abia, saro
sempre Labia*"
(Whether I have these
or not, I shall always
be a Labia). Malicious
gossip has suggested,
however, that he may
have subsequently
retrieved his treasures
from the water.

139

THE GHETTO

THE JEWS IN VENICE DURING THE 14TH AND 15TH CENTURIES.
The first signs of a Jewish presence in Venice date from the
early 14th century, when Jewish merchants first came to buy
and sell in the port and *fondachi*, without receiving the right
to settle permanently in the city. During the second half of the
century, the Jews began to establish themselves more or less

illegally, until the
Chioggia War of 1381
● *31* yielded a first
condotta. This
officially authorized
them to live in Venice
and to practise usury
and *strazziaria* (the
sale of secondhand
clothes and objects).
The *condotta*, which
defined the financial
conditions and status
under which they were
allowed to stay in the
city, was no more than

Inside the Schola
Spagnola.

**THE ORIGINS OF THE
WORD "GHETTO"**
In the 14th and 15th
centuries, foundries
were set up in
Cannaregio. Their
cinders were piled
nearby, on a spot
where new foundries
were to be built. The
Venetian word for "to
smelt" was *gettare*,
hence the name *geto
veccio* (old foundry)
for the first site, and
geto nuovo for the
second. With the
arrival of the Jews,
the meaning and
pronunciation
changed as the *ghetto*
became the place
assigned to them.

Circumcision
(late 18th century).

a renewable, temporary contract, however, and, on August 27,
1394, a decree was passed which stipulated that the Jews were
to be expelled from Venice at the end of the current *condotta*
– on February 20, 1397. From that time onwards, they were
permitted to stay for no more than 15 consecutive days, and
they also had to wear an emblem which would identify their
religion. The pretext for this decision came from certain
irregularities that had been uncovered in the management of
the Jewish *banchi,* but what really prompted it was the fear
that Jewish bankers and merchants would start to penetrate
into other sectors of Venetian commerce. Nevertheless, the
measure was deflected and the Jewish presence continued
undiminished through much of the following century until
1496, when a more restrictive order
was put into force which again
allowed Jews to stay in Venice for
only two weeks in every year.
**THE ESTABLISHING OF THE FIRST
GHETTO.** The war waged against
Venice by the allies of the League of
Cambrai, and the appalling Venetian
defeat at Agnadello in the spring of 1509 ● *33*, altered this
situation again. Fearing the advance of the Imperial army,
mainland Jews took refuge in Venice, where some of them
gave much-needed funds to the Republic, despite the severe
losses they had already suffered. Under these circumstances,
Venice as usual opted for political realism: she tolerated the
Jews, and at the same time proceeded to organize their
segregation from the rest of the population. On March 29,
1516, a substantial majority in the Senate approved Zaccaria
Dolfin's proposal that the Jews in Venice should move en bloc
to the Ghetto Nuovo, a sort of urban islet that was linked to
the rest of the city by two points of access which might be
closed at night. This decision meant the Jews could remain as
pawnbrokers and textile merchants, while still ensuring they

"All the forgotten diseases of the leproseries of the
Orient seemed to gnaw these blistered walls."

Théophile Gautier

were kept apart from the rest of the city. It ran contrary to the
tide of public opinion (fuelled by the sermons of the
Franciscans, who proclaimed that God would punish the city
if the Jews were admitted), while still taking shrewd account
of it, for the chosen site made it possible not only to protect
the Jews from violence and looting, but also to impose an
effective curfew upon them – and to keep them apart from the
rest of the Venetian population. As half-fortress and half-
gathering point, the Ghetto soon became the symbol of
Venice's ambiguous attitude; one which was prepared to
accept the Jews and to make the most of their skills, but at the
same time was still determined to demonstrate their
inferiority to Christians.

VENETIAN AMBIVALENCE. The Republic's
policy was most clearly demonstrated
when, in 1524, a group of patricians
proposed that a pawnshop should be
established in the city. This operation, by
lending money at a low rate of interest,
would have rendered the Jews
superfluous. But an alarmed Council of
Ten persuaded the patricians to drop
their project "on pain of death";
moreover, a decree was then passed
which forbade the Council to reconsider
the matter except with the unanimous
consent of all its members. Most wanted
the Jews to carry out the task of lending
money, because they could be easily
controlled and heavily taxed. The
condotte were regularly renewed. In
December 1571, during the crusade
against the Turks ● 36, in which Venice
played so prominent a part, a decision

was once more taken to expel the Jews; but this again was
never applied and, in 1573, a fresh *condotta* authorized them
to stay in Venice and to lend money at a maximum interest
rate of five per cent. After this there was no further talk of
driving the Jews from the city.

DAILY LIFE IN THE GHETTO. By consigning the Jews to the
Ghetto Nuovo, the Senate made what Brian Pullan has called
"the Venetians' contribution to the
language of persecution". From the
16th century onwards, the word *ghetto*
signified the segregation of the Jews in
Venice and gradually became a generic
term used all over Europe. After 1541,
the Jewish quarter was enlarged to
include the Ghetto Vecchio. In 1633,
the Ghetto Nuovissimo was also added
but, in spite of these extensions, the
population density remained very
high, and this explains the
relative tallness (for
Venice) of the buildings in
the Jewish quarter, which
frequently grew to heights
of six, or even nine stories.
The Jews were forbidden to

LA GIUDECCA ▲ *336*,
In 1515, Giorgio
Emo, a patrician, put
it to the Senate that
the population of
Jews, which had
grown, should be
consigned to this
island. But as troops
were billeted on the
Giudecca, the move
could have caused
trouble, and the idea
was dropped.

**THE GHETTO: A
SESTIERE WITH
A SOUL ✪**
You will not really
know Venice until you
have been to the
Ghetto, where lived
those who, materially
and intellectually,
contributed so much to
the richness of life in La
Serenissima. A short
ride in a vaporetto
(Line 1, along the
Grand Canal to the San
Marcuola halt) will take
you to this popular and
appealing quarter,
haunted by the shade of
Corto Maltese. A
hidden passage
interlinks all the
synagogues, among
which are the Schola
Levantina, a fine
Baroque building, and
the Museum of Hebrew
art, with its many
treasures.

The *aron* of Schola Spagnola, with the Ten Commandments.

THE CLOSURE OF THE GHETTO
The decree of 1516 stated that the Jews were "required to go without delay and to abide all together in the block of houses at the Ghetto, by San Girolamo . . . and in order to prevent them from moving about the streets at night . . . we decree that on the Ghetto Vecchio side, where there is a small bridge, and likewise at the other end of said bridge, two gates shall be raised, which shall be opened at dawn and closed again at midnight by four Christian sentries employed for the purpose and appointed by the Jews themselves at a wage that our college shall deem to be suitable." The entrance to the Ghetto on the Rio San Girolamo was also closed off, and the Jews were forbidden to leave the area during certain religious festivals.

leave their quarter during the night, or during Christian religious festivals; they also had to wear an identifying emblem, initially a yellow skullcap, then a turban or a hat, first yellow then red. Although they were placed under the control of a special magistrature, they were able to run their own affairs within the Ghetto. Butchers and bakers could ply their trades in the proscribed area according to the prescriptions of the Jewish faith. Community life was close-knit, and benevolent associations were as numerous as the synagogues, which were known as schole, like their Christian counterparts, the scuole ▲ *295*. The synagogues were usually on the upper floors of buildings with discreet façades: nothing on the outside gave any indication of the rich premises contained within. But the whole of Venice shared the same passion for music and theater, and the Campo del Ghetto Nuovo, although it housed no fewer than sixty tailors' shops and three moneylenders' offices and was full of busy crowds during the day, nevertheless contrived to double up as a venue for theatrical performances, which were often attended by Christians. Indeed, many of the Christians were happy to break the curfew during the feast of Purim, when there were masks and street dancing in the Ghetto, just as at Carnival time in the rest of Venice.

FROM THE FALL OF THE REPUBLIC TO MODERN TIMES. The gates of the Ghetto were finally demolished on June 10, 1797, during the French occupation, "so that there shall no longer be any apparent division between the citizens of this town". But, with the arrival of the Austrians, to whom Napoleon Bonaparte was soon to surrender the city, the Jews once again found that they were confined to the Ghetto in a kind of unofficial segregation. It was not until the Unification of Italy that Victor Emmanuel II was able to grant the Jews an equal status in law as the rest of his subjects. The history of the Jews of Venice was subsequently no different from that of all the other citizens, until the Fascist regime promulgated its racial laws and began to deport the Venetian Jews to concentration camps – a fact of which we are today reminded by a carved plaque on the wall of the Schola Spagnola.

THE SYNAGOGUES AND MUSEUM. In 1719 there were a total of nine schole; today there are just five remaining. Their names reflect something of the diversity which was to be found within the Jewish community in Venice.

In this scene from Luchino Visconti's 1954 masterpiece, *Senso*, Contessa Livia (Alida Valli) hurries through the labyrinthine Ghetto Nuovo (below) on a way to a tryst with her handsome young Austrian lover.

There was the SCHOLA GRANDE TEDESCA, which appeared on the Campo del Ghetto Nuovo in 1528; the SCHOLA CANTON (1532), which followed the Ashkenazi rite and was so named either after a family or because it stood in the corner of the piazza; and the SCHOLA ITALIANA (1575). The foundation dates of both the SCHOLA LEVANTINA (Eastern Mediterranean) and of the SCHOLA SPAGNOLA, or PONENTINA (Western Mediterranean) are rather less certain. Both were

THE OLD JEWISH CEMETERY
Goethe, Byron, Shelley, George Sand and Alfred de Musset were all fascinated by the melancholy beauty of this cemetery, abandoned

Sephardic and they stood on the Campiello del Ghetto Nuovo. The main halls of each of these synagogues are extremely impressive. The synagogue in the Ponentina was rebuilt in the 17th century by Longhena, but its rival can still boast a fine portal but and, on the inside, some 17th-century carved wood columns. Religious ceremonies are still conducted today in one or other of these two schole, depending on the season. The Schola Grande Tedesca contains a museum of Hebrew art on its ground floor which displays both religious and secular items that were collected from the 17th to 19th centuries. (After the Ponte del Ghetto Nuovo, follow the Fondamenta degli Ormesini, and then turn right at the second bridge into the Rio terrà Farsetti. At the Campiello dell'Anconeta take the Rio terrà del Cristo.)

in the 18th century, whose tombstones were gradually sinking into the sand and vegetation. In 1386, the Jews had obtained permission to bury the dead in this plot of ground by the Lagoon at San Nicolò di Lido. The brotherhood of the Misericordia was responsible for carrying out the burials, and every nation was allotted its own corner of the graveyard.

FROM SAN MARCUOLA TO SAN MARZIALE

THE CHURCH OF SAN MARCUOLA. This church's name is an odd contraction of Ermagora and Fortunato, the two saints to whom it was dedicated. Founded in about 1000, and rebuilt in the 12th century on a basilical plan, the church was rebuilt twice more in the 18th century. The  second rebuilding was supervised by Giorgio Massari; he made a large portal in the side of the church facing the Grand Canal, as part of a plan (never completed) to make this the main façade. Entering by the south portal, it is surprising to find the high altar not straight ahead but to the right. The altars are by Gianmaria Morlaiter, who made the high altar of La Salute ▲ *318*. Note also Tintoretto's *La Cena* (1547). In 1789 the San Marcuola quarter was seriously damaged by fire, and among the many buildings destroyed was the SCUOLA DEI LUCCHESI. (Turn right along the Rio terrà Dietro la Chiesa, cross the bridge on the Rio di San Marcuola and continue as far as the Via Larga Vendramin.)

PALAZZO VENDRAMIN-CALERGI. This is undoubtedly one of the noblest examples of Renaissance architecture in Venice. Francesco Sansovino, official chronicler of the Republic and son of the great architect, called it the finest structure on the Grand Canal. It was designed by Mauro Coducci; d'Annunzio has described its "ethereal aspect . . . like a sculpted cloud suspended on the water". The palace was completed in the early 16th century. Its owners, the Loredan family, were famous for their pride and, as if to refute this reputation, they had the Templars' motto of humility carved on the base of the façade. After passing through a succession of distinguished owners, the palace became the property of the Calergi, a great feudal family of Cretan origin, and was then passed on to their cousins the Vendramin. The composer Richard

The gate of SANTA MARIA DEI SERVI.

THE SCUOLA DEI LUCCHESI (Luccans) Many natives of Lucca were forced into exile when Castruccio Castracani took control of their city in 1317. According to the chronicles, thirty Luccan families and at least three hundred artisans arrived in Venice at this time, where they perfected (and perhaps introduced) the art of silk weaving. From the 14th century, these artisans had their own guild, which assembled at the Scuola del Volto Santo. This building burned down in the 1789 fire (see the painting on the right by Francesco Guardi). But the symbol of the Scuola dei Lucchesi, the *volto santo*, is still visible on some of the *patera* decorating the well and the entrance of the Corte del Volto Santo (which looks onto the Rio terrà della Maddalena).

Wagner lived and died here in 1883; bought by the city of Venice in 1946, the house was turned into a winter casino. (At the end of the Calle Larga Vendramin, turn right into the Rio terrà della Maddalena, the first street in Venice to be built over a filled-in canal, in 1398. At the end of this rio, turn right just before the bridge.)

THE CHURCH OF SANTA MARIA MADDALENA ● *83*. With its smooth, shadowless surfaces, this Neo-classical building clad in white marble is unique in Venice. Built by Tommaso Temanza in the second half of the 18th century, it replaced a 13th-century church. The exterior forms a perfect circle; the

interior is hexagonal, with four radial chapels. (After the Ponte Sant'Antonio, take the Salizzada Santa Fosca.)

CAMPO SANTA FOSCA ● *84*. A statue of the monk Paolo Sarpi stands at the center of this campo, with the CHURCH OF SANTA FOSCA to one side. Santa Fosca was founded in the 10th century, then rebuilt in 1297, its floorplan and orientation following Byzantine canons. It was demolished in 1679 to make way for a church which had a one (rather than the previous three) naves. Consecrated in 1733, it was completed by Domenico Rossi in 1741, but had to be restored again after a fire near the end of the century. To the left of the façade is a fine 15th-century brick campanile. (With the church on your right, pass the bridge and go straight on along the Calle Zancani, which leads to the church of San Marziale.)

THE CHURCH OF SANTA MARIA DEI SERVI. Nothing remains of the buildings that comprised the original 14th-century church and monastery here, except for a few vestiges such as the Gothic portal of the convent (in a private garden). Paolo Sarpi lived in the monastery and Veronese painted his *Supper at Simon Peter's House* (1570–6) for the refectory. This painting was later presented to Louis XIV by the Venetian Republic and is now at Versailles.

THE CHURCH OF SAN MARZIALE. According to legend, a boat ran aground here in 1286, near the church. It carried an image of the Virgin, placed there by a shepherd from Rimini; on the orders of the Doge the image was moved to the church. The present building dates from the 17th century. Inside are Tintoretto's *St Martial* and, in the sacristy, Titian's *Tobias and the Angel Gabriel* (1530). (With the church on your right, after the bridge turn left down the Fondamenta della Misericordia and take the Calle Larga, passing the Ponte dei More.)

THE DEATH OF WAGNER
This celebrated death in Venice inspired the Cuban writer Alejo Carpentier: "Passing by the Palazzo Vendramin-Calergi, Montezuma and Filomeno noticed some black figures carrying a coldly glinting metal coffin down to a gondola. 'It's a German, who died yesterday of apoplexy,' said the boatman, pausing for a moment. 'Now they are taking his remains back to his country. They say he wrote peculiar operas . . .' " (*Baroque concert*)

THE ATTACK ON PAOLO SARPI
The monk Paolo Sarpi (1552–1623) was a resolute opponent of Church interference in politics. He defended Venice at the risk of his own life when Rome laid an interdict on the city in 1606. On October 5, 1607, he was wounded by five unknown assailants; afterwards, he accused the Pope, claiming that he recognized the *stylus* (the style, but also the blade) of the Roman Curia.

145

SIOR ANTONIO RIOBA
Adorned in the last century with an iron nose, this statue, bearing a burden on its back, stands at the foot of the Ponte dei More. The Venetians invented a character for it, Sior Antonio Rioba, and used him as their mouthpiece when they wanted to criticize the government.

CAMPO DEI MORI

Beyond the Ponte dei More lies an intriguing "Venice within Venice".
CAMPO DEI MORI. The name of this campo probably alludes to the presence in the vicinity of the *fondaco,* and houses used by Arab merchants. Three 18th-century statues in front of the houses on the campo, and a fourth on the *fondaco,* are supposed to represent the three Moorish brothers, Rioba, Sandi and Afani. They were merchants who left Morea (the Peloponnese) to escape civil war. They arrived in Venice in 1112, where they acquired the name of Mastelli, purportedly because "they possessed thousands of buckets (*mastelli*) filled with gold sequins". The figure in a turban and oriental costume leading a camel, who inhabits the bas-relief on the façade of PALAZZO MASTELLI (on the Campo della Madonna dell'Orto), is a reference to the family's involvement in the spice trade. On the fondamenta, at the foot of the bridge, stands number 3399, Tintoretto's house, where he died in 1594.

MADONNA DELL'ORTO

THE CHURCH OF LA MADONNA DELL'ORTO. This church was dedicated to St Christopher (there is a statue of him by Bartolomeo Bon above the portal); it was rededicated to the Virgin after the discovery of a miraculous statue in a neighboring garden. The building was begun in the late 14th century and completed a hundred years later. It was restored by the British Save Venice Commission after the 1966 floods ■ *26.* Along its red brick façade are a frieze and garlands, ridge ornaments and niches containing statues of the twelve Apostles (from the workshops of the dalle Masegne). The elegant portal belongs to the transition period between Gothic and Renaissance. More than any other church in Venice, this is the shrine of Tintoretto, who is buried in the chapel to the right of the choir. While still a young man, he painted a *Last Judgment* and *Adoration of the Golden Calf* on the choir walls, *The Martyrdom of St Christopher* and the *Vision of the Holy Cross to St Peter* in the apse, and the *Presentation of Mary in the Temple* (above the entrance to the San Mauro chapel on the right of the nave). Also in the church are a masterpiece by Cima da Conegliano from his early days in Venice, *St John the Baptist among the Saints*, and a *Virgin and Child* by Giovanni Bellini in the Valier Chapel.

The Casino degli Spiriti.

SCUOLA DEI MERCANTI. An elegant CLOISTER of the former convent adjoins the church on one side, and on the other stands what was, after 1570, the headquarters of the SCUOLA DEI MERCANTI. As the owners of many houses in the Rialto, the commercial heart of the city, these merchants could, with the profits they made there, indulge in charitable works and assist widows and orphans. The interior was decorated with paintings by Tintoretto and Veronese, which were lost during the Napoleonic occupation of Venice. (Leave the campo, which has retained its original herring-bone brick paving, and turn right down the Fondamenta della Madonna dell'Orto.)

CORTE DEL CAVALLO. This courtyard owes its name to the workshop of Andrea del Verrochio and Alessandro Leopardi, in which was cast Bartolomeo Colleoni's famous bronze warhorse, which now stands at the center of the Campo Santi Giovanni e Paolo ▲ *157, 159*. (Retrace your steps and continue along the fondamenta.)

PALAZZO CONTARINI DAL ZAFFO. A patrician mansion dating from the late 16th century, the Palazzo Contarini dal Zaffo was famous for the literary debates which took place in its gardens and in the CASINO DEGLI SPIRITI – a small building at the end of the park overlooking the Sacca della Misericordia and the wide expanse of water beyond. Titian and Aretino, among others, took part in these intellectual joustings. The palazzo is now occupied by a charitable institution.

THE MISERICORDIA

SACCA DELLA MISERICORDIA. This is the "missing piece" of Venice, the cove in the northern laggon that was never filled in. (Beyond the bridge, continue on to the Fondamenta dell'Abbazia.) The SQUERO ● *69*, ▲ *324* here is now no more than a hangar. Like all *squeri*, it had living space and workshops. Squeri were always built on sloping ground at the water's edge. They are a little like mountain chalets; indeed the first Venetian shipwrights were carpenters from the villages of northern Italy. (Turn left.)

SCUOLA VECCHIA DELLA MISERICORDIA ● *86*. An elegant 14th–15th-century brick construction which was enlarged several times before being remodelled

"This is the derelict palazzo in which Tintoretto lived for 20 years, and later died. He was author of that *Crucifixion*, which contains so many figures bursting with life that one is at a loss to understand how they sprung from a single brain."
Maurice Barrès,
La Mort de Venise

THE COLLEONE ▲ *159* Andrea del Verrocchio was working on his equestrian statue of Colleone when he heard that another sculptor was to get the commission for the rider, and his work would be confined to the horse. He left Venice in a rage, but not before he had smashed the legs and head of his newly completed warhorse. Threatened with the death penalty, he replied that this would be a great pity . . . "since alive I can still make a more beautiful head for my horse". The authorities were charmed by his humor and aplomb, and doubled his fee.

in the Gothic style in about 1451. Also on the CAMPO DELL'ABBAZIA, one of the quietest and most picturesque squares in Venice with its herringbone paving, is the former CHURCH OF SANTA MARIA, called "*di val verde*" ▲ 295 after the island on which it was founded in the 10th century. Note the allegorical statues (by Clemente Moli) on the façade, and the portrait of the patrician Gaspare Moro, who paid for the church to be rebuilt (1651–9).

SCUOLA NUOVA. This was commissioned from Sansovino in 1534 by the brotherhood of La Misericordia, who sold their original building to the silk weavers' guild. It was 50 years before the interior was completed, and the exterior was never finished. (When you reach the PONTE CHIODO – the only bridge in Venice with no parapet – turn down the Fondamenta di San Felice and continue to the Strada Nuova.)

THE STRADA NUOVA

STRADA NUOVA. The Austrians planned to push this major arterial road through to the north of the city, but the project was not realized until 1871–2. Originally named Via Vittorio Emmanuele, it quickly became known as the "Strada Nuova". Running along the Grand Canal, it links the station with the Rialto Bridge. Today it is lined with shops and is very busy, especially at Christmas time and during the Carnival, when it is filled with multi-colored stalls.

THE CHURCH OF SAN FELICE. This 11th–12th-century church was demolished when it threatened to fall down and was rebuilt in 1531. It has a painting by Tintoretto, *St Demetrius and a Votary*. (Turn right and go on to the Ponte Pasqualigo.)

PALAZZO GIOVANELLI. This palace presents an early 15th-century Gothic façade on the Rio di Noale side. It was once famous for its art collection, assembled by the Giovanelli family, which included Giorgione's *Tempest* ▲ 307. It is now the office of a firm of auctioneers. (Turn back and take the Calle della Ca' d'Oro, to the right.)

THE CA' D'ORO: "A DIVINE PLAY OF AIR AND STONE". This mansion is, along with the Doge's Palace, the loveliest expression of the oriental, flowered Gothic style in Venice. Marius Contarini bought the site in 1412. He wanted his palace to be more splendid than all the others, so he involved himself closely in the works, which were carried out first by Lombard artisans directed by Matteo Raverti, and then by Venetians under Giovanni and Bartolomeo Bon. Before long the

Before the Campo della Misericordia, pause to admire the GOTHIC GATEWAY to the Corte Nuova. In its three-part lunette, the Madonna opens the folds of her cloak, receiving under her protection the genuflecting brotherhood of the Scuola Vecchia della Misericordia.

The intensely dramatic *St Sebastian* by Andrea Mantegna (1431–1506), on the first floor of the Ca' d'Oro.

> "You cannot imagine what an unhappy day I spent [...] before the Ca' d'Oro, vainly attempting to draw it while the workmen were hammering it down before my face."
>
> John Ruskin

building began to be called the "Golden House" (Ca' d'Oro). This gives some idea of the effect of its asymmetrical façade, on which a profusion of gilt was blended with polychrome marble and other adornments; and indeed it must have been staggering to have impressed a city as vivid and luxurious as 15th-century Venice. But decline quickly set in; the Ca' d'Oro changed hands many times and deteriorated over the centuries. It was almost a ruin when the Russian Prince Troubetskoy bought it in 1847 and set in motion a programme of ill-advised restoration. Finally, Baron Giorgio Franchetti, who acquired the building at the end of the century, reconverted the Ca' d'Oro to its original state; the façade recovered its brightness, and the courtyard its staircase and well. In 1916, Franchetti donated his collections, along with the palace, to the state. A museum was opened in 1927, which today contains Carpaccio's *Annunciation* and *Il Transito della Vergine*, Titian's *Venus* and Mantegna's *St Sebastian*. The Franchetti gallery also possesses rare examples of Gothic and Renaissance furniture, 15th- and 16th-century Flemish tapestries, and an interesting collection of medallions. The Ca' d'Oro, which was repeatedly altered this century, has been restored to its original splendor now that its marbles, which were damaged by pollution and the vibrations of the vaporetti, have been restored.

CAMPO SANTA SOFIA. The Church of SANTA SOFIA is only distinguishable by its square campanile, being otherwise invisible among the houses on the Strada Nuova. Near the traghetto, linking the campo to the Pescheria ▲ *285* on the other bank, is the PALAZZO SAGREDO, with its staircase and frescoes by Pietro Longhi (*La Caduta dei Giganti*, 1734).

A FAMOUS OWNER
In 1847, the Russian Prince Alexander Troubetskoy bought the Ca' d'Oro for the great ballerina Maria Taglioni, who collected palaces on the Grand Canal, and commissioned Meduna to restore it. The architect set about disfiguring the building before the horrified gaze of the art critic, John Ruskin, who was then staying in Venice. The "glorious" inside staircase was dismantled; the well, designed by Bartolomeo Bon, was sold; and the marbles of the façade were thrown away, along with the floor tiles.

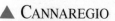

SANTI APOSTOLI

THE CHURCH OF SANTI APOSTOLI. According to legend, the original church was founded in the 9th century. Partly rebuilt in 1575 and restored several times, the present building owes its appearance to restoration work carried out in the mid-18th century. Of the 16th-century building only the CORNER CHAPEL remains today. Attributed to Mauro Coducci, it contains the tomb of Caterina, Queen of Cyprus ▲ *352.* The most notable pictures here are Veronese's *Manna from Heaven* and Tiepolo's *Communion of St Lucia.* The campanile ● *85* is one of the tallest in Venice, and has a tiny shop at its base. Aretino lived nearby, on Rio di San Giovanni Crisostomo, before moving to the Rialto. (With the church behind you, turn to face the Ponte Falier.)

PALAZZO FALIER ● *88.* This Venetian-Byzantine palace, which dates from the 13th century, was the home of the Doge Marin Falier, who was beheaded in 1355 after being found guilty of plotting against the Republic ▲ *232.* (Through the palace entrance, turn right, cross the Ponte San Giovanni Crisostomo, better known as the Ponte dei Giacatolli.)

The Church of San Giovanni Crisostomo, flanked by a campanile which was built between 1532 and 1590.

THE CHURCH OF SAN GIOVANNI CRISOSTOMO. Founded in the 11th century, San Giovanni Crisostomo was then rebuilt in the Renaissance style by Mauro Coducci (late 15th century). The façade is similar to that of San Zaccaria ▲ *171* and San Michele ▲ *153,* both of which were also designed by the same architect. Inside is one of Giovanni Bellini's final works, *St Jerome, St Christopher and St Louis of Toulouse* (1513). At the high altar is Sebastiano del Piombo's famous *St John Chrysostom and Saints* (1509–11). (Turn left.)

CORTE SECONDA DEL MILION ★. Marco Polo ▲ *281* lived in this small courtyard until the time of his death in January 1324; his house was subsequently burned down in 1596. The courtyard's name recalls the sobriquet that was given to the great explorer by his fellow Venetians, and also the story of his travels, which Marco Polo himself dictated to Rusticello of Pisa during his imprisonment by the Genoese in 1298. Rusticello transcribed the text into Old French, and this subsequently became the basis for the *Livre des Merveilles* (known as *Il Milione* in Italian). On the walls of the houses around here are some fine Venetian-Byzantine friezes and *patera.* (Pass behind the courtyard.)

TEATRO MALIBRAN. This theater is thought to stand partly on the site of Marco Polo's house, an unproven theory which is nevertheless commemorated by two plaques: an old one, in Latin, which is at 5864 Calle della Chiesa, and a more recent one opposite the Ponte del Teatro. Built by the Grimani family in 1677, the theater was inaugurated as the Teatro San Giovanni Crisostomo the following year. At that time it was the largest and most lavish of all the Venetian lyric theaters. After the opening of the Fenice ▲ *262* in 1792, the Malibran's repertoire was mainly confined to drama – until Gallo, who purchased it in 1819, once again brought operatic works to the program. It was during this time that the theater was renamed after its benefactor, the Spanish soprano Malibran. Since then it has been closed down several times, and work is still continuing after the fire of 1996. (Return to Campo San Giovanni Cristostomo, go back over the Ponte dei Giacattoli,

LA MALIBRAN
Maria Malibran (1808–36) arrived in Venice in 1835. She took lodgings at the Grand Hotel, near Palazzo Contarini-Fasan, where the legendary Desdemona is said to have spent her childhood. With an eye to Desdemona's story, Malibran elected to sing in Rossini's *Otello* at the Fenice. During her stay in Venice she heard that a small local theater was going bankrupt, and offered to sing there for nothing; however there was still not enough money, so Maria threw in the fee she received from the Fenice. In gratitude, the theater changed its name to Malibran.

and turn right down the Calle Boldù, which leads to the Campiello Santa Maria Nova.)
PALAZZO BEMBO-BOLDÙ. The façade of this Gothic building features a remarkable statue of Saturn, or Father Time. The figure is shown as an old man holding a solar disc. (Take the Calle Mirali on the left and pass the bridge.)
THE CHURCH OF SANTA MARIA DEI MIRACOLI ● *83* ★. This "precious jewel of the Renaissance" was built between 1481 and 1489 by Pietro Lombardo as a shrine in which to house Nicolò di Pietro's miracle-working *Virgin and Child*. The entire building is covered both inside and out with polychrome marble. The façade is encrusted with medallions, porphyry panels and green marble. The interior, is haloed in a soft light. The beautifully finished *coro pensile* (raised choir) was linked to the adjoining monastery until 1865 and is built over a kind of crypt. The curious bas-reliefs, which feature mermaids, Tritons, small animals, flowers and other figures, run the length of the pilasters and around the base of the church. The coffered ceiling is decorated with fifty panels depicting prophets and patriarchs.
PALAZZO SORANZO-BAROZZI. On the original door to this magnificent Gothic palace on the Fondamenta delle Erbe note the spy-hole and knocker. (Return to the apse of the church of the Miracoli, cross the bridge, diagonally cross the campo and take the little calle on the left.)
THE CHURCH OF SAN CANCIANO. Inside this frequently rebuilt sanctuary, the WIDMANN CHAPEL (built by Longhena and decorated in sumptuous Baroque style by Clemente Moli) is particularly worth a visit. The painters Jacopo da Ponte (known as Il Bassano), Leonardo Corona and Titian all died in this parish. (With the church façade on your left, cross the Campiello del Cason, then take the Rio terrà Santi Apostoli.)

The frozen Lagoon from the Fondamente Nuove (right).

On the façades of some of the houses in the Campo dei Gesuiti are inscriptions and insignia associated with the old guilds of *sartori* (tailors), *tessitori* (weavers) and *botteri* (coopers).

Young patricians used to play ball games on the Campo dei Gesuiti, but their habit upset the Jesuits, and in 1711 they were asked to find another location. Thenceforth the games were held at San Giacomo dell'Orio ▲ *349*, in the sestiere of Santa Croce. Rather different from early football ▲ *169*, the game involved teams of three men each. The batsman, who wore a studded armband, had to strike the ball while it was in flight, after it had been thrown by another player.

"On the walls and church squares, green and white marbles are set in one another to form blossoms and floral designs."
Hippolyte Taine, *Voyage en Italie*

THE JESUITS

ORATORIO DEI CROCIFERI. The order of the *Crociferi*, or Bearers of the Cross, were closely associated with the crusades, during which they wore a grey cross on their tunics. From the mid-12th century, they built a convent, church and hospice on this site. The buildings were burnt down in 1514 and were then rebuilt on a much larger scale. The hospice (which gave shelter to pilgrims and cripples) and the oratory were altered at the end of the 16th century on the intervention of the Doge Pasquale Cicogna. Palma the Younger was commissioned to paint a cycle of canvases which illustrated some of the high points in the history of the order. The artist responded with some of his finest work. Denounced for the laxness of its morals, the order was consequently suppressed in 1656 by Pope Alexander VII. A year later, the Jesuits (who had been driven out of Venice in 1606 as a result of the Republic's rift with Pope Paul V) returned to the city and purchased the Convent of the *Crociferi*.

THE CHURCH OF SANTA MARIA ASSUNTA, OR DEI GESUITI. In 1715, the Jesuits commissioned Domenico Rossi to build them a completely new sanctuary, but without changing the height of the building because a huge monument built by Sansovino for the Da Lezze family occupied the reverse of the façade. Rossi's church was completed in 1729; it took the form of a Latin cross and was decorated in lavish Baroque style. The church reflected favorably not only on the Jesuits, but also on the Manin family, which contributed large sums to the works, and thereby gained the right to burial in the choir, close to the high altar. After the suppression of the Jesuits in 1773, the convent served first as a public school and later, in 1807, as a barracks. With the rehabilitation of the order by Pius VII in 1814, Santa Maria Assunta once again

The cemetery gate of San Michele.

reverted to the Jesuits, who proceeded to build themselves another convent on the Fondamente Nuove. It is still occupied today by members of the order, and is the seat of the American Jesuit University. Inside Santa Maria Assunta are several masterpieces, notably Tintoretto's *Assumption of the Virgin*, and Titian's altarpiece *The Martyrdom of St Lawrence* in the transept, as well as canvases by Palma the Younger in the sacristy. Beneath a baldachin, on four wreathed columns in green and white marble, stands a colossal Baroque altar, whose tabernacle is encrusted with lapis lazuli. (Carry on towards the Fondamente Nuove and turn right. Take the first right-hand street, Calle della Pietà, as far as the Ramo del Tiziano on the left.)

TITIAN'S HOUSE. A plaque at number 5182–3 marks the site of the house where Titian lived, and in which he died in 1576. The Fondamente Nuove were not constructed until 1589, and thus during the artist's lifetime his house and garden would have looked directly on to the Lagoon. Returning to the Fondamente Nuove, you can board the ferry to Burano ▲ 370, Torcello ▲ 374, Murano ▲ 364, or San Michele.

THE ISLAND OF THE DEAD

THE CEMETERY OF SAN MICHELE. Before entering Venice proper, travellers and fishermen from Murano, Burano, Torcello or the other islands in the lagoon used to stop off at the two small islands just off the Fondamente Nuove – San Cristoforo della Pace and San Michele (which at one time was called "Cavana de Muran", or the Murano shelter). San Cristoforo was chosen as a site for a public cemetery in 1807 by the Napoleonic authorities. The architect Antonio Selva was commissioned to carry out this project, which was subsequently interrupted for a while

EZRA LOOMIS POUND
In 1908 Ezra Pound published his first collection of poems, *A Lume Spento*, in Venice. The theme of Venice recurs throughout Pound's masterpiece, the *Cantos*. He returned

to Italy in 1924, attracted by the Fascist ideas then current, and he lived in Venice from 1959 until the time of his death in 1972.

153

due to a lack of funds. In 1836 the canal between the two islets was filled in, but the building works were not finally completed until 1870. A plaque at the cemetery gate recalls that this island also served as a prison. Arrested in 1820 by the Austrian occupants of Venice, the Italian patriot Silvio Pellico, author of *My Prisons*, was held captive here after a year in the "Leads" ▲ 252. He was to spend the final period of his long imprisonment at the Spielberg near Brno, a Hapsburg state jail.

THE CHURCH AND MONASTERY OF SAN MICHELE. These two buildings, which stand at the cemetery entrance, were constructed between 1469 and 1535. The Renaissance church, in white Istrian stone, was the first of its kind designed by Mauro Coducci. In front of the main portal is the tombstone of Fra Paolo Sarpi, whose ashes were transported to the Church of Santa Maria dei Servi ▲ 145 in 1828. The cartographer Fra Mauro was a distinguished 15th-century inmate of the monastery. He was the author of a celebrated planisphere (which is now held at the Libreria Marciana ▲ 254). The small 15th-century Gothic CLOISTER is well worth seeing.

CAPPELLA EMILIANA. Built by Guglielmo dei Grigi, known as Guglielmo Bergamasco, this "round, white chapel, sculpted with shells and adorned with pink and green marble cabochons", as Michèle Manceaux describes it, is crowned by an unusual dome entirely covered with white stones.

DEATH IN VENICE. San Michele, hidden behind its pink walls and shaded by cypress trees, is one of the few cemeteries on earth to which the dead are brought by boat. In the old days, they would have been borne gently across the water from the city in funeral gondolas, which were richly decorated with gold-winged angels. These vessels were subsequently replaced by modern motorboats, which were fitted out as floating hearses. Today the island can accommodate no further graves, and Venice now has to send her dead to the mainland for burial.

THE TOMBS OF THE FAMOUS AT SAN MICHELE. In a section of the cemetery set apart for foreigners (Greek Square, XIV), among the tombs of Russian princesses and Greek queens, lie the mortal remains of the composer Igor Stravinsky (1882–1971) and Serge Diaghilev of the Russian Ballet (1872–1929). The grave of the American poet Ezra Pound (1885–1972) is located in square XV.

DIAGHILEV
In 1929, Diaghilev came to Venice. Convinced his end was near, he called his friend Misia Sert to join him. On August 18, he fell into a coma and died the following day. His body was put on a funeral gondola and carried across the Lagoon for burial.

Castello

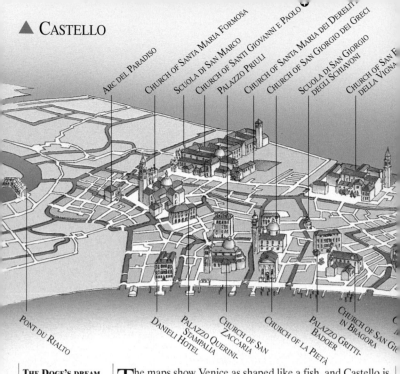

ARC DEL PARADISO
CHURCH OF SANTA MARIA FORMOSA
SCUOLA DI SAN MARCO
CHURCH OF SANTI GIOVANNI E PAOLO
PALAZZO PRIULI
CHURCH OF SANTA MARIA DEI DERELITI
CHURCH OF SAN GIORGIO DEI GRECI
SCUOLA DI SAN GIORGIO DEGLI SCHIAVONI
CHURCH OF SAN F DELLA VIGNA

PONT DU RIALTO
PALAZZO QUERINI-STAMPALIA
DANIELI HOTEL
CHURCH OF SAN ZACCARIA
CHURCH OF LA PIETÀ
PALAZZO GRITTI-BADOER
CHURCH OF SAN GIO IN BRAGORA

THE DOGE'S DREAM

Tradition has it that Giacomo Tiepolo, the 41st Doge of Venice (1229–49), had the following dream one night: a swamp area of the Lagoon, which later became Campo Santi Giovanni e Paolo, was covered with magnificent flowers. White doves with the sign of the cross on their heads flew overhead. Then he heard a voice saying: "I have chosen this place for my ministry." Having informed the senate of this divine message, the Doge obtained leave for the Dominicans to build a monastery on the spot. The order had been established in Venice for a decade, but they were living in difficult conditions, in tents under the portico of the Church of San Martino. The monastery church was dedicated, perhaps on the request of the Doge himself, to the martyred brothers John and Paul, who were put to death in Rome during the 4th century.

The maps show Venice as shaped like a fish, and Castello is its tail. It is the largest and most varied of the six sestieri and also, most importantly, the home of the Arsenal, which stands behind its high towers like a forbidden city within a city. The establishment of this naval dockyard on the Isole Gemini (twin islands) at the start of the 13th century was crucial to the area's development. All kinds of related activities grew up around what was to become the largest naval complex in Europe, along with the modest homes of dockworkers and sailors; later, foreign communities sprang up and even a few palazzos. The northern part of the sestiere was controlled by the Mendicant orders (Dominicans and Franciscans), whose charitable institutions (*ospedali*) proliferated. Their presence became an overwhelming feature of the area. The Arsenal lay halfway between the political and mercantile centers of San Marco and the Rialto to the west, and the religious center of the island of San Pietro to the east. Already, during the time of Aretino, a fortress (*castello*) had been built on San Pietro, from which the name of the sestiere probably derives. There was another island in the vicinity, known for centuries as l'Olivolo on account of its olive shape,

Veduta di SS Giovanni e Paolo.

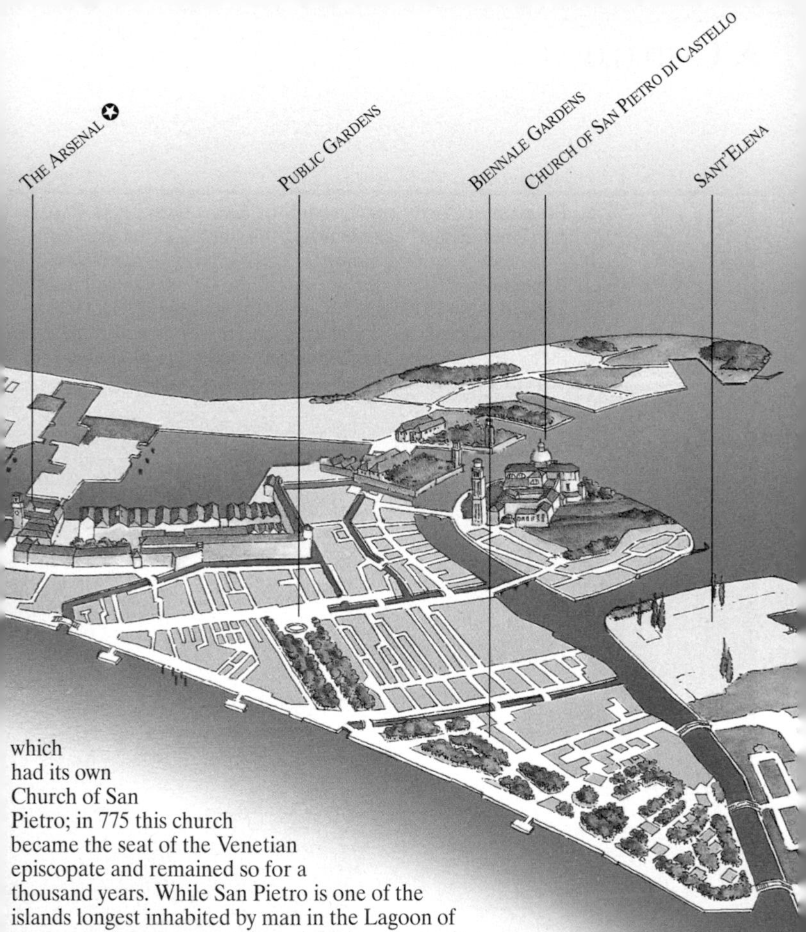

which
had its own
Church of San
Pietro; in 775 this church
became the seat of the Venetian
episcopate and remained so for a
thousand years. While San Pietro is one of the
islands longest inhabited by man in the Lagoon of
Venice, its neighbor Sant'Elena (which now constitutes the
most south-eastern point of the sestiere) was not built upon
until very late. Napoleonic town planning was responsible for
creating a whole series of public gardens here, which today
provide the location for the Venice Biennale, and he also

opened up the Via Eugenia,
now known as the Via
Garibaldi. In the great museum-
city that Venice has become
since the passing of her glory, in
this city where nothing can be
changed or taken away, Castello
is one of the few districts to
have been substantially modified in the 20th century – hence
the new quarters of Sant'Elena, Celestia and the south-
eastern tip of San Pietro.

SANTI GIOVANNI E PAOLO ● 78

THE CAMPO SAN ZANIPOLO, in the Venetian dialect a
contraction of the Christian names Giovanni and Paolo, was
proudly referred to by Venetians until the 19th century as the
Campo delle Maravege (campo of marvels). According to
some this was because of certain remarkable happenings that
occurred there. Other, however, believe that the name derives
from the campo's splendid monuments. At the center of the
square, which was paved in 1592 by Dominican friars, stands
the great equestrian statue of the *condottiere* Colleoni by
Andrea del Verrocchio.

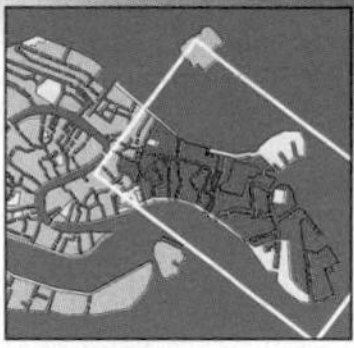

⏳ **One day**
◆ C D

**SANTI GIOVANNI
E PAOLO: A CAMPO
OF WONDERS ✪**
Verrocchio's
impressive statue of
Colleoni stands guard
before the pink brick
basilica. The interior is
a visual feast. Here is
the most important
collection of works by
Veronese in Venice
(in the Capella della
Rosario). The tombs
of the doges and other
leaders constitute a
comprehensive study
of statuary from the
Gothic through the
Rococo periods.

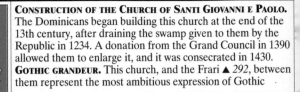

CONSTRUCTION OF THE CHURCH OF SANTI GIOVANNI E PAOLO.
The Dominicans began building this church at the end of the
13th century, after draining the swamp given to them by the
Republic in 1234. A donation from the Grand Council in 1390
allowed them to enlarge it, and it was consecrated in 1430.
GOTHIC GRANDEUR. This church, and the Frari ▲ *292*, between
them represent the most ambitious expression of Gothic

**MARSHES AND
LAGOON**
The strip of land
which extends from
the bridge across the
Rio dei Mendicanti to
the Fondamente
Nuove ▲ *153* was
reclaimed by
determined hard
work.

architecture in Venice. The five apses at the
rear of the building, like the façade with its
soaring central structure, are remarkable
examples of the architectural style of the 14th
century.The red brick main entrance, built in
1458 to plans drawn up by Antonio Gambello,
is representative of the transitional period
between Gothic and Renaissance. The
entrance is flanked by columns from a church
on Torcello which has now been demolished.
A VENETIAN PANTHEON. Like the Frari, SANTI GIOVANNI E
PAOLO is something of a memorial to the glories of Venice's
past. No fewer than twenty-five Doges, whose tombs were in
many cases sculpted by great masters such as Lombardo or
Giovanni Buora, lie buried in this sanctuary. It was here, from
the 15th century, that the funeral rites of the first magistrates
were invariably celebrated. The church also contains the
tombs of such legendary figures as Vettor Pisani, Ludovico
Diedo and Sebastiano Venier, the victor of Lepanto ● *36*.

"I stood in front of the Church of Saints John and Paul, contemplating the small head and square jaw of Bartolomeo Colleoni, the dreaded condottiere."

Henry James

There is even an urn containing the skin of Marcantonio Bragadin who, after the fall of Famagusta in 1571, the last Venetian citadel in Cyprus ● *33, 36*, was flayed alive by his Turkish captors.

THE TREASURES OF SANTI GIOVANNI E PAOLO. Among the most notable works of art in the church are a *Polyptych of St Vincent Ferrier* by Giovanni Bellini, *The Almsgiving of St Anthony* by Lorenzo Lotto, *St Dominic in Glory* by Piazzetta and, in the CAPPELLA DELLA ROSARIO, several paintings by Veronese. There is also an altarpiece by Longhena (1638) and a large narrative stained-glass window fashioned by the master glassblowers of Murano.

THE SCUOLA DI SAN MARCO ★ ● *86*

This charitable institution, founded in 1260, had many prominent Venetians among its members. First established in the Santa Croce quarter, it was transferred to the Campo Santi Giovanni e Paolo in 1437. In 1485 a fire destroyed the original wooden structure, which had a fine spiral staircase designed by Gentile Bellini. The reconstruction was assigned in 1489 to Pietro Lombardo, who was then working on the Doge's Palace ▲ *224*, and to Giovanni Buora. The two architects decided to retain the original plan of the building and place a smaller gallery for restricted meetings above the main hall, with its double row of columns. Mauro Coducci, who was later called in to mediate in a quarrel between the Grand Guardian of the brotherhood and the architects, himself ended up as the *proto* (commissioned architect) for the scuola. His contribution to the façade, which has a broad projecting portal, may be seen in its upper parts. In terms of its art treasures, the Scuola di San Marco was for many years the richest guild in Venice. It held the *Miracles of St Mark* by Tintoretto (now divided between the Accademia ▲ *301* and the Brera Museum in Milan), and canvases by Palma the Elder and Paris Bordone. In 1815 the Austrians demolished Coducci's monumental outside staircase, along with some of his other additions, and converted the building into a hospital, which it remains to this day. (Walk along the façade of the scuola.)

I MENDICANTI

THE CHURCH OF THE MENDICANTI. Now closed, this church was once dedicated to the patron saint of lepers who, until the 16th century, were treated in the same way as indigents in Venice. It was attached to the charity hospital, the two wings of which enclose it, The

THE CONDOTTIERE
Bartolomeo Colleoni was one of the most noteworthy figures in Italian political and social life during the 15th century. A *condottiere* from Bergamo, Colleoni reached the summit of his career when he was appointed to the permanent captain-general of the Venetian army. As a reward for his loyal service, the Republic gave him the fiefdom of Malpaga, on the Milanese border. But they failed to fulfill exactly all the conditions of Colleoni's will, by which he bequeathed his possessions to the Republic. One of these conditions was that a statue should be erected in his memory in Piazza San Marco soon after his death (1475). Since it was forbidden by law to build any monument in the great square, the Senate solved this dilemma by placing the statue in front of the Scuola Grande di San Marco. The figure was sculpted by the Tuscan artist Andrea del Verrocchio ▲ *147*, and then cast in bronze after his death by Alessandro Leopardi, who also added a pedestal and signed his name on the horse's girth. The statue of Colleoni was finally unveiled on March 21, 1496.

"The light from the bright sky reflected through to the courtyard. . . . In this small space, half-room, half-garden, the air was tepid, smelling of grapes. The silence was so complete that one heard the flutter of a bird hopping from perch to perch."

Hugo von Hofmannsthal, *Andreas*

I DERELITTI
With works of the 17th and 18th centuries, the church beside the hospice is a mini-museum. Note especially *The Sacrifice of Isaac* and *Two Apostles*, early works by Tiepolo. The church is directly accessible only when concerts are held or mass celebrated. Otherwise it is through the rest home, which includes the Ospedaletto.

architect was Scamozzi (1552–1616). The façade is by the Baroque architect Giuseppe Sardi (1673); though he followed Scamozzi's design, he still respected the church's original classical form. (Return to the campo and pass the church.)

I DERELITTI

BARBARIA DELLE TOLE. The street owes its name to the great timber warehouses (*tole* in Venetian) that once stood here. The term *barbaria* (Barbary) is more debatable; it may allude to the formerly somewhat lawless character of the place, to the tough lumberjacks from the mountains who handled the timber, or to its exportation to North Africa (Barbary), from where the Venetian word *barbe* (wooden planks) comes.

THE CHURCH OF SANTA MARIA DEI DERELITTI ● *83*. This is also known as the Church of the Ospedaletto, because it is an integral part of this nearby charitable institution. The façade (1670–2) and high altar were designed by Longhena. His forcefully projecting architectural elements lend emphasis to the whole, which is made more interesting by the grotesque masks, lion heads and caryatids in the façade's upper register (sculpted by Josse Le Court). Inside is *The Sacrifice of Isaac*, an early masterpiece by Giambattista Tiepolo.

THE OSPEDALETTO. The Republic created this institution in 1527 as a shelter for cripples, old people and indigent young women. In 1661 Sardi accepted the task of enlarging and restructuring the building, but he soon became embroiled in legal difficulties with his clients and was replaced by Longhena. Like many other institutions of its type, the Ospedaletto gradually changed its function with the passing of time. As in the Mendicanti ▲ *159*, the Incurabili ▲ *322* and the Pietà ▲ *174*, which housed poor or illegitimate girls, orphans and abandoned children, the education of the young inmates was heavily biased in favor of music. In the 18th century, these four *ospedali* became conservatories in all but name, with music taught by Venice's greatest masters; by the same token, the churches attached to the *ospedali* became concert halls, where talented pupils regularly performed.

TOWARDS SAN FRANCESCO DELLA VIGNA

THE FORMER CHURCH OF SANTA GIUSTINA. Today, the only vestige of what used to be a substantial religious complex of church and monastery is a mutilated 17th-century façade. The Church of Santa Giustina may date from as far back as the 9th century, although it first appears in Venetian chronicles during the 12th century. During the 15th and 17th centuries the building was extensively altered; then a bequest by Giovanni Soranzo, procurator of San Marco, made possible the construction of its celebrated façade. Work began in 1640

The Corte Nuova, photographed at the turn of the century.

under the direction of Baldassare Longhena. Four columns were raised in order to support a high coping, whose curvilinear pediment was then crammed with various statues of the benefactor and his children; they were removed in 1844, when the church was turned into a military school. On October 7 every year, the Doge attended Mass at Santa Giustina to give thanks for the victory of Lepanto ● *36*. (Walk from here along the Fondamenta Santa Giustina and the Calle San Francesco.)

SAN FRANCESCO DELLA VIGNA
In this zone of the Castello sestiere, the Venetian nobles used to practise archery and horsemanship.

THE CHURCH OF SAN FRANCESCO DELLA VIGNA. The name *della vigna* evokes the vineyards with which this site was once covered. In 1253 the vineyards were given to the Franciscans by Marco Ziani, son of the Doge Pietro Ziani. They built a monastery and church on the site. The church was rebuilt in 1534 by Jacopo Sansovino. It took the form of a Latin cross, with five chapels on either side of its nave. The façade (1562–72) is by Andrea Palladio, the architect of Il Redentore ▲ *338* and of San Giorgio Maggiore ▲ *340*. With his balanced, rational classicism, he created a harmonious scheme through a subtle play of triangles and rectangles. Inside is Veronese's altarpiece *Sacra Conversazione* (1562). Between the church and the Lagoon, the monastery with its three cloisters is one of the best examples of 14th-century Gothic in Venice.

PALAZZO GRITTI. This Renaissance building at the corner of the campo once belonged to the Doge Andrea Gritti. It was nicknamed "La Nunziatura", because the government bought it for use as a residence for papal nuncios under Pope Pius IV. Ceded to the Franciscans in the 19th century, it was linked to the convent by footbridge. (Pass beneath this footbridge, cross the bridge, take the little calle leading to the Salizzada San Francesco, then the Salizzada delle Gatte; this leads to the Campo delle Gatte, known as the CAMPIELLO UGO FOSCOLO, where a plaque marks the house of the poet Foscolo, who as an adolescent lived in Venice from 1792 to 1797. After the Ramo Ponte, turn right into the Salizzada Santa Giustina and take the Calle Zorzi, the last on the left, to the CORTE NUOVA. A tiny chapel nestles beneath the *sottoportego*. Walk down the right of the corte, cross the bridge, take the Fondamenta San Giorgio degli Schiavoni then cross the Ponte de la Comenda.)

The covered walkway that runs between the Palazzo Gritti and the Church of San Francesco della Vigna.

THE SCHIAVONIA
Dalmatia (which roughly corresponds to today's Croatia) was the first foreign region to be conquered by the Republic, and the first jewel in Venice's crown. It was much prized by succeeding generations.

SAINT GEORGE AND THE DRAGON
The lance emphasizes one of the diagonals which divide the painting shown below into four triangular masses – the monster and the city, the bone-strewn foreground, the knight on horseback and the

young girl, and the sky. Here, color acquires value in the overall construction, because each of these four zones has its own color scheme.

SAN GIORGIO DEGLI SCHIAVONI ★

SCUOLA SAN GIORGIO DEGLI SCHIAVONI. People from Dalmatia (Schiavoni) began to establish themselves in Venice at the start of the 15th century. Most were sailors or artisans, who quickly formed themselves into a scuola, the regulations (*mariegole*) of which were approved by the Council of Ten on May 19, 1485. The new scuola started out at the hospice of the Knights of Malta, who later allotted its members an altar of their own in the hospice church. The Dalmatian community grew rapidly in importance and eventually resolved to build its own headquarters. Between 1480 and 1501 the scuola raised a modest structure with a brick façade fronting the Fondamenta San Antonin. To decorate it, the Dalmatians commissioned ten paintings from Carpaccio, which they placed in a gallery on the upper floor. In 1551, the scuola was pulled down and rebuilt by Giovanni de Zan, but he decided to retain the original plan of two galleries and a sacristy. The paintings were moved to the ground floor, to the panelled gallery where they may be seen today. This scuola is one of the very few in Venice which has preserved its artistic heritage intact: moreover, it reveals a side to Venice that is unexpectedly tranquil and intimate.
CARPACCIO'S PAINTINGS ▲ *306.* Carpaccio's décor, created between 1502 and 1507, includes nine canvases that illustrate episodes from the lives of the three Dalmatian patron saints,

St George, St Tryphon and St Jerome. He took his theme from the *Golden Legend* of Jacobus de Voragine, Archbishop of Genoa, an excellent version of which (translated from

Latin by Nicolao Manerbi) was printed in Venice in 1475. The order in which the canvases are exhibited bears no relation to the chronological order in which they were painted. Thus the two paintings dedicated to St George (painted in 1507) are placed at the beginning of the cycle.

SAINT GEORGE. The *Golden Legend* relates that George, a tribune and native of Cappadocia, happened to pass through "Silcha, a provincial town in Libya". Here he saved the life of the king's daughter, who was about to be devoured by a dragon then terrorizing the neighborhood. After slaying this monster, the intrepid youth converted the entire local population to Christianity. Carpaccio's rendering of this tale is one of his most celebrated masterpieces: *St George and the Dragon*. In all the history of painting there is perhaps no handsomer St George than this young, blond knight, mounted on a black charger, whose silhouette against a clear background evokes a design from heraldry. The next painting shows the triumph of the knight finishing off the dragon in the town square.

OTHER WORKS. The two paintings that follow were the last that Carpaccio did for the Dalmatians. They represent *The Baptism of the King* and *The Miracle of St Tryphon*. This saint, a patron of the town of Cattaro on the east coast of the Adriatic, was born in Bithynia (in Asia Minor) and died a martyr. He is shown liberating the daughter of the Emperor Gordian from the clutches of the Devil. Next to this painting are the first two pictures commissioned from Carpaccio by the Scuola. These are the only ones that do not relate to patron saints of the Dalmatians: they are *The Vocation of Saint Matthew* and *Christ at Prayer on the Mount of Olives*.

THE SAINT JEROME TRILOGY. These three paintings, which date from 1502, are dedicated to St Jerome, father of the Vulgate Latin translation of the Bible and a reformer of the

THE VISION OF SAINT JEROME
Pure wealth of detail makes this work unique in the history of Venetian art.

The meticulousness and realism of the Flemish school are both to some extent echoed here, but they are expressed within an architectural concept of space which appears to have been a heritage of Tuscan art. Finally, there is exquisite color, which is always a fundamental component of Carpaccio's poetical insight.

THE DEATH OF SAINT JEROME
Here, the background is dominated by browns, while in the foreground monks in white and blue vestments form a circle around the body of the saint, suggested by a light stroke of the brush.

Christian liturgy. The first painting represents *The Miracle of the Lion*, with the saint seen pulling a thorn from a lion's paw. Although this event is supposed to have occurred in the East, the background depicts the Scuola and the Church of the Knights of Malta (the building on the right with the wooden porch). Next to it are *The Death of St Jerome* and a painting known as *The Vision of St Jerome*, which in fact is a representation of St Augustine hearing his own death announced by the voice of Jerome. In a concession to contemporary taste, the saint is portrayed with the features of Cardinal Bessarion, first patron of the Scuola ▲ *254*. (Take the Fondamenta dei Furlani and turn right onto the Salizzada dei Greci.)

SAN GIORGIO DEI GRECI ★

Standing out starkly in this quiet backwater, the buildings of the community form a tightly knit architectural ensemble and an enclave of silence and calm.

THE GREEK COMMUNITY. Already present in Venice from the early 11th century, Greeks began to arrive in substantial numbers during the 14th and 15th centuries under the pressure of Ottoman expansion. After the fall of Constantinople in 1453, a large proportion of Greek refugees were taken in by the Venetians; before long they formed the city's largest ethnic community after the Jews. About four thousand resident Greeks were counted by a census in the second half of the 15th century. Most of these were merchants, book publishers, artists, scribes and literary scholars. To begin with they were authorized to celebrate orthodox rites in several churches (among them San Stae ▲ *350*), but from 1470 onwards, a decree of the Council of Ten restricted them to a single chapel in the church of San Biagio. In 1526, the Greek community was given autonomous status vis-à-vis the patriarchate of Venice and authorized to celebrate its own orthodox cult. Permission was also given to the Greeks to acquire a large site beside the Rio di San Lorenzo. This they cleared, demolishing several buildings in the process, and then went on to build a church, a college, a scuola, a cemetery and a number of private houses. Most of this new complex was designed by Longhena. In 1678, the site was closed off on the Rio dei Greci side with a barrier which was designed by Longhena in such a way that it did not obstruct the view from the buildings.

The campanile, built between 1587 and 1592, leans to one side because of subsidence beneath its foundation.

THE CHURCH OF SAN GIORGIO DEI GRECI. The original architect of this church was Sante Lombardo, who was succeeded by Giannantonio Chiona in 1539. The simple, elegant lines of the façade resemble the work of Sansovino, the architect of the Libraria Marciana on St Mark's Square ▲ *254*. Distinctive elements on the inside are the women's stalls (above the entrance) and the iconostasis. Most of the icons here

The Madonna with the symbols of the Passion, an icon by Emmanuel Lombardos dating from the early 17th century.

were painted by Michele Damaskinos, a 16th-century Cretan artist and a fellow citizen and contemporary of Domenikos Theotokopoulos, better known as El Greco. The atmosphere in this church is perhaps more intimate than in other Venetian sanctuaries, and the Orthodox rites are still celebrated here, despite the fact that the Greek community in Venice has dwindled to barely a hundred souls.

SCUOLA DI SAN NICOLÒ DEI GRECI. Founded in 1498 to defend the rights of the Greek community, this scuola was first located at San Stae; after the acquisition of the Rio di San Lorenzo site, it moved to buildings of its own designed by Baldassare Longhena. Today, the scuola is an icon museum, containing one of the most important collections of its kind in Europe. It also possesses a number of other religious objects, many of which are marvels of Byzantine art, along with the works of celebrated Greek artists who lived in Venice (notably the 15th–17th century painters Michele Damaskinos, Giorgio Klotzas, Emmanuel Zane and the Cypriot Giovanni da Cipro).

THE HELLENIC INSTITUTE. This scholarly foundation occupies the Palazza Flanghini, a short distance farther on, which was formerly the Collegio Greco and was designed by Longhena. The Institute specializes in Byzantine and post-Byzantine studies, and has extraordinarily rich archives, as one would expect given the rôle played by Venice in the Mediterranean basin. They contain, among other things, some rare documents on Crete, the Ionian Islands, Cyprus and the Peloponnese, which for centuries were colonies of Venice in the Levant.

Inside the Church of San Giorgio dei Greci: the dome, the iconostasis and a detail of an icon.

This water-colored lithograph (opposite) by Joseph Nash shows the iconostasis as a partition dividing the nave of San Giorgio dei Greci from the choir, a feature which was obligatory in Greek Orthodox churches.

SANTA MARIA FORMOSA

On the Fondamenta dell'Osmarin, after the Ponte dei Greci, stands the 15th-century PALAZZO PRIULI. Originally decorated with frescoes by Palma the Elder, it still possesses a fine corner window. From the Fondamenta di San Severo, one can see the PALAZZO ZORZI (early 16th century) with its façade of Istrian stone. This palazzo is thought to be one of the last buildings designed by Mauro Coducci. (Take the Salizzada Zorzi to the RUGA GIUFFA, whose name derives from the presence of an Armenian community in Venice from the 16th century onwards.) At the corner of the Rio di Santa Maria Formosa and the Rio di San Severo, note the PALAZZO GRIMANI, formerly celebrated for its art collection, including works by Titian, Tintoretto, Veronese and Bassano. There were also some rare coins and Greek and Roman statues, but these were donated to the city of Venice in 1586 and two centuries later became the first treasures of the Museum of Archeology ▲ 255.

CAMPO SANTA MARIA FORMOSA. This campo, which cuts through the dense urban fabric of the Castello sestiere, is one of the largest open squares in Venice. Around it stand a variety of palaces. Immediately to the left of the Ruga Giuffa is the PALAZZO MALIPIERO-TREVISAN, which was mostly rebuilt at the start of the 16th century by the Trevisan family and boasts an all-white façade studded with medallions of porphyry and green marble. PALAZZO VITTURI, a 13th-century Venetian-Byzantine building, has a quadriform window with the point of each arch crowned by a *patera*, like the dot on an "i". Farther on, PALAZZO DONA has a 15th-century lunette in which an angel and *putti* brandish the arms of the Dona family. The corner of the campo is occupied by PALAZZO RUZZINI, with its elegant openwork balcony designed by Bartolomeo Manopola, one of the architects of the Doge's Palace. The Ruzzini, a rich family from Constantinople, built this mansion here after a fire destroyed their residence at San Giovanni Crisostomo.

THE CHURCH OF SANTA MARIA FORMOSA. Santa Maria Formosa is supposed to have been one of the eight sanctuaries founded in the 7th century by St Magnus, Bishop of Oderzo in Friuli. Using the foundations of the 11th-century building, the architect Mauro Coducci reconstructed the church in 1492 with three naves, giving it

THE SACK OF PALAZZO QUERINI-STAMPALIA
During Manin's provisional government ● *34*, ▲ *275*, the palace was the lodging of Jacopo Monico, patriarch of Venice, who lived on its upper floor. There was a rumor that the patriarch and a group of patricians favored the capitulation of the city. On August 3, 1849, a group of rioters penetrated the patriarch's apartments in his absence and wrecked the lower floor, which was the home of Count Giovanni, the last of the Querinis.

A canal adjoining the campo Santa Maria Formosa.

the form of a Latin cross. In 1542, the wealthy Cappello family built on a main façade as a memorial to Vincenzo Cappello, admiral of the Venetian fleet and conqueror of the Turks. In 1604, a second façade overlooking the campo was added: here again, three busts of the admiral attest to the contemporary fashion for transforming church fronts into monuments to individuals. The interior, characterized by an

CAMPO S.MARIA FORMOSA

odd chromatic play of grey and white, contains paintings by Bartolomeo Vivarini (*Triptych*, 1473), Palma the Younger, Palma the Elder and

Giambattista Tiepolo. The dome was rebuilt twice, after an earthquake in 1668, and after an Austrian bombardment in 1916. Numerous scuole and corporations had altars and chapels in the church, notably the SCUOLA DEI BOMBARDIERI (mortar manufacturers) and SCUOLA DEI CASSELLERI (artisans who made lavish nuptial chests for young brides). The CAMPANILE, which is decorated on all sides with geometrical motifs in relief, was designed by the priest Francesco Zucconi (1611–88). Its entrance is crowned with a grimacing face ● *84* which looks like the mask of an actor. This type of decoration became common in 17th-century Venice due to the success of a new theatrical genre, the melodrama. (Go round the church to the Campiello Querini-Stampalia.)

THE QUERINI-STAMPALIA FOUNDATION. Several members of the Querini family were banished from Venice for their part in the plot hatched against the Seignory in 1310 by Bajamonte Tiepolo ▲ *214*. They took refuge on Stampalia, a Greek island which they owned, and their branch of the patrician family became known thereafter as Querini-Stampalia. In 1868 the last bearer of the name, Count Giovanni, bequeathed his palace, complete with furniture, works of art and historical documents, to the city of Venice. His wish was that a library should be opened in his apartments, and that his collections should be properly preserved: in addition to the house, this man of science left a substantial sum of money to pay for his foundation. In accordance with the count's will, the Palazzo Querini-Stampalia now contains an immense library and museum. In rooms which were occupied during the mid-19th century by the patriarch of Venice, there is a collection of furniture, bibelots and sculptures. The picture gallery contains more than seven hundred works of the Venetian school, notably paintings by Pietro Longhi and a collection of canvases by Gabriele Bella illustrating the daily life of Venice during the 18th century. In the 1960's this Renaissance palace on the curve of the canal was restored and restructured by the architect Carlo Scarpa ▲ *346*, who added a little bridge spanning the canal and laid out new gardens. (Return to the campo.)

FEAST OF THE MARIAS
On January 30 every year, as a token of thanks to the *casselleri* for freeing some young girls who were kidnapped by pirates from Istria and Trieste in the 10th century, the Doge went to Santa Maria Formosa, where he was given two gilded straw hats (an example is at the Correr Museum). On the same occasion, the six sestieri endowed twelve poor but pretty girls, known as the "Marias"; they were dressed in rich clothes and paraded down the Grand Canal to San Pietro di Castello ▲ *182*.

The gardens of the Palazzo Querini-Stampalia, restored by Carlo Scarpa.

BELLA was born in Venice in 1730. In his modest but prolific work, he chronicled the customs and daily life of the Serene Republic at the time when Venice was at the height of her power. Bella's paintings are invariably enlivened by crowds of people and illustrate political institutions, official receptions, lay and religious feasts and public sports .

CEREMONIES OF VENICE
Following his election, the Doge mounted the *pozzetto*, which was carried shoulder high across Saint Mark's Square by the workers of the Arsenal (right). As he went among the crowd, he scattered coins that were newly minted with his effigy.

Gabriele Bella, a minor 18th-century artist in Venice, left a lively and candid portrait of public and political life in the city.

RECEPTIONS

In 1782, the heir to the throne of Russia and his wife visited Venice incognito, as the "Comte and Comtesse du Nord". They attended a concert given in their honor by the young orphans of the four *ospedali* (left).

GAMES

In order to keep themselves fit and active, Venetian nobles often played various types of ballgames. Spectators stood around the pitch, cheering on the players representing their particular faction.

RELIGIOUS FEASTS

The Good Friday procession (above), attended by patricians, members of the Scuole Grandi ▲ 295 and various prelates. The Church of San Geminiano, destroyed in 1808 to make way for Napoleon's new building, is in the background.

"After dinner, I went out by myself, into the heart of the enchanted city where I found myself wandering in strange regions like a character in the Arabian Nights. . . . I had plunged into a network of little alleys, *calli,* dissecting in all directions by their ramifications the quarter of Venice isolated between a canal and the lagoon, as if it had crystallized along these innumerable, slender, capillary lines. All of a sudden, at the end of one of those little streets, it seemed as though a bubble had occurred in the crystallized matter. A vast and splendid *campo* of which I could certainly never, in this network of little streets, have guessed the importance, or even found room for it, spread out before me flanked with charming palaces silvery in the moonlight. It was one of those architectural wholes towards which, in any other town, the streets converge, lead you and point the way. Here it seemed to be deliberately concealed in a labyrinth of alleys, like those palaces in oriental tales to which mysterious agents convey by night a person who, taken home again before daybreak, can never again find his way back to the magic dwelling which he ends by supposing that he visited only in a dream."

Marcel Proust,
Albertine Disparue

CALLE DEL PARADISO ● *93*. This calle, with overhanging buildings, is named after the lanterns with which it was decorated on Good Friday. The entrance is through a 15th-century Gothic archway, with a Madonna (between the arms of Foscari and Mocenigo) protecting a bride and groom. They are members of the families to whom the corner houses belonged. (Turn right into the Salizzada di San Lio, then left. At number 5484 in the CORTE PERINA stands the house of the painter Canaletto. Return toward the Salizzada San Lio.)

THE CHURCH OF SAN LIO. The original Church of St Catherine (9th century) was rebuilt in 1054 and dedicated to Pope Leo IX (*Lio*, in the Venetian dialect), who joined Venice in defending the cause of the Patriarch of Grado against the pretentions of Aquileia. The Renaissance GUSSONI CHAPEL, built by Pietro and Tullio Lombardo, contains *Saint James on the Road*, a late work by Titian, and *St Leo Exalting the Cross* and *Angels and Virtues* by Giandomenico Tiepolo. (From the Campo San Lio take the Calle della Fava, on the left.)

THE CHURCH OF SANTA MARIA DELLA CONSOLAZIONE. The original name of this church was "della Fava", prior to the construction of the present building, which was begun in 1704 by Gaspari and completed by Massari in 1750. It contains an

early work by Giambattista Tiepolo, *St Anne, the Virgin Child and St Joachim*, along with *The Madonna and St Philip Neri* by Piazzetta. This artist, who died in abject poverty, was buried in the tomb of his friend Giambattista Albrizzi. (Return to the Campiello Querini and from there take the Fondamenta del Rimedio.)

THE CHURCH OF SAN GIOVANNI NUOVO. This former church once housed the Guidi Museum, dedicated to the Roman painter Virgilio Guidi, who worked in Venice for many years. Baldassare Longhena lived and died in this parish. (Continue to Campo Santi Filippo e Giacomo, then follow Rughetta Sant'Apollonia as far as the bridge; from here you can see the Renaissance PALAZZO TREVISAN CAPPELLO, bought by Bianca Cappello ▲ *286*. Turn left before the bridge.)

PONTE DEL DIAVOLO

THE CLOISTER OF SANT'APOLLONIA. First dedicated to St Philip and St James, this church reverted to St Apollonia, patron of the linen weavers whose scuola was nearby. Today it is the Diocesan Museum of Religious Art, its collections consisting of pieces from Venice's deconsecrated churches. (Return to Campo Santi Fillippo e Giacomo and take the Salizzada San Provolo, which culminates in a florid Gothic portal with a Virgin and Child in its marble lunette.)

THE CHURCH OF SAN ZACCARIA

San Zaccaria stands on a campo whose gates were closed at night as the square was considered to be the private property of the nuns in the adjoining convent,

LA FAVA
The curious name of the Ponte della Fava was applied by extension to the church adjoining it. There are three theories about the origins of the word "fava": one, that it was the name of a local family; two, that a pastryshop here made special little cakes called *fave dolci* for All Souls' Day; and three, that a merchant of the quarter used to hide his contraband salt under a pile of broad beans (*fave*).

THE CLOISTER OF SANT'APOLLONIA
This cloister (12th–13th century), a unique example of Romanesque architecture in Venice, has remained intact, with its square floorplan, broad arches, colonnades of Istrian stone and brick paving, it has the air of a small campo in the center of which stands a well.

THE DOGE'S VISIT TO SAN ZACCARIA
Each year, the Doge went to San Zaccaria on the first Monday after Easter to pay homage to the nuns of the convent who gave up their vegetable garden to permit the enlargement of Saint Mark's Square ▲ *220*. Preceding him was an individual holding the ducal *corno* ▲ *231*. If tradition is to be believed, this hat was presented to one of the doges by Agnesina Morosini, who was Mother-Superior of the convent in the mid-9th century.

CALLE DELLE RASSE
In 1172, the Doge Vitale Michiel II was stabbed to death on the Riva degli Schiavoni, opposite the Calle delle Rasse, by an assassin who hid in the door of a house here. No subsequent doge was ever to pass down this dangerous alley again. Instead the Ponte della Canonica was built, so that state dignitaries could travel safely to the annual ceremony at San Zaccaria.

ARCHITECTURAL DEVELOPMENT. The Church of San Zaccaria was founded at the beginning of the 9th century, under the Doge Giustiniano Partecipazio. Towards the mid-10th century, the Byzantine basilica was radically altered and adapted in the Romanesque style. The crypt, which today is beneath the CHAPEL OF SAN TARASIO, dates from this era. The building as a whole was renovated between 1170 and 1174, at which time a campanile was added in alignment with the façade, to the right of the church. At the turn of the 14th century major new works were begun, at which time the building lost practically all of its Romanesque and Byzantine characteristics and became entirely Gothic. Yet the new Gothic choir and apses had scarcely been completed in 1443 when it was resolved not only to alter the building yet again, but also to build a new one on an adjoining site. As sometimes happens, the two churches, instead of being juxtaposed, became partially joined, as the left nave of the older edifice was confused with the right nave of the newer one. These works, begun in 1458, continued for about a century. At the death of the architect Antonio Gambello in 1481, Coducci took over and introduced various Renaissance elements, though without fundamentally modifying his predecessor's design. The church was consecrated in 1543.

PAINTINGS AT SAN ZACCARIA. Among the many works preserved in the church is an altarpiece by Giovanni Bellini (second altar on the left), entitled *The Holy Converse*, 1505. In the CHAPEL OF SAN TARASIO are frescoes by Andrea del Castagno, along with altar pieces (1442–4) by Antonio Vivarini and his brother-in-law Giovanni d'Alemagna.

THE BENEDICTINES. From its earliest beginnings, San Zaccaria was controlled by the nuns of the neighboring Benedictine convent, which explains the number and importance of the alterations made to it over the centuries. As one of the most favored institutions of the Venetian nobility, the convent of San Zaccaria was exceedingly rich; its

nuns, many of whom belonged to the wealthiest families in Venice, brought substantial endowments when they entered the convent and left it large sums when they died. It is known that the nuns of San Zaccaria lived very freely. In the 18th century the convent was a haunt of the Venetian beau monde, where balls, masquerades and theatrical performances were held and members of both sexes met and mingled.

> "It has high spirits or low, it is pale, or red, grey or pink, cold or warm [...] according to the weather or the hour."
>
> Henry James

RIVA DEGLI SCHIAVONI

The RIVA DEGLI SCHIAVONI runs alongside the edge of the basin of San Marco. This 550-yard quayside area, which today is invaded by souvenir stalls, was named in honour of the merchants of Dalmatia. By decree of the Senate, it was enlarged and then paved with Istrian stone between 1780 and 1782 by the architect Tommaso Temanza, at which time it also became one of Venice's favorite promenades.

THE GRAND HOTEL DANIELI. The former Palazzo Dandolo, built in the 14th century, is today one of the world's most famous hotels. Constructed at a time when the Republic was encouraging people to build palaces that would demonstrate the power and wealth of Venice, this building has changed hands many times over the centuries and at the time of the fall of the Republic was shared by several families. In 1822 it was rented by Giuseppe Dal Niel, who transformed it into an hotel before buying it outright, floor by floor, and becoming its sole owner in 1840. Named after Dal Niel, the hotel attracted a host of kings, princes, politicians and writers throughout the 19th century, to whom it offered unparalleled surroundings and comfort. Among the Danieli's famous guests were Kaiser Wilhelm of Prussia, Dickens, Wagner, Balzac, Proust, Debussy, Cocteau, George Sand and Alfred de Musset. In 1948, the construction of the Danielino, a modern annexe between the main hotel and the prison behind, caused a considerable furore. Today, the Danieli belongs to a large Italian hotel chain. Along one side of the hotel runs the CALLE DELLE RASSE, with its series of overhanging houses. The name "Rasse" derives from *rassa*, or *rascia*, a woollen fabric from Raska in Yugoslavia which was used to cover the *felze* (cabins) ● *57*, ▲ *190* of gondolas.

IN THE FOOTSTEPS OF DE MUSSET
Alfred de Musset and George Sand ended their famous love affair at the Hotel Danieli in 1834. De Musset, seriously ill, found out that Sand was

having an affair with his physician, Doctor Pagello, and returned by himself to Paris. After his death, Louise Colet traveled to Venice, where she had the owner of the hotel show her the room that was once occupied by the "sick young man with the blonde hair", an incident she recalls in *L'Italie des Italiens*.

The inscription on the plaque (right) on the south wall of the church in the Calle della Pietà is from Paul III's Papal Bull denouncing wealthy families who abandon their children at the Pietà (1548).

CLAUDIO MONTEVERDI Monteverdi was born in 1567 in Cremona.

LA PIETÀ AND RELIGIOUS MUSIC IN VENICE

THE CHURCH OF LA PIETÀ. In its present form, this church dates from the 18th century. It is the work of Giorgio Massari, who won a competition for its design in 1736. His plan, which can still be seen at the Correr Museum ▲ *246*, also included the adjoining orphanage but only a part of this was completed. The oval interior contains three frescoes by Tiepolo, Piazzetta's altarpiece *The Visitation*, and a high altar graced with statues by Gianmaria Morlaiter.

Distinguishing features of La Pietà are the absence of a chapel, the wrought-iron choirstalls, the vaulted ceiling which gives excellent acoustic effects, and the narthex which cuts all sound from the street outside. **ENTHUSIASM FOR MUSIC.** La Pietà fulfilled a double role as a place of worship and a concert hall. The church depended to a great extent on the orphanage next door, which from the 17th century onwards was a kind of conservatory in a city where, as Charles de Brosses noted, there was "an inconceivable passion for music", and whose primacy in the field was established by the masters of San Marco. **MUSICAL SUPREMACY.** In 1527, the Fleming Adriaan Willaert was appointed as Master of Music at the chapel of San Marco. On first seeing the basilica, he is said to have been stupefied . . . and convinced that his music was unsuitable for such a place. The two side naves each had their own organ, which probably gave Willaert the idea for a double choir to match. This innovation was to predominate in Europe right up to the time of Bach's *St Matthew Passion*, and its stereophonic effect was developed by Willaert's successors, Andrea and Giovanni Gabrieli. The voices of the choirs were answered by pealing trumpets placed in different places around the church; and after the arrival of Monteverdi ▲ *263*, the most famous of the masters of San Marco, the music achieved a quality that was maintained throughout the 17th century, at a time when Venetian opera was the rage of Europe.

He studied singing, the viola and musical composition. In 1590 he entered the service of the Duke of Mantua and, in 1613, was named Master of Music at the Chapel of San Marco, spending the last thirty years of his life in Venice. This was where he composed an immense body of religious music, of which little remains, as well as most of his operas. When he died in 1647, the city gave him a lavish funeral.

OSPEDALI AND PUBLIC CONCERTS IN THE 18TH CENTURY. The taste for music in Venice grew apace until the 18th century. In addition to the academies, and the private concerts which took place every night in one place or another around the city, the four *ospedali* ▲ *160, 322* also began to organize paying concerts, which were attended by select audiences; Jean-Jacques Rousseau attended a few of these during his stay in Venice in 1743–4. In Vivaldi's time, the Englishman Edward Wright wrote that ". . . every Sunday or feast-day, in the chapels of these hospices, concerts of vocal and instrumental music are given by the young girls of the institution; they stand in an upper gallery, and remain hidden from the view of their hearers by a grille of wrought iron. The organ and other instrumental parts are all played by these girls . . . " Each of these ensembles was composed of about forty inmates. They were trained to sing and play several instruments, and they were theoretically "cloistered like nuns" (de Brosses), but in practice the most gifted performers among them were permitted to sing outside their hospices, and even to teach music to the other girls. The success of such concerts was very considerable, and the profits they generated were so immense that the great masters such as Galuppi ▲ *263, 373* and Vivaldi welcomed the opportunity of directing them.

LA PIETÀ DURING THE 18TH CENTURY: VIVALDI'S OSPEDALE. From 1703, Vivaldi taught at the musical seminary of La Pietà, where he was the violin master and occasionally also the choirmaster and resident composer. This collaboration raised the prestige of the Ospedale, which consequently acquired a reputation for unrivalled musical skill. The bulk of Vivaldi's work (apart from his operas) was written for La Pietà, and no fewer than sixty of his religious works, including both the *Judith Triomphans* and the *Stabat Mater,* have survived down the years. Nevertheless Vivaldi, like Monteverdi, made his most significant contribution in the field of non-religious music. An incomparable virtuoso himself, he was the author of approximately 250 violin concertos which made him an outstanding master of the concerto for solo instrumentalists. Although La Pietà survived all the other *ospedali* by a hundred years, when it was finally closed towards the end of the 19th century it had become only a shadow of the institution which it had been during Vivaldi's time.

ANTONIO VIVALDI
The son of a San Marco violinist, Vivaldi was born on March 4, 1678. His was a musical education, though he was destined for the priesthood and ordained in 1703. But the man nicknamed "Prete rosso" on account of his red hair (or because of the red uniform he wore) soon distanced himself from the ministry, devoting his time to composition. Named violin master at La Pietà, in 1705 he published his first work and made his opera debut with *Ottone in villa*. Discovering a vocation for theater, he became director of Teatro Sant'Angelo in 1714. The successes that followed did not prevent him composing pieces for his favorite instrument, the violin. In 1740 he left Venice to offer his services to Charles VI, but the king died before his arrival. He went to the grave as a forgotten pauper the following year.

After the violent repression of the 1844 uprisings in Italy, the brothers Attilio (1810–44) and Emilio (1819–44) Bandiera attempted a landing in Calabria with a small band of followers. As former officers of the Imperial Austrian

Navy, they had joined Mazzini's Young Italy movement. The forlorn gesture of the brothers was intended as an example to their compatriots. They were captured and shot near Cosenza on July 25, 1844, with the cry of "Long live liberty. Long live the Motherland!" Later Mazzini was wrongly held responsible for their deaths.

A window of Palazzo Gritti-Badoer.

SAN GIOVANNI IN BRAGORA

Facing the church of the Pietà, pass to the right of it and cross the Ponte della Pietà to reach the PALAZZO NAVAGERO, which is famous for having been given to the poet Petrarch by the Republic between 1362 and 1365, in exchange for the gift of his manuscripts to the Libreria Marciana ▲ *254*. (Take the Calle del Dose, on the left.)

CAMPO BANDIERA E MORO. This square is named after the patriotic brothers Attilio and Emilio Bandiera (who lived at Palazzo Soderini, number 3618 here), and their friend Domenico Moro, who were shot by the Bourbons in 1844. The PALAZZO GRITTI-BADOER, rebuilt in the 15th century on much older foundations, is now a hotel (La Residenza), its grandeur giving it prominence among the other buildings here. The church stands slightly back from the campo.

THE CHURCH OF SAN GIOVANNI IN BRAGORA. The origin of the term *bragora* is much disputed. Some think it refers to a region of the Orient from which the relics of St John the Baptist are supposed to have come (the church is dedicated to him). Others believe it derives from two very ancient dialect words, *brago* (mud) and *gora* (stagnant canal), which describe the way the site probably looked in early times. Still others favor a derivation from *bragolare* (to fish), a simple allusion to daily life on the Gemini Islands which form the greater part of the sestiere. There is also a school of thought that traces it to the Greek *agora* (a town square). As to the church, local legend sets its foundation at the beginning of the 8th century, although it is first mentioned only in 1090. It owes its outer aspect to works begun in 1475, the façade reflecting the transitional period between Gothic and Renaissance. The interior was altered in the 18th century; the ceiling is designed like the hull of a ship, and there are vestiges of 15th-century frescoes on the walls. Paintings by Alvise Vivarini, Cima da Conegliano (a *Baptism of Christ*) and Palma the Younger can be seen here, along with the record of Vivaldi's christening. The composer, who was born in one of the houses in the campo, was baptized in one of the 15th-century fonts here. On the way out, note the well with its fine head of John the Baptist. (To the left of the church, take the Calle Crosera, then the Calle del Pestrin, the first on the right. Follow the fondamenta and cross the Ponte Storto.)

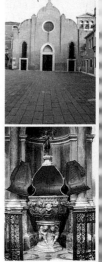

SAN MARTINO

THE CHURCH OF SAN MARTINO. This building was founded some time between the 7th and 8th centuries. The original Venetian-Byzantine church was demolished in 1540 and rebuilt by

La Residenza

Sansovino, who altered its orientation by 90 degrees and made it much larger. This indicates that the church and surrounding district were growing in importance with the development of the Arsenal nearby. St Martin, to whom it is dedicated, is the patron of an annual festival held on November 11, when the children of the city go from door to door collecting coins and drumming on saucepans. At Martinmas the pastryshops of Venice are filled with delicious cakes representing the saint on his horse, which are very popular with Venetian children. Antonio da Ponte, the architect of the Rialto Bridge ▲ 282, lived in this parish.

THE ARSENAL

Until 1808, the mid-16th century church of SANTA MARIA DELL'ARSENALE stood on the Campo dell'Arsenale, and was much frequented by sailors and local workmen. This church, which has now vanished, was attached to one of the two towers overlooking the docks and resembled a small classical temple.

THE FIRST ARSENAL. Venetian power overwhelmingly rested on the city's mastery of shipbuilding and the use of naval and merchant vessels. Nobody knows when the first arsenal was constructed; the usually quoted date of 1104 is not supported by any document. However, it is certain that an arsenal serving as a depot for arms, oars and rigging existed here in the early 13th century, which made it possible to repair and construct galleys. This first arsenal seems to have been the one described by Dante in the 21st canto of the *Inferno*: "For as at Venice, in the Arsenal, in winter-time, they boil the gummy pitch, to caulk such ships as need an overhaul; now that they cannot

QVOD . DVPLICI . HONORE . L . ETA .

COMMYNES IN VENICE
"Afterward they shewd me their arsenal, wherein they keep their galleys and do everything needful for their navy, which is the finest in the world today . . ." Thus Philippe de Commynes described the Arsenal in 1494, when he stayed in Venice as councillor and ambassador of Charles VIII of France, and reported on the attempts made by the Republic to organize a secret coalition against the French in the eastern Mediterranean.

THE ARSENAL: THE FINEST LIONS IN VENICE ○
The Arsenal is a military zone that is open to the public only for regattas and during the Biennale, or when exhibitions are held in the rope warehouse (the Tana). Debarred from entry, one can go no further than the gate, but what a gate! It is a Renaissance portal framed by two white marble lions, the finest in Venice.

177

PLANS
OF THE ARSENAL
In 1797–8 Maffioletti
drew three plans
of the Arsenal
(40 inches high by
56 inches wide)
to persuade the
Austrians to rebuild it.
The first plan (below
right) shows the
Arsenal as it looked
after the fall of the
Republic. The second
plan (right) shows its
state of destruction
after Napoleon
declared war on
Venice. The third
(not illustrated) sets
out a rebuilding
project.

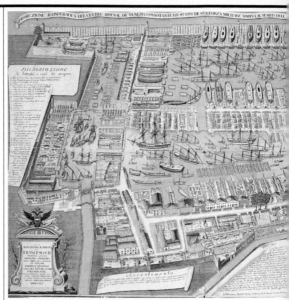

THE TWO LIONS
FROM GREECE
The statues of two
lions still guard the
entrance to the
Arsenal. They were
brought home from
Athens as booty by
Francesco Morosini
after the reconquest
of Morea in 1687.
The seated one was
once part of a
fountain at Piraeus.
The carved
inscription in runic

characters probably
refers to the brutal
repression of the
Greeks by the *vernighi*
(Scandinavian
mercenaries in the
pay of Byzantium)
in 1040.

sail – instead of
which one builds him
a new boat, one toils
to plug, seams
strained by many a
voyage, others stitch
canvas to patch a
tattered jib or lug,
hammer at the prow,
hammer at the stern,
or twine
ropes, or shave oars, refit and make all snug."
(translated by Dorothy L. Sayers)
Despite the beginnings of centralization, naval construction at
that time remained firmly linked to private initiative. It was
handled by the *squeri* ● 69 at various points around the city.
But the state fixed norms of construction and the Doge was
able, if any pressing need emerged, to requisition carpenters
and caulkers to work in the government shipyards.

A NEW ARSENAL. It was not until after 1320 that work
commenced on the new Arsenal. Its area
quadrupled in size and its role changed in
consequence. Previously the Arsenal had
been used for maintaining ships: now it
was also expected to construct them. The
"light galleys" (*galere sottili*) of the war
fleet were built here, as were the larger
merchant vessels (*da mercato*). These
ships were chartered to merchants, but they always remained
the property of the state which, when necessary, could
integrate them into its war fleet. When they carried precious
cargo, the ships travelled in convoys of eight to eleven vessels.
Meanwhile, "round ships" continued to be built in the private
shipyards, which still produced the main bulk of Venice's
seagoing tonnage.

> "Two mighty lions brought from Attica
> Stand guard beside the Arsenal;
> Peaceful they stand, and near the antique pair
> All is in size reduced, gate, tower and canal."
>
> Goethe

THE ARSENALOTTI. The *arsenalotti*, or arsenal workers, operated in teams. Each team was composed of a dozen carpenters, six sawyers, fifteen caulkers, their apprentices and one or two unskilled laborers; together, these men could float up to six large merchant galleys every two years. Every speciality had its foreman, and the work of the team was supervised by a general overseer. The management of the Arsenal was chiefly concerned with the materials and the quality of the finished product; it did not interfere with the practical process of shipbuilding. Constituting a kind of artisans' elite, the *arsenalotti* enjoyed huge prestige and benefits. Their skill as firefighters was much admired and they were always called upon when there was a fire in the city. The "Masters of the Arsenal" also formed the guard of honor at the Doge's Palace during the election of a new Doge, as well as manning the Bucintoro on major occasions. They constituted a reserve corps of non-commissioned officers, and many of them took part in sea-battles on the galleys they themselves had built. Lastly, they had rights to free or low-rent lodgings; this led to the construction of whole districts of houses in the vicinity of the Arsenal, which are among the earliest examples of "modular housing" attempted by mankind.

THE TANA. At the time of the expansion of the Arsenal in the early 14th century, a number of warehouses were built for storing and manufacturing ropes and cordage. These were incorporated into the Tana, which is 345 yards long by 22 yards wide, with 84 columns. The importing of hemp and tar was consigned to private entrepreneurs; inside the Tana, the hemp plants were carded and sorted, and the fibers separated. Once they had been spun, the fibers were either turned over to master-cordwainers who ran their own workshops, or else were made into ropes at the Tana itself.

THE ARSENALE NOVISSIMO. Faced with the Ottoman menace, and above all with the growing power of the Spanish fleet, in 1473 the Senate decided to build the Arsenale Novissimo, although the work was not completed until the beginning of the 16th century. With this addition, Venice was able to add a huge reserve to her existing stock of galleys. Some of these reserve vessels were kept afloat in the harbor and could be fitted for sea at only a moment's notice. Others stood in dry dock and could be relaunched after caulking. The process of building the galleys was not unlike an assembly line. The hulls were constructed in the new Arsenal and the Arsenale Novissimo before passing through a series of buildings in the old Arsenal where

PORTA MAGNA
The majestic gate of the Arsenal was the first piece of Venetian architecture to break with the Gothic tradition and imitate antiquity. Probably dating from about 1460, it was based on a drawing by Jacopo Bellini, and built by Antonio Gambello.

THE PELOPONNESIAC
Francesco Morosini ● *40* was the last Venetian to combine the offices of Doge and Supreme Commander of the Fleet. At the close of the 17th century, when Venice's status as a maritime power seemed to be undergoing a revival, Morosini won a series of battles against the Turks, and reconquered Attica and the Peloponnese, earning himself the sobriquet of "Peloponnesiac". Pictured above is a battle pitting Venetians against Turks in which "with a few galleys and four warships, Morosini put seventeen Turkish vessels to flight." He died while in office at Nauplis In 1694.

179

THE MERCHANT
GALLEY

**THE MERCHANT
GALLEY**
Although they were
equipped with sails,
the big Venetian
merchant galleys
continued to be
largely propelled by
oarsmen. Fast, fitted
with ornaments like

warships, always
traveling in convoy,
but incapable of
carrying heavy cargo,
these vessels were
usually reserved for
the transportation of
valuable goods. Given
the cost of their
armament, it was rare
for single individuals
to lease one of these
galleys alone – as a
rule, the merchants
tended to form
temporary
associations in order
to spread the cost.

they were fitted out with rigging, weaponry and victuals. Some
parts of them, which were made to very strict specifications,
were interchangeable – these included the masts, spars,
rowing benches and pulleys. In this way the size of Venice's
reserve of warships doubled from twenty-five to fifty vessels at
the close of the 15th century, and increased again to a
hundred ships in the mid-16th century. This total fell to about
fifty by 1633. The activity of the Arsenal
was at its height during the 1560's,
when it employed an average of
about two thousand workers.
This number would rise to
three thousand in times of
emergency. In 1570, in order
to counter the Ottoman offensive against Cyprus, a hundred
galleys were built in the space of two months, and at the
Battle of Lepanto ● *36*, no less than half the Christian fleet
which defeated the Turks consisted of ships that had been
built in the yards of Venice. On this occasion the Venetians
unveiled a brand new type of warship, the galleass, which was
the first galley of its kind to carry cannon on both sides.

GALLEYS AND SHIPS. The Venetians remained faithful to the
galley concept until the end of the 17th century, but by 1667
the Arsenal was already starting to turn out 70-gun ships of
the line according to the English pattern. In 1794 production
of a new type of ship, the 30- to 40-gun frigate, began in the
Arsenal. The yards also continued to produce better-
armed and larger sailing vessels than the traditional
galleys, which were finally abandoned in 1755.
Despite her steady decline, Venice remained the
most active naval dockyard in the Adriatic until
1797. The end of the Republic, brought by the
Napoleonic Wars and the Austrian occupation,
also marked the collapse of the Arsenal.

THE ARSENAL TODAY. The Arsenal is now a
navy base, functioning as a
roadstead for large
battleships and as dock.
However, it also has a
civilian use; a research
center and a society
concerned with the
preservation of antique
boats (not open to the
public) are based there.
(Follow the Fondamenta
dell'Arsenale, which leads
to the Campo San Biagio.)

THE NAVAL MUSEUM

Venice's Naval Museum
occupies the upper floor of
a warehouse annexe that is
situated beside the Rio
dell'Arsenale. Its
predecessor was the Casa
dei Modelli, which was
built by the government

towards the end of the 17th century in order to preserve models of the ships that were built in the shipyards of La Serenissima. Many of these models subsequently disappeared: first during the events of December 1797 and January 1798, when Napoleon's soldiers sacked the Arsenal and destroyed the Casa, and then again during the Second World War. Some of the Venetian maquettes may be seen today at the Musée de la Marine in Paris, while others, dating from the late 17th and early 18th centuries, have remained in Venice. The present museum was built on the initiative of the Austrian admiralty. It has about 25,000 objects on display, and these offer a microcosm of the history of the Venetian and Italian navies. Among other things there are collections of navigational instruments and uniforms, models of fortresses held by Venice throughout the Mediterranean, scale models of various types of vessels, such as the Bucintoro ● *38* and a 17th-century galleass. Among these scale models there is one particular curiosity: the *cammello*, which worked like a vise to grasp ships and raise them from the low waters of the Lagoon. However, the two *cortelà* (the decorated sides of a galley belonging to Lazzaro Mocenigo, which foundered by the Dardanelles in the 16th century) are unquestionably the most interesting exhibits here.

The emblem of the oar-makers.

TOWARDS VIA GARIBALDI

RIVA SAN BIAGIO. This wharf was originally used as an unloading and weighing area for imported goods. The original 11th-century Church of San Biagio situated here was, until the 16th century, the main sanctuary of Venice's Greek community ▲ *164*. (Cross the bridge).

RIVA DEI SETTE MARTIRI. Built in 1937, the original name of Riva dell'Impero was changed to Riva dei Sette Martiri in memory of seven Venetians who were shot by German soldiers during the Second World War.

VIA GARIBALDI. At 57 feet wide, this is the broadest street in the whole of Venice. It was created by filling in the Rio del Castello, and was opened by Napoleon during his visit to the city in 1807. It was originally called Via Eugenia, in honor of Eugène de Beauharnais, the French Viceroy of Italy; then it was renamed after Garibaldi, the hero of Italian unification, in 1867. On the right, at the beginning of this arterial road leading towards San Pietro di Castello, there is a plaque indicating the house of the navigators John and Sebastian Cabot, who were born in Chioggia ▲ *361*.

THE GALLEY OARSMEN
The most difficult problem to solve was that of finding crews to man Venice's ships, and in particular the oars. In the 13th and 14th centuries, to be a *galeotto* was still considered to be an honorable calling: but later it became more and more difficult to find free Venetians who were prepared to do this work. First Dalmatian and Greek volunteers were recruited, and then, in the second half of the 16th century, convicts were finally drafted to the galleys and kept chained to the benches. This innovation was championed in 1545 by Cristoforo da Canal, the first Venetian captain to put to sea in a galley rowed by convicts.

"IL CORSO"
Every Sunday during
Lent, until the start of
Holy Week, the
Venetians repaired to
the Church of San
Pietro di Castello,
where pardons were
awarded.

Following the
completion of the
religious ceremony,
which also gave the
women an excellent
opportunity to display
their finest jewelry,
everyone feasted on
frittele (fritters, the
traditional holiday
fare) and *zucca
barucca* (grilled
pumpkin), which they
washed down with
some Cypriot wine
and Malvasia, while a
corso was held on the
canal. In front of a
crowd which gathered
to watch on the parvis
of the church on the
bridge, the silk-clad
gondoliers would
engage in a sort of
contest, weaving their
vessels to and fro and
generally showing off
their skills with the
oar. Today's modern
regattas have evolved
from this very ancient
game.

SAN PIETRO DI CASTELLO

A wooden bridge leads from here to the island of San Pietro.
On this site, which has probably been inhabited since the 5th
or 6th century, there used to be a fortress (*castello*) whose
purpose was to protect the Realtine Islands from attackers
approaching from the sea. It was this *castello* which gave the
sestiere its name. Apparently there was also a line of

fortifications that stretched along the
basin as far as Santa Maria del Giglio ▲
264, at which point a chain barred the
entrance to the Grand Canal. From the
7th century until 1807, the island of San
Pietro was the seat of religious power in
Venice.

CAMPO SAN PIETRO. This campo is
unusual for Venice in that it is green, very
large, and directly adjoining the water.
Opposite the canal stands the church and
the PATRIARCHAL PALACE, whose
entrance bears the arms of the Patriarch
Lorenzo Priuli. The building was
converted into a barracks at the
beginning of the 19th century, by
Napoleonic decree.

THE CHURCH OF SAN PIETRO. The
Church of San Pietro was built during the
9th century. It played an important role
for hundreds of years as the seat of the
bishopric of Venice, which was
subordinate to the Patriarchate of Grado. Finally, in 1451,
Venice acquired her own patriarch, and the church became a
cathedral. Thus it remained until 1807, when the title was
passed to St Mark's. The Church of San Pietro had been
modified several times before Andrea Palladio was
commissioned to rebuild it in 1558. This operation was
completed by Francesco Smeraldi and
Giangirolamo Grapiglia who, as faithful
disciples of Palladio, appear to have
respected his plans to the letter. The
monumental high altar was executed in 1649
by Clemente Moli, from a design by
Baldassare Longhena, to whom we also owe
the design for the chapel dedicated to
Cardinal Francesco Vendramin (on the lower
left side.) The church also contains the so-
called CHAIR OF SAINT PETER, a marble
throne said to have been used by the apostle
in the Orient. Its back, curiously, consists of a
Muslim funeral stele covered in Arab
decorative motifs and verses from the Koran.

THE CAMPANILE. The construction of this
campanile (1463–74) had just been completed
when it was seriously damaged by lightning.
The repairs were assigned to Mauro Codussi in
1482 and, when he finished eight years later,
the result looked very different. The new
campanile was covered with Istrian stone and
sported a dome with a lead roof on a wooden structure.

CHURCH OF SAN
PIETRO DI CASTELLO

PUBLIC GARDENS

BIENNALE GARDENS

CHURCH OF SANT'ELENA

LA CERTOSA

This
dome was
replaced by a
polygonal tambour
roof in 1670. Each Saturday,
Venice's oldest market was held in the Cathedral square, most
of the customers being sailors from the port of San Nicolò di
Lido. Today there is just a series of *squeri* ● *69* on the Canal
San Pietro, along with workshops, pontoons, sheds, buoys and
moorings for small fishing boats and other vessels. (Return to
Via Garibaldi by the Fondamenta Quintavalle, the wooden
bridge of the same name, and the unassuming Fondamenta di
Sant'Anna.)

🚶 **Two hours**

◆ **D** D-E-F

In the area of the
public gardens
occupied by the
Biennale stand the
pavilions of the
various participating
countries. Many of
these were built by
some famous
architects, notably
Josef Hoffman

(Austria 1934),
Gerrit-Thomas
Rietveld (Holland
1954), Carlo Scarpa
(Venezuela 1954–6),
and Alvar Aalto
(Finland 1956). These
pavilions have had
the effect of
transforming the
gardens into a kind of
resumé of modern
architecture,
illustrating the
evolution of 20th-
century taste. They
come alive in the
autumn, when the
Biennale crowds
return. Shown above
are the American and
Italian pavilions.

Poster of
the first
Venice Biennale.

THE PUBLIC GARDENS

Napoleon drained a section of marshland and demolished
several churches to create these gardens, which became
Venice's favorite park. Concerts were performed here, the
central promenade was used for bicycle races (then a highly
novel pastime), and there was even a balloon ascent. Today,
most of the site is occupied by the Biennale. The main
entrance was designed by Gianantonio Selva (1810), who also
directed the rest of the works on the park. Opposite stands
the MONUMENT TO GIUSEPPE GARIBALDI (1885). Giambattista
Tiepolo was born in the Calle San Domenico, which
runs alongside the Gardens.

THE BIENNALE

THE BIRTH OF THE BIENNALE. A decision taken by
the communal administration of Venice, on April
19, 1893, decreed that an exhibition by Italian artists
should be mounted every two years, and this became
the catalyst for the creation of the Biennale. The
decree was changed in 1895 to include the exhibiting
of works by foreign artists as well, with certain
restrictions. Invited artists could only show a single
work; non-invited artists had to submit their
creations to a jury. The gardens of the Castello
sestiere were selected as the venue; an old merry-
go-round and the stable block which contained Toni the
elephant (a celebrated 19th-century attraction) were
demolished in order to make way for the Biennale. The first
exhibition, which opened on April 30, 1895, in the presence of
King Umberto I and Queen
Margherita, proved to be a huge
success: 200,000 visitors came to
see the pictures, no doubt
encouraged by the specially
cheap train fares and the free
entry to the exhibition.

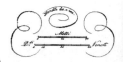

THE FIRST BIENNALES. At the
first exhibition, a painting by
Giacomo Grosso, *Il Supremo
Convegno*, representing a corpse
on a bier surrounded by five
nude women, raised such a furore
that the Patriarch of Venice (later Pope Pius X) had it
removed. The first Biennales were so oblivious to new trends
in art that, on April 27, 1910, a group of Futurist painters
climbed to the top of St Mark's clocktower in order to scatter
leaflets attacking Venice's addiction to the past and the
Biennale in general. After the First World War, the Biennale
became rather more receptive to modern art. The works of
Cézanne were shown there for the first time in 1920, at an
exhibition of Impressionists. Toulouse-Lautrec and Degas
followed in 1924.
THE FASCIST PERIOD. In 1930, the Italian state took over
control of the Biennale and divided it into several sections:
cinema, theater and music. In June 1934, Adolf Hitler visited
Venice and proclaimed his "disgust" with the degenerate art
shown at the Biennale.

THE POST-WAR BIENNALES. The first post-war Biennale took place in 1948 and was a crucial event. All the greatest artists of the day were represented: the Impressionists, the German artists banished by Nazism (notably Dix and Pechstein), Picasso, Klee, Schiele and Magritte, along with works from the Peggy Guggenheim Collection and the metaphysical painters (Carrà, Morandi and De Chirico).

THE BIENNALE AFTER 1960. In 1964, it was America's turn to produce a revolution in art, with the great exhibition that introduced Pop Art to Europe. "New democratic status" was introduced in 1973; a rather tardy expression of the principles of 1968, this sought to make the management of the Biennale more open, and to deprive critics, who might have a private stake in certain types of art, of their monopoly. During the 1970's, the Venice Biennales were organized around specific themes. The "Ambiente e Arte" exhibition on the environment took place in 1976 and was followed in 1977 by the

celebrated Biennale dedicated to dissidents in the East. But the new rules tended to favor the creation of lobbies which, coupled with the total inadequacy of Italian state funding, compromised the validity of the Biennale's programming and the effectiveness of its organization. Since the 1980's a growing campaign has sought to abolish the Biennale's status as a government institution controlled by political parties.

SANT'ELENA

Until the 19th century, Venice ended at the point of San Antonio – today's Public Gardens and site of the Biennale. The gardens are now connected by a bridge to the island of Sant'Elena, which owes its name to a convent and church containing the relics of the saint, brought from the East in the 13th century. The part of the Lagoon separating the island from the city was filled in during the last century. Modern Sant'Elena, which was developed only recently, has preserved plenty of green space by the water (the Rimembranze Park) and is the site of the Francesco Morosini Naval College and

the football stadium.

THE CHURCH OF SANT'ELENA. This church was founded in the second half of the 12th century. An Augustinian monastery was joined to it at a later date and, in 1439, works were begun to rebuild it in the Gothic

THE GARDENS
Linked to each other by paths and separated by hedges, the Biennale pavilions stand in the public gardens in which Wagner and Taine used to take the air, and where Théophile Gautier went to contemplate the pretty Venetian girls walking arm in arm.

THE BOOK PAVILION
Just opposite the Italian pavilion stands the 240 square yard Electa Book Pavilion (left), which was built by the architect James Stirling. This brand new, glass-sided structure, with its copper roof, was inspired by naval architecture and looks like nothing so much as a monster vaporetto. Inside the pavilion, art books and catalogues are displayed under wooden beams and rafters.

185

BIENNALE POSTERS
In order to conform with the tastes of the period, and the wishes of the organizers, the posters for the first contemporary Biennale favored stereotyped images of Venice which were familiar all over the world. This choice of graphics was in accord with goals which the Biennale had set itself, namely the development of tourism in Venice (the new luxury hotels at the Lido were built at this time) by organizing events which had international connotations. Thus the posters were commissioned from artists who shared the same objective; as to their texts, these endeavoured to attract visitors by advertising special rail ticket reductions and free admittance.

Poster for the Biennale of 1936.

style favored by the Benedictines, to whom the complex had been ceded by Pope Gregory XII. The Renaissance portal, by Antonio Rizzo, originally came from Sant'Aponal ▲ 286 and was only added in 1929. The sculptures in the LUNETTE depict Vettor Cappello, a hero of the Venetian navy who died in action against the Turks; this warrior is shown kneeling before the Madonna. Nothing of the convent remains today but a wing of the cloister, whose brick arches support a gallery. The campanile was rebuilt very recently.

Grand Canal

 From Santa Lucia Station
to St Mark's Square

 From St Mark's Square
to Santa Lucia Station

 Vaporetto stop

 Traghetto (a gondola which
crosses the river)

The *Canalazzo*, as the Venetians call it, traces a broad, inverted "S" shape, two and a half miles long, through the centre of Venice. Today's great waterway was originally the thoroughfare for merchant vessels on their way to and from the Rialto. Although the traffic is less dense than it used to be, the *Canalazzo* is still Venice's main street, with an unbroken sequence of palaces and churches on either side. The main façades of all these buildings overlook the water, and the best way to see them is from a gondola or vaporetto. Nothing seems to have been left out of this miraculous open-air stage, set for Venice's great regattas and festivals.

This painting shows the Church of Santa Lucia, which was demolished to make way for the railway station. The relics of St Lucia, who was martyred in Sicily, were moved to the Church of San Geremia, where they were placed in a glass coffin.

PALAZZO DIEDO

The Church of Santa Lucia, along with many Gothic and Renaissance palaces, was demolished in order to clear the way for the new station.

Venice was one of the obligatory stages of the Grand Tour, and so it attracted well-to-do travelers, artists and intellectuals of all nations bent on discovering both the Renaissance and their own romantic image of Italy.

THE STATION In 1846 Venice finally broke her thousand-year isolation from the rest of the world, when the railway bridge planned by the Austrians was completed.

GATEWAY TO VENICE

Venice is divided into six districts (*sestieri* in Venetian). The station quarter is called CANNAREGIO, a name that probably derives from the *canne* (rushes) that once grew here.

THE CHURCH OF THE SCALZI

The exiled Roman Discalced Carmelites commissioned Baldassare Longhena to build a church here in 1656. Thanks to Longhena the Grand Canal begins and ends with Baroque buildings. The rich decoration of the Scalzi included a fresco, *Il Trasporto della Casa di Loveto.* (1743), by Giambattista Tiepolo which was destroyed in 1915. The Ponte Miozzi, the stone bridge at the foot of the church was built in 1934, replacing the original iron bridge that spanned the canal from the early 19th century.

THE GRAND CANAL: SHOWCASE OF VENICE ✪

Whether traveling in a humble vaporetto or lording it in a taxi, sailing up or down the most famous waterway in the world is an experience that never palls. The colors, light and ambience change with every hour. Binoculars are very handy for picking out the sculptural detail of the palazzi.

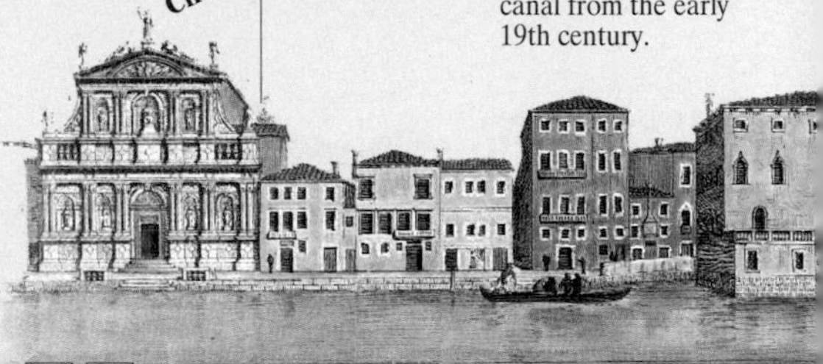

CHURCH OF THE SCALZI

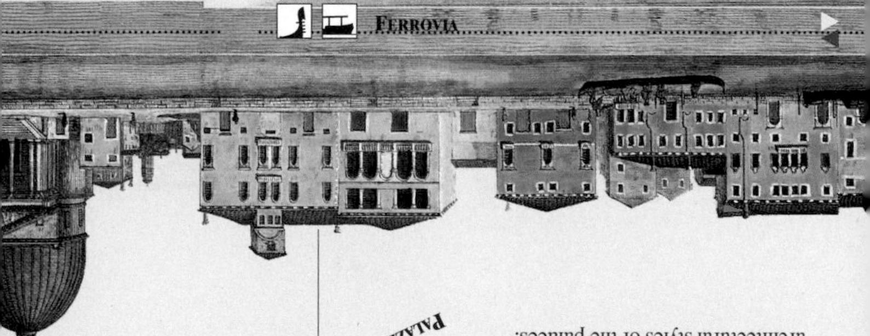

FERROVIA

PALAZZO FOSCARI-CONTARINI

VENETIAN WINDOWS

The immense variety of windows in the buildings along the Grand Canal reflects the many different architectural styles of the palaces.

CHURCH OF SAN SIMEONE PICCOLO

San Simeone Piccolo is an 18th-century imitation of the Pantheon in Rome, designed by Giovanni Scalfarotto. It has a copper dome and today is used as a concert hall.

CHURCH OF SIMEONE PICCOLO

189

> "The buildings lining each bank made one think of natural scenery, with the difference that the nature which created these possessed a human imagination."
>
> Marcel Proust

PALAZZO CALBO CROTTA

Just after the Bridge of the Scalzi stands the first palace of the Grand Canal, Palazzo Calbo Crotta. Originally Byzantine in style, but many times restored, the Calbo Crotta family home was filled with beautiful furniture which is now on display in the CA' REZZONICO, the great museum of 18th-century Venice ▲ *333*. Today it is better known as the Hotel Principe.

PALAZZO CALBO CROTTA

CHURCH OF SAN SIMEONE GRANDE

THE GONDOLAS

The special conditions of Venice led to the invention of the gondola – originally a richly decorated little craft. However an edict of the Seignory in the early 16th century limited their colour to black "with a view to avoiding unnecessary expense".

THE "FELZE"

Gondolas used to be closed in by *felze*, removable cabins with roofs like half-barrels. The *felze* also had a door with bas-reliefs and a small window at the side; very comfortable, with voluminous black fabric draped over their outsides, they were installed during the winter months and taken off every evening.

PALAZZO LABIA

Built for the wealthy Labia family, this is now the headquarters of Italian National Television. The interior is decorated with frescoes by Tiepolo. "The theme, which is the story of Cleopatra – an 18th-century Venetian Cleopatra – extends all round the walls of the apartment, then passes through the doors, under the marbles, and behind the imitation columns." (Guy de Maupassant)

The site of Palazzo Flangini was cleared in the 19th century.

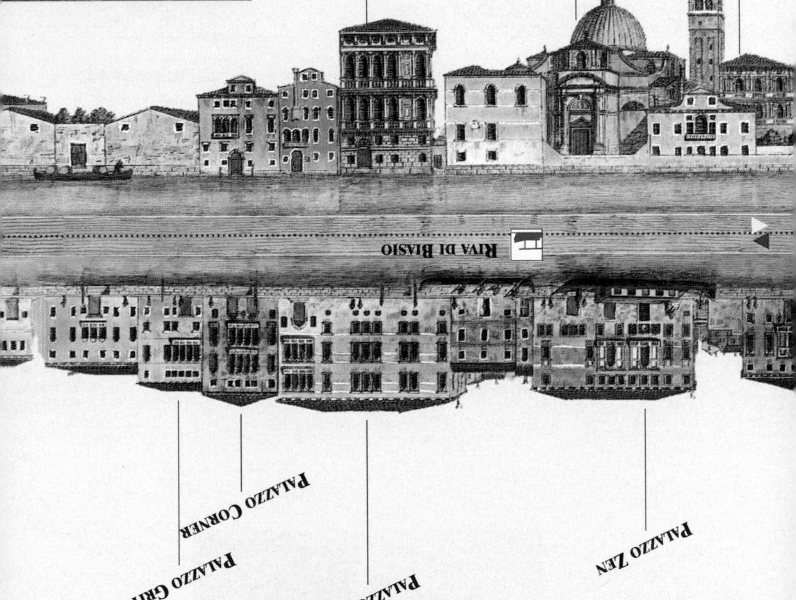

PALAZZO FLANGINI   CHURCH OF SAN GEREMIA   PALAZZO LABIA

RIVA DI BIASIO

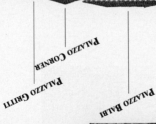

PALAZZO CORNER
PALAZZO GRITTI
PALAZZO BALBI
PALAZZO ZEN

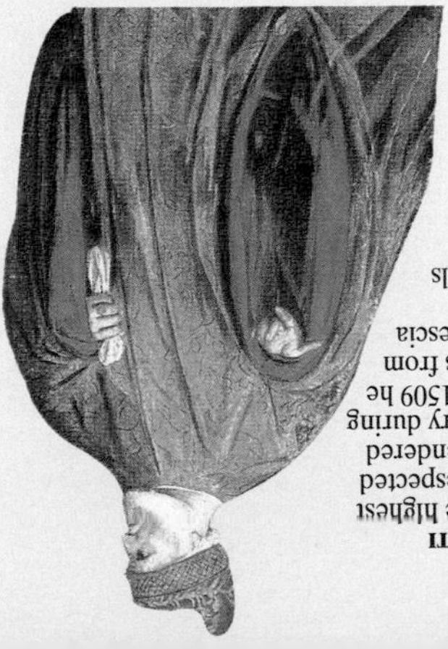

THE DOGE ANDREA GRITTI

Before his election to the highest office in 1523, the well-respected General Andrea Gritti rendered great service to his country during the Italian wars ● 33. In 1509 he drove the Imperial forces from Padua, and recovered Brescia from the French in 1512. He died of a surfeit of eels on Christmas Eve, 1538.

LA RIVA DI BIASIO

According to the chronicles of Venice, a diabolical butcher named Biasio opened a shop on the bank of the canal at this point and served human meat as a substitute for pork. He was condemned to death and beheaded between the two columns of the Piazzetta.

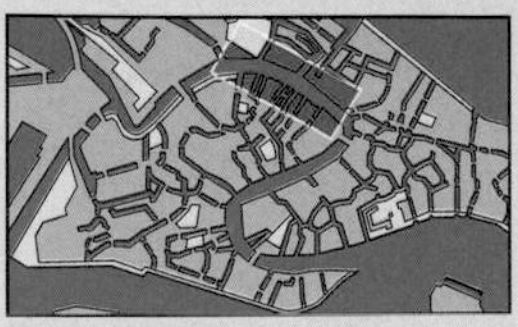

> "The Fondaco dei Turchi vanished behind them, its ivory surface wonderfully yellowed and worn, like the crumbling portico of some ruined mosque."
>
> Gabriele d'Annunzio

PALAZZO CORRER-CONTARINI
Known as the "House of Hearts" because of their heart-shaped blazons, these two palaces were acquired by the Contarinis in 1768, and a century later they passed into the hands of one of Garibaldi's generals.

PALAZZO CORRER-CONTARINI

PALAZZO GIOVANNELLI

PALAZZO GIOVANNELLI
Built in the first half of the 15th century, this Gothic palace acquired a large collection of paintings in the 18th century, including Giorgione's famous *Tempest* ▲ *307* (now in the Accademia ▲ *301*). Beside it, on a site which is now a garden, the sumptuous palace of the Bembo family once stood. It was demolished during the 19th century.

"A man's life often resembles these palaces of the Grand Canal, which begin at the base with an array of stones proudly sculpted in diamond points, and end with the upper floors hastily cobbled together from dried mud."

Paul Morand, *Venise*

192

ALTANE

Many Venetian palaces have *altane* – wooden roof terraces – on which the ladies of the nobility used to sit bleaching their hair according to an ancient formula.

VENETIAN BLEACH

"Take a full measure of the soap used for bleaching silk, and boil it with a little alum , . . next add two ounces of burned lead and boil the mixture until a piece of white fabric dipped in it turns black. Allow to cool . . . then add two ounces of powdered Damascus soap and leave in the sun."

Marinello

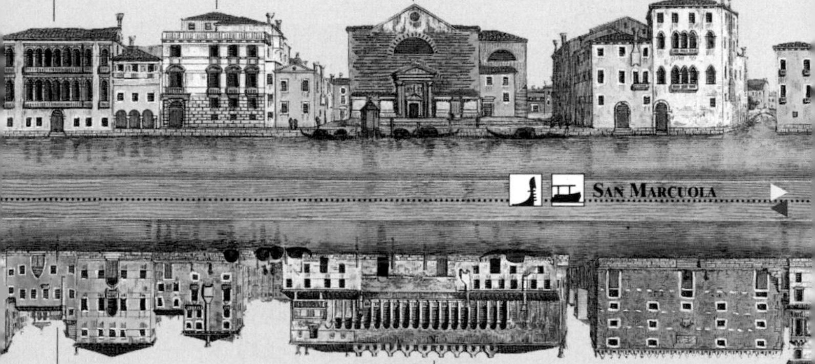

PALAZZO MARTINENGO-MARTELLI

This former palace was completely altered during the 19th century.

PALAZZO GRITTI

PALAZZO MARTINENGO-MARTELLI

CHURCH OF SAN MARCUOLA

SAN MARCUOLA ▶

▼

CHURCH OF SAN GIOVANNI DECOLLATO

FONDACO DEI TURCHI

DEPOSITO DEL MEGIO

DEPOSITO DEL MEGIO

This was one of the Republic's grain and flour stores, maintained in readiness for times of famine.

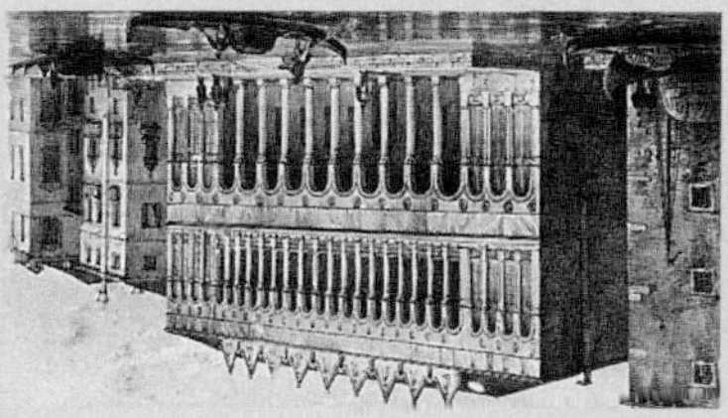

FONDACO DEI TURCHI

This Venetian-Byzantine building, one of the oldest in Venice, became the warehouse of the Republic's Turkish merchants in 1621 ▼ 347.

In the mid-19th century, a misguided restoration left the Fondaco dei Turchi with two incongruous side towers. Today it is used as the city's Natural History Museum.

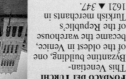

PALAZZO VENDRAMIN-CALERGI

Now the winter quarters of the municipal casino, this was the home of the composer Richard Wagner during the last months of his life. After he died on February 13, 1883, Wagner's body was taken to the station by gondola in the middle of the night, then shipped to Bayreuth for burial.

This majestic Renaissance palace was built in the early 16th century by the great architect Mauro Coducci, and became the property of the Duchesse de Berry in 1844. She also bought the Palazzo Marcello, named after the musician Benedetto Marcello, who was born there at the end of the 16th century.

PALAZZO VENDRAMIN-CALERGI

PALAZZO ERIZZO

PALAZZO EMO

PALAZZO MARCELLO

PALAZZO SORANZO

PALAZZO BELLONI-BATTAGIA

PALAZZO TRON

PALAZZO TRON

A late 16th-century construction, this little palace belonged to the Trons, a patrician family which only managed to produce a single doge. One of its more distinguished members was Andrea Tron, known as El Paron (the master), who attempted to reform the declining economy of Venice during the 18th century.

PALAZZO BELLONI-BATTAGIA

This building was commissioned from Longhena by Bortolo Belloni. His integration into the ranks of the Venetian patricians cost this wealthy merchant the sum of 150,000 ducats in 1647. Aside from their decorative function, the two *oculi* which stand above the palace signify the presence in the family of a *capitan da mar*, or admiral of the Venetian fleet.

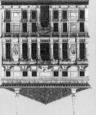

194

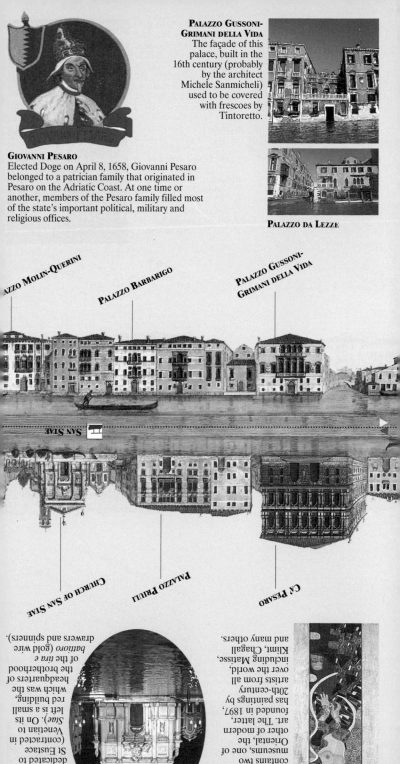

CA' PESARO ▲ 351

PALAZZO GUSSONI-GRIMANI DELLA VIDA
The façade of this palace, built in the 16th century (probably by the architect Michele Sanmicheli) used to be covered with frescoes by Tintoretto.

GIOVANNI PESARO
Elected Doge on April 8, 1658, Giovanni Pesaro belonged to a patrician family that originated in Pesaro on the Adriatic Coast. At one time or another, members of the Pesaro family filled most of the state's important political, military and religious offices.

PALAZZO DA LEZZE

PALAZZO MOLIN-QUERINI

PALAZZO BARBARIGO

PALAZZO GUSSONI-GRIMANI DELLA VIDA

SAN STAE

CHURCH OF SAN STAE

PALAZZO PRIULI

CA' PESARO

CHURCH OF SAN STAE
This church, said to have been founded in the 10th century, is dedicated to St Eustace (contracted in Venetian to Stae). On its left is a small red building, which was the headquarters of the brotherhood of the tira e battioro (gold wire drawers and spinners).

CA' PESARO
This palace, designed by Baldassare Longhena, today contains two museums, one of Oriental, the other of modern art. The latter, founded in 1897, has paintings by 20th-century artists from all over the world, including Matisse, Klimt, Chagall and many others.

THE FIFTH POPE
Carlo Rezzonico, who as Clement XIII was the fifth Venetian Pope, was born in 1693 in the 16th-century Palazzo Fontana.

As the most beautiful Flamboyant Gothic building in Venice, the Ca' d'Oro is a place of great subtlety and refinement, full of Byzantine overtones and delicate touches that might have been borrowed from the art of the goldsmith. It owes its name (House of Gold) to the gildings which originally embellished its façade. In 1916, Baron Giorgio Franchetti, the last private owner, bequeathed the Ca' d'Oro and its great collections of furniture, medals and paintings to the city of Venice.

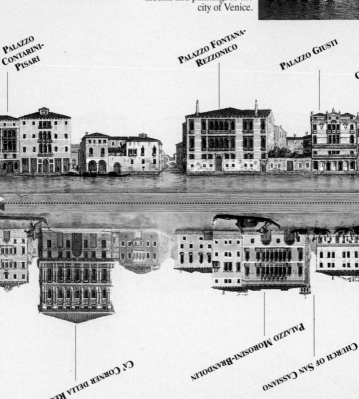

PALAZZO CONTARINI-PISARI

PALAZZO FONTANA-REZZONICO

PALAZZO GIUSTI

CA' D'O[RO]

PALAZZO MOROSINI-BRANDOLIN

CHURCH OF SAN CASSIANO

CA' CORNER DELLA REGINA

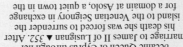

CA' CORNER DELLA REGINA
Caterina Cornaro was born in this palace in 1454; later she became Queen of Cyprus through her marriage to James II of Lusignan ▲ 352. After his death she was forced to surrender the island to the Venetian Seignory in exchange for a domain at Asolo, a quiet town in the province of Treviso. Received in Venice with every honor in 1489, Caterina reigned for 20 years thereafter over a court of great refinement at Asolo, which included (among others) the 16th-century poet and man of letters Pietro Bembo. The present palace was built by Domenico Rossi in the 18th century.

Among the collections of the Ca' d'Oro are some fragments of frescoes which adorned the FONDACO DEI TEDESCHI ▲ *276*. Artists involved in the project included Giorgione, who painted the side of the building facing the canal, and Titian.

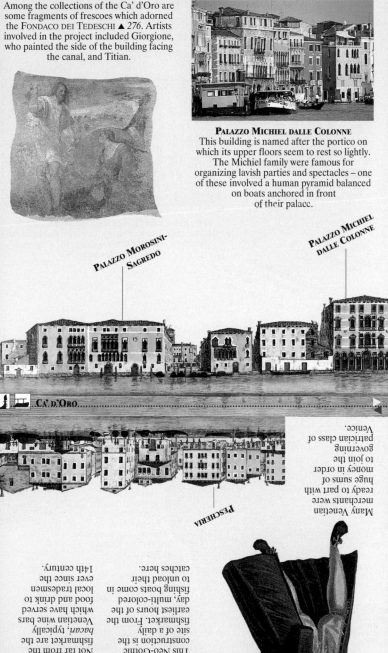

PALAZZO MICHIEL DALLE COLONNE

This building is named after the portico on which its upper floors seem to rest so lightly. The Michiel family were famous for organizing lavish parties and spectacles – one of these involved a human pyramid balanced on boats anchored in front of their palace.

PALAZZO MOROSINI-SAGREDO

PALAZZO MICHIEL DALLE COLONNE

CA' D'ORO

PESCHERIA

Many Venetian merchants were ready to part with huge sums of money in order to join the governing patrician class of Venice.

PESCHERIA ▲ 285 This Neo-Gothic construction is the site of a daily fishmarket. From the earliest hours of the day, multi-colored fishing boats come in to unload their catches here.

I BACARI ▲ 285 Not far from the fishmarket are the *bacari*, typically Venetian wine bars which have served food and drink to local tradesmen ever since the 14th century.

197

> "The houses of Venice are
> nostalgic for ships – hence
> their ground floors, which
> are so frequently awash."
>
> Paul Morand

Venetian-Byzantine detail of the
façade of the Ca' da Mosto.

CA' DA MOSTO

This 13th-century palace is one of Venice's oldest.
In 1432 the celebrated navigator Alvise da Mosto was
born here. Later he was to explore the west coast
of Africa in his caravelle.

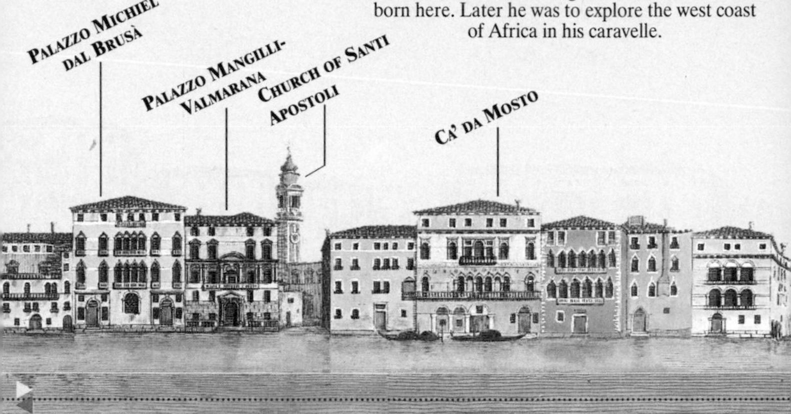

PALAZZO MICHIEL
DAL BRUSÀ

PALAZZO MANGILLI-
VALMARANA

CHURCH OF SANTI
APOSTOLI

CA' DA MOSTO

Among the street traders
of the 18th century was
the vegetable and
pumpkin-seller.
"The Venetians love
pumpkins, and the
pumpkin-seller displays
her wares like
leaves of yellow
wax, and slices
them into
pieces."
(Théophile
Gautier,
Voyage d'Italie)

"Venice . . . is one of those places
which I know before I see them,
and has always haunted me most
after the East."

Byron

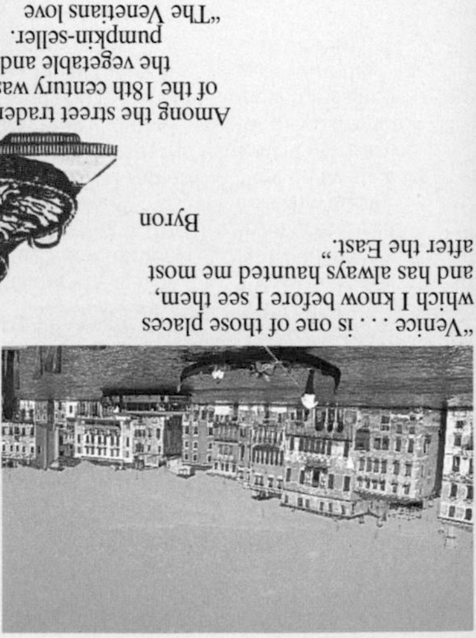

198

PALAZZO CIVRAN
Built in the 18th century on the site of a Gothic building.

PEACE IN A GONDOLA
According to legend, the daughter of the Doge Agnelo Partecipazio went on board a gondola in order to convince Pepin, son of Charlemagne, King of Italy, not to attack the Realtine Islands. The origins of the gondola must therefore go back at least a thousand years.

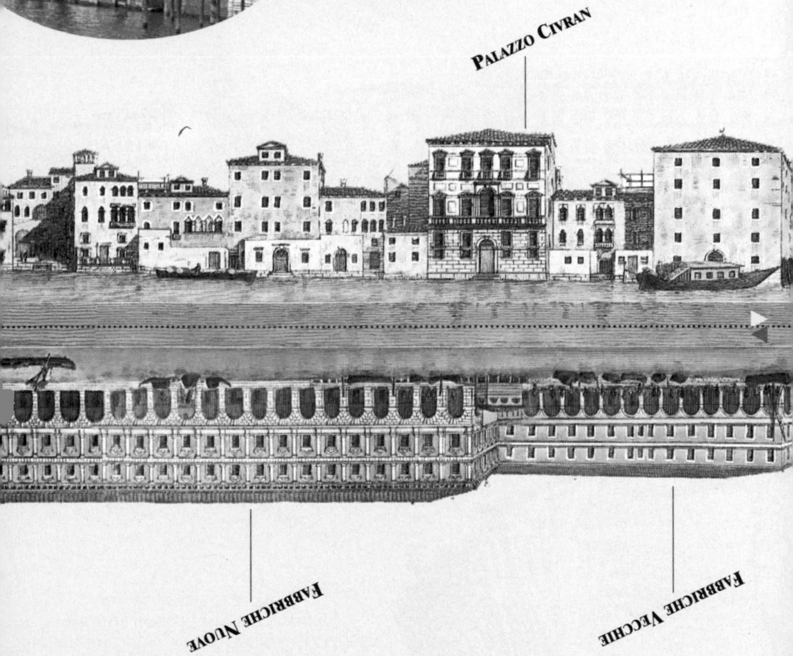

"These black gondolas slipping round the canals look like both coffins and cradles, the last and first resting-places of mankind."
Madame de Staël,
Corinne ou l'Italie

PALAZZO CIVRAN

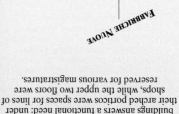

FABBRICHE NUOVE

FABBRICHE VECCHIE

MERCANTILE INSTITUTIONS
The institutions which administered the Republic's treasury and commerce were grouped in this part of the city. The FABBRICHE VECCHIE were built by

lo Scarpagnino for the offices of the tribunal, while the FABBRICHE NUOVE, built by Sansovino, were used for the trade ministry. Today the Fabbriche Nuove is the seat of the Venice assize court.

The construction of these two lengthy buildings answers a functional need: under their arched porticos were spaces for lines of shops, while the upper two floors were reserved for various magistratures.

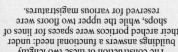

"The Rialto Bridge [...] is like a great horn pouring forth plenty from land and sea all over the surrounding waterfront."

Gabriele d'Annunzio

FONDACO DEI TEDESCHI

Before the central post office moved here, this palace was a warehouse used by the "German" merchants of Venice (that is the Germans, Hungarians, Austrians, and so on). In the 16th century its façade was covered in symbolic and allegorical frescoes by Giorgione and Titian ▲ 276.

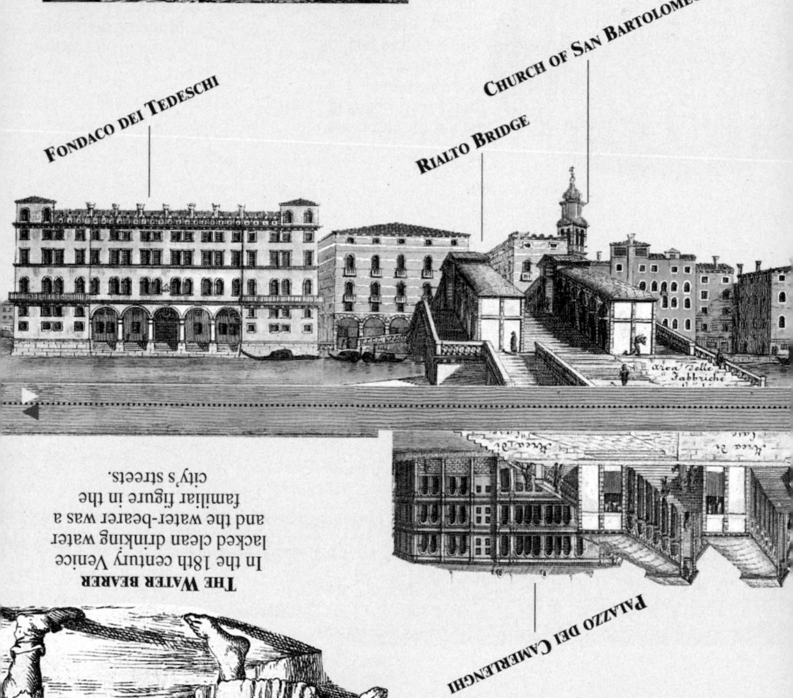

FONDACO DEI TEDESCHI

CHURCH OF SAN BARTOLOMEO

RIALTO BRIDGE

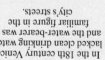

PALAZZO DEI CAMERLENGHI

THE WATER BEARER

In the 18th century Venice lacked clean drinking water and the water-bearer was a familiar figure in the city's streets.

THE RIALTO BRIDGE

This bridge was originally made of wood, with a central section that opened to allow galleys – and the Bucintoro – to pass through. It was rebuilt in stone in 1588–91 by Antonio da Ponte, after a long battle for the contract between the greatest architects of the 16th century (Michelangelo, Palladio and Sansovino). Today, the bridge is 92 feet long with a single arch, and is covered in souvenir stands ▲ 282.

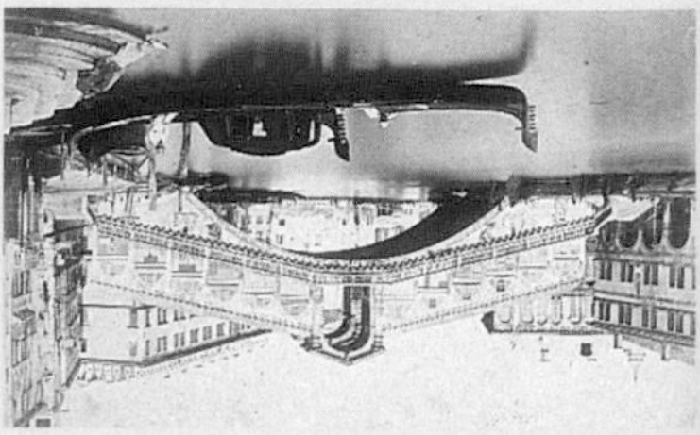

AROUND THE RIALTO

The Rialto area has been the heart of Venice and the city's commercial hub ever since the 9th century. For a thousand years now, this place has been aswarm with people shopping for vegetables, fish and flowers; grouped around it are Venice's most ancient buildings.

As it runs through the Rialto district, the Grand Canal is bordered by fondamente, which are quays along which one can walk and admire the palaces on either bank without taking a vaporetto.

PALAZZO BEMBO

RIALTO

PALAZZO BARBARIGO

FONDAMENTA DEL VIN

Multi-colored boats from the Lagoon bring fresh supplies to the Erberia and Pescheria markets every morning.

LA FONDAMENTA DEL VIN

Barrels of wine used to be unloaded along this quayside, but today it is mainly given over to tourist restaurants and souvenir stalls.

201

CA' LOREDAN AND CA' FARSETTI

These two palaces, built in the 13th century and extensively restored in the 16th, are now the offices of the Mayor of Venice. The salons of the Ca' Farsetti were a favorite haunt of the sculptor Antonio Canova.

ENRICO DANDOLO

The Doge of the Fourth Crusade ● *31* was born in a house that preceded the Casetta Dandolo, built in the 15th century.

This imposing white marble house was built by Michele Sanmicheli for Girolamo Grimani, Procurator of San Marco. Palazzo Grimani is now the seat of the Venice Court of Appeals.

PALAZZO CORNER-MARTINENGO-RAVA
(16th century)

PALAZZO GRIMANI
(16th century)

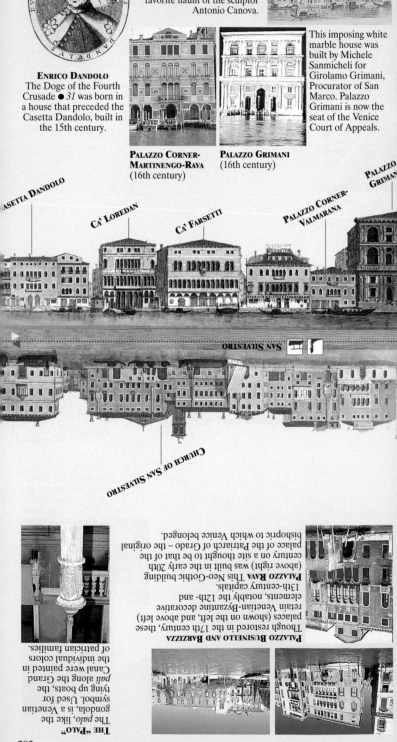

CASETTA DANDOLO

CA' LOREDAN

CA' FARSETTI

PALAZZO CORNER-VALMARANA

PALAZZO GRIMANI

SAN SILVESTRO

CHURCH OF SAN SILVESTRO

PALAZZO BUSINELLO AND BARIZIZZA Though restored in the 17th century, these palaces (shown on the left, and above left) retain Venetian-Byzantine decorative elements, notably the 12th- and 13th-century capitals.

PALAZZO RAVA This Neo-Gothic building (above right) was built in the early 20th century on a site thought to be that of the palace of the Patriarch of Grado – the original bishopric to which Venice belonged.

THE "PALO"
The *palo*, like the gondola, is a Venetian symbol. Used for tying up boats, the *pali* along the Grand Canal were painted in the individual colors of patrician families.

PALAZZO CORNER-CONTARINI DEI CAVALLI AND THE TWO TRON PALACES

The first, built in 1445, owes its name to the horses on the family coat of arms. The second is 19th-century Neo-Gothic, and the third is 15th-century and heavily restored.

LORD BYRON
(1788–1824)
Lord Byron was an habitué of the Contessa Marina Querini Benzon's literary salon.

PALAZZO BENZON was rebuilt during the 18th century.

The Comte de Chambord stayed at the Palazzo Benzon during the 19th century.

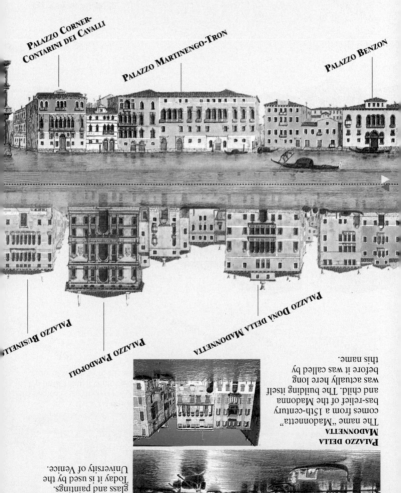

PALAZZO CORNER-CONTARINI DEI CAVALLI

PALAZZO MARTINENGO-TRON

PALAZZO BENZON

PALAZZO BUSINELLO

PALAZZO PAPADOPOLI

PALAZZO DONÀ DELLA MADONNETTA

PALAZZO DELLA MADONNETTA
The name "Madonnetta" comes from a 15th-century bas-relief of the Madonna and child. The building itself was actually here long before it was called by this name.

PALAZZO PAPADOPOLI
This palace was built in the mid-16th century for the Coccinas, a family of jewelers. In the 19th century it was purchased by the Papadopolis, who brought in a fine collection of coins, glass and paintings. Today it is used by the University of Venice.

203

Palazzo Corner-Spinelli

Built by Mauro Coducci, this building incorporates a number of Renaissance elements, foreshadowing Palazzo Vendramin-Calergi ▲ 90, 194. It belonged to Giovanni Corner, nephew of Caterina, Queen of Cyprus, before reverting to the Spinellis, a family grown rich in the silk trade. Today it is the headquarters of the RUBELLI fabrics firm.

Teatro Sant'Angelo

One of Venice's seven lyric theaters formerly stood on this site. Vivaldi created a number of operas there ▲ 175.

PALAZZO CORNER-SPINELLI

PALAZZO GARZONI

SANT'ANGELO

PALAZZO BERNARDO

PALAZZO DUBOIS

PALAZZO GRIMANI

PALAZZO BARBARIGO DELLA TERRAZZA

Palazzo Bernardo

This elegant 15th-century building has many decorative features in common with the Ca' d'Oro.

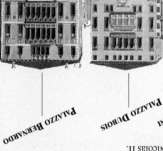

Palazzo Barbarigo della Terrazza

This palace is so called on account of the broad terrace at one side of it. Up until 1850, it contained a magnificent collection of paintings, most of which were eventually purchased by Czar Nicolas II.

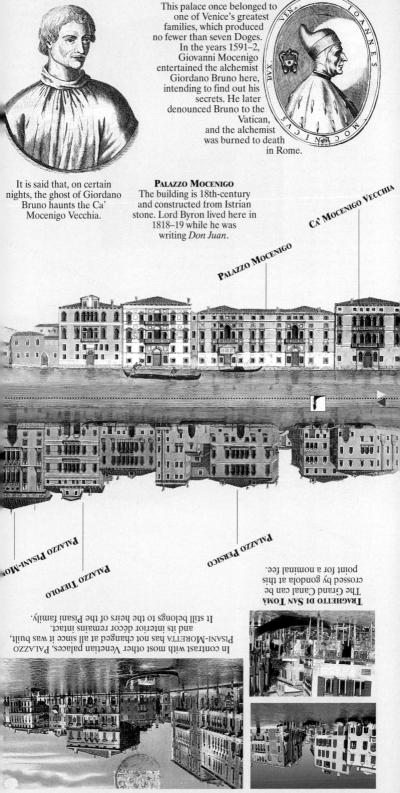

CA' MOCENIGO VECCHIA
This palace once belonged to one of Venice's greatest families, which produced no fewer than seven Doges. In the years 1591–2, Giovanni Mocenigo entertained the alchemist Giordano Bruno here, intending to find out his secrets. He later denounced Bruno to the Vatican, and the alchemist was burned to death in Rome.

It is said that, on certain nights, the ghost of Giordano Bruno haunts the Ca' Mocenigo Vecchia.

PALAZZO MOCENIGO
The building is 18th-century and constructed from Istrian stone. Lord Byron lived here in 1818–19 while he was writing *Don Juan*.

CA' MOCENIGO VECCHIA

PALAZZO MOCENIGO

PALAZZO PISANI-MORETTA

PALAZZO TIEPOLO

PALAZZO PERSICO

TRAGHETTO DI SAN TOMÀ
The Grand Canal can be crossed by gondola at this point for a nominal fee.

In contrast with most other Venetian palaces, PALAZZO PISANI-MORETTA has not changed at all since it was built, and its interior décor remains intact. It still belongs to the heirs of the Pisani family.

"The Grand Canal in Venice is the most wonderful thing on earth. No other city can offer a spectacle so beautiful, so strange, so fairylike ... Every palace there has a mirror in which to admire its own beauty, like a lovely woman. The magnificent reality is duplicated by a charming reflection. The water laps at the feet of each fine façade, lit by the pale-gold light of Venice and swayed in a second sky. The little boats and larger vessels which wait upon the water seem to have been placed there deliberately to make a foreground for decorators and watercolorists."

Théophile Gautier,
Voyage d'Italie

PALAZZO CONTARINI DELLE FIGURE

Built at the beginning of the 16th century, this building gets its name from the caryatids which hold up its balcony. It was commissioned by Jacopo Contarini, a great protector of artists and the patron of Palladio, architect of San Giorgio. At his death, Contarini left his fabulous art collection to the state.

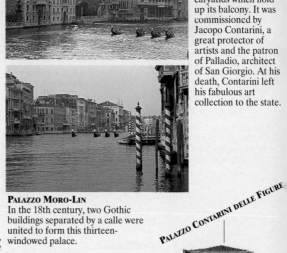

PALAZZO CONTARINI DELLE FIGURE

PALAZZO MORO-LIN
In the 18th century, two Gothic buildings separated by a calle were united to form this thirteen-windowed palace.

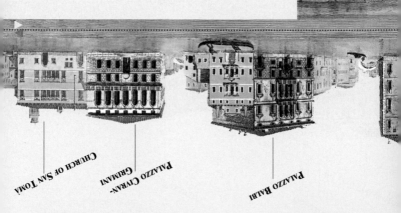

CHURCH OF SAN TOMA

PALAZZO CIVRAN-GRIMANI

PALAZZO BALBI

PALAZZO BALBI
With its magnificent position right on the curve of the Grand Canal, this much-painted building was commissioned in the 16th century by Nicolò Balbi. In 1807 Napoleon watched a regatta from here. Palazzo Balbi is now the seat of the Veneto Regional Council.

"All the balconies are crowded with pots of flowers; the flowers of Venice, sprung from warm loam and blossoming in the humid air, have a special freshness, a richness of substance, and a special heavy langor."

Georges Sand,
Lettres d'un voyageur

> "Every boat had its lantern. and the gondolas, moving rapidly along, were followed by tracks of light, which gleamed and played upon the waters."
>
> William Beckford

PALAZZO GRASSI ▲ 270
The last great 18th-century building to be constructed on the Grand Canal, Palazzo Grassi was designed by Giorgio Massari. In the 19th century it was the premises of the celebrated Degli Antoni bath-house, and in 1984 was bought and restored by the Fiat Foundation for use as an exhibition centre.

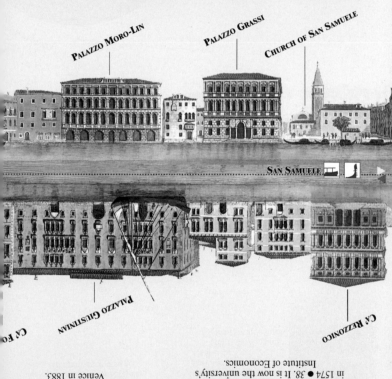

PALAZZO MORO-LIN

PALAZZO GRASSI

CHURCH OF SAN SAMUELE

SAN SAMUELE

CA' FO...

PALAZZO GIUSTINIAN

CA' REZZONICO

CA' FOSCARI
This majestic Gothic palace on the corner of the Rio Nuovo was built for the Doge Francesco Foscari. Because of its convenient location on the canal, the Republic used it to accommodate distinguished visitors, such as the French King Henri III in 1574 ● 38. It is now the university's Institute of Economics.

Wagner lived for seven months (1858–9) at PALAZZO GIUSTINIAN, where he composed the second act of *Tristan and Isolde*. He died in Venice in 1883.

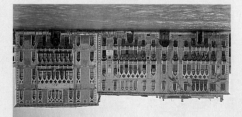

PALAZZO GIUSTINIAN-LOLIN

This 17th-century building, designed by Baldassare Longhena when he was a young man, was the home of the Duchess of Parma. Her brother, Count Henri de Bardi, brought back from India, China and Japan a collection of more than thirty thousand objects, which later formed the basis for Venice's Museum of Oriental Art (which is now in the Ca' Pesaro).

PALAZZO FALIER
(early 15th century)

THE "LIAGHI"

Palazzo Falier has two romantic *liaghi*, or covered balconies, on either side of its central windows. In the 19th century these typically Venetian features were restored, but their original structure was faithfully preserved.

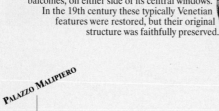

PALAZZO MALIPIERO   CA' DEL DUCA   PALAZZO FALIER

PALAZZO CONTARINI   PALAZZO MORO   PALAZZO LOREDAN

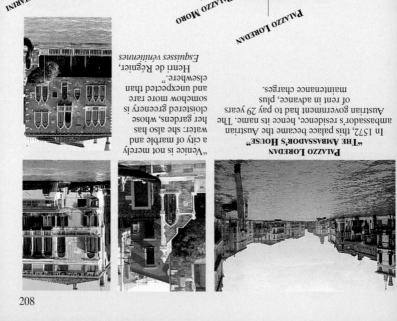

"Venice is not merely a city of marble and water: she also has her gardens, whose cloistered greenery is somehow more rare and unexpected than elsewhere."
Henri de Régnier, *Esquisses vénitiennes*

PALAZZO LOREDAN
"THE AMBASSADOR'S HOUSE"

In 1572, this palace became the Austrian ambassador's residence, hence its name. The Austrian government had to pay 29 years of rent in advance, plus maintenance charges.

> "Then my eyes [...] turned back to the Canal, where the boats went past, steered by adolescents in pink jackets and plumed caps."
> Marcel Proust

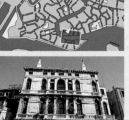

DORSODURO ▲ 297
This district takes its name from the notably hard subsoil on which it is built; it is among the less populous areas of Venice.

PALAZZO GIUSTINIAN-LOLIN
This palace is now the Levi Foundation Music Centre.

PALAZZO GIUSTINIAN-LOLIN

THE ACCADEMIA ▲ 301
The galleries of the Accademia at the former SCUOLA DELLA CARITÀ possess an incomparable collection of Venetian paintings, including works by all the great masters of the city (the Bellini brothers, Carpaccio, Giorgione, Titian, Veronese, Tintoretto, the 18th-century painters Longhi, Guardi and Tiepolo, and the landscapists). Other parts of the building are used by the Fine Arts Academy.

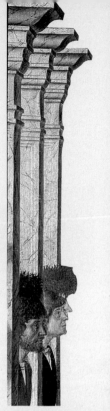

ACCADEMIA

PALAZZO CONTARINI DEGLI SCRIGNI

PALAZZO GAMBARA

PALAZZO QUERINI

CARITÀ

PALAZZO GAMBARA (late 17th century)

THE LEGEND OF SAINT URSULA
The Accademia contains the *Legend of St Ursula* cycle by the great Venetian painter Vittore Carpaccio ▲ 306. This series is made up of nine canvases tracing the life of the saint, eight of which portray scenes of the city in the 15th century, with its festivals, processions, palaces and interiors. A detail of the *Arrival of the Ambassadors*, c. 1500, is shown on the right. The scene is set in Brittany, but the sails, the gondolas skimming the Lagoon, the gentlemen's costumes and the design of the buildings leave no doubt that the artist was inspired by Venice.

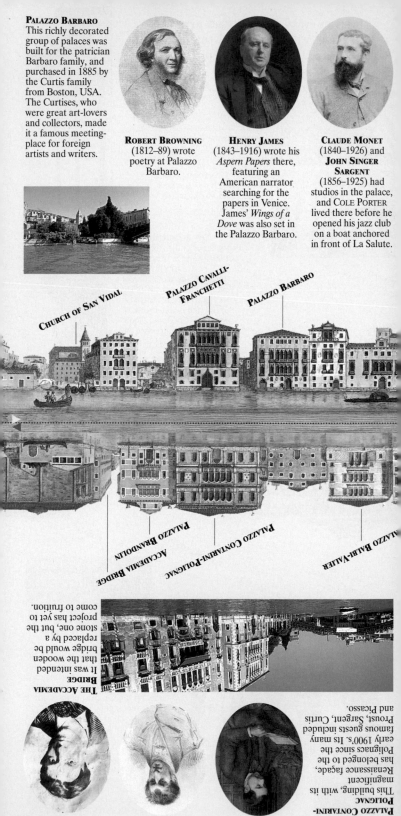

PALAZZO BARBARO
This richly decorated group of palaces was built for the patrician Barbaro family, and purchased in 1885 by the Curtis family from Boston, USA. The Curtises, who were great art-lovers and collectors, made it a famous meeting-place for foreign artists and writers.

ROBERT BROWNING (1812–89) wrote poetry at Palazzo Barbaro.

HENRY JAMES (1843–1916) wrote his *Aspern Papers* there, featuring an American narrator searching for the papers in Venice. James' *Wings of a Dove* was also set in the Palazzo Barbaro.

CLAUDE MONET (1840–1926) and **JOHN SINGER SARGENT** (1856–1925) had studios in the palace, and **COLE PORTER** lived there before he opened his jazz club on a boat anchored in front of La Salute.

CHURCH OF SAN VIDAL

PALAZZO CAVALLI-FRANCHETTI

PALAZZO BARBARO

PALAZZO BRANDOLIN

ACCADEMIA BRIDGE

PALAZZO CONTARINI-POLIGNAC

PALAZZO BALBI-VALIER

THE ACCADEMIA BRIDGE
It was intended that the wooden bridge would be replaced by a stone one, but the project has yet to come to fruition.

PALAZZO CONTARINI-POLIGNAC
This building, with its magnificent Renaissance façade, has belonged to the Polignacs since the early 1900's. Its many famous guests included Proust, Sargent, Curtis and Picasso.

CASETTA DELLE ROSE

The Casetta delle Rose, a small palace standing slightly back from the Canal, was the poet Gabriele d'Annunzio's home during the First World War. His jealous mistress, the actress Eleonora Duse, is said to have lodged in a palace on the opposite bank, in order to keep an eye on him.

PALAZZO CORNER DELLA CA' GRANDE

This majestic palace, built for a wealthy family by Jacopo Sansovino, owes its name to its sheer size. Famous for its rich interior, notably a bedroom decorated in cloth of gold, the Ca' Grande was bought by the Napoleonic government in 1812, and later restored for the Austrian administration. Today it houses the Prefecture of Venice.

"The gondolas rock at their berths, with a rhythm of calm, slow breathing. And their dry hawsers utter little cries."

André Suarès,
Voyage du Condottiere

PALAZZO CORNER DELLA CA' GRANDE

CASETTA DELLE ROSE

PALAZZO LOW...

CAMPO SAN VIO

PALAZZO BARBARIGO

PALAZZO DA MULA

CA' VENIER DEI LEONI

CA' VENIER DEI LEONI – THE PEGGY GUGGENHEIM FOUNDATION

This palace, with its unfinished ground floor, was bought by the wealthy American collector, Peggy Guggenheim, in 1951. On her death, it became the Guggenheim Foundation, containing one of Europe's greatest privately assembled collections of 20th-century art ▲ 316.

PALAZZO BARBARIGO

Lavishly decorated with mosaics by Carlini, this palace now belongs to a glass firm and is used to display its products.

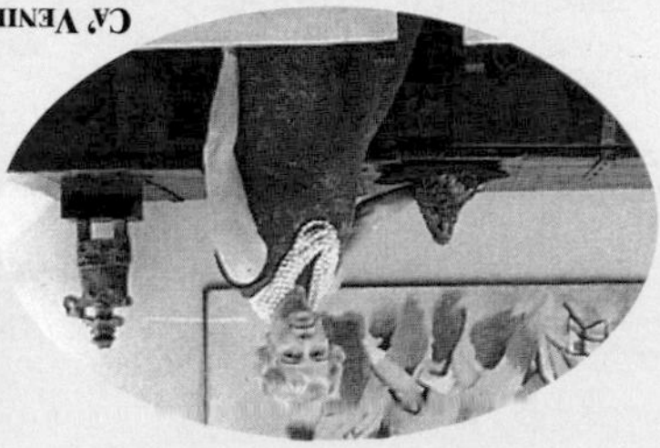

SANTA MARIA DEL GIGLIO
At Santa Maria del Giglio there is a traghetto which plies from bank to bank of the canal. For the Festival of La Salute on November 21 ● 49, ▲ 320, a bridge of boats is set up at this point, so the processions can make their way across.

THE GRITTI PALACE HOTEL
John Ruskin and his wife Effie rented a suite of rooms here during their second visit to Venice. Later, the Gritti became Hemingway's favorite Venetian hotel.

The terrace at the Gritti is famous as a place for breakfast.

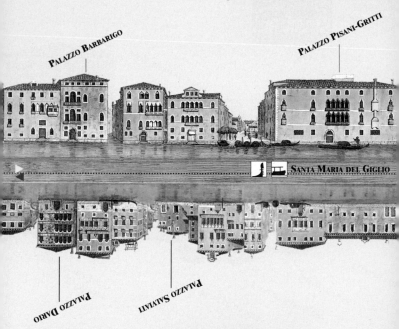

PALAZZO BARBARIGO

PALAZZO PISANI-GRITTI

SANTA MARIA DEL GIGLIO

PALAZZO DARIO

PALAZZO SALVIATI

PALAZZO DARIO
A Renaissance palace encrusted with polychrome marbles, the Palazzo Dario was the home of the French poet Henri de Régnier at the end of the last century.

PALAZZO SALVIATI
This palace now houses the exhibition rooms of the Salviati family, famous glassblowers from Murano.

CA' GENOVESE
In 1892, the second Gothic cloister of the San Gregorio Monastery was demolished to make way for this Neo-Gothic palace – one example of how little the artistic legacy of earlier centuries was valued during the 19th.

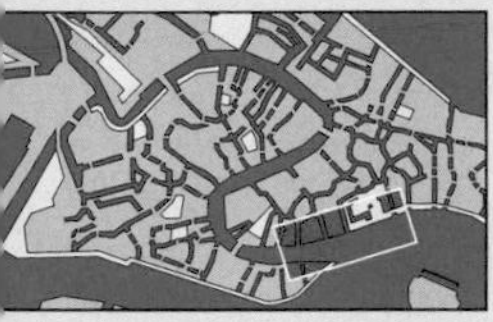

"The moorish gothic houses,
narrow as the jealous eyes
of othello, stand directly
on the canal."

Louis Aragon

THE HOUSE OF DESDEMONA
According to legend, Palazzo Contarini-Fasan was the house of Desdemona, a noble Venetian lady who fell victim to the mad jealousy of her husband, a member of the Moro family. William Shakespeare made her the tragic heroine of his play *Othello*.

PALAZZO FERRO-FINI

PALAZZO CONTARINI-FASAN

SALUTE

ABBEY OF SAN GREGORIO

BASILICA SANTA MARIA DELLA SALUTE

THE ABBEY OF SAN GREGORIO
(15th century)

THE BASILICA DELLA SALUTE
In 1630, plague struck Venice, and more than a third of the population succumbed to the "black death". On October 22, while the people were still counting their dead, the Senate commissioned Longhena to build a church in gratitude to the Virgin for bringing an end to the epidemic.

"Like an old lady on crutches, Venice rests on a forest of pilings . . . it took a million of them to build La Salute." (Paul Morand, *Venises*) Indeed, most of Venice's buildings are founded on pilings, which are set in the layer of *caranto* (clay and sand) and have gradually hardened into mineral form ● 97.

PALAZZO TIEPOLO
It is named after Bajamonte Tiepolo, who hatched a plot against the republic with Marco Querini in 1310. The plot failed and their houses were razed to the ground. In the 19th century, this palace was the Hotel Britannia. It is now the Regina e Europa.

PALAZZO GIUSTINIAN
During the 19th century this Gothic palace became the Hotel Europa. Verdi, Gautier and Proust all stayed there.

PALAZZO TREVES DEI BONFILI
The interior of this palace is redecorated throughout in the Neo-classical style.

PALAZZO TIEPOLO

PALAZZO TREVES DEI BONFILI

PALAZZO GIUST[...]

CHURCH OF SAN MOIS[...]

SEMINARIO PATRIARCALE

CUSTOMS POINT

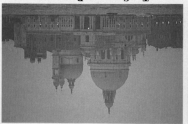

THE SEMINARIO PATRIARCALE
This building was constructed in the 1670's by Baldassarre Longhena. Today it is the home of the Manfrediana art gallery.

THE PALA D'ORO
To replace the tower that once defended the entrance to the Grand Canal, a belfry was erected with a bronze globe supported by two atlases and a weathervane (a statue of Fortune) by Bernardo Falcone.

After the customs point, the Grand Canal opens onto St Mark's Basin, where the full grandeur of Venice becomes apparent with views of the Doge's Palace, Piazza San Marco and the island of San Giorgio Maggiore.

PROUST delayed going to Venice for many years, because for him cities, like women, were best confined to dreams. But when he finally arrived he was not disappointed. Indeed he described the city lovingly and at length in his *Albertine Disparue* (*The Fugitive*).

HARRY'S BAR Frequented by Hemingway, this is one of the world's most famous café-restaurants.

PALAZZO ERIZZO   HARRY'S BAR   PALAZZO DEL MAGISTRATO   ROYAL GARDENS

SAN MARCO VALLARESSO

MONASTERY OF THE CYPRESSES

SAN GIORGIO MAGGIORE

340. The building is now owned by the Cini Foundation, which holds exhibitions there. The stunning view from the top of the campanile takes in the whole of Venice, the Giudecca and the lagoon.

In the mid-16th century, Andrea Palladio designed and partly completed the refectory, which was decorated with Veronese's *Marriage at Cana* (now in the Louvre), the church and the cloisters

SAN GIORGIO MAGGIORE

This green island, once known as "The Isle of Cypresses" was the site of a Benedictine monastery from the 10th century onwards.

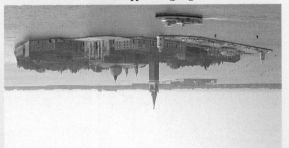

"Behind the rigid forest of ships riding at anchor, San Giorgio Maggiore appeared like a great pink galley, whose prow was turned to Fortune as she beckoned from her golden sphere."
Gabriele d'Annunzio, *Fire*

SAN MARCO ▲ 219

With its Byzantine basilica, Gothic palace and classical and Renaissance library, Piazza San Marco is a microcosm of differing styles. It is also a symbol of all earthly powers. Already a political and religious center, in the early 16th century it acquired a temple of culture, the Libreria Marciana, and a symbol of Venetian financial strength, the Zecca (Mint), looking on to the Lagoon.

THE ZECCA · **CAMPANILE** · **CLOCKTOWER**

THE PIAZZETTA
The high columns of red and grey granite standing on the Piazzetta mark the "gateway" to Venice, which could formerly be entered only by sea. At times when there were no state visitors, the space between the two columns became a free zone where gambling was tolerated.

" The admirable square sets forth its forest of columns, its Corinthian capitals, its statues and the noble variety of its classical forms. "
Hippolyte Taine, *Voyage en Italie*

THE DOGES
One hundred and sixteen Doges ruled the Serenissima from 726 AD to May 12, 1797, when the last Doge, Lodovico Manin, abandoned by his Council, gave his linen cap, worn under the ducal *corno*, to his valet. "Take it, I shall not be needing it again," he said.

THE LION OF VENICE

Venice chose as her emblem the Lion of St Mark the Evangelist, her patron saint. As the incarnation of the majesty of state, the lion standing on its hind legs and brandishing a sword became the city's defender and the symbol of her warlike strength.

> "And at night they sang in the gondolas,
> And in the barche with lanthorns;
> The prows rose silver on silver,
> taking light in the darkness."
>
> Ezra Pound

THE BRIDGE OF SIGHS

Built in the early 17th century, the Bridge of Sighs linked the jails of the Doge's Palace (the "Leads" and the "Wells") to a more recently constructed prison block.

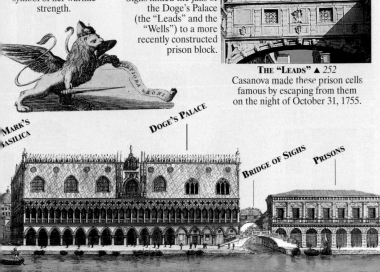

THE "LEADS" ▲ 252

Casanova made these prison cells famous by escaping from them on the night of October 31, 1755.

MARK'S BASILICA   DOGE'S PALACE   BRIDGE OF SIGHS   PRISONS

THE SCULPTURES OF THE DOGE'S PALACE

In the 14th and 15th centuries, both the Doge's Palace and the basilica were substantially altered. The palace was rebuilt in the Gothic style, with masterpieces of sculpture refining the effect produced by the fretwork of the façade. So that the basilica should not suffer by comparison, it was in turn covered with pointed features and sculptures in the new style.

THE DOGE'S PALACE

The Doge's residence, which formerly housed the administration of the Republic, was the heart of Venice for nearly seven centuries. The long history of the city is recorded in its richly decorated rooms ▼ 224.

CAFFÈ QUADRI

Opened in 1775 opposite Florian's, this café was one of the first in Venice to serve Turkish coffee.

Saint Mark's Square

**ST MARK'S SQUARE
(11TH CENTURY)**
At this stage the
square was divided in
two by Rio Batario.

★ Half a day
◆ C A5-A6-B5-B6

Called *piazza* (square) rather than
campo (field) in order to distinguish it
from the other open areas in Venice, this
"drawing room of Europe" (to use
Napoleon's phrase) has been at the heart
of Venetian life for more than a
thousand years. In
fact, the

1.

Piazza San Marco (St
Mark's Square) became the focus of the
major religious festivals ● *48*, games ● *50* and political
activities of the Serene Republic at a very early stage.
Like the Venetians themselves, for whom the square
has always been a favorite haunt,
tourists flock here in the
thousands every year.

3.

1. Procuratie Vecchie
2. Clocktower
3. Napoleon wing
4. Procuratie Nuove

THE FIRST SQUARE

Having abandoned
Malamocco for the
Rialto ● *30*, the Doges

5.

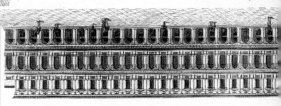

**ST MARK'S SQUARE:
SYMBOL OF THE
CITY ✪**
Even those who
consider themselves
hard to impress will
find this a breathtaking
sight. The whole
history of Venice, the
city at the crossroads
between East and
West, is concentrated
in St Mark's Square.
Climb the campanile
for an unparalled view
of the Lagoon and an
interesting angle on
the basilica. Then feast
your eyes on the
treasures of theDoge's
Palace and the
museums, visit the
prisons and linger on
the Bridge of Sighs.
The equally historic
saloons, bar and violins
of the Florian also
beckon.

St Mark's Square in
the 15th century, in
a manuscript of the
Duc d'Aumale, now
at Chantilly (right).

installed themselves at the junction of the area's two primary
waterways. The spot they chose became the administrative,
political and judicial heart of the Republic, though at the time
it looked very different from the San Marco we see today.
RIO BATARIO. A rio used to divide in two the space that is now
occupied by the square, making the original piazza little more
than the parvis of the basilica. The other side was taken up
by the vegetable gardens of the monastery of San Zaccaria
▲ *171*, with the little Church of San Geminiano in the center.
THE DOCK. A sheltered dock extended almost to the foot of the
basilica, effectively separating it from the Doge's Palace. The
basilica itself was flanked on its north-eastern side by the
Church of San Teodoro, dedicated to the city's
first patron saint, St Theodore.

ENLARGING SAN MARCO

The square was reorganized in the
12th century for the meeting of Pope
Alexander III and the Emperor
Barbarossa ● *30*, the foremost political
rivals of the time. The Rio Batario was
filled in, doubling the length of the square.

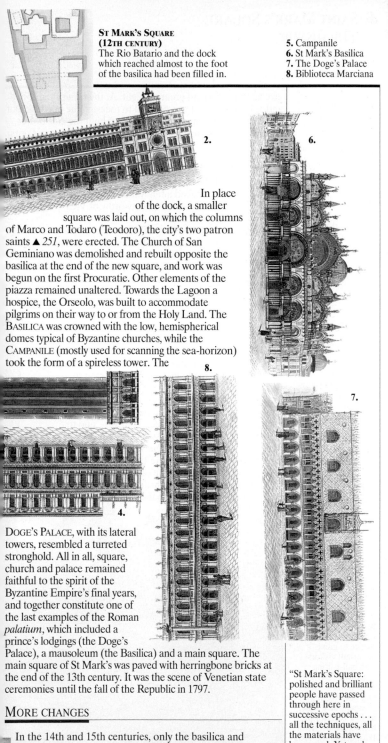

**ST MARK'S SQUARE
(12TH CENTURY)**
The Rio Batario and the dock
which reached almost to the foot
of the basilica had been filled in.

5. Campanile
6. St Mark's Basilica
7. The Doge's Palace
8. Biblioteca Marciana

2.

6.

In place
of the dock, a smaller
square was laid out, on which the columns
of Marco and Todaro (Teodoro), the city's two patron
saints ▲ *251*, were erected. The Church of San
Geminiano was demolished and rebuilt opposite the
basilica at the end of the new square, and work was
begun on the first Procuratie. Other elements of the
piazza remained unaltered. Towards the Lagoon a
hospice, the Orseolo, was built to accommodate
pilgrims on their way to or from the Holy Land. The
BASILICA was crowned with the low, hemispherical
domes typical of Byzantine churches, while the
CAMPANILE (mostly used for scanning the sea-horizon)
took the form of a spireless tower. The

8.

7.

4.

DOGE'S PALACE, with its lateral
towers, resembled a turreted
stronghold. All in all, square,
church and palace remained
faithful to the spirit of the
Byzantine Empire's final years,
and together constitute one of
the last examples of the Roman
palatium, which included a
prince's lodgings (the Doge's
Palace), a mausoleum (the Basilica) and a main square. The
main square of St Mark's was paved with herringbone bricks at
the end of the 13th century. It was the scene of Venetian state
ceremonies until the fall of the Republic in 1797.

MORE CHANGES

In the 14th and 15th centuries, only the basilica and
the Doge's Palace were substantially altered. The
palace was gradually transformed into the ensemble
we see today. To conform with the canons of Gothic
style (and to bear comparison with the palace) the
basilica was covered in pointed elements tending to

"St Mark's Square:
polished and brilliant
people have passed
through here in
successive epochs . . .
all the techniques, all
the materials have
been used. Yet each
new builder seems to
have put his faith in
his particular star."
Le Corbusier,
Propos d'urbanisme

221

"Around the buildings, the water, broad as a lake, weaves its magic setting of greenish and blueish hues, its mobile,

crystalline sea-green. A thousand ripples glint before the breeze, with sunshine sparkling at their crests . . . meantime the lustrous, luminous, enveloping sea penetrates Venice like a nimbus. And like a diamond in its setting, the Doge's Palace outshines all else."

Hippolyte Taine,
Voyage en Italie

BULL-BAITING
It was the custom in Venice to greet important visitors with bull-baiting sessions ● *50* (right) on St Mark's Square. One such baiting session, which was held in 1740 for the heir to the throne of Poland, and the 1782 celebration in honor of the Czarevitch ▲ *169*, became legendary in the annals of Venetian history.

give an impression of greater height. At the turn of the 15th and 16th centuries it was decided to redesign the north side of the square, after which Mauro Coducci built the clocktower and rebuilt the Procuratie Vecchie, which had only two floors.

THE ARCHITECTS OF THE PIAZZA

At the start of the 16th century, the Republic launched a renovation programme to make St Mark's Square worthy of Venice's greatness and power.

SANSOVINO. The project was assigned to Jacopo Tatti (better known as Sansovino) who worked on it without interruption for more than thirty years, beginning in 1529, and becoming a model "State Architect" in the process. Sansovino completed the Procuratie Vecchie on the west side of the square, restored the basilica and the campanile, reconstructed the Zecca and the Church of San Geminiano, and built the Loggetta. Lastly he constructed the Libreria, with its arcades and loggias opposite the Doge's Palace, and made the Piazzetta "fit rival to Michelangelo's Campidoglio" (W. Lotz).

SCAMOZZI. In the late 16th century the authorities committed themselves to the completion of Sansovino's Libreria – today the Biblioteca Marcian – and to rebuilding the entire south side of the Square. Vincenzo Scamozzi took charge of these works and erected the Procuratie Nuove; these were finished by Longhena, who attached them to the Church of San Geminiano. To make way for the new building, which was supposed "to give proper proportions to the square

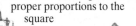

occupied by St Mark's Basilica, its principal element", the buildings of the Orseolo hospice were demolished because they were "too old and too ugly". When this was finished, St Mark's Square achieved its full magnificence, as Venice's "drawing room of Europe", public forum and theater.

THE FINAL TOUCHES

NEW PAVING. In 1723, Tirali was commissioned to change the paving of the square. He had just rebuilt the wall to the north of the basilica, placing two sculpted lions on either side of it – hence the name of Piazzetta dei Leoncini given to the little square adjoining it in 1722. He tore up the old brick pavement and replaced it with large slabs of trachyte, framed by bands of Istrian stone. His geometrical motifs follow the longitudinal axis of the square, heightening its effect of depth.

DEMOLITIONS AND RECONSTRUCTIONS. The only buildings which had not yet been tampered with were the 14th-century granaries (Granai di Terranova) next to the water after the Zecca. These were pulled down during the Napoleonic era to make way for the Royal Gardens (1808). A Napoleonic wing also displaced the Church of San Geminiano, and the Emperor's architects designed a new façade to the Doge's Palace on the Piazzetta dei Leoncini, which was completed between 1820 and 1843. A number of old houses were destroyed during this work, which radically altered the immediate area of the basilica.

THE THREE MASTS
"In the main square before the portal of St Mark's stand three tall ships' masts to which were attached three banners in red silk, picked out in rich gold, and at each side of the portal flew a lesser banner of like hue." *(Voyage to the Holy City of Jerusalem, Anon, 1480.)* On these three masts the banner of St Mark is still hoisted on feast days: the colors are still red and gold, but now they are surrounded by the colors of the Italian national flag. The masts stand on pedestals by Alessandro Leopardi. The one in the middle (1505) has a medallion with the effigy of Leonardo Loredan, Doge of Venice 1501–21.

"Venice, which is not a civilization, is yet something more than a city – like Alexandria or Byzantium. Since Venice revelled longer than any other place, and died wearing a mask, we should perhaps linger there awhile."
André Malraux,
L'Irréel

THE DOGE'S PALACE

THE STRONGHOLD. The original Doge's Palace was a square, fortress-like building with high walls, corner towers on the side nearest St Mark's Basin, and fortified

ACQUA ALTA ■ *26*
Because it stands nearer to sea-level than the other quarters of Venice, St Mark's Square is frequently flooded at times of *acqua alta* (high tide) – as shown here during the winter of 1911. This phenomenon is a serious problem, for which a solution has yet to be found.

gates. As the Doge's residence and the seat of the Venetian government and magistrature, it contained armories, courtrooms and dungeons. Between the 14th and the 16th centuries, this huge edifice was transformed into the building which we see now, after succumbing to a series of fires. But above all changes in the palace were brought on by necessity, as Venice grew richer and her empire expanded. Each organ of power (such as the Grand Council, the Senate, the Seignory and the Council of Ten) had to have a seat worthy of its dignity. Hence, the need to supply the Grand Council with a new chamber for its deliberations was the first goal of the reconstruction.

THE DOGE'S PALACE. Rebuilt (respectively) in 1340 and 1424, the two wings of the palace bordering St Mark's Basin and the Piazzetta are among the finest examples of Gothic architecture anywhere in the world. They testify to an uncommon degree of architectural skill because, in a kind of reversal of equilibrium, an airily light gallery and arcade are made to support the overwhelming mass of the upper masonry. Moreover, the building is adorned with beautiful 14th–15th-century capitals and corner figures (such as Bartolomeo Bon's early 15th-century *Judgement of Solomon*). The PORTA DELLA CARTA, a masterpiece of Flamboyant Gothic (named after the scribes who used to sit copying out petitions, both here and in the vicinity of the State Archives), leads through to the

FOSCARI PORTICO and thence to the palace's magnificent inner courtyard. This area was closed off by a Renaissance east wing designed by Antonio Rizzo (1483), from the base of which rises the SCALA DEI GIGANTI (Giants' Staircase), which was the scene of the Doges' inaugurations. Also designed by Antonio Rizzo in 1485, this staircase was decorated by Sansovino in the second half of the 16th century with the statues of Mars and Neptune, symbolizing Venice's domination of land and sea. The SCALA D'ORO (Gold Staircase), also by Sansovino, leads from the loggia floor to the upper levels of the building, past a riot of stuccos and frescoes.

THE INTERIOR OF THE PALACE. The rooms of the Doge's Palace were intended to illustrate the entire history of Venice, painted by some of her greatest 16th-century masters. Their work here defines Venice's greatest triumphs, from her mythical foundation and her institutions to her military victories. But more striking perhaps than the pictures of these great historical events is the vivid sense one has of the daily bustle that once enlivened the palace. The first floor was occupied by several minor institutions, namely the AVOGARIA (which examined cases at law), the CHANCELLERY, the CENSORS and the PROVVEDITORI DELLA MILIZIA DA MAR (which was in charge of equipping Venice's galleys). The GRAND COUNCIL held its sessions on the second floor, in the largest chamber of the palace. Tintoretto's magnificent late 15th-century *Paradise* (23 ft x 72 ft) dominates this chamber, the walls of which are covered with works by Veronese, Palma the Younger and Bassano, all of which extol the martial prowess of the Serene Republic. The same theme prevails in the BALLOT CHAMBER, where the votes of the Grand Council were counted and where the committee met to elect the

Doge. Just below the ceiling is a frieze containing the portraits of every one of Venice's Doges, whose apartments were also here. On the third floor, the SALA DELLE QUATTRO PORTE contains Tintoretto's ceiling illustrating the foundation of the city, *Jupiter leading Venice into the Adriatic*, 1577; after that is the SALA DEL COLLEGIO, where the Seignory met and foreign ambassadors were received. After the SENATE CHAMBER come the rooms used by the state security service – the COUNCIL OF TEN – which were decorated, like the SALA DEL COLLEGIO, by Veronese; the SALA DELLA BUSSOLA, with one of the boxes used for written denunciations which were formerly a common feature of the city; the SALA DEI TRE CAPI was the room used by the Council of Ten's "three heads", each of whom was chosen for a period of one month at a time; and lastly the room used by the STATE INQUISITORS. The tour ends with the palace's COLLECTION OF ARMS AND ARMOR, most of it captured from enemies.

PORTA DELLA CARTA
Recently restored, the elegant "paper doorway" to the Doge's Palace was made in the years following 1438 by the Bon brothers. The statues of Strength and Temperance in its lower section are attributed to Pietro Lombardo; those of Prudence and Charity are by Antonio Bregno. The statues of the Doge

Francesco Foscari and the winged lion, which were destroyed in 1797, were remade in 1885 by Luigi Ferrari.

BOSCH
In the TRE CAPI chamber hang several canvases commissioned from the Flemish painter Hieronymus Bosch.

FAÇADE OVERLOOKING THE PIAZZETTA
The refined colors, as well as the play of
light and shade on the Loggia Foscara and
the Gothic arcades, make this façade a
symbol of the majesty of the Venetian State.

The Grand Council and Senate made all the
decisions about works to be carried out on the
palace, clearly demonstrating that it was the
property of the Republic and not of the Doge.
While the names of the architects who applied
these decisions are not always known, the fame
of artisans, decorators and, above all, painters
who embellished the palace has long endured.

5. Square vestibule
6. Quattro Porte Chamber
7. College Antichamber
8. College Chamber
9. Senate Chamber
10. Chamber of the Council of Ten
11. Arms and armor
12. Tre Capi Chamber
13. Inquisitors' Chamber

1. Avogaria Chamber
2. Chancellery Chamber
3. Piovego Chamber
4. Giants' Staircase

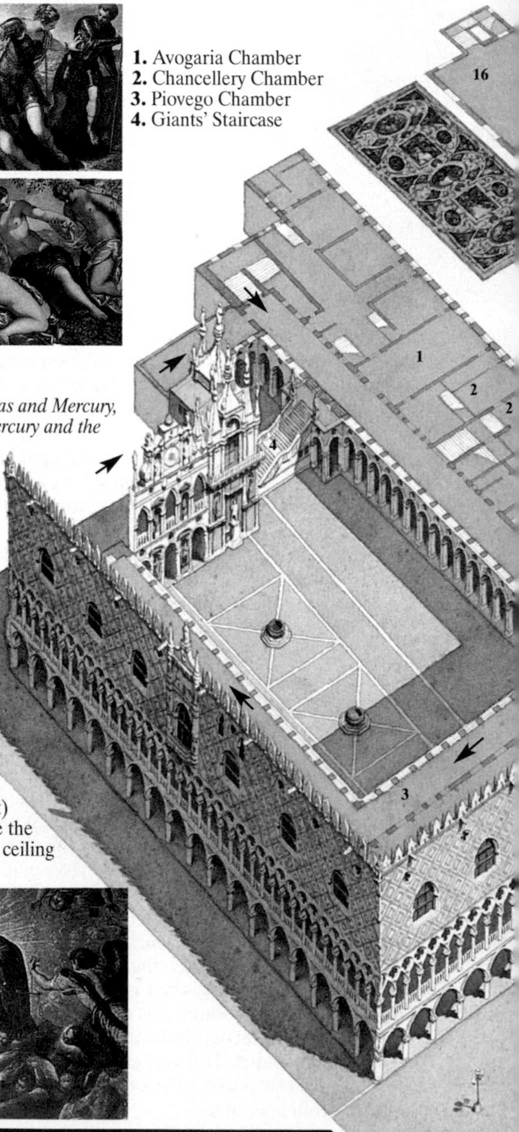

7. TINTORETTO
(College Antichamber)
The *Discovery of Ariadne, Pallas and Mercury,
The Strength of Vulcan* and *Mercury and the
Graces*. These four canvases,
painted in 1577–8, were
originally intended for the
square vestibule.

15. TINTORETTO
(Grand Council Chamber)
Paradise, painted 1588–94.
This grandiose work (23 x 72ft)
was commissioned to decorate the
walls of the chamber after the ceiling
was completed in 1584.

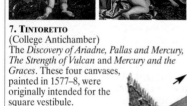

10. CEILING OF THE CHAMBER OF THE COUNCIL OF TEN
Decorated by Giambattista Ponchino and Veronese.

15. Grand Council Chamber
16. Ballot Chamber
17. Philosophers' Chamber
18. Doge's Apartments

14. The first floor of the Doge's Palace is linked to the Bridge of Sighs.

PORTA DELLA CARTA
The work of Giovanni and Bartolomeo Bon (1438).

BALCONY OF THE BALLOT CHAMBER
Designed by Scarpagnino and Sansovino (1536).

BRIDGE OF SIGHS
Built in 1600, by Antonio Contino.

BALCONY OF THE GRAND COUNCIL CHAMBER
The work of Dalle Masegne (1404).

From the 17th century onwards, the myth of the Venetian government spread throughout Europe, and its institutions became an obligatory reference point in every area of political thought. Travelers, ambassadors and men of letters all admired the stability of a regime that appeared to be unaffected by the passing of time, and in the eyes of political thinkers the Republic was a harmonious combination of monarchical, aristocratic and democratic principles, in the form of the Doge, the Senate and the Grand Council.

THE PATRICIAN CLASS
The members of noble families who were inscribed in the Golden Book (which recorded births and marriages) all had a lifetime seat on the Grand Council.

THE SENATE
Created in about 1255, the Senate numbered sixty members selected from the Grand Council and elected for one year. To these were added sixty more members (LA ZONTA), also elected by the Grand Council, and various magistrates who did not all have the right to vote. The senators had to be more than thirty years old and were the only magistrates who could be re-elected at the end of their term. As a kind of council of sages (made up of hot-blooded younger men, old men rendered prudent by long experience, and men in the prime of mid-life, calm and sure of themselves) the Senate debated the measures that should be taken by the government, provided the state with most of its higher civil servants, performed administrative functions and recommended "its" candidates for election to magisterial offices. These candidates were then confirmed by the Grand Council.

THE "BROGLIO"
Venetian elections were subject to widespread fraud. Before ballots were cast, members of the Grand Council milled about in front of the palace, on the *broglio*, and the most powerful attempted to buy the votes of impoverished nobles – the *barnabotti*. This practice became known as *broglio* – hence the Italian expression *imbroglio* (entanglement).

THE GRAND COUNCIL

This body was intended to represent the whole city of Venice. But in 1297, with the "Closure of the Grand Council" (*La Serrata del Gran Consiglio*) ● *31*, access to it was narrowed to life membership for the members of noble families only. The council, which numbered just over a thousand nobles in the 13th century, grew to twice that size in the 16th century. Extraordinary service to the Republic, or else the payment of a substantial sum to the government, could elevate certain commoners to membership of the Grand Council, with their names included in the Golden Book. The council could not initiate laws, but had the right to veto the more important ones. On the other hand, since it selected the members of future governments, it could also channel and legitimize an individual's political ambitions. The continuity of this self-perpetuating governing class was unique in Europe.

THE DOGE'S HATS

THE DOGE

The Doge of Venice personified the unity that existed in the Republic. Elected for life by the Grand Council, he was usually chosen from among the greatest Venetian families, and had to have attained a respectable age (often at least seventy). The Doge reigned rather than governed; his powers were limited and his actions severely controlled, even though in theory he had a say in all important decisions. He could not take any decision in the absence of his six councillors (one for each sestiere of the city). Indeed he did not even have the right to leave Venice, unless he was accompanied by two or more of these councillors.

THE "CORNO"

This hat, worn by the Doge, had a strange rounded peak and a broad band. It was covered in precious stones and was woven in cloth of silver and gold, on a base of velvet and damask.

In the Ballot Chamber of the Doge's Palace, the portrait of Falier is replaced by a black veil.

MARIN FALIER
After entering government service as a very young man, Marin Falier ended his long and brilliant career, at the age of seventy-six, decapitated by the executioner's sword. In 1355, just after his election as Doge, Falier led a popular conspiracy. Betrayed by a follower, he was sentenced by the Council of Ten, which he had controlled at the age of thirty. He was executed on April 17, 1355, in the courtyard of the Doge's Palace, and his head was displayed on the Piazzetta.

THE SEIGNORY
The Seignory consisted of the six councillors of the Doge and the three heads of the QUARANTIA (supreme tribunals which pronounced judgement in the civil and criminal appeal courts, and on the most serious penal offenses).

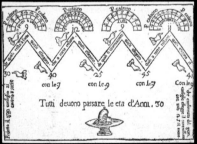

Tutti deuono passare le eta d'Anni. 30

THE APPORTIONING OF POWER WITHIN THE REPUBLIC
No single institution monopolized power, and no single decision making body could operate unchecked by another. The quick rotation of all offices – except those of the Doge and the nine procurators of St Mark's (State Treasurers) – made it difficult for a single individual or faction to appropriate power. The opposition did actually have a place in the system and did not need to plot its downfall in order to make itself heard, since everyone had a hand in the decision making process and in the election of magistrates. Moreover, the complexity of the authorities above the Grand Council level rendered personal ambition more or less futile. This system survived until 1797 and ensured the existence of a government that was as stable as it was effective.

THE COUNCIL OF TEN
Set up in 1310 after the conspiracy of Bajamonte Tiepolo ▲ *214*, the council of sixteen members (plus the Doge) was a permanent institution by the end of the 14th century.

The Doge's Palm Sunday procession. The original of this 16th-century engraving is more than 13 feet long.

Its members, chosen by the Grand Council and renewed a third at a time, were not permitted to be related to the Doge since their function was both to observe him and to work with him. The Seignory determined the order of the elections to the magistrature and made sure that they were carried out correctly, but it had to answer for its decisions to the Senate.

The Council's competence was extended from the domain of crimes against the state to cover all decisions requiring absolute secrecy. Often portrayed as a despotic power ruling the city, its real function was to prevent the ambition of influential citizens from threatening the State.

ELECTING THE DOGE

The ballot was secret with each voter slipping his fist into an urn to cast his vote. To be elected, a candidate needed to win a minimum of twenty-five votes.

Wax counters of three different colors were used as ballots, but then it was realized that the wax melted in the hand, so they were replaced by counters made of canvas. The counting was done with little modelled hands made of wood or gold.

THE "BALLOTINO"

For the final election, two nobles went to the basilica and picked out a ten-year-old boy from the crowd. This boy distributed the counters and added them up after the vote. He then remained in the Doge's service.

SAINT MARK'S BASILICA ★

THE EARLIEST BUILDINGS. In 828, two merchants returned to Venice from Alexandria with the mortal remains of St Mark The Evangelist. St Mark was immediately proclaimed patron saint of the city, replacing the Greek St Theodore, a change which probably symbolized Venice's desire to shake off the irksome tutelage of Byzantium ● *30*. Initially, the saint's relics were preserved in a hastily erected chapel inside the Doge's Palace, after which a church-mausoleum was built for them nearby in 832. In 976, the people rose in rebellion and burned both the palace and church, after which Pietro Orseolo had the sanctuary rebuilt and reconsecrated in 978. At the time, Venice's power and wealth were in full flush, and the whole city was gripped by construction fever. Having served the dual purpose of mausoleum and private chapel, fulfilling both a religious and a political function, the sanctuary of St Mark was finally demolished along with the neighboring Church of St Theodore to make way for a third and last building in 1063.

THE BYZANTINE BASILICA. Venice was already the gateway between the Orient and the West, though she still acknowledged the cultural supremacy of Byzantium. For this reason the city of the Doges produced a cathedral that was completely oriental in aspect, modelled on two basilicas in Constantinople – the Church of the Holy Apostles (now destroyed), and St Sophia. With its centralized, Greek cross floor plan, and its choir slightly raised to make space for a crypt ▲ *239* below, the basilica, consecrated in 1094, appeared structurally foursquare and robust on account of its brickwork and the cluster of low domes.

THE FAÇADES. Between the 11th and the 15th centuries, the basilica's aspect changed with the addition of a mass of ornament to its façades. Each of the original low domes was covered with a second cupola in wood, with a lead skin topped by a lantern and a gilded cross. The brickwork was concealed behind marble patterns, while in front of the main façade rose a double line of small columns that were topped by capitals, also of rare marble from the East. Leaf-work, aedicules and spires were grafted on to the arcades as Gothic additions, while the main portal was decorated with bas-reliefs representing the various crafts, and the signs of the zodiac. Towards the present Piazzetta dei Leoncini, an arch was constructed (the Arch of Sant'Alippio). Some of these ornamentations were bought or captured in distant Oriental countries by Venetian merchants, or else seized during wars and crusades. This was the case with the two pilasters from Acre, fine specimens of 6th-century Syrian art taken after the

The lame man gnawing his knuckles on the third arch is said to be a likeness of the architect of the basilica. Having fallen from the scaffolding in a transport of admiration for one of the domes, he is biting himself in rage because the church he built is not as beautiful as he hoped.

"The five domes of the basilica reigned in the sky like enormous bishops' mitres glittering with precious stones."
  Gabriele d'Annunzio

> "Abhorrent green, slippery city, whose Doges
> were old, and had ancient eyes."
>
> DH Lawrence

victory over the Genoese in the 13th century; and of the
TETRARCHS, an example of 4th-century Egyptian-Syrian
carving in porphyry which is still a part of the façade that
gives on to the Piazzetta.

**FIDELITY TO THE
ORIENTAL STYLE.** The
crowning of the
arcades, which allowed
the basilica to grow in
height and brought it
into harmony with the
Doge's Palace, was
really a concession to
Gothic art. The slow
process of covering the
façades led to a great mixture of styles. But perhaps the most
striking thing about St Mark's is its persistent Orientalism,
showing that although the balance of power between
Byzantium and Venice was changing in Venice's favor, the
Republic's taste in architecture was still Oriental. The city in
general, and St Mark's in particular, showed astounding
fidelity to Byzantium – or perhaps a desire to appropriate her
culture. This continuity is most evident in the use of mosaics, a
typically Byzantine trait; and the extravagant use of gold as
background, even on the façade. Thus the lunettes of the
upper register portray the *Deposition of Christ*, *Christ's
Descent into Limbo*, the *Resurrection*, and the *Ascension*; on
the lower register, the lunette of the main portal is filled by a
Last Judgement, and those of the side portals by pictures of
the transportation of the relics of St Mark. These decorations
were added quite late in the day, with the exception of the last
mosaic on the left (13th-century) representing the *Relics of St
Mark Transported into the Basilica*, which shows the building as
it was prior to the addition of its Gothic elements.

**THE PIETRA DEL
BANDO**
At the corner nearest
the Piazzetta is a
proclamation stone
(pietra del bando) like
the one at the Rialto
▲ *283*, made from a
piece of porphyry
brought from Syria in
the 13th century.
Government decrees
were announced from
here by a herald.

HIC DEFERT

OR P VSSÇIMARCI

THE PALA D'ORO ★
One of the richest pieces of goldwork in the world. Formerly this splendid altarpiece was only exhibited during major religious ceremonies; until 1836, its upper part could be folded forward by a complicated mechanism. The Pala has now been moved so that visitors can observe it without getting in the way of religious services.

THE GOLDEN SANCTUARY. You enter St Mark's through a narthex, which serves as a transitional space between the exterior portal (an open and light-filled area) and the interior, a place of serenity in which semi-darkness alternates with golden shafts of light. Far from revealing itself at a single glance, this secret, internalized space impinges very slowly on the consciousness. The first visual barrier you encounter is the iconostasis ▲ 165, like the narthex, a typical feature of Oriental churches. It is made of red marble with polychrome panels. Columns with capitals support its architrave, which is adorned with statues by the dalle Masegne that are masterpieces of 14th-century Gothic. Beyond these, on the high altar, glitters the PALA D'ORO, a 14th-century altarpiece of gold. About three thousand precious stones and eighty plaques of enamel, some from Constantinople, are set into a Gothic mounting, the work of a Siennese goldsmith in 1345. The upper register illustrates the principal festivals of the church. In the middle, Christ is conferring his blessing, surrounded by four prophets and the images of the Virgin, the Empress Irina and the Doge Ordelafo Falier (on the right). On either side are three tiers of angels, apostles and prophets. Apart from this altarpiece, the TREASURE OF ST MARK'S comprises a collection of icons and sacred objects, most of which came to Venice after the sack of Constantinople ● 31, and is displayed in what may have been a corner tower of the first Doge's Palace. The 12th-century PAVEMENT is of marble and mosaic with alternating animal shapes and geometrical designs, reflecting Byzantine taste ▲ 240.
MURAL MOSAICS. The work of decorating the inside of St Mark's proceeded for several hundred years until the building was covered in an astonishing 10,764 square feet of mosaic. Since this was intended to teach the faithful the rudiments of sacred history, the story is depicted on the walls of the church like a gigantic illuminated Bible. As in Byzantium, the figure of Christ has pride of place. Thus, beginning at the back of the basilica, the sequence is as follows: in the apse, Christ Pantocrator (11th-century, partially remade in the 16th century); in the first dome, Christ Emmanuel (the young Christ, 12th-century); at the crossing of the transept, the Ascension ▲ 240 (13th-century); and finally, the Pentecost (first half of the 12th-century). Though they may have been executed by local craftsmen, all these mosaics share a Byzantine stillness, with figures bearing no trace of individuality, and the general mass of subject matter in perfect balance. While the domes of the transept are dedicated to St John the Evangelist and St Leonard, along the main arches and vaults

DETAIL OF THE PALA D'ORO. Apparently when the two Venetian merchants Rustico and Buono brought the remains of the martyred St Mark from Alexandria, they hid them under a layer of pork so Muslim officials would not investigate too closely.

of the central nave run a series of episodes from evangelical history, regulated according to Byzantine iconographic canons to illustrate the principal festivals of the Christian Church. Thus the Passion (mid-13th century) appears on the main arch between the Ascension and Pentecost. This scene, in which the participants bear witness to Christ, shows the first stirrings of a taste for more sophisticated effects, with some angels revealing only part of their bodies. Elements from the Western, Romanesque and Gothic traditions have crept in here, as in the scene from the lives of Christ and the Virgin (right-hand nave and left-hand transept). The vision of the artists is more animated and more fluid: we are coming nearer to the 15th century and the close of the first and greatest period of St Mark's. Henceforth, mosaic art sought increasingly to compete with painting, introducing painterly relief and perspective. After a final

Part of the treasure.

THE LEGEND OF SAINT MARK
"Pax tibi Marce Evangeliste meus." "Peace be unto you, Mark my Evangelist." These were the words that were spoken by an angel to St Mark when he came to the

harmonious phase in the early 15th century, when they were influenced by Tuscan masters such as Paolo Uccello and Andrea del Castagno (see the four saints in the rear of the right transept), the mosaic artists were happy to copy cartoons supplied by the great masters of painting, applying canons that were ill-adapted to their technique. Nevertheless, there are other panels here that are well worth a look, notably the *Dance of Salome* (14th-century) in the baptistry, and a beautiful *Creation* (13th-century) in the Old Testament sequence that adorns the narthex.

Lagoon, thus apparently leaving the saint in no doubt that Venice would be his final resting-place. The theft of the relics was held to be justified, since it was considered to be no more than the fulfilment of a divine prediction.

The relics, which were brought from Egypt by merchants, had been hidden in the column of San Giacomo, near the altar, in order to foil the claims of the clergy of Alexandria. After their discovery, they were lodged in the crypt of the basilica.

ST MARK TAKING A SH[IP]
TO ALEXANDRIA
(Zen Chapel,
13th century)
The supple lines and
motifs of this mosai[c]
are in strong contras[t]
to the hieratic stiffne[ss]
of Byzantine art.

THE CRYPT OF THE BASILICA, with its central vaulting, harbored the relics of St Mark until 1811. Its heavy, archaic style is typical of the 11th century.

THE DISCOVERY OF THE BODY OF ST MARK, at which Doge Vitale Falier and a few members of the Seignory were present. This "miracle", which took place on June 25, 1094, is illustrated by a 13th-century mosaic on the west wall of the transept.

THE DANCE OF SALOME (baptistery). This fascinating image stands out from the rest of the mosaic cycle dealing with the life of John the Baptist (14th-century).

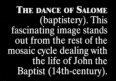

T JOHN among the guardian angels of the Seven Churches of the Orient (detail of the arch of the Apocalypse, completed in the 16th century by the Zuccato brothers, fter a drawing by ma the Younger.

THE CREATION OF EVE This is the 15th of the 24 concentric motifs in the dome of the Creation (13th century) at the south end of the narthex.

The Gothic treatment of Salome – who seduced Herod and so obtained the head of St John the Baptist – is a graceful, lascivious contrast to the Byzantine rigidity of the kings.

DETAIL FROM THE ARCH OF THE APOCALYPSE

CROSS-SECTION OF THE BASILICA, SHOWN LENGTHWISE

▲ SAINT MARK'S SQUARE
THE MOSAICS
OF THE BASILICA

POLYCHROME MARBLE MOSAICS
(12th century), cover the floor of the
basilica rather like a complicated
Oriental carpet. They are created
according to one of two distinct
techniques – the *opus tesselatum*, which
uses mosaic fragments of differing size
but regular shape, and the *opus sectile*,
a collection of tiny, irregular pieces of
stone. This latter technique was
generally used for geometrical and
animal motifs.

**THE DOME OF THE
ASCENSION,** at the crossing of
the nave and the transept,
represents a gold-clad Christ
in majesty who sits in a starry
sky surrounded by four
angels. Below, the Virgin
between two angels and the
twelve apostles (13th
century). Christ's image is
omnipresent in the basilica,
from the Child
Messiah of the
Emmanuel
Dome
through to
the Pantocrator
of the apse.

CHRIST'S ENTRY INTO JERUSALEM
This late 12th-century mosaic, which
adorns the main arch of the south
transept, is a faithful illustration of the
texts of the Gospels. Children are
shown crowding around the figure of
Christ and spreading their coats under
the hooves of his donkey.

**ST MARK MEDITATING
ON HIS GOSPEL**
(North-west side of the
Ascension dome.)
The patron saint of the
basilica is shown
adopting the pose of a
Byzantine scribe.

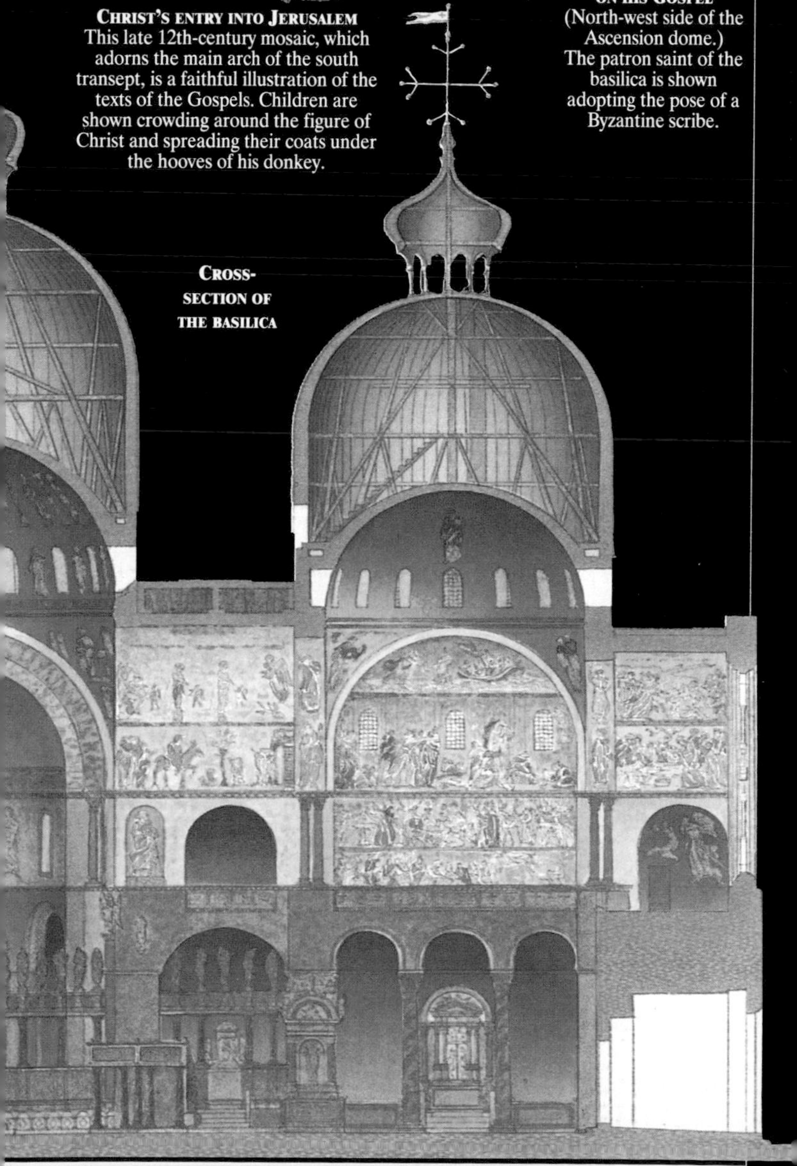

**CROSS-
SECTION OF
THE BASILICA**

ROMAN HORSES
According to a recent theory, the horses of St Mark's are Roman in origin, but with features borrowed from Greek art (the manes, for example) and dating from either the 2nd or 3rd century after Christ.

THE HORSES OF ST MARK

In the LOGGIA DEI CAVALLI is a copy of this celebrated quadriga of horses in gilded bronze, which seems so lifelike that the animals might at any moment "neigh and stamp their feet", as Petrarch wrote. Stored in a safe place during the two World Wars, their originals were recently taken down from the basilica, victims of pollution. After restoration, they were reinstalled under cover in an exhibition room.

A SYMBOL OF VENETIAN FREEDOM. The origins of the horses are hotly disputed. Are they Greek or Roman sculptures from

the fourth or third century BC, or are they from the time of Constantine (3rd century AD)? Another theory is that they were made by Lysippus, Alexander's court sculptor, but no-one now seriously believes the old contention that they came from Corinth. The most probable theory is that they once stood at the Hippodrome in Constantinople, while the only certainty is that they came to Venice in 1204 with other booty from the Crusades ● *31*. Fifty years later they were saved from oblivion by an anonymous ambassador from Florence, who saw them at the Arsenal. Subsequently it was suggested that they be placed on top of St Mark's, which was being repaired at the time. Once in place they quickly became the symbols of untrammelled Venice. But it seems to have been their destiny to be despoiled by occupying armies, for five centuries later they were once again removed, this time by Napoleon Bonaparte.

BONAPARTE AND THE HORSES OF SAINT MARK. In 1792, with all Europe in coalition against Revolutionary France, Venice opted to stay neutral, hoping the war would pass her by. The Republic was anyway no more than a shadow of its former self, and the city's fame only rested on the beauty of its palaces and churches, for Venetian military and naval power had vanished following the loss of Morea in 1718 ● *34*. The Doge Lodovico Manin and the Grand Council stuck to their neutral line until 1796, when the

THE HEADLESS HORSES
The horse-statues were cast in a metal of extraordinary composition – almost entirely pure copper, much more difficult to melt than ordinary bronze, but also much easier to gild. Each statue was cast in two sections, with the joint concealed by the collar. Some people think that they may have been dissected for transportation from Constantinople, and then arbitrarily reassembled on their arrival.

Directoire régime in France offered a full alliance; but ultimately the Republic could not prevent either Austrian or French troops from crossing Venetian territory. After his victory over the Austrians at Rivoli (January 14, 1797) Bonaparte decided to make peace with Vienna. Aware that his enemies would be reluctant to give up their positions on the left bank of the Rhine, he had the idea of offering them Venice in exchange. In the spring of 1797, French troops in the Veneto were attacked by

> "The four horses of Lysippus leapt into the clouds,
> arching their necks to which the gold still clung,
> proud to be yet in the sight of Man."
>
> Paul Morand

NAPOLEON IN VENICE
From November 29
to December 8, 1807,
Venice entertained
her sovereign, the
Emperor Napoleon.
Accompanied by
Prince Eugène ▲ 181,
he was welcomed
with enthusiasm
(eight years of
Austrian rule having
softened the memory
of six months'
occupation by the
French). Napoleon's
entire visit was a
succession of balls
and celebrations.

the population, and Bonaparte, refusing the apologies of the
Venetian Senate and demanding a change in the Republic's
constitution, marched on the city. On May 12, the Doge and
Grand Council resigned amid general panic. On May 16, a
municipality was chosen in the name of the people, and a
committee of public safety elected. At the request of this new
government, Bonaparte's soldiers occupied the city, while
Austria seized Istria and Dalmatia, Venetian territories
allotted to the Empire at the Leoben negotiations
before the Treaty of Campo Formio ● 34. At
the conclusion of this treaty (October 17,
1797) Bonaparte summarily informed the
Venetian envoy of his country's fate.
Thus, with a single stroke of a pen, and
no discussion of her secular rights, one of
Europe's oldest states was dismantled.
Before surrendering Venice to the Austrians
as the treaty required, the French systematically
looted all that they could carry. Among the treasures they
took (including paintings, the gilt of the Bucintoro ● 38, and
manuscripts) were the horses that had long been the symbol
of Venetian liberty. Brought to Paris, they were "harnessed"
to a chariot and installed in the Tuileries on the Arch of the
Carrousel. Austrian troops entered Venice on January 18,
1798, to be greeted as liberators, so great was Venetian hatred
for the nation that had betrayed them and pillaged the city.

**THE TREE OF
LIBERTY**
In May 1797, a bay
tree was planted on
St Mark's Square,
around which the
populace

danced the
Carmagnole.

But, on December 26, 1805,
Napoleon imposed the
Treaty of Presbourg on the
Holy Roman Empire in the
wake of his victory at
Austerlitz. By this treaty,
Venice and the Veneto
were incorporated
into the Kingdom of
Italy. The city reverted
to the French for
seven years, before
the final takeover
by Austria and the
return of the
quadriga and
other works of art
in 1815

A savage caricature
of Napoleon, with the
face portrayed as a
mass of corpses.

THE PROCURATIES

THE PROCURATORS OF THE REPUBLIC. The two long buildings of the Procuratie Vecchie and the Procuratie Nuove, which occupy the sides of St Mark's Square, formerly accommodated the offices of the Procurators of St Mark, the highest officials in the Republic, with the exception of the Doge. These magistrates and administrators of state property were nine in number, divided into teams of three: the *de supra* procurators, who attended the basilica and St Mark's Square, and the *de citra* and *de ultra* procurators, who looked after Venice's six sestieri.

THE PROCURATIE VECCHIE. In the 12th century, following the decision of the *de supra* procurators to install themselves near the basilica, the Procuratie Vecchie were constructed, only to be destroyed by fire and rebuilt in the 16th century. Bartolomeo Bon (seconded by Guglielmo dei Grigi) directed

INVESTITURE OF THE PROCURATOR
At this major event in Venetian life, the elected official gave bread to the poor and wine to the gondoliers, and threw parties for the nobility. He went in state to the basilica, where he swore an oath to do honor to his office before taking possession of an apartment in the Procuraties, which thenceforth bore his name.

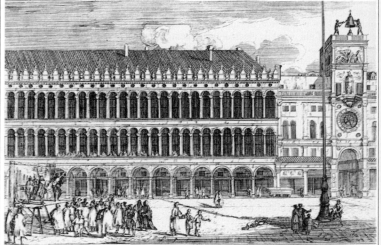

the works, according to a design by Coducci. The project stressed the functional nature of this building, which was intended above all to house offices – as it does to this day.

THE PROCURATIE NUOVE. With the development of the administrative activities of the procurators, there arose a need for a second building, the PROCURATIE NUOVE, on the site of the Orseolo hospice, a venerable institution which figures in Gentile Bellini's painting of *The Procession of Corpus Christi* ● 48. The works began in 1586 under Scamozzi's direction. Interrupted by the death of the architect in 1616, the buildings were finally completed by Longhena in 1640. The Procuratie Nuove were a part of the general reorganization of the square, which had been under way for some time ▲ 222. Their aspect was rather more official and sober than that of the Procuratie Vecchie. They also contained lodgings for the Procurators, who moved in reluctantly, since they were having to leave their splendid palaces for what they considered to be poky cubbyholes.

THE CAFÉS

THE BOTTEGHE DEL CAFFÈ. The first *bottega del caffè* opened under the Procuraties in 1683, and thereafter such cafés quickly multiplied. Many of them were similar to taverns, with low ceilings, no windows, poor lighting and the bare minimum of furniture. A century later, there were no fewer than twenty-four cafés situated on St Mark's Square alone, and they acquired such importance in Venetian life during the 18th century that Goldoni ▲ *291* had a café owner say in his *La Bottega del Caffè*: "My profession is necessary to the glory of our city, to men's health, and to the honest amusement of people who need to breathe easy for a spell." In due course, people of all ages and walks of life came to relax in these public places. But affinities, professional or otherwise, often tended to play a part in the choice of one café as against another. Patrons played cards, a passion with Venetians, in these establishments; likewise the cafés became the

traditional meeting place of lovers, so much so that the government, which had long sought to impose its control, decided to make them off-limits to women in 1767. Certain cafés also were known as the resort of men of letters.

FLORIAN'S. In 1720, an elegant new café was opened under the arcades of the Procuratie Nuove. It started out with a name that roughly translated as "Venice Triumphant", and which quickly reverted to the Café Florian in honor of its first owner, Floriano Francesconi. Venetian high society soon took the Florian to its heart: Goldoni was a regular habitué, as were the Gozzi brothers, Canova, and (a hundred years later) Balzac, who wrote of it: "Florian's is at once a stock exchange, a theater foyer, a reading room, a club, and a confessional, and it is so suited to the multiplicity of this nation's affairs that some Venetian women have no idea at all as to what kind of business their husbands conduct, because whenever a man has a letter to write, he goes to this café for the purpose." Today, as in the past, a half-hour spent on the terrace of Florian's, or in one of its magnificent coffee-rooms, is one of the greatest delights to be found in Venice.

AN ORIENTAL BEVERAGE
In 1585, the Venetian ambassador to Istanbul described before the Senate the customs of the Turks, who "drank a species of blackened water, drawn from a grain called *kahave*, which doth keep them awake." This grain, roasted and ground and viewed as a form of medicine, was sold in Venice from 1638

onwards at a very high price. But by 1676 it had become so popular that the Senate decided to impose a higher duty on its importation.

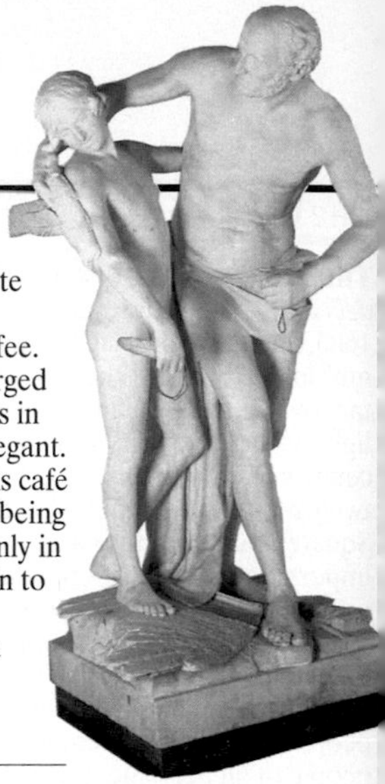

"DAEDALUS AND ICARUS"
This marble group (right) stands in the Throne Room and dates from 1778–9. It signals Canova's arrival as a sculptor and his passage from the Mannerism of the 18th-century to the Neo-classical style.

THE QUADRI. Opened in 1775 by Giorgio Quadri, a native of Corfu, this café, situated opposite Florian's was one of the first in Venice to serve real Turkish coffee. It would seem that Quadri enlarged and converted an older premises in order to make it rather more elegant. Nevertheless, for many years, his café had a bad reputation, its owner being constantly beset by creditors. Only in 1830 did the Quadri finally begin to attract the kind of elegant clientèle which may still be seen there today.

THE CORRER MUSEUM

FRANCESCO FOSCARI
Doge of Venice 1423–57.

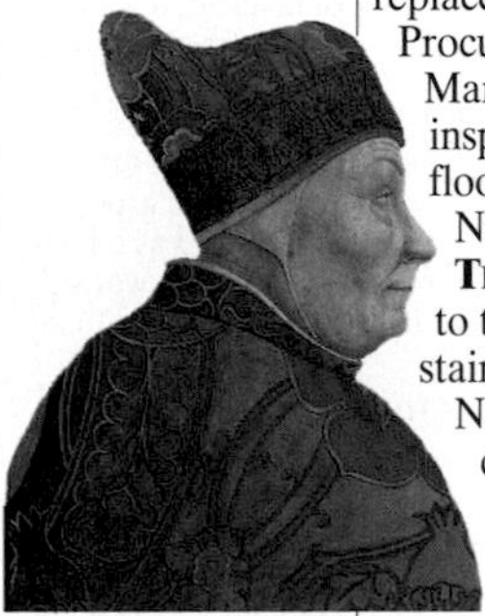

THE NAPOLEONIC WING. The construction of a building to close off the end of St Mark's Square began in about 1810, after the demolition of Jacopo Sansovino's 17th-century Church of San Geminiano. The new building not only replaced this church but also the respective wings of the Procuratie Vecchie and Nuove. It was designed by Giuseppe Maria Soli for the Napoleonic court, and it is clearly inspired by the Neo-classical Libreria Marciana, with a top floor that is adorned by statues and bas-reliefs glorifying Napoleon Bonaparte.

THE MUSEUM OF VENETIAN CIVILIZATION. The entrance to the Correr Museum is located at the top of the formal staircase which formerly led to the reception rooms of the Napoleonic wing. The latter only contains a part of the collections, the rest being exhibited in the Procuratie Vecchie. The museum itself owes its name to Teodoro Correr, a Venetian gentleman, who on his death in 1830 left his entire rich collection to the city of Venice. Opened in 1922, this "Museum of the City and Civilization of Venice" is made up of three main sections. On

SAN GEMINIANO
Sansovino completed the façade and dome of this church, which was begun in 1505 on far older foundations.

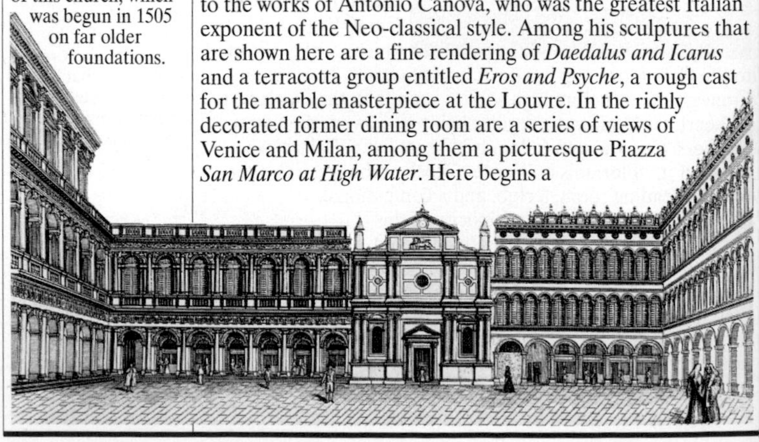

the first floor, after a suite of Neo-classical rooms, is the HISTORY SECTION. Beyond the Napoleonic loggia, frescoes by Giuseppe Borsato in the throne-room offer a fitting backdrop to the works of Antonio Canova, who was the greatest Italian exponent of the Neo-classical style. Among his sculptures that are shown here are a fine rendering of *Daedalus and Icarus* and a terracotta group entitled *Eros and Psyche*, a rough cast for the marble masterpiece at the Louvre. In the richly decorated former dining room are a series of views of Venice and Milan, among them a picturesque Piazza *San Marco at High Water*. Here begins a

The Napoleonic wing, seen from the
Basilica. The cornice bears images
from mythology and statues by
Domenico Banti and Antonio Bosa.
Below, the monumental main staircase,
designed by Giuseppe Maria Soli.

journey that travels through the history of Venice. The
visitor has barely had time in which to admire the marble
effigies of the Lion of St Mark, before the figure of the
Doge appears (represented by the *corno*, oath and
election to that office ▲ *231, 233*). After this comes a
representation of the principal feasts of Venice ● *48*
(Ascension, the Feast of the Redeemer ▲ *339*...), which
is followed by an evocation of the great offices of the
Republic by way of a display of the costumes that were
worn by its dignitaries – including the gown of mourning
that used to be worn by the Doge on Good Friday. Coins,
representations of the Bucintoro ● *38*, the Battle of
Lepanto ● *36* and a collection of arms and armor (in the
Morosini Room) all testify to the former vitality and
grandeur that was such a feature of Venice.

*The Man in the Red
Cap*, by Carpaccio.

THE PAINTINGS SECTION. On the
second floor, the picture gallery
demonstrates the great wealth
of Venetian painting that
existed in the 13th and
16th centuries. After sculpture's
adoption of a more realistic
style (as demonstrated in the
14th-century *Doge Antonio Venier*, by J delle Masegne), the
painters followed suit; hence Paolo Veneziano's Byzantine art
▲ *302* (*Six Saints*, late 14th-century) is close to Gothic, as in
Jesus Giving St Peter the Keys of Heaven (1369) by Lorenzo
Veneziano. But Byzantine art was soon to yield altogether, for
by the 14th century the problems of rendering space and light
in paint had been largely solved by the Renaissance. Each
artist was now able to express himself in his own idiom,
above all chromatically. There is a noteworthy contrast, for
example, to be found between the poignant tension of the
Pietà by the Ferraran Cosmè Tura (c.1468) and the golden
atmosphere and miniaturistic, rustic backdrop of the *Pietà*
of Antonello da Messina (1475–6). The room dedicated
to Bellini ▲ *304* contains some of the treasures that
were bequeathed by one of the most prolific of
Venice's artistic families, among them a
Transfiguration (1455–60) and a *Madonna and
Child* (1460–4) in which the delicate light
suffusing the work of Giovanni Bellini lends
great force to the serenity and poetry of his
art. Further on, with Carpaccio's
Courtesans (1510–15), the colors take
on a new gaiety and brightness. The
paintings section of the museum
ends with Lorenzo Lotto's *The
Madonna with the Christ Child at
her Breast*, c.1525, a canvas that is
full of tormented realism.

**MUSEUM OF THE
RISORGIMENTO.** Here the
collections of paintings and
objets d'art reflect the difficult
period between the fall of the
Republic in 1797, and Venice's
annexation to the Kingdom of
Italy in 1866 ● *35*.

In his *Eurydice* (1775)
Antonio Canova
gives proof of his
interest in the
Baroque style; there
is no indication here
of Neo-classicism, of
which he was to
become one of the
greatest exponents.

The Campanile

The Master of the House. From Coryate to Goethe, writers have advised visitors to Venice to climb the steps of St Mark's Campanile for its sublime view across the city and Lagoon. Standing where the Piazza meets the Piazzetta, this campanile is a full 315 feet high. It was built in the 8th century to serve as a guard tower for the dock ▲ *220*, the *paron di casa* (master of the house) as it is known to Venetians. It was then reconstructed, heightened and modified during the 12th, 14th and 16th centuries. It is crowned by a pyramid-shaped spire with a golden angel weathervane that turns with the wind. The campanile also contains the five bells of St Mark's, which can be heard across Venice tolling out the hours. In the time of the Republic, each bell had its own name: the big one was called Marangona (from the term for the widespread profession of carpenter, which was virtually a synonym for "worker" in Venice). Marangona was tolled morning and evening, to mark the beginning and end of each working day. The smallest bell, il Maleficio, announced death sentences, and La Nona marked the hour of the nones, while the Pregadi bell was rung to summon senators to the Doge's Palace. Finally, it was to the sound of La Trottiera that the magistrates made their way to the palace until the 14th century, no doubt trotting on horseback. On July 14, 1902, at 10 o'clock, the old campanile collapsed. Nobody was injured, but it totally demolished the nearby Loggetta of Sansovino. The decision was taken to rebuild the campanile "where it was, and like it was", using the original materials. The same applied to the Loggetta.

The Loggetta. This building replaced a *ridotto* ▲ *259*, which had itself supplanted some wooden shops. It was built by Sansovino between 1537 and 1549, and was completed by a terrace and balustrade in 1663. From 1569 the Loggetta was the barracks of the Guard of the Doge's Palace. With its three arcades separated by double columns, this building's small façade covered in mottled marble and allegorical figures representing Good Government (Apollo, Peace, Mercury and Minerva), made it possible to integrate the campanile with the rest of the piazza's architecture.

THE CLOCKTOWER

● 98

The clocktower stands on the north side of the square; the Merceria, Venice's principal shopping street, begins on the far side of its arch, to the left. A Renaissance building, the clocktower was constructed towards the end of the 15th century by Mauro Coducci. Later, in 1755, terraces were affixed to it by Giorgio Massari. The central corpus of the clocktower, which has remained unchanged since its construction, has three different registers directly above the arch. Each of them is heavily ornamented with colored décor and gilt. Immediately above the arch is the clock itself, a huge object made of gilt and blue enamel that rather resembles an eye watching over St Mark's Basin. In addition to the time, it also records the phases of the moon and of the zodiac. This clock is contemporary to the tower itself and was designed in order to assist people planning sea

voyages, providing information about the tides and the most favorable months for navigation. Higher up the façade, on either side of a niche containing a statue of the Madonna, are two little doors through which, at Ascensiontide ● 38, carved figures of the Three Kings were made to process. In the upper register stands a lion of St Mark against the backdrop of a starry sky. Finally, the whole tower is crowned by a celebrated pair of bronze figurines that are known as "The Moors", on account of their dark color. These automata, driven by a complex mechanism, indicate the hour of the day by striking a large bell.

THE CLOCKMAKERS
Paolo and Carlo Rainieri, who invented the mechanism which moves both the clock and the automata, were well rewarded by the Republic for their pains. Nevertheless, a later rumor had it that their eyes were put out, to prevent them reproducing a similar masterpiece elsewhere.

THE PIAZZETTA

The Piazzetta dei Leoncini is directly adjacent to St Mark's Square. It occupies the site of a dock that was here in the early days of the Republic ▲ 220, whose waters used to lap at the base of the campanile, and somehow it gives the illusion of being

THE LIONS OF THE REPUBLIC

The lion, one of the four winged creatures that appeared to the prophet Ezekiel, was taken as the sign of St Mark the Evangelist. In placing herself under this saint's protection, Venice adopted his symbol for her emblem. Thus the Republic secured a religious raison d'être and the winged lion became an omnipresent feature in the city – there are fourteen such lions to be counted on St Mark's Square alone. In sculpture, painting, manuscript illumination and ships' ensigns, the emblem of the Republic became famous throughout the known world. Its two principal attitudes were the *leone in moleca* (sitting) and the *leone andante* (walking). The hieratic position of the former represented the majesty of the state. The latter sometimes appeared with two feet on water and two on land, symbolizing the sovereignty of Venice over both elements. Portrayed with the open Bible – the Book of Wisdom – and the inscription *Clementia augustae*, it indicated the peace which Venice imposed within her territories. Finally, a lion with sword in paw and closed book signified the defender of the city in time of war. This was the symbol of Venice's military power, hence the inscription *Forteria leoni*.

> "The winged lion's marble piles,
> Where Venice sat in state, throned
> on her hundred isles!"
>
> Byron

the larger of the two squares. This may be because it is closed between the façade of the Doge's Palace to the east, and that of the Marciana to the west, with a long view across the open Lagoon at one end.

THE COLUMNS. At the open end of the Piazzetta, close to the water, stand two massive red and grey columns of Egyptian granite, known as the columns of Marco and Todaro. A third column was brought from the East with these two, but it fell into the sea and could not be recovered. According to tradition, the two survivors were set up on the Piazzetta in the 12th century by Niccolò Barattieri, the builder of the first wooden bridge at the Rialto. The columns were couched on octagonal plinths and crowned with Venetian-Byzantine capitals; the plinths were originally embellished with

sculptures representing the various crafts, which have now almost entirely disappeared. At the top of the column nearest the Libreria Marciana perches the image of Venice's first patron, the Greek warrior St Theodore, standing with one foot on a prostrate dragon who bears a more than passing resemblance to a crocodile. This is a copy; the original was taken away during the Second World War and now stands alone in the courtyard of the Doge's Palace. As a sculpture, it is an astonishing mixture. The fine marble head, thoroughly Greek in style, is either a portrait of Mithridates VI (132–63 BC), or perhaps of Ptolemy VI Philomotor (186–145 BC). The torso seems to have been part of a Roman statue from the time of Hadrian (2nd century AD), while the rest of the body and the crocodile are 14th-century additions by a Venetian sculptor. On the top of the second column is a winged Lion of St Mark, St Theodore's successor as patron saint of Venice. After a long and painstaking recent restoration, the lion was replaced here on St Mark's Day, April 25, 1991. It consists of a gigantic piece of bronze which was once covered in a skin of gold, if the early descriptions of it are to be credited. The lion weighs about 3 tons, and is 10 feet long. Nobody can agree about its origin, with some saying it is Etruscan, others that it is a specimen of 4th-century BC Sassanid art from Persia, and still others that it is Assyrian, from the 5th century BC! The most recent theory is that it is actually a Chinese chimera, and that the wings are a much later addition.

THE OFFICIAL GATEWAY TO VENICE. The two columns of the Piazzetta constituted Venice's traditional entrance at a time when the only way into the city was by sea. At times when the Republic was not entertaining official visitors, the space between the columns became the only "free zone" in the city, where games of chance were sanctioned; it was also the site of the scaffold, where executions took place after the dreaded Maleficio ▲ *250* had tolled in the campanile. Hence the persistent Venetian superstition that to pass between the two columns is to invite ill-fortune.

Turner ● *109*
and Venice
Light and water combine in Venice to create a restless magic. Whether veiled in mist, reddening at sunset, or ghostly under moonlight, all borderlines between dream and reality, present and past, are eradicated. It was this atmosphere of unearthliness that fascinated Turner, who in painting it rejected the representative style in favor of one approaching Impressionism.

The Italian comic actor Alberto Sordi, in *Venezia, la luna e tu* (1958).

The Prisons

The Doge's dungeons. At the time of the birth of the Venetian Republic, when the Doge's Palace was still no more than a fortress ▲ *224*, some space was naturally reserved there for prisoners. The later Gothic palace continued this tradition. But from the 14th century onwards the palace's tiny foetid cells, in which countless prisoners had both languished and died, were no longer sufficient to house all of the Republic's convicts. The government resolved to remedy this situation by adding some new cells, and eventually by building other prisons elsewhere. Although several attempts were made during the course of the 15th century to set up prisons outside the palace, it was not until the end of the following century that the idea finally came to anything. In 1580, it was resolved that new prison buildings should be built beyond the rio running alongside the Doge's Palace, close to the La Paglia bridge. The works were consigned to Antonio da Ponte, and then on his death in 1597, to Antonio Contin. By 1610 the job was finished, along with a bridge that linked the new prison to the Doge's Palace.

The Bridge of Sighs

The legend. It was not until the romantic 19th century that this famous bridge actually became known as the "Bridge of Sighs". One is supposed to look at it and at the same time imagine the "sigh heaved by a prisoner fresh from the courtroom of the palace, who crosses the canal by this bridge on his way to serve a long sentence in a foul, dank dungeon;

through the lattice window the wretch catches sight of the Lagoon, of the Island of San Giorgio, of the sky and the sunshine outside." This covered bridge, built in Istrian stone, with its frankly Baroque ornamentation, is made up of two corridors that are separated throughout their length by a partition wall. One of these corridors led to the courtrooms, and the other one to the Chamber of the Avogaria. In addition, these two corridors were also linked to the service staircase that leads from the "Wells" to the "Leads".

The Wells and the Leads. The construction of the new prisons answered some of the need to improve conditions of detention in Venice, given that the government had decreed that there should be sufficient space, air and light in the cells. Nevertheless, the Doge's Palace still contained

> "The ups and downs of Venice, where Human life oscillated for so long between two extremes, between *piombi* and *pozzi*, the leads above and the wells below."
>
> Paul Morand

dungeons in which prisoners' lives can only be described as miserable beyond belief. The nineteen cells of the WELLS were on the ground floor of the building, under the Chamber of the Avogaria. The Wells were narrow, dark, dank (on account of the nearby canal) and airless – hence their name. They were used from the 1530's until the end of the 18th century. The LEADS, by contrast, were situated just beneath the lead-covered roofs of the palace, just beside the TORTURE CHAMBER (*camera del tormento*). Probably built in the second half of the 15th century, they consisted of six or seven cells, in which were incarcerated special prisoners of the Council of Ten or of the Inquisitors, who were either awaiting judgement or else had already been convicted of minor offenses. These jails are

CASANOVA

Cross-section of the prisons, showing the celebrated Wells and

assumed – perhaps wrongly – to have contributed to the dismal reputation of Venetian justice; in any case they aroused the indignation of many writers, particularly during the 19th century. Their fame is largely due to the celebrated adventurer and libertine, Giovanni Giacomo Casanova de Seingalt, who described in his *Story of my Escape from the Leads of Venice* both the jail itself and the incredible manner of his getting out of it.

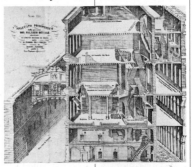

CASANOVA'S ESCAPE. Following his arrest on July 26, 1755, Casanova was immediately locked up in a cell inside the Leads. Manuzzi, a right-hand man of the State Inquisitor, had accused him of living a dissolute life, and of spreading anti-religious propaganda. Languishing in his tiny cell, in which there was no room even to stand up, Casanova quickly fell ill – but this did not stop him hatching his first plan of escape. On August 25, however, he was moved to a different cell, and so this plan was foiled. Undaunted, he worked out another scheme with the complicity of one of his cellmates, Father Balbi; his idea this time was to escape across the rooftops. During the night of October 31, he managed to slip out of his cell and onto the roof, afterwards climbing down through a skylight into an attic. From here he crossed through a number of small rooms on his way to the square room (SALA QUADRATA) that adjoins the Scala d'Oro. At this point he leaned out of a window and was seen by a guard who, taking him for an official left behind in the palace, opened the gates and let him out through the Porta della Carta. Hailing a gondola, Casanova made good his escape to the frontier, and then on to Munich and finally Paris. Twenty years later he returned to Venice once more, only to leave her again forever.

Leads. One can still see the two *bocci dei leone* in the Doge's Palace. One is in the courtyard, the other

in the Bussola chamber ▲ 225.

The walls of the Venetian prisons are covered in prisoners' graffiti, such as this example by Francesco Sforza.

The Libreria Marciana is one of Italy's largest libraries, containing more than a million volumes, priceless manuscripts, beautiful nautical charts and the famous 15th-century planisphere

THE LIBRERIA MARCIANA

THE ORIGINS OF THE LIBRARY. The gift of Petrarch – who bequeathed his library to the Republic in the 14th century – was followed, in 1468, by that of Cardinal Bessarion ▲ *164*, which included more than a thousand manuscripts. These two bequests formed the core of a huge state library for Venice, which subsequently became (along with the Library of Padua University) a depository for all books that were published in the Venetian state.

As the collection grew, so also did the need for a much larger building in which to house it. A site was duly chosen and the Libreria Marciana was built opposite the Doge's Palace.

by Fra Mauro ▲ *154*. It also contains the exquisite GRIMANI BREVIARY, a masterpiece which is illustrated with 110 Flemish miniatures (15th–16th century). At the entrance to the library stand two colossal caryatids (1553–5) by Alessandro Vittoria.

VENICE'S STATE ARCHITECT. The work began in 1537 and continued until 1554, directed by Jacopo Sansovino. This Tuscan architect, who escaped from Rome in 1527, became the principal exponent of the Republic's architectural and urban development aspirations. He had already been commissioned to complete the rearrangement of St Mark's Square, a prestigious exercise by which the state hoped to affirm its political clout. By rediscovering the architectural manner of the ancients and developing a grandiose "Roman" style that suited Venetian tradition, Sansovino fulfilled the wishes of the Serene Republic; he created around San Marco not only the Libreria Marciana, but also the Zecca, the loggia of the campanile and the Church of San Geminiano (since demolished). The Libreria, in particular, represents an essential element of his new style, with the Doric arcades of its ground floor, the series of windows adorning the loggia of its first floor, and its terrace, which appears as a counterpoint to the crenellations of the Doge's Palace. Despite a number of problems during its construction – the "Roman" arch collapsed in 1545, and Sansovino was arrested and obliged to rebuild the roof at his own expense – the Libreria remains one of his most sublime creations. He solved the problem of adapting his own architectural tenets to the site without upsetting its original balance.

EXALTATION OF KNOWLEDGE. The decoration of this temple of culture, originally meant to house a school of philosophy and rhetoric, exalts human knowledge in general and Venetian civilization in particular. The sculptures on the façade are by (among others) Minio, Vittoria and Ammanati, while the frescoes on the main staircase are by Battista Franco and Battista del Moro. The allegorical paintings in the main hall and vestibule (see Titian's *Wisdom* on the ceiling), represent a thoroughgoing manifesto of Venetian Mannerism.

MUSEUM OF ARCHEOLOGY

The collections of the Museum of Archeology are displayed in sections of the Libreria Marciana and the Procuratie Vecchie. Its two main resources come from donations that were made during the 16th century. In 1523, Cardinal Domenico Grimani, a celebrated humanist and theologian, presented the Seignory with his collection of Greek marbles, along with a magnificent library; and in 1593 his nephew Giovanni, the patriarch of Aquileia, made another significant bequest of original Greek art. Other donations were made during the 17th century, until eventually the museum's collection was acknowledged as one of the richest in the whole of northern Italy. With their Greek originals and Roman copies (which in many cases constitute vital evidence of works that have long since vanished) the museum's display rooms not only offer an overview of Greek art, but they also give us an insight into the tastes of past collectors. The room containing the Grimani statues, for example, is a monument to the admirable artistic sensibility of Giovanni Grimani, who somehow contrived to assemble a hoard of minor masterpieces dating from the 6th and 5th centuries before the birth of Christ. In addition to these works the museum also possesses an intriguing collection of medals and some splendid cameos – among them a Hellenic *Zeus with his Shield*. There are also some very fine portraits, an area in which ancient Rome excelled. Among the various busts on display, note especially the one entitled *Vitellius*, which is so realistic that for many years it was assumed to date from the Renaissance period.

THE MINT

LA ZECCA. The 9th-century mint in which the first Venetian coin was struck was located at San Bartolomeo, near the Rialto ▲ *276*. It was not until the end of the 13th century that a *zecca* (mint) was installed on St Mark's Square. The Zecca

The balustrade on top of the Libreria Marciana (above) is decorated with statues of mythological deities; there are three obelisks at the corners. This statuary is mostly by sculptors of the second half of the 16th century.

Among the painters chosen by Sansovino and Titian to decorate the Libreria Marciana were Veronese, Battista Franco, Andrea Meldolla, called lo Schiavone, and Giuseppe Porta, called Salviati. Each worked according to his own lights, and the result reflects the wealth and variety of Venetian Mannerism.

255

VENETIAN COINS
Of the 53 Doges, only Niccolò Tron in 1471 had coins struck with his effigy. Otherwise, the Doge's portraits did not appear on Venetian money; although the names were marked, the head was without individual features, a sign that Venice set more store by the Doge's office than by his person. The gold sequin bore the image of St Mark presenting a banner to a kneeling Doge, and on its reverse a Christ figure against a starred background. Other coins showed the Lion of St Mark, the Madonna, St Justine or an allegory of Justice. Under Doge Andrea Grimani (1521) a strange medal was struck, the *osella* ● *38* (derived from *osello*, the Venetian form of *uccello*, which means a bird). It was intended to replace the game with which the Doge used to regale Venice's more prominent citizens during certain festivals.

produced a coinage that was readily exchanged everywhere, because it originated in the richest city-state in Italy. On the other hand, it was a trifle drab to look at by comparison with the coinage of some other Italian states, which excelled in the realistic portraiture of princes – as in the Florentine florin. The most widespread coin, even after the appearance in the 16th century of gold ecus and heavy silver ducats, was always the sequin (called a ducat until 1540). The sequin came either in gold or in silver. The Zecca continued to function until 1870, some time after the collapse of the Venetian Republic. In the 16th century its old premises were replaced by the present building, designed by Sansovino. On the ground floor are a series of embossed arcades; on the upper floors, the façade is balanced throughout its length by windows, which lend emphasis to its ringed half-columns and imposing cornices. Since 1905, the mint building has been a part of the Libreria Marciana, its inner courtyard being covered over and used as a public reading room.

THE ROYAL GARDENS. These gardens were born of the Emperor Napoleon's wish to see a broad view from the windows of the Procuratie Nuove, which he had converted into a royal residence. To allow this view, the four huge, crenellated buildings of the Granai di Terranova (14th-century) were demolished in 1807. With these buildings, which formerly stood on the quayside beside the Zecca, vanished what had once been one of the largest grainstores in Europe.

San Marco

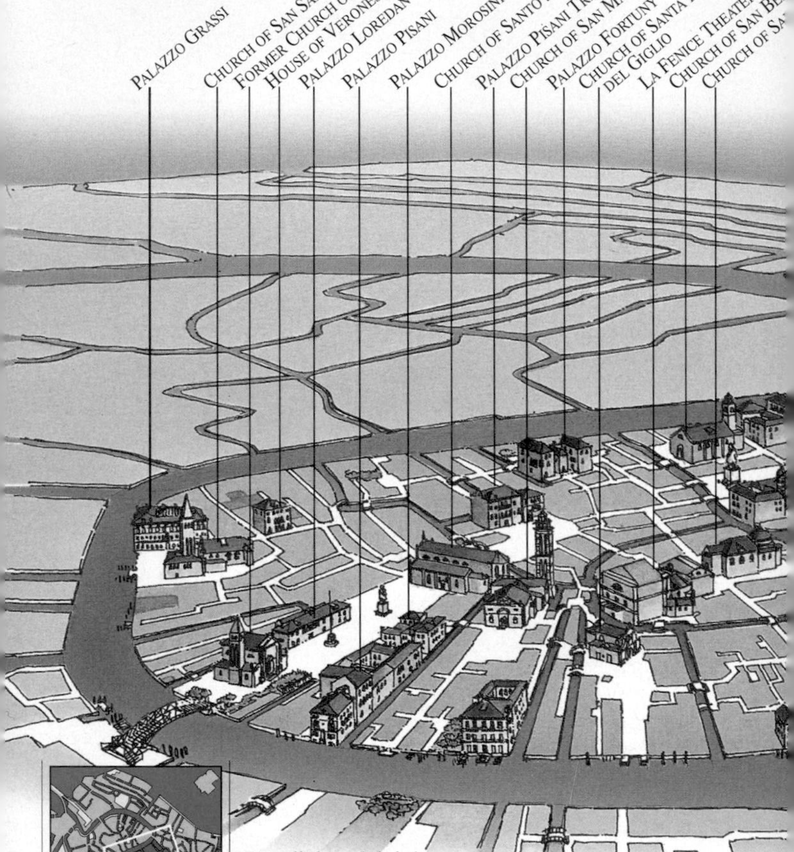

PALAZZO GRASSI
CHURCH OF SAN SAMUELE
FORMER CHURCH OF SAN VITALE
HOUSE OF VERONESE
PALAZZO LOREDAN
PALAZZO PISANI
PALAZZO MOROSINI
CHURCH OF SANTO STEFANO
PALAZZO PISANI TREVISAN
CHURCH OF SAN MAURIZIO
PALAZZO FORTUNY
CHURCH OF SANTA MARIA
DEL GIGLIO
LA FENICE THEATER
CHURCH OF SAN BEN
CHURCH OF SA

⏳ Half a day

◆ B C

CASINO VENIER ★
At the heart of the
Merceria, this small
apartment with its
stuccos and marble
floors has preserved
the atmosphere of the
original casini, where
masked Venetian
nobles came for
entertainment.
Casino Venier
belonged to Elena
Priuli, the wife of the
procurator Federico
Venier.

S mall though it is by
comparison with the other districts of
Venice, the sestiere of San Marco, at the heart of the city,
plays a crucial role in its cultural life, retaining considerable
importance because of its position between the Rialto ▲ *279*
and St Mark's Square ▲ *220*. Because it
is so central, and because it is semi-
enclosed by the southern loop of the
Grand Canal, this area was constantly
being altered until the beginning of the
19th century. In the past, construction,
demolition and reconstruction work was
always in progress in the vicinity of
St Mark's Square; today its maze of calli
(alleyways) is still packed with stalls and
workshops, magnificent patrician houses, museums, libraries
and theaters. Beyond these lie the broad light-flooded spaces
of the Campo Santo Stefano and the Campo Sant'Angelo, the
liveliest part of Venice's center, where the big hotels, banks,
travel agencies, antique shops, art galleries and booksellers
are all concentrated. (From the Piazzetta, take the
Fondamenta delle Farine to Calle Vallaresso).

HARRY'S BAR

**SESTIERE
DI
∩S.MARCO**

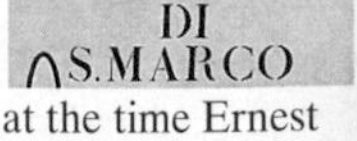

This celebrated restaurant and bar was
founded by Giuseppe Cipriani, who ran it at the time Ernest
Hemingway was staying in Venice. You can sample exquisite
tramezzini (sandwiches) and sip the famous Harry's Bar

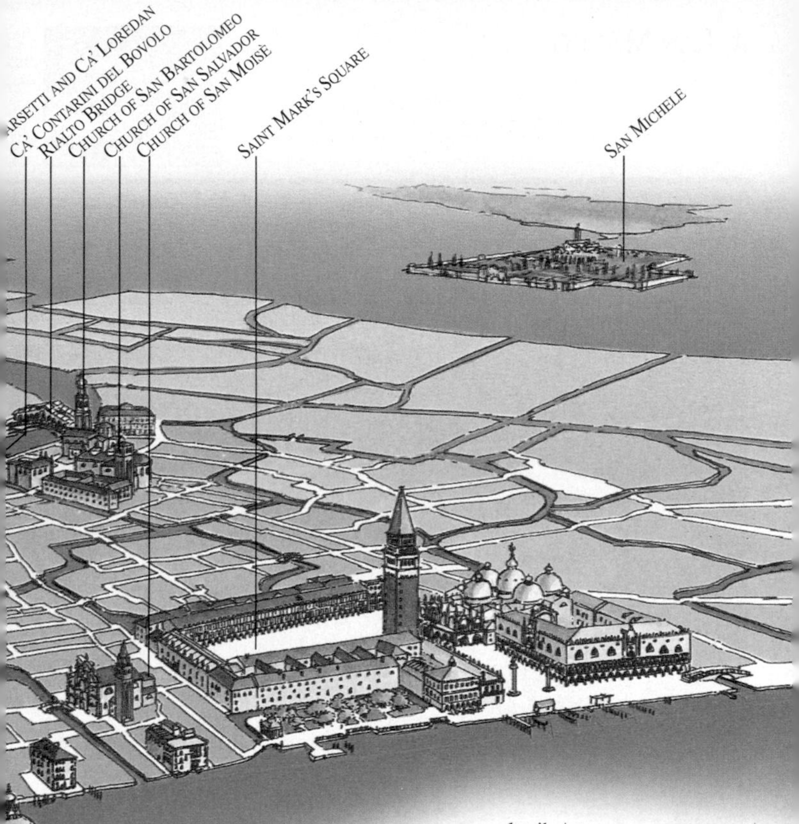

ARSETTI AND CA' LOREDAN
CA' CONTARINI DEL BOVOLO
RIALTO BRIDGE
CHURCH OF SAN BARTOLOMEO
CHURCH OF SAN SALVADOR
CHURCH OF SAN MOISÈ
SAINT MARK'S SQUARE
SAN MICHELE

cocktails of fruit juice and champagne, each named after one of Venice's great masters: for example, a Bellini (peach juice) or Tiziano (grape and pomegranate).

PALAZZO DANDOLO

A CELEBRATED RIDOTTO. In 1638, Marco Dandolo opened a public gaming room in his palace, which the Grand Council later described as a place of "solemn, continuous, universal and violent gambling". This *ridotto* was much frequented during carnival, when games of chance like *bassetta* and *faraone* were permitted. Ten rooms of the palace were devoted to this function; anyone might enter, but men were expected to wear the *bauto* ● *53*. In 1758, the Dandolo family commissioned the architect Bernardino Maccaruzzi and the painter Jacopo Guarana to renovate the old palace. Six smaller gaming rooms were built around the main hall: a pair of these were for dining, with wine, cheese, sausage and fruit in one, and tea, chocolate and coffee in the other ▲ *245*. On November 27, 1774, the Grand Council ordered the closure of the premises, because several families had been completely bankrupted there. The *ridotto* reopened under the French régime and was closed again by the Austrians. At the beginning of the 20th century one of

AN ESCORT TO THE RIDOTTO
The noblemen on their way to the *ridotto* wore the *bauto* and the white mask ● *53* so that they could go about the streets of Venice incognito. They took a lantern-bearer, or *codega*, who walked ahead of them.

This famous painting by Francesco Guardi shows a crowd of masked noblemen in the main hall of the Dandolo *ridotto*.

the most beautiful gaming rooms of the Palazzo Dandolo was turned into a cinema, and then converted into a theater in 1947. As such, it made a significant contribution to Venetian drama during a difficult period.

CASINI IN VENICE. The Grand Council's decision to close the *ridotto* on November 27, 1774, aroused strong protest, and the

THE LOTTERY
Introduced to Venice in 1522 by a certain Geronimo Bombarara, the idea of a lottery quickly spread among ordinary people, who were banned from the *ridotto*. In 1644 the government imposed a tax on the *loto*, and in 1734 it finally became a public institution.

gamblers simply decamped to resume play elsewhere. In theory, there had been free access to the *ridotto* for all, but in practice the stakes there were far too high for the gondoliers, artisans and servants to contemplate. As a result, ordinary people went to taverns to play cards or bet on the lottery; then, after the closure of the *ridotto*, the Venetian nobles duly followed suit, gravitating towards the city's cafés and casini. Casini were originally small apartments rented by patricians around St Mark's Square. Since they often had to attend Grand Council meetings, the patricians were obliged to wear their black robes constantly. This created a need for apartments near the palace where they could change clothes and relax – and they solved this problem by renting casini, under the arcades of the Procuratie ▲ *244*. The casini began as places of relaxation, but this soon changed and they became elegant bachelor apartments where people gathered to listen to music. With the 18th-century fashion for chinoiserie ● *45*, the décor and furnishings of the casini took on a strong flavor of the exotic and later, when gaming tables were installed, began to proliferate in earnest. The nobility had their own gaming houses, such as the CASINO DEI NOBILI at San Barnaba ▲ *334*, as did the ordinary people, who tended to favor casini outside Venice in places where there was also space to play ball games. From their beginnings around St Mark's Square, the casini spread through the neighboring parishes and beyond. The magistrates, forced to acknowledge

their inability to prevent gambling, instead began regulating and exploiting it with official gambling houses. (From Calle Vallaresso, take two lefts onto Calle del Ridotto.)

PALAZZO GIUSTINIAN

This Gothic palazzo (c.1474) fronting the Grand Canal is now the headquarters of the Venice Biennale ▲ *184*. For a while (c.1432) it was the home of the patriarch of San Pietro di Castello ▲ *182*, Lorenzo Giustiniani; later it passed to the Morosini family during the 17th century. It was then restored, and extensive additions were made to its façade. The interior still retains part of its original 17th-century decoration. (Return to the salizzada.)

SAN MOISÈ

THE CHURCH OF SAN MOISÈ. This church, originally dedicated to St Victor and probably founded in the 8th century, was rededicated to Moses after Moisè Venier paid for it to be rebuilt in the middle of the 9th century. A second rebuilding took place in the first half of the 11th century, after the church was destroyed by fire. It was not touched again until 1632, when the structure was completely changed. The present façade was built in 1668 by Alessandro Tremignon and paid for by a bequest from Vincenzo and Gerolamo Fini, who wanted their effigies placed within the church. Thus San Moisè became a kind of lavish mausoleum, filled with sculptures by the Flemish artist Meyring, a disciple of Bernini: many of these sculptures were removed in 1878. Today the interior is notable for its painting of *La Lavanda dei Piedi* by Tintoretto, and a *Last Supper* attributed to Palma the Younger. The celebrated courtesan Veronica Franco died in this parish in 1591, and is buried here. On the campo is one of Venice's better-known hotels, the BAUER GRÜNWALD. (Take the Calle Barozzi as far as the Corte del Teatro.)

SAN MOISÈ THEATER COURTYARD. This courtyard was the site of the first theater in Venice. Built in 1620 as a venue for comedies, the theater turned to opera a few years later with a performance of Monteverdi's *Arianna* ▲ *174, 263*. In the 18th century, several works by Vivaldi, Albinoni and Galuppi were performed there (the latter with librettos by Goldoni). A century later, the theater first premièred Rossini. Closed in 1820, it was reopened in 1871 as a puppet theater, before becoming a cinema and finally a private house.

PLAYING CARDS
They were kept in small lacquered wood boxes, and decorated with chinoiserie patterns ● *45*.

VERONICA FRANCO
This poetess and courtesan, who died age forty-five in the parish of San Moisè, left money to permit two ladies of her profession to marry or take the veil; if none were forthcoming, the cash was then intended to serve as a dowry for two young girls.

THE THEATER OF LA FENICE

THE BIRTH OF LA FENICE. In 1774, the San Benedetto Theater, which had been Venice's leading opera house for more than forty years, was burned to the ground. No sooner had it been rebuilt than a legal dispute broke out between the company managing it and the owners, the Venier family. The issue was decided in favor of the Veniers, with the result that the theater company decided to build a new opera house of its own on the Campo San Fantin. From the twenty-nine architectural plans which were submitted, the one by Gian Antonio Selva was chosen. The building works began in June 1790; by May 1792 the auditorium was completed. It was named *"La Fenice"* (The Phoenix), in an allusion to the

In 1808, when the French had been back in Venice for two years, Selva completed the Imperial box at La Fenice.

company's survival, first of the fire, then of expulsion from its former base. La Fenice was inaugurated on May 16, 1792 with an opera by Giovanni Paisiello entitled *I Giochi di Agrigento* (*Distractions of Agrigento*). The libretto was written by Alessandro Pepoli.

"SENSO"
The opening scenes of Visconti's *Senso* (center) based on the *Secret Journal of Countess Livia,* take place at La Fenice on May 27, 1866, during the Austrian occupation.
Towards the end of the third act of Verdi's *Il Trovatore*, the Italian patriots throw leaflets and tricolored cockades onto the stage and into the stalls, shouting "Viva Verdi"! (Viva Vittore-Emmanuelle, Rei d'Italia).

THE FAME OF LA FENICE. From the beginning of the 19th century, La Fenice acquired a European reputation. Rossini mounted two major productions in the theater and Bellini had two operas premièred there. Donizetti, fresh from his triumphs in Milan and Naples, returned to Venice – and La Fenice – in 1836, after an absence of seventeen years. Thus the three greatest Italian composers of the period each affirmed the theater's pre-eminence, but in December 1836 it was tragically burned down yet again. The following year Giambattista and Tommaso Meduna were commissioned to design a new theater, with décor by Tranquillo Orsi. La Fenice rose once again from its ashes on the evening of December 26, 1837.

VERDI AT LA FENICE. Verdi's association with La Fenice began in 1844, with a performance of *Hernani* during the Carnival season. Over the next thirteen years, the world premières of *Attila*, *Rigoletto*, *La Traviata* and *Simon Boccanegra* all took place there.

LA FENICE IN THE 20TH CENTURY. After a period of closure during the First World War, La Fenice again became the scene of intense activity, attracting the world's greatest singers and conductors. In 1930, the Biennale ▲ *184* initiated the First International Festival of Contemporary Music, which brought composers like Stravinsky and Britten, and more recently Berio, Nono and Bussotti, to write for La Fenice. Latterly, as part of the theater's bicentenary celebrations, La Fenice has put on a series of revivals of some of its greatest triumphs.

The phoenix, symbol of the theater, was a mythological bird reputed to rise from its own ashes: in the case of the theater which bore its name, this has already happened three times.

MONTEVERDI: THE FIRST GOLDEN AGE OF OPERA.

In 1607, Monteverdi's *Orfeo* was performed before the court of Mantua. The Florentines Peri and Caccini had previously sought to subordinate music to dramatic expression, with sterile and mechanical results. But with Monteverdi, the libretto remained intelligible, yet gained new meaning from the music, which the composer based entirely on emotional expression and the seductive power of the human voice. "With Monteverdi," wrote the French commentator Romain Rolland, "the cause of opera was won."

THE FIRST OPERA HOUSES. In 1637, the San Canciano Theater performed Europe's first opera before a paying public. The final works by Monteverdi were, of course, shown in Venice. Opera had at last emerged from the closed world of princely courts; it became a fiercely competitive business for several of the city's great families, who opened their own opera houses. Each year they mounted one or two seasons, hence the need for a constant renewal of the repertoire. This explains why the 17th-century Venetian school, represented by composers like Pier Francesco Cavalli and Marc'Antonio Cesti, was so prolific.

GRANDEUR AND DECADENCE. From the early 18th century, Venice gradually yielded operatic primacy to Naples, where Alessandro Scarlatti, the pioneer of *opera seria*, was making his mark and comic opera began to emerge in about 1730. This loss of primacy did not cause a decline. On the contrary, the new Venetian genre was represented by Galuppi ▲ *361*, who set to music three libretti by Goldoni ▲ *291*. Vivaldi ▲ *175* became director of the Sant'Angelo Theater and composed a number of operas, most of which are now lost. Venice still attracted composers, but its public grew fickle. In a city which saw the creation of 1,274 operas in little over a generation, reputations were as quickly forgotten as made.

THE BURNING OF LA FENICE
At 3am on the night of December 12–13, 1836, the alarm was sounded by the bells of the San Marco campanile ▲ *248* – the theater of La Fenice was in flames. On January 29, 1996, while in the process of restoration, the theater was once more the victim of fire. Distress was such that central government responded by allocating funds to cover two thirds of the reconstruction works, expecting to receive international donations sufficient to cover the remainder needed to complete the repairs to this outstanding opera house.

THE CURTAIN
In 1878, La Fenice commissioned a curtain with a historical theme from the painter Ermolao Paoletti. Paoletti chose a famous episode from Venetian history: the official welcome in front of the Doge's palace of the force that crushed the Turkish armada at Lepanto ● *36*.

SCUOLA DI SAN FANTIN
The guild of the Scuola di San Fantin (also known as the *Picai*, or "hanged men") had the duty of bringing solace to men condemned to death, and of following them in gloomy procession to the scaffold, dressed in black hoods.

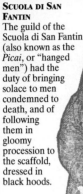

SAN FANTIN

THE CHURCH OF SAN FANTIN. This church stands opposite the entrance of La Fenice. Founded during the 9th century, and then reconstructed after a "miraculous" image of the Virgin was brought here from the Orient, the original sanctuary was demolished in 1506 along with its campanile. The following year the architect Scarpagnino began work on the building that we see today. The church was still unfinished when Scarpagnino died, but was completed by Sansovino in 1564. His contribution included the choir, with a dome resting on four grandiose Corinthian columns. On the walls, with their surface of white marble, hang two paintings by Palma the Younger, a *Deposition of Christ* (on the right-hand side) and *The Doge Luigi Mocenigo Kneeling in Gratitude for the Victory at Lepanto* (on the left).

THE SCUOLA. Built in 1471, the Scuola was redesigned at the close of the 16th century by Alessandro Vittoria. After the suppression of the guilds, in 1812 the building became the headquarters of the Ateneo Veneto (the Venetian Academy of Letters and Sciences). The ground floor gallery contains fourteen canvases by Palma the Younger, depicting the souls of the dead in purgatory. The reading room on the first floor, which has a ceiling decorated by the same artist, also contains a painting by Tintoretto entitled *Saint Jerome Receiving the Gifts of the Merchants*. (Rejoin the Calle XXII Marzo and then continue along the Calle dei Ostreghi).

TOWARDS THE CAMPO SANTO STEFANO

The Church and Campo San Maurizio.

SANTA MARIA DEL GIGLIO. This area is also known as Santa Maria Zobenigo, a name which has been distorted from that of a Slavic family, the Jubanicos, who once owned a sumptuous palace on the site. During the Festival of La Salute ● 49, ▲ 320 a wooden bridge is erected from the campo across the Grand Canal. At other times of the year one can cross the water on the traghetto ● 57, which has plied to and fro along this route ever since the 14th century. The CHURCH OF SANTA MARIA DEL GIGLIO owes its name to the lily which the Archangel is said to have carried at the Annunciation. It is also known as Santa Maria Zobenigo because the Jubanico family contributed generously to its foundation in the 10th century. It was completely rebuilt in the second half of the 17th century, at which time Antonio Barbaro, a high official in Dalmatia, commissioned Giuseppe Sardi to design the façade, donating thirty thousand ducats for the purpose. Inside the sanctuary are a number of paintings,

THE FAÇADE OF THE CHURCH OF SANTA MARIA ZOBENIGO
This is one of the most important examples of the Venetian Baroque style, with statues of the four Barbaro brothers (the one of Antonio Barbaro is by the Fleming Josse Le Court), and the allegorical figures of Glory, Fame and Wisdom extolling civil and military virtues. The base of the columns is carved with bas-reliefs representing naval battles, and maps of Zara, Candia, Padua, Rome, Corfu and Spalato (above). These allude to the military expeditions undertaken by the Barbaro family on behalf of Venice.

notably some portraits by Palma the Younger, Tintoretto's Evangelists (*Mark and John; Matthew and Luke*), and a *Virgin and Child with St John*, which has been attributed to Rubens (above). The 13th-century campanile fell down in 1775; it was never rebuilt, and today its base is occupied by shops.
CAMPO SAN MAURIZIO. This charming campo, which is dominated by the Church of San Maurizio, lies on the route between St Mark's Square ▲ *220* and the Grand Canal ▲ *187*. Founded in the 11th century, it was rebuilt in 1580 so that its façade overlooked the campo. In 1806, the church was demolished and rebuilt again by the architects Antonio Diedo and Giovanni Antonio Selva. To the right is the old SCUOLA DEGLI ALBANESI, the façade of which (1531) is decorated with classically inspired Renaissance bas-reliefs. Opposite the church is the PALAZZO BELLAVITE, built by a rich oil and flour merchant, Dionisio Bellavite. Because he wanted his façade to be as lavish as possible, no expense was spared, particularly with regard to the delicate working of the stone, which forms a lovely contrast to the frescoes by Veronese (c.1555) and a series of monochrome friezes of chubby cherubs and other allegorical figures. The poet Giorgio Baffo (1694–1768) lived in this palazzo at one time. He was famous for his lewd poems written in the Venetian dialect. Another famous occupant, in 1803, was the writer Alessandro Manzoni. (Continue along the Calle del Piovan and the Calle del Spezier.)

THE ANTIQUE MARKET
For those interested in antiques, there is a small market held in the Campo San Maurizio at various times of year, particularly at Easter and on All Saints' Day.

CAMPO SANTO STEFANO

CAMPO SANTO STEFANO

Today, this campo has lost none of its former liveliness. Up until 1802 it was the site of bull-running, ● *50*, which was then cancelled after one of the stands collapsed. In 1807, the Piazza San Marco market was moved to here, and in 1809 it was moved again – to San Polo ▲ *285*. During the time of the Republic, the campo was a favorite Venetian promenade, since it was still covered in grass – with the exception of a paved central avenue (the *liston*).

CAMPO SANTO STEFANO ★

Officially known as CAMPO MOROSINI, this open area lies at the heart of the most fashionable quarter of the city. At its center is a large STATUE (in itself a rarity for Venice) of Nicolò Tommaseo, the writer, patriot and leader of the Venetian uprising ● *34* ▲ *275* in 1848.

PALAZZO LOREDAN. In 1536, the Loredan family commissioned the architect Scarpagnino to rebuild this palazzo, which until that time had belonged to another great Venetian family, the Mocenigos. The long façade, with its broad, many-arched window, was once decorated with frescoes on Roman themes by Giallo Fiorentino and Giuseppe Porta. The palace was enlarged in 1618, a substantial reception hall being added on one wing. This new wing was adorned with a façade in Istrian stone, attributed by some to Palladio, although it is more likely to have been the work of his assistant, Giovanni Girolamo Grapiglia, who was the Loredan family's architect. In 1809 General d'Illiers, the first French governor of Venice, lived in the Palazzo Loredan. He had the reception hall decorated with frescoes, which were obliterated when the Austrians resumed control of the city. In 1840 Ferdinand I, Emperor of Austria, founded the Istituto Veneti di Scienze, Lettere ed Arti (the Venetian Institute of Science, Arts and Letters); the Palazzo Loredan became this institute's headquarters and has remained so ever since. It maintains a rich library, with one of the largest collections of periodicals in Italy.

PALAZZO MOROSINI. The Morosini family acquired this 14th-century palace in 1648. Its façade, then decorated with frescoes of scenes from antiquity by Antonio Aliense, was covered with stone to fit in with contemporary taste. At the close of the 17th century, Francesco Morosini ● *40* commissioned the family's architect, Antonio Gaspari, to undertake a fresh restoration (1688–94).

This was the origin of the Venetian expression "to go to the *liston*" (to go for a walk).

In the second courtyard of Palazzo Pisani – designed in the 18th century by the Paduan architect Girolamo Frigimelica – stands the mysterious statue of a veiled woman, whose identity has never been discovered, despite the best efforts of many researchers.

As a tribute to the owner's naval triumphs, a sea-horse's head was sculpted over the main doorway, with sea monsters above the side entrances. The illustrious client and his architect devised a project to unite the palace with a neighboring building belonging to the Morosini. The two houses shared a large courtyard, but their floor levels did not match; Gaspari corrected this, enriched the interiors with stucco, paintings and sculptures, and set aside a gallery in which the armor and war trophies of the Morosini family could be exhibited. At the end of the 18th century a further modernization was carried out by Gianantonio Selva, who removed the more baroque elements from the façade. In 1894 the Counts of Gattemburg (from Salzburg), who had inherited the palace, sold its precious collections at auction. The city of Venice acquired the collection of arms and armor, the archives and objects which had belonged to Francesco Morosini himself (now exhibited at the Correr Museum ▲ 246), and lastly a series of paintings by Pietro Longhi, now at the Ca' Rezzonico ▲ 332.

The inner courtyard of Palazzo Pisani, now the Conservatory of Music.

PALAZZO PISANI. This palace overlooks the Campiello Pisani, a delightful square in which lyrical plays and ballets are performed in summer. The building itself is one of the biggest in Venice, a charming mass of LOGGIAS, staircases, porticos and labyrinthine courtyards. Built in 1614–15, the Palazzo Pisani was designed around a splendid main courtyard surrounded by loggias, one above the next. In 1688 and 1716 the Pisanis acquired adjacent properties and enlarged their palace to plans by the Paduan architect Frigimelica. The result was completely faced with Istrian stone, and included a second main floor with a ballroom and library. The interior was decorated by the most prominent painters of the time – Guarana, Amigoni, Ricci, Pittoni and Tiepolo. In 1793 it was modernized by Bernardino Maccuruzzi, who added many more stucco features, particularly on the mezzanine floor. In 1880, after the death of Almoro, the last of the Pisanis, the palazzo became the headquarters of the BENEDETTO MARCELLO MUSIC

The campanile and the galleried clocktower ● 85, rising over the sacristy of the Church of Santo Stefano and the rooftops of one of Venice's busiest campi.

CONSERVATORY, an institute which owns a number of autographed manuscripts by Venetian composers.

THE CHURCH OF SANTO STEFANO. The façade of this church is immediately striking on account of its huge rose window and long side windows. However, the sculptures over the main portal, created in the workshop of Bartolomeo Bon, are its chief glory. Founded at the end of the 13th century by the Augustinians, and financed in part by the Republic, this Gothic church was altered in the early 18th century, when it was considerably lengthened. The apse was extended beyond the Rio

One of the two wells in Campo Santo Stefano.

The façade of the former Scuola dei Laneri still boasts a small 15th-century bas-relief in which the guild is seen gathered in adoration around the figure of Stephen, their patron saint.

del Santissimo di San Stefano, which was never filled in, so one can still pass beneath the church by boat, although there is little headroom. Inside, the principal feature is the ceiling, which looks like a richly decorated inverted ship's hull and is one of the few of this type still intact. The CORO DEI FRATI (monks' stalls) which faced the choir were dismantled in the 16th century and replaced in part behind the main altar. The church also boasts remarkable Lombard sculptures, and paintings by Bartolomeo Vivarini, Palma the Elder, Marieschi and Tintoretto, which were brought here over the centuries. Santo Stefano is the burial place of a number of people who performed great services to the Republic, foremost among them the Doge Francesco Morosini ● *40*. The church's convent buildings, which stand between it and the Campo Sant'Angelo, are built around a cloister restructured by lo Scarpagnino.

SCUOLA DEI LANERI. This building opposite the main entrance to the church was built with help from the Augustinians in 1437, then enlarged in 1473. The former Scuola di Santo Stefano, founded on March 3, 1298, became the Scuola dei Laneri di Santo Stefano after it was taken over in 1506 by an influx of merchants and artisans trading in woollen goods (*laneri*). At this time the scuola acquired five canvases (1511–20) by Carpaccio representing episodes in the life of St Stephen; one of them was lost and the other four were dispersed during the 19th century. In the second half of the 18th century, the corporation went through a deep crisis in which the scuola had to lease its chapel to a cheese merchant to survive. By the time of its abolition by Napoleonic decree in 1806, it had effectively ceased to exist. Today, heavily altered and two floors taller than before, the old building is occupied by a restaurant.

THE FORMER CHURCH OF SAN VITALE. This church was founded in 1084 under the Doge Vitale Falieri and was restored many times before being completely rebuilt in 1696 by the architect Antonio Gaspari. Its façade was originally designed to celebrate the exploits of Francesco Morosini, but was ultimately executed in the Palladian style by Andrea Tirali, who added a row of Corinthian columns. Inside, on a wall at the far end of the nave, hang two later works by Carpaccio: *Saint Vitale on Horseback* and *Four Saints Adoring the Virgin*. No longer used for worship, the church is now the headquarters of the Unione Cattolica dei Artisti Italiani, which holds exhibitions of its members' work. On St Vitale's day, the clergy of the parish used to go in

On the small Campo San Vitale, opposite the galleries of the Accademia ▲ *301*,

there stands a charming brightly colored palazzo, which is now the German Embassy.

procession to the ferry pier, where they met the clergy of neighboring San Trovaso ▲ *324*, presented them with a bouquet of flowers, and accompanied them back to San Vitale to say mass. This courtesy was returned by the San Trovaso clergy every June 16, on the feast day of San Gervasio and San Protasio.

TOWARDS SAN SAMUELE

CAMPO SANT'ANGELO. This campo owes its name to a church, dedicated to St Michael the Archangel, which was demolished in 1837. In the ORATORIO DELLA SANTISSIMA ANNUNZIATA is an *Annunciation* by Palma the Younger and a 16th-century wooden crucifix. The quarter was mainly inhabited by nobles and their palaces may be seen round the campo. Among these is PALAZZO DUODO where the musician Domenico Cimarosa (formerly Catherine the Great's Master of Music at her chapel in St Petersburg) died in 1801. There is also the 15th-century PALAZZO GRITTI, with its façade presaging the Renaissance style, and PALAZZO PISANI. Originally built for the Trevisan family, the latter passed to the Pisanis in the second half of the 17th century. In terms of style it belongs to the period just after Longhena, who was its original architect. A series of details (heads on the keystones of arches, balustrades and the general handling of the stonework) suggest the work of Domenico Rossi, or at least of his school. The interior of the palace has remained unaltered, but its original sumptuous furnishings have now vanished.

THE HOUSE OF VERONESE ▲ *310*. At 3338 Salizzado San Samuele stands the building in which the "magician of color" (to borrow a phrase from Giulio Lorenzetti) lived from 1583 until his death. Paolo Caliari, who was probably a native of Verona (hence his surname of "Veronese"), arrived in Venice in 1553. In the spring of 1588, while walking in a religious procession through Treviso, he went down with a violent fever. He was immediately taken to Venice, where he died a week later on April 19. Veronese is buried in the Church of San Sebastiano ▲ *326*, at the foot of the organ which he had decorated.

"Flag stones, walls, paved enclosed courtyards; all around are closed-up houses, making triangles or squares bulging outward in obedience to the need for more space, and to the flukes and accidents of building; and in the center is a delicately worked well-head with sculpted lions and naked figurines disporting themselves at its rim."
  Hippolyte Taine,
  Voyage en Italie

On the *altane* (wooden terraces) "balanced on the rooftops with the lightness and sureness of birds' nests" (Pier-Maria Pasinetti), the ladies of Venice would sit bleaching their hair blond using the ancient mixture of unguents

based on sulphur or lead mixed with alum.

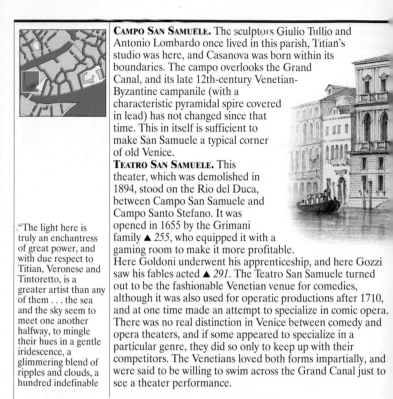

CAMPO SAN SAMUELE. The sculptors Giulio Tullio and Antonio Lombardo once lived in this parish, Titian's studio was here, and Casanova was born within its boundaries. The campo overlooks the Grand Canal, and its late 12th-century Venetian-Byzantine campanile (with a characteristic pyramidal spire covered in lead) has not changed since that time. This in itself is sufficient to make San Samuele a typical corner of old Venice.

TEATRO SAN SAMUELE. This theater, which was demolished in 1894, stood on the Rio del Duca, between Campo San Samuele and Campo Santo Stefano. It was opened in 1655 by the Grimani family ▲ *255*, who equipped it with a gaming room to make it more profitable. Here Goldoni underwent his apprenticeship, and here Gozzi saw his fables acted ▲ *291*. The Teatro San Samuele turned out to be the fashionable Venetian venue for comedies, although it was also used for operatic productions after 1710, and at one time made an attempt to specialize in comic opera. There was no real distinction in Venice between comedy and opera theaters, and if some appeared to specialize in a particular genre, they did so only to keep up with their competitors. The Venetians loved both forms impartially, and were said to be willing to swim across the Grand Canal just to see a theater performance.

"The light here is truly an enchantress of great power, and with due respect to Titian, Veronese and Tintoretto, is a greater artist than any of them . . . the sea and the sky seem to meet one another halfway, to mingle their hues in a gentle iridescence, a glimmering blend of ripples and clouds, a hundred indefinable

points of light, and then to cast this fine weave upon all visible objects."

Henry James

PALAZZO GRASSI

THE LAST OF THE GREAT VENETIAN PALACES. Palazzo Grassi was built for the powerful family of that name, who came from Chioggia, though their origins were Bolognese. In 1718, the Grassi joined the ranks of the patricians of Venice after contributing sixty thousand ducats to the final war against the Turks ● *34*. Their palace remains an important example of 18th-century civil architecture and is, chronologically, the last in the long line of great Venetian mansions. To build it, the Grassi commissioned the architect Giorgio Massari, who had just successfully completed the Ca' Rezzonico on the other side of the Grand Canal ▲ *332*. Massari, a pupil of Longhena, anticipated the rise of Neo-classicism with his plan for an imposing, stylistically perfect but somewhat cold building. A majestic staircase leads from the entrance hall to the main salon on the *piano nobile*, then on to various other rooms on succeeding floors. The walls are decorated with frescoes by Michelangelo Morleiter, in which picturesque groups of figures dressed in 18th-century costume lean over a trompe l'oeil balcony. Some of the rooms still have their original décors of stucco and fresco done by the school of Tiepolo. Elsewhere, Fabio Canal's work glorifies the Grassi – who eventually died out in

> "Between the still-slumbering walls of brick and marble, beneath the ribbon of the sky, more and more brightly gleamed the ribbon of the   water."
>
> Gabriele d'Annunzio

THE SECRET STAIRCASES
Giorgio Massari, who designed the Palazzo Grassi (the last major building on the Grand Canal), is said to have added a number of secret staircases, in which lovers could conceal themselves.

the 1830s, leaving their palace to the Counts Tornielli. Later it was sold to the celebrated operatic tenor Poggi, then served a while as a hotel before being turned into the celebrated degli Antoni bathhouse – drawing its water from the Grand Canal. For a number of years thereafter it was the headquarters of the International Art Center, which mounted performances in the palace's 18th-century open-air garden theater.

THE RESTORATION OF PALAZZO GRASSI. After surviving several more owners, the palace was bought by Fiat in 1984, with a view to setting up a center for cultural, artistic and scientific activities. For this purpose, the company had the building radically restored by the architects Gae Aulenti and Antonio Foscari. Their work was guided by three imperatives: to re-establish a sound structure for the palace, to respect its innate character, and to make it more suitable for exhibitions. It was designed so that light would flood in everywhere and the central courtyard was covered by a glass roof. Color, too, was freely used – pink for the walls, pale green for the *boiseries*. In the stairway, as in the first-floor rooms, the frescoes and painted ceilings have been preserved in their original state.

MAJOR EVENTS AT PALAZZO GRASSI. The restored palace was inaugurated in May 1986 with an exhibition entitled "Futurisms". A year later came an exhibition on Arcimboldo and the transformation of the human face in art between the 16th and 20th centuries. Since then, Palazzo Grassi has

hosted a wide range of exhibitions, from the Phoenicians to modern art and Italian art 1900–45. There have also been shows dedicated to the Celts, Leonardo da Vinci, Andy Warhol, Marcel Duchamp, the Venetian and northern European painting. (Return via the Campo Santo Stefano, then along Calle dei Frati; at the end of Campo Sant'Angelo, turn left into Calle degli Avocati, then take the Calle Pesaro on the right.)

Since the restoration of the Palazzo Grassi, a wide variety of major exhibitions has been organized there every year.

Towards the Rialto Bridge

PALAZZO FORTUNY, OR PESARO, OR DEGLI ORFEI. (Number 3958 on Campo San Benedetto.) This imposing building was originally the property of the Pesaros, a rich merchant family which supplied Venice with a succession of politicians and admirals ▲ *195*. The palace dates from the end of the 15th century and is a superb example of Decorated Gothic, enriched with Renaissance elements. The building is arranged around two inner courtyards which are so huge that, in the 16th century, theatrical performances were regularly held in them. Its façades, which overlook the campo and Rio di Ca' Michiel, contain two rows of gemelled windows, with balconies supported by lions. The first and second floors each have their own *portego*, a salon which measures no less than 51 feet in length. The palace is also known as PALAZZO DEGLI ORFEI (Palace of the Orpheans) because, after the Pesaro family had departed to the new quarters which they had built at San Stae ▲ *351*, it became the headquarters of a famous philharmonic society called the Orphean Academy, which organized

balls and concerts. Later, the palace came into the hands of the Apollinea Academy, which subsequently moved to La Fenice ▲ *262*. At the end of the 19th century the building was finally purchased by MARIANO FORTUNY Y MADRAZO (1871–1949), painter, photographer, fabric designer, couturier and inventor of genius. Fortuny was born in Granada. Following the death of his father, a famous painter and collector of fabrics, he moved to Venice in 1889. Ten years later he took over Palazzo Pesaro, divided up the space with hangings, covered the walls with fabrics, and then set up a workshop on the first floor, which he filled with works of art. The second floor was reserved for his studio; an excellent physicist and chemist, Fortuny worked constantly at his many inventions. He devised new lighting systems for the theater, and also a reflective, moveable dome, which helped to give a sky-like illusion of depth. It was also for the theater that he created his first female dancers' costume, the "Knossos scarf", in 1906. The following year he introduced his first "Delphos dress" (facing page), in pleated silk. Its name was a homage to the statue of the *Charioteer of Delphi*, and the dress was inspired by the linen *chitons* of ancient Greece. The pleating was done by a process which was patented by Fortuny in 1909, in which the folds were set by hand into moistened fabric, then sewn in place and finally sealed with a hot iron.

On February 19, 1515, the Compagnie della Calza degli Immortali put on a performance of Plautus' *Miles Gloriosus* in the main courtyard of Palazzo Pesaro, which was hung with rich fabrics for the occasion. Among the audience that day were the family of Doge Leonardo Loredan, the Ambassador of the King of France, and many noble ladies.

> "Fortuny's dresses, which combine originality with
> fidelity to the past, bear decorative witness [...]
> to Venice's debt to the Orient."
>
> Marcel Proust

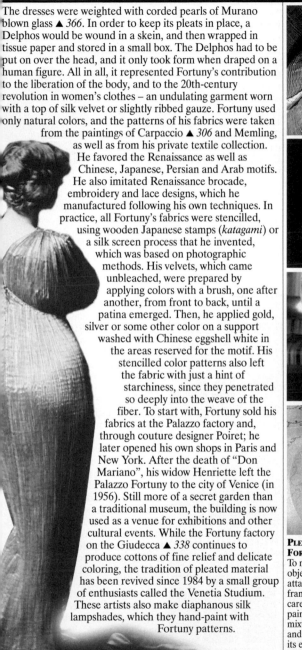

The dresses were weighted with corded pearls of Murano blown glass ▲ 366. In order to keep its pleats in place, a Delphos would be wound in a skein, and then wrapped in tissue paper and stored in a small box. The Delphos had to be put on over the head, and it only took form when draped on a human figure. All in all, it represented Fortuny's contribution to the liberation of the body, and to the 20th-century revolution in women's clothes – an undulating garment worn with a top of silk velvet or slightly ribbed gauze. Fortuny used only natural colors, and the patterns of his fabrics were taken from the paintings of Carpaccio ▲ 306 and Memling, as well as from his private textile collection. He favored the Renaissance as well as Chinese, Japanese, Persian and Arab motifs. He also imitated Renaissance brocade, embroidery and lace designs, which he manufactured following his own techniques. In practice, all Fortuny's fabrics were stencilled, using wooden Japanese stamps (*katagami*) or a silk screen process that he invented, which was based on photographic methods. His velvets, which came unbleached, were prepared by applying colors with a brush, one after another, from front to back, until a patina emerged. Then, he applied gold, silver or some other color on a support washed with Chinese eggshell white in the areas reserved for the motif. His stencilled color patterns also left the fabric with just a hint of starchiness, since they penetrated so deeply into the weave of the fiber. To start with, Fortuny sold his fabrics at the Palazzo factory and, through couture designer Poiret; he later opened his own shops in Paris and New York. After the death of "Don Mariano", his widow Henriette left the Palazzo Fortuny to the city of Venice (in 1956). Still more of a secret garden than a traditional museum, the building is now used as a venue for exhibitions and other cultural events. While the Fortuny factory on the Giudecca ▲ 338 continues to produce cottons of fine relief and delicate coloring, the tradition of pleated material has been revived since 1984 by a small group of enthusiasts called the Venetia Studium. These artists also make diaphanous silk lampshades, which they hand-paint with Fortuny patterns.

PLEATED SILK AND FORTUNY LAMPS
To make these fragile objects, the silk is attached to a brass framework, then carefully hand-painted with a mixture of silver, oil and color; after that its edges are trimmed with Murano glass beads. A single one of these lamps can represent a week's hard work for ten people.

273

IL BOVOLO
The semicircular arches of this spiral staircase give it an airy quality; its construction appears to reproduce the classic Byzantine stairway-tower, in the style of the period. It is said to be Renaissance in its columns, Gothic in its method of construction, and half Venetian-Byzantine, half Renaissance in its form. It is thought that Giovanni Candi was the architect.

THE CHURCH OF SAN BENEDETTO. The present building dates from 1685. On the lower left-hand side of the aisle hangs Giambattista Tiepolo's *Saint Francis de Paule*, which has been heavily restored. (Take the Salizzada del Teatro, then Calle San Paternian.)

CAMPO MANIN. This campo received its name after 1875, at the suggestion of the patriot Giorgio Casarin, to honor the memory of Daniele Manin, leader of the 1848 Venice uprising ● *34*. The Savings Bank building here is one of the very few modern constructions in Venice (1968).

CA' CONTARINI DEL BOVOLO. This palace, which is a mixture of Renaissance and Gothic, could not be confused with any other. In the late 15th century, with a view to enlarging his home, Pietro Contarini added a series of loggias to it, which were linked together by a round tower with a spiral staircase. This tower so caught the imagination of the Venetians that they nicknamed the palazzo "Contarini del Bovolo" (of the snail). It was later converted into an hotel during the 19th century, then converted back to private use again. Today it is the headquarters of an organization which oversees the city's educational foundations. (Return to Campo Manin, then follow the Ramo della Salizzada.)

THE CHURCH OF SAN LUCA. San Luca features an altarpiece by Veronese, *The Virgin Appearing to Saint Luke*, at its high altar, and a *Virgin and Saints* by Palma the Younger. The writer Aretino is buried in this church. He is said to have died laughing, having been provoked by an obscene remark made about his sister (1556).

CAMPO SAN LUCA. This campo is a popular and lively meeting place for the city's young people. The marble plinth in the middle of the square is supposed to mark the exact center point of Venice; since it bears the arms of the Scuola della Carità and of various painters, it may refer to Bajamonte Tiepolo's conspiracy ▲ *214*, which his colleagues contrived to foil. (Continue along Calle del Forno, Calle del Teatro and Calle dell'Ovo.)

THE CHURCH OF SAN SALVADOR. No more can be seen of this church than the façade and part of the apse, because it is otherwise blocked by the adjacent monastery, whose monks were once notorious for their "licentiousness". Legend has it that a pre-8th century chapel once stood on this spot, but no church or monastery is mentioned

During the period of the Republic, Venice was subdivided into about seventy different parishes (*parrocchie*).

before the 11th century. The church was consecrated in 1177 by Pope Alexander III in person, when he came to Venice in order to conclude the peace treaty with the Emperor Barbarossa ● *30*. The architectural ensemble was restructured at the start of the 16th century. Begun by Giorgio Spavento in 1506, the works were continued under the direction of Tullio Lombardo. Finally Jacopo Sansovino added the two cloisters at the end of the Calle dell'Ovo and completed the main church between 1530 and 1534. San Salvador, which was much admired at the time for its modernity, has one grave defect, namely its lack of light. To compensate for this, Scamozzi placed a lantern in each of its domes (1569). The three-part façade, with its matching doorway, was designed by Giuseppe Sardi. Among the many monuments inside is that of the Doge Francesco Venier by Sansovino. He also contributed the altar in the CHAPEL OF ST AUGUSTIN which harbors Titian's retable, *The Annunciation*.

SCUOLA DI SAN TEODORO ● *87*. This building is said to date back to the time when St Theodore was still the patron saint of Venice ▲ *251*. But the first real mention of it does not come until 1258, at which time it was attached to the Church of San Salvador. With its pupils increasing in number, the scuola moved into a part of the monastery, but when the monks decided to restructure their building, the members of the scuola were obliged to move once again. On April 8, 1551, the scuola took possession of its new premises, and in December of that same year it was assigned an altar (to the left of the high altar) in the church. Then, in 1552 the guild was designated a "Scuola Grande" ▲ *295*, and so needed a building worthy of the new title. Several contiguous sites were bought and, in 1576, Antonio Sardi and his son Giuseppe won a competition for the architectural contract. Longhena then completed the second floor of the façade, which looks out on to the Calle dell'Ovo. After its suppression in 1806, the scuola was stripped of many of its art treasures, but it did retain its ceilings by Giovanni Segala and Giacomo Filippo Parodi. The building subsequently went through a number of successive identities as a repository for archives, an antique shop, a cinema and then a furniture warehouse, before the scuola was finally reconstituted in 1960. Today, the guild is responsible for running the building once again, and uses it to stage commercial and cultural exhibitions. (Take the Calle Larga Mazzini towards the Grand Canal, passing in front of Palazzo Dolfin-Manin, which was once the property of Ludovico Manin, the last Doge of Venice, and is now a branch of the Bank of Italy. From here, continue along the Riva del Ferro.)

DANIELE MANIN ● *34*

Born in Venice on May 13, 1804, Manin became a lawyer after completing his studies in Padua. In 1840 he began to take an interest in the

politics of the Republic, and in January 1848 he was arrested with Nicolò Tommaseo ▲ *266*. Two months later he was set free by the insurgents, who occupied the Arsenale. In the evening of March 22, the Austrians surrendered, and Manin became President of the short-lived Republic. An advocate of all-out resistance to the powerful Austrian forces, he was given full powers in August; but Austria was determined to reconquer Venice and on August 24, 1849, Manin's government was forced to capitulate. He died in exile in Paris, in 1857.

On December 20, 1883 a monument to Carlo Goldoni ▲ 291 was erected on Campo San Bartolomeo. The cast, of bronze, was made by the sculptor Dal Zotto.

CAMPO SAN BARTOLOMEO. Originally a market area, this campo is still a popular meeting place for Venetians. During the 9th century a little church dedicated to St Demetrius stood here, which was rebuilt in the 12th century and given the name of San Bartolomeo Apostolo. With the development of the Rialto quarter ▲ 279, the church gained in importance, but it remained half-hidden by new construction; today we can only see its side entrance and campanile. It was not until some radical restoration work had taken place in 1723 that San Bartolomeo assumed its present form. For a while the church possessed a painting by Albrecht Dürer, *The Feast of the Rosary*, which was commissioned from the artist by the German community in Venice. This passed into the collection of Emperor Rudolph II in 1606, and is now at the National Museum in Prague. San Bartolomeo is now deconsecrated and is used as a site for temporary exhibitions.

FONDACO DEI TEDESCHI. The term *fondaco* or *fontego* comes from the Arabic word *fonduc*, which means an inn, a warehouse, or a place for commercial transactions. Built in 1228, this building was occupied by the accountants and experts who oversaw the commercial activity of the Rialto. When trade with northern Europe became vital to Venetian interests, it was reserved for the use of German merchants. At about this time the *fondaco* was transformed into a market and, when the original building was destroyed by fire, the city replaced it between 1506 and 1508 with the huge two-hundred-room building which we see today. Its coping, portico and two small corner-towers (destroyed in 1838) were all copied from older Venetian-Byzantine models, while its overall plan and façades are both clearly Renaissance in style. Giorgione and the young Titian decorated the latter between 1508 and 1509. It would appear that the two painters' cycle of frescoes alluded to the solidity and stability of the Republic of St Mark, which was founded on the twin principles of peace and justice. Giorgione painted the allegory of peace on the main façade, while Titian took care of Justice, producing an allegory of *Judith*. Only a few restored fragments of these works survive today, and they can be viewed in the Ca' d'Oro ▲ 148, 196. In 1806, Napoleon put an abrupt end to the activities of the Germans in the *fondaco* and turned the building into a customs house. Since 1870, it has served as the city of Venice's Central Post Office.

San Polo

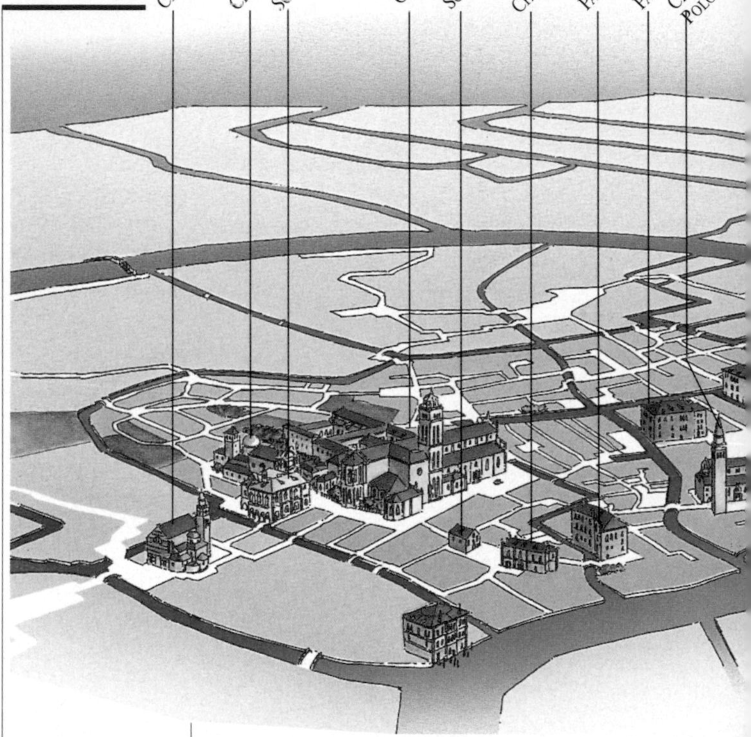

CHURCH OF SAN PANTALON
CHURCH OF SAN ROCCO ✪
SCUOLA DI SAN ROCCO ✪
CHURCH OF SANTA MARIA GLORIOSA DEI FRARI ✪
SCUOLA DEI CALEGHERI
CHURCH OF SAN TOMÀ
PALAZZO CENTANI
PALAZZO CORNER-M
CHURCH OF S
POLO

URBAN DEVELOPMENT
During the 9th and 10th centuries, the Rialto area consisted of little more than a cluster of small islands which were set in the midst of sandbanks and marshland. Then, between the 10th and 11th centuries, the land was progressively drained and a new commercial center grew up beside the Grand Canal, crisscrossed by numerous footpaths.

Enclosed by the wide loop of the Grand Canal, the 84-acre sestiere of San Polo is Venice's smallest district. To the east it includes the Rialto, one of the city's livelier zones and certainly one of its most ancient; indeed the very name "Rialto" harks back to Venice's remote origins. In the 9th century there was a small settlement in the middle of the lagoon, called *Rivoaltus* (upper bank) because the land there was higher than elsewhere and thus less prone to flooding. After the year 810, the Doge moved his residence to Malamocco ● *30*, which became the heart of the new state. It extended over a cluster of small islands (the Realtine Islands) and at its center was the Rio Businiacus, the future Grand Canal, and the two sestieri known to us today as San Marco and San Polo. Only the left bank was to retain the name of "Rialto" when the city of Venice was undergoing its greatest expansion two centuries later. Another century passed; then, in 1097, the main market which had been located on the right bank was moved to the island opposite, to a site beside the waterway. During the 12th century, a pontoon of boats was thrown across the Grand Canal to link the two banks together; it was subsequently replaced by a wooden bridge some time between 1200 and 1260. At that time a major

PALAZZO BERNARDO · PALAZZI SORANZO · PALAZZO ALBRIZZI · PALAZZO TIEPOLO MAFFETTI · CHURCH OF SANT'APONAL · CHURCH OF SAN CASSIANO · CHURCH OF SAN SILVESTRO · PESCHERIA · FABBRICHE NUOVE · CHURCH OF SAN GIACOMO DI RIALTO · PALAZZO DEI CAMERLENGHI · RIALTO BRIDGE

🚶 1/2 journée

◆ B A D6-E6-F6

THE RIALTO: CONSTANTLY BUZZING ✪

In the morning, the Rialto is filled with Venetians buying fruit and vegetables, making their way past tourists who come to take pictures of this colorful market. Later, the Rialto fills with souvenir merchants. At night, the bridge is perfect for moonlight strolls. In summer, open-air concerts take place outside the neo-Gothic fish market.

THE BURNING OF THE RIALTO

The chronicle of Marin Sanudo, a learned patrician who

commercial zone grew up around the market, and the Rialto became the hub of a great trading city. In time the urban fabric of the sestiere grew denser, the buildings taller, and new structures filled surrounding empty spaces. By the end of the 15th century, the quarter had acquired strong individual characteristics. On January 10, 1514, a fire reduced most of the Rialto to ruins; but the magistrates refused to abandon the area and commercial life quickly recovered. New houses were built on the foundations of old ones, a process that took more than eighteen years to complete. The east side of the district, where palaces stand beside humbler dwellings and churches are set on little campi, was complemented (to the west of the Rio di San Polo) by a more open area boasting major religious edifices and scuole – the Frari, San Rocco and San Giovanni Evangelista.

owned an *osteria* on the Rialto, relates how a fire ravaged the district during one night in 1514. The flames were spread by the high winds; the lumber stores, which were stacked high with wood, were destroyed one after another, while some citizens took advantage of the chaos to loot the premises of others. Only the little Church of San Giacometto escaped unscathed from the flames.

THE RIALTO, HOME OF COMMERCIAL VENICE

THE HEART OF THE BUSINESS DISTRICT. As well as its wholesale and retail traders, its workshops and stores selling luxury products (especially spices and fine fabrics), between the 13th and 15th centuries the Rialto area also contained the city's main trade-related legal authorities, private and public banking houses, marine insurance agencies and even a kind of commodity stock market. From dawn till dusk, the area was a hive of commercial activity. Men of all nations met and mingled beneath the Rialto's arcades, in the *fondachi* ● 89 or else in one of the myriad of picturesquely-named *osterie*.

▲ SAN POLO

Emblems
of the merchants.

A colony of the
Serene Republic.

The moneychangers,
and then the bankers,
set up shop at the
Rialto. The area was
policed day and night,
with extra protection
when funds were
moved from the
Banco di Giro to the
Zecca ▲ 255: at such
times, shopkeepers
armed themselves
and stood guard in
front of their shops.

Every form of business and barter was
conducted here. Quantities of grain were
bought and sold on a daily basis, as were
slaves, despite a series of strict bans on
the slave trade. In addition the Rialto
had its own corps of artisans, among
them jewelers, woodcarvers and
madonneri (painters of madonnas).

THE MAGISTRACIES. In the mid-13th
century, a magistracy was created in
order to oversee the affairs of the Rialto
district. Its officers had to swear an oath
not to yield to any form of pressure, and
to think only of the best interests of the
Seignory when they granted leases on
warehouses, shops and stalls. Additional
magistracies were set up until the 15th
century – notably fiscal and financial
organizations and offices assigned to
regulate the various professions and
corporations.

THE BANKS. The necessities of commerce
prompted the creation of banks, which
naturally enough began to cluster around
what had become the main trading
quarter of Venice. The first banks to
appear (in about 1157) were private ones,
and thereafter the banker's calling remained a prerogative of
the nobility until the great wave of bankruptcies in 1584. The
first state bank, the Banco di Piazza, was founded four years
later. The Banco di Giro (deposit bank), which stood beside
the Church of San Giacomo, appeared in 1619.

FOREIGNERS IN THE RIALTO. As a major port and crossroads
between East and West, Venice was a cosmopolitan city. It
was in the Venetian interest to welcome foreigners, since they
made such an obvious contribution to the city's prosperity,
and the Republic instituted highly tolerant laws in respect of
them. While foreigners had to submit to Venetian law in
matters such as taxation, merchants of the Rialto had the
freedom to manage their premises as they liked, whether they
were Venetians, Turks, Germans or any other nationality.

THE ERA OF TRADE. With her attention still firmly fixed on the
Orient, Venice grew bolder as her power increased. Although
the Venetians benefited from immense privileges within the
Byzantine Empire, and had taken advantage of the Crusades
to open new outposts throughout the Mediterranean,
unbounded greed eventually drove them to seize a quarter of
the Emperor's territories in 1204 ● *31*. However, the
Byzantines reconquered Constantinople in 1261; after
banishing the Venetians, they transferred their former
privileges to the Genoese. This setback did not discourage
the merchants of Venice, as the exploits of the Polo
family show. Full of confidence and enterprise, the
Polos set out from Venice to penetrate deep into the
East; clearly, the relative peace which existed in Asia,
unified by Genghis Khan, and the high taxation on
merchandise transported through Muslim countries,
were enough incentive for merchants to go to the Far
East on their own account.

> "As sailors and merchants, town-builders and
> politicians, the Venetians were the forerunners
> and the youth of today's civilization."
>
> Le Corbusier

MARCO POLO

FIRST VOYAGE OF THE POLOS (1265).
Niccolo and Maffeo Polo set out on
their first voyage in a vessel full of
merchandise for Constantinople; like
many of their fellow citizens, they
maintained a trading house there.
They then sailed on into the Black
Sea, where they bartered their goods
for Russian and Turkish products
before penetrating the lands of the
East, where they met the Great
Khan. After this they returned to Italy before setting out
again, this time taking the young Marco Polo with them.

MARCO POLO IN CHINA (1271–95).
The three men completed
the long journey out almost entirely by land, and presented
themselves to the Mongol Emperor on arrival in northern
China. Genghis Khan made friends with Marco, appointing
him governor of the Yangzhou region. Though the
commercial goal that had motivated his family was mostly
put aside from this time on, Marco continued to observe
China with the practised eye of a merchant and of an
excellent administrator. He was amazed by the variety
and abundance of the products available in Quinzai,
now known as Hangchow. He chronicled the imports
and exports, the taxes levied, and the city's methods
of administration. His attention was also drawn to
products readily available in China, which he
thought vital to the West: sugar, spices (especially
pepper, which was abundant), silk and cotton, the
trade in which had so enriched his native Venice.

THE RETURN OF MARCO POLO
After 25 years in
China, Marco Polo
returned to Venice in
1295 and lived there
largely unknown to
his fellow citizens. He
had left his native city
at a very early age
and now, though he
spoke many other
languages, had
trouble expressing
himself in his mother
tongue. We would
probably never have
heard of Marco Polo
had he not been
imprisoned for a spell
in Genoa, where he
related his
adventures to
a cellmate,
Rusticello
of Pisa
▲ 150.

THE RIALTO

THE RIALTO BRIDGE. This was the first construction to span the Grand Canal, and it remained the only link between the two sides of the waterway until the 19th century. The first boat-bridge, which appeared around 1172, was superseded by a wooden construction between 1200 and 1260. But, after three successive wooden bridges collapsed, it was decided in 1524 that a permanent stone bridge should be erected. In 1557 the Republic launched a competition for the building contract, in which Palladio, Vignola, Sansovino, Scamozzi and Michelangelo all took part. But the project was endlessly delayed by a shortage of money and disagreements about the form that the bridge should take: how many arches should it have? Five, three, or one? Finally, in 1588, a one-arch bridge was settled upon, following a design submitted by an architect, Da Ponte, whose name seemed to predestine him for the work. The subsequent construction work was difficult, given the instability of the site and the height (25 feet) required to allow galleys to pass safely beneath. In 1591, the work was completed and the bridge finally opened. The overhanging portico is a later addition, and shelters two rows of luxury boutiques which are much favored by tourists today. In 1977, the Rialto Bridge was entirely restored by the Venezia Nostra Committee.

PALAZZO DEI DIECI SAVI. This palace, which stands on the left at the foot of the bridge, was built in 1521 by Antonio Abbondi (Lo Scarpagnino). Formerly the city's main tax office, it is now occupied by the municipal waterboard.

PALAZZO DEI CAMERLENGHI. Between 1525 and 1528 Guglielmo dei Grigi, who belonged to a family of Lombard master-builders, constructed an elegant palace by the Rialto; today, unfortunately, it is no more than a shadow of its former self. The *camerlenghi* (magistrates responsible for collecting state taxes), had their offices in this building, hence its name. The first floor was occupied by the Republic's treasury, and

on the ground floor were the cells in which tax-evaders were imprisoned. The paintings of the Palazzo Camerlenghi were dispersed during the Napoleonic occupation and are now mostly to be found at the Cini Foundation on the island of San Giorgio ▲ *342.*

THE BRIDGE OF WOOD
The first wooden bridge at the Rialto was burned down during a rebellion in 1310 by retreating supporters of Bajamonte Tiepolo ▲ *214.* Its successor collapsed in 1444 under the

weight of a crowd that had come to attend the marriage of the Marchioness of Ferrara. So a third bridge was built, a magnificent, solidly-based piece of construction with two central spars that could be raised to allow the passage of tall ships. This bridge was included by Carpaccio in his *Miracle of the True Cross* (opposite). At the start of the 16th century, it was in such bad shape that it had to be partly restored – in vain, for it later collapsed entirely.

RUGA DEGLI ORESI. This alley was formerly occupied by a number of gold and silver workers (*oresi*, in the Venetian dialect). The Sottoportico di Rialto, which adjoins it, is still full of jewelry stores.

THE CHURCH OF SAN GIACOMO DI RIALTO. Affectionately known as "San Giacometto" because it is so small, this church in the form of a Greek Cross is the oldest in Venice. According to legend it was founded in the 5th century, but a date somewhere between the 11th and 12th centuries would probably be nearer the truth. In 1587 its floor was raised and the dome and arches restored, but the Doge, who traditionally worshipped there once a year on Ash Wednesday, ordered the builders on no account to meddle with the form of the sanctuary. Of the original church, only the Greek marble columns of the naves and the chapters ornamented with sculpted foliage remain. These probably derive from other more ancient Venetian-Byzantine structures. The façade, which is dominated by an arcaded clocktower ● 85 in Istrian stone, is the product of many alterations: since the 14th century it has had a large clock in its center (rebuilt in 1749). As for the wooden portico, this was added in the 15th century and restored in 1758.

THE "GOBBO DI RIALTO"
This little statue, sculpted by Pietro da Salo in 1541, shows a man holding up a flight of stairs. The figure was known as the "hunchback" (*gobbo*) though he is

merely bent beneath his burden, seen as an allegory of the heavy taxes imposed on Venetians. Nearby is the Pietra del bando, a pink granite podium from which government decrees were proclaimed.

A WARNING TO MERCHANTS
As Venice's commercial activities were mostly clustered around the Church of San Giacomo di Rialto, the outer wall of the apse was inscribed with an exhortation to merchants to be honest, not to cheat on weights and measures, and to draw up fair contracts.

THE FABBRICHE VECCHIE. This arcaded building (1520–2) was completed by Scarpagnino at the same time as his reconstruction of the entire district following the great fire of 1514. Formerly the seat of the trade, navigation and food supply administrations, it is now Venice's main tribunal.

SOTTOPORTICO DEL BANCO DI GIRO. Merchants used to gather for business under this portico, which adjoined the offices of the Banco di Giro. The giro system allowed people to transfer money from one account to another without

During the 19th century, people would travel for many miles in order to buy the aromatic and medicinal herbs, flowers and fruit on the stalls of the Erberia market.

having to carry it on their person. The sums involved would be inscribed on the banker's register as an order of payment, which would have to be presented by the party himself; the money would then be "transferred" to the account which was to be credited. Since the bank register was an officially notarized document, no receipt was required.

THE ERBERIA. Casanova, in his twelve-volume autobiography *History of My Life* (1826–38), had this to say about the Erberia: "It is so-called because it is positively the market for herbs, fruit and flowers. Those who go there early in the morning say they do so for the innocent pleasure of seeing the arrival of all kinds of green herbs, and of fruits and flowers in season. These are brought in by the inhabitants of the little islands surrounding the capital, and are sold at low prices to the main retailers." Today there are retail markets in the Erberia from 9am to 11am. These are so delightful, even out of season, that they always attract large crowds of people. Prices are much lower here than elsewhere, which is quite important in an island city like Venice, where fresh produce is necessarily expensive because of the considerable cost of transport. The wholesale markets that Casanova so admired have now moved to Tronchetto, near the Piazzale Roma.

The seller of bussolai *● 76 and other sweetmeats: hers was one of many street trades plied in Venice in the 18th century.*

THE FABBRICHE NUOVE. This long building stands on the curve of the Grand Canal. Built between 1553 and 1555 by Sansovino, it used to be the headquarters of the trade administration and it is now the Assize Court.

CAMPO DELLA PESCHERIA. There has been a fish market on this site for a thousand years. The sunlight has barely begun to glimmer on the canal and on the still-wet pavement of the market, when the first brightly painted boats arrive and the air fills with the fishermens' shouts. The *bragozzi* ▲ *360* and

the *topi* ● *73* tie up at the fondamenta in apparent confusion, though in fact every mooring is strictly allocated. Then the fishermen bring their catch ashore, swapping banter in the strange dialect of Venice, with its bitten-off vowel sounds and musical cadences that differ depending on which sestiere one comes from. After the fishermen come the lighters, filled with fruit and vegetables for the Erberia. By 8.30am the stalls are laid out and ready for business: by 12.00pm the stallholders are packed and gone, and the marketplace is left to the cats. On summer evenings, concerts and theatrical performances are often held here, or near the ferry landing stage. The Campo della Pescheria is one of the few points at which one can walk along the bank of the Grand Canal. To do so, take the RIVA DELL'OLIO, so named because oil used to be brought ashore there. Other names for this stretch are the Fondamenta dei Sagomatori (a reference to the measures used for casks of oil), or the Fondamenta del Legno, because wood was also unloaded at this wharf. (Return to the Campo della Pescheria and turn off down the Calle delle Beccarie.)

CAMPO DELLE BECCARIE. This area, which once housed the public abattoirs, is now full of traditional Venetian *bacari*, and is much favored as a rendezvous by the local tradesmen. In fact anybody in Venice with someone to meet for an aperitif could well invite them into one of the wine bars here to share an *ombra*. This strange expression for a glass of wine – white wine, for preference – is said to have originated in St Mark's Square, where wine from the barrel used to be sold at the foot of the campanile. As the sun moved across the sky, the trestle-tables, demi-johns and kegs would all be moved in concert, to keep the wine cool and in the shade. Another school of thought believes that the phrase means the "shadow of a litre", in other words a small quantity of wine. The local habit is to drink one's *ombra* with *cicchetti*, or snacks. Of these there is a wide range, notably meatballs (*polpettine*), portions of fried fish or vegetables, hard-boiled eggs, or creamy fish paste on toast. These delicacies are generally eaten while standing up. (After the bridge and the Campo delle Beccarie, turn left along the Calle dei Botteri, and then right into Calle Corpus Domini Cristi.)

FONDACO DEI TEDESCHI
Located in the San Marco sestiere, but visible from the Rialto Bridge, this former warehouse of Venice's German merchant community is now the city's central Post Office ▲ *200, 276.*

The Pescheria and the landing-stage for the ferry to Campo Santa Sofia ▲ *149.*

Campo San Giacomo di Rialto, with its market. At the far end, the Church of San Giacometto, with its characteristic galleried clocktower.

DAUGHTER OF THE REPUBLIC
Already the widow of another

Florentine, the Venetian aristocrat Bianca Cappello married Francesco dei Medici in 1578. Venice was delighted with the match, giving her the title of "Daughter of the Republic"; in return, Bianca served her country well. Nevertheless when she and her husband were poisoned by Cardinal Ferdinand di Medici in 1587, Venice bowed to Florentine pressure and forbade citizens to wear mourning. In Florence the "traitor" Cardinal refused to allow Bianca to be buried in the Medici family vault.

RIVA DEL VIN

FROM THE RIALTO TO CAMPO SAN POLO

CAMPO SAN CASSIANO. This zone developed independently of the Rialto market, and was not directly linked to it until 1436. A few wealthy families pooled their funds to build the CHURCH OF SAN CASSIANO at the start of the 9th century, on the site of an oratory dedicated to St Cecilia. All that remains of this Venetian-Byzantine sanctuary is the pair of marble pilasters in the doorway; inside are several paintings by Tintoretto. There used to be two "very beautiful theaters" in the vicinity, "which were large enough to contain great concourses of spectators, and in which comedies were played at carnival time, as is the custom of this city" (Sanudo). One became the first paying theater in Europe open to the general public, by a decree of the Council of Ten in 1636. It was demolished in 1812. (Return to the Campo delle Beccarie, then take the Ruga degli Speziali and the Ruga Vecchia San Giovanni; turn left into Calle Toscana, then left again into Calle dei Preti).

THE CHURCH OF SAN GIOVANNI ELEMOSINARIO. The Church of San Giovanni was founded towards the end of the 9th century, then reconstructed to plans by Scarpagnino after the fire of 1514. The interior, shaped like a Greek Cross, has the sobriety of the high Renaissance. The choir contains an altarpiece by Titian, *San Giovanni Elemosinario* (c.1545). In the CAPELLA DEI CORRIERI is one of Pordenone's greatest works, *Saint Catherine, Saint Sebastian and Saint Roch*. This church was formerly under the special protection of the Doge, who went to Mass there every Wednesday. Thus it is no surprise that the arms of the Doge Michele Steno are engraved on its campanile. (Continue straight on along the Ruga Vecchia San Giovanni.)

THE CHURCH OF SANT'APONAL. Built by a family from Ravenna in the 11th century, this church was dedicated to the patron saint of that town, St Apollinarius, and was totally rebuilt in the 15th century in the late Gothic style. Deconsecrated in 1810, it was used successively as a mill, a night-shelter for the poor, and a prison: for the latter purpose, four large windows were knocked through its façade. Finally, the building was put up for auction and repurchased for Christian worship, and it was reopened in 1851. At that time, it still possessed the 13th-century bas-relief which stood over the little door of its campanile: a "Leone a moleca" (a lion clutching a closed Bible). Today it is closed again. (Continue into the Calle del Luganegher.)

CAMPO SAN SILVESTRO. Though now no more than a thoroughfare, this campo was once full of stalls and workshops, and was directly linked to the Grand Canal by a rio (since filled in). The present CHURCH dates from the 19th century, when it replaced a building founded in the 9th

century, of which the only remaining trace is a fragment of a
column topped by a Venetian-Byzantine capital that has been
incorporated into the outer wall facing the rio terrà. Inside is
a *Baptism of Christ* by Tintoretto: facing the porch is the
CA' VALIER, which was formerly decorated with 17th-century
frescoes by Taddeo Longhi. This may have been the home of
the painter Giorgione, unless (as some say) he lived at
number 1099. (Continue along Sottoportico del Traghetto.)
RIVA DEL VIN. This fondamenta is one of the rare stretches of
walkway beside the Grand Canal (along with the Riva
dell'Olio and the Riva del Carbon opposite). It is so named
because it was once an unloading point for wine barrels on
their way to the various warehouses and *bacari* of the district.
(Return to Campo Sant'Aponal. Take the Calle Bianca
Capello – named after the famous noble Venetian lady who
was born here – continue to PALAZZO MOLIN-CAPELLO, then
take the Calle Banco Salviati).

PALAZZO ALBRIZZI. Belying its very sober exterior, on the
inside the Palazzo Albrizzi is one of the most sumptuous
houses in the whole of Venice – a maze of white-and-gold
rooms filled with voluptuous stucco. The Albrizzi family came
to Venice from Bergamo in the 16th century and acquired
great wealth by trading in oils and fabrics. In 1648 they began
purchasing this palace, floor by floor, embellishing it as they
went. The final section of it passed into their hands in 1692. It
was in this house that Isabella Teotochi, with whom the poet
Ugo Foscolo was infatuated during his stay in
Venice, held her literary salon at the
start of the 19th century following
her marriage to Count
Albrizzi ▲ 171. Here
Isabella regularly received
Pindemonte, Alfieri and
Canova, who in 1812
sculpted her for a
Head of Helen, which
is still to be seen in
the palace.

**FONDAMENTA DELLA
TETTE.** One may be
forgiven for wondering
just how this fondamenta
and the bridge nearby
acquired their peculiar
name, since *tette* is a slang
Italian term for breasts. The
reason is simply that the
fondamenta marked the
limit of the area in which
prostitutes were authorized
to solicit customers, which
they did by exhibiting their
bare breasts from the
balconies. If local legend is
to be believed, a law
against homosexuality
or transvestitism
lay at the root
of this custom.

**THE PROSTITUTES OF
VENICE**
In a city as rich as
Venice, all the
pleasures of the flesh
were bound to be
readily available, and
the repressive laws of
the Republic had
little or no effect on
the matter. According
to Marin Sanudo, at
the beginning of the
16th century there
were no fewer than
11,654 prostitutes
working in Venice, a
considerable number
in view of the total
population of
100,000. The
prostitutes lived close
by the Rialto. Their
highest category, the
courtesans, lived in
sumptuous
apartments, dressed
with elegance, were
accomplished
musicians and were
familiar with the
wealthiest patrician
families.

CAMPO SAN POLO
As in Venice's other major piazzas, bull-baitings were frequently held in the Campo San Polo ● *50* and were very

popular. The Compagnia della Calza (literally, the company of the stockings), jovial bands of young men who were identified by the different emblems on their hose, were responsible for organizing these events, which usually took place over Carnival. Oxen were generally used instead of bulls, so as to keep accidents to a minimum.

AROUND CAMPO SAN POLO

THE CAMPO. Campo San Polo, with its brick paving, is one of the oldest and widest squares in the whole of Venice. In the past it must have looked somewhat different, because the Canal Sant'Antonio formerly lay in front of the buildings which now divide it from the Soranzo Palazzi. This watercourse was filled in between 1750 and 1761, and the little bridges which once gave direct access to the palaces were subsequently demolished. Because it is situated at the heart of this crowded quarter, the campo was formerly the scene of religious and lay ceremonies, of preachings, bull-runnings, balls, banquets, theatrical performances and masked galas during Carnival time. Since 1977, this function has been resumed and now Campo San Polo is not only one of the principal Carnival venues, but it is also used as a venue for screening films during the Venice Film Festival ▲ *356*.

PALAZZO MAFFETTI-TIEPOLO (number 1957). Built during the 14th century, this palace was reconstructed in the baroque style by Massari during the 18th century. A staircase decorated with stucco, multi-colored marble and faded frescoes, along with bas-reliefs and garlands over the doors, give some idea of what the decoration by Domenico Rossi must have been like.

THE SORANZO PALAZZI. These two palaces, fused into one by the Soranzo family, are the principal buildings on the campo. Looking at the geminate window on the first floor, one is tempted to date the palace on the left somewhere around the mid-14th century; yet its two doorways with their sculpted lintels seem older. The right-hand palace, with its eight-arched window, has features that clearly indicate the 15th century. Tradition has it that frescoes by Giorgione once adorned the façade but, if so, no trace of them remains today. Casanova entered this house as a humble violinist and came out of it ennobled, having been adopted within by a sick senator to whom he had rendered a service.

PALAZZO CORNER-MOCENIGO (number 2128). Palazzo Corner-Mocenigo was built for Giovanni Cornaro by the architect Michele Sanmicheli, in

order to replace a palace that was destroyed by fire in 1535. Although it was described at the time as "magnificent and very rich", the structure has always been considered a trifle big for Venice, at six storeys high. Today it houses the Guardia di Finanza.

THE CHURCH OF SAN POLO. Rebuilt several times, this building is now a hotchpotch of different styles. The two openings in the façade, and the fragments of cornices and pilasters on the same side as the entrance, are vestiges of the primitive church that stood here in the 9th century. The wooden ceiling (uncovered recently during renovation work), the rose-window and the side portal, are obviously the result of work undertaken in the 14th and 15th centuries to graft Gothic elements on to the original Byzantine building. The arrangement of the interior again reveals a Byzantine concept of space, despite the alterations made by Davide Rossi in 1804 with a view to adapting the church to Neo-classical canons. There are paintings by Tintoretto (including a *Last Supper*), Veronese, Palma the Younger, and Giandomenico Tiepolo (fourteen canvases of the *Way of the Cross*). The CAMPANILE (1365) stands in front of the church in the Salizzada di San Polo. Two face-to-face stone lions stand over the church entrance: one clutches a serpent in its claws, the other a man's head. This is said to be an allegory on the condemnation to death of Doge Falier.

PALAZZO BERNARDO. Standing slightly apart in the Calle Bernardo is this fine example of flowery Venetian Gothic (1422). Do not miss the magnificent spiral staircase in the inner courtyard. (Continue straight on, then turn left along the Rio terrà San Secondo.)

THE PRINTING HOUSE OF ALDO MANUTIUS THE ELDER. Apparently number 2311 of this rio terrà was where the humanist Aldo Manutius the Elder founded his printshop at the turn of the 16th century; and here the Aldine Academy met to decide what texts they should print, Erasmus himself being among their number. Manutius left the quarter towards the end of his life. He went to live at San Paternino, where he is buried, and where Paola and Aldo the Younger carried on his work. (Take the Rio terrà Primo, turn right and continue along the Calle San Boldo.)

CAMPO SAN BOLDO. Built in the 18th century, PALAZZO GRIMANI has rather strangely engulfed the tower of the campanile. Though converted into a part of the house, it remains the last vestige of the church which was destroyed in 1826. On the other side of the rio one can hire boats at different types for reasonable prices. (Go back to Campo San Polo, then along Salizzada di San Polo and Calle dei Saoneri, then turning left and then right.)

L'ARTE
DELLA
STAMPA
NEL
RINASCIMENTO ITALIANO
VENEZIA

ALDVS PIVS MANVTIVS·R·

VENEZIA MDCCCXCIV
FERD. ONGANIA, Editore

LORENZACCIO
On February 26, 1546, Lorenzo de' Medici (Alfred de Musset's *Lorenzaccio*) was assassinated on Campo San Polo. He had come to Venice under the assumed name of Messer Dario, after killing his cousin Alessandro de' Medici, Duke of Florence. Lorenzo's

other cousin, Cosimo, succeeded to the dukedom and sent two hired assassins to Venice to avenge his brother. The killers eventually stabbed Lorenzo to death in the street, along with his uncle Alessandro Soderini. After this they sought asylum in the Spanish Embassy. Curiously enough, the Venetian government took no action against the pair.

ALDO MANUTIUS
Born in about 1450, Manutius started out as a Greek tutor to the Prince de Carpi, and he did not actually become a publisher in Venice until he was forty years old. At that time the city was a world center for publishing – the pocket edition and italic script were both invented there, by Manutius. The Aldine Press quickly flooded the fast-growing book market with a series of classical texts in both Latin and Greek, which were edited by famous scholars.

Chamber music at the Ca' Goldoni.

In the beautiful courtyard of the Palazzo Centani (the other name for the Ca' Goldoni) there is an open staircase that dates from the 15th century. At the center of the courtyard is a traditional well.

THE HOUSE OF GOLDONI ★

This 15th-century building, with its elegant Gothic façade overlooking the Rio San Tomà, was the birthplace of Carlo Goldoni. Goldoni, who has often been called the "Italian Molière", stated that he was born during the Carnival "in the year 1707, in a great and beautiful house between the Nomboli and Donna Onesta bridges, on the corner of the Calle della Ca' Centani, in the parish of San Tommaso". The house, which was bequeathed to the city in 1931, has been used as an institute of dramatic studies and a museum since 1952.

THE COMMEDIA DELL'ARTE.

From the mid-16th century onwards, a new theatrical genre began to develop which was much more focused on stagecraft than had been the case hitherto. The actors learned to combine the skills of acrobats, mime artists and singers, and they improvised their parts each night on the basis of a simple plot (the *canevas*) and a "formula" of tirades, soliloquies and *lazzi* – scene substitutions, mimicry and jokes which could be adapted to suit any comedy. The plots, which were generally inspired by classical comedy, in time became very similar to one another. In fact the great novelty of this comedy of improvisation – and one of the reasons for its huge success – was the introduction of "fixed" rôles, played by actors with masks. In other words, each actor gave up the pretence of renewing his part every night, instead limiting himself to a single character. Before long, the actors became known by the names of their masks alone.

> "I have never witnessed such an ecstasy of joy as that shown by the audience when they saw themselves and their families so realistically portrayed on the stage. They shouted with laughter from beginning to end."
>
> Goethe

THE MASKS.

In Commedia dell'Arte the same roles occur again and again. First of all, there are the two manservants, or *zanni* (from the name "Giovanni" ● 42), who are HARLEQUIN AND BRIGHELLA. At the beginning of the piece, both are equally coarse, lazy and greedy. Before long, however, Brighella becomes crafty, skilled at setting up traps and stratagems. Harlequin, who starts out dressed in white, is the acrobat of the troupe who makes everyone laugh with his antics: he is often the butt and victim of Brighella. "His garments are those of a poor wretch who picks up odds and ends of rags to clothe himself" (Goldoni). Then come the two "dotards": PANTALON ● 42, an old Venetian merchant whose function is to obstruct the aspirations of the young lovers and the plots of the servants, and BALANZON, a doctor-at-law who is his complement.

Balanzon is a pedant who lards his speeches with hopelessly muddled quotes and Latin tags. These "masks" are accompanied by lovers and servants, whose characters all derive from traditional comedy.

CARLO GOLDONI'S REFORMS.

After studying law, Goldoni came to practise in Venice, continuing to do so off and on until 1748. As a young man he was enchanted by the theater, and began to write tragi-comedies and burlesques soon after meeting Giuseppe Imer, who was acting at the Teatro San Samuele in 1734. By the time Goldoni met Girolamo Medebach in 1745, his apprenticeship was complete. He had just written *The Servant of Two Masters*; Medebach, who had become director of the Teatro Sant'Angelo, engaged him as a full-time author for his theater troupe. As it turned out Goldoni became one of the first authors to make a living from his writing. Little by little, he was able to "reform" the Commedia dell'Arte which, since it depended purely on the skills of the actor, was at the mercy of any weakness he might exhibit. Goldoni returned to the written text: "I quietly sought the freedom to write whole plays of my own, and despite the hampering effect of the masks I quite quickly succeeded in doing so." His method was to describe in detail the daily life of Venice and to satirize the manners of his time. In 1753, he produced *La Locandiera*, then left Medebach to work for the Teatro San Luca. Gradually he gave more importance in his plays to ordinary individuals, satirizing the laziness of the aristocracy. In 1757, he quarrelled with CARLO GOZZI, who saw in Goldoni's work an "instrument of social subversion". Meanwhile Goldoni constantly renewed his repertoire to compete with other theaters. This was the period of his greatest success: *I Rusteghi* (1760), the trilogy of *La Villegiatura* (1761) and *Le Baruffe Chiozzotte* (1762). In 1762 he was invited to Paris by the Comédie Italienne; bidding farewell to Venice with *Una delle ultime sere de Carnevale* (One of the Last Nights of Carnival), Goldoni left for the French capital, where he wrote practically nothing but *canevas* comedies. He taught Italian at the royal court and received the king's protection; but the Revolution deprived him of his pension, which was only restored to him on February 7, 1793 – the day after his death.

CARLO GOZZI
Born in Venice on December 13, 1720, Gozzi grew up in a highly literate family. From the mid-century onwards, he pursued a career in the theater, declaring his total opposition to the innovations of Goldoni. In his early work, this quarrelsome polemicist set out to show that he could arouse the interest of the public with simple plots relying on improvisations within the Commedia dell'Arte framework. Later, he reduced his emphasis on improvisation, offering an approach to theater that was based on imagination and wonder, as opposed to Goldoni's realism. In 1761 he mounted *The Love of Three Oranges* at the Teatro San Samuele, a play holding Goldoni up to ridicule. A conservative in art and politics,

Gozzi witnessed the decline and fall of Venice, dying at the age of eighty-six in 1806.

CAMPO SAN TOMÀ. THE CHURCH OF SAN TOMÀ has existed since the 10th century and took its present form in 1742. The 14th-century CAMPANILE was demolished because of its faulty foundations, and the present smaller one erected in its place. Opposite the church stands the old SCUOLA DEI CALEGHERI (shoemakers). Note the bas-relief over the doorway and the "lunette" containing Pietro Lombardo's *Saint Mark Healing the Shoemaker Aniano*. The shoemakers' guild, which acquired the building in 1446, had more than 1,500 members in the 18th century and operated in 400 workshops.

THE FRARI AND SAN ROCCO: PANTHEON OF VENICE ✪
To visit the pantheon of illustrious Venetians, (among them Monteverdi), alight from the vaporetto (no. 1 or 82) at the San Toma halt). While the spirit of Titian pervades the Frari, there is an entire interior by Tintoretto in the Scuola Grande di San Rocco: mirrors allow you to admire the ceiling without craning your neck! Then, after so much beauty, unwind with an ice-cold ombra (a local white wine) in one of the many bacari (typical Venetian bistros).

SANTA MARIA GLORIOSA DEI FRARI ★   ● 82

THE FRANCISCAN CHURCH. Around 1222, the Franciscans established themselves in Venice. They lived on charity and occasional jobs, sheltering in churches and convents until the state presented them with a former Benedictine abbey. In 1236, a site adjoining the abbey was given to the Franciscans, along with a handsome donation from the Doge Jacopo Tiepolo. Here they built the Convent and Church of Santa Maria Gloriosa, known as the Frari (a distortion of *frati*, brothers). Work on the church began in 1250 and was completed about 1330; the result was a building which was smaller than the future basilica, and oriented in a different direction. Donations from great Venetian families made it possible to enlarge and embellish this structure in the mid-14th century; it was then demolished at the start of the 15th century, to make way for

the new basilica, a huge mass of brick punctuated by features of white marble.
THE INTERIOR. The Frari is a pantheon of the glories of Venice, the city's largest place of worship and one of the largest ever built by a religious order. At the center of the church is the ancient CORO DEI FRATI, a choir of 124 wooden stalls sculpted by Marco Cozzi (1468). Preserved intact, these stalls form an ensemble that has no equal in Venice. At the bottom of the central apse, framed by the arch of the high altar, hangs Titian's *Assumption* (1516–18). On either side are six smaller apsidal chapels, reserved for certain guilds and noble families, who decorated them at their own expense. On the left side of the transept is the CAPELLA CORNER (c.1420), dedicated to St Mark the Evangelist. On the altar here stands a triptych of *Saint Mark and Three Saints* (1474) by Bartolomeo Vivarini.

THE LETTUCE OF THE FRARI
The Oratorio della Lattuga (lettuce) was founded in 1332 by Niccolò Lion who, if tradition be believed, built it after he was miraculously cured by a lettuce. Gravely ill, he suddenly craved one in the middle of the night, and it was found in the Frari's kitchen garden.

"The "Tomb of Canova", by Canova, cannot be missed; consummate in science, intolerable in affectation, ridiculous in conception, null and void to the uttermost in invention and feeling."

John Ruskin

Above the font is a fine wooden statuette of St John the Baptist, by Sansovino; and in the chapel to the side is the tomb of Monteverdi, ▲ *174, 263*. There is another wooden statuette of St John the Baptist in the chapel adjoining the high altar, which is the only work of the Florentine master Donatello to be found in Venice. By way of the sacristy, at the end of the right-hand extension of the transept, one can reach the Capella Pesaro, which contains a glorious triptych by Giovanni Bellini. In the chapter-house some of the treasures of the basilica are exhibited, along with a *Virgin* by the great 14th-century master Paolo Veneziano; and in the nave, above the PESARO ALTAR, is a masterpiece by Titian, the *Ca' Pesaro Altarpiece*. Further on is the MONUMENT OF ANTONIO CANOVA, who died in Venice in 1822. This Neo-classical pyramid was designed by the artist himself in honor of Titian, but was never realized in the sculptor's lifetime. It was finally executed by his pupils in 1827 and contains Canova's mummified heart in an urn of porphyry. In front of this is the MONUMENT TO TITIAN, who died of the plague in 1576 after asking to be buried in the Frari. This, too, was erected by Canova's disciples. In addition to these, the basilica contains a number of monuments to various Doges, notably Francesco Foscari, who is portrayed lying beneath stone drapes held by two knights bearing the dead man's coat of arms.

THE CAMPANILE. Situated at the junction of the transept and the left-hand nave, the 262-foot campanile of the Frari was constructed between 1391 and 1396 according to plans by Jacopo Celega. It is one of the tallest in Venice.

THE ARCHIVES. The city's archives occupy both the former convent of the Frari and the old oratory of San Niccolò della Lattuga. The immense convent, a center of sanctity, faith, science and the arts in Venice, had by the 16th century achieved a size commensurate with the role played in the life of the city by the Franciscan community. As an architectural complex, it is focused around two cloisters. The CLOISTER OF THE HOLY TRINITY, with its 17th-century portico, was renovated in 1713 by Father Antonio Pittoni, who erected a monumental Baroque well at its center. The CLOISTER OF SAINT ANTHONY was designed by the school of Sansovino. The convent, which was closed by a Napoleonic decree in 1806, was used as a barracks until 1815, when it became a repository for the State Archives. In its three hundred-odd rooms are packed about fifteen million volumes, which record the entire history of La Serenissima,

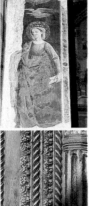

Detail of the frescoes in the basilica (opposite and below).

Detail of the portal of the basilica.

THE "ASSUMPTION" ★ by Titian.

THE DOGE'S VISIT
On St Roch's day, the heads of the scuola entertained the Doge and the officers of the Seignory: the *guardian grande* presented a bunch of flowers to the Doge and stood at his side, while the *sottoguardiano* did the same for the Seignory and the assembled ambassadors. Then the other members of the scuola offered bouquets to the

Doge's retinue. Next the Doge advanced to the high altar, where mass was celebrated by the chaplain of the scuola; this was followed by a ceremony in which servants placed candles on silver platters and distributed them to the assembled company. Afterwards the official cortège repaired to a side room of the scuola to pay homage to the holy relics, visited the Church of the Frari and returned in gilded *peatoni* to the Doge's Palace.

SAN ROCCO

During the 14th century and after, San Rocco was venerated throughout Europe as a protector against the plague, but especially so in Venice, which was a frequent prey to epidemics. Having concluded that the plague of 1575–6 was brought to an end by his intercession, the state decreed that the feast of San Rocco (August 16) should be marked with a great ceremony in his church. On that day, paintings were exhibited in the piazza outside, which the Doge would admire after attending Mass.

THE CHURCH. San Rocco was built in about 1489 by Bartolomeo Bon, an architect who worked in the Renaissance style of Coducci. Its present appearance is the result of two major 18th-century modifications, when the façade with its bas-relief by Gianmaria Morleiter (*San Rocco Tending the Sick*) was rebuilt. Tintoretto painted an *Annunciation* and several episodes in the life of the saint which are now in the church, notably *Presentation of San Rocco to the Pope*.

THE SCUOLA GRANDE ★, ● 87. The Scuola di San Rocco, which gave great help to the sick during times of plague, was declared a Scuola Grande by the Council of Ten in 1489. In the same year, Bartolomeo Bon was given the task of constructing the scuola's first headquarters; not long after, as the scuola continued to prosper, a second building was commissioned from him. After 1524, Bon's work was continued by a series of architects, among them Sante Lombardo, Lo Scarpagnino and Giangiacomo dei Grigi. Despite all these contributions, the façade gives a remarkable impression of homogeneity. Fortunately San Rocco was spared when Napoleon closed the other scuole in 1806, and today is chiefly famous for its interior décor, which includes about fifty works executed by Tintoretto between 1564 and 1587. In the LOWER GALLERY are episodes from the life of the Virgin. The pictures in the MAIN UPPER GALLERY illustrate the links between Old and New Testaments, while exalting the activities of the scuola. On the ceiling of the ALBERGO ROOM are allegories of the Scuole Grande around *San Rocco in Glory*. The side walls are painted with the figures of two prophets: one has his eyes turned toward the *Crucifixion* on the wall at the end of the room, while the other

> "It is not immortality that we breathe at the Scuola di San Rocco, but conscious, reluctant mortality."
>
> Henry James

Tintoretto's *Annunciation* (ground floor gallery). Here the beams of light draw the eye to the face of the Virgin, which is the focal point of the entire scene.

COMPETING MASTERS

Once the decision had been made to decorate the ceiling of the Albergo's main hall with a scene of *Saint Roch in glory*, a competition was launched in 1564 in which all the greatest painters of Venice took part. Tintoretto won by a stratagem: apparently he presented the jury with a completed work, which (against all the rules) he unrolled on the ceiling, proclaiming that this was his way of going about his work, and that if the other competitors had been honest, they would have done likewise. Not surprisingly there was an outcry, upon which Tintoretto offered his work free of charge to San Rocco, as a gesture of devotion. The competition was cancelled, and the contract to decorate the hall was given to Tintoretto. In three years, he completed all of the canvases now to be seen on the walls and ceiling. After making a number of other donations, he proposed in 1577 to decorate the entire building against a life annuity of a hundred ducats. By 1581 he had completed the paintings in the upper room; then, between 1583 and 1587, he added the eight paintings in the lower rooms.

contemplates three episodes from the Passion of Christ to the left.

SAN GIOVANNI EVANGELISTA. Behind the Frari, facing the CHURCH OF SAN GIOVANNI EVANGELISTA, is the scuola of the same name. The members

of this guild were established here from 1307. They enlarged their building in the 15th century. It still has a superb Renaissance portal in marble by Pietro Lombardo (1481), and its "lunette" is crowned by an eagle, the symbol of St John the Evangelist. In 1512 the church was restructured by Coducci, who rebuilt the façade and created the monumental staircase.

THE SCUOLE ● *86*

The term *scuola* (from the Latin *schola*, a corporation or guild) in Venice designates a form of association between lay citizens. The scuole were corporations that combined devotion and mutual assistance; sometimes they were linked to professions. Their members met in churches under the protection of a patron saint, worshipping and participating in public ceremonies together. At the beginning of the 16th century, five of these guilds had the title of scuola grande: Santa Maria della Carità ▲ *300*, San Giovanni Evangelista, Santa Maria in Valverde, San Marco, and San Rocco. In 1552, the Council of Ten accorded this title to a sixth guild: that of San Teodoro ▲ *275*. Each of these main scuole had between five and six hundred members; the smaller ones, of which

Emblems of scuole grandi San Giovanni Elemosinario and Santa Maria della Misericordia.

In Gentile Bellini's *Procession of Corpus Christi* ● *48*, the scuole grandi walk in procession with their holy relics. In the foreground are the members of the Scuola San Giovanni Evangelista, who commissioned this painting.

there were about a hundred, had far fewer. The origins of all – and especially of the scuole grandi – went back to the 13th-century movement of the Flagellants, who castigated themselves in public to expiate the sins of the world and appease the wrath of God. The Flagellants, who appeared in Italy around 1260, quickly gained influence among the brotherhoods which the mendicant orders established among the lay populations of the cities. In Venice, the oldest scuola was that of Santa Maria della Carità, whose statutes (*mariegole*) went back precisely to the month of December 1260. The other scuole grandi appeared a little later. Apart from their religious function, the scuole fulfilled a role of mutual assistance: members knew that their scuole would procure them free lodging or money for their daughters' dowries, should they stand in need of such assistance. Some scuole even paid the doctors who visited the indigent sick, to whom they gave medicines free of charge. Thus even the poorest could obtain work or count on a regular distribution of alms. This social activity meant that the scuole played an important part in the life of the city. In effect, while politics as such had been the exclusive province of patricians ever since the closure of the Grand Council ● *31*, the direction of the scuole was barred to them; only merchants, artisans, state functionaries, advocates, notaries or doctors could occupy a position of responsibility in a scuola. Moreover, the scuole received immense donations, which they regularly invested in state loans or property development. So rich and powerful did they become that in the military and financial domains they amounted to a state within a state, with responsibilities ranging from recruiting men to row Venice's galleys, to financing her military expeditions. Thus the scuole gave citizens a way of influencing political events, while forming a link between the wealthier sectors of society and the lower orders. As such they were a highly effective instrument of social cohesion.

Dorsoduro

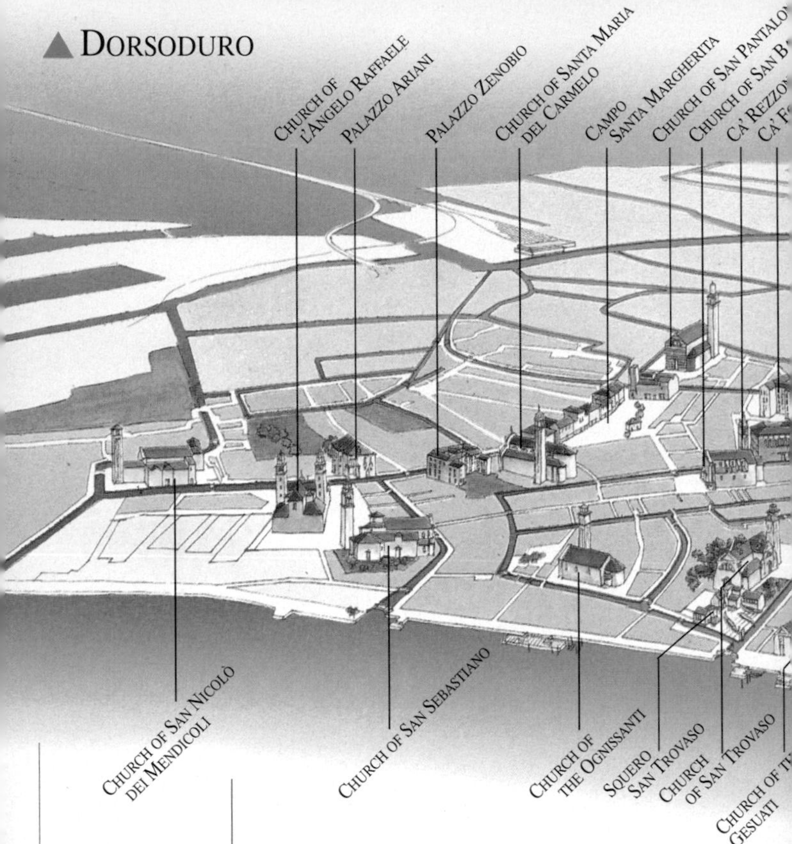

CHURCH OF L'ANGELO RAFFAELE
PALAZZO ARIANI
PALAZZO ZENOBIO
CHURCH OF SANTA MARIA DEL CARMELO
CAMPO SANTA MARGHERITA
CHURCH OF SAN PANTALON
CHURCH OF SAN B
CÀ REZZONICO
CÀ F

CHURCH OF SAN NICOLÒ DEI MENDICOLI
CHURCH OF SAN SEBASTIANO
CHURCH OF THE OGNISSANTI
SQUERO SAN TROVASO
CHURCH OF SAN TROVASO
CHURCH OF TH GESUATI

🚶 One day
◆ B

The sestiere of Dorsoduro covers Venice's southern flank; as an administrative area, it occupies 230 acres, including the island of Giudecca. The name means "spine" (hard back) and refers to the quality of the soil, which is higher above sea-level and more stable than that in the other quarters of the city. Although it is apart from the main orbit of the Rialto ▲ 279 and San Marco ▲ 220, Dorsoduro contains a number of monuments which rank among the most interesting in the whole of Venice. Building in this area began on the western side, with the first two poles of attraction forming during the 7th century around the Churches of l'Angelo Raffaele and San Nicolò dei Mendicoli. During the 11th century, new urban nuclei emerged in the central part of Dorsoduro, growing steadily with the establishment, between the 13th and 16th centuries, of religious complexes in the central-to-west zone and along the banks of the Grand Canal. In the two centuries that followed, Dorsoduro acquired both dignity and status, with the lavish rebuilding of many of its churches and the construction of magnificent palaces. The skyline was radically changed by the building of La Salute and the Zattere. During the 19th century, after the establishment of the Accademia at La Carità, and the construction of a new bridge, the sestiere became one of the areas most favored by wealthy foreign residents; later,

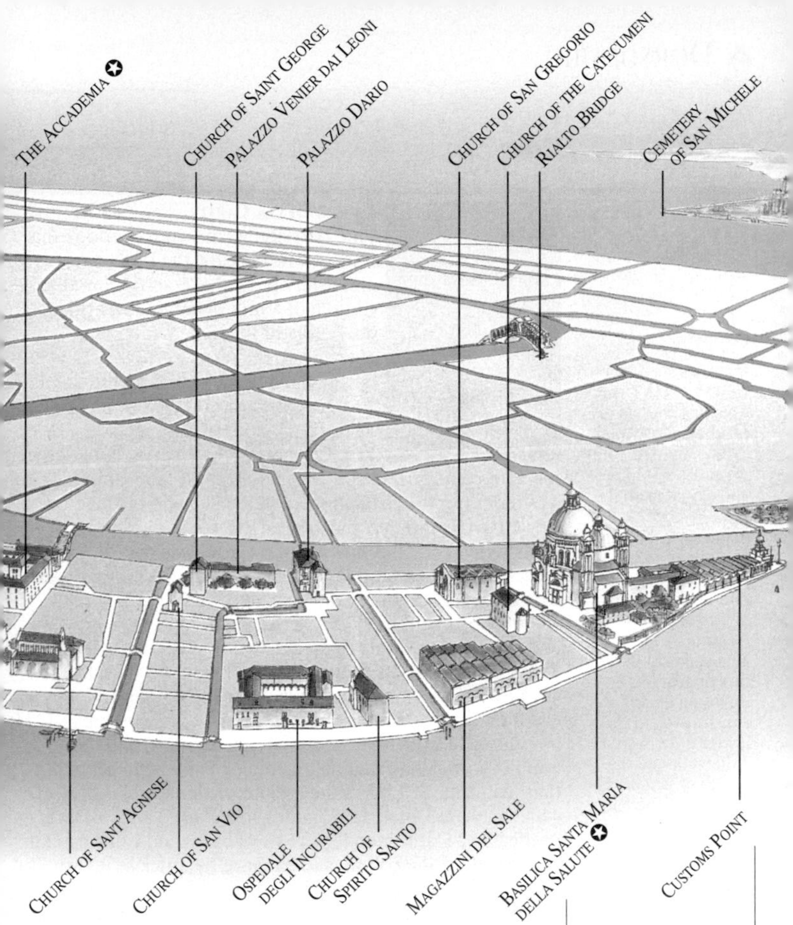

CHURCH OF SAINT GEORGE

PALAZZO VENIER DAI LEONI

PALAZZO DARIO

CHURCH OF SAN GREGORIO

CHURCH OF THE CATECUMENI

RIALTO BRIDGE

CEMETERY OF SAN MICHELE

CHURCH OF SANT'AGNESE

CHURCH OF SAN VIO

OSPEDALE DEGLI INCURABILI

CHURCH OF SPIRITO SANTO

MAGAZZINI DEL SALE

BASILICA SANTA MARIA DELLA SALUTE ✪

CUSTOMS POINT

in the second half of the century, the construction of the merchant shipping docks galvanized industrial development on the western end of the sestiere.

THE ACCADEMIA

PONTE DELL'ACCADEMIA. From 1488 onwards, Venetians cherished the hope that a stone bridge might one day be built between Campo San Vitale ▲ *268* and Campo della Carità. But it was not until the 19th century and the time of the Austrian occupation ● *34* that the English architect Neville was able to realize his plans for a steel bridge. This was inaugurated on November 20, 1854, then demolished during the Fascist era and replaced, after a national contest, by a wooden bridge. The wooden bridge deteriorated rapidly, however, and another contest was held in 1985. But, although a wide variety of architects came up with some original ideas (one being a transparent bridge which was supposed to minimize the impact on the surrounding area), in the end the municipality decided to duplicate the previous design,

Along the Dorsoduro stretch of the Grand Canal, there stands an uninterrupted series of sumptuous palaces.

CAMPO DELLA CARITÀ
This was once an off-the-beaten-track campo, bordered on two sides by water and closed in on the third by now-demolished buildings. It was an isolated place of prayer and pilgrimage. But the arrival of the Accademia in 1807 changed both its function and its atmosphere; and the construction of the bridge in 1854 created a direct link to the center of Venice. The filling in of the Rio della Carità (1839) and the Rio di Sant'Agnese (1863), along with the appearance of a vaporetto line (1881), completed this development. Today the campo is very busy in the daylight hours, with students attending courses at the Academy of Arts and visitors coming to the museum; at night it falls silent, since nobody lives here.

CAMPO DELLA CARITÀ. The Academy of Fine Arts and its museum overlook this square. They occupy the former monastery of the Lateran Canons, the Church of Santa Maria della Carità and the scuola of the same name. The entrance to the faculty is by way of a portico linking the church to the scuola, and the entrance to the museum is through the door of the scuola.

THE CHURCH OF LA CARITÀ. Founded in the 12th century, this church (like the monastery adjoining it) was rebuilt in the years immediately following 1441, with a single nave and polygonal apses. One would hardly guess from the way it looks now that La Carità was once one of the most interesting examples of Gothic architecture in Venice. The truth is that it has been spoiled several times, notably when it became the seat of the Academy, and its interior was divided into two floors to create class and exhibition rooms.

THE CONVENT OF LA CARITÀ. This convent was founded in 1134 by the Lateran Canons when they first established their order in Venice. With the election of a Venetian Pope in 1434, new opportunities were opened to the Canons, and they became sufficiently wealthy to employ Palladio to rebuild their convent. In 1555–6 the architect submitted his project, which included an atrium leading to a cloister with a Doric portico and Corinthian loggia; stone bases and stone capitals were used for the columns to enhance the brick structure. But lack of funds prevented the work from being completed, and in 1630 the building was partly destroyed by fire. Finally the operations carried out in the 19th century left nothing of the original building save the right-hand side of the cloister.

SCUOLA DI SANTA MARIA DELLA CARITÀ ● 87. The Scuola Santa Maria, in existence since 1260, was one of the earliest guilds to receive the title of Scuola Grande ▲ 295. Its members first met on the Giudecca, and then in the Cannaregio district, before they acquired these premises close to the monastery of La Carità. Later on, the monks found themselves short of money and in 1344 were persuaded to part with the piece of land on which the scuola was built. In 1442 the

order received the pope's financial aid and sought to enlarge its church; but the scuola resisted stoutly and undertook an expansion of its own, at the same time renovating the interior of its existing building. Thereafter the scuola remained unaltered until the mid-18th century, when it was given a new façade designed by Giorgio Massari and built by Maccaruzzi. Finally, when the Academy was installed there in the mid-19th century, the entire premises were adapted to this new function. Part of the artistic heritage of the scuola has remained, notably a *Madonna and Saints* by Antonio Vivarini and Giovanni d'Alemagna, and a *Presentation of Mary in the Temple* by Titian. The latter is an allegory of the duty the old scuola set itself, which was each year to supply dowries to twenty poor girls of an age to marry.

THE ACCADEMIA GALLERIES. The Academy of Fine Arts was created by a decree of the Senate on September 24, 1750, and placed under the responsibility first of Giambattista Piazzetta and then of Giambattista Tiepolo. In 1807 it was reorganized with an art gallery of its own. This gallery had a dual function: to provide examples to the pupils, and to house the artistic heritage of the public buildings dispersed by the fall of the Republic ● *34*, as well as the treasures of the convents, monasteries and churches recently suppressed by Napoleonic decree. The Academy was established at La Carità. On August 10, 1817, its galleries were opened to the public and thereafter its exhibition space grew steadily. At the end of the Second World War the great architect Carlo Scarpa ▲ *346* redesigned the Academy with the collaboration of the curator, and today it offers the most complete panorama of Venetian painting in existence. The original kernel of its collection, which consisted of pictures given to the Academy by the artists themselves in the late 18th century, along with a few works that formerly belonged to the Republic, has been enriched beyond measure by religious treasures, private legacies, restitutions and purchases. Among its collection of primitives are pieces by Paolo and Lorenzo Veneziano and Michele Giambono. The 15th century is represented by Giovanni Bellini and Carpaccio; and the 16th by Giorgione, Titian, Tintoretto, Veronese, Bassano and Lorenzo Lotto, as well as many other remarkable (if not so famous) painters. Equally well represented are the 17th and 18th centuries, with paintings by Tiepolo, Piazzetta and Longhi, and many delicate pastels by Rosalba Carriera. The collection of drawings includes several masterpieces by Leonardo da Vinci and an entire sketchbook by Canaletto. The pages that follow show a selection of major works by some of these painters which can be seen at the Academy; some of these illustrations are accompanied by other pictures by the same artists which are still kept in the churches and scuole of Venice, and which may help to give a more comprehensive idea of each master's style.

THE ACCADEMIA : TITIAN'S RICH TONES, LONGHI'S MASKS ✪
The golden age of Venetian painting was brought about by that sublime trio Titian, Tintoretto and Veronese, and others, from Bellini to Giorgione and Guardi. The most remarkable thing is that you only have to look outside to see a living Canaletto, and today's carnival masks come straight out of the genre scenes of Pietro Longhi.

THE DOOR OF THE ACCADEMIA
Sculptures of St Leonard and St Christopher, the patrons of the brotherhood of La Carità, stand on either side of this door. In the niche above it sits the Madonna, surrounded by members of the guild. Beyond the portico of the Academy is an inner courtyard, which was once shared by the scuola and the convent. There is a carving on the well of a cross held by two figures: this is the emblem of the Scuola della Carità.

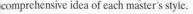

LORENZO VENEZIANO
was active between
1357 and 1372.
Apprenticed to Paolo
Veneziano (no
relation) he later
moved to Bologna
and Verona,
where Gothic art
was flourishing.

PAOLO VENEZIANO
(c.1290–c.1360)
was the principal figure
in 14th-century
Venetian art. He is
thought to have been
responsible for
introducing the taste
for polyptychs to
Venice. The
replacement of mural
mosaics by polyptychs
is a major phenomenon
of Venetian art; no
longer would sacred
images be inaccessibly
placed on high walls
and vaultings – they
would instead be visible
at eye-level. This
implied a completely
different relationship
between man and
things sacred. Venetian
art was progressively
breaking loose from
the influence of
Byzantium, which was
more hieratic in its
outlook. The works of
Paolo are especially
striking for their
radiant colors, as in his
Coronation of the Virgin
(above, detail). The
sweetness of the
figures' expressions is
only matched by their
refinement and
elegance.

MICHELE GIAMBONO,
whose career lasted
from 1420 until 1462,
was unmoved by the
new influences of the
Renaissance,
preferring instead
to raise his own
archaic style to near-
perfect levels.

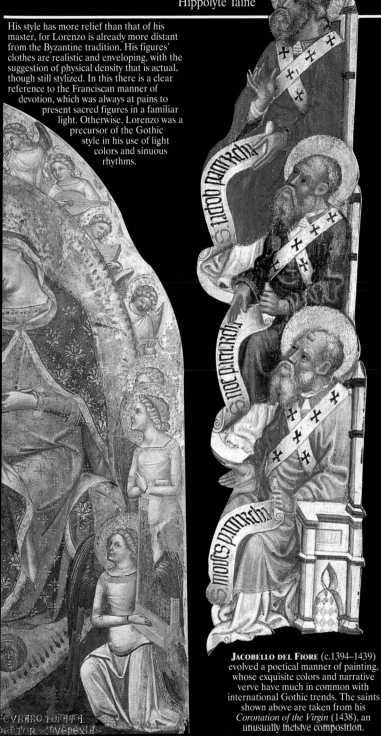

"Here, as everywhere else, the new art was born of the Byzantine tradition."

Hippolyte Taine

His style has more relief than that of his master, for Lorenzo is already more distant from the Byzantine tradition. His figures' clothes are realistic and enveloping, with the suggestion of physical density that is actual, though still stylized. In this there is a clear reference to the Franciscan manner of devotion, which was always at pains to present sacred figures in a familiar light. Otherwise, Lorenzo was a precursor of the Gothic style in his use of light colors and sinuous rhythms.

JACOBELLO DEL FIORE (c.1394–1439) evolved a poetical manner of painting, whose exquisite colors and narrative verve have much in common with international Gothic trends. The saints shown above are taken from his *Coronation of the Virgin* (1438), an unusually incisive composition.

303

GIOVANNI BELLINI

Without breaking his ties with tradition, Giovanni Bellini revitalized Venetian painting, first by placing his figures in precise perspectives and then by opening up their backgrounds to include landscapes and clear rocky vistas. In his carefully framed altarpiece at San Giobbe (c.1487), a major work completed at the height of his career, Giovanni heightens his perspective with a coffered ceiling resting on pillars that are identical to those of the altar itself. Behind the group of figures is a niche-like apse which fades into the shadows. Giovanni saw this picture as an extension of real space, occupied by figures that were not only majestic but also aglow with human warmth. Yet the Virgin herself somehow remains aloof from the rest of the scene, and this icon-like detachment bears the stamp of Venice's Byzantine legacy.

The work of Giovanni Bellini (c.1433?–1516) is peopled by Madonnas, infant Christs and pietàs, all permeated by a sense of deep human melancholy.

"LA PIETÀ"

Here Bellini's interest in landscape is evident. Against the backdrop of a walled city (Vicenza) he places the body of Christ in the arms of the Virgin, whose face is worn with age and suffering.

> "Bellini's virgins are certainly the loveliest,
> the most human, the tenderest and
> most delicate known to man."
>
> Marcel Brion

GENTILE BELLINI
Gentile, brother of
Giovanni, became a
portraitist and
painter of Venice's
ceremonies. At the
same time, he was
also adept at the
traditional Venetian
art of story painting,
usually on a huge
canvas, which was
commissioned by
one of the scuolas to
tell the story of a
saint, or of some
miracle wrought
by a relic.

*Miracle of the Cross at
the Bridge of San
Lorenzo,* by Gentile.

In the *Altarpiece of
San Zaccaria*, the
forms are relaxed and
supple and the colors
dazzling.

**"ALTARPIECE OF
SAN ZACCARIA"**
▲ *171* Here
Giovanni (then
aged 75)
developed and
deepened his
investigation of
the relationship
between color and
light. The
composition is
basically the same
as that of his San
Giobbe altarpiece,
except insofar as
the architecture is
opened up at the
sides to admit
light and reveal a
background
landscape.

THE SAINT URSULA CYCLE ★

Painted for the Scuola di Sant'Orsola between 1490 and 1500, this is Carpaccio's most extensive series. In these nine canvases, he was freely inspired by 15th-century stories of the life of St Ursula, a Breton princess who agreed to marry an English prince on condition that he convert to Christianity and go with her on a pilgrimage to Rome accompanied by ten thousand virgins. The entire group was massacred by the Huns at Cologne on the return journey.

"THE TRIUMPH OF SAINT GEORGE" ▲ 163

A second cycle of paintings, partly devoted to the Dalmatian St George, was created by Carpaccio for the Scuola di San Giorgio degli Schiavoni.

Vittore Carpaccio was born in Venice in about 1465 and died c.1526.

"THE TEMPEST"

The spendours of nature and man's harmonious, poetic relationship to it are the true subjects of Giorgione's canvas.

"LA VECCHIA"

A symbolic representation of the passing of beauty, this painting is an explicit invitation to ponder mankind's destiny. The inscription reads "With time".

> "From Giorgione onwards, the Venetian school delved deep; to form, which satisfies the mind, it preferred color – form's rival."
>
> René Huyghe

GIORGIONE
Born c.1478 at Castelfranco Veneto, Giorgione died in Venice in 1510. He perfected a way to extract undreamed-of luminosity from paint glaze, which created effects of atmospheric transparency. His themes were largely humanist in inspiration.

"THE ARRIVAL OF THE AMBASSADORS" shows Carpaccio's prodigious ability to encapsulate a story in paint.

The Presentation of Mary at the Temple (1539) was Titian's sole concession to the genre of story painting, which had been epitomized by the work of Gentile Bellini and Vittore Carpaccio, and which had largely fallen into disuse by the 16th century. Conforming to the aesthetic ideals of the Venetian school, Titian gave priority to color, using its power to stress the monumentality of his images.

THE DEATH OF TITIAN

This painting by Alexandre Jean-Baptiste Hesse, now at the Louvre, is a homage to the great master. In July 1576, Titian's son Orazio fell sick with the plague and was removed to the *lazaretto*. Left alone, Titian died on 27 August of "high fever", which may also have been the plague. However, he was spared the common grave used for victims of the epidemic, and interred at the Frari.

"[Titian] walks in step with nature: hence each
one of his figures is alive and in motion,
with flesh that quivers."

Giorgio Vasari

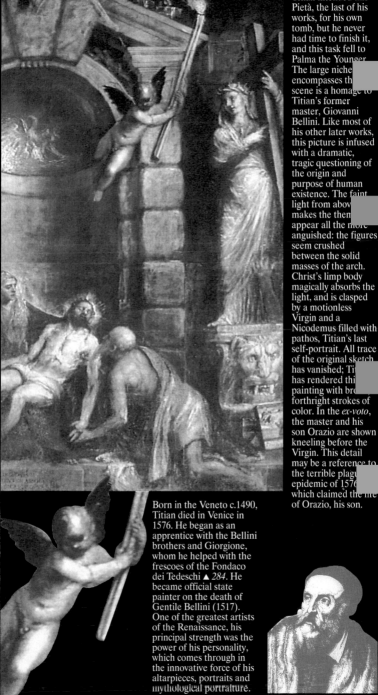

"LA PIETÀ" (1576)
Titian intended this
Pietà, the last of his
works, for his own
tomb, but he never
had time to finish it,
and this task fell to
Palma the Younger.
The large niche
encompasses the
scene is a homage to
Titian's former
master, Giovanni
Bellini. Like most of
his other later works,
this picture is infused
with a dramatic,
tragic questioning of
the origin and
purpose of human
existence. The faint
light from above
makes the theme
appear all the more
anguished: the figures
seem crushed
between the solid
masses of the arch.
Christ's limp body
magically absorbs the
light, and is clasped
by a motionless
Virgin and a
Nicodemus filled with
pathos, Titian's last
self-portrait. All trace
of the original sketch
has vanished; Titian
has rendered this
painting with broad,
forthright strokes of
color. In the *ex-voto*,
the master and his
son Orazio are shown
kneeling before the
Virgin. This detail
may be a reference to
the terrible plague
epidemic of 1576
which claimed the life
of Orazio, his son.

Born in the Veneto c.1490,
Titian died in Venice in
1576. He began as an
apprentice with the Bellini
brothers and Giorgione,
whom he helped with the
frescoes of the Fondaco
dei Tedeschi ▲ *284*. He
became official state
painter on the death of
Gentile Bellini (1517).
One of the greatest artists
of the Renaissance, his
principal strength was the
power of his personality,
which comes through in
the innovative force of his
altarpieces, portraits and
mythological portraiture.

VERONESE
(1528–88)
Following the death of Titian, Veronese became the official state painter of the Republic. With his penchant for Palladian décors and architecture, he created some lavish stage sets for his figures. The dazzling quality of light and color in his compositions give them great power, as in this allegory of Venice in the Doge's Palace (below).

This *Last Supper* was renamed *The Feast at the House of Levi* after Veronese was prosecuted for introducing humble characters into the scene of the Holy Sacrament.

The Flight into Egypt (1583–7) is one of a series of paintings composed by Tintoretto for San Rocco ▲ *294*.

In the *Translation of the Body of Saint Mark* (1552–65), a stormy light bathes the scene, revealing the importance of light in the creation of dramatic tension. The construction in perspective (left) shows Tintoretto's close attention to architectural forms.

"A fine excess of fantasy and sheer mastery seized the artist [Veronese] and drove him to push the resemblance of bodies and objects to the brink of trompe l'oeil."

Paul Valéry

Jacopo Robusti, known as **TINTORETTO**, was born in Venice in 1518 and died there in 1594. He soon moved away from the Venetian tradition to concentrate on Mannerism. Restless by nature, he fashioned means of expression of new force, using light and chiaroscuro to heighten his dramatic effects.

PIETRO LONGHI
(Venice, 1702–85)
An attentive observer
of contemporary life,
Longhi was
principally a genre
painter.

In his
smaller
pictures,
which are
both vivid
and harmonious,
he sketched the
aristocrats and salons
of the 18th century, as
in *The Dancing
Lesson* (above), along
with the everyday life
of Venice. The spirit
of Longhi's work has
been justly compared
to Carlo Goldoni's
theater ▲ *290*.

ALESSANDRO LONGHI
(Venice, 1733–1813)
A disciple of his
father, Alessandro
enlarged his slender
figures and
transposed them into
portraits. His father's
sharp eye and
expressiveness are
equally evident in the
work of the son, as
demonstrated in
*The Family of
the Procurator
Pisani,*
(above).

ROSALBA CARRIERA
(1675–1757) was a portrait
painter who worked
particularly in pastels. She
achieved spectacular
success throughout
Europe.

> "Elegant and stylish, like Watteau or Boucher, Tiepolo's principal asset was nonetheless an admirable and invincible ability to charm."
>
> Guy de Maupassant

GIAMBATTISTA TIEPOLO (1696–1770) worked with prodigious speed, which sometimes exposed him to the charge of carelessness. An admirer of Veronese, he broke free of academic precepts in about 1725 and began to investigate Rococo.

He introduced new accents to painting, with his penchant for triumphal allegories, both sacred and profane. Tiepolo's colors have silvery nuances; his subject matter has a sensual overlay, and his light is full of rich impasto. Left, *The Exaltation of the Cross.*

In a move away from the traditional landscape in perspective, Francesco Guardi evolved an "impressionist" vision in his landscape work. His drawings are often handled with quivering touches, the line rapid and sharp; his paintings convey an emotional, vibrant atmosphere. Below, *The Fire at San Marcuola.*

FRANCESCO GUARDI (1712–93) was the more famous of the two Guardi brothers. His views of the city make him perhaps the last painter-poet of 18th-century Venice. His work, in which he shows an acute sense of the ephemeral and a melancholy that borders on the romantic, is unusual for a period in which Neo-classicism was very much the fashion.

Antonio Canal, known as **CANALETTO** (1697–1768), began painting views of Venice after spending the years 1716–19 in Rome, where he was influenced by the landscape painters Gian Paolo Pannini and Gaspar van Wittel. Much admired by the English nobility, to whom he was introduced by Joseph Smith, a future British consul in Venice, Canaletto's name quickly became synonymous with the city. He honed his technique, his style of expression, his faultless sense of perspective and his photographic eye; at the same time his rendering of light was incomparably limpid, and his colors were as clear as his spatial sense was true. Following a long stay in London, he returned to Venice in 1756.

One of Canaletto's last paintings (above) is an academic study of a portico (1765), a trial piece which won him election as a member of the Academy. For this reason it is somewhat dry and technical. Strange as it may seem, there are very few views of Venice by Canaletto which are still on display in the city.

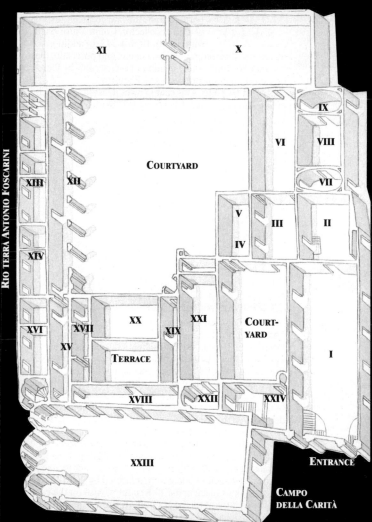

PLAN OF THE ACCADEMIA

I. Venetian painters: 14th century
II. Giovanni Bellini, Cima da Conegliano
III. Late 15th–early 16th century
IV. Italian painters: 15th century
V. Giovanni Bellini and Giorgione
VI. 16th century
VII. Lorenzo Lotto, GG Savoldo
VIII. Palma the Elder
IX. 16th-century schools of painting
X. Titian, Veronese and Tintoretto
XI. Veronese, Tintoretto and GB Tiepolo
XII. 18th-century landscape painters

XIII. Tintoretto, Bassano
XIV. Renovators of the 17th century
XV. Minor painters of the 18th century
XVI. Giambattista Piazzetta
XVII. Longhi, Canaletto, Carriera, Guardi
XVIII. 18th-century painters and engravers
XIX. 15th-century painters
XX. Gentile Bellini and Vittorio Carpaccio
XXI. Vittorio Carpaccio
XXII. Bookshop
XXIII. Venetian painters: 15th century
XXIV. Albergo Room, Titian

PALAZZO DARIO
The Palazzo Dario is said to bring ill-luck to its owners. This legend does not seem to have affected the French poet Henri de Régnier, who lived there from 1899 to 1901; and certainly not the palace's

present owner, the Italian industrialist Raul Gardini.

JACKSON POLLOCK
Much influenced by his encounter with the European Surrealists during the war, the principal representative of American Abstract Expressionism worked on huge canvases, which he spread out on the floor and covered in paint from a dripping bucket.

FROM SAN VIO TO SAN GREGORIO

CAMPO S. VIO

PALAZZO CINI. At number 864 on La Piscina Forner stands the late 16th-century mansion of a great collector, Count Vittorio Cini, who died in 1977 ▲ *342*. In addition to quantities of furniture, ivories, enamel and porcelain, there are a number of remarkable paintings here, notably by Piero della Francesca, Sandro Botticelli and Pontormo.

CAMPO DI SAN VIO. This campo owes its name to the Church of San Vio (Venetian street slang for "Santi-Vito-e-

Modesto"), which stood here until the 19th century. San Vio was the scene of an annual celebration of the thwarting of Bajamonte Tiepolo's St Vitus' Day conspiracy on June 15, 1310 ▲ *214*; the Doge, with the Seignory, representatives of the scuole grandi and other Venetian institutions, would arrive along the Grand Canal to attend mass and a banquet at San Vio. To make it easier for them to disembark, the buildings which closed off the campo on the canal side were demolished; hence its peculiar look of a lengthy rectangle completely open to the water. The old church, probably founded in the 10th century, was rebuilt at the same time and enriched by items from Bajamonte Tiepolo's palace, which was dismantled after his plot was exposed. A cross and *patera* from the original building were inherited by the votive chapel which took its place in the 19th century. Also on the campo is the little CHURCH OF SAINT GEORGE THE EVANGELIST. (Take the Calle della Chiesa and the Fondamenta Venier.)

PALAZZO VENIER DEI LEONI (GUGGENHEIM FOUNDATION) ★. A wrought-iron gate marks the way in to the Peggy Guggenheim Foundation. Work on the original Palazzo Venier, designed by Lorenzo Boschetti, was begun in 1749 but never got beyond the first floor – earning the palace the sobriquet of "nonfinito". The extent of the first floor, and (even better) a wooden

maquette at the Correr Museum ▲ *246,* give an idea of what the palace would have looked like had it been completed. Finished or not, it was home to the illustrious Venier family, which had entered the ranks of the nobility in 1297 and over the centuries gave Venice no fewer than three Doges, including the great Sebastiano Venier, Supreme Commander of the Christian Fleet at Lepanto ● *36.* Yielding to the 18th-century penchant for the unusual, the Venier family surrounded themselves with exotic animals, even keeping a chained lion in the courtyard of the palace, hence its nickname, "Ca' Venier dei Leoni". In 1949 the American collector Peggy Guggenheim bought the property, made her home there and opened an art gallery. In 1976, a few years before her death, she donated the palace and contents to the Solomon R Guggenheim Foundation of New York, which has administered both the Guggenheim Museum in Venice and in Manhattan (assembled by Peggy Guggenheim's uncle) ever since. The Ca' Venier today contains one of the most important collections of modern art in the world. The entire avant-garde of the first half of the 20th century is represented here, especially the Surrealists. The gardens are filled with sculptures, and temporary exhibitions are regularly held at the museum.

PALAZZO DARIO ★. In 1490, Giovanni Dario, the ambassador to Constantinople, received a large cash reward for his part in convincing the Turks to ratify a treaty. The construction of a palace naturally followed, with the work directed by Pietro Lombardo and his team of stonemasons and carvers. Lombardo, always more concerned with the interaction of surfaces than with volumes, adopted a mainly pictorial approach to the façades. By covering them with medallions of colored marble, he transformed the exterior into an exercise in décor which gave no inkling of how the palace was organized inside. Sadly, extensive changes in the 19th century have perverted the Palazzo Dario almost beyond recognition. (Continue on along the Calle Barbaro.)

THE CHURCH AND CONVENT OF SAN GREGORIO. The old church here was rebuilt between 1445 and 1461, and is now the restoration center of the government's "Superintendance" of galleries and works of art in the Venice region. The monastery was rebuilt a hundred years earlier, and is now a private house.

PEGGY GUGGENHEIM
Born in New York in 1898, she became interested in avant-garde painting at an early age. She left the USA for Europe in 1921. In 1938 she opened the Guggenheim-Jeune Gallery in London. She travelled throughout Europe, unconcerned by the threat of war, but in the end the Nazi advance forced her to return to America, where she founded a new gallery, Art of this Century, in 1942. In the same year she began her short-lived marriage to Max Ernst. By 1949 she was back in Venice, where the Biennale gave her a special pavilion to show her collection. The exhibition was a huge success: Peggy Guggenheim fell in love with Venice and stayed there until her death in 1979, becoming an honorary citizen of the city.

THE "ORECCHIONI" OF LA SALUTE
The exterior and interior of this basilica are very different. The inside is austere, while the outside is exuberant with statues (no fewer than 125 of them) and ornaments. The great volutes of the façade serve as buttresses to the dome, and are affectionately referred to by the Venetians as *"orecchioni"* (big ears).

SANTA MARIA DELLA SALUTE: A MUCH-LOVED VENETIAN FESTIVAL ✪
Venice is at its best in the fall, and November 21 is the best day to visit the Baroque church of Santa Maria Della Salute. That day, a procession is held to commemorate the intercession of the Mother of Mercy during the great plague of 1630. For the occasion a pontoon of boats spans the Grand Canal.Then the party begins and everyone tucks into fritelle (fritters).

THE BASILICA OF SANTA MARIA DELLA SALUTE. On October 22, 1630, the Senate decided to build a church in honor of the Madonna, in order to mark the end of a plague which had devastated the city. The site of the new sanctuary was one of the finest in Venice, adjoining St Mark's Basin. Its first stone was laid on April 1, 1631, before the Seignory had even chosen an architectural design from the various basilical and central models on offer. In the end, a central plan was decided upon, submitted by the thirty-two-year-old Baldassare Longhena, for whom this was to be the first major architectural commission. At that time, neither Bernini nor Borromini had yet undertaken any work of importance, so Longhena's project was entirely revolutionary, as he himself was the first to acknowledge. The effect was all the more striking in that his huge octagonal construction (which was covered in Istrian stone, crowned with two domes and flanked by a pair of campaniles) was made to rise out of such unassuming urban surroundings. On the outside of the building, half-columns resting on massive pedestals and a gigantic staircase distinguished the main Palladian façade from the seven other sides of the basic octagon. Inside, six chapels were clustered around the central space, which was crowned with a tall dome supported by eight enormous pillars. The second dome (over the choir) was built on a much smaller scale. At a later stage Longhena designed the high altar, which is brought to life with statues by Josse Le Court (1670). After the death of Longhena, his work was completed by Antonio Gaspari

> "The classic Salute waits like some great lady on the threshold of her salon [...] with her domes and scrolls, her scolloped buttresses forming a pompous crown."
>
> Henry James

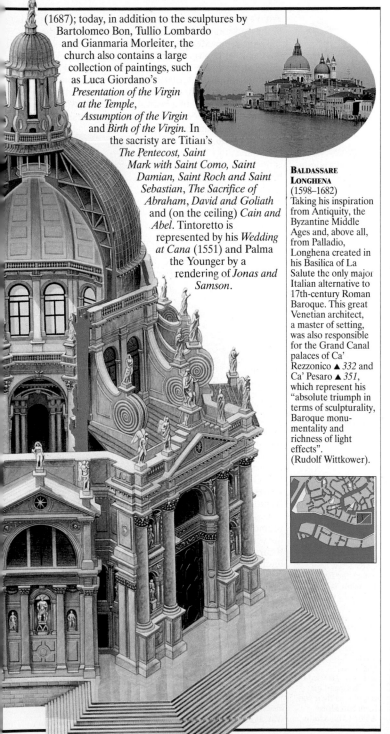

(1687); today, in addition to the sculptures by Bartolomeo Bon, Tullio Lombardo and Gianmaria Morleiter, the church also contains a large collection of paintings, such as Luca Giordano's *Presentation of the Virgin at the Temple*, *Assumption of the Virgin* and *Birth of the Virgin*. In the sacristy are Titian's *The Pentecost, Saint Mark with Saint Como, Saint Damian, Saint Roch and Saint Sebastian*, *The Sacrifice of Abraham*, *David and Goliath* and (on the ceiling) *Cain and Abel*. Tintoretto is represented by his *Wedding at Cana* (1551) and Palma the Younger by a rendering of *Jonas and Samson*.

BALDASSARE LONGHENA (1598–1682) Taking his inspiration from Antiquity, the Byzantine Middle Ages and, above all, from Palladio, Longhena created in his Basilica of La Salute the only major Italian alternative to 17th-century Roman Baroque. This great Venetian architect, a master of setting, was also responsible for the Grand Canal palaces of Ca' Rezzonico ▲ *332* and Ca' Pesaro ▲ *351*, which represent his "absolute triumph in terms of sculpturality, Baroque monumentality and richness of light effects". (Rudolf Wittkower).

319

THE FESTIVAL OF LA SALUTE ● 49. On November 21 (the day of the Presentation of the Virgin at the Temple) in the year 1687, the Doge Marcantonio Giustinian swore a solemn oath that henceforth, every year on the same date, the Venetians would repair to the Church of La Salute as a token of their devotion and their eternal gratitude to the Madonna for bringing an end to the plague which had ravaged the city. This oath forms the basis of a festival which, along with the Festival of the Redeemer ▲ *339,* is among Venice's most characteristic religious occasions. Still popular even today, this ceremony has been

THE PLAGUE DOCTOR
This costume was invented in the 16th century by the French physician Charles de Lorme. The plague doctor, masked like a huge bird with spectacles and a beak filled with medicinal herbs and essences, visited the sick in the times of plague that so frequently afflicted Venice. He also wore gloves and a long linen or canvas coat soaked in wax, and he carried a stick with which he raised the bedcovers and clothing of the plague victims – expecting, somewhat naïvely, to be protected from contagion by all this paraphernalia.

faithfully (and most sincerely) observed by many subsequent generations of Venetians; in it were united both their religious faith and the sentiment that they belonged to a community whose past glories were now reawakening after a dark interlude. Traditionally, on this day the gondoliers bring their oars to be blessed by a priest, who stands on the steps of the basilica.
CAMPO DELLA SALUTE. On the actual day of the Festival of La Salute, the campo is entirely occupied by stalls selling candles, religious images, toys and freshly cooked pastries. The promenade between the basilica and the Grand Canal quayside was built in 1681.
SEMINARIO PATRIARCHALE. This seminary stands beside the basilica, on a part of the site that was formerly occupied by the buildings of La Trinità (these were demolished so as to make way for La Salute). This ancient complex formerly included a Gothic scuola and a Venetian-Byzantine church dating from the 11th or 12th century and ceded to the Teutonic knights by the Republic in exchange for their assistance during the war against Genoa ● *31.*

THE WOODEN BRIDGE
Today as in the past, and here as at Il Redentore ▲ *338,* a temporary bridge is built across the Grand Canal a few days before the Festival of La Salute is held. Originally the bridge rested on boats (right); today it is supported by pontoons. Crossing the canal opposite Santa Maria del Giglio ▲ *264,* this walkway was used by the Doge and his retenue on their way from San Moisè ▲ *261* to La Salute.

> "The statue of Fortune, in the form of a weathervane standing atop the world, gives a true idea of the perceptions of the time, and of the hopes and ideals of the last days of Venice."
>
> John Ruskin

After the suppression of the Knights, Pope Clement VIII decided in 1596 to establish a seminary directed by monks and dedicated to the education of orphans. When La Salute was built, this seminary was reconstructed by Longhena. Abandoned when the monks were forced to leave the city by Napoleonic edict, the building was ultimately placed at the disposal of the Seminario Patriarcale by the Austrians in 1815. Today it contains a museum and the Manfrediniana picture gallery, created by Marchese Federico Manfredini (1743–1829). (Continue along the Fondamenta della Salute.)

THE CUSTOMS POINT

When the original customs post near San Biagio ▲ *181* became inadequate to handle the volume of goods entering Venice, the Republic decided to establish a *dogana di terrà* (land-based customs post) to check imports from the mainland on the Riva del Vin ▲ *287*, near the Rialto, and a *dogana di mare* (sea customs) at the end of the Dorsoduro sestiere. The latter was built in the 15th century: its role was to investigate the ships which entered the port of San Nicolò before they dropped anchor in St Mark's Basin in front of the Doge's Palace. Between 1677 and 1682, the customs buildings were reconstructed by Giuseppe Benoni, who won a contest for the project in 1677. For the warehouses, Benoni held to a strictly parallel distribution of buildings behind a continuous façade. Instead of the crenellated tower which stood at the point of the sestiere until the beginning of the 16th century, he erected a lower construction in the shape of an L, with a portico and a small white tower. The roof-ridge of the customs house is topped by bronze statues bearing a golden ball, on which stands a statue of *Fortune* which was sculpted by Bernardo Falcone.

THE ZATTERE

This broad quayside was built following a decree promulgated on February 8, 1516. In 1640, an order was given by Giovanni Valier and Giuseppe Barbarigo, the administrators of timber and forestry for the Republic that, from that time onwards, all cargoes of wood were to be unloaded at this point. Since lumber came from the Forests of the Cadore to Venice by flotation (*zattera*) on the current of the River Piave, the quay was named "Zattere". Beginning at the customs point and ending at Santa Marta, this area now constitutes a delightful promenade which was a favorite place of the American poet Ezra Pound ▲ *153*, who customarily spent six months of each year in the city. The second half of the walk is full of cafés with delightful terraces that extend on rafts over the water; these are particularly pleasant during warm weather because they face south. Here you can be sure of the best Gianduiotto ice-cream in Venice – a delicious blend of chocolate, honey, hazelnuts and whipped cream. (Take the Rio terrà ai Saloni.)

THE CUSTOMS POINT
This is the small triangular area at the very tip of the Dorsoduro sestiere. It was also called La Trinità, as were the church and the scuola on the same site, and *Punta del sale*, after the many old salt depots of the Zattere.

THE ZATTERE: A STROLL ON THE QUAYSIDE AND DELECTABLE ICES ✪
Strolling along the south-facing Zattere, which runs between La Salute and the harbor, is a favorite occupation with Venetians. Café terraces on piles reach right onto the water. It is good place in which to relax in the sun or to enjoy lunch in the open air. Not to mention the perfect opportunity to try a homemade ice cream at Nico or Aldo. For those who love architecture, there is the church of Gesuati, which is a harmonious blend of the classical Palladian style and Baroque, decorated by Tiepolo.

THE CHURCH AND HOSPICE OF THE CATECUMENI. The government of the Republic automatically gave asylum to all infidels who were prepared to renounce their faith. A large number of prisoners ready to do this were taken at the Battle of Lepanto ● *36* and installed in a group of houses in the vicinity of the old *dogana di mar*; nearby an oratory dedicated to John the Baptist was constructed. A century and a half later, in 1727, the architect Giorgio Massari was commissioned to design a new building for neophytes. On the rio terrà side, the wings of the hospice enfold the Corinthian pilasters and triangular pediment of the church façade; elsewhere it extends around a courtyard and an elegant little cloister with a portico. (Return to the Zattere.)

MAGAZZINI DEL SALE. This was where salt, Venice's only raw material, was stored. To judge by the acreage of saltpans, the industry must once have been a thriving one; certainly the levy raised on the mineral by the *proveditore* was one of the Republic's most important sources of revenue. The Biennale ▲ *184* at one time used these old warehouses as exhibition halls.

MAGAZZINI DEL SALE
Built in the 14th century and restored during the Austrian occupation ● *34*, these depots stood on the Giudecca Canal. Nowadays, the Società Remiera Bucintoro puts up its boats there between regattas ● *55*.

THE CHURCH AND CONVENT OF SPIRITO SANTO. The Santo Spirito Church and Convent were founded in 1483 by Maria Caroldo, a Dominican nun belonging to the order of St Catherine of Siena. The convent quickly attracted rumors of scandal, its foundress being accused of having a priest as a lover and of squandering the funds of the community. The punishment imposed on her does not appear to have acted as a deterrent, however, because other scandals also broke out in the convent during the 16th century, and the Inquisition had to step in several times to restore order. At about the time that the Fondamenta delle Zattere was created, the religious complex was rebuilt, with a new rectangular cloister and portico in place of the former monastery and church. On a newly acquired site, another church was built to face the fondamenta, on which, in 1506, the neighboring Scuola dello Spirito Santo had already been installed. This scuola was suppressed in 1810 and its premises were then turned into a warehouse. The sanctuary contains Palma the Younger's *Marriage of the Virgin*.

The Churches of the Gesuati and Santa Maria della Visitazione.

OSPEDALE DEGLI INCURABILI. A charitable institution of the Venetian government, the Ospedale degli Incurabili was financed by the city's noble families and the rich bourgeoisie; one of the obligations of the dominant classes was to bear the cost of foundations such as these. It

> "The palaces and churches, in their great masses,
> rise light and miraculous like the harmonious
> dream creations of some young god."
>
> Ivan Turgenev

would seem that, during the 16th century, the hospice was reserved for incurable syphilitics, but very soon after it was also taking in abandoned children. Like the Pietà ▲ *174*, the Derelitti ▲ *160* and the Mendicanti ▲ *159*, the Incurabili became a kind of music conservatory. In 1527 a program of restructuring was begun, which was not completed until 1591. The buildings were arranged around a broad rectangular courtyard containing a church which was destroyed in 1831. Transformed into a hospital (1807), and then into a barracks (1831), they were used until very recently as a center for the re-education of minors. (Take the Rio terrà dei Gesuati.)

THE CHURCH OF SANT'AGNESE. In contrast to many other Venetian churches, the 11th–12th century Sant'Agnese has only partially changed over the years. Although its structure has been modified and its interior décor destroyed, the organization of the inner space remains basically that of a Byzantine basilica. Closed in 1810, it was reopened for worship towards the middle of the 19th century and then became the oratory of the adjoining College of Cavanis. (Return to the Zattere.)

I GESUATI
Inspired by the classical Palladian manner, the Church of the Gesuati has a façade with four gigantic Corinthian half-columns, crowned by a cornice and a triangular pediment with an oval at its center.

THE CHURCH OF THE GESUATI. The order of the Gesuati, dedicated to hospital service, was suppressed in 1668 on the grounds of immorality; as a result its headquarters on the Zattere (the Convent and Church of Santa Maria della Visitazione) reverted to the Dominicans. In 1724 the latter commissioned Giorgio Massari to build a new church and convent on an intermediate property, barely touching the original Renaissance ensemble. While the architect was working on his project, the monks managed to raise sufficient alms and donations to complete a church (1726–36). The interior of this building is made up of a single nave, or rather a long rectangle with rounded ends and three chapels on each side. The vault is pierced with large half-moon windows, while a dome with a lantern light in its center soars over the choir. Most of the statuary is by Gianmaria Morleiter, while the paintings are by Sebastiano Ricci, Giambattista Piazzetta and Giambattista Tiepolo, and deal mostly with subjects relevant to the Dominican tradition. Ricci created an altarpiece of *Pius V with Saint Thomas and Saint Peter the Martyr*; Piazzetta, in another altar painting, has depicted three Dominicans, Saint Vincenzo Ferrer, Giacinto and Luigi Beltran. Tiepolo's contribution included episodes in the life of St Dominic in the small side panels of the ceiling, as well as the *Institution of the Rosary* in the central panels. This shows the Virgin's

Mist over the Zattere, beside the Incurabili.

PALAZZO CONTARINI CORFU
Where it stands on the junction of Rio di San Trovaso and the Grand Canal, the distinctive feature of this palace is its little corner tower. The Contarini family bore the surname of dagli Scrigni, a reference to the many jewel caskets said to be hidden in the walls of their villa near Padua.

apparition to Dominic with a rosary in her hand, followed by the saint's popularization of this convenient new way of praying. She proffers her rosary to Dominic, whose figure stands out starkly black and white against a background of vivid color; at the base of the composition, the faithful await the saint's transmission of the Virgin's gift. Also by Tiepolo is the altarpiece of three much-venerated Dominican saints – Catherine of Siena, Rose of Lima and Agnes of Montepulciano. Taken as a whole, this decorative ensemble confirms the Gesuati as one of the loveliest expressions of Rococo art in Venice.

THE CONVENT OF THE GESUATI. Due to a lack of funds, the convent here was not begun until 1751. Over the years the part of it directly behind the church was nearly completed; but the newer and much larger buildings planned for the area between this first edifice and Santa Maria della Visitazione have remained unfinished.

SANTA MARIA DELLA VISITAZIONE. This tiny church, which was reconstructed between 1494 and 1524, stands adjacent to the Church of the Gesuati. Its most notable features are a fine façade in the style of Lombardo, an early 16th-century cloister, and, near the entrance, the lion's mouth into which people dropped nasty notes denouncing one another to the authorities.

SAN TROVASO ★

"SQUERO" ● *69*. A curious sight awaits you as you round the corner of Rio Trovaso and Rio Ognissanti. Here you might think yourself not in a great and populous city, but in some corner of an Alpine village. There are three buildings, curiously built of wood; one even has a long balcony not unlike the ones on chalets in the Dolomites. The two taller buildings serve as living quarters, while the third is a

workshop fronting a small dock. It transpires that this is the oldest of the *squeri* (gondola boatyards) still in existence; it has been here since the 17th century. Though they are now very rare, the *squeri* ▲ *147* of Venice formerly numbered in the hundreds and could be found in every part of the city. Before the Arsenal ▲ *177*

Only two or three gondolas are built each year in each one of the *squeri*; but every vessel then requires some major maintenance. Every fourteen years, the axis of a gondola needs to be realigned.

monopolized the shipbuilding industry, these yards built and repaired boats of every size and description. Today the *squeri* are restricted to gondolas, and this one is the busiest of all. Despite the high cost of building a gondola (each costs about twenty million lire) the yard has enough advance orders to keep it working for ten years. The only difficulty it faces is a shortage of craftsmen.

RIO DI SAN TROVASO. As the link between Venice's two main arteries, the Grand Canal and the Giudecca Canal, this

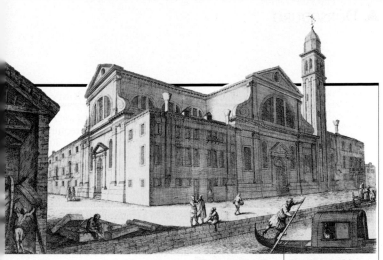

waterway has always carried heavy boat traffic. It was lined with splendid houses and some even finer gardens. Some of these gardens are no longer what they were, but nonetheless they count among the last of their size in Venice.

THE CHURCH OF SAN TROVASO. The word "Trovaso" is yet another baffling Venetian elision, in this case of the names of "Gervasio e Protasio". Founded in the 9th or 10th century, it was several times altered before being totally reconstructed at the end of the 16th century along Palladian lines. The main façade overlooking the Rio degli Ognissanti is divided into two registers. Two slender wings, defined by pilasters with Corinthian capitals, flank the central part of the building,

The Church of San Trovaso and its two entrances, one overlooking the campo, the other facing the river.

which has a broad half-moon window topped by a triangular tympanum. The rear façade is much the same. The floorplan takes the form of a Latin cross with a single nave and side-chapels. *Joachim Driven from the Temple* (in the choir), *The Temptation of Saint Anthony* (in the Milledonne Chapel), *The Last Supper* and *Christ Washing the Feet of the Leper* (in the Chapel of the Sacrament) are all by Tintoretto, with the possible exception of the last, which is merely attributed to him. Other treasures at San Trovaso are Palma the Younger's *Deposition from the Cross* and *Birth of the Virgin*, *Saint Chrysogonus Mounted on a Horse* by Giambono (15th century), and a magnificent Renaissance bas-relief of *Angels Bearing the Symbols of Christ's Passion*, surrounded by other angels with musical instruments, which is in the Clary Chapel.

CAMPO SAN TROVASO. As often happens in Venice, the Church of San Trovaso juts fairly extensively into its campo and effectively divides it into two parts. Each of these parts has its own well, the most interesting being the raised white-stone one in Campo San Trovaso proper. The Venetians, who were unable to reach the water table by digging, were obliged for many centuries to make do with rainwater supplemented by fresh supplies brought by ship from the mainland ● *81*.

THE "SQUERAROLO"
The supply of timber for Venice's naval industry came from the mountains of the Cadore. After the close of the 16th century, the wood was sent exclusively to the Zattere. Naturally enough, the inhabitants of the Cadore region excelled in everything to do with wood and the working of wood. They became the first *squeraroli* (owners of *squeri*) and built vessels in their yards that looked not unlike the houses they lived in.

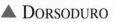

RIO DELL'ARZERE
Behind the Angelo Raffaele, a bridge spans this rio bearing the three escutcheons of the "Proveditore".

The area is an old one, traditionally occupied by fisherfolk who kept it busy and lively. In the early morning the fishermen would return here to sell their catch at the quayside.

THE CHURCH AND CONVENT OF THE OGNISSANTI

This part of Dorsoduro was virtually deserted when its religious occupation began. In the early 15th century, a group of Benedictine nuns abandoned their convent on Torcello as the island had become unhealthy due to malaria ▲ *374* and their buildings were no longer inhabitable. So they established themselves at Dorsoduro. A new church had already been built when the nuns acquired a "miraculous" image of the Virgin in 1472. This stroke of fortune brought in much-needed cash to enable them to rebuild and enlarge the church and convent. But the order was not very wealthy, and work advanced so slowly that the second church was not consecrated until 1586. After the suppression of the order in the 19th century, the church and convent lay abandoned until GB Giustinian transformed them into a home for old men. It is now a hospital (the Ospedale Giustinian).

THE CHURCH OF SAN SEBASTIANO
With their dazzling colors, daring effects of foreshortening and exuberant ornamentation, Veronese's decorations inside this church are uniquely beautiful.

THE ANGELO RAFFAELE QUARTER

THE CHURCH OF SAN SEBASTIANO ★.
This church, built in the 16th century by Lo Scarpagnino, has a modest exterior. Inside is one of the finest cycles of paintings by Veronese to be found in Venice. He began with the sacristy in 1555, decorating its ceiling with a scene of the *Crowning of the Virgin*, complete with images of the Four Evangelists. The following year he tackled the nave, completing the three major scenes from the life of Esther framed on the ceiling. The frescoes of the *Annunciation*, St Sibyl, and other saints were finished in 1558; the whole cycle was completed in 1565, with two great canvases for the main chapel: *San Marco e Marcellano esortati al martirio da San Sebastiano,* and *Il Martiro da San Sebastiano*. At his own request, Veronese is buried in this church. His tomb is marked

> "It is charming to disembark at the polished steps of a little campo – a sunny, shabby square with an old well in the middle, an old church on one side and tall Venetian windows looking down."

Henry James

by a plaque, at the foot of the organ, which he decorated thirty years before his death ▲ *269*.

THE CHURCH OF L'ANGELO RAFFAELE. There was a place of worship on this spot as early as the 7th century; several times rebuilt, it was given its present dimensions in 1618 by the architect Francesco Contino, though the façade is somewhat later (1735). A group over the portal featuring the Angel Raphael and Prophet Tobias invites the visitor to enter. Above the entrance on the inside, five panels showing episodes from the life of Tobias extend to the organ loft. These were executed in about 1749 by one of the greatest proponents of Venetian Rococo, Gianantonio Guardi (1698–1760), brother of Francesco; they are considered his masterworks. The theme of the angel Raphael is echoed at the back of the choir in a work by Michelangelo Morleiter (1729–1806). A local story has it that two lacemakers living near the Church of l'Angelo Raffaele made a collar out of snow-white strands of hair, and it was worn by Louis XIV at his Coronation.

"I NICOLOTTI" ▲ *334*
The Nicolotti were one of the city's two factions. The day they elected their leader, the *gastaldo*, was a holiday, and the mast used to fly their banner stands in the middle of the campo to this day.

I MENDICOLI

I Mendicoli is one of the outer districts of Dorsoduro, which today is mostly occupied by ordinary working people. It owes its name of Mendicoli (beggars) to the poverty of its original inhabitants, who were mainly artisans and fishermen.

SAN NICOLÒ DEI MENDICOLI. The simplicity of this church is as charming as it is rare in Venice. Far from the political and economic hubs of the city, and thus deprived of the donations and benefits normally conferred by wealthy parishioners, it has changed little over the centuries. According to tradition, San Nicolò was founded in the 7th century by a group of Paduans displaced by the Lombard invasion; it was rebuilt in the 12th century, and the central part of the façade with its gemelled window dates from this era. The 15th-century portico is one of only two its kind in Venice (with that of San Giacometto ▲ *283*) to have survived; apparently *pinzocchere* (zealots) were in the habit of spending long hours doing penance here. The central apse of the interior, with its Byzantine cornice, is the most ancient feature of the church.

San Nicolò in gloria, de Lorenzo Lotto (détail).

PALAZZO ZENOBIO
This building is unusual for Venice, since it has two wings on the side of its garden (one of the loveliest in the city). At the close of the 18th century, the building was further adorned with a pavilion designed by Temanza, which was used for its archives and library.

FONDAMENTA BRIATI

THE FONDAMENTA. This is named in honor of the glassmaker Giuseppe Briati (1686–1772). In the 18th century the Venetian glass industry was in deep crisis ▲ 366, for while the craftsmen of Murano clung to traditional local methods, the rest of Europe had become infatuated with the robust cut-glass of Bohemia and Silesia. After a visit to Prague, Briati returned to Murano in 1730 and set up a works specializing in Bohemian-style glassware, obtaining from the Council of Ten a monopoly to produce it. But the other glassmakers resented Briati and attacked his workshop; Briati sought permission to move his business into Venice, finally alighting here.

PALAZZO ARIANI. The façade of this building offers one of the most attractive examples of Venetian Gothic to be seen in the

city. The rest is constructed in the L-shape which is so typical of 14th-century palaces, with a fine courtyard and an outside staircase. The Ariani family fortune lay in the increasing amount of traffic on the river passing through Fusina. At the time of the "closure" of the Grand Council ● 31, the Arianis were invited to join the patricians of Venice, despite their bourgeois Istrian origins. A century later they were excluded, after an obscure squabble over a bad debt, and were never again reinstated.

PALAZZO ZENOBIO ★   ▲ 383

The Palazzo Zenobio was built at the close of the 17th century by the architect Antonio Gaspari. Today it is recognized as one of the most significant examples of Baroque architecture in the city. Its white façade, which is topped by a large curvilinear tympanum broken in the middle in the Romanesque manner, is something of a novelty for Venice. Though he himself had been a pupil and colleague of

Longhena, Gaspari seems to have preferred in this case to seek inspiration in the work of the great architect Francesco Borromini, whose style he sought to bring to the city. The interior has the special charm common to nearly all Venetian palaces built at that time. The landscapes of its *portego* were executed by one of the first artists to specialize in views of Venice, Luca Carlevaris, who was protected for many years by the patrician Zenobios. The trompe-l'oeil architectural perspectives enlarging the already enormous space of the ballroom, served three decades later as a model for the artists decorating a similar room at the Ca' Rezzonico. Over the entrance of this ballroom, adorned with undulating gold and white stucco, is the tribune where the orchestra sat. In the 19th century, Palazzo Zenobio was acquired by the Armenian brotherhood, founded by Méchitar, which converted it into a college for young people of Armenian origin ● *328*.

INTERIOR OF PALAZZO ZENOBIO (above)

PALAZZO ARIANI
The incomparable stone arabesques of this palazzo's six ogival windows add much to the

I CARMINI

SANTA MARIA DEL CARMELO (I CARMINI).
Though the Campo Santa Margherita was already a self-contained urban entity, the immediate environs of the future church were still deserted when work began on it. This may explain why two exits were planned, one towards Santa Margherita and the other towards the future Campo dei Carmini. Begun in 1286, the works were finished in 1348. In the early 16th century, the façade was rebuilt in Renaissance style, and between 1653 and 1674 wooden panelling was installed in the nave to cover Gothic features, some of which are still visible elsewhere in the church. Between the nave and choir are two choristers' galleries decorated with episodes from the life of Christ (Andrea Schiavone, 16th-century). Among other works, the church has a *Nativity* (c.1509) by Cima da Conegliano (right-hand nave, second altar) and *Saint Nicolas in Glory between Saint John the Baptist and Saint Lucy,* an altarpiece painted by Lorenzo Lotto c.1529 (left-hand nave, adjoining the side portal). There used to be a passage from the sacristy to the convent cloister. This elegant Renaissance building is now the seat of the Art Institute. (Entrance to the right of the church.)
SCUOLA GRANDE DEI CARMINI ★. From its beginnings in Palestine, the Order of Our Lady of Mount Carmel began to

spread to the West in 1235. Forty years later it was formed into a confraternity of women known as the *pinzocchere dei Carmini* (Carmelite zealots), who carried a scapular showing the image of the Virgin. The Virgin herself is said to have appeared to The Blessed Simon Stock to assure him of the perpetuity of the Carmelite order; as a consequence it was opened to males in 1595. The Counter Reformation was a time of great

splendour of its unique façade. At one time, the building was very richly decorated, but many of its paintings and tapestries were sold abroad. After their family's exclusion, several of the Ariani attempted to regain admittance to the Grand Council with results that were sometimes dramatic. One family member had counted on his military exploits during the Genoese war to bring him back into favor, and when this did not happen he abandoned his wife and children, took religious orders, and left Venice for ever.

Courtyard
of Ca' Foscari.

expansion for the Carmelites because of the development of the cult of Mary as a counterweight to Protestantism, and by 1675 their order embraced no fewer than 75,000 members. The Carmelite church was their Venetian headquarters until 1625, at which time they purchased several other adjoining buildings and hired the architect Cantello to convert them. Following the acquisition of the corner building in 1667, Longhena was called in to unify the ensemble. In 1767 the order became a scuola grande ▲ 295, which was suppressed in 1806, then revived again in 1840. The fame of this scuola today lies in the decoration of its upper gallery, executed by Giambattista Tiepolo between 1739 and 1749; the middle of the ceiling is taken up by a rendering of *Our Lady of Mount Carmel Appearing to the Blessed Simon Stock*, with allegories of virtue and scenes from the life of the Virgin all around it. In the archive room there is a *Judith and Holophernes* by Giambattista Piazzetta (c.1743).

AROUND CAMPO SANTA MARGHERITA ★

CAMPO SANTA MARGHERITA. This is one of the liveliest squares in Venice. In place of the present Rio terrà Canal and Rio terrà della Scoazzera, there used to be a canal with a dumping ground beside it. This made the campo very much a working people's zone: the few patrician mansions here are all on the Rio di Santa Margherita side, and are all pre-15th century. They include two small Gothic palaces (one of which has an overhanging Tuscan roof, a rarity for Venice), and the lovely PALAZZO FOSCOLO-CORNER, which was worked on in the late 14th century by the Celegas, who were the architects of the Campanile of the Frari ▲ 293. Their contribution was probably no more than an adjustment, because most of the elements here (the gateway, for instance, with its Byzantine lunette) definitely date from the 13th century. The far side of the campo is closed off by the Church of Santa Margherita, which is now part of the university. The campanile to the side has at its foot some splendid Baroque sculptures in marble, notably a fearsome dragon. In the middle of the campo is the SCUOLA DEI VAROTERI, or Furriers' Guild, formed during the 13th century. The bas-relief (1501) over the door here was brought from the Furriers' previous headquarters in the Cannaregio district.

CAMPO SANTA MARGHERITA
During the warmer months of the year, it is a particular delight to sit in one of the many tree-shaded cafés around this broad campo. Plays and musical festivals are often held here.

THE CHURCH OF SAN PANTALON. The first church on this site, dating from the 11th century, was demolished in the 17th century and rebuilt between 1668 and 1686 by Francesco Comino, an architect from Treviso. Comino reoriented its façade away from the canal and toward the campo, but it was never completed. The interior, which has a single vaulted nave and side chapels, is a perfect example of the Baroque ideal; in a stunning tour de force of perspective, the painted vault duplicates and prolongs the architecture of the nave, and abounds elsewhere in daring effects of foreshortening. The decoration of the choir by Gianantonio Fumiani

The picturesque Campo Santa Margherita, with its many shops, is also the scene of a daily fish and vegetable market.

(1650–1710) is in the same spirit, and the paintings include the *Miracle of Saint Pantalon* (1587) by Veronese, the *Crowning of the Virgin* (1444), an altarpiece by Antonio Vivarini and Giovanni d'Alemagna, and a triptych attributed to Paolo Veneziano (in the Sacro Chiodo chapel).

CA' FOSCARI. The building of the palace known as Ca' Foscari coincided with the start of the process of transforming the Grand Canal, which reached its height in the Renaissance and Baroque periods. Built by the Giustinian family at the turn of the 14th and 15th centuries, the original palace was flanked by two towers that were a characteristic of Venice's most ancient *fondachi*. It was purchased in 1428 by the Seignory, which presented it to one of the generals of the Republic, the Marchese di Mantua; it then seems to have passed to Francesco Sforza in 1439. In 1452 it was bought at auction by the Doge Francesco Foscari, who demolished it and raised the present building instead. According to Ruskin, Ca' Foscari is "the noblest example in Venice of the 15th-century Gothic style". The openwork décor of the windows counterbalances the massive size of the palace and its foursquare shape. On the landward side, the gateway is embellished with *putti* bearing the arms of Foscari. Francesco Foscari himself died in November 1457, aged 84, just a few days after he had been relieved of his office by the Council of Ten. Twice he had seen his only son banished from Venice for corruption, murder and treason, an episode which inspired Byron's historical drama *The Two Foscari*. His dogate was one of the longest in the city's history (1423–57) and, despite opposition, had successfully inaugurated the policy of expansion on the mainland ● *32*. By the 19th century Ca' Foscari was in a pitiful state of repair, so much so that it had to be bought and restored by the municipal authorities. Today it is the principal seat of the university, and adjoins the headquarters of the Venice Fire Department.

THE CEILINGS OF SAN PANTALON
This ceiling carries the largest painted decoration ever laid on canvas. It depicts the martyrdom of Pantalon, physician of the Emperor Diocletian, who was put to death for converting to Christianity. Fumiani worked on it from 1680 to 1704, filling forty panels mounted on wooden frames. Legend has it that the artist was killed in a fall from his scaffolding, and was buried in the church.

CA' REZZONICO

FROM LONGHENA TO MASSARI. Around 1667, the procurator Filippo Bon commissioned Baldassare Longhena to build a palace in place of two houses he owned at San Barnaba. Only the first floor and *piano nobile* were completed by the architect's death in 1682, after which the work ceased because the Bon family fell into serious financial straits. For over seventy years the palace remained covered with a temporary wooden roof, for its owners had been bled dry by the expense of building the first half. Finally, in 1751, they gave up and sold the unfinished building to the wealthy Rezzonico family. In his original design Longhena appears to have sought a classical balance of simplicity and formality; the ground floor was done in bossage stonework, and the first floor had windows with key arches embellished by masks (inspired by the Marciana ▲ *254*). Massari, who was engaged by the Rezzonicos to complete the second floor, replaced Longhena's half-columns with pilasters and tempered some of the original austerity with small oval windows. Inside, Massari's influence is more powerful. The traditional Venetian *portego* ● *88* was supposed to cross from one side of a palace to the other. Here it was reduced to leave room on the canal side for a ballroom two floors high. The fitting out of grandiose reception rooms on the *piano nobile* and the new use given to the mezzanine floor (changed from the original offices to winter living quarters) also reflect the development of a patrician way of life increasingly geared to luxury.

THE APOGEE OF THE REZZONICOS. The Rezzonico family originally came from Como; they joined the Venetian nobility in 1687 in exchange for the 100,000 ducats they contributed to pay for the war in Crete ● *34*. For Giambattista Rezzonico, the acquisition of the palace of San Barnaba was the confirmation of this new social position. And

PIETRO LONGHI ▲ *312*
The museum's collections contain paintings by 18th century Venetian masters such as Rosalba Carriera, Tiepolo and Guardi . . . not forgetting Pietro Longhi. This "Molière among painters", as André Chastel has described him, contrived to record Venetian society at the height of its glory, portraying the city's inhabitants like so many actors in a play. In *La Cioccolata del mattino* (1775–80), (below) the figures

appear as if they are on stage, with the priest on the left, and the lady lounging in bed at the center with her *cavaliere* standing behind.

then, barely two years after the completion of the palace, his son Carlo, bishop of Padua, was elected Pope. The Venetians, scarcely able to contain their delight at the prospect of a Venetian reigning at the Vatican, awarded the title of Knights of St Mark to the Rezzonicos, an honor that had previously been strictly reserved to the three most ancient patrician families. The Pope responded by presenting the Republic with the order of the Golden Rose; and in 1769, the year of his death, Ca' Rezzonico was chosen as the venue for a reception

in honor of Emperor Joseph II. It was the scene of many similar balls and receptions before the collapse of the Republic, which was followed in 1810 by the death of the last Rezzonico and the

dispersal of his goods and furniture. Ca' Rezzonico then went through a series of different owners before it was bought by the Italian state for conversion into a museum (1934).

THE MUSEUM OF 18TH-CENTURY DECORATIVE ARTS ★, ● 44.
Opened to the public in 1936, the collections at Ca' Rezzonico include paintings, pieces of furniture, faïence and porcelain from a number of different palaces. On the first floor, the ballroom and a smaller adjoining room (the "Brustolon" room) are devoted to work commissioned from the celebrated cabinet maker Andrea Brustolon by Pietro Venier. The most spectacular piece is an extravagant console table held up by a statue of Hercules set between Cerberus and the Hydra. A *Nuptial Allegory* painted by Giambattista Tiepolo on the ceiling of the Nuptial Room for the wedding of Ludovico Rezzonico and Faustina Savorgnan in 1758, is matched by another Tiepolo masterpiece, the *Allegory of Merit*, in the Throne Room. To get from one to the other, the visitor must pass through the Pastel Room (several works by Rosalba Carriera) and the Tapestry Room with its Flemish hangings. Here the *ciocche* (chandeliers in the shape of bouquets of flowers), the looking glasses and the mirrored wall-brackets constitute the glassmakers' contribution to the original 18th-century décor, the most extravagant *cioccha* of all being a 20-branched specimen (left) by Giuseppe Briati ▲ 328. On the second floor, the rooms called "Villa Zianigo" are devoted to a cycle of frescoes painted by Giandomenico Tiepolo just after the fall of the Republic for his country house near Mirano; and farther on a blend of Rococo and chinoiserie characterizes the "Green Laquer Room", while the "Alcove Room" is a faithful reconstitution of an 18th-century bedroom, dressing-room and boudoir. Every element is here, down to a fifty-eight-piece silver *nécessaire*. Lastly, an 18th-century puppet theater and a reconstituted 18th-century pharmacy are displayed on the third floor.

The furniture of Andrea Brustolon (1662–1735) owes much to Baroque statuary, particularly in its combination of boxwood and ebony.

CARLO REZZONICO
Born in 1693 in a Grand Canal palazzo, ▲ 196, he became the fifth Venetian Pope under the name of Clément XIII.

THE "FELZE"
A small wooden cabin used as a cover for gondolas ● 57.

In a scene from his sentimental comedy *Summertime* (1955), David Lean had Katharine Hepburn fall into the Rio di San Barnaba.

NICOLOTTI AND CASTELLANI
The caps and sashes of the Nicolotti ▲ 327 were black; those of their sworn enemies, the Castellani, were red.

SAN BARNABA

CAMPO SAN BARNABA. The parish of San Barnaba was founded during the early 9th century, when the Doge was decamping from Malamocco in favor of Venice ● 30. Its center grew from a group of houses on the southern side of the campo, which in fact shared the characteristics of the oldest campi – a simple rectangle bounded by a canal, with a church at one end. Today's Church of San Barnaba has a classic façade of half-columns and Corinthian capitals, built in the 18th century. By contrast the campanile has remained almost unaltered since its construction around the year 1000, with the exception of a conical spire that was added in the 14th century and which makes it one of Venice's more interesting silhouettes. It was from this parish of San Barnaba, where many of them lived, that the impoverished nobility of the city got their nickname of *barnabotti* ▲ 226. The Casino dei Nobili was formerly in the sottoportico San Barnaba (on the right as you face the church) which was known as the *sottoportico del casin* in consequence. At the fall of the Republic, San Barnaba was still a refuge for ruined nobles, who were given free lodgings here. Nowadays one of its more singular features is a brightly colored barge that is tied up to the fondamenta, from which fruit and vegetables are sold.

PONTE DEI PUGNI. Although any bridge in Venice could become a battleground for brawling factions, some of them were specially favored: thus the Ponte della Guerra at San Zulian, the Ponte della Guerra at Santa Fosca, and the Ponte dei Pugni (literally, Bridge of Fists), where prints marking the dividing lines can still be seen. The district-by-district rivalries of Venice broadly separated the city into two clans: the Castellani, who lived in the sestieri of Castello, San Marco and part of Dorsoduro, and the Nicolotti, who hailed from Cannaregio, San Polo, Santa Croce and the parish of San Nicolò dei Mendicoli ▲ 327. Tradition has it that this rivalry first came into existence before the city itself, when the two mainland towns of Heracleia and Jesolo migrated en bloc into the Lagoon bringing an old quarrel with them. Whether or not this is actually true, the factions of Venice liked nothing better than to engage in regular pitched battles, which the government was unable – or unwilling – to prevent. It should not be forgotten, of course, that it was in the Republic's interest to have seasoned fighting-men at the ready in case of war; moreover it was highly convenient that

Men who fell in the water during the struggle could return to their places in the ranks by passing over the boats of the spectators, or by clambering onto the nearest bridge. As the fight went on, the crowd grew progressively more excited, and since many of the spectators were perched on balconies and *altane*, it was not unusual to see stones, rooftiles, chairs and boiling water showered down on the combatants below. As a rule the brawl tended to spread to the packed throngs along the canalsides and on the boats.

one side could be played off against the other to head off a united rebellion. Thus the government opted to feed the rivalry by imposing its own rules of engagement. The brawls usually took place on the bridges; they were permitted by law between September and Christmas, and they were precisely regulated. First of all, a challenge was issued, then "godfathers" were chosen as referees, and a bridge was selected for the encounter. On the appointed day, the factions turned out with their "godfathers" and formed ranks amid the din of castanets, trumpets and drums. Then, harking back to the days of chivalry, collective and individual challenges would be heralded; prior to a more general scrimmage, the best fighters of either faction were in the habit of duelling one to one, or in *mostre* (combats of two against two). After this the *guerra* commenced in earnest, with the two factions charging the bridge with the aim of taking possession and holding it. The subsequent mêlée might go on for several hours, after which a toll of a dozen men killed was considered nothing out of the ordinary. Until the 16th century, the two sides fought with their bare knuckles or else with rushes, double pointed, tipped with steel and then hardened by immersion in boiling water. In the latter case, they also wore breastplates, helmets and gauntlets. But the rushes eventually caused too many casualties, and so were banned in favor of fisticuffs – until 1705, when the Council of Ten promulgated its umpteenth decree that outlawed this factional brawling. For some obscure reason this decree appears to have had its effect, though all of those that had gone before it had been completely ignored.

PITCHED BATTLES
The last pitched battle where steel-tipped rushes were used was in 1574 during a visit by Henri III of France. Six hundred men were involved, and the carnage was so great that the king had it stopped.

335

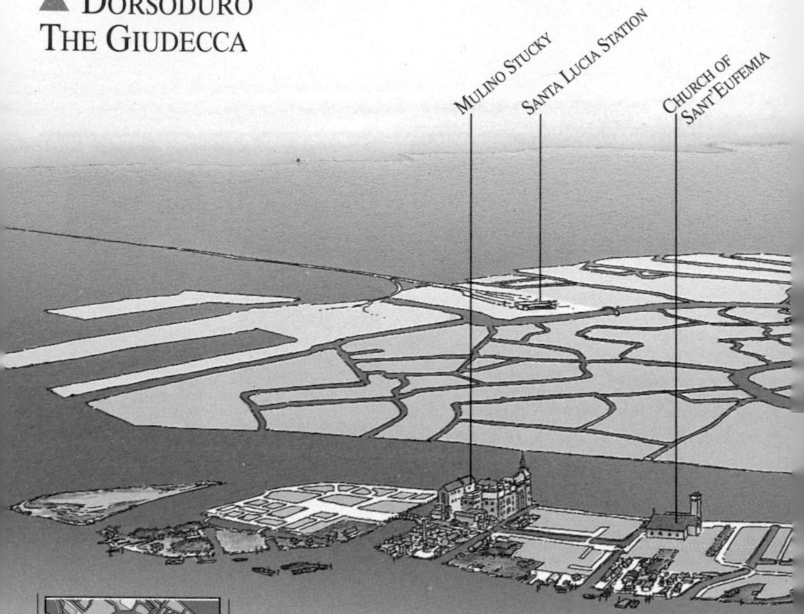

MULINO STUCKY SANTA LUCIA STATION CHURCH OF SANT'EUFEMIA

🚋 **Two minutes**
⏳ **Two hours**

"There is only one street on the island of Spinalunga . . . with blind alleys running out of it like the teeth of a comb."

Frederick Rolfe,
*Desire and Pursuit
of the Whole*

THE GIUDECCA ★

THE HISTORY OF THE ISLAND. Originally called Vigano, after the early name of the Giudecca Canal, or else *Spinalunga* ("long spine") on account of its fishbone shape, this island owes its present sobriquet to the word *giudicato*, referring to a 9th-century judgement passed on dissident families, banishing them from Venice and assigning them certain parts of the "Giudecca" in which to live. The name has nothing to do with the presence of a Jewish community, as is commonly thought. In the 14th and 15th centuries, major palaces were built along the Giudecca Canal. On the other side of the island facing the Lagoon, the only buildings were monasteries hidden in the greenery (there were about seven of them, mostly now destroyed), and a few small palaces here and there, occupied by schools of philosophy and literature. At that time, and for several centuries, the Giudecca was a resort for wealthy patricians, who maintained villas and gardens there, which is why it was regularly visited by famous men like Michelangelo. Already the island possessed, in Sant'Eufemia, one of the oldest churches in Venice; in the 16th century it was further enriched by the Churches of Il Redentore and

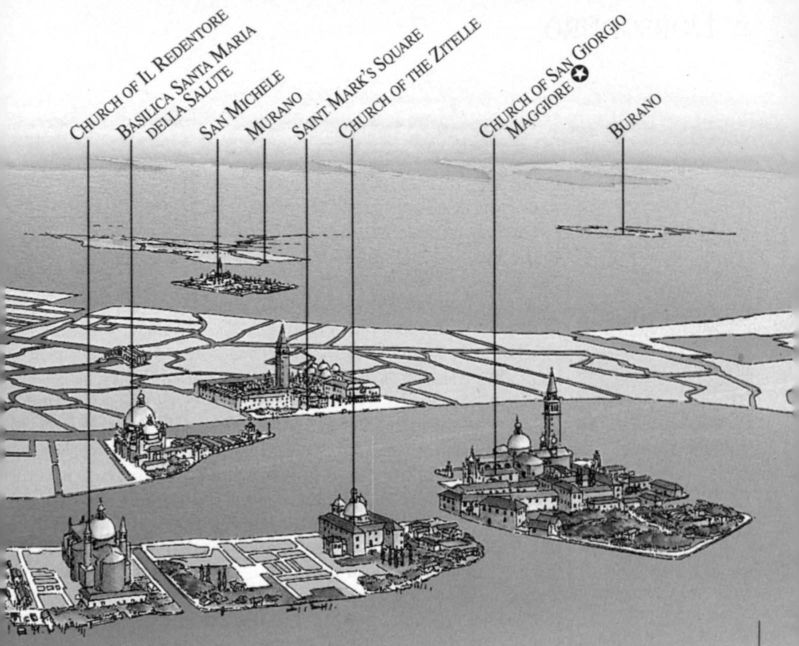

CHURCH OF IL REDENTORE
BASILICA SANTA MARIA DELLA SALUTE
SAN MICHELE
MURANO
SAINT MARK'S SQUARE
CHURCH OF THE ZITELLE
CHURCH OF SAN GIORGIO MAGGIORE ✪
BURANO

the Zitelle, both of which were designed by Palladio, the greatest architect of his time. In the 19th century, various industries were established on the Giudecca with a view to resuscitating the Venetian economy. Factories were set up; some moved into the surviving religious buildings. Little trace remains today of all this activity save gutted hulks like the highly visible Mulino Stucky. In the 20th century the Giudecca has remained on the fringes of Venice, to some extent ignored by the worlds of industry and commerce. Recently, it has drawn considerable profit from a program of decentralization.

FROM SANT'EUFEMIA TO MULINO STUCKY

THE CHURCH OF SANT'EUFEMIA.
Founded in the 9th century and dedicated (according to the 14th-century chronicles) to one of the four martyrs of Aquileia, Sant'Eufemia has been much altered over the years. The 18th century, in particular, has left its mark on the interior. The side portal (1596) came from the demolished Church of San Biagio e Cataldo on the island. The triple-naved basilica plan of Sant'Eufemia harks back to the 11th century, and some of its capitals are Venetian-Byzantine. On the first altar in the right-hand nave is *San Rocco and the Angel* by Bartolomeo Vivarini (1480); on the altar of the left-hand nave is a Pietà sculpture by Gianmaria Morleiter (18th century). After major restoration work in the 18th century by the Neo-classical architect Tommaso Temanza, the church was decorated in 1764 by Canaletto, then aged nineteen. For his frescoes, the young painter took the work of Giambattista Tiepolo at the Gesuati as his model, covering the ceiling of the naves with a *Santa Eufemia in Glory* (center), a *Baptism of the Saint* (left) and an *Episode from the Life of the Saint* (right). A short walk

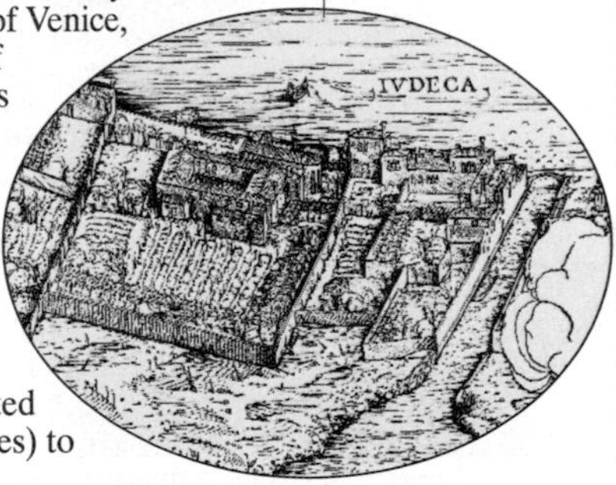

The Giudecca has lost most of its old gardens, which can be seen here on De Barberi's magnificent map (c.1500). They have since made way for new buildings.

along the Fondamenta del Rio di Sant'Eufemia leads to the charming presbytery garden, which is full of roses in the spring. (Take the Fondamenta San Biagio.) Note in passing PALAZZO FOSCARI (number 795), a flowered Gothic building that dates from the 15th century, with two *piani nobili* each with a set of four windows (one set is three-cusped, the other topped with ornamental capitals).

MULINO STUCKY. In 1883, Giovanni Stucky established several mills at the western end of the Giudecca. His business was so successful that in 1895 he decided to enlarge it still further. The project submitted by a Hanoverian architect to satisfy Stucky's grandiose vision caused much bafflement, but Stucky found an infallible way to overcome the reservations of the municipality: he simply threatened to fire all his workers if he did not get his way. Around the huge new factory a number of lesser buildings used for subsidiary industries began to cluster; but the whole enterprise fell into decline after Stucky himself was murdered by one of his employees in 1910. The firm was

With the Mulino Stucky, Northern architecture made an incongruous entry into the Venetian skyline. But, not unlike the British House of Commons, it is now a familiar feature of the city.

finally closed down in 1954. The Mulino, whose condition today is nothing less than catastrophic, is to be transformed into a "multifunctional center". Returning by the same road, look out for the FORTUNY FABRIC FACTORY (number 804) ▲ *273*, founded in 1919 and enlarged in 1920, which today employs thirty people and exports its products all over the world. Number 801 is a former brewery; through its gates, one can see that the central building here apes the Neo-Gothic style of the Mulino Stucky. (Return to the Fondamenta del Rio di Sant'Eufemia and continue straight on.)

FROM SANT'EUFEMIA TO ZITELLE

THE CHURCH OF IL REDENTORE. By the time the Senate voted in September 1576 to build a church dedicated to the Redeemer if Venice was freed from the plague, a quarter of the city's population had already perished. The death rate fell dramatically in the ensuing bitter winter. In February, Andrea Palladio was chosen as architect for the new church, and a green site was allocated on the north side of the Giudecca that was visible from every side of St Mark's Basin. Palladio had already left a strong impression on this panorama with his Church of San Giorgio. The works began in 1577 and were completed in 1592 by Antonio da Ponte after Palladio's death in 1580. The late 17th-century statues on the outside are by the school of Josse Le Court; inside, the single nave is lined with intercommunicating chapels. The altarpieces were commissioned by the Senate from the best available artists and conform to an agreed pattern: on the right, the *Nativity* (Francesco Bassano), the *Baptism of Christ* (School of Verona), *The Flagellation* (School of Tintoretto); on the left, *The Deposition* (Palma the Younger), *The Resurrection* (Francesco Bassano) and *The*

The Church of the Redeemer, Il Redentore, "is Palladio's most accomplished and beautiful work in Venice". (Terisio Pignatti)

Ascension (probably by Domenico Tintoretto). The canvases on the reverse wall of the façade are later, while the Baroque high altar dates from the late 17th century. Behind the altar, beyond the five tall Doric columns, are the monks' stalls and there are sacristies at either side of the choir. The one on the right is open to visitors; it contains several Venetian masterworks, notably Veronese's *Baptism of Christ* and two very beautiful 18th-century reliquaries. In the monastery precinct is the Church of Santa Maria dei Angeli, the first Capucin sanctuary on the Giudecca (c.1560), along with the old monks' pharmacy, which is full of china and alchemical instruments from the 17th and 18th centuries.

CASA DEI TRE OCI. This odd Neo-Gothic house was built by a painter at the beginning of this century. It owes its name to its three round windows.

THE CHURCH OF THE ZITELLE. Designed by Palladio and completed in 1586, the Church of the Zitelle has a façade with a central tympanum flanked by two pinnacle turrets. Its interior is polygonal, with a large dome. It has been altered so as make it suitable for concerts, seminars and other events. Its name alludes to the girls, who were poor but honest, and taken into the adjoining convent in the 18th century, where they produced the highly prized "Venice point" lace. Nearby is the 14th-century house of the family of Alvise da Mosto, the celebrated 15th-century navigator.

HOTEL CIPRIANI. The Cipriani stands on the south-eastern shore of the Giudecca, in its own park; it also boasts its own heated seawater swimming pool. There is no fondamenta along the south shore, but on the way back to Sant'Eufemia try cutting through the middle of the island, which turns out to be a busy working-class area. Head first for the old naval dockyard, near the Rio del Ponte Lungo; then for the Junghans watch factory, founded in 1878 (the building has been converted into flats). From here, continue past the Corti Grandi, which were the headquarters of the Venetian coconut-fiber industry between 1878 and 1950.

FESTIVAL OF THE REDEEMER ● 49
After the first stone of the church was laid on July 21, 1577, the Doge Alvise Mocenigo and the patriarch went to visit the site. A bridge of boats was organized to enable people to join the ceremony, and so the Feast of the Redeemer began. Every year, the Doge, high officials, clergy and population of Venice processed across the canal on a bridge of boats from the Zattere. During the Republic, the ceremonies lasted three days: the secular festival on Saturday, the procession on Sunday, with Monday a day on which everyone enjoyed themselves on the island. The Festival of the Redeemer is still held on the third Sunday in July, with the patriarch's procession and mass in the church. There is firework display the evening before.

339

Two minutes

One hour

◆ D A4-A5-A6-B4-B5-B6

SAN GIORGIO MAGGIORE ★

HISTORY. The site of San Giorgio Maggiore appears to have been used in Roman times. In 982, the Benedictines established themselves there, and soon enough the island, known as the "Green Isle" or the "Isle of Cypresses" (a description shared by a cloister in the monastery), became one of the Republic's most favored locations for distinguished foreign visitors. Its position in St Mark's Basin opposite the Piazzetta ▲ 249 made it a strategic point controlling the traffic between the lagoon and the canals crisscrossing the city. After the fall of the Republic, it was turned into a free port; a new harbor was constructed in 1812, and subsequently the island became the headquarters of the artillery before

returning to its original cultural vocation thanks to the Cini Foundation. Administratively, it is a part of the San Marco sestiere ▲ 258.

THE CHURCH OF SAN GIORGIO MAGGIORE. This church looks out over St Mark's Basin, of which it is one of the principal architectural components. Begun by Andrea Palladio in 1566, it was completed a quarter of a century later by Simone Sorella. For the façade Palladio borrowed a number of elements from classic pagan temples, such as a triangular pediment and a large *pronaos* (portico) with four columns, completed on the sides with half-pediments and pilasters. On the inside is a striking atmosphere of serenity and harmony, mostly due to the light flooding the building through broad window apertures inspired by Roman baths. The inner walls are covered with stucco and Istrian stone of perfect smoothness; and at the rear of the building, four steps and a balustrade mark off the monks' stalls from the square choir, which has columns at each of its four corners. It was always the custom that on St Stephen's Day (December 26) the Doge came to hear Mass at San Giorgio, sung by a double choir of St Marks' choristers and the Benedictine monks of the adjacent monastery. Palladio

The Church of San Giorgio and the Cypress cloister.

SAN GIORGIO MAGGIORE, ISLAND OF CYPRESSES ✪
The island of San Giorgio, which can be seen from St Mark's Square, is well worth a visit. It can be reached by vaporetto (no. 82). The finely proportioned church is by Palladio, who also designed the Cypress cloister in the monastery (note the superb Baroque staircase). From the top of the bell tower (take the lift) there is an unusual view of the Lagoon and its host of small islands.

took this into account in his design for the stalls, which were completed by Gaspare Gatti in collaboration with Albert van der Brulle, who also executed the bas-reliefs of episodes from the life of St Benedict (1594–8). The choir is decorated with canvases by Tintoretto: *Manna from Heaven* (left-hand wall) and *The Last Supper* (right-hand wall). On the high altar is a bronze group by Girolamo Campagna (1591–3) who also sculpted the marble of the second altar to the left. A door to the right of the choir leads through to the conclave room where Pius VII was elected Pope in the last century. Here there is an altar-piece by Carpaccio (1516) of St George and the Dragon, rather later than the one in San Giorgio degli Schiavoni ▲ *162*. On the way out, note Sebastiano Ricci's *Madonna* (1708, in the chapel to the right of the choir), a 15th-century crucifix in polychrome wood (second altar to the left) and an *Adoration of the Shepherds* by Jacopo Bassano (first chapel to the right). In the 17th century four works by Giulio del Moro were added to the façade; these were the statues of St George and St Stephen (to whom the church is dedicated) and the funerary monuments of the Doges Tribuno Memmo and Sebastiano Ziani. Anyone wishing to contemplate the most beautiful view of the Lagoon to be seen from any point in Venice should climb to the top of the great campanile, erected by Scalfarotto in 1726.

THE MONASTERY OF SAN GIORGIO. In 829, Doge Partecipazio could already refer in his will to a "Church of San Giorgio". In 982, the Doge Tribuno Memmo gave the island to Giovanni Morosini, a noble who had joined the Benedictine order, with the proviso that the church should still depend on St Mark's. In return, the monks undertook to drain the surrounding marshes and repair a mill. The monastery was reconstructed by order of Pietro Ziani, a former Doge, who retired there. At the start of the 15th century, the reorganization of the

The monumental double-sided staircase which leads from Palladio's cloister to the priest's apartments was designed by Longhena. The statue by the Paliari brothers in the niche on the landing represents an allegory of the Serene Republic.

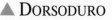

The Palladian façade of San Giorgio, directly opposite the Piazzetta ▲ 249, has been reproduced by countless painters.

THE LIBRARY
Today the library of San Giorgio boasts over a hundred thousand volumes, as well as two globes constructed in the early 18th century by

a Franciscan cosmographer, Father Vincenzo Coronelli.

Benedictines into the congregation of St Justina prompted dissension, with some monks concerned at the consequences of a change in their relation to the Venetian government. This was resolved in 1430, when Doge Foscari decided the monastery should accept the congregation in exchange for a pledge of loyalty to the Republic. In cultural terms, the monastery retained close links with Florence and Padua: to such effect that Cosimo de' Medici, banished from Florence

in 1433, took refuge at San Giorgio, bringing with him the architect Michelozzo. A library was built (demolished in 1614) on his orders and at his expense, which had a great influence on the Venetian masters. Towards the end of the 15th century, the architectural ensemble of San Giorgio Maggiore was radically altered. The Gothic church had overlooked the cypress cloister, facing the center of the island and the monastery. Its replacement faced the other way, toward St Mark's Basin. A new dormitory and "laurel" cloister designed by the Buoras, and a refectory by Palladio were added in 1561. Palladio continued to work at the monastery until his death.

THE CINI FOUNDATION. In 1951, the art patron Count Vittorio Cini chose the Monastery of San Giorgio as headquarters for his foundation, which he named after his son Giorgio Cini, killed in a flying accident. Since then the rooms of the old building have been filled with permanent collections of paintings, furniture and other items. Concerts, seminars and exhibitions also take place in this important arts center.

THE TEATRO VERDE. Vittorio Cini was also behind the construction of this Greek-style open-air theater, called "green" because it is set in the middle of a large garden. Closed in 1974, it was reopened in 1999 on the occasion of the Biennale ▲ 184 of dance, drama and music.

Santa Croce

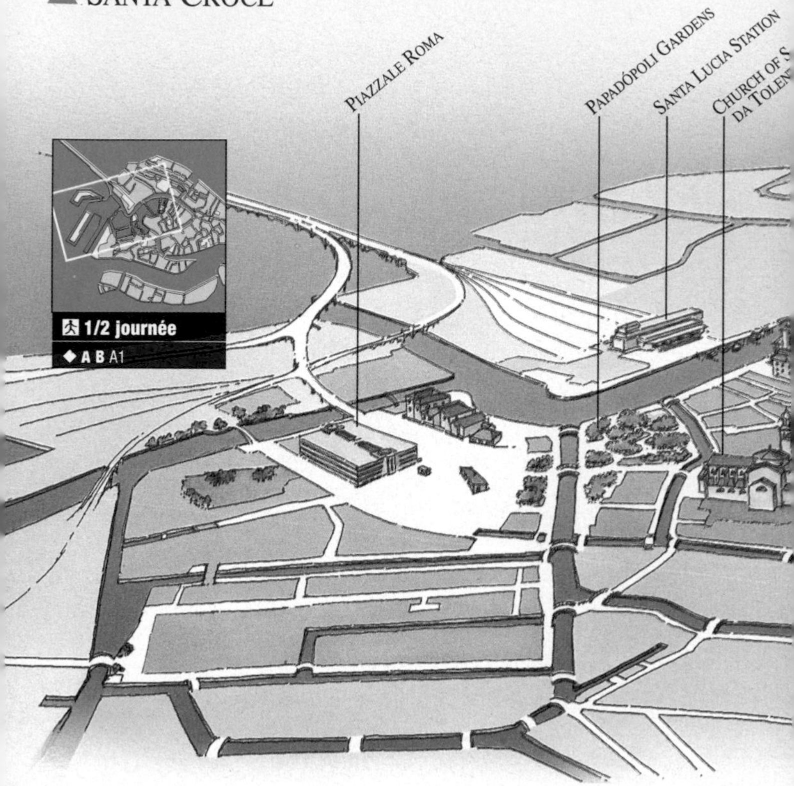

PIAZZALE ROMA

PAPADÓPOLI GARDENS

SANTA LUCIA STATION

CHURCH OF S.
DA TOLEN

1/2 journée
◆ A B A1

The creation of the tram line that runs between Venice and the mainland eventually meant that the Piazzale Roma had to be equipped with multi-storey garages. After this came the excavation of the Rio Nuovo (which was completed in 1938) to link the Piazzale with the

station, the center of the city and the Lido ▲ *354*. Since the garages were inadequate and expensive, another parking area was created just a few years ago in the Tronchetto area.

The sestiere of Santa Croce, in the northwest of Venice, covers ninety-four acres. It has two very distinct areas. The east side is very old and typically Venetian; to walk here is to be, to some extent, away from the crowds, in a minor area of Venice – but one which nevertheless can boast some of the loveliest palaces on the Grand Canal. The western part is completely different. During the last two centuries, industrial complexes have appeared in the old buildings, and in some cases have replaced them; at the same time, this part of the sestiere has grown in size with the filling-in of large expanses of water (notably the port area and the Tronchetto).

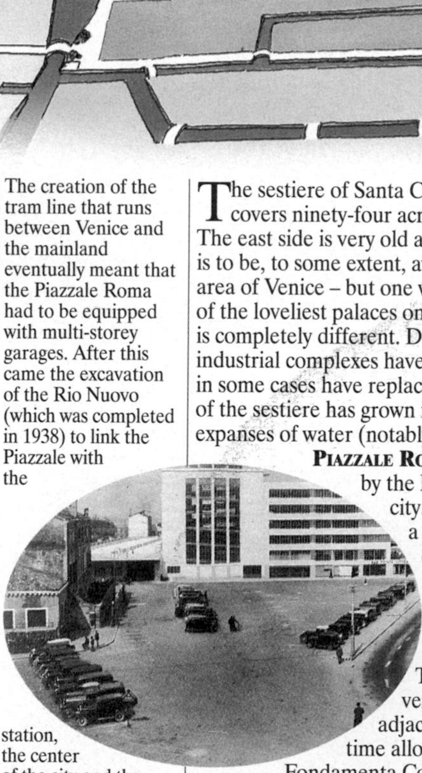

PIAZZALE ROMA. Coming to Venice by car, it is by the Piazzale Roma that one enters the city. The piazzale has been remodeled, a process that has entailed the demolition of several buildings and the modernization of the trolleybus terminus. Coaches stop there just long enough to take up or set down visitors, but go to park in the Tronchetto. Vehicles may make very brief stop and in the small adjacent parking lot the maxiumum time allowed is 30 minutes. (From the Fondamenta Cossetti, cross the elegant stone bridge that spans the Rio Nuovo.)

THE PAPADÓPOLI GARDENS. In 1810, a number of buildings were demolished to make way for these gardens; among them were the Church and Monastery of Santa Croce, which stood on the junction of the Grand Canal and the Rio dei Tolentini, and which had given the sestiere its name. (Cross the Ponte dei Tolentini.)

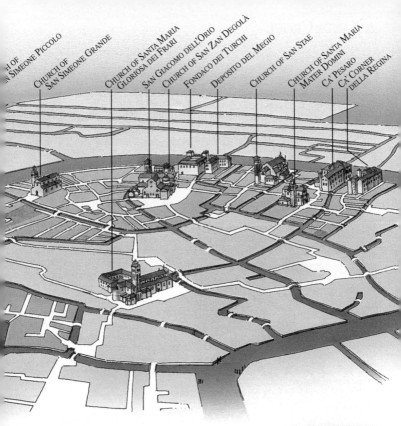

THE TOLENTINI

THE CHURCH OF SAN NICOLÒ DA TOLENTINO. In 1527, when Rome was sacked by the troops of Charles V, the Theatine Order (founded just a few years earlier by St Gaetan de Tiène and Jean-Pierrc Carafa) sought and found asylum in Venice. The following year, their congregation established itself in an oratory which adjoined the Church of San Pantalon ▲ *330*, and which was dedicated to San Nicolò da Tolentino. Towards the end of the century, it was decided that the ensemble should have rather different architectural proportions, and so a new church and monastery were planned. The project was initially entrusted to Scamozzi, but after a disagreement with his employers, the Theatines themselves decided to take control of the works. The new church was duly consecrated in 1602. Its interior consists of a single nave with three side-chapels. Until the 18th century there was a dome above the transept; this was then demolished and replaced with a flat ceiling decorated with frescoes by Gerolamo Mengozzi Colonna and Gaetano Zompini. On the outside, the roof was covered with tiles in the usual way. Just like those in the side-chapels, the altars in the two main chapels at the ends of the transept were paid for by wealthy Venetian families. The high altar was

The Piazzale Roma quarter.

"Shadows ripple on the bridges, and on the distant water vessels move: you can hear them puffing and blowing, and their wake churns the water right up to our canal."

Jean Giono,
Voyage en Italie

The door of the Architecture Faculty.

commissioned from Longhena in 1661, who subcontracted it to the sculptor Josse Le Court. The interior of the church was finally completed in 1671. Thirty years later, the Theatine order set about constructing a façade, which was executed between 1706 and 1714 by Andrea Tirali and paid for by the patrician Alvise Da Mosto. Its principal features are an eight-columned Corinthian portico and a Palladian pediment.

THE MONASTERY. The monastery was begun at the same time as the church, but was not completed until the first decades of the 17th century. The cloister is broad and elegant, standing

to the left of the church almost back-to-back with its choir. The LIBRARY and REFECTORY were also built to the same impressive proportions. Today these premises are the seat of Venice's architectural faculty, which is one of the foremost institutions of its kind in Italy; it has a main entrance designed by Carlo Scarpa who, like many other great Italian architects, was once a teacher here.

SAN SIMEONE

THE CHURCH OF SANTI SIMEONE E GIUDA APOSTOLI. To distinguish it from its close neighbor, this church is still known as San Simeone Piccolo (the Lesser), despite the fact that it was much enlarged during the 18th century. Giovanni Scalfarotto designed and built it between 1718 and 1778 on a carefully integrated plan; its dome is immense and has much in common with the Neo-classical church of La Salute ▲ 318. The entrance portico consists of Corinthian columns with corner pillars which are crowned by a triangular tympanum in marble. At present, the church is not in use as a place of worship. (Continue to the Ponte dei Scalzi, then take the Calle Longa Chioverette, and then the Calle Bergama, and finally cross the little bridge.)

CARLO SCARPA (1906–78)
Carlo Scarpa taught architecture in Venice from 1926 onwards. His special interest was in museums and exhibitions: he was responsible for the Venezuelan pavilion at the Biennale ▲ 184, the Canova Museum in Possagno, the restoration of the Palazzo Querini-Stampalia ▲ 167, and the Castelveccio Museum in Verona.

SAN SIMEONE PROFETA (OR SAN SIMEONE GRANDE). Founded in 967, San Simeone Grande was rebuilt at the beginning of the 18th century by Domenico Margutti, and then again by Giorgio Massari in 1755. Massari added the Rosary altar and a façade, the stylistic unity of which was comprehensively wrecked by an 1861 restoration. San Simeone Grande is constructed along the lines of a basilica; it contains several paintings by Palma the Younger, as well as a fine monument to St Simon (1318) which reflects the influence of the school of Pisa. The second altar on the left belonged for a while to

the
SCUOLA DEI
GARZOTTI, the
woolcarders' guild,
whose workshops once lined
the Fondamenta del Rio Marin.
The original pavement, which was
covered-over in 1630 by order of the
public health magistrate because a plague
victim had been buried there, has now been
uncovered and is well worth a visit. The portico
against the left-hand side of the church contains a 15th-
century tombstone on which is carved the image of a praying
bishop. The campanile was rebuilt during the 18th century in
more modest dimensions. (Take the Lista Vecchia dei Bari;
after the Campiello Riello, turn left into the Rio terrà, then
right into the Calle Bemba.)

SAN ZAN DEGOLÀ

CAMPO SAN ZAN DEGOLÀ. This campo, with its church in one
corner and the canal of the same name in front, has always
been a quiet place slightly apart from the bustle of Venice –
this was so even when the Fondaco dei Turchi attracted
hordes of merchants. The transformation of the adjoining
areas has had little effect on this atmosphere of calm.
THE CHURCH OF SAN ZAN DEGOLÀ. Dedicated to the
decapitated St John, the origins of this church are very
ancient. Starting as a simple oratory in the 7th and 8th
centuries, by 1007 it had become a parish church. The Venier
family is thought to have paid for the building, which was
restored by the Pesaros in the 13th century. Today its
proportions still offer a precise idea of Venetian-Byzantine
notions of architecture, despite changes
made to the apse and façade in the 18th
century. The triple-naved basilical
interior has a keel-vaulted ceiling, while
the simple volutes on the façade
accomplish a graceful marriage between
the two wings of the church and its taller
central body. San Zan Degolà was closed
during the Napoleonic occupation
because of fears it might collapse, then
reopened after restoration work in 1818.

FONDACO DEI TURCHI ★ ● 89, ▲ 193

THE RECONSTRUCTION OF A VENETIAN-BYZANTINE PALACE.
This building, which began as a palace, was so badly damaged
that it had to be compely rebuilt in the 1860's. The result was
a construction sumptuously coated in marble, with the same
expansive Venetian-Byzantine façade as its predecessor: a
long portico on the ground floor, arcades on the upper floors

**SAN ZAN
DEGOLÀ**
In 1358, on San
Giovanni Decollato's
day, the Venetians
defeated the Genoese
at Negroponte.

Inside, Venetian-
Byzantine capitals
crown the Greek
marble columns;
vestiges of Byzantine
frescoes have been
discovered in a side-
chapel.

347

**THE TURKS'
WAREHOUSE**
Even when she was at
war with the
Ottomans, Venice
maintained
commercial
links with

merchants.
The Turks' fondaco
had its doors and
windows closed off,
Muslim-style, and
contained a mosque
and a bath-house. At
the same time, it
served as a
warehouse, trade
center and a bazaar
controlled by a special
magistrature. There
was one restriction
(all imported goods
had to be sold in
Venice), one
interdiction (no entry
for Christian women
and boys) and one
special security
measure (merchants
had to deposit their
money and weapons
on arrival).

and two crenellated towers on either side. Materials from the
old building were re-used and old documents and pictures
referred to in this rebuilding, even though the project as a
whole was not scientifically planned.

THE ORIGINAL BUILDING. The first palace was probably built in
the early 13th century by Giacomo Palmieri, a former consul
of Pesaro on the Adriatic coast, who took refuge in
Venice and founded one of the city's greatest patrician
and mercantile families, the Pesaros ▲ 195. On the
canal side the original building had a long portico,
where merchandise could be conveniently loaded
and unloaded – a typical arrangement in Venice
where great houses often doubled as warehouses
▲ 104. It was one of the largest establishments
on the Grand Canal; indeed in 1381 the state
purchased it as a gift for Nicolas d'Este, Marquis
of Ferrara, as a reward for his loyalty during the
Chioggia War ● 31. From that time, the palace
was what might be called an occasional property of
the d'Este; Venice would confiscate it when relations
with Ferrara were bad, and give it back when they
improved.

THE TURKS. In 1621 the Seignory rented the palace to
Ottoman merchants as their main business locale, with a view
to monitoring their activities. Major alterations were made to
create twenty-four shops on the premises, to which were
added fifty-two bedrooms along with quarters for servants. At
this time the building became known as the Fondaco dei
Turchi (the Turks' Warehouse). Later, as trade with the East
began to decline, the palace was abandoned by its Ottoman
occupants and fell into ruin.

THE MUSEUM. In 1880 the municipality purchased the
Fondaco and restored it. In 1924, after a spell as the Correr
Museum (1898–1922), this former palace became Venice's
Museum of Natural History, and it has been ever
since.

DEPOSITO DEL MEGIO

This austere brick building was one of the many depots in which the Republic stored its grain and flour during times of war and famine. Its date of construction remains unknown, but it is mentioned in an account of the 1346 famine. After being completely remodeled on the inside, it was recently turned over for use as a public school. (Take the Calle del Megio and the Calle Larga.)

CAMPO SAN GIACOMO DELL'ORIO ★

TEATRO ANATOMICO. From the 16th century onwards, this building, which is situated on the north side of the campo (number 1507), was a kind of medical center where many distinguished doctors from Bologna and elsewhere came in order to teach. Today it is a private residence.

THE CHURCH OF SAN GIACOMO DELL'ORIO. This church was built during the 9th and 10th centuries and reconstructed in 1225. It retains a number of its Byzantine traits, despite a series of modifications that have taken place over the years. Between the end of the 14th century and the beginning of the 15th, a broad transept was grafted on to the three-nave basilical plan of the old church. A number of elements (columns, capitals and arches) were also recast in the Gothic style. In 1549 the CHAPEL OF THE SACRAMENT was added to the right of the choir, and the apses were restored in the style of the Renaissance. The brick CAMPANILE dates from 1225. (Return to the Calle Larga and turn right after the bridge into the Calle del Tintor, then turn left into the Salizzada San Stae.)

CAMPO SAN GIACOMO DELL'ORIO
Different explanations have been given for this campo's strange name. The simplest is that it derives from a laurel tree (*lauro*) which once grew next to the church. Another, more fantastical, has it descending through a series of distortions from the word *lupo* (wolf), since packs of wolves used to overrun the area in the dim and distant past. According to yet another theory, the church was named San Giacomo dal Rio (St James of the River) to distinguish it from its namesakes on the Rialto ▲ *283* and the Giudecca. But the most likely derivation is that "Orio" comes from *luprio* (a piece of dry land emerging from a swamp). During the 18th century, the campo was roughly paved over.

PALAZZO MOCENIGO ★

THE MOCENIGO FAMILY. The Mocenigos, who were Lombards by origin, were nonetheless established in Venice for so long that at an early date they were already among the city's oldest patrician families. One branch of the family resided in the San Stae quarter. Having acquired several neighboring houses, Alvise the First, who had been a *proveditore generale* (military governor) in Dalmatia, set about enlarging the family home towards the end of the 16th century. The result was a traditional palazzo, featuring a main hall (*portego*) in its central block ▲ *88*. At the beginning of the 18th century, this building was once again enlarged on its right-hand side, where the *salizzada* is situated today.

THE CENTER FOR THE HISTORY OF COSTUME. When he bequeathed his palace to the city in 1954, Alvise Mocenigo presented the museums of Venice with a doubly remarkable asset. The interiors, for one thing, were completely intact; and for another the furniture and the interior still measured up to the standards of elegance that had prevailed in the great houses of the 18th century. A new library and museum have been installed since the legacy came into effect. The latter contains 5th–7th century Coptic textiles, Italian and French fabrics from the 14th–19th centuries, and 18th–19th century costumes. Palazzo Mocenigo also houses the Vittorio Cini collection of religious drapery and woven fabrics from many different sources. (Continue along the Salizzada San Stae.)

Palazzo Mocenigo was decorated with Rococo frescoes by Jacopo Guarana and Agostino Mengozzi Colonna in 1787; their theme was the apotheosis of the Mocenigo family.

THE "CARRO"
The Pesaros got their fortune and nickname "Pesaro del Carro" from the *carro*, a kind of chariot which they invented to transport boats between the river and the Lagoon. With the construction of locks, the family received dues from the vessels passing through. In 1613, this was appropriated by the State, but the Pesaros were well compensated.

SAN STAE

THE CHURCH OF SAN STAE. Following the destruction of the Venetian-Byzantine church, a replacement was built in 1678 overlooking the Grand Canal. In general, this church (designed by Giovanni Grassi) shows a strong Palladian influence. Its single nave is joined to a deep apse and six side-chapels, the ceiling is vaulted, and all along the walls a heavy coping is supported by stout columns. With its four pillars crowned by a triangular tympanum, Domenico Rossi's façade is likewise thoroughly Palladian. Inside are paintings by Piazzetta, Tiepolo and Ricci.

SCUOLA DEI TIRAORO E BATTILORO ● 87.

To the left of the church stands an elegant construction dating from 1711, which was formerly the headquarters of the goldsmiths' and silversmiths' guild. An exhibition room was installed here in 1876 after the suppression of the scuola. (Cross the bridge and turn left down the Calle Pesaro.)

CA' PESARO ★   ● 91, ▲ 195

THE PATRICIAN PALACE. In 1628, after they had acquired three contiguous palaces, the Pesaros began to unite them into a single building. Leonardo Pesaro inherited the property and set about completing this work, beginning in 1652. The idea of his architect, Longhena, was to create a hall on the ground floor giving on to the Grand Canal, with reception rooms above. To reach the upper floors, he designed a majestic staircase in the center of the building. The lavish wall-facing of the façade was finished in 1679; with its play of chiaroscuro, exuberant sculptures and diamond-point bossage, this

represents a high point in the progress of Venetian Baroque. The deaths of Leonardo Pesaro and Longhena in 1682 brought work to a brief halt, but shortly afterwards it was resumed and the first floor was completed. Gaspari, who took over from Longhena, finished the second floor in 1710, having displaced Longhena's central staircase to the side of the hall, thereby releasing plenty of space.

THE MUSEUM OF MODERN ART. The Veronese Duke of La Masa bought Ca' Pesaro in the 19th century. His widow created a foundation with the aim of exhibiting the work of Venetian artists who lacked the means to make themselves known, before offering the building to the city in 1889. In 1902 the municipality installed a Modern Art Gallery; between 1910 and 1920, exhibitions were organized there which challenged the conformism of the Biennale ▲ 184 and gave artists a chance to express themselves. Today the gallery possesses canvasses by many of the great artists of the 19th and 20th centuries.

THE MUSEUM OF ORIENTAL ART. Partly composed of the collections of Henri de Bourbon-Parme, a great traveller and ethnologist who lived for many years in Venice, this museum has also found a home in the Ca' Pesaro. (Continue along the Fondamenta Ca' Pesaro.)

PALAZZO AGNUSDIO

This building stands at the foot of the Ponte di Forner, number 2060. Three elements of the original 14th-century Gothic palace survive: the five ogival windows, with sculpted representations of the Annunciation and the symbols of the Evangelists above; the landward door

PALAZZO MOCENIGO
Antonio Corradini's frame for a portrait of the magistrate Giulio Contarini da San Beneto bears an allegory of Justice, symbolizing his office within the Republic.

PALAZZO AGNUSDIO
The landward door of this palazzo is surmounted by a 15th-century lunette, which features two angels holding the family's coat of arms. Among the symbols of the Evangelists that can be seen above the windows are the Bull of St Luke and the Lion of St Mark ▲ 250.

with its angel in majesty, encircled by a 13th-century Romanesque frieze; and the waterside door, crowned by a *patera* featuring the mystical Lamb of God – after which the palace is named. (Take the Fondamenta Rimpetto Ca' Mocenigo as far as the Campiello Spezier, then follow the Calle della Chiesa.)

SANTA MARIA MATER DOMINI

The north side of Campo Santa Maria Mater Domini is distinctive for the remains of buildings which date back to the Byzantine era.

CHURCH OF SANTA MARIA MATER DOMINI. According to tradition, the first church on this site was built in 960. It became a parish church in the 11th century, and adopted its present name, abandoning that of Santa Cristina. In the early 16th century the old Byzantine structure was demolished to make way for a Renaissance edifice with a Greek Cross floorplan, four corner chapels and a dome. Two classic volutes bind the lower register of the façade to its Corinthian columns and to the upper register, which consists of a triangular tympanum. (Cross the Ponte Santa Maria Mater Domini.)

THE QUEEN OF CYPRUS
In the 15th century, Venice – which had designs on Cyprus – took advantage of a quarrel over the succession between the two sons of the dead king, John II of Lusignan.

PALAZZO GOZZI. At number 2269 on Ramo Calle della Regina stands the palace of the Gozzi brothers. The onslaught led by Carlo Gozzi against the playwright Goldoni was the central event in Venetian theater during the 18th century ▲ *291*. His brother Gasparo Gozzi was a talented moralist and humorist, who satirized many aspects of Venetian daily life in the press, particularly in the popular *Gazzetta Veneta*. (Continue along Calle della Regina and Calle di Ca' Corner.)

CA' CORNER DELLA REGINA ▲ 196

A 14th-century Gothic palace on this site was the birthplace in 1454 of the celebrated Queen of Cyprus, Caterina Corner. At the beginning of the 17th century her descendants acquired some adjacent buildings, before purchasing Palazzo Grimani on the narrow Calle della Rosa in 1678.

The old king's bastard, James II, appealed to Venice for help, and Caterina Corner was sent to marry him. Widowed within a year of her wedding in 1472, she usurped the Cypriot throne with the help of the Venetian Seignory. But, in 1489, she was recalled to Venice, and had to surrender the island. On June 1, she landed at St Mark's Basin and was received with the honours due to a great monarch.

In 1700 the Corners commissioned the family architect, Domenico Rossi, to rebuild the palace. The old structure was duly demolished and the first stone of the new one laid in 1724. Rossi's plans envisaged a building on a scale that would rival the Ca' Pesaro ▲ *195, 351* but his project was only partially completed. The façade as it survives today is fascinating on account of its elongated form and extended balcony. After Rossi's death, Francesco Bagnolo enlarged the palace on the landward side between the Calle della Rosa and the Calle della Regina, and in the final quarter of the century the interior was decorated with a series of new frescoes. The last of the Corners died in the 19th century, and afterwards the palace passed through many hands before it was finally bought by the Biennale ▲ *184* in 1975 and turned into a depository for archives.

Lido, Chioggia

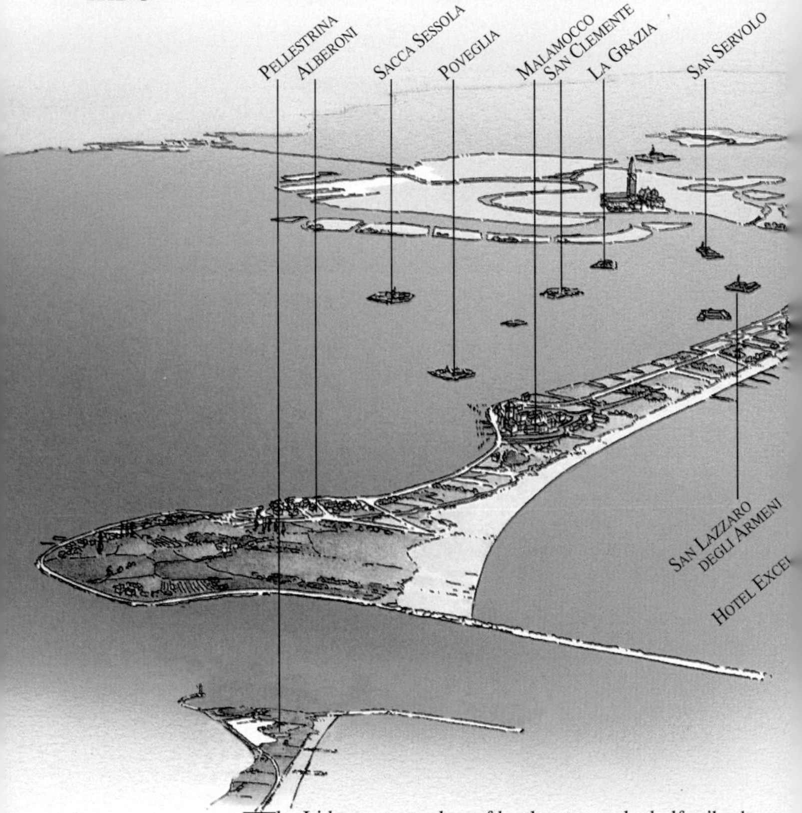

▲ LIDO

PELLESTRINA
ALBERONI
SACCA SESSOLA
POVEGLIA
MALAMOCCO
SAN CLEMENTE
LA GRAZIA
SAN SERVOLO

SAN LAZZARO
DEGLI ARMENI

HOTEL EXCEL

The Lido, a narrow bar of land seven and a half miles long and two and a half miles wide at its broadest point, lies between the Lagoon and the sea. Its long beaches of fine sand, so close to Venice, were "discovered" in the mid-19th century, when Byron, Shelley,

"After an hour, we arrive at the Lido, that long bank of sand which protects Venice from the open sea. At its center stands a church and a village, with vegetable gardens all around . . . on the left, an avenue of trees, old, but renewed by the coming of spring . . . we go forward and three hundred paces farther on we meet the open sea – no longer inert and lake-like as in Venice, but thundering with the perpetual rush and retreat of the ocean, the boil and foam of the waves. And all along the length of this strip of sand there is no-one to be seen . . ."

Hippolyte Taine,
Voyage en Italie

Musset and many of the other romantic writers raved about them. During the late 19th century, buildings began to appear on the Lido, which gradually became both a residential suburb of Venice and a fashionable resort. There are few traces of the past here now; apart from Malamocco ● *30* – with its fine campanile similar to that of San Marco ▲ *248* – only the remains of a church and convent, and of Fort San Nicolò, which controlled the entrance to the Lagoon, testify to an earlier occupation.

🕐 **Half a day**

THE LIDO PROMENADE. There is a car-ferry to the Lido from Tronchetto; otherwise most visitors tend to use public transport. Bicycles and tandems can be rented on the spot on the corner of the Gran Viale and Via Zara. The Lido's main avenue is lined with villas, gardens and elegant shops, and leads through to the open sea. From the Piazzale Bucintoro, you can either go left along the Lungomare Gabriele d'Annunzio and continue on to the military and civilian beaches of San Nicolò as far as the lighthouse, or else you can turn right

along the Lungomare Guglielmo Marconi. This route passes the splendid GRAND HOTEL DES BAINS, which was much frequented in the last century by rich European families. The hero of Thomas Mann's *Death in Venice* stayed in this hotel, which also features strongly in Luchino Visconti's film of the same title. After this you come to the CASINO, CINEMA FESTIVAL PALACE, and the GRAND HOTEL EXCELSIOR. Parallel to the Lungomare Marconi, the Via Sandro Gallo links Piazzale Santa Maria Elisabetta to Malamocco, between the sea and Lagoon. Beyond this is the small district of ALBERONI – one of the few places on the

Lagoon where one can ride and play golf – which is so named on account of the trees (*alberi*) surrounding the fort. The Lido is very different from the city of Venice in aspect, because it consists almost entirely of Neo-Gothic, Neo-Byzantine or Liberty-style villas. Nonetheless, there are one or two interesting monuments to be found here: notably the CHURCH OF SANTA MARIA ELISABETTA (mid-16th century), the CHURCH AND CONVENT OF SAN NICOLÒ with its 16th-century cloister and adjoining planetarium, the church at NOTRE-DAME-DE-LA-VICTOIRE (1925) and the JEWISH CEMETERY, a forest of 16th- and 17th century tombstones ▲ *143*.

THE GRAND HOTEL EXCELSIOR
At the southern end of the Lido stands the odd-looking, Neo-Moorish Grand Hotel Excelsior, side by side with the Grand Hotel des Bains. The residents of this legendary palace are the rich and famous (especially those who come for the Film Festival) and they are here to breathe the sea air and savour the hotel's atmosphere of turn-of-the-century grandeur. In such surroundings it is easy to imagine the aristocrats of the 1890's, sitting elegantly bored under their parasols while their sailor-suited offspring gambolled in the healthy fresh air.

LA MOSTRA : VENICE, CITY OF THE CINEMA

Many hundreds of movies and television films have been made about Venice, or with Venice providing the backdrop. Some would even say that the city has seen too many films and too few masterpieces – although among the latter have been works by Visconti, Antonioni, Fritz Lang, Ernst Lubitsch, Orson Welles and Joseph Losey. It is certainly true that international productions do tend to feature the same houses and public places over and over again, but how could a city as mythical as Venice escape such constant repetition of this kind? It is quite certain that St Mark's Square, the Rialto Bridge, the Bridge of Sighs, the Carnival, gondolas and the pigeons will always symbolize Venice, both in reality and on celluloid.

THE ORIGINS OF LA MOSTRA. The objective of the Festival of International Cinematographic Art, which was inaugurated on the Lido on August 6, 1932, was "to raise the new art of the cinema to a level with the other arts". The new festival was organized within the framework of the Biennale ▲ 184, which already included world-ranking practitioners in music and the figurative arts. The success of the film festival, which was the first of its kind, was so great that the organizers quickly decided to make it a permanent feature of the Biennale's programme, with competing films. The following year, prizes were given, and three years after that the PALAZZO DELLA CINEMA, the present headquarters of the Festival, was built close to the Hotel Excelsior. At that time Italy was a Fascist state; nevertheless the cinema in Venice was relatively unconstrained, at least until 1939. Directors such as John Ford, Joseph von Sternberg, Frank Capra and Jean Renoir brought luster to the competition for best film, encouraging critics to give an intellectual basis to the new art – indeed the first history of the cinema in Italian was eventually written by a Venetian, Francesco Pasinetti.

However during the period of Mussolini's dictatorship and the Second World War, the festival fell into neglect; between 1942 and 1945 nothing was achieved.

THE FESTIVAL AFTER THE WAR. During this period, La Mostra gave prominence to Neo-Realism in the cinema, with films like Rossellini's *Paisa*. A rival festival festival at Cannes was founded in 1946, but Venice for a while managed to hold its own by mounting retrospectives of the work of great directors.

PALAZZO DELLA CINEMA
Designed by the architect Luigi Quagliata, the Palace of the Cinema was built in 1936. Today, it looks as though the Venice Film Festival will have to move to another building, designed by the Madrid architect Rafael Moneo.

CARDBOARD VENICE
The myth of Venice is so strong that film makers do not always take the trouble to go there on location. In Berlin, Vienna and Hollywood cardboard Venices have been built especially for films, and some people found them better than the original. One example is in the operetta *Top Hat* (1935), directed by Mark Sandrich, in which Fred Astaire and Ginger Rogers tap dance in kitsch surroundings.

FROM THE 1950's TO THE PERIOD OF DISPUTE.

FROM THE 1950's TO THE PERIOD OF DISPUTE. All that glistened was not gold for the Mostra during the 1950's; commercial and political interference combined to penalize "controversial" film directors, even though the excellent health of the film industry in general contrived to obscure the defects of the Venice Film Festival. The high point in its history came with the revelation of the film cultures of Japan, India, the USSR and South America, along with the emergence and affirmation of new directions in international cinema. The reputation of the festival was particularly high between 1963 and 1968, under the enlightened guidance of Luigi Chiarini, when it regained all of its former weight and prestige as a showcase and a laboratory for the cinematographic arts. These were the years of the "Nouvelle Vague", when the most coveted film awards were won by such

Poster for the first Venice Film Festival (August 6, 1932).

COMPLICITY

In 1991, the director Federico Fellini presented the Golden Lion to Marcello Mastroianni, his favorite actor, in recognition of his career achievements. Among many films, the pair made *La Dolce Vita* (1960), *Eight and a half* (1963), *La Cité des Femmes* (1980) and *Ginger and Fred* (1985). Mastroianni (born in 1924) has also made films with other great Italian directors such as Antonioni, Visconti, Scola, the Taviani brothers, Marco Ferreri . . . and has had an international career with films directed by Boorman (*Leo the Last*, 1970), Demy (*L'Evénement le Plus Important*, 1972), Polanski

names as Resnais, Tarkowski, Godard, Antonioni, Pasolini, Bresson, Kluge, Buñuel, Bellochio and Visconti. Nevertheless some violent objections and disputes arose, with the result that many of the Festival's awards were spurned. The Biennale was forced into a long period of reform, remaining in a semi-paralyzed state until the late 1970's, when Carlo Lizzani took over and became its director.

THE VENICE FILM FESTIVAL TODAY. Today the Golden Lion awards have been re-established at the Venice Film Festival, although the Biennale and the city of Venice have both still had their difficulties. There are many more competing festivals in existence today, and anyway the cinema is no longer the force that it was. Sixty years after its foundation, the Festival is once again attempting to move its locale and to change its habits, notably by a reduction in its bureaucratic procedures.

(*What?*, 1972), Mikhalkov (*Les Yeux Noirs*, 1987) and Chalonge (*Les Voleurs d'Enfants*, 1991).

🚲 **Half a day**

THE PELLESTRINA COAST
Along this long, narrow ribbon of land run the *murazzi*, giant embankments built in the 18th century to protect Venice and the Lagoon. The idea was first put forward by the geographer Vincenzo Coronelli in 1716, but it was not until April 24, 1744, that the Republic finally made its decision to go ahead. The work lasted from 1751 to 1782. The embankment was 46 feet thick at its base and 13 feet high; originally it was 12½ miles long, extending right up to the Lido.

CHIOGGIA   CATHEDRAL OF SANTA MARIA

Perhaps the most agreeable way to travel between Venice and Chioggia is by bicycle – you can rent one at the Lido and then follow the coastline. Your first stop will be the ALBERONI ▲ *355*, where there is a ferry to San Pietro in Volta. The countryside around here is typical of the area, and famous for its fishing; cross from San Pietro to the main road along the MURAZZI, continuing to Pellestrina, where there is a ferry to Chioggia.

HISTORY

FROM THE ORIGINS OF CHIOGGIA TO THE 14TH CENTURY. According to legend, the city of Chioggia (which was formerly one of the busiest fishing ports in the Adriatic) was founded by Clodius, a companion of Aeneas, hence its antique name of Clodia. This account is probably fairly close to the truth; in any case, the origins of Chioggia are extraordinarily ancient. The locality had been inhabited for many centuries prior to the era of Roman domination (first century BC). Pliny the Elder (23–79 AD) mentions it in his *Naturalis Historiae*. Under the Romans, Chioggia became an important port astride the sea and river routes to Padua; later its isolated position between the Adriatic and the Lagoon made it a safe haven for mainland refugees who were seeking shelter during the Barbarian invasions ● *30*. In the 9th century, the town was destroyed by the armies of Pepin, son of Charlemagne and King of Italy, then immediately rebuilt. The subsequent *Pactum*

SOTTOMARINA   PELLESTRINA   LIDO   VENICE

Fishing nets ■ 23.

Clodiae defined the territory belonging to Chioggia and its relationship with the Realtine Islands, and for many years the town had its own government, laws and councils. In the 11th and 12th centuries, the exploitation of its salt pans brought about a period of economic expansion, during which the town was transformed into an urban conglomerate. In the 12th century, the salt pans numbered more than seventy, and the salt was exported to many regions of Italy and abroad. The city and the surrounding countryside became very wealthy as a result.

THE WAR WITH GENOA AND THE END OF CHIOGGIA'S AUTONOMY ● *31.*
The salt boom lasted until the 14th century, when Chioggia was once again sacked during Venice's war with Genoa. Later it was to be the scene of a decisive battle which brought to an end a hundred years of conflict between these two great maritime powers over the monopoly of trade with the Levant. In 1378, Chioggia was taken by the Genoese, and the security of the Lagoon was seriously threatened; but in 1380 the Venetians recovered it again and defeated their commercial rivals once and for all. Thereafter the fate of Chioggia was bound to that of Venice, although it continued, as in the past, to claim autonomous status.

THE FISHMARKET
This was the earliest fishmarket in the Lagoon and still takes place every day except Mondays.

THE FISHING FLEET

CHIOGGIA'S FISHERMEN. The waters around Chioggia have always been rich fishing grounds, and after the decline of its salt industry the island reverted naturally to fishing as its principal resource. Some of the boats that were used by the Chioggiotti have since become famous; among them the

THE "BRAGOZZO"
This flat-bottomed boat is designed for fishing on the sea-bottom. Its length varies from 30 to 50 feet, and its width from 7 to 10 feet. Its decoration is very distinctive, for not an inch of the *bragozzo* is left unadorned. Its trapezoid sail is highly colored and its construction and embellishment are carried out with religious care. The central part tends to be yellow, orange or white, while the broader lower part may be white, blue or yellow. In the center of the sail are heraldic emblems, both religious and profane, and their variety is infinite. Some have religious themes – the Virgin, Christ on the cross, patron saints; others refer to nature (suns, moons, compass-cards) or bear monograms, symbols or designs related to the names, qualities or defects of the owner (the *paron*) or his family. On the beautiful black hull, the waterline is marked by a white or reddish-brown line. On the inside of the stern are inscribed various formulae invoking divine protection for the boat and those who sail in her. Almost without exception, the *bragozzi* seem to recall the splendid galleys which were once the pride and joy of the Venetian navy.

tartana (used for drag-netting), which was supplanted in the second half of the 18th century by the *bragozzo*. Since even today the Chioggiotti live mostly on the high seas, it is hardly surprising that their houses are small and modest affairs; their main interest is their boat, which is both their instrument of work and their families' most cherished possession. Here and there across the island one may still see the occasional palace, and there are plenty of churches as well. But still the most charming features of Chioggia are its attractive position, its air of vitality and its cheery disorderliness.

THE CHIOGGIOTTI OF THE PAST. During the course of the 19th century, Venetian painters such as Guglielmo Ciardi, Ettore Tito and Italico Brass came often to Chioggia in order to paint the island's fisherfolk, and their work exudes the relaxed and sunny atmosphere that was a feature of the island before the coming of the motor car. At that time the women of the island wore a nun-like traditional costume, a

feature of which was a white half-length apron that was tied in front, and which could be raised to head level and drawn tight around the face. Chioggia is also the setting for one of Goldoni's most famous plays, *Le Baruffe Chiozzotte* ▲ 291, which was written in 1762, and in which the playwright casts an ironic eye over the island and its inhabitants. But Chioggia has done more than just inspire agreeable paintings and comedies: it is also the birthplace of such important figures as John Cabot ▲ 181, who discovered Canada in the 15th century, and also Rosalba Carriera (1675–1757) ▲ 312, a painter who was greatly honored by the French when she visited Paris in 1720–1.

THE FISHERMEN'S GUILD
Nobody knows exactly when the fishermen of Venice first organized themselves into a guild. But it would seem that the Venetian Republic quickly sought to assert control over the profession, which was of vital importance to Venice's economy. On the other hand, a decree of September 5, 1536, handed down by the Council of Sages, stipulated that the representatives of the fishermen's guild should take part in all sessions dealing with problems having to do with the Lagoon. Clearly, they knew the subject better than anyone else!

AROUND CHIOGGIA

THE GEOGRAPHY. Chioggia occupies two long, parallel islands, with the Canal della Vena passing in between them. A number of calli cross the canal and the main street (Corso del Popolo) at right angles, giving the town a distinctive aspect. Even though it has been destroyed and rebuilt several times, Chioggia has always clung to its regular chequerboard town plan, which may well reflect its Roman past. Moreover, from Roman times onward there was always a CHIOGGIA MAGGIORE and a CHIOGGIA MINORE. After the war of 1379–80, only the former was reconstructed. Today the site of Chioggia Minore is filled by the SOTTOMARINA resort, which is linked to Chioggia Maggiore by a bridge across the Lagoon.

PIAZZETTA VIGO. On this little piazza is a column surmounted

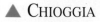

"The sails of Chioggia have the same red paintings with red backgrounds as the shrouds of the Incas . . ."

Paul Morand, *Venises*

THE LIONS OF THE REPUBLIC
The Venetians customarily set up a stone lion, symbol of the Republic, in each one of their territorial possessions. Thus, at the entrance to Chioggia, as at the entrance to Venice on by a winged lion, symbolizing the island's bond with Venice.

CANAL DELLA VENA. The many bridges that cross the Canal della Vena offer a fine view; also here is the 18th-century PALAZZO GRASSI, where Pope Pius VI stayed when he halted at Chioggia on his journey to Vienna.

CORSO DEL POPOLO. This "avenue" alongside the canal has a succession of arcades running

along one side of it. The most interesting building is the old GRANAIO (grainstore, 1322). Modernized in the 19th century in company with many of Chioggia's other monuments, the Granaio has now been converted into a fishmarket; it does still retain some of its original features (such as corbels, pilasters and arches). See also the bas-relief *Virgin and Child* by Sansovino (16th century).

the Piazzetta ▲ *249*, we are greeted by the statue of a winged lion.

THE CATHEDRAL OF SANTA MARIA. Farther along the island is the massive Cathedral of Santa Maria, with its characteristic square campanile (1347–50). Founded in the 11th century and consecrated as a cathedral in 1110, Santa Maria was destroyed by fire in 1623 and reconstructed by Longhena. Work continued until 1647, and even by then the façade had not been completed. The building itself is basilical in form featuring three naves; it contains works by Palma the Younger, Giambattista Piazzetta and Giambattista Tiepolo.

CAMPO DEL DUOMO. On this campo stands the little church of SAN MARTINO (1392), one of the few 14th-century buildings in Chioggia to have escaped destruction and alteration. It was built of brick after the Chioggia war, as a memorial to the churches of Chioggia Minore destroyed during that conflict; its principal treasure is a 14th-century polyptych attributed to one of the earliest painters of the Venetian School, Paolo Veneziano. (Follow the Corso to the last bridge over the Canal della Vena: cross to the Canal San Domenico. From here the PONTELUNGO links Chioggia with the mainland.)

The canals of Chioggia.

THE CHURCH OF SAN DOMENICO. This building stands on an islet right at the end of the Canal San Domenico. Founded in the 13th century, it was then restored during the 19th century. The church contains a painting of *St Paul* by Carpaccio.

The Islands

**THE ISLANDS:
DIVERSITY IN
THE LAGOON ✪**
The ubiquitous
vaporetto (nos. 12,
14 or 52) also serves
the north of the
Lagoon. At Murano,
visit the glassblowing
workshops: you are
guaranteed not to
return without a
souvenir. Burano
is the center of
Venetian lacemaking:
lacemakers can be
seen at work in their
doorways, a sight that
never fails to get
cameras clicking.
Torcello seems to be a
haven of peace that is
filled with birdsong.
Be sure to see the
fabulous mosaics in
the cathedral.

CHURCH OF SANTA MARIA
DEGLI ANGELI

CHURCH OF
SAN PIETRO MARTIRE

A fragment of the
magnificent floor of
the Basilica Santa
Maria e San Donato.

**THE BARBARIGO
ALTARPIECE** (right)
This painting, which
hangs in the Church
of San Pietro Martire,
was commissioned in
the 15th century from
Giovanni Bellini (who
was then the official
state painter of
Venice ▲ 304). The
subject – the Doge
Agostino Barbarigo
presented to the
Virgin of St Mark's
and St Augustine –
and the presence of
the arms of the
Barbarigo family
indicate that this
canvas originated in
the Doge's private
palace.

HISTORY

THE ORIGINS. The island of Murano, the largest of
the islands in the Lagoon, is about a mile across the
water from Venice and was already inhabited in
Roman times. Refugees from Altino escaped here
during the Barbarian invasions and gave the island
the name of "Ammurianum", after one of the gates
of the city they had left. Men and women from
Oderzo later joined these settlers and, by the 7th and
8th centuries, the island's port of Sant'Erasmo was an
important calling-place for merchant ships.
A PROSPEROUS ISLAND. Until the 10th century, Murano was a
trading center in its own right, whose salt pans, water-mills
and fishing fleet made it an economic force to be reckoned
with. So densely was the island populated that, by the 11th
century, the Doges were encouraging islanders to move to
Venice (Dorsoduro). After the 13th century, Murano passed
under the jurisdiction of a *podesta* chosen from the ranks of
the Venetian patricians, but despite this it continued to have
its own Grand Council (along with a smaller council which

Palazzo Giustinian, now the Glass Museum.

dealt with the *podesta*) and thus governed itself more or less according to its own laws. To these institutions were added offices like that of the *camerlengo* ▲ *282* (treasurer) and the *nuncio*, a kind of ambassador to Venice who took care of the island's interests in the city. Murano shared with Venice the much-prized right to strike its own gold (*oselle*) and silver coinage ▲ *256*.

A GLASS CENTER AND RESORT. By the end of the 13th century Murano was specializing in the manufacture of glass. This came about because, in 1291, all the glassmakers in Venice were asked to move to Murano as a security precaution, since the city (then constructed almost entirely of wood) lived in mortal fear of fire. Glass production became such a thriving industry at Murano that, from the 15th to the end of the 17th century, the island was Europe's principal supplier. At this time it also became a popular resort for Venetian noblemen, who built "country houses" there, which in fact were sumptuous palaces surrounded by beautiful gardens.

LANDSCAPE OF THE ISLAND. For many centuries the geography of Murano remained virtually unaltered and, at the close of the 18th century, its little town still contained more canals than streets and more pleasure gardens and vegetable plots than buildings. But, during the 19th century, all this began to change; the vegetable plots were built over, and two of the island's inlets were filled with earth in order to create new residential areas (Sacca Serenella and Sacca San Mattio).

MURANO GLASS ● 58

A TRADITION ROOTED IN ANTIQUITY. The origins of glassmaking are clearly very ancient in the Lagoon; excavations have yielded fragments of objects dating back as far as the Roman era. But it was not until the late 10th and early 11th centuries that glass production really took root in Venice itself, and the glassmakers quickly organized themselves into a guild; soon after, in 1291, they moved en bloc to Murano.

A SUMMER RESORT
During the 16th century, Murano became one of the city's principal summer resorts. The countryside, transformed into an oasis by years of patient work, was full of charm with fresh-water wells, vegetable gardens, orchards and vines. Little by little the island acquired palaces and pleasure gardens filled with rare plants from the Orient, Africa and the New World. It was in surroundings like these that the poetess Gaspara Stampa fell in love with Count de Collalto, and Aretino read aloud his bawdy stories. But after a while the Venetians discovered the countryside of Treviso and the banks of the Brenta, and Murano was left to its green orchards.

Contemporary objects from the Murano glassworks.

THE BAROVIER CUP
Now preserved in the glass museum, this is perhaps the most famous wedding cup in the world. Made of enameled blown glass, it is a perfect example of 15th-century art. The exterior was decorated by the daughter of Angelo Barovier, which explains its name.

The support, in dark blue, is embellished with effigies of the bride and groom, as well as with allegorical scenes showing young girls beside a fountain and gentlemen hunting.

EARLY GROWTH. From the mid-14th century onwards, the artisans of Murano started to sell their products abroad. They quickly gained a reputation for producing small pearls of glass, and for the mirrors which became a major Murano export during the course of the 15th century. Within fifty years the island's glasswork had lost much of its utilitarian character and had become a fully fledged art form.

NEW COMPONENTS FOR GLASS. During the 15th and 16th centuries, the glassmakers of Murano became increasingly preoccupied with the materials that they were using in order to manufacture their products. First of all they evolved ENAMELED GLASS, which came in mostly dark colors and which Murano continued to manufacture for export long after the Venetian fashion for it had faded. Then there was CRYSTALLINE GLASS, a kind of glass (not crystal) that had a remarkable degree of transparency; AVENTURINE GLASS (gold flux), which was invented at Murano; and other types of glass which resembled gemstones, such as CHALCEDONY GLASS. The workshops also resuscitated *milfiori*, a very ancient technique by which baguettes of colored glass were combined with transparent glass. Finally, there was also a considerable production of objects in *lattimo*, an opaque and milky type of glass, and *latticino*, a skillful blend of *lattimo* and clear glass.

THE STATUS OF THE GLASSMAKERS. Because of the growing importance of the glass industry, its artisans had to submit to severe political restrictions in order to balance their very considerable privileges. By contrast with the rest of Europe, Venice did not require a man to belong to a glassmaking family as a condition for learning the art. Any talented apprentice could rise, step by step, through the ranks, to become a master glassmaker. However, the glassmakers were forbidden to emigrate from Venice on pain of sequestration of all their goods. Nevertheless, it is known that in the 16th century several glassmakers did succeed in setting up factories in Northern Europe, where they also flourished.

NEW FORMS. During the 17th and 18th centuries, the search for new shapes in glass became paramount at Murano. Venetian mirrors and chandeliers had become so successful in Europe that Louis XIV was obliged to found a competitive glassworks in France in order to limit the huge expense of importing the Venetian product. At the same time, major innovations were being made in Northern Europe with the development of crystal production and techniques for glass-engraving. Soon Venice found itself imitating Bohemian glass-crystal: in 1730 Giuseppe Briati founded a factory whose goal was to rival the products of the North. But the results were disappointing, because fine Venetian crystal was found to be unsuitable for cutting or facetting.

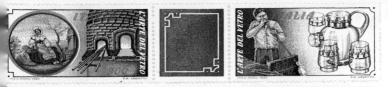

THE GLASS MUSEUM. The only institution of its type in Italy, the Glass Museum now occupies Palazzo Giustinian, one of the largest palaces in the Lagoon and the former seat of the bishopric. The museum is composed of three separate sections: the first houses the archeological collection and displays precious examples of Egyptian and Dalmatian glass; the second contains pieces manufactured between the 18th

and 19th centuries; and the third offers examples of contemporary and industrial glass products. All three are well worth a visit, but the most interesting rooms are unquestionably those in the second section, because they give a clear idea of how tastes and techniques have evolved within the glass industry, how the various instruments on display were used, and how the different phases of glass manufacture, ● *58*, succeeded one another throughout the years.

EXPLORING THE ISLAND

A CLUSTER OF ISLANDS. The map shows that the organization of the urban center of Murano is almost identical to that of the city of Venice itself, consisting of ten separate islands grouped around a grand canal, which is proportionally much wider than the one in the city, and which is known by three different names at different stages along its course: the Canal San Giovanni, Canal Ponte Longo and Canal dei Angeli.

THE GLASSWORKS RESIDENCE. If Rio dei Vetrai is primarily medieval in its aspect, and notwithstanding the presence of a number of later structures, this is due to the survival of a specific type of building – the glassworks residence. These houses served as homes for the glassworks owners, and they also doubled up as workshops and warehouses for the storing of raw materials. Among the better examples of this type of construction are the CASA DEGLI OBIZZI E DEI SODECI and the PALAZZETTO CORNER, both with their series of columns and their three-cusped Gothic windows.

THE "CORSO"
On Ascension Day, when the Doge "married" the sea ● *38*, a *corso* or regatta took place at Murano. At this time boats with oarsmen dressed in gold livery gathered in the island's grand canal, and an extravagantly dressed crowd assembled to watch the gorgeous procession. Today, a regatta is held at Murano on the first Sunday in July.

"This cup was truly very beautiful . . . in its hollow it preserved the living breath of a human being, and its clearness rivalled that of the water and the skies; its violet fringe resembled the jelly-fish which float in the sea, simple, pure, with no ornament other than this sea-fringe and no members other than its foot, its stem and its lip."
Gabriele d'Annunzio, *Fire*

DETAIL OF THE PAVEMENT
The vase (above) from which the two peacocks drink, echoes a pagan theme that was fairly common in the Orient – the symbol of the spring of life.

THE TREASURES OF MURANO. At the end of the fondamenta, on the left, is the CHURCH OF SAN PIETRO MARTIRE. Here, the Renaissance colonnades, paintings and carved wood altar front (representing episodes from the life of St John the Baptist) are well worth the detour. Farther along the Canal dei Angeli stands the PALAZZO DA MULA, whose façade contains a wealth of Byzantine, Gothic and Renaissance features. Beyond Palazzo Giustinian is PALAZZO TREVISAN ▲ 90, a solid Palladian-style building crowned with a cornice, and with an exterior that used to be decorated with frescoes.

CHURCH OF SANTA MARIA E SAN DONATO ★

THE FOUNDATION. This church is not only the most attractive building on the island, but also one of the oldest in the whole of the Lagoon; its pavement alone is well worth the journey from Venice. The foundation of a Sanctuary of Santa Maria here goes back to the 7th century, although the building itself was rebuilt and reconsecrated to the Madonna and San Donato when the latter's corpse was brought to Murano from Cephalonia in 1125. The interior recalls the Byzantine atmosphere of San Marco ▲ 236, although it is full of Romanesque influences from the mainland.

THE EXTERIOR. Santa Maria e San Donato has been subjected to some ill-advised restoration work, which has led among other things to the creation of new windows as an "interpretation" of its style. The simplicity of the façade, which looks out on to a small, quiet campo, is in strong contrast to the richness of the apse; although in all fairness a portico and baptistery were originally planned for

The church is positioned so as to display its
most beautiful feature, the apse, to those
arriving by sea.

the church front but were
never realized. The portal is
crowned by a bas-relief of *San
Donato and Votary* from the late
14th–early 15th century. In the
buttresses supporting the church's central
structure are fragments of pilasters from the ruins
of Altino (2nd century).

THE REFLECTED APSE. With the customary
Venetian awareness of the interplay between water
and architecture, the church is so oriented in order to
show its best point, a magnificent apse, to the people
arriving from its seaward side. Atop the fine brick
structure reflected in the water stands a line of blind
arches, which are echoed by a gallery just above.
Between these two levels runs a series of triangles,
like the teeth of a saw: these are variously
decorated with crosses, flowers and animals. This
decoration, along with the rhythm of the columns and the
Istrian stone parapets of the gallery above, lend the whole a
kind of aerial grace.

THE INTERIOR. Inside, Santa Maria e San Donato is built on
the lines of a basilica, with three naves separated by two rows
of five columns in Greek marble. The keel vaulting, which was
constructed at the beginning of the 15th century, is one of the
most interesting features here. By the high altar are the
RELICS OF SAN DONATO. Above the arcades of the main nave
runs a BAS-RELIEF with, at one point, a winged lion separated
from a wine cask by two escutcheons. According to the local
legend, a cask like this at Burano used to fill up of its own
accord with sacramental wine, but only while the cask was
kept here beside the relics of St Alban. The prodigy ceased to
occur in 1543 when the inhabitants of Murano insisted that
the cask be brought to their island. As to the mosaics, note in
the apse a large blue figure of THE
VIRGIN AT PRAYER (called a
theotocos by the Greeks) which
stands out against a gold
background: and, above all, the
marble-mosaic pavement.

One of the two
peacocks (below) and
a chalice (far left) in
the entrance to the
main nave.

**THE PAVEMENT
OF SAN DONATO**
This floor has the
"softness of an
oriental carpet",
made of "... narrow
bands of marble,
finely knotted and
woven into diamond
shapes." (Pietro
Toesca) It also
reserves several
surprises for anyone
who cares to look at it
closely. Both in its
design and in its
technique, it is similar
to the pavement of St
Mark's ▲ 240. Among
other features, it
carries an inscription
showing the date of
its completion (1140),
a vignette of two
roosters carrying a
dead fox (symbolizing
the triumph of
Christian vigilance
over paganism and
luxury) and a
fragment of mosaic
depicting a pair of
crickets.

369

🚤 **Forty-two minutes**
⛰ **Half a day**

LACE AND THE SEA
The story goes that a sailor, leaving his fiancée at Burano, set out on a voyage and came to a place that was inhabited by mermaids. Bewitched, the rest of the ship's crew leaped into the water, but the lover resisted the lure of the mermaids' song. The queen of the mermaids, touched by his constancy, shook her tail and whipped up a crown of sea foam, which took solid form and became a bridal veil for the sailor's distant betrothed. Later the young girls of the island copied the veil with needle and thread. Although a fable, there is certainly some truth in the notion that Burano lace is connected with the sea, for its complex stitching and weaving derive from the techniques used for making fish nets.

HISTORY

Like the other islands in the Lagoon, Burano has probably been inhabited since Roman times, well before the Lombards established themselves in the mainland cities during the 6th century. When they did so, the inhabitants of Altino took refuge on the island, which they called Boreana, after one of the gates of their native city which had faced northwards and through which the *bora,* or north wind, blew. The island was already fully occupied in the year 1000, and has remained so ever since. For centuries it remained subordinate to Torcello (from which it was administered) and Mazzorbo nearby. Burano was referred to as a simple village, while its neighbors had the status of towns. However, the island began to gain importance in the 16th century when it became a center for lacemaking; moreover, its inhabitants were spared the ravages of malaria, which became a serious threat elsewhere as the marshes advanced further into the Lagoon. This was because Burano was providentially sited in the path of the wind and well away from stagnant waters. Anyway, the lace industry prospered, and the island had a period of glory which lasted until the end of the 18th century. With the collapse of the Republic, Burano joined the other island communities in decline. Named as capital of the islands in the northern part of the lagoon in the 19th century, it finally became an integral part of Venice in 1923.

THE ISLAND OF LACE ● *60*

The streets of Burano are full of women doing embroidery, but there are practically none to be found who still know the true art of Burano – lacemaking. Apart from the fact that the profession is "deadly to the sight", it requires astonishing skill and patience to make lace, which was formerly one of Venice's most valued products.

TORCELLO

CHURCH OF SAN MARTINO

THE BEGINNINGS OF
LACEMAKING IN THE LAGOON. As early as the 15th century, women were making lace in the convents, charitable institutions and private houses of Venice, and also on the surrounding islands. But it was not until the mid-16th century and the invention of the *punto in aria* that the art of lacemaking with a needle was born, and immediately became the speciality of Burano.

THE VALUE OF LACE. As an accessory to fashion, fine lace symbolized the highest social status. The extreme refinement of Burano work was very popular among the princes, nobles and wealthy bourgeois of Europe; so popular, in fact, that a school of lacemaking had to be created to meet the growing demand. While Burano evolved lacemaking with needles alone, Chioggia ▲ 358 and Pellestrina developed a different product, which was made with lace bobbins. A number of manuals with illustrated designs for lace and embroidery were printed in Venice. So

FRENCH LACE
Louis XIV's minister Colbert employed lacemakers from Burano to launch the industry in France. This led to the invention of a new type of lace to rival that of Burano, known as that "noblest and most Italian variety."

THE PAINTED ISLAND
With its small, brightly colored

great was the enthusiasm for Burano lace that, in the mid-17th century, attempts were made to imitate it abroad; notably in France, with Louis XIV's creation in August 1665 of a "Manufacture Royale des Dentelles Françaises".

WHIMS OF THE 18TH CENTURY. Foreign competition eventually took its toll on Burano, along with the various difficulties brought about by the social, political and commercial decline of the Republic of Venice. By the 18th century Burano lace had lost much of its cachet and was perilously close to extinction.

THE REBIRTH OF THE LACE INDUSTRY. Towards the close of the 19th century an attempt was made to revive Burano lacemaking. In 1872, Contessa Marcello opened a lacemaking school at Burano under the aegis of Queen Margarita of Italy. Francesca Memo, known as La Scarpaiola, was at that time the only person left alive on the island who still knew the secret of *punto in aria*; she was brought in to teach the art to others, and before long the commercial production of lace had begun once again.

houses bathed in sunlight, Burano has always attracted artists and painters. Before the First World War, the "Burano School" of painting evolved here; its members combined a grainy surface and strong use of color with a complete lack of respect for the academic rules of painting. Among them was the great Gino Rossi. Many paintings of the Burano School hang in one of Venice's more unusual galleries, namely the Restaurant Da Romano on Burano's via Galuppi. This celebrated trattoria first instigated the Burano art prize, which was inaugurated in 1947.

THE 20TH CENTURY. By the beginning of the 20th century Venice and the islands between them employed some five thousand lacemakers in seven major factories. The Burano school opened a shop on St Mark's Square, with branches at Chioggia and Jesolo. To survive, Burano was gradually obliged to produce more lace of inferior quality. The Fascist regime attempted to revive the old standards and restore the island's reputation for quality by offering financial aid and publishing advertisements in the press, but to no avail; the debts grew and standards continued to decline. Nowadays, real Burano lace is a phenomenally expensive luxury, since it takes three years for ten women to make a single tablecloth. The last of the lacemakers who still work in the great tradition of the island now firmly believe that "their art will die with them".

BURANO'S COLORS

Situated some six miles from Venice, Burano looks completely different from the other islands of the Lagoon. There are no imposing palaces here, but rather uniform ranks of houses that are all the same height and all painted in bright colors. They are small, one or two floors only, with façades and simple square windows all alike. There is no exterior ornament except bright color to distinguish one from the next. The job of repainting the houses in these deep reds, vivid yellows and intense blues was left to the women, since the men were usually away at sea. Tradition has it that these bright colors helped the sailors to recognize their homes from many miles off, as they sailed back toward the island. Today the boats still move up and down the canals and wait in lines, side by side, at their moorings along the bank. The nets hang drying in tiny backyards or in front of the houses. All of these images are a part of the island's landscape, as are the groups of women who sit gossiping or embroidering on their doorsteps, and whose voices represent the authentic sound of Burano.

A WALK ACROSS THE ISLAND

TO THE CENTER OF THE ISLAND. Walk along the Rio di Mezzo, then take the Via Galuppi to the square which is also dedicated to Burano's most famous son, the musician Baldassare Galuppi (1706–85), known as Il Buranello. The whole of this route is occupied by shops selling lace (most of it made in China). On the square are the only two large pieces of architecture on the island which have been spared demolition: these are the ORATORIO SANTA BARBARA (17th century) and the CHURCH OF SAN MARTINO (16th century), flanked by its 18th-century CAMPANILE. The façade of this church has, oddly, no door. Inside, among other things are a *Crucifixion* by Tiepolo (1725) and a *Miracle of Saint Alban* attributed to Zanchi. This picture was inspired by a legend which is very popular on Burano: apparently the sea threw up at this site a kind of casket made of stone, which the fishermen were unable to shift. To everyone's astonishment, however, some children succeeded where their elders had failed, and when the casket was opened it was found to contain relics of St Alban, St Dominic and St Orso, which were carried in procession across the island. On the square, the former Palace of the Podesta (14th century) contains the MUSEUM AND SCHOOL OF LACEMAKING. This museum commemorates three centuries of the art and has more than 68,000 pieces of lace on display. But only the 20th-century pieces come directly from Burano, since the older ones are all from Venetian public and private collections. The museum, which was created in order to promote the kind of quality lacemaking that has been all but eliminated by machine-made products, is now managed on a co-operative basis by ten lacemakers.

SECRET BURANO. If you leave the square and wander farther afield on the island, you will discover its quiet, secret places, shimmering with light and color. Look especially for Campo della Pescheria, Rio della Giudecca, or (in the north of Burano) Rio Mandracchio.

"On the thresholds of the small houses along the canal and in the narrow streets, one can see the lacemakers about their famous craft, using not a spindle but a simple needle

and thread."
Maurice Barrès,
La Mort de Venise

The vivid colors of the housefronts are all the more striking because their doors and windows are outlined in white. Perhaps in reaction to the unbroken greyness of the winter days, the Buranese sometimes cover their doors with strange geometrical motifs that bear an uncanny resemblance to modern works of art.

Forty minutes

Two hours

The visitor who comes to Torcello from Murano and Burano cannot fail to fall under its strange spell. For Torcello, lost in its solitude at the heart of the Lagoon, was once a thriving town in its own right, and is now no more than a ghost of its former self.

HISTORY

"An unearthly silence reigns over this place, where nature is so abundant that the works of man scarcely affect it."

Georges Sand,
Lettres d'un voyageur

THE ORIGINS. The beginnings of Torcello are linked to the history of Altino and the Barbarian invasions of the 5th and 7th centuries. The word *torcello* comes from the name of a gate or tower at Altino, or perhaps from the ramparts and defensive towers by which that city was probably surrounded.

THE AUTONOMY OF TORCELLO. In the 7th century, the Bishop of Altino decamped, along with the entire population of the town, to Torcello – bringing with him the relics of Altino's first bishop, St Eliodorus, who thus became the patron saint of the island. Little by little Torcello acquired a degree of administrative autonomy to go with its growing political independence from Byzantium; as a result it prospered within the confederation of islands which were eventually to form the Venetian state. During the 10th century, Torcello had about ten thousand inhabitants, with no fewer than ten churches and several convents. At that time it was the richest and most powerful island in the Lagoon, and a trading outpost of considerable importance.

The Agnus Dei – detail of a mosaic in the right-hand apsidal chapel of Santa Maria Assunta.

DECLINE. Thereafter Torcello fell into decline, and eventually had to submit to the jurisdiction of a Venetian *podesta* – though this dignitary was still nominated by the island's own Grand Council. Between the 14th and 16th century its decline was accelerated by the action of two rivers, the Sile and the Dese, which slowly transformed the water around Torcello into a malarial swamp. Their beds were not diverted until the 17th century.

THE CATHEDRAL
On the side of this cathedral, with its somewhat stark exterior, are curious stone shutters that move on stone hinges. Ruskin thought that the overall effect of this building was more like a storm refuge somewhere in the Alps rather than a cathedral in a populous area.

The inhabitants were forced by this scourge to move to Murano or Venice, and the former urban center was gradually dismantled. At the end of this long process Torcello was left almost deserted, and even today its population does not exceed sixty souls.

THE RELIGIOUS COMPLEX

There are no calles on Torcello, but merely a road which passes among fields and a few houses. After crossing the PONTE DEL DIAVOLO (built, according to tradition, in a single night), you arrive on the piazza where there is a marble seat known as the THRONE OF ATTILA, formerly used by the bishop or by the representative of the secular power. Here also is a large complex of religious buildings, comprising three separate edifices that are linked by a portico. This ensemble was designed to symbolize the progress of the Christian believer: the baptistry represents his birth and childhood, the cathedral the course of his life, and the church (where a canonized martyr lies entombed) symbolizes his death and transition into paradise.

THE BAPTISTRY. Only a few vestiges remain of the 7th-century building which once stood in front of the cathedral. Its circular ground-plan, punctuated by eight columns, was probably modeled on the architecture of Roman baths.

THE CATHEDRAL OF SANTA MARIA ASSUNTA ★. If one is to believe the inscription to the left of the choir, this cathedral is the oldest Venetian monument in existence. The first written record in the history of Venice is here, indicating the year 639 as its date of foundation. It was considerably modified in the 9th and 11th centuries; the church increased in length, the apses were reconstructed. The central apse was raised, as was the choir, and beneath these a crypt was dug. Today what remains of the ancient pavement can be viewed (through a pair of grilles) at a depth of some eight inches below the present one. In the 14th century the portico was linked to that of the adjoining Santa Fosca. Inside,

"THE LAST JUDGEMENT" ★
The two final registers show, on the left, the blessed entering paradise (detail below), and on the right the anguish of the damned, who writhe in a river of fire which flows from the feet of Christ. From top to base and from left to right, are the proud, the lustful, the gluttonous, the wrathful, the covetous, the miserly and the slothful.

THE MOSAICS
Torcello is one of the finest examples of the taste and style of Byzantium grafted onto the tradition of the Lagoon, with a severe, bald exterior contrasting with an interior aglitter with fiery mosaics.

THE APOSTLES
In the hollow of the main apse, a double procession of the apostles marches at the feet of the Virgin (facing, detail on the right). This is the conventional form of representation established in Byzantium for main apses during the 9th century, with the difference that the Virgin is not accompanied here by the archangels Michael and Gabriel.

376

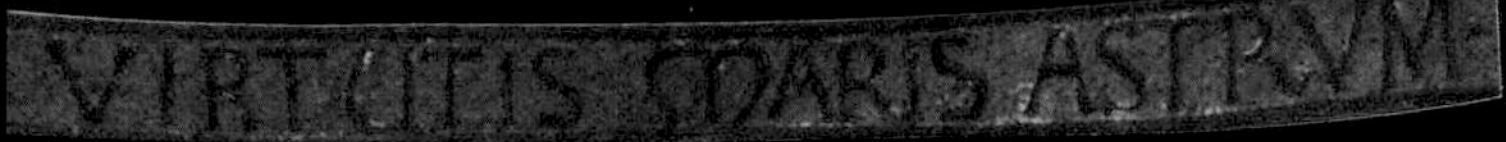

Inscription in the apse dividing the
Virgin from the Twelve Apostles.

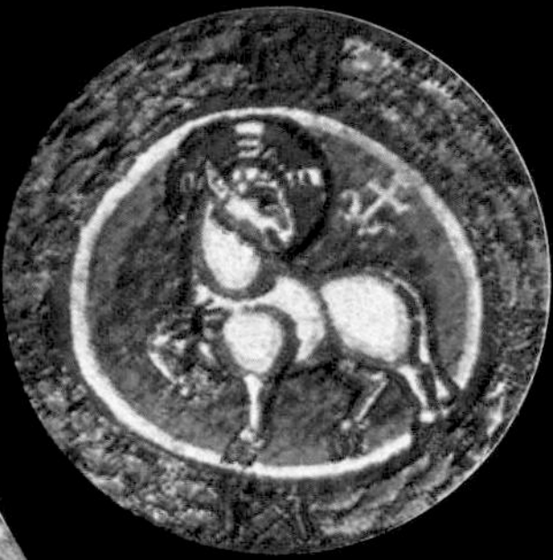

THE LAMB OF GOD
On the vault of the
right-hand apsidal
chapel, above the image
of Christ, four angels
support a medallion
depicting an Agnus Dei
against a blue
background. This
ancient image (11th-
century) was copied
from the Church of San
Vitale at Ravenna.

RIGHT-HAND APSIDAL
CHAPEL
Christ with his hand
raised in blessing sits
enthroned between the
archangels Gabriel
and Michael. Below
are the four doctors of
the Church
(Ambrose, Augustine,
Gregory and Martin).
This group, which
like the Agnus Dei
was inspired by the
school of Ravenna,
was completed in
864, at which time
the two side apses
were opened. It
was extensively
reworked in the
12th and 13th
centuries, and little
remains of the
original décor.

THE VIRGIN AND CHILD
The tall figure of the Virgin
stands out forcefully against a
broad golden background in
the hollow of the apse, "as if
haloed in lunar light".
In this 12th–13th century
mosaic, Mary carries a
handkerchief in one hand,
the symbol of the *mater
dolorosa*. The Child clasps
the rolls of the law.

According to one interesting theory, related by the art historian Lauritzen, the dome which was to have crowned the Church of Santa Fosca was never finished because "... the Greek workers who began the building left the site halfway through, leaving its completion to local masons who were incapable of raising a dome ..."

Two small 14th-century palaces stand opposite the churches. These are the PALAZZO DELL'ARCHIVO, whose portico contains fragments from Altino, and the PALAZZO DEL CONSIGLIO, with its Gothic outside staircase leading to the first floor. These two palaces house the MUSEO DELL'ESTUARIO, which contains precious objects found in excavations here, as well as archeological evidence of Torcello's origins from Altino and two paintings by Veronese.

the three naves separated by two rows of nine columns stretch away toward their respective apses. The beautiful marble mosaics, the priceless iconostasis, and a ceremonial episcopal throne at the end of the choir combine to create an atmosphere that is quite extraordinary. With its marble panels separated by slender columns, the iconostasis of Santa Maria Assunta is undoubtedly among the loveliest traceries of stone ever produced by Byzantine art. Whether lions or peacocks, the animal shapes that inhabit it all strike heraldic poses; thus the peacocks are seen drinking at a fountain, the symbol of divine grace. At the foot of the altar is a marble Roman sarcophagus containing the relics of St Eliodorus. Apart from the mosaics in the apses, note the immense LAST JUDGEMENT (11th–12th century) on the reverse of the façade. This picture-narrative extends over six registers and should be viewed in order from top to bottom. First comes the crucifixion, followed by the descent into Limbo; Jesus in triumph towers over the conquered Lucifer, hurls down the Gates of Hell and seizes Adam by the arm. Eve stands in the background, and on either side of the panel are the archangels Michael and Gabriel. At the third level Jesus is seen in glory in his mandorla of light, flanked by the Virgin and John the Baptist. Next is a scene of the throne prepared for the Last Judgement; two angels, to the left and right, call upon the dead, who are yielded up from the bowels of the earth and the stomach of wild animals and sea monsters. Finally, in the last two registers, the elect are sorted from the damned after their souls have been placed in the balance.

SANTA FOSCA. This church, constructed in the form of a Greek cross, was erected between the 11th and 12th centuries. It probably began as a *martyrium*, or sanctuary for the relics of martyrs. Today it is shaped as an octagon surrounded by a portico, whose raised arches rest on columns with Venetian-Byzantine capitals. With its double row of blind arcades and saw-tooth motif, the apse and its two accompanying chapels are strongly reminiscent of San Donato on Murano ▲ *368*. So movingly simple is Santa Fosca that it borders on the abstract; in fact it is the perfect expression of the Byzantine idea of space emerging from structural coherence and unity. To crown it all, the church is bathed in a light of unearthly clarity.

The Lagoon

SACCA SESSOLA
POVEGLIA
SANTO SPIRITO
SAN CLEMENTE
LA GRAZIA
SAN GIORGIO MAGGIORE
MURANO
LAZZARETTO VECCHIO
SAN SERVOLO
SAN LAZZARO
DEGLI ARME

HUNTING IN THE LAGOON

The wooded edges and marshlands of the Lagoon used to be a sporting paradise, swarming with pheasants, partridges, deer, wild boar and foxes. They were used by the nobility, for whom hunting and shooting were favorite pastimes, as Longhi's painting shows. Hunting was viewed by the Venetians as a useful, healthy occupation and with time it became the excuse for excursions to the *casoni*, the thatched hunting lodges on wooden pilings that were so characteristic of the Lagoon foreshore. Later, much of the countryside was stripped of woodland and cultivated, but the *valli* (reserves) and the *barene* (mudflats) ■ *18* continued to attract both hunters and game.

The smaller islands around Venice can be split between the northern and southern parts of the Lagoon. Some can be reached by public transport and others not. If you have money and time, you can rent a boat from one of the *fitabarche*, as the boat rental sites are called, and tour around those islands within rowing distance – or motor distance – of the city. It is essential to buy a chart to look out for the markers, and to follow the *bricole* (mooring posts) ■ *24* and buoys indicating the navigable channels. The visitor confined to the vaporetto must use his imagination and perhaps an old map like the one drawn by Bordoni in the 16th century ("Venezia e le isole") to identify the places he will not put into. Then he will see how the scope of Venice itself expands in his mind's eye, how the islands rise, like pearls on a necklace, around the city, and how Venice is the rational focus of a far larger Lagoon. Everything had a place in the web that vanished in the 19th century with the linking of the city to the mainland by railway bridge, and the dredging of a canal between the city and Lido. This created a direct route from Mestre (and subsequently Marghera) by way of San Marco to the open sea. All the little

islands not directly linked to the historic center were abruptly excluded from the economic life of Venice, and then abandoned by their inhabitants. Today, of the thirty-four islands in the Lagoon (which belong to the Italian state, the city of Venice or private individuals) at least a score are totally abandoned. There is a sense in which all once enjoyed equal importance since none could be reached except by boat, although each had specific functions according to its position. The most densely populated islands lay along the main arteries between the sea and *terra firma*; the convents and monasteries clustered around Venice; near the Lido and port entrances stood the defensive and military installations and the quarantine stations.

TIMBER FOR VENICE
In the 11th–12th century, wood became indispensable to the urban and economic development of Venice. As an entirely artificial town, the city required an enormous quantity of wood for building purposes, and in the 13th century virtually everything there was made of it, including houses (hence the frequent fires), bollards, pilings indicating navigable channels and mooring posts. The lumber trade grew apace, augmented by the needs of a powerful fleet. Once the woodland on the islands had succumbed to uninterrupted logging, the Venetians turned instead to the huge forests along the Istrian Coast, shipping lumber from the Cadore and Belluno regions in Northern Italy.

THE NORTHERN LAGOON

MAZZORBO. Today, Mazzorbo is made up of vines, orchards, fruit gardens and a handful of houses, though it was once a place of commercial importance. Its name has connotations of grandeur, since *maiurbium* in Latin means "greater city". It is linked to Burano by a long wooden bridge ▲ *370* and now has just a few hundred residents. Its monasteries, churches and palaces have all been destroyed, but a few Gothic houses still stand along the canal (which is served by a vaporetto).

Sarcophagus of the Egyptian Prince Nehmekhet (c.1000 BC) in the library of the museum at San Lazzaro degli Armeni.

Lazzaretto Nuovo.

"The Lagoon and the mist swallowed up all shapes and all colors. Only the groups of worshippers stood out against the grey monotony of the scene: they looked like monks moving along a way covered in ashes."
Gabriele d'Annunzio, *Fire*

Likewise, Mazzorbo still has its 14th-century CHURCH OF SANTA CATERINA, a blend of Gothic and Romanesque, with a picturesque campanile covered in greenery and the oldest bell in the Lagoon (1318).

SAN FRANCESCO DEL DESERTO. South of Burano is one of the Lagoon's loveliest and quietest spots, San Francesco del Deserto, the "monastery-island". According to legend, St Francis of Assisi passed through here on his way back from the Middle East, where he had been to preach the Gospel. As the saint approached the island a storm that was raging suddenly dropped and the birds began to sing. Whatever the reason, a group of Franciscans established themselves here in the 13th century. Two hundred years later they abandoned the monastery, only to return in the mid-19th century. Thus San Francesco del Deserto has maintained its original function and to this day is run by the same religious community, which admits visitors to admire the serene beauty of its cloisters, trees and cultivated land. Above all, San Francesco del Deserto is a haven of greenery and tranquility.

LE VIGNOLE AND SANT'ERASMO. These two islands are the market gardens of the estuary; they face the port of the Lido, and for centuries have supplied Venice with delicious fresh vegetables, notably *spareselle* and *castradure* (slender green asparagus and baby artichokes, obtainable at the Erberia ▲ *284*). For centuries Le Vignole and Sant' Erasmo were used as summer resorts; today the Venetians still like to go on excursions to them by boat, and maybe take a meal in one of the taverns. Of the two, only SANT' ERASMO is open to visitors; it is also larger than its neighbor. These huge market gardening centers used to be surrounded with fortifications, the size of which can be gauged by the ruins of the so-called TOWER OF MAXIMILIAN. The islands played their part in the general defensive plan of Venice, as did the FORT OF SANT'ANDREA, built in the 16th century by the brilliant state architect Sanmicheli. His stout Renaissance bastions, designed to impede a sea-borne attack, are now in a woeful state of repair and in some places have completely collapsed. Also worthy of mention are the islands of MADONNA DEL MONTE and SAN GIACOMO IN PALUDO (visible from the Murano–Burano vaporetto), which little by little have sunk into the Lagoon. No trace remains of the monasteries that once stood on them – the ruins you see are of a gunpowder magazine and a military barracks dating from the 18th and 19th centuries.

San Lazzaro
degli Armeni.

LAZZARETTO NUOVO. Hermits were the first permanent inhabitants of this island, before 1486 when it became a *lazzaretto* (quarantine station) where goods that might carry infection from their country of origin were stored. In 1576, about ten thousand people were isolated here, and those who developed the plague were transferred to the Lazzaretto Vecchio. Next the island was completely evacuated until the 19th century, when it became a military site with a fortress. Since then, it has been overwhelmed by wild vegetation and today the buildings on it are steadily falling into ruin.

THE SOUTHERN LAGOON

SAN LAZZARO DEGLI ARMENI. A monastery has survived on this island (left), which was much loved by Lord Byron. Indeed it is one of the few places in or around Venice that has not been altered from its original function over the years. Monks first arrived here during the 12th century and built a leper colony. After that, the island was more or less abandoned until 1717, when the Venetian Republic gave it to the Armenian monk Manug de Pierre, known as Mechitar the Consoler ▲ *329*, who had escaped from the Turks. Mechitar founded a new community on the site, using and adapting the existing buildings. Today, about thirty fathers and seminarists live permanently in the monastery, whose goal is to preserve Armenian culture. There is a museum in the monastery, a picture gallery, a late 18th-century printing press which is the only one of its kind in the world and a rich library containing more than 150,000 volumes and also a precious collection of illuminated manuscripts. All around it is a huge garden, where peacocks wander among the rare flowers and plants.

SAN CLEMENTE AND SAN SERVOLO. These two islands, whose history is linked to religious orders, are among those which were, until recently, used for hospital and quarantine purposes. SAN CLEMENTE (above) was once the site of a charity hospital and a stopping place for pilgrims to the Holy Land; later it was changed into a hermitage. A number of distinguished guests of the Republic have stayed here, most

"We slipped along a narrow canal, past half-drowned land and rotted greenery, from which great birds rose and flapped away. All around us were poles standing in the water to direct the boatmen: they looked like marks left on a sublime painting, to guide some inept copyist."

Maurice Barrès, *La Mort de Venise*

LORD BYRON
A complete room in the museum of San Lazzaro degli Armeni is devoted to Lord Byron, who regularly visited the convent in order to study the Armenian language.

SAN CLEMENTE
This aerial photograph clearly shows the walls built along the edge of the island against the sea. The buildings were all erected after 1834.

Isla della Grazia.

The islands of the Lazzaretto Vecchio, facing the Lido, were once a haven for pilgrims en route to the Holy Land.

notably the Duke of Mantua who brought the plague with him in 1630. After this, the island was used as a powder magazine, until, in 1834, the Austrian government established a lunatic asylum there. This became a specialist hospital, which closed in the 1950s. It was sold at the end of the 1990s, and there are plans to convert it into tourist accommodation. A Benedictine monastery was established on SAN SERVOLO during the 8th century, but in the first half of the 18th century this was turned into a psychiatric institution. Today its buildings are empty; they stand within a large park planted with trees and flowers which has been left in a state of complete abandon. Since 1977 the island has housed a center for training craftsmen in the restoration of historic monuments.

SANTA MARIA DELLA GRAZIA OR DELLA CAVANA. Santa Maria is linked to San Zaccaria by a vaporetto service. Formerly it too offered shelter to pilgrims on their way to or from the Holy Land. Later, churches and monasteries were built here, but after their abolition by Napoleon a powder magazine and then a hospital were built in their place. In early 1999, the last of the hospital patients were transferred to the hospital of Santi Giovanni e Paolo.

LAZZARETTO VECCHIO. Lazzaretto Vecchio used to have its own church dedicated to St Mary of Nazareth (whose name was distorted first into *nazaretum*, then into *lazzaretto*). It was a quarantine station for plague victims during the first great epidemic of the 14th century. Later it was used as a military depot, and was abandoned in the early 19th century. Today it is a center for stray dogs, financed and run by volunteers.

SANTO SPIRITO AND POVEGLIA. These two islands, which lie opposite the Lido behind San Clemente and La Grazia, once possessed some great art treasures. SANTO SPIRITO, today little more than a wasteland, had a church designed by Sansovino which was decorated with works by Palma the Elder and Titian, masterpieces that are now, for the most part, to be seen in the church of La Salute ▲ *318*. Like Poveglia, it was variously used during the last two centuries as a barracks and munitions depot, and today it is dismally run-down.

POVEGLIA, a former residence of the Doge's entourage which was abandoned in the 14th century, looks altogether better, with well-maintained gardens and vineyards. A youth hostel is to open there. At the tip of the island stands a curious octagonal construction, formerly a part of the defensive system installed throughout the Lagoon by the Venetian government.

Practical information

◆ GETTING THERE

ADDRESSES

→ IN LONDON
■ **Italian Embassy**
14 Three Kings' Yard
London
W1Y 2EH
Tel. 020 7312 2200
Fax 020 7499 2283
e-mail: *emblondon@
embitaly.org.uk*
■ **Italian Cultural
Institute**
39 Belgrave Square
London
SW1X 8HX
Tel. 020 7235 1461
Fax 020 7235 4618
e-mail:
*ici@italcultur.org.
uk*

→ IN NEW YORK
■ **Italian Consulate**
690 Park Ave.
New York
10021-5044
Tel. 212 737 9100
(or 439 8600)
Fax 212 249 4945
*www.italconsulnyc.
org*
■ **Italian Cultural
Institute**
686 Park Ave.
New York
10021-5009
Tel. 212 879 4242
Fax 212 861 4018
www.italcultny.org

→ TOURIST
INFORMATION ON
THE INTERNET
■ **Italian National
Tourist Office
(ENIT)**
www.enit.it
In Italian but
gives access to
2 other sites:
www.enit.it/Musei
(museums in Italy),
*www.enit.it/Avveni
menti*
(cultural events,
etc.)
e-mail: *sedecentrale.
enit@interbusiness.
it*
■ **Italian Tourist
Web Guide**
www.itwg.com
■ **Arcanet
Italian museums**
*www.arcanet.it/
cultura/musei-it*
(Italian and English)
*www.repubblica.it/
servizi_new/servizi*
(science and
culture)

ANIMALS

→ CERTIFICATES
Certificates of
origin, vaccinations
and good health
issued maximum
one month
before arrival.
Certificates of
rabies vaccination
issued maximum
11 months prior to
arrival.

MONEY

→ CURRENCY
The Italian
monetary unit
is the lira (lire).
£1 = 2,996 lire
$1 = 2,127 lire
You can change
money upon
arrival, but you
should bear
in mind that
automatic machines
and travel agents
charge less
favorable rates.

→ CREDIT CARDS
Practically all
cash dispensers
in Venice accept
credit cards,
including Visa,
MasterCard and
American Express.

FORMALITIES

→ DOCUMENTS
Valid ID cards or
passports needed
for European Union
members.
US visitors need a
valid passport to
enter Italy for 90
days and should
register with the
police 3 days
before entering
the country.
Carry photo
ID at all times.

→ DRIVING
DOCUMENTS
Valid driving
license, car
registration papers
and proof of
insurance. An
International
Driver's Permit is
recommended.
■ **American AA**
Tel. 1 800 564 6222
■ **AA (UK)**
Tel. 0870 550 0600

WHEN TO GO?
Visit in the spring or
in the fall to avoid
the summer heat
(up to 85°F) and
crowds. In winter
temperatures
vary between
41°F and 30°F.
Beware of the
acqua alta: do not
be caught by the
high tides which
overrun St Mark's
Square, especially in
summer and in
winter ▲ *26, 224.*

HEALTH
Form E111, issued by
EU Health Authorities
countries, entitles
members to
emergency medical
treatment.
Non-EU members
must take out
personal medical
insurance.

TELEPHONE

→ TO CALL VENICE
FROM THE UK
AND US
■ 00 (UK)/011 (US) +
39 + 041 (code for
Venice) and the
number you wish
to call.

ELECTRICITY
Alternating current
220 volts. Take
an adapter with
you for personal
appliances such as
hairdryers or electric
shavers as Italian
plugs have rounded
pins.

TRAVEL

→ BY AIR
■ **Alitalia**
Tel. 08705 448 259
www.alitalia.com
(UK)
Return fares range
from £119 (apex) to
£638 (business).
Tel. 1 800 223 5730
*www.alitaliausa.
com*
(US)
■ **American Airlines**
via London
Tel. 1 800 433 7300
■ **United Airlines** via
Frankfurt
Tel. 1 800 538 2929
Prices range from

$457 (apex) to
$5,100 (business).
■ **British Airways**
Tel. 0345 222 111
*www.britishairways.
com*
Flights from
London Heathrow
Return £124 (apex)
to £638 (club)

→ USEFUL WEBSITES
*www.cheapflights.
com*
www.ebookers.com
www.ryanair.com
www.go.com
www.expedia.com

→ BY COACH
Eurolines
Tel. 01582 40 45 11
www.eurolines.co.uk
Departure from
Victoria coach
station at 9am on
Mon., Wed., Fri. and
Sat., arriving in
Venice at 1pm the
following day.
Return fares range
from £69–£79
(promotional)
to £129–£139
(normal), according
to season.

→ BY ORIENT-EXPRESS
Reservations:
Tel. 020 7928 60 00
(London)
Departs: 3 or 4
times a month on
Thur. or Sun.),
leaving London
Victoria station at
noon and arriving in
Venice at 5.35pm
the following day.
Single fare: £1,165
Return fare: £1,690

→ BY TRAIN
Take the Eurostar
from London
Waterloo to
Paris Gare du
Nord, then take a
day or night train
to Venice from
Gare de Lyon.
■ **Information**
International
Rail Enquiries
(London):
Tel. 0990 848 848
Eurostar (London):
Tel. 01233 617 575
www.eurostar.com
SNCF (Paris)
Tel. 0836 35 35 35
www.sncf.fr

THE A TO Z TO STAYING IN VENICE ◆

Addresses – arrival – celebrations and festivals – cost of living – emergency services – exchange – food specialties – getting around – leisure – mail – markets – newspapers – opening times – police stations – public conveniences – public holidays – reductions – shows – sizes – telephone – tourist offices – transport

ADDRESSES
■ **UK consulate**
Accademia
Dorsoduro 1051
30123 Venice
Tel. 041 522 7207
■ **American Consulate-General**
Via Principe
Amedeo 2
Milan 20121
Tel. 026 596 561

ARRIVAL
→ **MARCO POLO INTERNATIONAL AIRPORT**
■ **Information**
Airport
Tel. 041 260 92 60
Italtravel (airline)
San Marco 72/b
Tel. 041 528 96 56
■ **Transfer to the city center**
Eight miles from the city center.
By water-taxi
Fare: around
130,000 lire.
Duration: 20 mins.
Bus no. 5
Fare: 1,500 lire.
Duration: 20 mins.
Arrival point:
Piazzale Roma.
By motoscafo (boat)
Information
about schedules:
Tel. 041 528 78 86.
Fare: 17,000 lire.
Duration: 1 hour.
Arrival point:
St Mark's Square.
By airport shuttle
Fare: 6,000 lire.
Departs: every hour
Duration: 20 mins.
Arrival point:
Piazzale Roma.

→ **SANTA LUCIA STATION**
■ **Information**
Santa Lucia and
Mestre stations
Tel. 041 71 55 55
Open 7.10am–
9.30pm.
■ **To St Mark's Square**
Motoscafo no. 82
Vaporetto no. 1

CELEBRATIONS AND FESTIVALS
■ **Feb.** Carnaval
■ **March**
Su e zo per i ponti
(Marathon)
■ **25 April**
St Mark's Day (the

patron saint of the city)
■ **May**
Ascension Day
Vogalonga ● *55*
■ **June–Sep.**
Art Fair ▲ *184*
■ **July**
Celebration of the Redeemer;
Murano boat race.
■ **Aug.**
Celebration of the Madone de Pellestrina;
August boat race;
Arte antica a Venezia (International Antique Fair), which lasts 10 days to the end of the month at Zitelle, on Giudecca Island.
■ **Sep.**
La Mostra Internazionale d'Arte Cinematografica (international film festival) at the Palazzo del Cinema (Lungomare Marconi, Lido) and lasts for 10 days.
Tel. 041 526 87 00
Information:
Ufficio attività d'istituto, Ca' Giustinian,
San Marco (tel. 041 521 87 11). The winner is awarded the famous Golden Lion; historical boat race; Burano boat race.
■ **Oct.**
Sant'Erasmo boat race; Venice Marathon.
■ **Nov. 21**
Celebration of the Madone de la Salute ● *49*.

COST OF LIVING
COFFEE
1,300–2,000 lire
"UN'OMBRA"
1,600–2,000 lire
TRAMEZZINO
1,500–3,000 lire
MUSEUMS
3,000–10,000 lire
THEATER
25,000–100,000 lire
MEALS
30,000–80,000 lire
DOUBLE ROOM
70,000–200,000 lire
and over

EMERGENCY SERVICES

Useful numbers
Emergency services: 113
Medical emergencies: 118
Hydroambulances: 523 00 00
Drugstores open 24 hours a day: 238 11 30
Police: 112
Fire service: 115

Note: The numbers in the box above can be dialed free of charge from any public telephone.

→ **DRUGSTORES**
Usual opening times: Mon.–Fri. 8.30am–12.30pm and 3.30–7.30pm. Closed Sat.–Sun.

→ **HOSPITALS**
■ **Al Mar hospital**
Lido
Tel. 041 526 17 50
■ **Fatebenefra private hospital**
Madonna dell'Orto
Cannaregio 3458
Tel. 041 78 31 11
Emergencies (no charge)
■ **Public hospital Santi Giovanni e Paolo**
Castello
Tel. 041 529 45 17/ 42 23

EXCHANGE
Exchange bureaux can be found in most banks, at the station and airport.
Warning: It is illegal to change money on the street.

FOOD SPECIALTIES
Baccalà mantecato: dried, filleted, unsalted northern fish in olive oil, turned into a paste. *Fegato alla veneziana:* thinly sliced veal liver marinated in vinegar water then fried with onion. *Ombra:* glass of red or white wine, generally quite

light, served with *cicheto,* appetizers, or fried sardines.

GETTING AROUND
Venetians do not go by *calle* (streets). They use the bridges, buildings or boutiques nearest the address required as reference points. A *calle* can have the same name in several *sestiere* (each of the six sections of Venice: Cannaregio, Castello, Dorsoduro, San Marco, San Polo and Santa Croce). Each section is given a specific numbering system. The same applies to Isola della Giudecca, Isola di Sant'Elena and Isola si Sacca Fisola.
Tip: Get as many details as possible before setting off to look for a place.

LEISURE
→ **APT (AZIENDA DI PROMOZIONE TURISTICA)**
San Marco 71/f
Tel. 041 520 89 64
For visits to the various islands in the Lagoon. Take a full day to visit the three main islands: Murano, Burano and Torcello.
→ **EOLO**
Tel. 041 71 63 04
Cruises around the Lagoon in a typical *bragozzo.* Delicious cuisine.
→ **SIOR BEPI**
Castello 2127A
Tel. 03 472 682 027
Cruises around the Lagoon in a *bragozzo.*

MAIL
→ **POST OFFICES**
Usual opening times: 8.30am–1pm.
■ **Main post office**
Fondaco dei Tedeschi, near the Rialto.

→ **SENDING MAIL**
■ **To send something from Venice to the rest of Italy**

◆ THE A TO Z TO STAYING IN VENICE

Letter, postcard: 800 lire.
Regular postal order: 5,000-10,000 lire.
■ **To send something from Venice to Europe**
Letter, postcard: 900 lire.
Express: + 3,600 lire. Registered mail with acknowledgement of receipt: + 4,900 lire. Regular postal order: 6,300–10,000 lire. Money transfer (into account): 6,500 lire.

MARKETS
Set up in the morning on the city's open squares (*campi*). Many are around the Rialto.
■ **Campo della Pescheria**
Fish market. Daily except Sun. and Mon.
■ **Canal at the end of Via Garibaldi**
(Near the Arsenal) Vegetable market set up on boats. Daily (except Sun.).
■ **Erberia**
Around the Rialto. Wholesale and retail herb, fruit and flower market. Prices are cheaper. Daily except Sun.

NEWSPAPERS ● 76
→ **FOREIGN NEWSPAPERS**
Sold at the station and at newsagents' in tourist areas.

→ **LOCAL NEWSPAPERS**
Il Gazzettino, Veneto's daily; *La Nuova Venezia*, another daily; *Venezia News*, monthly cultural review; *Artshow*, free monthly guide to art exhibitions (*www.undo.net/arts how*); *Un Ospite di Venezia*, free bilingual (Italian/ English), pocket-size review of cultural events; *Venezia da Vivere*, free quarterly review in Italian, listing concerts and

alternative exhibitions.

OPENING TIMES
→ **BANKS**
Usually open Mon.–Fri. 8.30am– 1.30pm and 3–4pm. Closed Sat.–Sun.
→ **CHURCHES**
Open mornings and evenings. Opening times may vary according to seasons, services and security arrangements. Churches belonging to the Chorus route ◆ *410* are open Mon.–Sat. 10am– 5pm, Sun. 1–5pm. This route gives access to 13 churches (admission to 1 church: 3,000 lire, or to 6 churches within 48 hours: 15,000 lire).

POLICE STATIONS
San Marco 996 Tel. 041 522 54 34 Giudecca 543 Tel. 041 522 41 46

PUBLIC CONVENIENCES
Found on the first floor of buildings and fully automatic. A few are equipped for disabled visitors. **Cost:** 500–1,000 lire. Some also have shower facilities. **Cost:** 3,000–4,000 lire.
■ **Cannaregio**
Santa Lucia Station *Shower facilities available.*
Campo San Leonardo *Automatic toilets.*
■ **Castello**
Campo Bandiera e Moro *Shower facilities available.*
■ **Murano**
Piazza Colonna
■ **Santa Croce**
Piazzale Roma Giardini Papadopoli
■ **San Marco**
Calle della Bissa Giardini Ex Reali Calle dell' Ascensione *Shower facilities available.*

■ **San Polo**
Campo San Polo *For men only.*
Campo Nuovo Rialto

PUBLIC HOLIDAYS
■ Jan. 1 New Year's Day
■ Jan. 6 La Befana, Epiphany
■ Easter Monday
■ Apr. 25 St Mark's Day
■ May 1 Labor Day
■ Aug. 15 Ferragosto (Assumption)
■ Nov. 1 Ognissanti (All Saints)
■ Dec. 8 Immaculate Conception
■ Dec. 25 Christmas
■ Dec. 26 Santo Stefano (St Stephen's Day)

REDUCTIONS
→ **CTS CARDS**
The Centro Turistico Studentesco e Giovanile offers foreign visitors cards entitling them to reductions in many museums, bars and hotels, as well as reduced fares on certain plane and train journeys.
■ **Ostelli card**
Gives access to youth hostels.
■ **Agis card**
Offers reductions in movie theaters.
■ **"Under-26" youth card**
For non-student foreign visitors who are under 26. Cost: 20,000 lire.
■ **Member card**
For foreign visitors over the age of 26. Tarif: 45,000 lire.
■ **Group cards**
For school groups, professional organizations, etc. Valid Jan. 1–Dec. 31.
■ **Information**
Dorsoduro Ca' Foscari 3252 Tel. 041 520 56 60

→ **ROLLING/VENICE**
Card available to those between the

ages of 14 and 29, entitling them to certain reductions and facilities, as well as giving them access to certain establishments such as hotels. Cost: 5,000–10,000 lire.
■ **Information**
Tel. 041 534 69 30

→ **«CARTA GIOVANI»**
Free, personal "young person's card" reserved for those aged 14 to 29, and issued by tourist offices. Entitles the holder to reductions in museums and movie theaters, as well as some stores and restaurants.

SHOWS
→ **CASINO MUNICIPAL**
Lungomare G. Marconi, Lido 4 Tel. 041 526 06 25 From Oct. to Mar., the casino is located at Palazzo Vendramin-Calergi, Cannaregio 2040. Tel. 041 529 71 11

→ **GOLDONI THEATER**
San Marco 4650/b Tel. 041 520 75 83

SIZES
Italian sizes are different from British and US sizes.
■ **Women's skirts/dresses**
UK 10 (US 8) is an Italian 36; UK 12 (US 10) Italian 38 etc.
■ **Men's pants**
UK/US 38 is an Italian 46; UK/US 40 is an Italian 48, etc.

TELEPHONE

City code for Venice: 041 Information: 12 Collect calls from Venice: 170

→ **TO CALL THE UK FROM VENICE**
Dial 00 + 44 + the number you wish to call, omitting the intial 0.

THE A TO Z TO STAYING IN VENICE ◆

Addresses – arrival – celebrations and festivals – cost of living – emergency services – exchange – food specialties – getting around – leisure – mail – markets – newspapers – opening times – police stations – public conveniences – public holidays – reductions – shows – sizes – telephone – tourist offices – transport

→ **TO CALL THE US FROM VENICE**
Dial 00 + 1 + the number you wish to call.

→ **PUBLIC TELEPHONES**
Long-distance calls within Italy as well as international calls can be made from public telephones with 100, 200 and 500 lire coins, tokens, credit cards or telephone cards.

→ **RATES**
■ **Local calls (TUT)**
200 lire when the call is answered, then 200 lire per unit.
■ **National calls**
400 lire when the call is answered, then 200 lire per unit.

→ **TELEPHONE CARDS Information**
Tel. 167 293 822
24 hours a day, with English answering service.
■ **International (with code)**
12,500-, 25,000-, 50,000- and 100,000-lire cards available.
Dial the access code (Italy, 1740) for vocal service in Italian and English.
■ **National**
5,000-, 10,000- and 15,000-lire cards available.

→**TELECOM CENTERS**
In these you pay at the counter once you have made your call. This makes international calls a lot easier.
■ **With operator**
Near Campo San Bartolomeo, next to Fontego dei Tedeschi.
■ **Without operator**
Campo San Luca (fax facilities as well). Ruga Rialto (Rialto Bridge, on the market side), and at Santa Lucia station.

→ **UNITS**
Peak time:
1 unit = 3 mins and 10 secs,
Mon.–Fri. 8am–6.30pm and Sat. 8am–1pm.
Off-peak time:
1 unit = 6 mins and 40 secs,
Mon.–Fri. 6.30pm–8am, Sat.–Sun. and public hols. 1pm–8am.

TOURIST OFFICES
■ **Castello**
Calle del Rimedio, 4421
Tel. 041 529 87 11
Fax 041 523 03 99
■ **Lido**
Gran Viale Santa Maria Elisabetta, 6/a
Tel. 041 526 57 21
Fax 041 529 87 20
■ **San Marco**
Calle dell'Ascensione, 71
Tel. 041 522 63 56
Fax 041 529 87 30

TRANSPORT
→ **INFORMATION OFFICE FOR ALL TYPES OF TRANSPORT**
Piazzale Roma
Tel. 041 528 78 86
Open 8am–8pm.

→ **BICYCLES (FOR HIRE)**
Bruno Lazzari
Gran Viale Santa Maria Elisabetta
Lido 21/b
Tel. 041 526 80 19
Open 8.30am–7.30pm. Closed Sat. pm and Sun. in low season.
Giorgio Barbieri
Via Zara, Lido 5
Tel. 041 526 14 90
Open daily 8.30am–8pm.
Closed in winter.

→ **GONDOLAS** ● *68, 70*
Practically only used by tourists. In summer traffic jams are not uncommon on the smaller canals, giving rise to well-orchestrated abuse-throwing amongst the gondoliers.
■ **Fare**
A fixed fare is

charged, not per person. A gondola ride (6 people minimum) costs:
■ **50 mins**
120,000 lire (daytime),
150,000 lire (8pm–8am).
■ **Additional 25 mins**
60,000 lire (daytime),
75,000 lire (8pm–8am).
■ **Stops and reservations**
Bacino Orseolo
Tel. 041 528 93 16
Calle Valaresso
Tel. 041 520 61 20
San Marco
Tel. 041 520 06 85
Riva degli Schiavoni (Danieli Hotel)
Tel. 041 522 22 54
Ferrovia
Tel. 041 71 85 43
Santa Maria del Giglio
Tel. 041 522 20 73
San Tomà
Tel. 041 520 52 75
Santa Sofia
Tel. 041 522 28 44
Riva del Carbon-Rialto
Tel. 041 522 49 04

→ **MOTOSCAFO**
Starting from Piazzale Roma, it covers quite a large area. Two lines circle around Venice: Lines 51–52 (green circular), Lines 41–42 (red circular). Also stops at Murano and the Lido.

→ **TRAGHETTO**
Gondola linking one side of the Grand Canal to the other at 7 different points. Standing is compulsory.
Fare: 750 lire per person.

→ **VAPORETTO** ● *72*
Eight lines operate from Santa Lucia station. Line 1 (*accelerata*), the slowest, stops at 16 different points, past all the palazzi along the Grand Canal. During the day, the *accelerata*

runs every 10 mins; at night, it's every 20 mins and becomes Line N. Line 82 links St Mark's Square to Giudecca, via the Rialto and the Piazzale Roma at 6 different points. Lines 3 and 4 (*turistica*), operating in summer, link Tronchetto to San Zaccaria, following the Grand Canal first, then that of Giudecca on the way back.
Lines 12 and 14 serve Murano, Burano and Torcello respectively from the Fondamenta Nuove and San Zaccaria via the Lido at specific times.
■ **Tickets**
Sold at the vaporetti ticket offices.
City-pass: book of 20 tickets valid from 1 to 3 days, or weekly pass.
■ **Fare**
Charged according to the line not to the distance traveled.
Cost: between 1,000 and 4,500 lire.

→ **WATER-TAXIS**
■ **Fares**
City center (around 80,000 lire from Piazzale Roma to San Marco, for instance).
Various supplements may be charged for luggage, etc.
Warning:
Always ask the fare before getting into a water-taxi.
■ **Radio-Taxis**
Central tel.:
041 522 23 03 or 522 85 38
■ **Stations**
Airport
Tel. 041 541 50 84
Lido
Tel. 041 526 00 59
Rialto
Tel. 041 523 05 75
San Marco
Tel. 041 522 97 50
Sotoriva
Tel. 041 520 95 86

◆ HOTELS

⬚ < 80,000 lire
⬚ 80,000–220,000 lire
⬚ 220,000–600,000 lire
⬚ > 600,000 lire

The ▲ symbol refers to the Itineraries section; the ◆ refers to the maps
A list of symbols can be found on page 385.

BURANO

**Locanda-Ristorante
Raspo de Ua ***
Piazza Galuppi 560
Tel. 041 73 00 95
Closed Nov. 15–
Dec. 15.
*Housed within a
very old palazzo, a
small 6-bedroom
hotel with plenty
of charm. A favorite
with painters.*
⬚

CANNAREGIO

Adriatico **
◆ A A5
Lista di Spagna 224
Tel. 041 71 51 76
Fax 041 71 72 75
*Near the station.
Rooms clean and
reasonable.*
⬚⬚

**Albergo Bernardi
Semenzato ****
◆ C A2
Santi Apostoli
4363/4366
Tel. 041 522 72 57
Fax 041 522 24 24
*Warm, friendly
welcome. Charming
rooms with exposed
beams.*
⬚⬚

Albergo Santa Lucia *
◆ A B5
Lista di Spagna
Calle Misericordia
358
Tel./fax 041 71 51 80
Closed Dec.–Jan.
Open New Year's
Day.
*Hidden in a small,
quiet alley, this is a
charming 15-room
pensione where
you can count on a
warm reception. In
summer breakfast is
served in the
garden. Excellent
value, with pretty,
sunny bedrooms.*
⬚⬚

Amadeus **
◆ A B5
Lista di Spagna 227
Tel. 041 71 53 00
Fax 041 524 08 41
*Luxury hotel
situated near the
station, overlooking
a lively street.*
⬚⬚⬚

Caprera **
◆ A A3-B3
Cannaregio 219/220
Tel. 041 71 52 71
Fax 041 71 59 27
*Small, well-kept
family hotel.*
⬚

Florida **
◆ A F5
Calle Priuli 105
Tel. 041 71 52 53
Fax 041 71 80 88
Closed Nov. 15–
Dec. 15.
*A quiet hotel, facing
the Scalzi bridge.*
⬚⬚

Giorgione ***
◆ C A2
Calle Larga dei
Proverbi
(Santi Apostoli) 4587
Tel. 041 522 58 10
Fax 041 523 90 92
*A comfortable,
tastefully decorated
hotel, with a pretty
garden. Reception
somewhat cool.*
⬚⬚⬚

Hesperia **
◆ A A3-B3
Cannaregio 459
Tel. 041 71 60 01
Fax 041 71 51 12
Closed Dec.
*View over the
Cannaregio Canal.
Delightful owner.
Small restaurant, Il
Melograno, nearby.*
⬚⬚⬚⬚

La Forcola **
◆ A C4
Ponte
dell'Anconetta
2356
Tel. 041 524 14 84
Fax 041 524 53 80
*Fine hotel located in
a palazzo, by a
canal.*
⬚⬚

**La Locanda
di Orsaria ****
◆ A F5
Calle Priuli 103
(near the station)
Tel. 041 71 52 54
Fax 041 71 54 33
*This small family
hotel overlooks a
quiet street.
Beautiful, spacious
rooms with*

*individual safe
deposit boxes.*
⬚⬚⬚

Leonardo Venezia **
◆ A C3-C4
Calle della Masena
1385
Tel. 041 71 86 66
Fax 041 524 40 18
*Typical Venetian
pensione, run
by a charming
proprietress. Cozy
rooms and friendly
reception. This is an
excellent hotel in an
area of Venice that
has all too many
characterless ones.*
⬚⬚

Marte *
Ponte delle Guglie
338
Tel. 041 71 63 51
Fax 041 72 06 42
*Near the station.
A recently
renovated but
characterless
palazzo with sunny
and spacious rooms.
View across the
canal and the Ponte
delle Guglie.
Reception rather
cool.*
⬚⬚⬚

**Silva Ariel
Hotel ***
◆ A C3-C4
Calle della Masena
1391/a
Tel./fax 041 72 03 26
*All rooms with en-
suite bathrooms.
Pleasant garden
where breakfast is
served in summer.*
⬚⬚⬚⬚

Villa Rosa *
◆ A A5
Lista di Spagna
Calle Misericordia
389
Tel. 041 71 65 69
Fax 041 71 65 69
Closed Nov.–Dec. 15,
Jan.
*This pink-painted
pensione at the end
of a secluded alley
gives the impression
of being in a quite
different quarter of
Venice, far from
the busy station.
This is a charming,*

*welcoming hotel.
Very good value.
Reductions on
presentation of this
guidebook.*
⬚⬚⬚

CASTELLO

Albergo Corona *
◆ C B3
San Filippo
e Giacomo Calle
Corona 4464
Top floor
Tel. 041 522 91 74
Closed 1 week in
Jan.
*A charming little
hotel with pretty
bedrooms and a
view across the
rooftops. Very
reasonable prices.*
⬚⬚⬚

Alloggi Silva *
Fondamenta
del Remedio 4423
Tel. 041 522 76 43
Fax 041 528 68 17
Closed in Nov.
*Good value. Nine
small but pleasant
rooms. Those on
the upper floors
are brighter and
more airy.*
⬚⬚

Al Piave **
◆ C B4
Ruga Giuffa
4838/4840
Tel. 041 528 51 74
Fax 041 523 85 12
Closed 3 weeks in
Jan.
*Located in a typical
lively area of Venice.
Family hotel,
but a somewhat
unfriendly reception.*
⬚⬚⬚

Bisanzio **
◆ C D5
Calle della Pietà
3651
Tel. 041 520 31 00
Fax 041 520 41 14
Open all year round.
*Very quiet hotel.
The rooms are
attractive, with
terraces attached.*
⬚⬚⬚⬚

Casa Fontana **
◆ C B5
Campo San Provolo
4701

Tel. 041 522 05 79
Fax 041 523 10 40
*Charming family
hotel near San
Zaccaria. Additional
beds available for
children.*
□□⊡⊠⊠⊡

Casa Verardo *
◆ C B5
San Filippo e
Giacomo Ponte
Storto 4765
Tel. 041 528 61 27
Fax 041 523 27 65
*Entirely renovated
in the Venetian
style, this hotel is
owned by a
charming young
couple who
welcome you to
their "home".*
□□⊠⊠⊡

Da Bruno **
◆ C A4
San Lio 5726/a
Tel. 041 523 04 52
Fax 041 522 11 57
Closed 1 month in
winter.
*Reasonable hotel
with a small terrace.*
□⊡

Danieli ***
▲ 173 ◆ C B6
Riva degli Schiavoni,
4196
Tel. 041 522 64 80
Fax 041 520 02 08
*World-famous
palazzo of
breathtaking beauty
and comfort. Simple
and friendly service.*
□□⊠⊠⊞

Foresteria Valdese
◆ C B4
Calle Lunga Santa
Maria Formosa 5170
Tel./fax 041 528 67 97
Open 9am–1pm
and 6–8pm.
Closed Nov. 15–
Jan. 1.
*Advanced booking
recommended.
The hotel is mostly
occupied by young
people and groups
from Switzerland.
Bedrooms,
dormitories and
apartments for
4 to 5 people.
Modestly equipped.*
□⊠⊡

Locanda Canal *
◆ C B5
Fondamenta
del Rimedio 4422/c
(near St Mark's
Square)
Tel. 041 523 45 38
Fax 041 241 91 38
Closed Dec. 23–
Jan. 31.
*During the tourist
season, a two-night
minimum stay is
enforced. A small,
unpretentious, quiet
and comfortable
pensione.*
⊡⊠⊡

Londra Palace **
◆ C B6-D6
Riva degli Schiavoni
4171
Tel. 041 520 05 33
Fax 041 522 50 32
*Superb setting
and friendly,
attentive service.
This is a big hotel
that offers a number
of extras, such as
free entry to the
casino, and use of a
car for the day.
There is a 20%
reduction for
children under 7.
(See also Restaurant
Do Leoni).*
□□⊠⊠⊞

Metropole **
◆ C B6-D6
Riva degli Schiavoni
4149
Tel. 041 520 50 44
Fax 041 522 36 79
*A beautiful hotel,
very comfortable
and full of charm.
Splendid views
across the Lagoon
and inner
courtyards. Two*

*small conference/
banqueting rooms.
All bedrooms have
bathrooms with
marble baths.*
□⊡⊠⊠⊡

Paganelli *
Riva degli Schiavoni
4182/4687
Tel. 041 522 43 24
Fax 041 523 92 67
*The modest
entrance conceals
a small, gracious
hotel with beautiful,
spacious rooms.
Reasonably priced.
Ask for rooms
in the quieter
annex.*
□⊡⊠⊠⊡

Rio *
◆ C B5
Campo San Filippo
e Giacomo 4556
Tel. 041 523 48 10
Fax 041 520 82 22
*Modern interior,
recently decorated,
in this quiet hotel,
with a view across
the campo.*
□⊡⊡⊡

Santa Marina *
◆ C A3
Campo Santa
Marina 6068
Tel. 041 523 92 02
Fax 041 520 09 07
*This recently built
hotel is located near
the Rialto, on a
pleasant and quiet
square. Friendly
reception. In
summer breakfast
is served outside.
Extra beds available
for children in
rooms.*
□⊡⊠⊡

Savoia e Jolanda *
◆ C B6-D6
Riva degli Schiavoni
4187
Tel. 041 520 66 44
Fax 041 520 74 94
*A well-located
hotel, comfortable
but lacking in
character.*
□⊡⊡⊠⊡

Scandinavia **
◆ C B4
Campo Santa Maria
Formosa 5240
Tel. 041 522 35 07
Fax 041 523 52 32
*Venetian-style hotel
located on one of
the most beautiful
spots in Venice,
near St Mark's
Square. Safe-
deposit boxes in all
the rooms.*
□⊡⊡

CHIOGGIA

Bellevue *
Lungomare
Adriatico 22
Sottomarina
Tel. 041 40 50 17
Fax 041 40 14 39
*Located in a very
lively quarter.
Modern,
comfortable rooms
with views of the
sea. Restaurant,
games room, billiard
room.*
□⊠⊠⊡

Bristol **
Lungomare
Adriatico 46
Sottomarina
Tel. 041 554 03 89
Fax 041 554 18 13
Closed Nov.–Feb.
*The best hotel in
Chioggia, with
garden, swimming
pool and private
beach. Taverna
for dancing in the
evenings. Full-
board possible.*
□⊡P⊠⊠⊡

Capinera *
Lungomare
Adriatico 12
Sottomarina
Tel. 041 550 60 38
Fax 041 550 65 20
Closed Nov.–May
*Very quiet hotel-
restaurant. Rooms*

⊡ < 80,000 lire
⊡ 80,000–220,000 lire
⊠ 220,000–600,000 lire
⊞ > 600,000 lire

overlooking a garden on one side of the hotel and overlooking the sea on the other. Private beach. Reductions for children. *Full board is available.*
⊠ 🅿 🗭 ⊡

Gambero d'Oro ***
Viale Venezia 1
Sottomarina
Tel. 041 550 04 24
Fax 041 40 30 54
Small hotel-restaurant close to the seafront. Pleasant and quiet.
⊡ ⊡ 🏠 🅿 ⊡

Grand'Italia ****
Piazza Vigo 1
Tel. 041 40 05 15
Fax 041 40 01 85
Pretty hotel in Chioggia's historic center, close to the landing stage.
🅿 ⊠

Touring ***
Lungomare
Adriatico 44
Sottomarina
Tel. 041 554 05 04
Fax 041 554 17 46
Closed Nov.–Feb., except during the Carnival.
Close to the seafront, with private beach and pleasant rooms. Good value.
⊡ 🅿 🗭 ⊡

▆▆▆ DORSODURO ▆▆▆
Accademia-Villa Maravege ***
◆ B C4
Fondamenta Bollani 1058
Tel. 041 521 01 88
Fax 041 523 91 52
Well-known, attractive 17th-century villa. Delightful gardens. Avoid the rooms in the noisy annex. Reserve well in advance.
⊡ 🗭 ⊠

Agli Alboretti **
◆ B C5
Accademia 884
Tel. 041 523 00 58
Fax 041 521 01 58

A cosy, paneled hotel with simple bedrooms – come here for peace and quiet, or if La Galleria is full.
⊡ ⫿⫿ 🏠 ⊡

Alla Salute da Cici **
◆ B F5
Fondamenta Ca' Bala, Salute 222
Tel. 041 523 54 04
Fax 041 522 22 71
Closed Nov. to Christmas.
Quiet pensione with garden, in a pretty palazzo close to La Salute.
🗮 🏠 🗭 ⊡

American ***
San Vio 628
Tel. 041 520 47 33
Fax 041 520 40 48
Reasonably priced but banal rooms. Some overlook a canal.
⊡ ⊡ ⊠

Foresteria Domus Cavanis
◆ B C5
Rio Terrà Antonio Foscarini 912/a
Tel./fax 041 528 73 74
Closed Oct.–May.
A religious foyer reserved for students under 25. Plenty of cheap, basic rooms. Shower on the landing.
⊡ ⊡

La Calcina ***
◆ B D6-F6
Zattere 780
Tel. 041 520 64 66
Fax 041 522 70 45
Attractive pensione with a magnificent view across to the Giudecca. Carefully restored, it has retained all its charm. Spacious, sunny rooms. Friendly welcome.
⊡ 🗭 🗭 ⊡

La Galleria *
◆ B C5
Accademia 878/a
Tel./fax 041 520 41 72
Stunning pensione located in an 18th-century palazzo, with a superb view

of the Grand Canal and Accademia. Excellent value, though rather noisy.
⊡ 🄲 ⊡ ⊠ 🗭 ⊡

Locanda Montin *
◆ B B4
Fondamenta di Borgo 1147
Tel. 041 522 71 51
Fax 041 520 02 55
The ideal pensione, on the banks of a beautiful canal, with a garden. We recommend that you reserve well in advance.
⊡

Messner **
Dorsoduro 216
Tel. 041 522 74 43
Fax 041 522 72 66
Hotel with garden in a pleasant, tranquil quarter.
⊡ ⫿⫿ ⊡

Pantalon ***
Ca' Foscari 3941/3942
Tel. 041 71 08 96
Fax 041 71 86 83
Entirely renovated. Each room has a minibar and a safe-deposit box. Air conditioning. Small pets accepted.
⊡ 🄲 ⊡ ⊠

Pausania ***
◆ B A4-B4
Fondamenta Gherardini 2824
Tel. 041 522 20 83
Fax 041 522 29 89
Elegant and sunny hotel situated in a 14th-century palazzo. Extremely popular with tour operators, but the prices remain excessively high.
⊡ ⊡ ⊠ ⊠

Seguso **
◆ B D6-F6
Zattere 779
Tel. 041 528 68 58
Fax 041 522 23 40
Closed Dec.–Feb.
Almost an institution, with the faded charm of an authentic turn-of-the-century pensione. Fine

view across to the Giudecca. Reductions for children under 3. Half-board only.
⊡ ⊠ 🗭 ⊠

Tivoli **
◆ B B2
Crosera S. Pantalon 3838
Tel. 041 524 24 60
Fax 041 522 26 56
Impersonal hotel with only the most basic comforts, but it is conveniently situated close to the major monuments and the vaporetto.
⊡ 🄲 ⊡

▆▆▆ GIUDECCA ▆▆▆
Cipriani ****
Fondamenta San Giovanni 10
Tel. 041 520 77 44
Fax 041 520 39 30
Closed Nov. 15–Mar. 15.
Luxury complex with private tennis court, Olympic seawater swimming pool, sumptuous bedrooms, private moorings. The restaurant has an excellent reputation (see Restaurants).
⊡ ⊡ 🎇 🗭 ⊞

Istituto Suore Canossiane
Ponte Piccolo 428
Tel. 041 522 21 57
Open 3–10pm.
A religious institution close to Sant'Eufemia, with two dormitories for women only.
🗭 ⊡

Youth hostel
Ostello Venezia
Fondamenta delle Zitelle 86
Tel. 041 523 82 11
Fax 041 523 56 89
Open 7.30–9am and 1–11.30pm.
Leave your card in the morning. Groups must reserve by fax. Youth card essential for this pearl among youth

hostels. Dormitories
with 16 beds.
Breakfast and bed
linen included.
▨▩▣

LIDO

**Atlanta Augustus
*****
Via Lepanto 15
Tel. 041 526 05 69
Fax 041 526 56 04
*Simple, clean rooms
in this small, well-
kept 1930s style
hotel.*
▣

Cristallo **
Gran Viale
Santa Maria
Elisabetta 51
Tel. 041 526 52 93
Fax 041 526 56 15
Closed in winter,
except during
Christmas and the
Carnival.
*On the Lido's
liveliest boulevard.
Convenient garden
and bathing cabins
reserved in summer
for hotel guests.
Reductions for
children.*
▣▨▣

**Grand Hôtel
des Bains ******
Lungomare Marconi
17
Tel. 041 526 59 21
Fax 041 526 01 13
Closed Nov.–May.
*Internationally
famous hotel,
immortalized by
Thomas Mann (and
Luchino Visconti)
as the setting for
Death in Venice.
Park, swimming
pool, private beach,
various sports.
The hotel is free
for children under
the age of 6.*
▣▣▨▣▨▨▦

Excelsior *****
Lungomare Marconi
41
Tel. 041 526 02 01
Fax 041 526 72 76
Closed Nov.–March
*This early 20th-
century hotel is a
mixture of Moorish,
Byzantine and
Gothic styles. It is*

the headquarters
of the jury of La
Mostra del Cinema
and is situated near
the casino and the
beach.
▣▣▨▦

La Pergola *
Via Cipro 15
Tel. 041 526 07 84
*A delightful family-
run guesthouse
with modern décor
and rooms
overlooking
the garden.*
▨▣

Le Garzette
Lungomare Alberoni
32
Tel. 041 73 10 78
Closed Dec. 15–
Jan. 15.
*Authentic farm
close to the sea
and to the golf
club. It offers
breathtaking views
over the Lagoon
and the Adriatic.
Five double rooms
with bath. Half-
board available.
Family cuisine is
served, based on
vegetables picked
fresh from the
garden and fish.
Reservations
recommended.*
▨▣

Reiter **
Gran Viale 57/b
Tel. 041 526 01 07
Fax 041 526 14 91
*This hotel-
restaurant has now
been completely
renovated. Double
rooms with
views on to the
garden.*
▨▣

Rigel ***
Via Dandolo 13
Tel. 041 526 88 10
Fax 041 276 00 77
Closed Nov.–
Carnival.
*A quiet hotel with
its own garden.
Meals are available
for groups only.
Only five minutes
away from the
landing stage.*
▣▣

Stella **
Via Sandro Gallo
111
Tel. 041 526 07 45
Fax 041 526 10 81
Closed Nov.–March,
except during the
Carnival.
*Parking lot and
garden. Five
minutes from the
casino. Breakfast
included.*
▣▨▣▣

Vianello **
Via Casa Rossa
10/14
Tel./fax 041 73 10 72
Closed Nov.–March
*Hotel with garden.
Possibility of half-
board.*
▣▣

Villa Aurora **
Riviera San Nicolò 11
Tel. 041 526 05 19
Fax 041 526 86 27
Closed Jan. 8–
Carnival.
*Quiet hotel-
restaurant, with a
terrific view over
the Lagoon.*
▨▨▣

Villa Cipro **
Via Zara 2
Tel. 041 526 14 08
Fax 041 276 01 76
*Modern hotel with
a small garden.*
▣

Villa delle Palme *
Via Dandolo 12
Tel. 041 242 13 12
*Fine "Liberty"-style
villa. Some rooms
have balconies
overlooking the
garden. Quiet
and close to the
beach.*
▣▣

Villa Pannonia ***
Via Doge D. Michiel
48
Tel. 041 526 01 62
Fax 041 526 52 77
Closed for one week
at Christmas.
*1900s hotel-
restaurant with
garden. Breakfast
included. Reductions
available for
children.*
▣▨▣

Villa Tiziana***
Via A. Gritti 3
Tel. 041 526 11 52
Fax 041 526 21 45
Closed Nov.–March,
except during the
Carnival.
*Quiet villa with
garden, 50 yards
from the sea.
Private beach.*
▣▨▦

MURANO

Pensione al Soffiador
Viale Bressagio
10/11
Tel./fax 041 73 94 30
Closed Dec. 15–
Jan. 15.
*Also a fish restaurant
at lunchtime.
Excellent value.*
▣▣

SAN MARCO

Ai Do Mori *
◆ C A5-B5
Calle Larga
San Marco 658
Tel. 041 520 48 17
Fax 041 520 53 28
Closed Jan. 7–31.
*Close to St Mark's;
quiet and
comfortable. View
of the campanile
and basilica. One
room offering a
view across the
rooftops is reserved
for painters.
Friendly reception.
No charge for
children under the
age of 3.*
▣▣▨▨▣

Ala ***
◆ A E4
Campo Santa Maria
del Giglio
Tel. 041 520 83 33
Fax 041 520 63 90
*Near the Church of
Santa Maria del
Giglio. Some of
the rooms are very
beautiful, with
antique furniture
and décor.*
▣▣▨▣▣

Al Gazzetino *
◆ C A4
Calle de Mezo
4971
Tel. 041 528 65 23
Fax 041 522 33 14
*Small hotel-
restaurant, next to*

393

⊡ < 80,000 lire
⊡ 80,000–220,000 lire
⊡ 220,000–600,000 lire
⊞ > 600,000 lire

San Salvador, with a view looking across the canal. Additional beds for children available. Small pets are accepted.
⊡ ⅏ ✕ ⊡

All'Angelo ***
◆ C A5-B5
Calle Larga San Marco 403
Tel. 041 520 92 99
Fax 041 523 19 43
Fine stone staircase and majestic hallway; rooms clean but rather lacking in character (30% reduction for children).
⊡ C ✕ ⊡

Ateneo ***
◆ B F3
Campo San Fantin 1876
Tel. 041 520 07 77
Fax 041 522 85 50
This recently restored hotel is comfortable but rather impersonal. Accessible by gondola.
⊡ C ⊡ ⊡

Bauer Grünwald e Grand Hotel *****
◆ C F4
Campo San Moisè 1459
Tel. 041 520 70 22
Fax 041 520 75 57
Very close to St Mark's and accessible by gondola. Most of the hotel is post-war and ponderous, but its 230 rooms of all different styles have a certain class. The old part of the hotel dates from the 12th century. There is also a view across the Grand Canal. Free of charge for children under 3 and reductions for children under 7.
⊡ C ⊡ ✕ ⅏ ⊡

Bonvecchiati ***
◆ B F2
Calle Goldoni 4488
Tel. 041 528 50 17
Fax 041 528 52 30

A charming hotel with a fine glass roof. Many paintings, most of which were given to a former owner (who also ran the Alla Colomba restaurant) in lieu of payment (modern art 1940–50). Cosmopolitan clientele. Reductions for children under 12.
⊡ C ⊡ ✕ ⊡

Casa Petrarca *
Calle delle Schiavine 4386
◆ B F3
Tel./fax 041 520 04 30
Charming little guest-house – a home from home with a very charming owner. Ideal accommodation for students in the center of Venice.
C ⊡

Cavalletto e Doge Orseolo ****
◆ C A5
Calle Cavalletto 1107
Tel. 041 520 09 55
Fax 041 523 81 84
Discreetly luxurious hotel, in a typically Venetian setting overlooking a gondola mooring. Rooms are expensive but charming and very spacious. Close to St Mark's Square.
⊡ C ⊡ ✕ ⅏ ⊡

Centauro **
◆ C E4
Calle della Vida 4297
Tel. 041 522 58 32
Fax 041 523 91 51
In a quiet, secluded corner, right in the heart of Venice. Views of the canal, or across the city's rooftops.
⊡ C ⊡

Città di Milano **
◆ C A4
Campiello San Zulian 590
Tel. 041 522 70 02
Fax 041 522 78 34

Between the Rialto and St Mark's Square, on the quiet, delightful Campo San Zulian.
⊡ C ⊡

Concordia ****
◆ C A5-B5
Calle Larga San Marco 367
Tel. 041 520 68 66
Fax 041 520 67 75
Modern, centrally located hotel, with pseudo-Venetian décor. Comfortable but without much charm. This is the only lodging house with a view directly on to St Mark's Square. Free accommodation for children under 10.
⊡ C ⊡ ✕ ⅏ ⊡

Diana **
◆ C A5
Calle Specchieri 449
Tel. 041 520 69 11
Fax 041 523 87 63
A small hotel with five bedrooms. Breakfast included.
⊡ C ⊡

Europa e Regina ****
◆ B F4
Via XXII Marzo 2159
Tel. 041 520 04 77
Fax 041 523 15 33
This superbly sumptuous palazzo tends to be full throughout the year. Beautiful terrace overlooking the Grand Canal and the Basilica Santa Maria della Salute. Attentive service.
⊡ C ⊡ ⅏ ⊡

Firenze ***
◆ B F4
Corte Foscara 1490
(behind the Salizada San Moisè)
Tel. 041 522 28 58
Fax 041 520 26 68
Three minutes from St Mark's Square. Entirely restored, this hotel boasts an elevator (extremely

rare in Venice). Pleasant roof terrace with a beautiful view over the city where breakfast is served in summer. Air-conditioning in summer. All the rooms have safe-deposit boxes.
⊡ C ⊡ ⅏ ⊡

Flora ***
◆ A A6
Calle Bergamaschi 2283/a
Tel. 041 520 58 44
Fax 041 522 82 17
Charming, slightly run-down hotel, with magnificent Liberty-style staircase and inner courtyard. In summer, breakfast is served on a pleasant patio.
⊡ C ⅏ ⊡

Gorizia alla Valigia **
◆ C A5
Calle dei Fabbri 4696/a
Tel. 041 522 37 37
Fax 041 521 27 89
Closed Jan.
Some of the rooms here are very small indeed. The collection of pictures is not very good, but suffices to lend this hotel a note of kitsch. Reductions for children under 6.
⊡ C ⊡ ✕ ⊡

Gritti Palace Hotel *****
▲ 212 ◆ B E4
Campo Santa Maria del Giglio 2467
Tel. 041 79 46 11
Fax 041 520 09 42
This palace, named after the 15th-century Doge Andrea Gritti, is one of the most famous in Venice. Luxurious and sophisticated, the Gritti Palace Hotel offers Sheraton services such as garages on the Piazzale Roma

and shuttle transfers to the airport. The rooms overlook the Grand Canal. Free for children under 6.
▢▢▢▢▢▢▢

Istituto Ciliota
◆ B D3
Calle Muneghe 2976
Tel. 041 520 48 88
Religious establishment admitting women only. Open to female tourists from mid-June to mid-Sep. (open until 11.30pm). Reductions for students on presentation of a student card.
▢▢

La Fenice e Des Artistes ***
◆ B E3
Campiello della Fenice 1936
Tel. 041 523 23 33
Fax 041 520 37 21
Charming, old-fashioned hotel. Breakfast is served in an enclosed garden.
▢▢▢▢

Lisbona ***
◆ B E4-F4
Calle Larga XXII Marzo
Tel. 041 528 67 74
Fax 041 520 70 61
This hotel, in the Venetian style, is located opposite San Moisè, in the "sotoportego" of the gondoliers, five minutes from St Mark's Square. Adjoining rooms and additional beds for children available. Safe-deposit box and minibar in each room. Small pets are accepted.
▢▢▢▢▢

Locanda Fiorita *
◆ B D3-D4
San Marco 3457/a
Tel. 041 523 47 54
Fax 041 522 80 43
A delightful,

BAUER GRÜNWALD HOTEL

EUROPA E REGINA HOTEL

GRITTI PALACE HOTEL

MONACO E GRAN CANAL HOTEL

friendly hotel, at the back of the Campo Santo Stefano. Warm welcome.
▢▢

Luna Hotel Baglioni ****
◆ C A6
Calle Larga de l'Ascension 1243
Tel. 041 528 98 40
Fax 041 528 71 60
Open all year round. *This building originated in the 12th century as a Templars' hospice and was later converted into a convent. Magnificent marble inner courtyard. Luxury hotel restaurant. Splendid salon decorated with school of Tiepolo frescoes.*
▢▢▢▢▢▢

Mercurio **
◆ B F3
Calle del Fruttarol 1848
Tel. 041 522 09 47
Fax 041 528 52 70
Unpretentious hotel close to La Fenice theater and renovated in 1996. Friendly reception.
▢▢▢▢

Monaco e Gran Canal ****
◆ C A6
Calle Vallaresso 1325
Tel. 041 520 02 11
Fax 041 520 05 01
Superb palace dating back from the end of the 18th century and overlooking the Grand Canal, but somewhat soulless.
▢▢▢▢▢▢

Orion **
◆ C A5
Calle Spadaria 700/a
Tel. 041 522 30 53
Fax 041 523 88 66
18 rooms.
▢▢▢▢

◆ HOTELS

⬚ < 80,000 lire
⬚ 80,000–220,000 lire
⬚ 220,000–600,000 lire
⊞ > 600,000 lire

Rialto *
◆ B F1
Riva del Ferro
5149
Tel. 041 520 91 66
Fax 041 523 89 58
*Near the Rialto.
Well-situated but
somewhat noisy.
Comfortable rooms.*
⬚⬚⬚⬚⬚

San Gallo *
Campo San Gallo
1093/a
Tel. 041 522 73 11
Fax 041 522 57 02
*Venetian-style décor.
The rooms are
pleasant although
rather small.
Stunning terrace.*
⬚⬚⬚⬚

San Giorgio **
◆ B D3
Rio terrà della
Mandola 3781
Tel. 041 523 58 35
Fax 041 522 80 72
*Excellent pensione,
efficiently run by
a young couple.
Tasteful décor,
with replicas of
17th-century
furniture as well as
some family pieces.*
⬚⬚⬚⬚

San Marco *
◆ C A5-A6
Place Saint-Marc 877
Ponte dei Dai
Tel. 041 520 42 77
Fax 041 523 84 47
*A characterless but
well-located and
modern hotel on
the edge of
St Mark's Square.
Many rooms.*
⬚⬚⬚⬚

San Salvador **
Calle Galiazzo 5264
Tel. 041 528 91 47
*Family pensione,
young clientele.*
⬚⬚

San Samuele **
◆ B D3
Salizada
San Samuele 3358
Tel./fax 041 522
80 45
*Ideal location,
3 minutes' walk
from the
Accademia. Family*

*hotel with slightly
run-down décor.
Rooms are
comfortable,
spacious, simple
and clean.*
⬚⬚⬚⬚

San Zulian *
◆ C A5
Calle San Zulian
534/535
Tel. 041 522 58 72
Fax 041 523 22 65
*Quiet, comfortable
rooms.*
⬚⬚⬚⬚

**Saturnia
e International *****
◆ B E4-F4
Calle Larga XXII
Marzo 2398
Tel. 041 520 83 77
Fax 041 520 71 31
*Palazzo once
owned by the Doge
Pisani family. The
entrance hall is a
little overwhelming,
but decorated
with splendid 14th-
century bas-reliefs.
Interior courtyard.*
⬚⬚

Albergo Guerrato **
◆ A E5-F5
Calle drio la Scimia
240/a
Tel. 041 522 71 31
Fax 041 528 59 27
*Fifty yards from the
Rialto, a hotel run
by a delightful
couple. Friendly
reception and sunny,
large rooms which
can accommodate
large families.
Copious breakfast.
An excellent choice.*
⬚⬚⬚

Alex **
◆ B C1
Rio terrà Frari
2606
Tel./fax 041 523 13 41
Closed Jan.
*A small hotel with
pleasant rooms.*
⬚⬚

**Casa dello Studente-
Domus Civica** ◆ B B1
San Rocco 3082
Tel. 041 71 02 05
Open 7.30am–
11.30pm.

Closed Oct.15–
June 15.
*Cheap, spacious
rooms for students
in the university
area. Reductions for
holders of youth
cards.*
⬚

Carpaccio *
◆B D4
San Polo 2765
Tel. 041 523 59 46
Fax 041 524 21 34
Closed end Nov.–
March 15.
*A small hotel near
San Tomà, quiet
and well-run, but
rather expensive.*
⬚⬚⬚⬚⬚

Hotel Iris **
◆ B C2
San Tomà 2910/a
Near Frari
Tel./fax 041 522
28 82
*Adequate rooms,
some overlooking
a small canal, and
others overlooking
the hotel's garden-
restaurant.*
⬚⬚

Locanda Sturion *
◆ B F1
Calle dello Sturion
679
Tel. 041 523 62 43
Fax 041 522 83 78
*One of the oldest
locandas in Venice.
Very well-run.
Centrally located
near the Rialto and
Grand Canal. Elderly
people may find
the staircase leading
up to the reception
difficult to
negotiate. Triple
rooms available for
families with
children.*
⬚⬚⬚⬚

Marconi *
◆ B F1
Fondamenta del Vin
729
Tel. 041 522 20 68
Fax 041 522 97 00
*Fifteenth-century
palazzo with small
rooms, pleasant
service. Free for
children under 10.*
⬚⬚⬚⬚⬚

Ai Due Fanali *
◆ A B6
Campo San Simeon
Grando 946
Tel. 041 71 84 90
Fax 041 71 83 44
Closed Jan. but
open for New Year.
*Decent rooms on a
quiet square beside
the church. Some
rooms overlook
the Grand Canal.
Reductions of 20
to 25% for students
out of season.*
⬚⬚⬚

Airone **
◆ A A6
Santa Croce 557
Tel. 041 520 49 91
Fax 041 520 48 00
*Situated opposite
the station, this
hotel overlooks the
Grand Canal. Free
for children under
the age of 6.*
⬚⬚⬚

Al Gallo *
◆ B A1
Calle Amai 197/g
Tel. 041 523 67 61
Fax 041 522 81 88
Closed Nov. 15–Dec.
15.
*This tiny guesthouse
has 7 rooms and
rudimentary
comforts. Pleasant
service and prices
that seem to
fluctuate according
to the owner's whim.
No charge for babies.*
⬚⬚

Al Sole *
Santa Croce 136
Tel. 041 71 08 44
Fax 041 71 43 98
Closed Nov.–March
except during the
Carnival.
*A Venetian palazzo
with beautifully
decorated rooms
and a view over a
small canal. Free
for children under 2.*
⬚⬚⬚

Canal e Walter *
Santa Croce 553
Tel. 041 523 84 80
Fax 041 523 91 06
*Near the station,
this establishment*

consists of two
renovated hotels.
Decent rooms
and an interior
garden.

Casa Peron *
◆ B B2
Salizada
San Pantalon 84/85
Tel. 041 71 10 38
Closed in Jan. after
Epiphany.
*Though rather plain,
this hotel is ideal for
small groups and
students. Located in
the lively university
quarter. Breakfast
included.*
*The hotel's annex is
very cheap for
Venice, but there
are no showers and
breakfast is not
included.*

Gardena ****
◆ A A6-B A1
Fondamenta
dei Tolentini 239
Tel. 041 220 50 00
Fax 041 220 50 20
Very good location

and friendly
reception.

Locanda Stefania *
◆ A A6-B A1
Fondamenta dei
Tolentini 181/a
Tel. 041 520 37 57
*Mainly occupied by
Venetian students
throughout the
academic year, but
welcomes tourists
from mid-June until
mid-Sep.*

Marin *
◆ A A6
San Simeone Piccolo
670/b
Tel. 041 71 80 22
Fax 041 72 14 85
Closed Nov.
*Located in a quiet,
residential area.
Charming owners.
Family atmosphere
and 16th-century
fresco in the dining
room.*

San Cassiano *****
Calle Rosa 2232
Tel. 041 524 17 68

Fax 041 72 10 33
*Elegant and
very comfortable
palazzo dating
from the 14th-
century, with good
period furniture.
Polite service and an
international
clientele.*

Sofitel ******
◆ B A1
Santa Croce 245
Giardini Papadopoli
Tel. 041 71 04 00
Fax 041 71 03 94
*Close to the station,
with comfortable
modern rooms.
Free for children
under the age
of 12.*

TORCELLO
**Locanda
Cipriani *******
Torcello Island
Tel. 041 73 01 50
Fax 041 73 54 33
*A 4-bedroom hotel
in the middle of this
tiny island where
Hemingway
used to come.*

Excellent food.
Currently closed for
renovation.

AROUND VENICE
MESTRE
**Camping
Alba d'Oro ********
Via Triestina 214/b
Ca' Noghera
Tel. 541 51 02
Closed Oct.–March
*Luxury campsite
situated about 1
hour from the
station. Bungalows
and trailers.*

TREPORTI
**Camping Marina
di Venezia********
Punta Sabbioni,
Via Montello 6
Tel. 530 09 55
Fax 96 60 36
Closed Oct. 31–
April 1.
*This site offers
luxury camping: it is
well-equipped and
has a fine private
beach to boot.
Stores, restaurants,
bars, pizzeria.
Bungalows
and trailers.*

◆ RESTAURANTS

The ▲ symbol refers to the Itineraries section; the ◆ refers to the maps
A list of symbols can be found on page 385.

■ < 35,000 lire
■ 35,000–45,000 lire
■ 45,000–90,000 lire
⊞ > 90,000 lire

BURANO

Da Romano ("Tre Stelle da Romano")
Via Baldassare Galuppi 221
Tel. 041 73 00 30
Open noon–2.30pm and 6.30–9pm.
Closed Tue., Sun. dinner, Dec. 15–Carnival.
One of Venice's finest fish restaurants, with paintings by artists who have visited at one time or another. Reserve at weekends. Specialties: fresh fish and fish risotti.
■ ■

Gatto Nero-Da Ruggero
Fondamenta della Giudecca 88
Tel. 041 73 01 20
Open 9am–4pm and 6–10pm.
Closed Mon. and Jan. after Epiphany.
A typical local restaurant recommended by many food guides. The picture collection is the chef's pride and joy. Clients of all types. Specializes in fish only (risotto alla buranella).
■ ■

CANNAREGIO

Ai 40 Ladroni
◆ A C2–AC3
Fondamenta della Sensa 3253
Tel. 041 71 57 36
Open 9am–midnight.
Closed Mon., at Christmas and 3 weeks in Aug.
Popular restaurant serving fine Venetian specialties. Friendly atmosphere.
■ ■

Alla Vedova
◆ A E5
Ramo Ca' d'Oro 3912/3952
Tel. 041 528 53 24
Open 11.30am–3pm and 6–11pm.
Closed Thur. in winter.

Popular with Venetians for pre-dinner drinks. Specialties (fish, fried vegetables and Venetian dishes) at the bar or tables.
■

Al Milion
◆ C A3
Corte Al Milion, San Giovanni Grisostomo 5841
Tel. 041 522 93 02
Open 11am–2pm and 6–10pm.
Closed Wed.
Venetian specialties at the bar or at one of the small wooden tables in this charming tavern. Specialties include fegato alla veneziana and seppie alla veneziana.
⊠ ■

Antica Mola
◆ A C3–AD3
Fondamenta degli Ormesini 2800
Tel. 041 71 74 92
Open daily 8am–midnight.
Charming and hospitable, off the tourist circuit. Typical Venetian cuisine. Specialties: baccala (cod) and risotti.
■ ■

Fiaschetteria Toscana
◆ C A3
San Giovanni Grisostomo 5719
Tel. 041 528 52 81
Open 12.30–2.30pm and 7.30–10.30pm.
Closed Tue.
Close to the Rialto, in a lively neighborhood. An excellent fish restaurant serving Venetian and Italian specialties.
■ ■

L'Iguana
◆ A E4
Fondamenta della Misericordia 2515
Open 8am–3pm and 6pm–1am.
Closed Tue. (except in summer) and Jan.
Mexican restaurant

– only seats 35 indoors. In summer, there are tables in the garden.
■ ■

CASTELLO

Al Covo
Campiello della Pescaria 3968
Tel. 041 522 38 12
Open 12.30–2.15pm and 7.30–10.15pm.
Closed Wed., Thur., Jan. and 15 days Aug.
Stylish restaurant with a wooden bar and Murano glass bottles. The food is all freshly made on the premises. 140 different wines.
■ ■

Al Mascaron
◆ C B4
Calle Lunga Santa Maria Formosa 5225
Tel. 041 522 59 95
Open 11am–3pm, 6.30pm–12.30am.
Closed Sun. and Dec.–Jan.
Furnished in the style of a 19th-century Venetian tavern. Both locals and tourists share good, traditional cuisine in a young, relaxed atmosphere.
■

Alle Testiere
◆ C B4
Calle del Mondo Nuovo 5801
Tel. 041 522 72 20
Open 11am–3pm and 6–10pm.
Closed Sun.
Enjoy an ombra with cichetti, or fish.
■

Cip Ciap
◆ C B4
Ponte del Mondo Nuovo 5799
Tel. 041 523 66 21
Open 7am–9pm.
Closed Tue.
Also called La Bottega della Pizza, this popular establishment offers a wide choice of pizzas by the slice. Try the famous Disco Volante, which the padrone will tailor

to your tastes, simply by looking at your face. Take away only.
■ ■

Corte Sconta
◆ C D5-E5
Calle del Pestrin 3886
Tel. 041 522 70 24
Open 12.30–2pm and 7.30–10pm.
Closed Sun.–Mon., Jan. 7–Feb. 7, and July 20–Aug. 20.
This beautiful old osteria has become very fashionable – reservations are essential. Good fish cuisine, but expensive, and the servings are parsimonious. Specialties include: sepia eggs, granzeole and sampietro alle erbe.
■ ■

Danieli Terrazza
◆ C C6-D6
Riva degli Schiavoni 4196
Tel. 041 522 64 80
Open noon–3pm and 7–10.30pm.
The most luxurious, if not the most beautiful restaurant in Venice. Highly reputed cuisine and friendly service. On the top floor of the Danieli hotel, it has a magnificent view across the Lagoon. Specialties: branzino al forno, granzeole con polenta, gamberetti.
■ ▩ ⊞

Da Remigio
◆ C D5
Salizada dei Greci 3416
Tel. 041 523 00 89
Open 12.30–2.30pm and 7.30–10pm.
Closed Mon. eve. and Tue.
Unfrequented by tourists, this popular trattoria serves simple, reasonably priced food to inhabitants of the Castello quarter. Friendly service but a little slow.

Book at least 4 days in advance.
◻▣

Do Leoni
◆ C C6-D6
Riva degli Schiavoni 4171
Tel. 041 520 05 33
Open noon–3.30pm and 7.30–11.30pm.
Closed Tue.
Overlooking the Grand Canal, the Londra Palace's high-class restaurant offers Venetian and international cuisine. À la carte menu only in the evening. Video bar after 11pm.
◻◙▩▦

La Grande Muraglia
◆ C E6
Calle Morosini 3958
Tel. 041 523 23 82
Open noon–3pm and 7pm–midnight.
Closed Mon. out of season.
A reasonably priced Chinese restaurant.
◻▣

Trattoria Ai Tosi
◆ D C3-D3
Secco Marina 738
Tel. 041 523 71 02
Open 9.30am–11.30pm.
Closed Wed.
Located in a lively area, between Via Garibaldi and the Biennale, this friendly trattoria is popular with Venetians.
▣

Trattoria Alla Rivetta
◆ C C5
Salizada San Provolo 4625
Tel. 041 528 73 026
Open 10am–10pm.
Closed Mon., and July 15–Aug. 15.
Typical fish restaurant. Throughout the summer, Venetians tend to abandon this place to the tourists. As waiters are rushed off their feet, check your bill carefully. Specialties include fried

calamari, grilled sole and spaghetti alle vongole.
▣

CHIOGGIA

Al Bersagliere
Via Cesare Battisti 293
Tel. 041 40 10 44
Open noon–3pm and 7–10pm.
Closed Tue.
Very good fish restaurant.
◻▣

Antico Toro
Corso del Popolo 1306
Tel. 041 40 05 60
Closed Wed.
Traditional dishes from Chioggia.
▣

El Gato
Corso del Popolo-Campo Sant'Andrea 653
Tel. 041 40 18 06
Open noon–2.30pm and 7–10.30pm.
Closed Mon. and Jan.
Highly praised fish restaurant. Fine dining room with arcades and pleasant atmosphere. Specialties: polenta, lumachine di mare, spaghetti with mussels.
◻▣

La Bella Venezia
Calle Corona 51
Tel. 041 40 05 00
Open 10am–3pm and 7–10pm.
Closed Thur. and Jan.
This restaurant has an excellent reputation for its fish dishes. Very pleasant garden and spacious reception room.
◻▣

Mano Amica
Corso del Popolo 1340, corner of Piazzetta Vico
Tel. 041 40 17 21
Closed Mon.
Family-run restaurant serving fish specialties.
◻▣

DORSODURO

Agli Alboretti
◆ B C5-C4
Accademia 882
Tel. 041 523 00 58
Open 7–11pm.
Closed Wed. and 3 weeks in Jan. and Aug.
Very well-located gastronomic restaurant beside the Accademia and close to the Grand Canal. Plush atmosphere. Rather expensive. Specialties: hot avocado and shrimp.
◻ⓒ▣

Ai Gondolieri
Fondamenta dell'Ospedaletto 366
Tel. 041 528 63 96
RESTAURANT: open noon–3pm and 7.30–10pm.
BAR: open 10am–4pm and 7–10pm.
Closed Tue. and end July–Aug. 15.
Enormous, delicious panini; relaxed, friendly atmosphere. Restaurant: exquisite food, especially good meat dishes and fresh vegetables. Impressive wine list. Quite expensive.
▦

Al Profeta
◆ B A4
Calle Lunga Santa Barnaba 2671
Tel. 041 523 74 66
Open noon–3pm and 6.30–11pm.
Closed Mon.
Young, unpretentious pizzeria with an attractive garden.
ⓒ▣

Al Sole di Napoli
◆ B B3
Campo Santa Margherita 3023
Tel. 041 528 56 86
Open noon–2.30pm and 6.30–10.30pm.
Closed Thur. and Dec. 6–Jan. 6.
Basic restaurant, reasonably priced pizzas. Terrace on

the square in the summer.
◻▩▣

Antica Locanda Montin
◆ B B4-B5
Fondamenta Eremite 1147
Tel. 041 522 71 51
Open 12.30–2.30pm and 7.30–10pm.
Closed Tue. eve., Wed., Jan. 7–20 and 10 days in Aug.
Immortalized by d'Annunzio. Still retains its magical and nostalgic atmosphere, though slightly spoiled now by the numerous group tours. Specialties: grigliata dell'Adriatico, coda di rospo ai ferri.
◻▩▣

Antico Capon
◆ B B3
Campo Santa Margherita 3004
Tel. 041 528 52 52
Open noon–midnight.
Closed Wed. winter.
Overlooking one of the biggest squares in Venice, the terrace of this gastronomic restaurant is flooded with sunshine in summer.
◻▣

Crepizza
◆ B B2
San Pantalon 3757
Tel. 041 524 22 36
Open 9.30am–3.30pm, 6.30–11pm.
Closed Tue.
One of Venice's few crêperies.
◻▣

Da Gianni
◆ B D6-F6
Zattere 918
Tel. 041 523 72 10
Open 7.30am–11pm.
Closed Wed. and Jan.
Restaurant directly overlooking the Giudecca. Service can be rather curt. Specialties include carpaccio e parmigiano, seppie alla Veneziana.
◻▩▣

◆ RESTAURANTS

■ < 35,000 lire
■ 35,000–45,000 lire
■ 45,000–90,000 lire
■ > 90,000 lire

Incontro
Dorsoduro 3062
Tel. 041 522 24 04
Open noon–3pm
and 7.30–10.30pm.
Closed Mon.
*Young friendly
atmosphere.
Specialty: sardines,
ravioli with goat's
cheese, grated
orange peel and
saffron.*
■ ■

La Dolce Vita
◆ B A3-B3
Rio terrà della
Scoazera 2894
Tel. 041 523 11 15
Open noon–3pm
and 7pm–2am.
Closed Sun.
*A small, friendly
restaurant serving
pasta, pizzas and
salads. Largely
patronized by a
young clientele.*
■

La Furatola
◆ B A4-B4
Calle Lunga Santa
Barnaba 2870/a
Tel. 041 520 85 94
Open noon–3pm
and 7–9.30pm.
Closed Wed. eve.
and Thur.
*Specialties: fish and
seafood (extra
fresh).*
■

La Sosta
◆ B B3
Campo S.
Margherita 3019
Tel. 041 528 52 55
Open 7am–1am
(summer) and 7am–
8.30pm (winter).
Closed Sun.
Snack bar.
■

Linea d'Ombra
◆ B D6-F6
Zattere 19
Tel. 041 528 52 59
Closed Sun. eve.
and Wed.
*Excellent cuisine in a
delightful setting:
fireplace, wood-
paneling, latticed
windows. Terrace
with a view over the
Giudecca.*
■

Riviera
◆ B D6-F6
Fondamenta delle
Zattere 1473
Tel. 041 522 76 21
Open May 16–
Oct. 14: Tue.–Sat.
noon–2.30pm, 7.30–
9.15pm; Sun. noon–
2.30pm. Oct. 15–
May 15: Tue., Thur.,
Sun. noon–2.30pm;
Fri.–Sat. noon–
2.30pm and
7.30–9.15pm.
*In summer, sit on
the terrace on
Fondamenta delle
Zattere, at the far
end of the Stazione
Marittima.*
■

Taverna San Trovaso
◆ B C4-C5
Fondamenta Priuli
1016
Tel. 041 520 37 03
Open noon–3pm
and 7–10pm.
Closed Mon.
*Authentic restaurant
with good food and
impeccable service.
Specialties: fish and
pizzas.*
■ ■

Cipriani
Giudecca 10
Tel. 041 520 77 44
Open 12.30–2.30pm
and 8–10.30pm.
Closed Nov. 15–
Feb. 25.
*Restaurant in
the refined hotel
of the same name.
Superb location,
terrace open
in summer;
delicious antipasti.
Specialties: Venetian
and international
dishes.*
■ ■ ■

Harry's Dolci
◆ B A6
Fondamenta San
Biagio 773
Tel. 041 522 48 44
Open noon–3pm
and 7.30–10.30pm.
Closed Tue. and
Nov.–March.
*Less expensive
than Harry's Bar,
with a fine terrace
overlooking the*

*canal. Delicious
pastries served
outside lunch and
dinner hours. All
Cipriani products
can be bought.*
■ ■ ■

L'Altanella
Calle delle Erbe 268
Tel. 041 522 77 80
Open 12.30–2pm
and 7.30–9pm.
Closed Mon.–Tue.,
Aug. 1–15 and
Jan. 1–15.
*Authentic Venetian
restaurant. In
summer, the terrace
by the canal is
covered in flowers.
Specialties: fish
(grilled monkfish in
particular) and
Venetian-style sepia.*
■ ■

Belvedere
Piazzale Santa
Maria Elisabetta 4
Tel. 041 526 01 15
Open noon–2.30pm
and 7–10pm.
Closed Mon.
*This little family
restaurant is not
much to look at
and is relatively
expensive. Still, it
appears popular
with Venetians.*
■ ■ ■

Da Andri
Via Lepanto 21
Tel. 041 526 54 82
Open 12.30–4pm.
Closed Mon.–Tue.
and Jan.–Feb.
*Located beside
the canal in a busy
spot, especially in
summer. Specialty:
fresh fish.*
■

Da Cicio
Via Sandro Gallo
241
Tel. 041 526 06 49
Open 6am–11pm.
Closed Tue.
*Small, typically
Venetian restaurant
accessible by
vaporetto and bus.
Renowned for its
simple, fresh food.
Specialty: fish.*
■ ■ ■

Da Nane
San Pietro in Volta,
Pellestrina 282
Tel. 041 527 91 10
Open noon–2pm
and 7–9pm.
Closed Mon. and Feb.
*Authentic restaurant
with an excellent
reputation in
the middle of a
fishing village.
Terrace in summer.
Specialties: pasticcio
di pesce, risotto
di seppioline and
fresh fish.*
■ ■ ■

Da Valentino
Via Sandro Gallo 81
Tel. 041 526 01 28
Open 12.30–2.30pm
and 7.30–11pm.
Closed Mon.
from April–Oct.,
Mon.–Wed.
from Nov.–March.
*Good restaurant.
The menu features
fresh, locally caught
fish and varies daily
according to the
morning's catch.
In winter, it includes
duck from the
Lagoon. Specialties:
grilled fish and
risotto.*
■ ■

Favorita
Via F. Duodo 33
Tel. 041 526 16 26
Open 12.30–3pm
and 7.30pm–
midnight.
Closed Mon. and Jan.
*Excellent fish
restaurant.
Exclusively Venetian
cooking. Terrace and
piano bar open in
summer.*
■ ■

**Pizzeria-Restaurant
Venezia 2000**
Lungomare
D'Annunzio 2
Tel. 041 526 81 21
Open 8am–2.30pm
and 5–11pm.
Closed Mon. out
of season and
Dec. 15– Jan. 15.
*Terrace with a view
of the Adriatic.
International cuisine
and pizzas.*
■ ■ ■

**Self Service
Gran Viale**
Gran Viale Santa
Maria Elisabetta 10/b
Tel. 041 526 03 22
Open 9am–1am.
Closed Wed.
*International
restaurant-cafeteria.*
▣ ▪

MURANO

Trattoria al Corallo
Fondamenta Vetrai
73
Tel. 041 73 96 36
Open noon–3pm
and 4–8pm.
Closed Tue. and
Dec. 15–Jan. 15.
*Pleasant atmosphere
and friendly service.
Meals at tables or
at the bar.
Specialty: fish.
Excellent value.*
▣ ▪

**Trattoria
Busa alla Torre**
Campo Santo
Stefano 3
Tel. 041 73 96 62
Open 11.45am–
3.30pm.
Closed Mon. and
Jan. 10–31.
*The oldest private
mansion in Murano
(11th-century).
Fish restaurant.*
▣ ▪

**Trattoria
Valmarana**
Fondamenta
Navagero 31
Tel. 041 73 93 13
Open 11.30am–3pm.
Open evenings by
reservation for
groups only.
Closed Wed. and Jan.
*Specialties: delicious
rombo, fresh fish
and grilled meat.*
▣ ▪ ▪

SAN MARCO

Agli Assassini
◆ B E3
Rio terrà degli
Assassini 3695
Tel. 041 528 79 86
Open 11.30am–3pm
and 6.30–11.30pm.
Closed Sun.

Al Bacaretto
◆ B D3
Salizada San

Samuele 3447
Tel. 041 528 93 36
Open 7am–10.30pm.
Closed Sun. and
Aug.
*Regular clientele of
artists and students.
An old Venetian
house simply
decorated and
pleasantly located
(Calle Larga). The
terrace, open in
summer, can hold up
to 20 people. Typical
Venetian dishes,
also breakfasts and
cichetti.*
▣ ⬆ ▪

Al Graspo de Ua
◆ B F1
Calle dei Bombaseri
5094
Tel. 041 522 36 47
Open noon–3pm
and 7–11pm.

MUSICIANS, ST MARK'S SQUARE

THE GRAND CANAL, NEAR THE RIALTO

Closed Mon.–Tue.
*Near the Rialto, a
venerable Venetian
tavern that has
become a
fashionable fish
restaurant. Reserve
well in advance.*
▣ ▪

Alla Botteghe
◆ B D3
Calle delle
Botteghe 3454
Tel. 041 522 81 81
Open 8am–8pm.
Closed Sun.
Spritz and cichetti.

Antica Carbonera
Calle Bembo 4648
Tel. 041 522 54 79
Closed Tue.
*Trattoria of long-
standing tradition.*
▪

Antico Martini
◆ B F3
Campo San Fantin
1983
Tel. 041 522 41 21
Open noon–2.30pm
and 7–11.45pm.
Closed Tue.
*This highly regarded
traditional Italian
restaurant was
founded in 1720.
Terrace. Throughout
the winter months
open evenings only.
Specialties include
risotto and fegato
alla Veneziana.*
▣ C ▦

Caravella
◆ B E4-F4
Calle Larga XXII
Marzo 2397
Tel. 041 520 89 01
Open noon–3pm
and 7pm–midnight.
*Cozy, intimate
restaurant serving
international and
Venetian food of an
exceptionally high
quality. Nautical
varnished wood
décor. Specialties:
risotto alle seppie,
bigoli in salsa.*
▣ ▣ ▦ ▦

Club del Doge
◆ A E2
Campo Santa Maria
del Giglio 2467
Tel. 041 79 46 11
Open 8–11am,
12.15–2.30pm and
7.15–10.30pm.
*Gourmet restaurant
belonging to the
Gritti Palace Hotel.
Superb décor and
view over the Grand
Canal and the
Basilica of Santa
Maria della Salute
from the terrace.*
▣ C ▦ ▦

Da Arturo
◆ B E3
Calle degli Assassini
3656
Tel. 041 528 69 74
Open noon–2.30pm
and 7–11pm.
Closed Sun., Aug.
and before the
Carnival.
*Ernesto, the
charming owner,
has a loyal Venetian
clientele. Specialties
include the meat
dishes and misto
di verdure.*
C ▪

Da Ivo
◆ B F3
Ramo dei Fuseri 1809
Tel. 041 528 50 04
Open noon–2.30pm
and 7–11.45pm.
Closed Sun. and
from Jan. 7–31.
*Small, friendly and
luxurious restaurant
close to La Fenice.
Rustic décor and
some private dining
rooms overlooking
the canal. Tuscan,
Florentine
and Venetian
specialties are on
offer. Dinner
reservations are
essential.*
▣ C ▦ ▪

Da Raffaele
◆ B E4
Fondamenta
delle Ostreghe 2347
Tel. 041 523 23 17
Open 9am–4pm and
6pm–midnight.
Closed Thur. and
Dec. 15–Jan. 31.
High-class

■ < 35,000 lire
⊠ 35,000–45,000 lire
⊠ 45,000–90,000 lire
⊞ > 90,000 lire

restaurant with a magnificent dining room, collection of arms and armor. Terrace open in summer. Specialties: risotto, rombo alla Raffaele.
■ ◉ ⊠ ⊞

Devil's Forest
◆ C A4
Calle dei Stagnieri 5184
Tel. 041 520 06 23
Open 8am–midnight.
A modern, pub-style establishment near the Rialto frequented by a young clientele. Original salads, delicious and inventive tramezzini. Extensive wines and beers.
◉ ◘

Do Forni
◆ C A5
Calle dei Specchieri 468
Tel. 041 523 21 48
Open daily noon–3.30pm and 7pm–midnight.
Thirties décor bar, similar to that in the Orient Express. Although in a busy tourist area, it is favored by wealthy Venetians and Italians.
■ ◉ ⊞

Fiore
◆ B D3
Calle delle Botteghe 3461
Tel. 041 523 53 10
Open 9.30am–11pm.
Charming bacaro where Venetian cuisine is served throughout the day. Good choice of wines and cichetti at the bar.
◘

Harry's Bar
◆ C A6 ▲ 215, 258
Calle Vallaresso 1323
Tel. 041 528 57 77
Open 10.30am–11pm.
Closed Mon.
One of the few places that remains

resolutely authentic, despite the assaults of time and publicity. Chic, simple but extremely expensive and constantly packed. Venetian specialties, low-calorie dishes and grilled fish.
■ ◉ ⊠ ⊞

La Colomba
◆ B F3
Piscina di Frezzeria 1665
Tel. 041 522 11 75
Open noon–3pm and 7–11pm.
Closed Wed. except in May–June, Sep.–Oct.

HARRY'S BAR

Luxury restaurant near La Fenice frequented by local and foreign artists. Priceless collection of paintings (De Chirico, Chagall, Picasso and many others paid for their meals here with pictures). Specialties include fish dishes.
■ ◉ ⊞

La Mansarde and Al Teatro
◆ B F3
Ramo Feretta Campo San Fantin 1912/18
Tel. 041 522 10 52
Fax 041 523 72 14
RESTAURANT (*La Mansarde*): open 11am–4pm, 7pm–midnight.
CAFÉ-BAR (*Al Teatro*): open 7.30am–midnight. Reservations essential.
This more or less private club (apply to Al Teatro for membership) is

located on the 5th floor. Terrace and a magnificent view over Venice. Open after the theater. Clientele of artists.
■ ◉ ⊠ ⊠

McDonald's
◆ B E2-F2
Campo San Luca
Open 10am–10pm.
Two other branches: one at Campo San Bartolomeo and the other near San Felice, along the Strada Nuova.
◉ ◘

Rosa Salva
◆ C A5
Calle Fiubera 951
Tel. 041 521 05 44
Open 7.30am–8pm.
This bar is owned by a family of caterers and confectioners who enjoy a high reputation in Venice. They own three other cafés, located respectively at Campo San Luca, Merceria and Campo San Giovanni e Paolo (with tables on the square) and serving tramezzini, savory pies and cakes.
◘

Rosticceria Al Teatro Goldoni
◆ B F2
San Marco 47/47
Tel. 041 522 24 46
Open 8am–10pm.
Closed 15 days in Aug., and Wed. out of season.
Self-service canteen on the 1st floor, restaurant on 2nd.
■ ◉ ◘

Rosticceria San Bartolomeo
◆ B F1
Calle della Bissa 5424
Tel. 041 522 35 69
Open 9am–2.30pm and 5–9pm.
Closed Mon.
Self-service restaurant serving Venetian dishes. Fast and cheap.
■ ◉ ◘

Terrazza Tiepolo
◆ B F4
Calle Larga XXII Marzo 2159
Tel. 041 520 04 77
Open 7–10.30am, noon–2.30pm and 7–10pm.
The restaurant of the luxury Europa e Regina hotel has a terrace overlooking the Grand Canal and offers a remarkable view of the Basilica of Santa Maria della Salute. Terrace open in summer. Cosmopolitan clientele. Italian and international cuisine.
■ ◉ ⊠ ⊞

Vino Vino
◆ B F3-F4
Ponte delle Veste 2007/a
Tel. 041 523 70 27
Open 10.30am–midnight.
Closed Tue.
Near La Fenice theater; a variety of wines are available at this friendly bar, along with typically Venetian snacks (before 9pm). Relaxed atmosphere, youthful clientele.
■ ◉ ◘

▰▰▰ SAN POLO

Alla Madonna
◆ B F1
San Polo 594
Tel. 041 522 38 24
Closed Wed.
Near the Rialto. Popular with Venetians. Large crowded dining room. Italian and Venetian specialties.
⊠

Al Peoceto Risorto
◆ A E6
Calle Donzella 249
Tel. 041 522 59 53
Open noon–3pm and 7–10pm.
Closed Thur. pm, Fri. and Aug.
Formerly a fishermen's tavern, this venerable restaurant has had many moments of glory – Jean

Cocteau, Josephine Baker, Eisenhower and Elizabeth II have all dined here. Specialties: fish and seafood.
🔲🏛

Antica Osteria Uga Rialto
◆ B F1
Ruga San Giovanni 692
Tel. 041 521 12 43
Open 10am–11pm.
Closed Sun.
Good choice of wines, cichetti and Venetian dishes. The restaurant tends to be crowded at lunchtime as it is only 5 mins from the Rialto.
🔲🍴

Antiche Carampane
Rio terrà delle Carampane 1911
Tel. 041 524 01 65
Open noon–3.30pm and 7.30–11pm.
Closed Sun. eve., Mon. and Aug.
A small fish restaurant that is full of charm. Reservations are recommended.
🔲🏛

Da Fiore
◆ B D1
Calle del Scaleter 2202 (near the Campo San Polo)
Tel. 041 72 13 08
Open 12.30–2.30pm and 7.45–10pm.
Closed Sun.–Mon., Christmas and 3 weeks in Aug.
Excellent, but expensive, restaurant that is much appreciated by Venetians and tourists alike. Reserve well in advance. Specialties: risotto con scampi or seppie.
🔲🎪

Da Ignazio
◆ B F1
Calle dei Saoneri 2749
Tel. 041 523 48 52

Open noon–3pm and 7–10pm.
Closed Sat. and 15 days at end of July and at beg. of March.
Small trattoria near the Rialto. Friendly service and excellent, unpretentious food. In summer, there is a terrace and arbor.
🔲🏛

Due Colonne
Campo Sant'Agostin 2343
Tel. 041 524 06 85
Open noon–3pm and 7–11pm.
Closed Sun.
Friendly pizzeria offering a great range of pizzas.
🔲

Osteria Antico Dolo
◆ A B6-C6
Calle Ruga Vecchia 778
Tel. 041 522 65 46
Open 10am–3.30pm and 6.30–10pm.
Closed Sun.
A 130-year-old bacaro offering a wide choice of wines and cichetti. Specialties: tripparissa and Venetian dishes.
🏛

Pizzeria da Sandro
◆ B D1
San Polo 1473 (a few steps away from Campo San Polo)
Tel. 041 523 48 94
Open 11.30am–11pm. Closed Fri.
Good pizzas. Pleasant terrace in the summer.
🔲

━━━ SANTA CROCE ━━━
Ae Oche
◆ A C6-D6
Calle del Tintor 1552/a
Tel. 041 524 11 61
Open 7pm–midnight.
Closed Mon. Nov.–March.
Good location. Lively restaurant

with very friendly service. Young clientele. Reserve at weekends. The menu runs to 70 pizzas: delicious and good value.
🔲🔳

Al Gallo
◆ A 1
Calle Amai 197/e
Tel. 041 520 59 53
Excellent pizzas.
🔳

Antica Besseta
Salizada Zusto 1395
Tel. 041 72 16 87
Open 12.30–2.30pm and 7–9.30pm.
Closed Tue.–Wed. and July 20–end Aug.
This restaurant is somewhat isolated but it is still a favorite with the locals. Traditional cuisine. We recommend that you reserve in advance. Specialties: risi e bisi and fish dishes.
🏛

Latteria Berengo
◆ A A6-B A1
Fondamenta dei Tolentini
Two generations of milkmen have been running this store, which makes up sandwiches according to clients' specifications and then prices them by weight. Good, cheap sandwiches, popular with students and local residents.
🔳

La Zucca
◆ A C6
S. Giacomo dell'Orio 1762
Tel. 041 524 15 70
Open noon–3pm and 7–11.30pm.
Closed Sun.
This popular restaurant can only seat up to 25 people. The menu always carries one or two

vegetarian dishes. Specialties: pasta and pumpkin soup.
🔲🔳

Nono Risorto
Sottoportego Siora Bettina 2338
Tel. 041 524 11 69
Open noon–2.30pm and 7pm–1am.
Closed Wed.
Restaurant with a pleasant garden. Specialties: fish dishes, pizza.
🔳

Trattoria Al Ponte
Ponte di Lazzarin Giuliano e Giovanni 1666, San Giacomo dell'Orio
Tel. 041 71 97 77
Open 8am–1am.
Closed Sat. eve.–Sun., Aug. and 1 weekend in Jan.
Small, lively brasserie that often gets crowded at lunchtime. It has a great atmosphere.
🔲🔳

Vecio Frittolin
◆ A D6
Calle Regina 2262
Tel. 041 522 28 81
Open 11.30am–3.30pm and 6pm–midnight.
Closed Sun. eve. and Mon.
Dishes served according to whatever fresh market produce is available. Popular with Venetians.
🔲🔳

━━━ TORCELLO ━━━
Locanda Cipriani
Torcello Island
Tel. 041 73 01 50
Open noon–3pm and 7–9pm.
Closed Tue. and Nov. 15–Feb. 15.
Often crowded in summer. Excellent cuisine, pleasant and restful surroundings. Specialty: risotto alla torcellana.
🔲🔳

◆ BARS AND NIGHTLIFE

The ▲ symbol refers to the Itineraries section; the ◆ refers to the maps
A list of symbols can be found on page 385.

CANNAREGIO

Bar Cicchetto
◆ A A5
Calle Misericordia
367/a
Tel. 041 71 60 37
Open Mon.–Fri.
7.30am– 8.30pm,
Sat. 7.30am–4pm.
Closed Sun.
Tramezzini *and*
cicchetti.

Bar Gelateria Da Nini
Ponte delle Guglie
1306
Tel. 041 71 78 94
Open 5am–midnight
(in season); 5am–
10pm (out of
season).
Closed Thur.
*A lively bar, favored
by younger
Venetians. Delicious
hot chocolate.*
🎵 ▣

Canottieri
◆ A A3
San Giobbe 690
Tel. 041 71 79 99
Open 6.30pm–2am.
Closed Sun.
*Live concerts on
Thur. Cabaret
on Tue.*
🎵

**Cantina Vecia
Carbonera**
◆ A D4
Rio terà della
Maddalena 2329
Tel. 041 71 03 76
Open Tue.–Thur.,
Sun. 9am–2.30pm
and 5pm–1am;
Fri.–Sat. 9am–
2.30pm and
5pm–2.30am.
Closed Mon.
*Osteria with a great
range of wines,
beers and* cichetti.
*Friendly, youthful
atmosphere.
Popular with locals.*

Casanova Music Café
◆ A E5
Strada Nuova 158/a
Tel. 041 275 01 99

Circolo Ai Miracoli
Cannaregio 6075
Tel. 041 523 06 16
Open 5pm–
midnight.
Closed Tue., and
July–Aug.

*Classical music, art
and photography
exhibitions, book
signings, poetry
readings and recitals.*
🎵

Enoteca Boldrin
San Canciano 5550
Tel. 041 523 78 59
Open 9am–9pm.
Closed Sun.
*Self-service at
lunchtime. Good
wines. Friendly
atmosphere.*

Giubagio
◆ C B1
Fondamenta Nuove
5039
Tel. 041 523 60 84
Open 6.30pm–9pm.
*Friendly bar serving
excellent sandwiches
and tramezzini.*

Il Paradiso Perduto
◆ A E4
Fondamenta
Misericordia 2540
Tel. 041 72 05 81
Open 7pm–1am.
Closed Wed.
*A restaurant-bar
much favored by
Venetians.
Expensive, but has a
great atmosphere
thanks to the jazz
and poetry.*
🎵

CASTELLO

**Bar Pasticceria
Didovich**
◆ C A3-B3
Campo Santa
Marina 5909
Tel. 041 523 00 17
Open 7.30am–8pm.
Closed Sun.
*Café-pâtisserie well
known for its
quality products.
Terrace on the
square in summer.*

**Birreria Forst Da
Ernesto e Riccardo**
◆ C B5-B6
Calle delle Rasse 4540
Tel. 041 523 05 57
Open 10am–11.30pm.
Closed Sat. out of
season.
*Frequented by
tourists and
Venetians. Whole
grain, rye bread and
toasted sandwiches.*
▣ 🎵

CHIOGGIA

**Astoria
American Disco Bar**
Lungomare Adriatico
Sottomarina
Tel. 041 554 18 41
Open daily 8.45am–
3am.
*Trendy nightclub
with American-style
snack bar. Open-air
discotheque at night
in summer.*
🎵

Hijack
Viale Padova 18
Sottomarina
Tel. 041 554 01 70
Open 10pm–4am.
Closed weekdays
in winter.
*Large discotheque
with garden,
American bar, snack
bar and restaurant.*
🎵

Tomato
Lungomare
Adriatico
Sottomarina
Tel. 041 554 03 10
Open until 3am.
*Pizzeria and
pleasant café.
Discotheque
at night (open-air in
summer) playing
Latin American and
other live or DJ
music.*
🎵

DORSODURO

**Ai Do Draghi
(Bar Rosso)**
◆ C B3
Campo Santa
Margherita 3665
Tel. 041 528 97 31
Open 8am–9pm.
Closed Sat.
afternoon and Sun.
in winter, and
15 days in Aug.
*Known also as Bar
Rosso because of its
location, in former
days, next to the
headquarters of the
Communist Party.
Small dining
room and terrace
in the summer.
Very lively at
lunchtime. Excellent
toasted sandwiches,
crostini and
tramezzini.*
▣ 🎵

Alla Bauta
◆ B A2
Fondamenta del
Gaffaro
Open 7.30am–8pm.
Closed Sat. pm, Sun.
*Snack-bar with
terrace overlooking
the canal, popular
with Venetians at
lunchtime. Excellent
sandwiches.*
▣

**Antica Osteria
Veneziana (Da
Sandro)**
◆ B A4
Calle Lunga San
Barnaba 2753/a
Tel. 041 522 19 51
Open 7.30am–2am.
Closed Sun.
Tramezzini, cichetti.

Bar Salus
Rio terrà Ponte
dei Pugni 3112
Tel. 041 528 52 79
Open 7am–2am.
Closed Sun.
*Very popular bar in
summer. Terrace
stays open late.*

Codroma
◆ B A3
Ponte del Soccorso
2540
Tel. 041 520 41 61
Open until 1.30am.
Closed Thur.
*Pleasant osteria,
usually full. Popular
place to play bar
games: chess,
backgammon and
cards. Lively jazz
ambience. Wines
and* cichetti.
🎵 ▣ ▣ ♨

Gelateria Causin
◆ B B3
Campo Santa
Margherita 2996
Open 8.30am–8pm.
Closed Sat.
*Ice cream makers for
three generations.
This is an institution
in Venice. Delicious
ice creams, made the
old-fashioned way.*

Il Caffè
◆ B B3
Campo Santa
Margherita
Tel. 041 528 79 38
Open 8am–midnight.

Closed Sun.
*Attractive terrace.
Ideal place to stop
for a quick drink.*

LIDO

Bistrot de Venise
Calle dei Fabbri 4685
Tel. 041 520 22 44
Fax 041 523 66 51
*www.bistrotdevenise.
com*
Open daily
9am–1am.
*Popular with
Venetians. French
and Venetian cuisine
and a young, lively
atmosphere. Always
crowded. Concert
every Mon. evening.
Temporary painting
exhibitions and
literary evenings.*
▣

Bounty Bar
Gran Viale 6/b
Tel. 041 276 00 83
Open 7am–midnight.
Closed Thur.
*Elegant snack-bar,
with nautical décor.
Tea room serving
Venetian pastries,
cantuccini alla
mandorle and pies.*

Club 22
Lungomare Marconi
22
Tel. 041 521 10 11
Small discotheque.

SAN MARCO

Brasilia
◆ B D3
Calle della Verona
3658
Tel. 041 523 99 18
Open 7.30am–8pm.
*Friendly welcome.
Sandwiches,
tramezzini, savory
pies, cakes, fresh
vegetable and fruit
salads, fruit juices. In
winter hot
chocolate with fresh
cream prepared to a
traditional recipe.*

Devil's Forest
◆ B D3
Calle dei Stagnieri
5181
Tel. 041 520 06 23
Open 8am–midnight.
Closed Mon.
*Lively pub close
to Campo San*

Bartolomeo. Popular
meeting place for
young Venetians in
the evening. Food
available.

Enoteca Al Volto
◆ B E2-F2
Calle Cavalli-San Luca
Tel. 041 522 89 45
Open 9am–2.30pm
and 5–10.30pm.
Closed Sun.
*Typical bacaro with
excellent wines and
cichetti. Young
clientele.*

Florian
▲ 245 ◆ C A6
St Mark's Square 56
Tel. 041 528 53 38
Open 9am–midnight.
Closed Wed.

*One of the oldest
(founded in 1720)
and best-known
cafés in Venice and
Italy. 18th-century
marble guéridon
tables and paintings.
Impeccable service,
exorbitant prices.*
▣

Haig's
◆ A E4
Campo Santa Maria
del Giglio 2477
Tel. 041 523 23 68
Open noon–5am.
Closed Wed. winter.
*One of Venice's
choicest and most
expensive bars.*
▣

Harry's Bar
◆ C A6 ▲ 215, 258
Calle Vallaresso 1323
Tel. 041 528 57 77
Open 10.30am–
10.30pm.
Closed Mon.
*Founded by
Giuseppe Cipriani
and frequented in
its early days by
Hemingway, Harry's
is an institution,*

along with its
trademark, the
Bellini cocktail
(champagne and
fresh white peach
juice). See also
Restaurants.*
▣ ▨

Lavena
◆ C A5-A6
St Marks' Square
133–134
Tel. 041 522 40 70
Open 9.30am–1am.
Closed Tue. winter.
*Luxury tearoom
founded in 1750.
Wagner was a
habitué between
1879 and 1883.
18th-century décor,
with Venetian glass
chandelier, mirrors
and marble.*
▣ ♫

Martini Scala Club
Campiello San
Gaetano
Tel. 041 522 41 21
Open 10pm–3.30am
(in season);
9.30pm–3.30am
(out of season).
Closed Tue.
*Piano bar decorated
with oriental rugs. A
convenient place to
dine after taking in
a show.*
▣ ♫ ▦

Quadri
◆ C A5-A6 ▲ 246
St Mark's Square 120
Tel. 041 522 21 05
Open 9am–midnight.
Closed Mon. out of
season.
*Historic café,
founded in 1638.
Like Florian, Quadri
has seen many
celebrated guests
(Stendhal, Byron,
Dumas and Proust
among them).
Concerts on the
terrace in summer.*
▣ ♫

Vino Vino
◆ B E5
Calle del Cafetier
2007
Tel. 041 523 70 27
Open 10.30am–
midnight.
Closed Tue.
Pleasant spot for a

quiet drink or a bite
to eat. See also
Restaurants.*
▣

SAN POLO

Caffè Blue Music Bar
Calle della Crosera
3778
Open 8am–2am.
Closed Sun.
*Lively student bar.
Serves sandwiches.*
♫

Caffè dei Frari-Toppo
◆ B C1-C2
Ponte dei Frari 2564
Tel. 041 524 18 77
Open Mon.–Fri.
7am–midnight,
Sat. 8am–8.30pm.
Closed Sun.
*Opposite the Church
of the Frari, a bar on
two levels patronized
by a young clientele.*

Cantina Do Mori
◆ B D1
San Polo 429
Tel. 041 522 54 01
Open 8.30am–
1.30pm and
5–8.30pm.
Closed Sun. and
Wed. afternoon.
*Bacaro favored by
Venetians. Good
choice of Italian
and local wines.
Selection of cichetti.*

Cantina Do Spade
Calle do Spade 860
Tel. 041 521 05 74
Open 9am–2pm and
5pm–midnight.
Closed Sun. and Aug.
*Typical bacaro,
opened in 1475.
Many wines.
Excellent cichetti
made with game.*

SANTA CROCE

Ai Postali
◆ A B6
Rio Marin 821
Tel. 041 71 51 56
Open 10am–3pm
and 6pm–2am.
Closed Tue. out of
season.
*A small wine bar
serving sandwiches
and crêpes. Lively
clientele of Venetian
and foreign
students. Highly
original décor.*

◆ SHOPPING

The ▲ symbol refers to the Itineraries section; the ◆ refers to the maps
A list of symbols can be found on on page 385.

Scuola dei Merletti
Piazza Galuppi,
Burano 183
*Works by the
cooperative's
lacemakers.
Lace museum.*

Coin
Cannaregio 5787
Open 9.30am–1pm
and 3.30–7.30pm.
Closed Sun.–
Mon. am.
Department store.

Marchini
◆ C A3
Salizada San
Giovanni
Grisostomo
Tel. 041 528 52 73
Open 7.15am–
8.30pm.
*One of three
pâtisseries owned
by the Marchini
family. The other
two are located
respectively in San
Marco and at Ponte
delle Paste (Calle
Carminati) near
Campo San Lio in
Castello (also a café).*

Lele Nason
◆ C B1
Calle del Fumo,
Cannaregio 5306/b
Tel. 041 522 81 13
Open 9am–7pm.
Closed Sun.
Mirrors, masks.

Orsoni
Sotoportego dei
Vedei 1045
*Mosaic workshop
created in 1888.
Commissioned by
Catalan architect
Gaudí for the
decoration of the
Sagrada Familia,
in Barcelona.*

Santagostino
◆ A C2
Fondamenta della
Sensa,
Cannaregio 3272
*Founded in 1952,
this reputable
mosaic workshop
has restored the
clocktower as well as
the tiles on the first
floor of Ca' d'Oro.*

Standa
Cannaregio 3659
Open daily 8.30am–
7.20pm.
Closed Christmas,
Jan. 1, Easter,
May 1.
Department store.

Cipolato Sigifredo
◆ C A4
San Lio, Castello 5336
Tel. 041 522 84 37
Open 11am–7.30pm.
Closed Sun.
Goldsmith.

**Laboratorio
Artigiano Maschere**
◆ C C3
Barbaria delle Tole
6656
*Superb masks made
of Roman paste or
leather, designed by
Giorgio Clanett.*

**Paolo Brandolisio
and Spazio Legno**
◆ C E5
San Martino 3865
*Master makers of
traditional Venetian
crafts, including oars.*

**Santi Giovanni e
Paolo**
◆ C C3
Barbaria de le Tole
Castello 6358
Tel. 041 522 96 59
Bookstore.

Canestrelli
Campiello Barbaro
Dorsoduro 364
*One of the last
gilders in Venice.
Top-quality
restoration of
paintings, furniture
and mirrors.*

Ca' Macana
Dorsoduro 3172
*This workshop and
store specializes in
porcelain and fabric
masks.*

**Causin Caffé
Gelati**
◆ B B3
Campo Santa
Margherita 2996
Tel. 041 523 60 91
Open 8am–9pm.
Closed Sat. and Aug.
Ice cream makers.

Il Doge
◆ B B3
Rio terrà Canal
Tel. 041 523 46 07
Ice cream makers.

Nico Gelati
◆ B D6-F6
Zattere, Dorsoduro
922
Tel. 041 522 52 93
Open 7am–10pm.
Closed Thur. and
Dec. 20–Jan. 20.
*One of the most
famous ice cream
makers in Venice.
Don't miss the
gianduiotto and the
Coppa Cardinale.*

Norelene
Calle della Chiesa
727
*Dyed and printed
silk, velvet and
cotton by Hélène
and Nora Ferruzzi.
Here traditional
meets modern.*

Archimede Seguso
Fondamenta
Serenella 18
*Renowned since
1946 for their
filigree glass work
and for latticino.
Lamps, decorative
plates and vases with
a contemporary
design.*

Barovier e Toso
Fondamenta Vetrai
28
*Blown-glass
objects designed
by famous
contemporary
artists.*

Alberto Valese-Ebrù
◆ B D3
Salizzada San
Samuele 3135/Santo
Stefano 3471/Calle
della Fenice 1920
*Famous marbled
paper. Other
beautiful objects
designed and made
by this reputed
paper-maker and
binder include
maps, books,
diaries, as well as
marbled plaster
sculptures.*

Archimede Seguso
◆ C A5-A6
Piazza San Marco
143
*Objects from
the workshop
of the same
name in Murano
sold here.*

**Ars Nova/Venetia
Studium**
◆ B E4-F4
Calle XXII Marzo
*Huge choice of
shawls, pocket
handkerchieves and
cushions.*

Attilio Codognato
◆ C A5-A6
San Marco 1295
*Antique dealers
specializing in
jewelry.*

Arte Contini
◆ C A5-A6
San Marco 2765
Tel. 041 520 49 42
Open 10am–1pm
and 3.30–7.30pm.
Closed Sun.
*Conceptual and
abstract art; great
20th-century
masters.*

Bac Art Studio
◆ C A5-A6
San Marco 2663
Tel. 041 522 81 71
Open 10am–1pm
and 3–7pm.
Closed Sun.
*Drawings, original
and multiple
editions.*

Bugno et Samueli
◆ B F3
Campo San Fantin
San Marco 1996/a
Tel. 041 523 13 05
Fax 041 523 03 60
Open 10.30am–
12.30pm and
4–7.30pm.
Closed Sun.–
Mon. am.
Art gallery.

Colussi Il Fornaio
◆ C A5-A6
San Marco 4579
Tel. 041 522 26 59
Open 8am–1.30pm
and 4.30–8pm.
Closed Sun.
*Bakers and
cakemakers.*

Fantoni
◆ B F2
Salizada San Luca
San Marco 4121
Tel. 041 522 07 00
*Fine books on
Venetian art and
exhibition catalogs.*

Gianni Cavalier
◆ B D3-D4
Campo Santo
Stefano, San Marco
2863
*One of the last
gilders and lacquer
specialists in Venice.*

Herriz
◆ B E4-F4
Calle XXII Marzo,
San Marco 2381
*Famous names in
jewelry from 1900
to 1950 (1920–1930
in particular).*

Jesurum
◆ C A5-A6
Piazza San Marco
(store)
San Marco 4856
(exhibition room).
*Lace manufacturers
located in the
former 13th-century
church of Sant'
Apollonia since
1869. Shirts, table
and bedlinen, etc.,
hand-embroidered.*

Livio de Marchi
◆ B D3
San Samuele 3157
Tel. 041 528 56 94
Open 8am–6.30pm.
Closed Sun.
*Wood sculptures
inspired by everyday
objects.*

Luciano Filippi
Calle della Bissa
5458
Tel. 041 523 69 16
Open 8.30am–
12.30pm and
3–7.30pm.
*Reproductions of
old Venetian texts.*

Marchini
Calle del Spezier 2769
Tel. 041 522 91 09
Open 8.30am–
8.30pm. Closed Tue.
*Cakemakers
renowned for the
quality of their
products.*

Navigliovenezia
◆ C A5-A6
San Marco 1632
Tel. 041 522 76 34
Open 10.30am–
12.30pm and
4.30–7.30pm.
Closed Mon. am
and public hols.
Art gallery.

Missiaglia
Piazza San Marco
125
*These jewelers,
founded in 1836,
are famous
throughout
Italy for their
silver objects and
jewelry.*

Mondonovo
Dorsoduro 3063
*Over 300 models
of masks are
displayed in
Giano Lovato's
boutique.*

Paolin
◆ B D3-D4
Campo San Stefano,
San Marco 2962
Tel. 041 522 55 76
Open 7.30am–
midnight;
out of season:
7am–8.30pm.
Closed Dec.–Jan.
Ice cream makers.

Paolo Olbi
◆ B E3
Calle della Mandola
San Marco 3653
Tel. 041 528 50 25
Open 9.30am–
12.30pm and
5.30–7.30pm.
Closed Mon. am.
*Drawing books,
diaries, marbled
paper, paper or
leather objects at
reasonable prices.*

Peggy Stuffi
◆ C A5
Calle Fiubera
San Marco 819
*Renowned restorers
of lacquered
furniture. Specialists
in antique fans.*

Prova d'Artista
◆ C A5-A6
San Marco 1994/b
Tel. 041 522 48 12
Open 11am–1pm

and 4.30–7.30pm.
Closed Sun.–
Mon. am.
*Prints by
international
artists.*

Rubelli
Campo San Gallo,
San Marco 1089
*Damask, brocade
and velvet have
been hand-woven
here since 1858.
When the last two
weavers retire, the
workshop will be
turned into a
museum.*

Santo Stefano
◆ B D3-D4
Campo San Stefano,
San Marco 2953
Tel. 041 523 45 18
Open 10.30am–
12.30pm and 4–7pm.
Closed Sun.
*Contemporary
figurative art.*

Valese Fonditori
◆ C A5
Calle Fiubera
San Marco 793
Tel. 041 522 72 82
Open 10.30am–
7.30pm; out of
season: closed
12.30–3pm.
Closed Sun.
*Foundry selling the
well-known "Venice
lions".*

Veneziartigiana
◆ C A5-B5
Calle Larga 412
Tel. 041 523 50 32
Open 9.30am–11pm
March–Nov.
Out of season:
closed Mon. am.
Crafts.

Venice Design 2
◆ C A6
Calle Valaresso
Tel. 041 523 90 82
Open 10am–1pm
and 3–7.30pm.
Closed Tue.
*Modern and
contemporary
paintings and
sculptures.*

V Trois
◆ B E4
Campo San
Maurizio

San Marco 2666
*Antique dealer with
exclusive rights to
the valuable Fortuny
fabrics (£100 per
yard).*

SAN POLO

Cicogna
◆ C B26
Campo San Tomà,
San Polo 2867
*Michel Cicogna has
restored furniture
exhibited at Ca'
Rezzonico and at
the Museum of 18th-
century Venetian
decorative arts.*

Ex Libris
◆ B D1
San Polo 1462
Tel. 041 522 40 04
Open 10am–7pm.
Closed Sun.
Marbled paper.

Gilberto Penzo
◆ B C1-C2
Calle dei Saoneri
2681
*Scale models of
traditional Venetian
boats.*

Mascari la Drogheria
◆ B D1
San Polo 381
Tel. 041 522 97 62
Open 8am–1pm
and 4.30–7pm.
Closed Wed.
Venetian groceries.

SANTA CROCE

Bevilacqua
Campiello della
Comare
Santa Croce 1320
*Sumptuous
fabrics hand-
woven here since
1875.*

Da Carlo Pistacchi
Rio terrà dei
Nomboli
*Delicious ice
cream.*

Mare di Carta
◆ B A1
Fondamenta dei
Tolentini 222
Tel. 041 71 63 04
Fax 041 275 62 07
www.maredicarta.
com
*International
nautical bookstore.*

◆ PLACES TO VISIT

The ▲ symbol refers to the Itineraries section, while the ◆ refers to the maps
A list of symbols can be found on page 385.

VENICE

ARCHEOLOGICAL MUSEUM Place Saint-Marc 52 Tel. 041 522 59 78	Open 9am–2pm. May be open in the afternoon from April to Sep. Roman copies of Greek and Egyptian statues.	▲ 255 ◆ C A3
ARCHIVIO R. MAESTRO **LIBRARY** Ghetto Vecchio 1189 Tel. 041 71 88 33	Open Mon., Wed. and Fri. 9am–1pm; Tue., Thur. 2–6pm; Sat. by appointment. Library of the Jewish community.	▲ 140 ◆ A B3
BASILICA OF SANTA **MARIA DELLA SALUTE** Campo della Salute Tel. 041 73 12 68	Visit the basilica on Nov. 21 (the saints day), much celebrated by Venetians.	▲ 318 ◆ B F5
CA' D'ORO **GALLERIA FRANCHETTI** Tel. 041 522 23 49	Open 9am–2pm (ticket office closes at 1.30pm). This superb Gothic palace contains the art collection of Baron Franchetti (13th- and 15th-century paintings).	▲ 148 ◆ A E5
CA' DEL DUCA San Marco 3052	Visits by prior arrangement. 18th-century Venetian and German porcelain. Oriental art.	▲ 208 ◆ B C4
CA' FOSCARI	Houses some of the university's departments.	▲ 331 ◆ B C3
CA' PESARO **(MUSEUM OF MODERN ART)** Fondamenta Mocenigo, San Stae 2076 Tel. 041 72 11 27	Currently closed for restoration; due to reopen in 2001. Permanent modern art exhibition on the first floor of this palazzo. Temporary exhibitions are also held on the second floor.	▲ 351 ◆ A D5
CA' PESARO (MUSEUM OF ORIENTAL ART) Fondamenta Mocenigo, San Stae Tel. 041 524 11 73	Open 9am–2pm. Closed Mon. Situated on the 4th floor of Palazzo Pesaro. The largest collection of Oriental art in Europe.	▲ 351 ◆ A D5
CA' REZZONICO Calle San Barnaba Tel. 041 241 01 00	Currently closed for restoration. Due to reopen in 2001. Superb collection of lacquered furniture and paintings dating from the 18th century. There is also a reconstruction of an 18th-century pharmacy.	▲ 332 ◆ B C4
CAPPELLA EMILIANA San Michele Cemetery	Open April–Sep. 8am–6pm; Oct.–March 8am–4pm.	▲ 154 C D-E-F
CHURCH OF L'ANGELO RAFFAELE Campo l'Angelo Raffaele Tel. 041 522 85 48	Open morning and afternoon. Times may vary.	▲ 327
CHURCH OF SAN BARNABA Campo San Barnaba	Open morning and afternoon. Times may vary.	▲ 334 ◆ B B4
CHURCH OF SAN BARTOLOMEO Campo San Bartolomeo	Converted into an art gallery and used for temporary exhibitions.	▲ 276 ◆ B F1
CHURCH OF SAN BENEDETTO Campo San Benedetto	Closed.	▲ 274 ◆ B D2
CHURCH OF SAN CANCIANO Campo San Canciano Tel. 041 523 52 93	Open morning and afternoon. Times may vary.	▲ 151 ◆ C A2
CHURCH OF SAN CASSIANO Campo San Cassiano Tel. 041 72 14 08	Open morning and afternoon. Times may vary.	▲ 286 ◆ A E6
CHURCH OF SAN FANTIN Campo San Fantin Tel. 041 523 52 36	Open morning and afternoon. Times may vary.	▲ 264 ◆ B F3
CHURCH OF SAN FELICE Campo e fondamenta San Felice Tel. 041 522 17 51	Open morning and afternoon. Times may vary.	▲ 148 ◆ A E5
CHURCH OF SAN FRANCESCO **DELLA VIGNA** Campo San Francesco della Vigna Tel. 041 520 61 02	Open morning and afternoon. Times may vary.	▲ 161 ◆ C E3
CHURCH OF SAN GEREMIA Campo San Geremia Tel. 041 71 61 81	Open morning and afternoon. Times may vary.	▲ 138 ◆ B B4-5
CHURCH OF SAN GIACOMETTO **(SAN GIACOMO DI RIALTO)** Campo San Giacomo	Open morning and afternoon. Times may vary.	▲ 283 ◆ B F1

CHURCH OF SAN GIACOMO DELL'ORIO Campo San Giacomo dell'Orio Tel. 041 524 06 72	*Chorus route: Open Mon.–Sat. 10am–5pm, Sun. 1–5pm.*	▲ *319* ◆ A C6
CHURCH OF SAN GIOBBE Campo San Giobbe Tel. 041 524 18 89	*Open morning and afternoon. Times may vary.*	▲ *139*
CHURCH OF SAN GIORGIO DEI GRECI Calle dei Greci 3419 Tel. 041 522 54 46	*Greek orthodox church. Call for information on times of liturgy.*	▲ *164* ◆ C C5
CHURCH OF SAN GIORGIO MAGGIORE San Giorgio Maggiore Island Tel. 041 528 99 00	*Open 9am–5.30pm (until 7pm in high season). A mass takes place with Gregorian chants each Sun. at 11am. There is also a monastery on the island of San Giorgio Maggiore. Superb view over the Lagoon from the belltower.*	▲ *340* ◆D A-B4
CHURCH OF SAN GIOVANNI ELEMOSINARIO San Polo	*Closed. The portico is behind railings, encased between two houses; you can get a glimpse of it from the Ruga Vecchia San Giovanni.*	▲ *286* ◆ B E-F1
CHURCH OF SAN GIOVANNI EVANGELISTA Campiello della Scuola (Near the Frari) Tel. 041 71 82 34	*Open to the public when seminars, congresses and concerts are being held.*	▲ *295* ◆ B C1
CHURCH OF SAN GIOVANNI CRISOSTOMO Campo San Giovanni Crisostomo Tel. 041 522 71 55	*Open morning and afternoon. Times may vary.*	▲ *150* ◆ C A3
CHURCH OF SAN GIOVANNI IN BRAGORA Campo Bandiera e Moro Tel. 041 520 59 06	*Open morning and afternoon. Times may vary.*	▲ *176* ◆ C D5
CHURCH OF SAN GIOVANNI NUOVO	*Closed.*	▲ *171* ◆ C B5
CHURCH AND CONVENT OF SAN GREGORIO Campo San Gregorio (Near the Salute)	*Closed. It has now been turned into a restoration workshop for museum paintings.*	▲ *317* ◆ B E5
CHURCH OF SAN LIO Campo San Lio	*Open morning and afternoon. Times may vary.*	▲ *171* ◆ C C4
CHURCH OF SAN LUCA San Marco 4040 Tel. 041 522 95 66	*Open morning and afternoon. Times may vary.*	▲ *274* ◆ B F2
CHURCH OF SAN MARCUOLA Campo San Marcuola Tel. 041 71 38 72	*Open morning and afternoon. Times may vary.*	▲ *144* ◆ A C4
CHURCH OF SAN MARTINO Campo San Martino Tel. 041 523 04 87	*Open morning and afternoon. Times may vary.*	▲ *176* ◆ C E5
CHURCH OF SAN MARZIALE Campo San Marziale Tel. 041 71 99 33	*Open morning and afternoon. Times may vary.*	▲ *145* ◆ A E4
CHURCH OF SAN MAURIZIO Campo San Maurizio	*Houses exhibitions.*	▲ *265* ◆ B E4
CHURCH OF SAN MOISÈ Campo San Moisè Tel. 041 528 58 40	*Currently closed for restoration.*	▲ *261* ◆ B F4
CHURCH OF SAN NICOLÒ DEI MENDICOLI Campo San Nicolò Tel. 041 275 03 82	*Open morning and afternoon. Times may vary.*	▲ *327*
CHURCH OF SAN NICOLÒ DA TOLENTINO Campo dei Tolentino 265 Tel. 041 71 08 06	*The convent next door is the University's center for architecture studies.*	▲ *345* ◆ B A1
CHURCH OF SAN PANTALON Campo San Pantalon	*Open morning and afternoon. Times may vary.*	▲ *330* ◆ B B2
CHURCH OF SAN PIETRO DI CASTELLO San Pietro di Castello Island (Behind the Arsenal) Tel. 041 523 51 37	*Chorus route: Open Mon.–Sat. 10am–5pm, Sun. 1–5pm.*	▲ *182* ◆ D D2

◆ PLACES TO VISIT

CHURCH OF SAN POLO Campo San Polo Tel. 041 523 76 31	*Chorus route:* *Open Mon.–Sat. 10am–5pm,* *Sun. 1–5pm.*	▲ 289 ◆ B D1
CHURCH OF SAN ROCCO Campo San Rocco	*Recently restored.*	▲ 294 ◆ B B1
CHURCH OF SAN SALVADOR Merceria San Salvador Tel. 041 523 67 17	*Open morning and afternoon. Times may vary.*	▲ 274 ◆ B F2
CHURCH OF SAN SAMUELE Campo San Samuele	*This church is used as an exhibition room for sale items produced by the Foundation based in the Palazzo Grassi.*	▲ 269 ◆ B C3
CHURCH OF SAN SILVESTRO Rio Terrà San Silvestro Tel. 041 523 80 90	*Open morning and afternoon. Times may vary.*	▲ 286 ◆ B E1
CHURCH OF SAN SIMEONE GRANDE **(SAN SIMEONE PROFETA)** Campo San Simeone Santa Croce 919 Tel. 041 71 89 21	*Open morning and afternoon. Times may vary.*	▲ 346 ◆ A B6
CHURCH OF SAN SIMEONE PICCOLO **(SANTI SIMEONE E GUIDA APOSTOLI)** Campo Nuova San Simeone	*Open morning and afternoon. Times may vary.*	▲ 346 ◆ A A6
CHURCH OF SAN STAE Campo San Stae	*Chorus route:* *Open Mon.–Sat. 10am–5pm, Sun. 1–5pm.* *Classical music concerts Sat. and Sun.*	▲ 350 ◆ A D5
CHURCH OF SAN TOMÀ Campo San Tomà	*Currently closed for restoration.*	▲ 292 ◆ B C2
CHURCH OF SAN VITALE Campo San Stefano	*The annex is used as an art gallery.*	▲ 268 ◆ B D4
CHURCH OF SAN ZAN DEGOLÀ **(SAN GIOVANNI DECOLLATO)** Campo San Zan Degolà	*Currently closed for restoration.*	▲ 347 ◆ A C5
CHURCH OF SANT'AGNESE Campo Sant'Agnese	*Used for oratories.*	▲ 323 ◆ B C5
CHURCH OF SANT'ALVISE Campo Sant'Alvise Tel. 041 524 46 64	*Chorus route:* *Open Mon.–Sat. 10am–5pm, Sun. 1–5pm.*	▲ 350 ◆ A D2
CHURCH OF SANT'APONAL Campo Sant' Aponal	*Closed.*	▲ 286 ◆ B E1
CHURCH OF SANT'ELENA Campo della Chiesa	*Open morning and afternoon. Times may vary.*	▲ 185 ◆ D F5
CHURCH OF SANT'EUFEMIA Fondamenta Sant'Eufemia 680 Tel. 041 522 58 48	*Open morning and afternoon. Times may vary.*	▲ 337
CHURCH OF SANTA FOSCA Campo Santa Fosca	*Open morning and afternoon. Times may vary.*	▲ 145 ◆ A E4
CHURCH OF SANTA GIUSTINA Campo Santa Giustina	*Only the façade is genuinely old.* *It is now a high school.*	▲ 160 ◆ C D3
CHURCH OF SANTA MARIA **DEI DERELITTI** Salizada Santi Giovanni e Pado	*Open morning and afternoon. Times may vary.* *Concerts are sometimes held here in the afternoon or in the evening.*	▲ 160 ◆ C C3
CHURCH OF SANTA MARIA **DEI MIRACOLI** Campo dei Miracoli	*Chorus route:* *Open Mon.–Sat. 10am–5pm,* *Sun. 1–5pm.*	▲ 151 ◆ C A3
CHURCH OF SANTA MARIA **DEI SERVI**	*A jewel of a church since its renovation. The convent has been converted into a students' residence.*	▲ 145 ◆ A D4
CHURCH OF SANTA MARIA **DEL GIGLIO** Campo Santa Maria Zobenigo Tel. 041 522 57 39	*Chorus route:* *Open Mon.–Sat. 10am–5pm, Sun. 1–5pm.*	▲ 264 ◆ B E4
CHURCH OF SANTA MARIA **DELLA CONSOLAZIONE (DELLA FAVA)** Campo della Fava 5503 Tel. 041 522 46 01	*Open morning and afternoon. Times may vary.*	▲ 171 ◆ C A4
CHURCH OF SANTA MARIA **DELLA MISERICORDIA (DI VAL VERDE)** Campo dell'Abbazia	*Open morning and afternoon. Times may vary.*	▲ 148 ◆ A F4
CHURCH OF SANTA MARIA FORMOSA Campo Santa Maria Formosa Tel. 041 523 46 45	*Chorus route:* *Open Mon.–Sat. 10am–5pm, Sun. 1–5pm.* *Concerts are sometimes held here in the evening.*	▲ 166 ◆ C B4

CHURCH OF SANTA MARIA MADDALENA Rio Terrà Santa Maria Maddalena	*Currently closed for restoration.*	▲ *145* ◆ D D4
CHURCH OF SANTA MARIA MATER DOMINI Campo Santa Maria Mater Domini	*Open morning and afternoon. Times may vary.*	▲ *352* ◆ A D6
CHURCH OF SANTA SOFIA Strada Nuova Campo Santa Sofia	*Open morning and afternoon. Times may vary.*	▲ *149* ◆A F5F6
CHURCH OF SANTA ZACCARIA Campo Santa Zaccaria Tel. 041 522 12 57	*Beautiful altarpiece by Bellini.*	▲ *172* ◆ C C5
CHURCH OF SANTI APOSTOLI Campo Santi Apostoli Tel. 041 523 82 97	*Open morning and afternoon. Times may vary.*	▲ *150* ◆ A F6
CHURCH OF SANTO STEFANO Campo Santo Stefano 3825 Tel. 041 522 23 62	*Chorus route:* *Open Mon.–Sat. 10am–5pm, Sun. 1–5pm.* *Regular concerts and recitals are held in this church.*	▲ *267* ◆ B D3
CHURCH AND CONVENT OF SPIRITO SANTO Fondamenta Zattere del Spirito Santo	*Open morning and afternoon. Times may vary.*	▲ *322* ◆ B E6
CHURCH OF THE CARMINI **(SANTA MARIA DEL CARMELO)** Campo dei Carmini Tel. 041 522 65 53	*Chorus route:* *Open Mon.–Sat. 10am–5pm;* *Sun. 1–5pm.* *Concerts are held on some evenings.*	▲ *329* ◆ B A3
CHURCH OF THE FRARI **(SANTA MARIA GLORIOSA DEI FRARI)** Campo dei Frari Tel. 041 522 26 37	*Open morning and afternoon. Times may vary.*	▲ *292* ◆ B C2
CHURCH OF THE GESUITI **(SANTA MARIA DEL ROSARIO)** Fondamenta Zattere dei Gesuiti Tel. 041 523 06 25	*Chorus route:* *Open Mon.–Sat. 10am–5pm,* *Sun. 1–5pm.*	▲ *323* ◆ B C6
CHURCH OF THE GESUITI **(SANTA MARIA ASSUNTA)** Campo dei Gesuiti Tel. 041 523 16 10	*Chorus route:* *Open Mon.–Sat. 10am–5pm,* *Sun. 1–5pm.*	▲ *152* ◆ C A1
CHURCH OF THE MENDICANTI Fondamenta dei Mendicanti	*Annex of the Santi Giovanni e Paolo hospital.* *Rarely open (only for funerals).*	▲ *159* ◆ C C2
CHURCH OF LA CARITÀ Campo della Carita	*Open morning and afternoon. Times may vary.*	▲ *300* ◆ B C5
CHURCH OF LA MADONNA DELL'ORTO Campo Madonna dell'Orto Tel. 041 71 99 33	*Open for the 6.30pm service.*	▲ *146* ◆ A E2
CHURCH OF LA PIETÀ Riva degli Schiavoni	*To arrange visits, contact the Istituto Santa Maria* *della Pietà. Concerts are held here some evenings.*	▲ *174* ◆ C C6
CHURCH OF THE OGNISSANTI Fondamenta degli Ognissanti	*This church houses the Giustinian hospital.*	▲ *326* ◆ B A5
CHURCH OF IL REDENTORE Campo Redentore Tel. 041 523 14 15	*Chorus route:* *Open Mon–Sat. 10am–5pm,* *Sun. 1–5pm.*	▲ *338*
CHURCH OF THE SCALZI **(SANTA MARIA DI NAZARETTA)** Fondamenta Scalzi Tel. 041 71 51 15	*Open morning and afternoon. Times may vary.* *Situated near the station.*	▲ *138* ◆ A A5
CHURCH OF THE ZITELLE **(SANTA MARIA DELLA PRESENTAZIONE)** Fondamenta delle Zitelle	*This church has been beautifully restored and is* *now used for congresses and exhibitions.*	▲ *339*
CINI FOUNDATION San Giorgio Maggiore Island Tel. 041 528 99 00	*Open when seminars, congresses or concerts are* *being held. The superb open-air Teatro Verde has* *been reopened.*	▲ *342* ◆ D B4-5
CINI FOUNDATION, LIBRARY OF San Giorgio Maggiore Island Tel. 041 528 99 00	*Open 9am–12.30pm.* *Closed Sat.–Sun. and public hols.* *Reserved for students.*	▲ *342* ◆ D B4-5
CLOCKTOWER Merceria, St Mark's Square	*The tower will be opened to the public in 2001.* *The clock has been restored.*	▲ *249* ◆ C A5
CONVENT OF LA CARITÀ	*Main office for the galleries of the Accademia and* *of the Accademia di Belle Arti.*	▲ *300* ◆ B C5
CONVENT SAN GIORGIO	*Open when seminars, congresses and concerts are* *being held. State school.*	▲ *341* ◆ D A-B4

◆ PLACES TO VISIT

CORRER MUSEUM Place Saint-Marc 52 Tel. 041 522 56 25	*Library: open to the public Mon., Wed., Fri.* *8.30am–1.30pm; Tue.–Wed.,Thur. 8.30am–5pm.* *Museum: open 10am–5pm all year round.* *You can buy a single ticket which allows entrance* *to both the Museum and to the Doge's Palace.* *2nd floor: historical collections (history of the* *Venetian Republic); 3rd floor: masterpieces from* *the Italian Renaissance (inlcuding works by* *Bellini, Carpaccio, A. da Messina, Lorenzo* *Cotto, etc.). Temporary exhibitions are also held* *here from time to time.* *Open June–Sep. 10am–7pm; Oct.–May* *10am–4.30pm. Closed Sat. and Jewish hols.*	▲ *246* ◆ **C** A6
DEPOSITO DEL MEGIO	*Open morning and afternoon. Times may vary.*	▲ *349* ◆ **A** C-D5
DOGE'S PALACE Piazzetta San Marco Tel. 041 522 49 51	*Open Nov.–March 9am–5pm (ticket offices close at* *3.30pm); April–Oct. 9am–7pm (ticket offices close* *at 5.30pm). Closed Jan. 1, May and Christmas hols.* *For guided tours reserve by telephone.*	▲ *224* ◆ **C** B6
CENTRE FOR THE HISTORY OF COSTUME (PALAZZO MOCENIGO) Santa Croce 992 Tel. 041 72 17 98	*Open 8.30am–1.30pm. Closed Sun. and public hols.* *This imposing palace houses a collection of Coptic* *fabrics (5th–7th centuries), French and Italian* *fabrics (14th-19th centuries) and costumes from* *the 18th and 19th centuries. Library.*	▲ *350* ◆ **A** D6
FENICE (LA)	*Currently closed for restoration.* *Due to reopen in 2001.*	▲ *262* ◆ **B** E3
FONDACO DEI TEDESCHI (POSTE CENTRALI) Via Rialto Tel. 041 271 71 11 Venice's main post office	*Open 8am–7pm. Closed Sun.* *To visit this building you must write to the* *Direzione Provinciale for authorization. Free* *exhibitions are held in the inner courtyard of this* *16th-century palace.*	▲ *276* ◆ **B** F1
FONDACO DEI TURCHI (MUSEUM OF NATURAL HISTORY) Fondaco dei Turchi 730 Tel. 041 72 18 52	*Curently closed for restoration; due to reopen end* *of 2001. The façade facing the Grand Canal has* *been renovated.*	▲ *347* ◆ **A** C5
GALLERIES OF THE ACCADEMIA Ponte dell'Accademia Tel. 041 522 22 47	*Open Tue.–Fri. 9am–7pm;* *Sat.–Mon. and public hols. 9am–2pm.*	▲ *301* ◆ **B** C5
GHETTO (THE)	*Jewish quarter.*	▲ *140* ◆ **A** C3
HEBREW ART MUSEUM Campo Ghetto Nuovo 2902/b Tel. 041 71 53 59	*Guided tours in English and Italian hourly from* *10.30am until 1.30pm. Exhibition of religious objects,* *furniture and collection of embroidered fabrics.*	▲ *143* ◆ **A** C3
HELLENIC INSTITUTE Castello 3412 Tel. 041 522 65 81	*Open 9am–1pm.* *Closed Sun. and public hols.*	▲ *165* ◆ **C** C5
MARCIANA LIBRARY (LIBRERIA MARCIANA) Piazzetta San Marco 7 Tel. 041 520 87 88	*Open Mon.–Fri. 9am–7pm.* *Visits by appointment from Mon. to Sat.* *Access to reading rooms on presentation of ID.* *Passes are available for one or several days.*	▲ *254* ◆ **C** A6
MULINO STUCKY Giudecc	*Being rebuilt. Residences and a congress center are* *on the agenda.*	▲ *338*
NAVAL MUSEUM Campo San Biagio Arsenale 2148 Tel. 041 520 02 76	*Open 9am–1pm.* *Closed public hols.* *Interesting collection of scale models of Venetian* *boats.*	▲ *180* ◆ **D** A2
ORATORIO DEI CROCIFERI Campo dei Gesuiti	*Building with tall chimneys opposite the Church of* *the Gesuiti.*	▲ *152* ◆ **C** A1
OSPEDALETTO Salizzada Santi Giovanni e Pado	*Open Thur.–Sat. 4–7pm.* *Fine 18th-century music room decorated with* *frescoes by Jacopo Guarana.*	▲ *160* ◆**C** C3
PAPADÓPOLI GARDENS Behind the Piazzale Roma		▲ *344* ◆ **B** A1
PALAZZO AGNUSDIO Santa Croce 2060	*Private palazzo, near the Museo Ca'Pesaro.*	▲ *351* ◆ **A** D6
PALAZZO ALBRIZZI Cannaregio 4118	*Head office of a German-Italian association that* *organizes exhibitions and concerts.*	▲ *287* ◆ **B** D1
PALAZZO ARIANI Fondamenta Briati Santa Croce	*Private palazzo near the Church of the Carmini.*	▲ *328*

PALAZZO BERNARDO Calle Bernardo	*Private palazzo situated behind the Campo San Polo.*	▲ *289* ◆ B D1
PALAZZO BEMBO-BOLDÙ Cannaregio 5999	*Private palazzo situated behind the Campo San Cancian.*	▲ *151* ◆ C A3
PALAZZO DEI CAMERLENGHI Left of the Rialto Bridge, on the market side	*Public administration building.*	▲ *282* ◆ B F1
PALAZZO CENTANI CA' GOLDONI Campo San Tomà 2794 Tel. 041 523 63 53	*Library: open 8.30am–1.30pm. Closed public hols. Only opened to drama students and theater specialists. Museum: currently closed for restoration.*	▲ *290* ◆ B C2
PALAZZO CINI San Vio 864 Tel. 041 521 07 55	*Remarkable, comprehensive collection of Venetian paintings. Open Aug. 31–Nov. 30 10am–1pm and 2–6pm. Closed Mon.*	▲ *316* ◆ B D5
PALAZZO CONTARINI-CORFU (PESARO DAGLI SCRIGNI) At the corner of the Grand Canal and the Rio San Trovaso	*Private palazzo. Can be seen from the Grand Canal.*	▲ *324* ◆ B C4
PALAZZO CONTARINI DAL BOVOLO Calle della Vida, San Marco 4299	*Due to reopen in 2002.*	▲ *274* ◆ B F3
PALAZZO CONTARINI DEL ZAFFO Cannaregio, near the Church of the Madonna dell'Orto	*Nursing home. Can be seen from the vaporetto that runs along the north side of the city.*	▲ *147* ◆ A E3
PALAZZO CORNER MOCENIGO Campo San Polo 2128	*Head office of the Guardia di Finanza.*	▲ *288* ◆ B D1
PALAZZO DANDOLO Behind St Mark's Square	*The Al Ridotto theater has been closed.*	▲ *259* ◆ C A5
PALAZZO DARIO Dorsoduro	*Private palazzo. Fine façade on the Grand Canal side.*	▲ *317* ◆B E5
PALAZZO DEI DIECI SAVI Fondamenta del Vin, Rialto	*Head office of the Magistrato alle acque.*	▲ *282* ◆ B F1
PALAZZO FALIER Ponte SS. Apostoli	*Private palazzo.*	▲ *150* ◆ C A2
PALAZZO FORTUNY (PESARO DEGLI ORFEI) Campo San Benedetto 3780 Tel. 041 520 09 95	*Currently closed for restoration; due to reopen in 2004.* *Temporary exhibitions are still held here.* *Exhibition of dresses and fabrics by M. Fortuny.*	▲ *272* ◆ B E2-3
PALAZZO GIOVANELLI San Felice	*Private palazzo, near the Ca'd'Oro.*	▲ *148* ◆ A C5
PALAZZO GOZZI Santa Croce	*Private palazzo.*	▲ *352* ◆ A D6
PALAZZO GRASSI Campo San Samuele 3231 Tel. 041 523 16 80	*Opening times vary according to exhibitions. Exhibitions of modern and contemporary art and antiques organized by a private foundation.*	▲ *270* ◆ BC3
PALAZZO GRITTI Castello	*Franciscan convent, near the Church of San Francesco della Vigna.*	▲ *161* ◆ D A2
PALAZZO LABIA Campo San Geremia Tel. 041 78 11 11	*The RAI's head office.* *Visits by prior arrangement only* *(Tel. 041 524 28 12).*	▲ *138* ◆ A B4
PALAZZO LOREDAN Campo San Stefano	*Head office of the cultural institution, Istituto Veneto.*	▲ *266* ◆ B D4
PALAZZO MAFFETTI-TIEPOLO San Polo 1957	*Private palazzo.*	▲ *288* ◆ B D1
PALAZZO MOROSINI Campo San Stefano	*Head office of the Consorzio Venezia Nuova.*	▲ *266* ◆ B D4
PALAZZO PISANI Campo San Stefano	*Conservatory of music.*	▲ *267* ◆ B D4
PALAZZO SAGREDO Cannaregio	*Private palazzo near the Ca'd'Oro.*	▲ *149* ◆ A E6
PALAZZI SORANZO Campo San Polo	*Private palazzo.*	▲ *288* ◆ B D1
PALAZZO SORANZO-BAROZZI Cannaregio Fondamenta Sanudo	*Private palazzo.*	▲ *151* ◆ C AB-3
PALAZZO VENDRAMIN-CALERGI San Marcuola Cannaregio 2040 Tel. 041 529 71 11	*Winter casino.* *Open Oct.–March.*	▲ *144* ◆ A D4-5
PALAZZO ZENOBIO-COLLEGIO ARMENO Fondamenta del Soccorso 2596 Tel. 041 522 87 70	*Visits by prior arrangement only.*	▲ *328* ◆ B A3 ◆ B D-E5

◆ PLACES TO VISIT

PEGGY GUGGENHEIM FOUNDATION **(PALAZZO VENIER DEI LEONI)** San Gregorio 701 Tel. 041 520 62 88	*Open all year round 11am–6pm. Closed Tue.* *One of the most remarkable private collections of* *modern art in the world. Temporary exhibitions.*	▲ *316* ◆ **B** D-E5
PINACOTECA MANFREDINIANA Campo della Salute	*Situated in the convent.* *Closed to the public.*	▲ *321* ◆ **B** F5
PRISONS (THE) At the Bridge of Sighs Information at the entrance of the Doges' Palace Tel. 041 522 49 51	*Visits by appointment only (Apply to Monsignore* *G. Bertoli).* *Open Nov.–March 9am–5pm (ticket offices close at* *3.30pm); April–Oct. 9am–7pm (ticket offices close* *at 5.30pm). Closed Jan. 1, May 1 and Christmas* *hols.Tours of the main chambers (Grand Council,* *Senate) and of the prisons, including the Bridge of* *Sighs. Guided tours of the Leads in Italian twice* *daily (10am and noon).*	▲ *252* ◆ **C** B6
QUERINI-STAMPILIA FOUNDATION Campo Querini 4778 Tel. 041 271 14 11	*Pinacoteca: open Tue.–Fri. 10am–1pm and 3–6pm;* *Sat.–Sun. 10am–1pm and 3–10pm. A large* *collection of 16th- and 18th-century paintings is* *housed on the 3rd floor of the Foundation.* *Library: open Mon.–Sat. 4–11.30pm;* *Sun. 3–7pm (access to card holders only).*	▲ *167* ◆ **C** B1
ST MARK'S BASILICA, **PALA D'ORO AND TREASURE** St Mark's Square Tel. 041 522 56 97 (Sacristy), 041 522 52 05 (Procuratoria di San Marco)	*Chorus route:* *Open Mon.–Sat. 10am–5pm; Sun. 1–5pm.* *Apart from the golden altarpiece, the basilica* *houses a beautiful collection of objects in silver* *and gold.*	▲ *234* ◆ **C** A5
ST MARK'S CLOCKTOWER St Mark's Square Tel. 041 522 40 64 Info. 041 522 52 05	*Open 9am–8pm (summer); 10am–4pm (winter).*	▲ *248* ◆ **C** A6
SAN MICHELE CEMETERY	*Private.*	▲ *153* ◆ **C** D2
SANT'APOLLONIA CLOISTERS Sacred Art Museum of the Diocese	*Open daily. Romanesque-style cloisters.* *Museum open daily 10.30am–12.30pm.*	▲ *171* ◆ **C** B5
SCUOLA DEI LANERI Santo Stefano	*Open April–Sep. 8am–6pm; Oct.–March 8am–4pm.*	▲ *268* ◆ **B** D3
SCUOLA DEI MERCANTI Campo della Madonna dell'Orto		▲ *147* ◆ **A** E2
SCUOLA GRANDE DEI CARMINI Campo dei Carmini 2617 Tel. 041 528 94 20	*Art school. The cloister may be visited during the* *school's opening hours.* *Many works by Tiepolo.*	▲ *329* ◆ **B** A3
SCUOLA GRANDE DI SAN ROCCO Campo San Rocco Tel. 041 523 48 64	*Open March–Nov. daily 9am–5.30pm;* *Dec.–Feb. Mon.–Fri. 10am–1pm; Sat.–Sun.* *10am–4pm. Collection of fifty works by Tintoretto.*	▲ *294* ◆ **B** B2
SCUOLA NUOVA Fondamenta della Misericordia	*Situated next door to the Church of the* *Misericordia.*	▲ *148* ◆ **A** E4
SCUOLA SAN GIORGIO DEGLI SCHIAVONI Calle Furlani Tel. 041 522 88 28	*Open May–Oct. 9.30am–12.30pm, 3.30–6.30pm;* *Nov.–April 10am–12.30pm and 3–6pm. Closed* *Sun. pm–Mon. Don't miss the Carpaccio series here.*	▲ *162* ◆ **C** D4
SCUOLA DI SAN MARCO Campo San Giovanni e Paolo	*Public hospital, to the left of the cathedral.*	▲ *159* ◆ **C** B3
SCUOLA DI SAN NICOLÒ DEI GRECI Ponte dei Greci	*Museum of icons.*	▲ *165* ◆ **C** C5
SCUOLA DI SANTA MARIA DELLA CARITÀ Campo de l'Accademia	*Galleries of the Accademia.*	▲ *300* ◆ **B** C5
SCUOLA DI SAN TEODORO Campo San Salvador	*Art exhibition hall.*	▲ *275* ◆ **B** F2
SCUOLA VECCHIA **DELLA MISERICORDIA** Campo dell'Abbazia	*Closed.*	▲ *148* ◆ **A** F4
STATE ARCHIVES Campo dei Frari 3002 Tel. 041 522 22 81	*Open Mon., Fri.–Sat. 8.30am–2pm;* *Tue.–Thur. 8.30am–6pm.* *Closed Sun. and public hols.* *The cloisters are open to the public when* *temporary exhibitions are on. A thousand years of* *Venetian history is displayed here.*	▲ *293* ◆ **B** C1
TEATRO MALIBRAN Corte del Milion	*Currently closed for restoration.* *Due to reopen in Sep. 2000.*	▲ *150* ◆ **C** A3

TEATRO ANATOMICO Campo San Giacomo dell'Orio	*Private.*	▲ *349* ◆ A C6
TEATRO VERDE Île San Giorgio Maggiore	*The theater, which was restored, was open for the 1999 Dance, Theater and Music Festival.*	▲ *342* ◆D B6
TITIAN'S HOUSE Ramo del Tiziano 5182/3 Cannaregio	*Near the Fondamenta Nuove.*	▲ *153* ◆C B1
TOTEM IN CANALE GALLERIES Accademia 878 Tel. 041 522 36 41	*Open Mon.–Sat. 10am–1pm, 3–7pm;* *Sun. from April–Sep: opening times may vary.* *Contemporary and African art gallery.*	◆ B D3
VERONESE'S HOUSE Salizzada San Samuele 3338 San Marco		▲ *269* ◆ B D3

THE ISLANDS

BURANO

CHURCH OF SAN MARTINO Via Galuppi 20	*Open morning and afternoon. Times may vary.*	▲ *373*
MUSEUM AND SCHOOL OF LACEMAKING Piazza Galuppi Tel. 041 73 00 34	*Open Tue.–Sat. 9am–6pm; Sun. 10am–4pm.* *Lace Museum and cooperative, where lacemakers can be seen at work.*	▲ *373*

CHIOGGIA

CATHEDRAL OF SANTA MARIA Calle Duomo 77 Tel. 041 40 04 96	*Open Sat. 3–6pm; Sun. 8am–noon, 4–6pm. Opens half an hour later in summer and on public hols.* *Undergoing restoration works.*	▲ *362*
CHURCH OF SAN DOMENICO Canal San Domenico Tel. 041 40 35 26	*Open 7.30am–noon, 4–8pm;* *7.30am–noon, 3–6pm (out of season).* *Founded in the 13th century and restored in the 19th century, this church contains a magnificent painting of St Paul by Carpaccio.*	▲ *362*
CHURCH OF SAN MARTINO Sottomarina Tel. 041 40 00 54	*Open 4–10pm; 6.30am–12.30pm and 2.30–8pm (out of season).*	▲ *362*
PALAZZO GRASSI Riva Vena	*Now a hospital.*	▲ *362*

LIDO

CHURCH AND CONVENT OF SAN NICOLÒ Riviera San Nicolò 26 Tel. 041 526 02 41	*Open morning and afternoon. Times may vary.* *The celebration of the Ascension (Sensa), and of the union between Venice and the sea, is held outside this church.*	▲ *355*
CHURCH OF SANTA MARIA ELISABETTA Piazzale Santa Maria Elisabetta Tel. 041 526 00 72	*Open morning and afternoon. Times may vary.*	▲ *355*
JEWISH CEMETERY Via Cipro 70 Tel. 041 526 01 42	*Open 9.30am–2.30pm.* *Closed Sat. and Jewish hols.* *16th- and 17th-century tombs.*	▲ *355*

MURANO

CHURCH OF SANTA MARIA E SAN DONATO Campo San Donato Tel. 041 73 90 56	*Open morning and afternoon. Times may vary.*	▲ *368*
GLASS MUSEUM (PALAZZO GIUSTINIAN) Fondamenta Giustinian 8 Tel. 041 73 95 86	*Open all year round 10am–5pm.* *Closed Wed., May 1, Christmas and Jan. 1.* *The Museo Vetrario Antico and the Museo Vetrario Moderno have both been restored and combined into one museum.*	▲ *367*

TORCELLO

CATHEDRAL OF TORCELLO (SANTA MARIA ASSUNTA)	*Open 10am–12.30pm, 2–5pm. Concerts are held here.*	▲ *375*
CHURCH OF SANTA FOSCA	*Open 10am–12.30pm, 2–5pm.*	▲ *376*

◆ BIBLIOGRAPHY

ESSENTIAL

◆ BLUE GUIDE: *Venice*, 1980
◆ GRUNDY (M.): *Venice, An Anthology Guide*, London, 1976
◆ HONOUR (H.): The Companion Guide to Venice, London, 1965
◆ LINKS (J.G.): *Venice for Pleasure*, London, 1966
◆ LORENZETTI (G.): *Venice and Its Lagoon*, Rome, 1961
◆ MCCARTHY (M.): *Venice Observed*, Penguin Books, New York, 1982
◆ MORRIS (J.): *Venice*, London, 1960; also *The Venetian Empire*, London 1980
◆ NORWICH (J. J.): *The History of Venice*, London 1988.
◆ PIGNATTI (T.): *Venice*, London, 1960
◆ SHAW-KENNEDY (R.): *Art and Architecture in Venice. The Venice in Peril Guide*, London, 1972

GENERAL

◆ BERTUZZI (F.): *Couleur de Venise*, Mengès, Paris, 1986
◆ BELLAVITIS (G.), ROMANELLI (G.): *Venezia*, Laterza, Bari, 1985
◆ BRILLI (A.): *Le Voyage d'Italie*, Flammarion, Paris, 1989
◆ CANESI, (M.): *Venise*, De Vecchi, 1986
◆ FRANZOI (U.), Di Stefano (D.): *Le Chiese di Venezia*, Azienda Autonoma Soggiorno e Turismo, Venice, 1976
◆ MASIERO (F.): *Venise vue du ciel*, Gallimard, Paris, 1991
◆ PEROCCO (G.), SALVADORI (A.): *Civiltà di Venezia*, 3 vol., La Stamperia di Venezia, 1979
◆ PIGNATTI (T.): *Venezia, Mille Anni d'Arte*, Arsenale Editrice, Venice, 1989
◆ *Storia della cultura veneta*, col., Neri Pozza, Vicenza, 1976-86, 6 vol.
◆ *Venezia, città industriale*, col., Marsilio, Venice, 1980

NATURE

◆ BERENGO (G.G.), MOLDI-RAVENNA (C.), SAMMARTINI (T.): *Giardini segreti a Venezia*, Arsenale Editrice, Venice, 1988
◆ *Laguna, Conservazione di un Ecosistema*, Arsenale Editrice, Venice, s. d.
◆ *Laguna tra fiumi e mare*, Filippi Editore, Venice, 1982
◆ *La Salvaguardia fisica della Laguna* (catalogue of the exhibition), Comune di Venezia, 1983

HISTORY

◆ BENZONI (G.): *I dogi*, Electa, Milan, 1982
◆ BERENGO (M.): *La società veneta alla fine del '700*, Firenze, 1970
◆ BERNARDELLO (A.), BRUNELLO (P.), GINSBERG (P.): *Venezia 1848-1849, La rivoluzione e la difesa*, Comune di Venezia, Stamperia di Venezia, 1980
◆ BETTINI (S.): *Venezia. Dalla prima crociata alla conquista di Costantinopoli del 1204*, Firenze, 1966
◆ BETTINI (S.): *Venezia. Nascita di una città*, Milan, 1978
◆ BRAUDEL (F.), QUILICI (F.): *Venise*, Arthaud, Paris, 1984
◆ BRAUDEL (F.): *La Méditerranée et Le Monde Méditerranéen à l'Epoque de Philippe II*, Tr. Sian Reynolds, 2 vols, London and New York, 1973
◆ BRAUNSTEIN (P.), DELORT (R.): *Venise: portrait historique d'une cité*, Seuil, Paris, 1971
◆ BROWN (H.): *Studies in the History of Venice, 2 vols*, London 1907
◆ CAMBRIDGE MEDIEVAL HISTORY *Vol V, Venice sections* by R. Cessi
◆ CALIMANI (R.): *Histoire du ghetto de Venise*, Stock, Paris, 1988
◆ CARILE (C.), FEDALTO (G.): *Le origini di Venezia*, Patron, Bologna, 1978
◆ CESSI (R.): *Storia della Repubblica di Venezia*, Giunti-Martello, Firenze, 2 vol., 1991
◆ CESSI (R.), ALBERTI (A.): *Rialto. L'Isola, il ponte, il mercato*, Zanichelli, Bologna, 1934
◆ CHAMBERS (D.S.): *The Imperial Age of Venice, 1380-1580*, London 1970
◆ COLIN (R.-P.): *Les Privilèges du Chaos: la Mort à Venise et l'esprit décadent*, Le Lérot, Aigre, 1991
◆ COMISSO (G.): *Les Agents secrets de Venise: 1705-1797*, Le Promeneur, Paris, 1990
◆ COMISSO (G.): *Les Ambassadeurs vénitiens*, Le Promeneur, Paris, 1989

◆ CONCINA (E.): *Venezia nell'età moderna*, Venice, 1989
◆ COZZI (G.), KNAPTON (M.): *La repubblica di Venezia nell'età moderna-Dalla guerra di Chioggia al recupero della Terraferma*, UTET, Turin, 1986
◆ COZZI (G.): *Repubblica di Venezia e Stati Italiani. Politica e Giustizia dal secolo XVI al secolo XVIII*, Einaudi, Turin, 1982
◆ CURIEL (R.), COOPERMAN (B.): *Le Ghetto de Venise*, Herscher, Paris, 1990
◆ DA MOSTO (A.): *I Dogi di Venezia*, Martello, Milan, 1960
◆ DAVID (J.C.): *The Decline of the Venetian Nobility as a Ruling Class*, Baltimore 1962
◆ DIEHL (C.): *La République de Venise*, Flammarion, Paris, 1985
◆ DRÈGE (J.-P.): *Marco Polo et la route de la soie*, Découvertes, Gallimard, Paris, 1989
◆ DUBY (G.), LOBRICHON (G.): *L'Histoire de Venise par la peinture*, Belfond, Paris, 1991
◆ FINLAY (R.): *Politics in Renaissance Venice*, New Brunswick, 1980
◆ FORTIS (U.): *Ebrei e Sinagoghe*, Storti, Venice, 1973
◆ GEORGELIN (J.): *Venise au siècle des lumières: 1669-1797*, EHESS, Paris, 1978
◆ HALE (J.R.): *Ed., Renaissance Venice*, London 1973
◆ HAZLITT (W.C.): *History of the Origin and Rise of the Venetian Republic, 2 vols*, London 1900
◆ HOCQUET (J.-C.): *Le Sel et la fortune de Venise*, Presses Universitaires de Lille, 1982
◆ JONARD (N.): *La vie quotidienne à Venise au XVIIIe siècle*, Hachette, Paris, 1965
◆ KNEZEVICH (M.): *Il magnifico principe di Venezia. Norme e tradizioni legate al dogado*, Storti, Venice, 1986
◆ KOFMAN (S.): *Conversions: le marchand de Venise sous le signe de Saturne*, Galilée, Paris, 1987
◆ LANE (F.C.): *Venice, a Maritime Republic*, Baltimore, 1966
◆ LANE (F.C.): *Venice and History*, Baltimore 1966

◆ LANE (F.C.): *Venetian Ships and Shipbuilders of the Renaissance*, Baltimore 1934
◆ LAURITZEN (P.L.): *The Palaces of Venice*, London,1978
◆ LAURITZEN (P.L.): *Venice*, London, 1978
◆ LONGWORTH (P.): *The Rise and Fall of Venice*, London, 1974
◆ LOWRY (M.): *Le Monde d'Alde Manuce: imprimeurs, hommes d'affaires et intellectuels dans la Venise de la Renaissance*, Promodis, Cercle de la Librairie, Paris, 1989
◆ MCNEIL (W.H.): *Venice, the Hinge of Europe 1081-1797*, University of Chicago, 1974
◆ MONNIER (P.): *Venise au XVIIIe siècle*, Complexe, Brussels, 1982
◆ PULLAN (B.): *Rich and Poor in Renaissance Venice*, Oxford, 1971
◆ *Rinascimento Europeo e Rinascimento Veneziano* (a cura di V. Branca), col., Venice, 1977
◆ TENENTI (A.): *Naufrages, corsaires et assurances maritimes à Venise d'après les notaires Catti et Spinelli: 1592-1609*, EHESS, Paris, 1959
◆ THIRIET (F.): *Registres des délibérations du Sénat de Venise concernant la Romanie*, EHESS, Paris, vol.1: 1958, vol. 2: 1959, vol.3: 1961
◆ THIRIET (F.): *Histoire de Venise*, PUF, Paris, 1985
◆ TUCCI (U.): *Mercanti, Navi e Monete nel Cinquecento Veneziano*, Bologna, 1981
◆ VALENSI (L.): *Venise et la Sublime Porte: la naissance du despote*, Hachette, Paris, 1987
◆ *Venezia e la peste*, col., Venice, 1979
◆ WOWTHORNE (S.T.): *Venetian Opera in the 17th. Century*, Oxford University Press, 1954
◆ ZORZI (A.): *La République du lion: histoire de Venise*, Perrin, Paris, 1988
◆ ZORZI (A.): *Une cité, une république, un empire*, Nathan, Paris, 1980
◆ ZYSBERG (A.), BURLET (R.): *Gloire et misère des galères*, Découvertes, Gallimard, Paris, 1987

416

TRADITIONS

◆ ALBERICI (C.): *Il Mobile Veneto*, Electa, Milan, 1980

◆ ARTHUS-BERTRAND (Y.): *Safari vénitien: carnaval de Venise*, Laffont, Paris, 1985

◆ BAROVIER MENTASTI (R.): *Il vetro veneziano*, Electa, Milan, 1982

◆ BAROVIER MENTASTI (R.), DORIGATO (A.), GASPARETTO (A.), TONINATO (T.): *Mille anni di arte del vetro a Venezia* -- catalogo della Mostra, Albrizzi, Venice, 1982

◆ BRAZOLO (U. dei): *La Gondola*, Canova, Treviso, 1979

◆ BRUNELLO (F.): *Arti e mestieri a Venezia nel Medioevo e nel Rinascimento*, Neri Pozza, Vicenza, 1981

◆ BUSETTO (G.): *Cronaca veneziana – Feste e vita quotidiana nella Venezia del Settecento*, Fondazione Scientifica Querini-Stampalia, Venice, 1991

◆ BUTAZZI (G.), MONTI (P.): *Venezia e la sua gondola*, Görlich, Milan, 1974

◆ CERVIN (R. de): *Bateaux et batellerie de Venise*, Vilo, Paris, 1978

◆ CLAUSEL (J.): *Venise exquise: propos de tables et de recettes*, Laffont, Paris, 1990

◆ DOIZY (M.-A.), IPERT (S.): *Le papier marbré*, Technorama, Paris, 1985

◆ FABRE (D.): *Carnaval ou la fête à l'envers*, Découvertes, Gallimard, Paris, 1992

◆ FIORIN, (A., a cura di): *Fanti e Denari*, Arsenale Editrice, Venice, 1989

◆ FRAIGNEAU (A.): *Les Enfants de Venise*, Arléa, Paris, 1988

◆ GHIRARDINI (G.): *El parlar figurato*, Venice, 1980

◆ LAROCHE (R. de), LABAT (J.-M.): *Chats de Venise*, Casterman, Paris, 1991

◆ *La voga alla veneta*, col., Comune di Venezia, Assessorato Turismo e Sport, 1983

◆ LEVI-PISETZKY (R.): *Il Costume e la Moda nella Società Italiana*, Einaudi, Turin, 1978

◆ MAFFIOLI (G.): *La Cucina Veneziana*, Padua, 1962

◆ MARIACHER (G.), VALERI (D.): *Il Settecento veneziano a Ca' Rezzonico*, Sadea/Sansoni, Firenze, 1966

◆ MENEN (A.): *Vivre Venise*, Mengès, Paris, 1978

◆ MORAZZONI (G.): *Mobili veneziani laccati*, Milan, 1954

◆ REATO (D.): *Histoire du Carnaval de Venise*, Oréa-Marco-Polo, Bordeaux, 1991

◆ ROMANELLI (S.), PEDROCCO (S.): *Bissone, Peote e gallegianti*, Alfieri, Venice, 1980

◆ SALVAGGION (N.), SAVELLA (A.), GRANZOTTO (G.): *Le Carnaval de Venise*, Amilcare Pizzi, 1986

◆ TAMASSIA-MAZZAROTTO (B.): *Le Feste Veneziane*, Sansoni, Firenze, 1961

◆ TASSINI (G.): *Curiosità veneziane*, Filippi Editore, Venice, new ed. 1990

◆ VEDRENNE (E.): *Demeures secrètes de Venise*, Albin Michel, Paris, 1990

◆ VITOUX (F.), DARBLAY (J.): *L'Art de vivre à Venise*, Flammarion, Paris, 1990

◆ ZANELLI (G., a cura di): *Squeraroli e squeri*, Ente per la conservazione della Gondola e la tutela del Gondoliere, Venice, 1986

◆ ZORZI (A.): *Venetia Felix, Gabriel Bella cronista della Serenissima*, Franco Maria Ricci, Milan, 1989

ART/ARCHITECTURE

◆ ACKERMANN (J.S.): *Palladio*, Turin, 1972

◆ ARSLAN (E.): *Venezia Gotica*, Venice, 1970

◆ BALISTRERI (C.): *Case Veneziane a loggia*, Cluva universitaria, Venice, 1986

◆ BARRAL I ALTET (X.): *Les Mosaïques de pavement médiévales de Venise, Murano, Torcello*, Picard, Paris, 1985

◆ BASSI (E.): *Architettura del Sei e Settecento a Venezia*, Filippi Editore, Venice, s.d.

◆ BASSI (E.): *Palazzi di Venezia*, Stamperia di Venezia, Venice, 1976

◆ BRUSATIN (M.): *Venezia nel Settecento. Stato, Architettura, Territorio*, Einaudi, Turin, 1980

◆ BRUYÈRE (A.), STAINER (M.): *Sols: Saint-Marc, Venise*, Imprimerie Nationale, Paris, 1989

◆ CHASTEL (A.): *Italie. Renaissance méridionale, 1460-1500*, L'Univers des Formes, Gallimard, Paris, 1965

◆ CONCINA (E.): *Structure urbaine et fonctions des bâtiments du XIe au XVe siècle*, UNESCO-Save Venice Inc., 1981

◆ CONSTANT (C.):*Guida a Palladio*, Lidiarte, Berlin, 1889

◆ CRISTINELLI (G.): *Baldassare Longhena... Architetto del Seicento a Venezia*, Venice, 1978

◆ FAURE (E.): *Histoire de l'art, 1909*, 3 vol., Folio, Gallimard, Paris, 1988

◆ FONTANA (G.J.): *Cento palazzi tra i più celebri di Venezia*, Venice, 1865

◆ GIANIGHIAN (N., a cura di): *Dietro i Palazzi, Tre secoli di architettura minore a Venezia, 1492-1803*, Arsenale Editrice, Venice

◆ GRANDESSO (E.): *I Portali Medievali di Venezia*, Helvetia, Venice, 1988

◆ HELLENKEMPER (G.): *La Création du monde: les mosaïques de Saint-Marc à Venise*, Le Cerf, Paris, 1986

◆ HEYNDENREICH (L.H.): *Italie: éclosion de la Renaissance, 1400-1460*, L'Univers des Formes, Gallimard, Paris, 1972

◆ LECLERC (H.): *Venise baroque et l'opéra*, Armand Colin, Paris, 1987

◆ *Le Trésor de Saint-Marc de Venise*, Musées Nationaux, col., Paris, 1984

◆ LEVI (C.A.): *I Campanili di Venezia*, Venice, 1980

◆ LIEBERMAN (R.): *L'Architettura del Rinascimento a Venezia*, Becocci, Firenze, 1982

◆ *L'Immagine e il mito di Venezia nel cinema*, col., Comune di Venice, 1983

◆ MARETTO (P.): *La Casa Veneziana nella storia della città, dalle origini all'Ottocento*, Marsilio, Venice, 1986

◆ MARETTO (P.): *L'Edilizia Gotica Veneziana*, Venice,1978

◆ MARIACHER (G.): *Il Sansovino*, Milan, 1962

◆ MCANDREW (J.): *Venetian Architecture of the Early Renaissance* M.I.T., Cambridge, Mass., 1980

◆ MURARO (M.): *La vita nelle pietre*, Arsenale Editrice, Verona, 1985

◆ MURARO (M.), GRABAR (A.): *Les Trésors de Venise*, Skira, 1007

◆ MURATORI (S.): *Studi per un'operante storia urbana di Venezia*, Rome, 1960

◆ MURRAY (P.): *Architettura del Rinascimento*, Electa, Milan

◆ NORBERG-SCHULZ (C.): *Architettura Occidentale*, Milan, 1981

◆ PIGNATTI (T.): *Le Scuole di Venezia*, Milan, 1981

◆ PIZZARRELLO (U.), CAPITANIO (E.): *Guida alla città di Venezia*, L'Altra Riva, Venice, 4 vol.,1986-1990

◆ PUPPI (L.): *A. Palladio*, Milan, 1973

◆ RIZZI (A.): *Vere da pozzo di Venezia*, La stamperia di Venezia, Venice, 1981

◆ RIZZO (T.): *I Ponti di Venezia*, Newton Compton, Rome, 1983

◆ RUSKIN (J.): *The Stones of Venice*, 3 Vols., London, 1851-3

◆ RUSKIN (J.): *St. Mark's Rest*, London, 1877

◆ SALVADORI (A.): *Architect's Guide to Venice*, Canal Libri, Venice, 1990

◆ SCARABELLO (G.), MORACHIELLO (P.): *Venise: Guide historique et culturel*, Larousse, Paris, 1988

◆ TAFURI (M.): *Venezia e il Rinascimento*, Einaudi, Turin, 1985

◆ TRINCANATO (E.R.), FRANZOI (U.): *Venise au fil du temps*, Joël Cluenot, Boulogne-Billancourt, 1971

◆ WITTKOWER (R.): *Art et architecture en Italie 1600-1750 – L'âge du baroque*, Hazan, Paris, 1991

◆ ZORZI (A.):*Venezia Scomparsa*, Electa, Milan, 1984

PAINTERS

◆ BURCKHARDT (J.): *Pale d'Altare del Rinascimento*, Cantini, Firenze, 1988

◆ DE VACCHI (P.), BERNARI (C.): *Tintoretto*, Rizzoli, Milan, 1970

◆ FIOCCO (G.): *La Pittura Veneziana del '600 e '700*, Verona, 1929

◆ HOCHMANN (M.): *Peintres et commanditaires à Venise (1540-1628)*, Ecole Française de Rome, 1992

◆ HONOUR (H.), Fleming (J.): *The Venetian Hours of Henry James, Whistler and Sargent*, Walter Books Ltd, London, 1991

◆ BIBLIOGRAPHY

◆ Huse (N.), Wolters (W.): *Venezia. L'Arte del Rinascimento*, Venice, 1989
◆ *La Pittura nel Voneto: il Quattrocento*, Electa, Milan, 1987
◆ Levey (M.): *Painting in 18th Century Venice*, University of London, 1959
◆ Logan (O.): *Culture and Society in Venice 1470-1790*, Batsford, London, 1972
◆ Longhi (R.): *Viatico per cinque secoli di Pittura Veneziana*, Firenze, 1946
◆ Nepi-Sciré (G.): *I Capolavori dell'Arte Veneziana, Le Gallerie dell'Accademia*, Arsenale Editrice, Venice, 1991
◆ Olivari (M.), *Giovanni Bellini*, Scala, Firenze, 1990
◆ Olivato (L.), Puppi (L.): *Mauro Codussi*, Rome, 1971
◆ Pallucchini (R.): *L'Opera Completa di Giambattista Tiepolo*, Milan, 1968
◆ Pallucchini (R.): *La Pittura Veneziana del '700*, Instituto per la collaborazione culturale, Venice-Rome, 1960
◆ Pallucchini (R.): *La Pittura Veneziana del Trecento*, Venice, 1964
◆ Pallucchini (R.), Rossi (P.): *Tintoretto, le Opere Sacre e Profane*, Alfieri Electa, Milan, 1982
◆ Pignatti (T.): *Giovanni Bellini, l'opera completa*, Rizzoli, Milan, 1969
◆ Pignatti (T.): *L'Opera completa di Pietro Longhi*, Venice, 1974
◆ Pignatti (T.): *Origini della Pittura Veneziana*, Istituto Italiano di Arti Grafiche, Bergamo, 1961
◆ Pignatti (T.): *Paolo Veronese, l'opera completa*, Alfieri, Venice, 1978
◆ Pignatti (T.): *Carpaccio*, Skira, Geneva, 1958
◆ Piguet (P.): *Monet et Venise*, Herscher, 1988
◆ Schultz (J.): *Venetian Painted Ceilings of the Renaissance*, University of California, Berkeley
◆ Stainton (L.): *Turner in Venice*, British Museum 1985
◆ *The Genius of Venice (1500-1600)*, (catalogue of the exhibition), Royal Academy of Arts, London, 1983
◆ *Tiziano* (catalogue of the exhibition), Marsilio,

Venice, 1990
◆ Vasari (G.): *Le Vite de Più Eccelenti Architetti, Pittori et Scultori Italiani, Firenze, 1550*, Einaudi, Turin, new ed. 1986 (Lives of the most eminent Italian architects, painters and sculptors)
◆ Zampetti (P., a cura di): *Guardi*, Venice, 1965
◆ Zeri (F., a cura di): *La Pittura del Quattrocento*, Milan, 1987
◆ Zorzi (L.): *Carpaccio et la représentation de sainte Ursule*, Hazan, Paris, 1991
◆ Zuffi (S.): *Giorgione*, Arnoldo Mondadori Arte, Milan, 1991

LITERATURE

◆ Aragon (L.): *Les Voyageurs de l'impériale*, Folio, Gallimard, Paris, 1972
◆ Balzac (H. de): *Massimilla Doni*, José Corti, Paris, 1964
◆ Barrès (M.): *La Mort de Venise*, Christian Pirot, Saint-Cyr-sur-Loire, 1990
◆ Boito (C.): *Senso*, Actes Sud, Arles, 1983
◆ Brosses (C. de): *Lettres familières d'Italie*, Mercure de France, Paris, 1986
◆ Butor (M.): *Description de Saint Marc*, Gallimard, Paris, 1963
◆ Byron (Lord): *Beppo, A Venetian Story*
◆ Byron (Lord): *Childe Harold's Pilgrimage*
◆ Calvino (I.): *Contes populaires italiens*, Denoël, Paris, 1984
◆ Carpentier (A.): *Concert baroque*, Folio, Gallimard, Paris, 1978
◆ Casanova (G.J.): *Memoirs*
◆ Chase (J.H.): *See Venice and Die*
◆ Chateaubriand (F.-R. de): *Voyages en Italie*, la Pléiade, Gallimard, Paris, 1969
◆ Chateaubriand (F.-R. de): *Mémoires d'outre-tombe*, la Pléiade, Gallimard, Paris, 1950
◆ Comisso (G.): *Les Agents secrets de Venise*, Le Promeneur, Paris, 1990
◆ Comisso (G.): *Les Ambassadeurs vénitiens*, Le Promeneur, Paris, 1989
◆ D'Annunzio (G.): *Il Fuoco*, 1900
◆ D'Annunzio (G.): *Notturno*, Mondadori, Milan, 1975
◆ Dickens (C.): *Pictures from Italy*, Baudry's

European Library, London, 1846
◆ Drodskij (J.): *Fondamenta degli Incurabili*, Adelphi, Milanı, 1991
◆ Du Bellay (J.): *Les regrets*, Poésie Gallimard, Paris, 1975
◆ Fruttero (C.) et Lucentini (F.): *L'Amant sans domicile fixe*, Seuil, Paris, 1989
◆ Gautier (T.): *Voyage en Italie*, Fasquelle, Paris, 1930
◆ Giono (J.): *Voyage en Italie*, Folio, Gallimard, 1953
◆ Goethe (J. W. von): *Voyage en Italie*, Slatkine Reprints, 1990
◆ Goldoni (C.): *Dramatic Works and Memoirs*
◆ Guilloux (L.): *Parpagnacco ou la conjuration*, Gallimard, Paris, 1954
◆ Hemingway (E.): *Across the River and into the Trees*, Cape, London, 1952
◆ Hofmannsthal (H. von): *Andreas*, L'Imaginaire, Gallimard, Paris, 1970
◆ James (H.): *The Wings of the Dove*
◆ James (H.): *The Difference*
◆ James (H.): *The Aspern Papers*
◆ Lawrence (D.H.): *Lady Chatterley's Lover*
◆ Malraux (A.): *L'irréel*, Livres d'Art, Gallimard, Paris, 1974
◆ Mann (T.): *Death in Venice*
◆ Mauriac (F.): *Le Mal*, la Pléiade, Gallimard, *Paris*, 1963
◆ Montaigne (M. de): *Journal de voyage*, Folio, Gallimard, Paris, 1983
◆ Montesquieu (C. de): *Lettres persanes*, Folio, Gallimard, Paris, 1973
◆ Morand (P.): *Venises*, L'Imaginaire, Gallimard, Paris, 1971
◆ Musset (A. de): *Oeuvres complètes*, la Pléiade, Gallimard, Paris, 1938
◆ Pasinetti (P.-M.): *De Venise à Venise*, Liana Levi, Paris, 1984
◆ Pasinetti (P.-M.): *Le Pont de l'Accademia*, Calmann-Levy, Paris, 1970
◆ Pasinetti (P.-M.): *Rouge vénitien*, Albin Michel, Paris, 1963
◆ Pound (E.): *Cantos*
◆ Pratt (H.): *Fable de Venise*, Casterman, Paris, 1984
◆ Proust (M.): *Albertine*

disparue, Folio, Gallimard, Paris, 1989
◆ Régnier (H. de): *Esquisses vénitiennes*, Complexe, Brussels, 1991
◆ Rilke (R.-M.): *Les Cahiers de Malte Laurids Brigge*, Gallimard, Paris, 1991
◆ Romain (J.) et Zweig (S.): *Volpone*, Gallimard, Paris, 1950
◆ Rousseau (J.-J.): *Les Confessions*, Folio, Gallimard, Paris, 1973
◆ Sand (G.): *Consuelo*, Glénat, Paris, 1991
◆ Sand (G.): *Lettre d'un voyageur*, la Pléiade, Gallimard, Paris, 1971
◆ Sartre (J.-P.): *Situations IV*, Gallimard, Paris, 1964
◆ Shakespeare (W.): *The Merchant of Venice*
◆ Shakespeare (W.): *Othello*
◆ Shelley (P. B.): *Collected Works*
◆ Sollers (P.): *La Fête à Venise*, Gallimard, Paris, 1990
◆ Staël (Mme. de): *Corinne ou l'Italie*, Folio, Gallimard, Paris, 1985
◆ Stendhal: *Chroniques italiennes*, Folio, Gallimard, Paris, 1986
◆ Stendhal: *Œuvres intimes*, la Pléiade, Gallimard, Paris, 1982
◆ Stendhal: *Voyages en Italie*, la Pléiade, Gallimard, Paris, 1973
◆ Suarès (A.): *Le Voyage du condottiere*, Granit, 1985
◆ Wagner (R.): *My Life*

EXPLORING VENICE

◆ Arthus-Bertrand (Y.), Le Guelbout (P.): *Venise vue du ciel*, Chêne, Paris, 1988
◆ Bellavitis (G.): *L'Arsenale di Venezia. Storia di una grande struttura urbana*, Marsilio, Venice, 1983
◆ Bergamo (S.): *La Basilica dei Frari*, Venice, 1983
◆ Bertoli (B.), Niero (A.): *I Mosaici di San Marco*, Electa, Milan, 1987
◆ Bonechi (E.): *Un jour à Venise*, Bonechi-Edizioni Il turismo, 1988
◆ Broccato (C.): *L'Antico Cimitero Ebraico di San Nicolò del Lido a Venezia*, Venice, 1992
◆ Brunetti (M.): *Santa Maria del Giglio, vulgo Zobenigo, nell'arte e nella storia*, Venice, 1952
◆ Concina (E.): *Chioggia*, Canova,

Treviso, 1977
◆ *Dal Museo alla Città*, a cura della Soprintendenza ai Beni Artistici e Storici di Venice 1980-1990
◆ DAMERINI (G.): *L'Isola e il Cenobio di San Giorgio Maggiore*, Firenze, 1968
◆ DAZZI (M.), MERKEL (E.): *Catalogo della Pinacoteca della Fondazione Scientifica Querini Stampalia*, Neri Pozza, Vicenza, 1979
◆ DE COSTER (L.), VRANCKX (G.): *16 promenades dans Venise*, Editions Universitaires, Begedis, 1987
◆ DOLCETTA (M.), ORLANDI (F.): *Di Isola in Isola*, Brentani, Dolo, 1983
◆ DORIGATO (A.): *Il Museo Vetrario di Murano*, Electa, Milan, 1986
◆ FLINT (L.), CHILS (E.): *Collezione Peggy Guggenheim*, Mondadori/Solomon R. Guggenheim Foundation, 1986
◆ FONTANA (P.): *Les jours et les nuits de Venise*, Nathan, Paris, 1991
◆ *Fortuny nella Belle Epoque*, col., Electa, Milan, 1984
◆ FRANZOI (U.): *L'Armeria del Palazzo Ducale a Venezia*, Canova, Treviso, 1990
◆ FRANZOI (U.), PIGNATTI (T.), WOLTERS (W.): *Il Palazzo Ducale di Venezia*, Canova, Treviso, 1990
◆ FRANZOI (U.): *Itinerari segreti nel Palazzo Ducale a Venezia*, Canova, Treviso, 1983
◆ FRANZOI (U.): *Le Palais ducal de Venise*, Storti, Venice, 1978
◆ FROSINI (P.), NORDIO (M.): *Venise porte a porte*, FMR, Paris, 1981
◆ GASCAR (P.): *Saint-Marc*, Delpire, Zurich, 1964
◆ GRAMIGNA (S.), PERISSA (A.): *Scuole di Arti, Mestiere e*

Devozione a Venezia, Arsenale Editrice, Venice, 1981
◆ *Itinerari Veneziani*, col., Comune di Venezia, 1983-1992
◆ JOUFFROY (A.): *Libre Venise*, Bordas, Paris, 1980
◆ MANGINI (N.): *I Teatri di Venezia*, Mursia, Milan, 1974
◆ MARABINI (J.): *Venise*, Seuil, Paris, 1988
◆ MASIERO (F.): *Le Isole delle Lagune Venete*, Mursia, Milan, 1981-85
◆ MAUPAS (C.): *A Venise*, Hachette, Paris, 1989
◆ NIERO (A.): *La Chiesa dei Carmini*, Venice, 1965
◆ NIERO (A.): *La Chiesa di San Giacomo dell'Orio*, Venezia Sacra, 1990
◆ NIERO (A.): *La Basilique de Torcello et Santa Fosca*, Ardo Editori d'Arte, Venise, s.d.
◆ PERRY (M.): *La Basilica dei SS. Maria e Donato di Murano*, Parrocchia della Basilica, 1984, 2nd edit.
◆ *Piazza San Marco. l'Architettura, la storia, le funzioni*, Marsilio, Venice, 1970
◆ PIGNATTI (T. a cura di): *Gran teatro La Fenice*, Marsilio, Venice, 1981
◆ PIGNATTI (T.), Le Scuole di Venezia, Electa, Milan, 1981
◆ PIZZARELLO (U.), FONTANA (V.): *Pietre e Legni dell'Arsenale di Venezia*, L'Altra Riva, Venice, 1983
◆ POLACCO (R.): *La Cattedrale di Torcello*, L'Altra Riva – Canova, Venice-Treviso, 1961
◆ POLACCO (R.): *La Cattedrale di Torcello*, Treviso-Venice, 1981
◆ RAMOS (M.-J.): *Venise*, Marcus, Paris, 1989
◆ REINISH SULLAM (G.): *Il Ghetto di Venezia*, Carucci, Roma, 1985
◆ REZVANI (S.): Venise: avec Rezvani, Autrement, Paris, 1985
◆ RIBADEAU-DUMAS (F.): *Les Mystères de Venise*

ou les secrets de la Sérénissime, Albin Michel, Paris, 1978
◆ RIZZI (P), MARTINO (E. di): *Storia della Biennale, 1895-1982*, Electa, Milan, 1902
◆ ROMANELLI (G.): *Le Musée Correr*, Electa, Milan, 1984
◆ ROMANELLI (G.): PEDROCCO (F.): *Ca' Rezzonico*, Electa, Milan, 1991
◆ ROMANELLI (G.): *Venezia Ottocento*, Officina, Rome, 1977
◆ ROITER (F.): *Venise, guide photographique*, Co-Grot, 1984
◆ ROSA SALVA (P.), SEMENZATO (M.): *Laguna di Venezia – Itinerari*, Cassa di Risparmio di Venezia, Fondo Mondiale per la Natura (W.W.F.), sezione di Venezia (s.d.)
◆ SALZANO (E.): *Venise, portrait d'une ville: atlas aérien, portrait d'une ville à l'échelle 1/1000e*, Gallimard, Paris, 1990
◆ TRICANATO (F. R.): *Il Palazzo Ducale di Venezia*, Florence, 1966
◆ TRICANATO (E.R.): *Venezia Minore*, Milano, 1948
◆ VALCANOVER (F.): *Ca' d'Oro – La Galerie Giorgio Franchetti*, Electa, Milan, 1991
◆ VAROTTO (A.): *Venise 360°*, Glénat, Paris, 1987
◆ *Venezia una guida per la città – Tre itinerari inconsueti*, col., Comune di Venezia, Assessorato al Turismo, Venice, 1985
◆ VIANELLO (R.): *La Giudecca*, Venice, 1966
◆ WOLTERS (W.): *Storia e politica nei dipinti di Palazzo Ducale*, Arsenale Editrice, Venice, 1987
◆ ZANDER RUDENSTINE (A.): *Peggy Guggenheim Collection*, Venice, Harry N. Abrams, Inc., Publishers, New York and the Solomon R. Guggenheim Foundation, N.Y., 1985

◆ ZORZI (A.): *Canal Grande*, Rizzoli, Milan, 1991
◆ ZORZI (A.), MARTON (P.): *Les palais vénitiens*, Mengès, Paris, 1989

REVUES

◆ *Dentelles et broderies, Antiquités et Objets d'art*, Fabbri, Paris, 1991
◆ *Isole di Venezia*, Bell'Italia, Giorgio Mondadori, numéro spécial, septembre 1990
◆ *Italie: Monuments Historiques*, Paris, n°149, janvier-février 1987
◆ *La Marine de Venise*, Time-Life, 1981
◆ LAMBERT (E.), MATTHIEUSSENT (E.): *Venise et les Vénitiens*, Autrement, hors-série n°4, 1985
◆ *Le mobilier italien, Antiquités et Objets d'art*, Fabbri, Paris, 1991
◆ *Le verre, Antiquités et Objets d'art*, Fabbri, Paris, 1991
◆ *Lustres, lampes, lampadaires, Antiquités et Objets d'art*, Fabbri, Paris, 1991
◆ MENEN (A.): *Venise*, Time-Life, 1976.
◆ *Venise, un voyage intime*, Autrement, hors-série n° 14, octobre 1985, Paris
◆ *Venezia*, Meridiani, Domus, n. 1, 1986

CHILDREN

◆ CALVINO (I.): *Le palais du sieur mort*, Folio Junior, Gallimard, Paris, 1982
◆ DEL TORRE (C. et G.), BATTISTON (M.-B.): *La Cité des doges au xve siècle*, Venise, Albin Michel Jeunesse, Paris, 1989
◆ SCUTARI (A.), PEZZETTA (E.): *Scolta che te conto, Storia di Venezia*, Filippi Editore, Venice, 1982
◆ VENTURA (P.): *Venise: naissance d'une cité*, Nathan, Paris, 1988

◆ LIST OF ILLUSTRATIONS

LIST OF ILLUSTRATIONS ◆

◆ LIST OF ILLUSTRATIONS

LIST OF ILLUSTRATIONS ◆

◆ LIST OF ILLUSTRATIONS

LIST OF ILLUSTRATIONS ◆

◆ LIST OF ILLUSTRATIONS

The publishers wish to extend their thanks to the following individuals, whose help in compiling this book has been invaluable:
Padre Raffaele Andonian (Palazzo Zenobio, Armenian College),
S Graziano Arici,
S Jacopo Barovier,
S Bertarello,
S Oswaldo Böhm,
Dott. Giorgio Buseto (Curator of the Querini-Stampalia Foundation),
S Paolo Canestrelli,
S Cassio (Correr Museum),
Sra Antonietta dell Toffola,
S Roberto Fontanari (Accademia),
Sa. Margusta Lazzari (Querini-Stampalia Foundation),
Dott.essa Lunardon (Church of Santa Maria dei Dereletti e Ospedaletto),
S Antonio Menegnolo (Loggia of the Houses of St Mark/Procuratoria of St Mark),
Elisabetta Navarbi (La Fenice Theater),
Prof Giandomenico Romanelli (Curator of the Correr Museum),
Patriarchal Chancellor Mario Ronzini (Church of San Giovanni in Bragora),
Sa Rossi (Assistant director of the Biblioteca Marciana),
Dott Francesco Semenzato,
S Francesco Turio Böhm,
Sa Vianello (Querini-Stampalia Foundation),
Sa Nanni Wurmibrand,
Dott Marino Zorzi (Curator of the Biblioteca Marciana).

In some cases we have been unable to contact the heirs to certain copyrighted documents, or their publishers; an account remains open for them at our offices.

◆ GLOSSARY

A

ACQUA ALTA: High water.
ALTANA: A sort of wooden platform or terrace, built on a roof, like a bird's nest.
ARSENALOTTI: The workers in the old Arsenal dockyards.

B

BACARO: Wine bar.
BAICOLI: Small Venetian cakes.
BALLOTINO: Child selected to draw the ballots during the election of the Doge.
BARENE: Salt flats in the Venetian Lagoon.
BAUTA: Garment worn during Carnival, consisting of a black silk hood with a lace cloak.
BISSONA: A boat with eight oarsmen, which features in the Venice Historical Regatta.
BRAGOZZO: Chioggia. Typical fishing boat.
BRICOLA: Cluster of pilings in the Lagoon, positioned to mark navigable channels. The term also applies to mooring-posts.
BUSSOLAI: Small Venitian cakes.

C

CA': Abbreviation for casa, house.
CALLE: Alley, street or space between houses in Venice. A small calle is called a calletta.
CAMERLENGHI: The treasurers of the former Venetian Republic.
CAMPO: "Field"; this term applies to all Venice's open spaces, with only St Mark's Square being allowed the title of piazza. The campi used to be covered in grass and planted with trees. A campiello is a small square.
CANALE: Canal.
CANALAZZO: The Grand Canal.
CAORLINA: A boat rowed by six oarsmen.
CASINO: Gaming house
CICHETTI: Snacks and hors d'oeuvres, usually consumed in bacari.
CONTRADA: Parish.
CORNO: The Doge's hat.
CORSO: Originally a race between competing gondoliers.
CORTE: A courtyard shared by several

houses; a public area, as opposed to the cortile, which is the private courtyard of a palace.
CORTELÀ: Decorated sides of a galley.
CROSERA: A junction of several calli.

D

DESDOTONA: A boat with eighteen oarsmen, which features in the Venice Historical Regatta.
DOGE: Head of the Venetian Republic, elected for life.

E

ERBERIA: Fruit and vegetable market at the Rialto.

F

FELZE: Small box-like cabins, which used to be placed on gondolas during the winter.
FERRO: Gondola figurehead.
FONDACO: Warehouse-residence, where merchants both lived and stored their goods.
FONDAMENTA: Quay alongside a canal.
FONTEGO: See fondaco.
FORCOLA: Rowlock of gondola.
FRITTELLE: Fritters.

G

GONDOLIN: Racing gondola.

L

LIAGO: Broad covered balcony.
LISTA: A part of a street which was formerly attached to a foreign embassy, hence outside Venetian territory.

M

MARIEGOLE: "Mother rules" of a guild or brotherhood.
MASCARETA: Light racing skiff, usually reserved for women competitors.
MOTOSCAFO: Launch; a smaller version of the vaporetto.
MURAZZO: Sea wall between the Lagoon and the Adriatic.

O

OMBRA: A glass of wine, as served in the bacari.

OSELLA: A commemorative medallion.
OSPEDALE: Hospice for abandoned children, usually offering a musical education.

P

PARROCCHIA: During the Republic, Venice was subdivided into about seventy parishes: their numbers were reduced after Napoleon's appropriation of the city.
PESCHERIA: The Rialto fish market.
PIANO NOBILE: First floor of a palace.
PIAZZA: St Mark's Square (only).
PIAZZETTA: Small square adjoining St Mark's.
PISCINA: An arm of the Lagoon which was originally used by Venetian children as a bathing place (nowadays the piscinas are surrounded by buildings, or have been filled in).
PONTILE: Landing stage for vaporetti and motoscafi.
PORTEGO: Main salon, covering the entire width of the piano nobile of a palace.
PUPARIN: Long Lagoon boat.

R

RAMO: A very short calle, often a dead end.
RIDOTTO: Gaming house, place of entertainment in Venice.
RIO: Canal. There are only three "canals", properly speaking, in Venice – the Cannaregio canal, the Grand Canal and the Giudecca Canal.
RIO TERRÀ: A filled-in rio, now a street.
RIVA: Bank.
RUGA: From the French "rue", a street; in Venice, a straight calle full of boutiques.
RUGHETTA: Short ruga.

S

SACCA: A large piscina. More recently, a part of the Lagoon which has been filled in.
SALIZZADA: Paved main thoroughfare; as a rule, the ordinary calli were not paved.

SANDALO DA S'CIOPO: A small, light boat with a flat bottom.
SANPIEROTA: Very stable Lagoon vessel.
S'CIOPON: See Sandalo da s'ciopo.
SCUOLA: Professional corporation or religious brotherhood.
SESTIERE: One of the six sections of Venice, dating from about 1170.
SOTTOPORTEGO: Portion of a street passing through a building.
SQUERO: Private boatyard, where traditional gondolas are built.
STAZIO: Landing stage for gondolas.

T

TABARRO: Voluminous cape worn during Carnival.
TOLE: Lumber yards.
TOPO: Sailing vessel, used for fishing in the Lagoon.
TRAGHETTO: Publicly maintained gondola with two oarsmen: also, point at which the Grand Canal can be crossed.

V

VAPORETTO: Venetian public transport along the Grand Canal.
VIA: Street.
VOGALONGA: Nineteen-mile boat race.

Z

ZATTERE: Quay in the Dorsoduro sestiere where barges of produce were unloaded.
ZUCCA: Pumpkin.

INDEX ◆

◆ INDEX

◆ INDEX

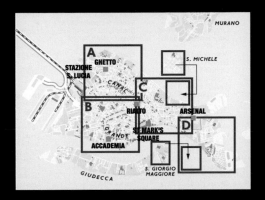

Map section

Key

Freeway
Expressway
Main road
Railroad
Ferry link
Cemetery
Airport

Fondamenta: f. Salizzanda: s. Terrà: t.
Rio: r. Sottoportico: sp.

437

◆ CANNAREGIO, SANTA CROCE

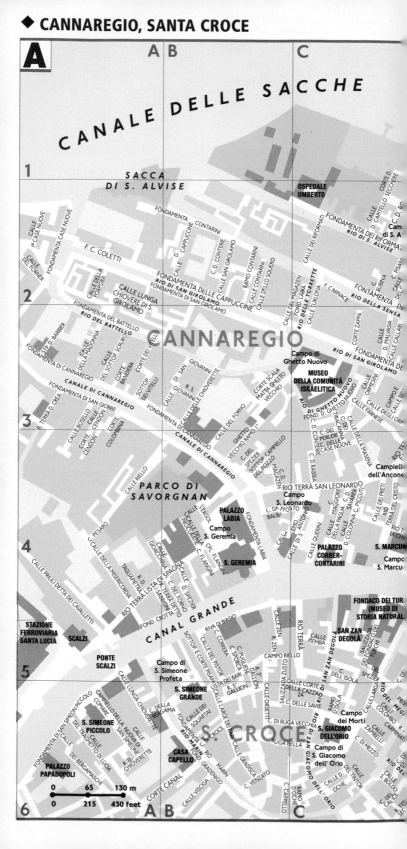

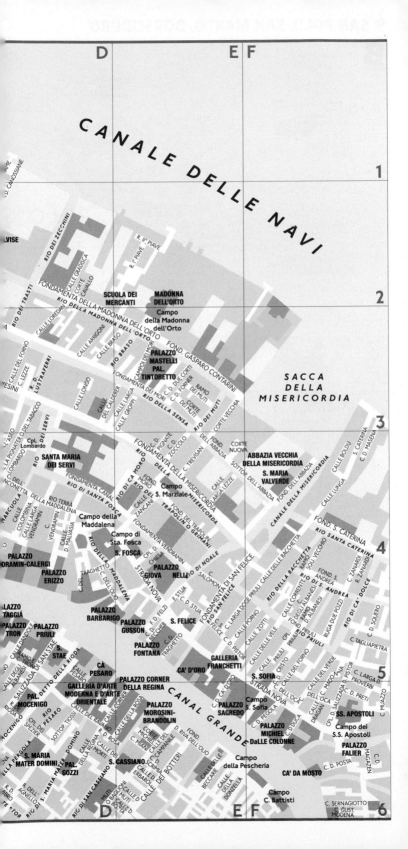

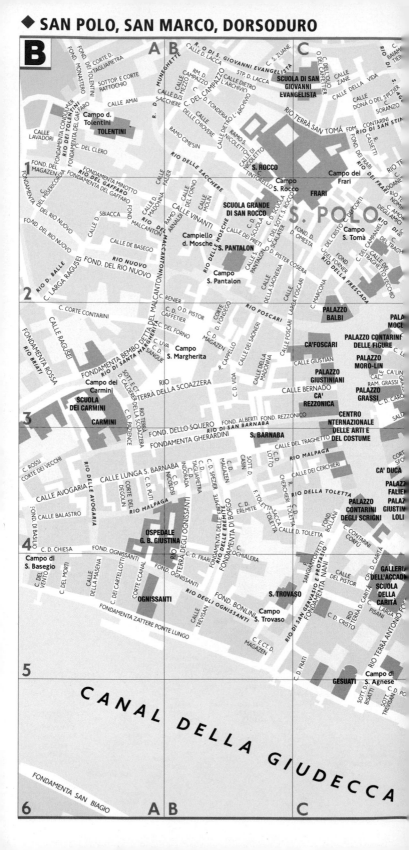

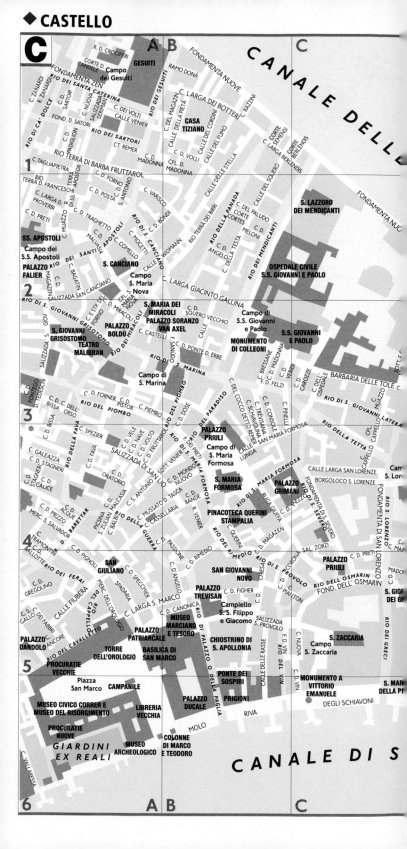

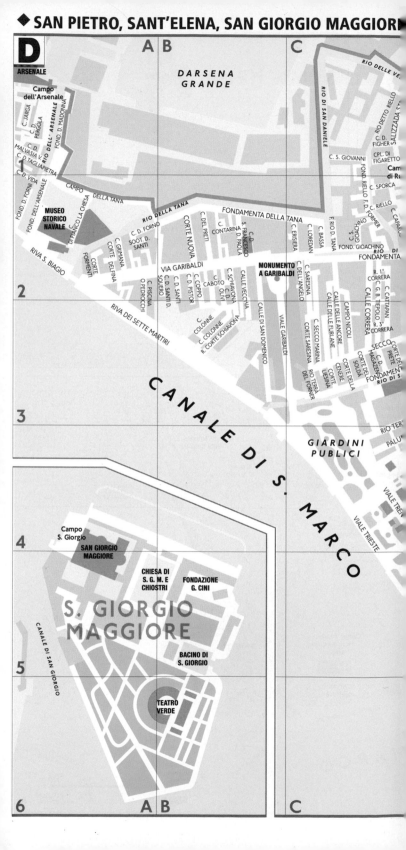

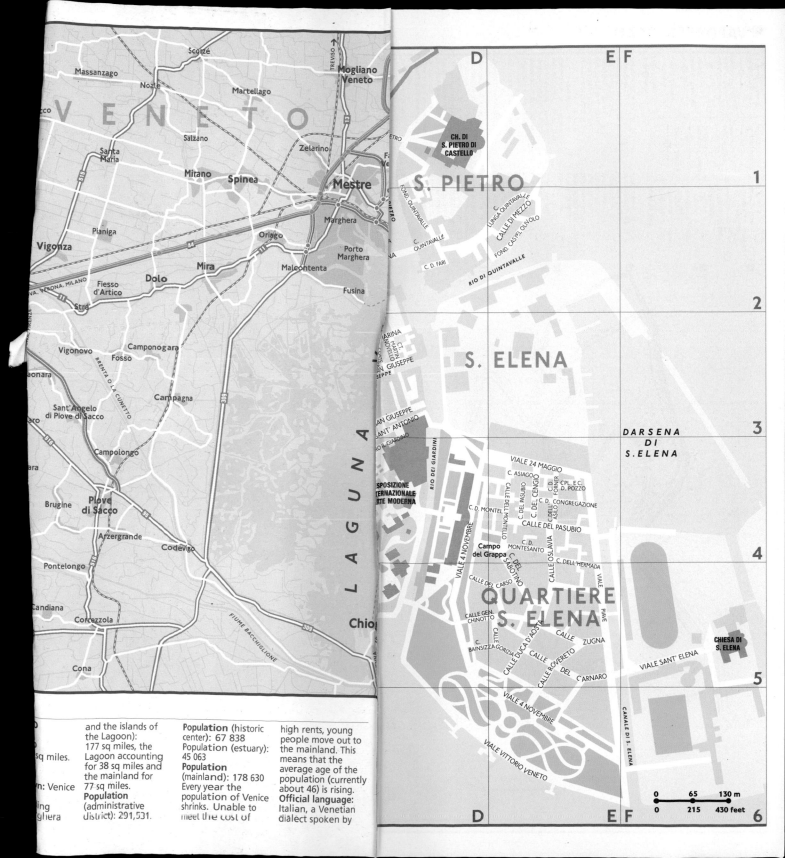

and the islands of the Lagoon): 177 sq miles, the Lagoon accounting for 38 sq miles and the mainland for 77 sq miles.

...wn: Venice

Population (administrative district): 291,531.

Population (historic center): 67 838
Population (estuary): 45 063
Population (mainland): 178 630
Every year the population of Venice shrinks. Unable to meet the cost of

high rents, young people move out to the mainland. This means that the average age of the population (currently about 46) is rising.
Official language: Italian, a Venetian dialect spoken by

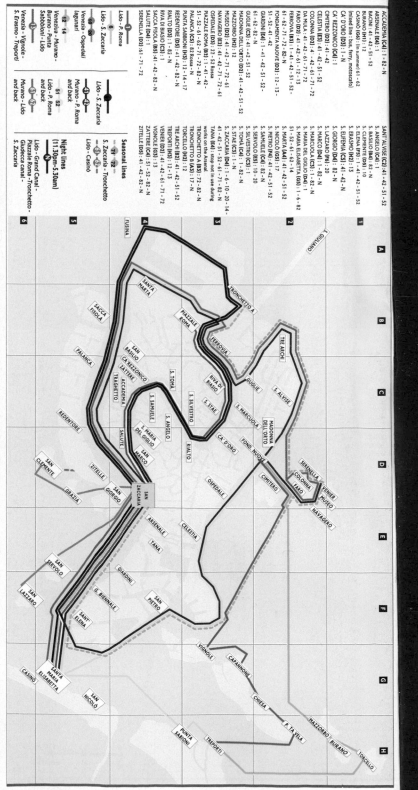

ACCADEMIA (C4): 1 - 82 - N
ARSENALE (E4): 1
BACINI (A1): 41 - 42 - 51 - 52
BURANO (H1): 12
CASINO (G6): (in summer) 61 - 62
CASINO (G6): (limited line : bus, ferry, motoscafo)
CA' REZZONICO (C4): 1
CA' D'ORO (D3): 1 - N
CIMITERO (D2): 41 - 42
COLONNA (D2): 41 - 42 - 51 - 52
CELESTIA (E3): 41 - 42 - 61 - 71 - 72
DA MULA : 41 - 42 - 61 - 12 - 13
FARO (D2): 41 - 42 - 51 - 52
FERROVIA (B3): 1 - 41 - 42 - 51 - 52 -
61 - 62 - 71 - 72 - 82 - N
FONDAMENTA NUOVE (D2): 12 - 13 -
51 - 52 - 41 - 42
GIARDINI (E4): 1 - 41 - 42 - 51 - 52 -
61 - 62 - 82 - N
GUGLIE (C3): 41 - 42 - 51 - 52
MADONNA DELL'ORTO (D2): 41 - 42 - 51 - 52
MAZZORBO (H2): 12
MUSEO (D2): 41 - 42 - 71 - 72 - 61
NAVAGERO (E2): 41 - 42 - 71 - 72 - 61
OSPEDALE (D3): 23 - 52 Rossa
PIAZZALE ROMA (B3): 1 - 41 - 42 -
51 - 52 - 61 - 62 - 71 - 72 - 82 - N
PALANCA (C3): 82 Rossa - N
PUNTA SABBIONI (H3): 12 - 14 - 17
REDENTORE (D3): 41 - 42 - 82 - N
RIALTO (D3): 1 - 82 - N
RIVA DI BIASIO (C3): 1
SACCA FISOLA (B3): 41 - 42 - 82 - N
SALUTE (D4): 1
SERENELLA (D2): 61 - 71 - 72

SANT'ALVISE (C2): 41 - 42 - 51 - 52
S. ANGELO (C4): 1
S. BASILIO (B4): 82 - N
S. CLEMENTE (D5): 82 - N
S. ELENA (F4): 1 - 41 - 42 - 51 - 52
S. ERASMO (H2): 13
S. EUFEMIA (C3): 41 - 42 - N
S. GIORGIO (D4): 82 - N
S. LAZZARO (D4): 20
S. MARCO (D4): 1 - 82 - N
S. MARCUOLA (C3): 1 - 82 - N
S. MARIA DEL GIGLIO (D4): 1
S. MARIA ELISABETTA (G3): 1 - 6 - 82
S. MARTA (A4): 41 - 42 - 51 - 52
S. NICOLO (G3): 17
S. PIETRO (F4): 41 - 42 - 51 - 52
S. SAMUELE (C4): 82 - N
S. SERVOLO (E5): 10 - 20
S. SILVESTRO (C3): 1
S. TOMA (C4): 1 - 82 - N
S. STAE (C3): 1 - N
S. ZACCARIA (D4): 1 - 6 - 10 - 20 - 14 -
41 - 42 - 51 - 52 - 61 - 71 - 82 - N
TANA (E4): stop not in use during
works on the Arsenal
TRONCHETTO A (B3): 72 - 82 - N
TRONCHETTO B (A3): 17 - N
TORCELLO (H2): 12
TRE ARCHI (B3): 41 - 42 - 51 - 52
TREPORTI (H3): 12 - 13
VENIER (D2): 41 - 42 - 61 - 71 - 72
VIGNOLE (G3): 13
ZATTERE (C4): 51 - 52 - 82 - N
ZITELLE (C4): 41 - 42 - 82 - N

Seasonal lines

 6
Lido - P. Roma

 Lido - S. Zaccaria

 12 - 14
Venezia - Murano -
Burano - Punta
Sabbioni - Lido

 Venezia - Vignole -
S. Erasmo - Treporti

 Lido - S. Zaccaria

 Lido - Casinò

 6
Venezia - Ospedali
lagunari

 51 - 52
Murano
and back

 Murano - P. Roma
and back

 Lido - P. Roma
and back

 Murano - Lido
and back

Night lines
(11.30pm–5.30am)

 N
Lido - Grand Canal -
Piazzale Roma -Tronchetto -
Giudecca canal -
S. Zaccaria

FACTS AND
FIGURES
■ THE VENETO
Area: 7088
Population
445,2793.
Largest tow
■ VENICE
Area (includ
Mestre, Ma